ATLAS'S BONES

THE AFRICAN FOUNDATIONS OF EUROPE

Atlas's Bones

D. Vance Smith

THE UNIVERSITY OF CHICAGO PRESS
Chicago and London

The University of Chicago Press, Chicago 60637
The University of Chicago Press, Ltd., London
© 2025 by The University of Chicago
All rights reserved. No part of this book may be used or reproduced in any manner whatsoever without written permission, except in the case of brief quotations in critical articles and reviews. For more information, contact the University of Chicago Press, 1427 East 60th Street, Chicago, IL 60637.
Published 2025
Printed in the United States of America

34 33 32 31 30 29 28 27 26 25   1 2 3 4 5

ISBN-13: 978-0-226-83030-8 (cloth)
ISBN-13: 978-0-226-84043-7 (ebook)
DOI: https://doi.org/10.7208/chicago/9780226840437.001.0001

The University of Chicago Press gratefully acknowledges the generous support of Princeton University toward the publication of this book.

Library of Congress Control Number: 2025021654

♾ This paper meets the requirements of ANSI/NISO Z39.48-1992 (Permanence of Paper).

Authorized Representative for EU General Product Safety Regulation (GPSR) queries: **Easy Access System Europe**—Mustamäe tee 50, 10621 Tallinn, Estonia, gpsr.requests@easproject.com
Any other queries: https://press.uchicago.edu/press/contact.html

FOR OLIVIA,
who was fascinated by Carthage

Contents

PREFACE · AN ATLAS FOR THIS BOOK *xi*
INTRODUCTION *1*
African History and White Noise *1*
"Africa," the Fallout of Metonymy *4*
All of Africa *8*

I. Ancient and Medieval: Reading Africa

CHAPTER ONE · EGYPT, THE EXCEPTION *23*
Africa, the Continent *23*
Alexander the Great African *25*
The Libyan God of Europe *29*
The Fluid Land *33*
Egypt in Medieval Europe *37*
Moses the African *40*
Alexander's African Romance *46*
Egyptology's History of Europe *52*
Egypt Theory *64*

CHAPTER TWO · AFRICA, FULCRUM OF EPIC *71*
Mythic Landing: The *Iliad*, the *Argonautica*,
the *Pharsalia*, the *Aeneid* *71*
Britain's African Foundations: Geoffrey of Monmouth *89*
The African Invention of England *95*

CHAPTER THREE · THE SPECTER OF CARTHAGE *103*
Carthage the Symptom: Virgil, Silius Italicus, Horace, Freud *103*
Carthage and African Identities: Sallust,
Tertullian, Augustine *110*
Augustine's Scandalous Carthaginian Theory *117*

The Dream of Scipio Africanus: Cicero and Macrobius *122*
Petrarch's Modern Africa *125*
Chaucer and the African *132*

CHAPTER FOUR · GHOSTS OF LANGUAGE:
PUNIC, LYBIC, AFRICAN MYTH *147*

The African Tumor in Language *147*
Martianus Capella: In the Palace of Myth *152*
Fulgentius: Africa's Mythic Language *156*
Libyc, the Purest Language *164*
The Symbolic Violence of Lost Languages: Bourdieu *170*
Our Most Secret Writing: Assia Djebar *175*

II. Medieval and Modern: Writing Africa

CHAPTER FIVE · ALLEGORY OF TWO AFRICAN CITIES *181*

Auerbach in Alexandria *181*
Auerbach in Carthage *191*

CHAPTER SIX · THE KING'S AFRICAN BODIES *201*

Kantorowicz's African Body *201*
Mystical Kings, European and African *211*
Anthropology's Divine Kings and Colonial Rule:
Leo Frobenius and Max Gluckman *219*

CHAPTER SEVEN · KENYA'S MEDIEVAL CHARTER *233*

The Feudal Metaphor *233*
Medieval Land Law in Africa *237*
How Oxford Medievalists Ruled the World *248*
Independent Feudalism *251*
Kenyatta and Malinowski Imagine Land *255*
Ngũgĩ wa Thiong'o: Land before Time *264*

CHAPTER EIGHT · FANON OUTSIDE HISTORY:
MANICHEISM, AUGUSTINE, AND HEGEL *271*

Which Manicheism? *271*
Manicheism and Dialectic *281*
Struggling with Augustine, Then and Now *293*

CHAPTER NINE · ZIMBABWE AND THE
FEAR OF THE MEDIEVAL *303*

The Specter of Carthage, Again *303*
Picturesque Archaeology *310*

Barbarian Invasions: Rhodes's Gibbon *314*
The Inconvenience of the Medieval *323*

CODA · THE NEW DIVINE KINGS *335*

Acknowledgments *347*
Notes *351*
Index *395*

Preface

An Atlas for This Book

> mons factus Atlas: nam barba comaeque
> in silvas abeunt, iuga sunt umerique manusque,
> quod caput ante fuit, summo est in monte cacumen,
> ossa lapis fiunt; tum partes altus in omnes
> crevit in inmensum (sic, di, statuistis) et omne
> cum tot sideribus caelum requievit in illo.

[Straightway Atlas became a mountain huge, as the giant had been; his beard and hair were changed to trees, his shoulders and arms to spreading ridges; what had been his head was now the mountain's top, and his bones were changed to stones. Then he grew to monstrous size in all his parts—for so, O gods, ye had willed it—and the whole heaven with all its stars rested upon his head.]

OVID, *Metamorphoses*, Bk. IV, 657–662.

History has simplified

him. Its elegies had blinded me with the temporal
lament for a smoky Troy, but where coral died
it feeds on its death, the bones branch into more coral,

and contradiction begins.

DEREK WOLCOTT, *Omeros*

Atlas was an African. In Greek mythology he was a Titan, a primeval god, who stands at the western edge of the world—that is, on the Atlantic shore of Africa—and holds up the entire cosmos. According to Ovid, he was turned into stone when he looked at Medusa's head, and became the Atlas Mountains. Atlas was also (remember this is myth) the king of the Mauri people, whose name became a catchall in early modern Europe for Africans, Maghrebians, Iberians, and anyone whose skin was darker than a Northern European: a Moor. King Atlas was legendary for the invention of astronomy (in his career as a mythical giant he held the stars), and for his deep knowledge of philosophy, mathematics, and geography. We still call a collection of maps an atlas; Gerardus Mercator, who created the form of the modern world map, first used the name in the title of his survey of the entire universe.

This mythical African, in other words, became the literal foundation of the world. According to the Greeks themselves, he was one of the founders of Western knowledge. The myth of Atlas, in all its complexity and profundity, is the foundation of this book, which tells the story of Atlas over and over. It is the story of the importance of Africa, not just in its own deep stories, but in the ancient and medieval archives of Europeans themselves. The great poet Petrarch placed the palace of Truth on the summit of the Atlas Mountains. This book is also (especially in its second half) the story of the millions of Africans whose bones lie buried on three continents, or at the bottom of the Atlantic, to ensure European and American dominance in the era of imperialism and colonialism. Atlas's presence at the foundation of the world becomes forgotten; as Derek Wolcott's *Omeros* says, "History simplified him." But in Ovid's short story, and in the story of its forgetting, lies the tangle of history's bones: the ironies, the blindnesses, the fantasies of the oppressors and the oppressed. "The bones branch," says *Omeros*, "and contradiction begins."

Introduction

L'Europe est une périphérie d'Afrique.

OUSMANE SEMBÈNE

African History and White Noise

In an age when white supremacists claim that Africans do not share the "common unconscious" of Western culture, this book argues that Africa is, in fact, the foundation of its "common unconscious."[1] The first half of this book examines the ideas, the art, the mythology, and the forms of writing that shaped much of the intellectual culture of Europe in the Middle Ages and well beyond. Africa's influence has been forgotten. The British Museum, for example, has put its Africa exhibit in the basement. But the basement is also the foundation; Africa is the heart, the origin, the true homeland, of much of the European culture that the rest of the museum celebrates. This book is the story of the deep influence of Africa, and of the way Europe has forgotten it. It is the story, indeed, of the way Africa gave birth to the modern world, and of how the modern world forgot not only Africa's history—but its own. When Hegel declared that Africa has no history, he did not mention that the most influential work *on* history was written by an African 1,400 years earlier.

People forget—or never knew—that the most brilliant thinker of late antiquity, Augustine, was African. When they remember that he was, they might protest that being African did not really matter to him. But it did. This book shows that Africanness was a deep force moving through his life. It shaped his thinking in profound ways, but because it took place at such depths, it has not always been visible on the surface.

There are many other Augustines. There are Africans who shaped what became European literature, political theory, even Roman Catholicism. They did so *as* Africans, and the "forgotten" continent of Africa became one of the most important sites by which, and against which, European culture defined itself. The inventor of the King Arthur legend, Geoffrey of Monmouth, describes how an African army saved the Anglo-Saxons and how Stonehenge itself came from Africa. The most influential poet of love in the Middle Ages, Francis Petrarch, believed his most important achievement—and the first real "modern" work—was his epic *Africa*. It is little read today, even by medievalists, and most of them think it is bad. Its neglect, and perhaps even the judgment of its quality, reveal much about how Africa's importance has been forgotten.

How *did* this forgetting happen? That is one of the twin threads of this book, which traces the clamor of European thinkers drowning out Africans, starting in Rome after the fall of Carthage in 146 BCE. By the epoch of imperialism, this clamor had become so loud that virtually none of the many voices in the African foundations of Europe could still be heard. Imperial policymakers, anthropologists, missionaries, and administrators came to believe that (because it was "backward") Africa was stuck in the "Middle Ages"—that is, their *own* Middle Ages.

One of the tragic ironies of colonialism is that European colonizers believed that because Africans had no history, they could impose one on it. If Africa had no history, it might as well begin with the Middle Ages. This very idea weaponized the discipline of medieval studies as the agent of colonialism. English medievalists, especially at Oxford, became some of the most important policymakers and administrators in African colonies. And, indeed, many of the "problems" of postindependence African nations can be laid at the feet of men trained in the study of the *European* Middle Ages. Part of the tragedy of Europe's legacy in Africa is that it strove to implant a European idea of historical progress. Colonizers were morally—even religiously—convinced that what Europe had to offer would fill a sizable void in African cultures. That moral conviction was only possible because of the massive forgetting of how important Africa had been in the history not just of Europe but also of the world. Well into the Middle Ages itself, Europeans recognized that Africa was a central and foundational part of their own history and culture, even an important part of how they imagined themselves as Europeans.

This book's goal is to show how much Africa has given to the world over the millennia. My job has been made easier since I started the project because of a number of popular programs and books on African civilizations. The best known is Henry Louis Gates's PBS series *Africa's Great Civilizations*, a gorgeous survey of some of the continent's most spectacular cultural monuments. There have been important recent books that survey the cultural heights of ancient and medieval Africa: F. X. Fauvelle's *The Golden Rhinoceros*; the collection of essays *Great Kingdoms of Africa*; Michael Gomez's *African Dominion: A New History of Empire in Early and Medieval West Africa*; and Howard W. French's *Born in Blackness: Africa, Africans, and the Making of the Modern World*.[2] Three recent blockbuster exhibitions have given a fuller picture of the cultural sophistication of premodern Africa: *Caravans of Gold: Fragments in Time* (at Northwestern University, the Aga Khan Museum in Toronto, and the Smithsonian, 2019–2022); *Sahel: Art and Empires on the Shores of the Sahara* (Metropolitan Museum, 2020); and *Africa and Byzantium* (Metropolitan Museum, 2022–2023).

This book covers only a part of what it could. Here are some major omissions. I do not know Arabic, and there are other scholars far better prepared to write about Islam in Africa. There is, for example, already one important book on Islamic North Africa's global importance: Michael Gomez's *African Dominion*. There is not enough on Ethiopia in this book; I simply do not know as much as I should. But medieval Ethiopia has recently become an important academic field in its own right, and there are and will be books that will remind us of Ethiopia's significance. There is little here on West Africa; again, I do not know what I should, but here there is also a rich history. I drafted much of a chapter on South Africa but realized that South Africa's colonial entanglement in medieval European constitutional and religious history is so deep that a single chapter would not be enough. Suffice it to say that the theology of apartheid in the Dutch Reformed Church comes from xenophobic manifestations of medieval theology, and that Jan Smuts, the Afrikaner first Prime Minister of the Republic of South Africa, was the best student of the Cambridge medieval constitutional historian F. W. Maitland.

There are numerous examples, not just of the vitality of premodern Africa, but also of its global importance. The Apostle Mark helped establish Christianity before it spread in Europe north of the Alps; the Ethiopian church may be as old as the Ethiopian who talked to Philip about the book of Isaiah (Acts 8:26–39). An international culture flourishing on the east coast of Africa during the European Middle Ages controlled the trade of gold from further south, and its trade and political networks from the Gulf of Persia to the interior of Africa created what has been called the largest "cultural continuum" in the world at the time.[3]

"Africa," the Fallout of Metonymy

As this book will show, for centuries Europe was intimately acquainted with Africa. Europeans knew that their history overlapped with Africa's. They even celebrated the foundational role that Africa played in European culture. But at some point Africa began to recede from Europe. The ninety-six miles between Sicily and Tunisia became an ocean away, then a world away, then a millennium away.

Even as precise maps of the African coastline were being drawn by Italian and Spanish merchants in the thirteenth century, a new map was being drawn that divided Europe and Africa not by religion, culture, or politics, but by race.[4] It has not always been clear in more recent history that the division is racial, because racism needs to rely on other reasonings to explain itself. Hegel, celebrated for his vision of a world made up of "pure" dialectical relations, divides Africa into three parts. The first two are, in fact, not "really" Africa: Egypt, an important civilization in its own right, and North Africa, which is part of Europe. The rest is "Africa proper," cut off by the Sahara and mountains. The essence of the continent is, for Hegel, its Blackness, the "peculiarly African character." He's not talking in the nostalgic, aestheticized way of colonialists like Isak Dinesen (*Out of Africa*) or Kuki Gallman (*I Dreamed of Africa*), taking in land, animals, and people in a single dreamy gaze. No, Hegel is specifically talking about the people, in terms that suggest they have failed at being people. He no longer refers to them as Africans, but as "Negroes," beings he claims have no "reverence and morality," "nothing harmonious with humanity."

Strangely for something that is its "proper" self (*eigentlich*, its own), Hegel defines Africa "proper" in terms of what it is not. This Africa is not something that the rest of Africa is (civilized or European); it is not something that the rest of humanity is (reverential and moral). Africa "proper" is not even Africa, strictly speaking—it is the people who live in it. Hegel's capture of a continent in a web of negations formed a philosophical tradition, Afropessimism, that still declares the impossibility of thinking Blackness outside of its origins in white metaphysics, since it is defined from the beginning as a negation: what is not white.

Hegel's infamous passage is paradoxically lucid about the insidious ways racism creeps into discourses about Africa. Or, rather, how it does not creep. It often pushes its discourse into the world and returns to its hiding places. One of these hiding places is the Sahara Desert, as we've seen. That cartographical division remains one of the most consistent tropes in talking about Africa. Both the World Bank and the International Monetary Fund continue to treat all of sub-Saharan Africa as a single economic unit, although they don't agree on which countries it includes.[5] Neither institution is clear about why they divide Africa like this; one of the few discussions in an IMF report says it's because sub-Saharan countries share the same "stage" of economic and political "development," similar "climactic conditions," and the same "level of human development."[6]

That definition is simply a bland office-park version of Hegel. It says something sweeping about all of sub-Saharan Africa and then immediately disavows it ("In many other ways, however..."). Neoliberal institutions like the IMF and the World Bank might not champion Hegel's goal for the world—freedom of the spirit—but they still assume that the world *has* a common goal, that what matters most is progress toward something, the development of some latent capacity that needs to be realized. This goal is just as insistently a Western one today as it was in the era of colonization, when colonization was justified as the moral imperative to "civilize" Africa. In all of these cases, Africa is put on a schedule: it needs to "catch up" with the West, and it needs to be made modern.

We will see in this book how the idea of European modernity sharpens itself against the notion of an Africa that seems stuck in the past. Yet it is a past that exists only in the European imagination. For me, the most shocking moment in the passage from the IMF report is the rapid and casual invocation of a "level of human development." I don't know if an actual explanation of what that means would blunt its implications. It's apparently not the same thing as economic or political development, both of which the report at least defines in rudimentary ways. It might be related to "human capital," which the report invokes without much explanation in its larger discussion of the economic foundations of sub-Saharan Africa. But that phrase "level of human development" is chilling in a less clinical way. It's hard to decouple it—to put it as blandly as possible—from a basic assumption that sub-Saharan Africans are less evolved than people elsewhere, even the people who share the northern part of their continent. The very assignation of tens of millions of people in dozens of countries to the single category of a "level of human development" is as broadly sweeping and, when it comes out into the open, as racist, as Hegel's diatribe about the "peculiarly African character."

It's my contention in this book that to divide Africa into North Africa and sub-Saharan Africa is to make an invidious distinction that begins with, and powerfully reinforces, a modern European division of Africa by race. We tend to resist less when a part of Europe, or a part of its history, comes to stand for all of Europe. The philosopher Martin Heidegger said that philosophy was "Greek in its nature," but that only meant that it was fundamentally "Western-European."[7] It doesn't matter how Heidegger justifies that leap; it's one that is so common that it's almost a fundamental feature of the idea of Europe and the West. American jurisprudence is conducted in buildings that might have stood in classical Greece.

In European philosophy and culture, "Greece" is a metonymy, a part that stands for the whole. North Africa is a similar metonymy: it is, as Hegel says, European. Sub-Saharan Africa, however, does not have a comparable rhetorical figure. It is a part of Africa that is simply apart. It is the fallout of metonymy, a part that is left over when sub-Saharan Africa is excluded from North Africa and becomes "proper" Africa, precisely by being *less* than the whole of Africa.

In rhetoric, the "proper" (Hegel's *eigentum*) is the thing itself, represented by a sign that means no more than the thing it represents. But proper Africa is a sign that does not participate in the system of other signs—another way of saying, that is, language. It is closed up, Hegel says; it has no part of History; it is hidden in Night. Proper Africa is, in Hegel's terms, not a sign at all, but a symbol. There is "no natural bond between the signifier and the signified." It is arbitrary, it can be changed. But "in the symbol the original characters (*eigene Bestimmtheit*) (in essence and conception) of the visible object are more or less identical with the content which it bears as symbol."[8] Africa is just itself. Nothing more can be said about it. It resists, one could say more theoretically, discourse. At the end of his discussion, Hegel says we will "leave Africa, not to mention it again." We will see later that leaving Africa is not as easy as that. Hegel, after all, didn't leave *all* of Africa behind—just the part south of the Sahara. The great medieval Italian poet Francis Petrarch obsessed over a poem about Africa for so long that finally the Augustine in his mind has to tell him: "Leave Africa."

Introduction 7

So: what is Africa? How much of it has been forgotten? What parts of it are the true Africa? To a large extent, what we mean by Africa depends on *when* we mean. The name was first used for the province created (in northern Tunisia and part of Libya) when Rome destroyed Carthage. The Romans added a second province in Numidia and Mauretania (to the west), and Augustus merged the two (now called *Africa Vetus* and *Africa Nova*) into a single province, *Africa Proconsularis*. But "Africa" was a name that began to slide across the rest of the continent, just as the Greek name "Libya" had done. In his influential description of the world, the classical geographer Claudius Ptolemy's section on Libya includes much of Africa. Perhaps "includes" isn't the best word, because to the west and south it gets vague: to the south of Ethiopia, Ptolemy says, "the geography is unknown."[9] It wasn't until Bartolomeu Dias sailed around the Cape of Good Hope in 1488 that Western geographers knew how far Africa extended to the south.

Classical geography divided the world into three parts: Asia, Europe, and what Latin writers beginning with Strabo began to call "Africa," which was thought to be the same size as Europe.[10] Even after Europeans knew how far to the south Africa extended, however, Ptolemy's "unknown geography" covers what Hegel thought of as the "proper" Africa, namely everything below the Sahara.

But even Africa above the Sahara slides off and on the continent. Egypt, as we will see in the first chapter, is considered to be geographically in Africa, but not always culturally. It has at times been put in Asia: in the classical era the Nile was seen as the best place to divide the continents of Africa and Asia. Part of Egypt at least—most notably, Alexandria—was firmly on *Africa terra*. Its border with Africa drifted both west and east over the millennia, and in the eighteenth century began to drift into Europe and Asia. Much of the impetus behind this drift has to do with race.

When Napoleon invaded Egypt, he took a small army of scholars who eventually produced the massive multivolume *Description de l'Égypte*, a project that supported the contention that the great monuments of Egypt could not have been made by a Black race. To be precise, the *Description* refers to *the* Black race (*la race nègre*), as if all of the people of Africa can be reduced to a single category: anything that isn't "Egyptian" becomes merely Black.[11] It dismisses earlier opinions that many of the monuments of Egypt *were* built by Black people. Those arguments were based on physiognomic racism, the notion that the traits of "Black" people were visible. The builders, per the *Description*, seem to be more like the present-day Copts, whom many people, it says, believe are the descendants of the ancient Egyptians. The *Description* cordons Egypt off from the rest of Africa with a string of false premises, aesthetic impressions, and special pleading. Or, to put it more succinctly: of racisms. This string will be broken by other racisms, as we will see. Other Egyptologists used the same evidence to argue that ancient Egyptians "raced" the peoples outside of Egypt to shore up notions of Egyptian cultural and political dominance. Egypt, indeed, is the flash point of some of the most rancorous debates over the contributions of Africans to world culture. Those debates are propelled by the question of what race ancient Egyptians were. Rather than discuss the exchange, influence, and synthesis of African cultures over millennia, most public debates have focused simply on the DNA of mummies. More interesting questions of what social relations may have been like or how extensively Nubia, "Ethiopia," and Libya interacted with Egypt have either been suspended or overlooked. Egypt was and still is immensely important *in* Africa.

All of Africa

The Pan-African movement that began in the United States in the nineteenth century and was the founding ideology of anti-colonialism across the African continent had as one of its aims the reclaiming of Egypt for Africa. One of Pan-Africanism's methods was to delegitimize white supremacy by recreating the histories that had been obscured by slavery and modern racism. As more Africans joined the movement, this historical work began to extend further back in time, and to increasingly focus on Africa, a focus that came to be known as Afrocentrism. The first modern Afrocentric historiography is often regarded as Africanus Horton's 1868 *Vindication of the African Race*. "Why should not the same race who governed Egypt once," Horton said, "once more stand on their legs and endeavor to raise their characters in the scale of the civilized world?"[12]

A young Senegalese student in Paris, Cheikh Anta Diop, helped to form the first Pan-African Student Congress in 1951, and went on to write some of the most influential Afrocentric works, beginning with *Nations nègres et culture* in 1954. His work is best known for its insistence not only that Egypt is a part of Africa, but also that Africa is really the origin of the Egypt that Europe has thought of as the *exception* to Africa. Diop's insistence that Egypt is African enfolded the argument that Egyptians were, therefore, Black. His work lies behind contemporary diasporan identifications with Egypt as the Black origin of worldwide knowledges. Although Diop influenced entire movements in Africa and throughout the diaspora, his work did not have much traction in Western scholarly journals and was largely overlooked by white Western scholars.

One exception was the Cornell University scholar Martin Bernal, whose *Black Athena* appeared in 1987. It was celebrated by Africanists and postcolonialists, but it triggered a response from (mostly) classicists, led by the Wellesley College professor Mary Lefkowitz. Her 1996 *Not Out of Africa: How Afrocentrism Became an Excuse to Teach Myth as History* wears its outrage in its title, and the scolding tone dominated much of the subsequent critique of Diop and Bernal. The pressure of Afrocentrism contributed to the polarization of Classics departments in particular, and to recent excavations of the pervasive Eurocentric, white roots of the modern study of the Classics—essentially a vindication of Bernal's argument that the "Aryan Model" had shaped the modern study of the ancient world. It may be incidental that Bernal was a white Englishman, but it isn't incidental that he was trained as a Sinologist. He was a double outsider, in other words, to Africa, but an insider to the Western and white world of scholarship. Because he was not trained in African languages, much of Bernal's central evidence, which is linguistic, is shaky. Nevertheless, his work was taken up in ways that were both more extensive than Diop's and more tolerant. In its June 22, 2013, obituary, the *New York Times* said that Bernal's book had "ignited the debate" over the African origins of civilization, as if Diop had not been writing about it for forty years already.[13]

My discussion of Afrocentric scholarship is informed by the effect the work of Diop and Bernal, and the strident reactions to it, had on the *popular* conception of African history. There has been so much important Afrocentric work done since Bernal's book came out that it is impossible simply to dismiss it, as happened with both Diop and Bernal. I celebrate this work and am inspired by it. But my purpose in this book, although it is allied with Afrocentric projects, is not only to recover more of the rich African past. It is also to show *how much knowledge of Africa there has always been in Europe*—and how deeply Europeans have engaged with

Africa. More precisely, this book discusses the many ways that Europeans in the Middle Ages (and to a lesser extent premodern Europe) wrote about the historical legacy of Africa in their own world.

This book will turn again and again to the European Middle Ages. There are two reasons for this. The Middle Ages, like Africa, holds a place in the Western imagination as backward, primitive—by definition, not modern. Until recently, when there has been an explosion of work on the Global Middle Ages, many scholars of the period assumed that medieval Europe was, for the most part, cut off from the other continents. The extent of Europe's involvement in the rest of the world is now better understood than it was even ten years ago. This book adds to that repository of knowledge, but it argues that the inter-involvement of Africa and Europe was more profound than just the exchange of goods and the reports of various travelers. Africa was not only known to Europeans, but played a profound role in how Europeans imagined both the world and themselves.

The other reason for the importance of the Middle Ages is that it completed the logical circle of colonialism. Precisely because Africa was considered backward, Europeans used the Middle Ages as a kind of archive to understand the "backwardness" of Africa. They went further: part of the civilizing mission of imperialism had the eventual goal of bringing Africa into the modern era. Medieval forms of law and social structure would place Africa on a developmental timeline that would end in something like European modernity.

As we will see in later chapters, another powerful, and closely related, circular logic that governed European ideas about Africa and Africans was race. Recent work in medieval studies has complicated the idea that European racism is a modern phenomenon. It does not, as Sierra Lomuto put it, "exclusively belong to a scientific discourse that postdates our premodern period of study," nor does it "begin and end with skin color or biological markers of difference. . . . It is malleable because its constitutive parts are themselves malleable."[14] Geraldine Heng's 2018 *The Invention of Race in the European Middle Ages* argues that the assumption that racism was not fully activated until the Atlantic slave trade obscures the many ways in which practices of exclusion, oppression, and othering in the Middle Ages are, in fact, what we now recognize as racism. Heng's work shows how the Crusades turned Muslims into the demonized other, and how that racialized discourse shaped the representation of non-

European—or, rather, non-white populations—in literature, polemic, and theology. The work of scholars like Cord Whitaker shows how deeply the culture of white medieval Europe drew on the negative associations of Blackness to construct its identity.[15] For the most part, this work has shown how Africa and Africans are a recurrent figure of the racial other in the development of this European discourse. That is certainly true, and there are abundant examples of African armies in literature listing terrifying, barely civilized warriors from the edges of the world.

But what this book shows, I hope, is that, along with the historical diminution of the cultural and religious difference of Africa to the single datum of a racial Black other, Europeans also thought about Africa and Africans in complex, nuanced, and profound ways. That is partly because when medieval Europeans thought about "the world" they were using tools and ideas that came from Africa itself. So, rather than think of Africa solely as the site of Blackness in the European imagination, I would like to explore, along with this, the many ways that Africa was *familiar* to Europe and not just its increasingly othered, unknown continent. Here is one example from far-flung Britain.

In the General Prologue of *The Canterbury Tales*, Geoffrey Chaucer describes a knight who has returned from a years-long series of adventures that included fighting in "Tramyssene" (Tlemcen in modern Algeria) and for the "Belmarye," that is, the Banū Marīn, rulers of the Marinid empire in Morocco. Both were important for establishing trade networks with Europe. Tlemcen was the principal port for Italian and Spanish gold traders in the thirteenth and fourteenth centuries. Pisa signed a treaty of friendship in the 1130s with Tlemcen. The Marinid dynasty controlled much of the trade in gold from the Empire of Mali, one of the richest sources in the world. Mansa Musa, the ruler of Mali, took so much gold with him on his *hajj* to Mecca in 1324 that he depressed the value of the dinar in Cairo for years. The true extent and the immense importance of the trans-Saharan trade networks is becoming increasingly clear. The landmark exhibition in 2019, *Caravans of Gold*, is the fullest account yet of this trans-Saharan trade, which extended from today's Ghana and Burkina Faso across Africa and Europe.

The extensive trade and cultural interactions between Africans and Europeans over these centuries complicates the counter-trend of increasing European racism. Africans may have become increasingly othered in the era of the Crusades, but Africa and Africans remained an integral part of the cultural imaginary of Europe, not just a site on which Europe projected xenophobic forms of ethnic and religious identity. It is undeniably true that crusade polemic uses crudely racial, binary terms, but in reading "Europe's" encounter with "Africa" in the premodern period, we run the risk of being unable to break out of the manichaeism of later periods, or from writers who are intensely invested in depicting a world violently divided into Black and white.

In Geraldine Heng's book, the encounter of peoples tends to be depicted as a binary confrontation between sides in a religious war, yet in the terms of the modern phenomenon of colonialism. The chronicler Fulcher of Chartres's account of the First Crusade describes, Heng says, the "expropriation of land and resources; the creation of colonial elites, a subject class ('servants'), and intergenerational transfers of colonial privilege ('inheritance'); a mystified politics of language and of sexual and ethnoracial relations; even the pleasures of going native, and complacent self-congratulation by colonial masters secure in the rightness of their destiny" (126). After the First Crusade, the East was ruled (partially, and briefly) by Westerners, and their right to occupation was underpinned by the very divine legitimation that Fulcher is praising. Yet the power relations are a bit more nuanced. It is true, as Heng suggests, that "Reading Fulcher *now* with the unavoidable knowledge of later, newer colonizations—accruing different moments of the colonial *now*—makes us alive to the modernity of the past, to the panoply of resources that can be amassed to mystify operations of power" (126).

But if anything, Fulcher's passage should complicate contemporary notions of what Heng calls "the resilience of colonial dialect," not simply reveal its persistence over time. Some of the features in the passage that Heng points to are indeed the product, quite literally, of the colonial moment—that is, of the 1969 English translation of Fulcher that Heng uses.[16] Where the translation refers to the languages and lineages that "both races" now share, Fulcher's Latin text uses the term *natio*. It is not clear what, precisely, the two "nations" are, unless it is those born, to stress the etymological sense of *natio*, in the East, and those born in the West. The politics of social relations here is certainly "mystified," and Heng's book is excellent about the ways in which religious discourse is deployed throughout the Middle Ages to mystify social relations. But it is not as precisely situated in the politics of "ethno*racial* relations," with the glaring exception of the "Saracens," with which "we" (per Fulcher) now intermarry,[17] as it might seem at first. Heng's "subject class" is invoked by the term "servants" in the translation, but Fulcher refers to the *familia* in Latin, a capacious term that means members of a household, including blood relations.

I am not suggesting that the discourse of race or class does not operate in Fulcher's description, but rather that its complexities demand closer historicization. That close attention to history includes moments close to our own. The process of "going native" that Heng refers to complicates her own argument in two ways. First, it was usually used by colonizers to refer to a supposed *violation* of the process of colonization. It described, and in some places still describes, a betrayal of the cultural values of the colonizers, usually when a colonist married or had affairs with Indigenous people, or lived too much like them: it is the same thing as "letting the side down."[18]

It is hard to reimagine the events that medieval writers describe outside of nineteenth- and twentieth-century fantasies of racialized East-West relations. But we now have a clearer sense of how pervasive and powerful those fantasies were, both because of the horrific reemergence of racist nationalisms in our time, and the critical work of decolonial and indigenous studies.

All of this makes it difficult to recognize how people in the Middle Ages may have already thought beyond the binaries that we tend to attribute to them. North Africa didn't just become the "other" after the First Crusade. It also stood at the foundation of European formations of political destiny and identity, and it hovered over literary discourse like a specter. More precisely, it underpinned and structured visions of both political and cultural permanence in the later European Middle Ages.

A poem, *Carmen in Victoriam Pisanorum*, celebrates the victory of Pisa and Genoa over the port of Mahdia, the capital of Ifriqia (literally, "Africa," although in this case it meant northern Tunisia) in 1087. It complains that the ruler of Mahdia was harassing all of Italy and "pillaging Roman territory as far as Alexandria."[19] The extent of Mahdia's military threat is exaggerated, but it did affect trade networks between Pisa and North Africa. These networks were so important that several churches in and near Pisa were decorated with ceramic bowls from Tunisia.[20] One of the many inscriptions on the exterior of the Pisa Duomo mentions a large bronze statue that was captured in North Africa, which might perhaps be the famous griffin that stood on top of a column on the roof.[21] It is clear that, from an economic, and perhaps cultural, perspective, Pisa was at least as interested in North Africa as Mahdia was interested in Italy.

Altercations over the years only underscore how long the trading relationship existed between Pisa and the cities of North Africa. In 1200, the Tunisians seized goods belonging to Pisan merchants, in revenge for Pisan piracy. Surviving letters between Tunisian and Pisan merchants suggest that the seizure was more of a warning gesture than a complete severing of trade relations: Tunisian merchants reassured their Pisan counterparts that their goods were safe, and that they anticipated an eventual return to normal trade.[22]

Trade with North Africa, in substantial part, made Pisa wealthy; during the eleventh and twelfth centuries, it became one of the major maritime powers of the Mediterranean. Pisa's North African trade in the Middle Ages also contributed to the development of modern mathematics. The Fibonacci sequence was discovered by Leonardo Fibonacci, who lived in the Algerian port of Béjaïa, where his father was a customs official for Pisa, and where Leonardo learned to do mathematics with Arabic numerals.

Although the *Carmen in Victoriam Pisanorum* opens with a reference to trade, it represents Pisa's war with Mahdia as religious. Indeed, the war has sometimes been described as the precursor to the First Crusade, which was launched just eight years later (a later raid on Mahdia by a Franco-Genoan expedition in 1390 is, on the other hand, sometimes called the *last* crusade).[23] It is, indeed, a bit difficult to distinguish the Pisan/Genoan attack from a crusade. Later texts justify it as a religious war, aiming to take back an Africa where Christ had been denied.[24] The *Montecassino Chronicle* says that the idea of the expedition originated in papal councils, that Pope Victor III gathered an Italian army, and that he promised the soldiers full remission of their sins for participating.[25] The *Carmen*, written a few years after the campaign, is more direct about its purpose: to defeat Islam in Africa. It describes Mahdia's ruler as an impious Saracen, similar to the Antichrist; its people are the enemies of the Creator, and they deny the doctrines of the Trinity and the Incarnate Word.

The *Carmen* often refers to the enemy as Saracens or pagans, blanket terms that cover a multitude of ethnic and cultural differences. But at times it shows a greater erudition and awareness of the complex relation between Islam and Christianity. The *Carmen* calls the enemy, who invoke Muhammad, "Agareni": the descendants of Hagar, the Egyptian concubine whom Abraham drove into the desert. The epithet indicates a certain awareness of the roots of Islam in Judaism, an awareness that is usually absent from popular literature about Islam in medieval Europe. The epithet is far more common in Greek than it is in Latin; the poet clearly knows more about the cultural situation of Muslims in North Africa and the Byzantine world than do most European authors of the time (and later times, too).[26] Although the poem seems to use crude demonizations of Islam—it calls Timinus, the ruler of Mahdia, a serpent and the Antichrist—it also betrays a sophisticated, scholarly understanding of the relation between Christianity and Islam. Muhammad himself is not a demon or a monster, as in most popular medieval European representations: he is an arch-heretic, a heresiarch (st. 52). That careful relegation of Islam to a heresy rather than paganism (except when the poem earlier calls the Mahdianites pagans) suggests a nuanced and theologically sophisticated understanding of Islam of the kind based on actual readings of the Qur'an.[27]

The poem is attuned to the situation of Islam in Africa. It does fault "Africa, which denied [or killed] Christ" (Mahdia is on Cape Africa), but it also compares the Pisans to the Israelites defeating the Pharoah again (*iterum*) and taking the Egyptian gold with them (st. 68). Poetic license identifies a town in Tunisia with Egypt, more than 1100 miles to the east. The analogy is tempting in multiple ways: the Pisans, like the Israelites, says the poem, fled across the sea, and were rescued by the miraculous appearance of fresh water, just as Moses drew water from the rock.

This extended analogy underscores the poem's acute consciousness of what it means, on multiple cultural and historical levels, to confront a city in Africa. The most remarkable example of this is its comparison of the current heresy in North Africa (Islam) with one of the most prominent heresies of the past: Arianism. Muhammad, says the *Carmen*, is a heresiarch greater than Arius. Not only does this comparison put Islam within the orbit of Christianity, it also reminds readers that North Africa is historically a site of heresy. The dominant—that is, hegemonic—form of Christianity practiced throughout North Africa under the Vandals was Arianism, which Vandal rulers used to distinguish their North African dominion from Rome and the influence of Nicene Christians.[28] But the *Carmen*'s identification of Arianism with Mahdia is more specific even than that: Arius himself was North African, a Berber who may have been born in Libya. In that case, the *Carmen*'s reference to the "Africa" that denied Christ might not be just a reference to Islam's denial of the doctrine of the incarnation, but also to *Arianism*'s denial of Christ's divinity. Islam in Africa, from this perspective, is nothing new: it is merely a restatement of a recurrent heresy, one that might justify—if for the sake of orthodoxy alone—the permanent presence of orthodox Christians in North Africa.

The poem's geopolitics might seem less sweeping. Pisa is concerned with a single city led astray by one bad ruler. The name "Africa" could refer just to Mahdia.[29] But it is difficult to know where to stop: is the poem being precise about its aspiration to dominate just one town, or is it—not very subtly—also dreaming about dominating a larger part of the continent? The poem uses another African city in just that way, treating it as a metonymy for all of Africa.

That city is Carthage. As we will see, almost from the moment of its destruction, Carthage came to stand not just for the continent but also for the fate of civilization itself. The Greek historian Polybius reports that Scipio Africanus the Younger (who acquired the name "Africanus" when he conquered Carthage) gazed over the wreckage of the city, musing about the eventual fate of Rome. Contemplating Carthage encouraged thinking on a world-historical level, and it is therefore not surprising that the author of the *Carmen* used Carthage as a symbol of the importance of the Pisan victory over Mahdia. Pisa, the poem begins, will achieve the same glory in conquering Mahdia that the Romans once gained in conquering Carthage. Whatever else the war may have been about—protection from Mahdian marauding, the assertion of trading rights, the overcoming of Islam and heresy—it was also Pisa's claim to have taken the place of Rome on the world stage by conquering another African city.

Whether or not Pisa's victory represents the first steps of modern European colonization on the African continent, the deep history that the poem invokes suggests a different strategy of historical, cultural, and sovereign legitimation than the particular binarisms of the later crusade period in imagining the Muslim world (what Heng nicely calls "Islamdom") as a whole.

Mahdia, Ifriqia, Africa might be enemies of Europe. But enemies are complex things. There's even a certain necessity for them. Augustine argued that the fear of Carthage as an enemy (the *metus hostilis*) is what made the Roman republic great. The Hundred Years War between England and France created an extraordinarily fertile environment for English literature, as Ardis Butterfield showed in *The Familiar Enemy:*

Chaucer, Language, and Nation in the Hundred Years War (2010). The greatest works in Middle English came out of it, most notably Chaucer's, with its rich awareness of French literature. That century-long encounter with the enemy helped to shape English literature in general. As we will see, Carthage stood in relationship not just to Rome but also to Europe for hundreds of years, and its erstwhile status as an enemy to medieval Europe's foundational city resulted in some of Europe's most important and complex ideas.

My professional training focused on these ideas. My main interest in graduate school was the intellectual history of the Middle Ages, the way in which the traditions of philosophy influenced literature. I thought of this as a kind of anthropology, a way of understanding the culture of a world that was distant from mine in time. I don't know why Europe in particular caught my attention. Part of the reason, which I intuited at the time, was a kind of demure Oedipal reaction: my father is a cultural anthropologist whose work began—and continues still—in contemporary Africa. I chose Europe and a time well before his. I eventually wrote three books on literature in medieval Europe and edited others. This is my first book on Africa, but this is far from the first time I've thought about Africa.

I think it's necessary to talk about this because I am yet another white person writing about Africa. I hope the evidence of Africa's influence on the world in this book stands on its own. But I am aware that I will always be outside, not just the embodied experience of even my closest boyhood friends in Africa, but outside the long, intimate, and often complex family histories of those friends—and all that that means—for thinking the world from Africa.

I am from Africa. I did not, however, grow up in it like most white people did. When I started high school in Kenya, I was one of two white boys. The other was five years older, and we never talked. From Second Form on, I was the only white boy. My school was founded as an alternative to English schools like Rugby and Winchester, so white settlers didn't have to send their sons to England to learn how to rule colonies. But despite the replacement of white with Black students, the old system was intact when I started. The structural brutality that was designed to mold British white boys into a colonial elite was then shaping a new Kenyan elite. All of my classmates suffered humiliation and pain for the first two years, no matter how important their parents were. Each of us was singled out for punishment because of what made each of us different. We needed to be less different. My difference needed more attention: I represented the lingering colonizer. All of us incurred some degree of trauma but, just as the founders of those schools intended, that trauma forged us into a brotherhood that remains strong after forty years. I wrote this book because these brothers encouraged me to. I've been sharing parts of it with them for eight years now, and am grateful for their enthusiasm to hear more.

My parents were American but went to South Africa at a young age and fought against the emerging system of apartheid. My father and S. E. M. Pheko of the Pan-Africanist Congress of Azania published a newspaper for Black South Africans with the pointed title *Our Africa*. It was closed down after numerous difficulties with the South African government, and by the American mission that bankrolled it because they thought it was too incendiary.

My parents had some limited immunity from the apartheid government because they were Americans, but Pheko was arrested the day I was born. My mother had to take a taxi home because my father was at the detention center being interviewed by the police. Shortly after that, my parents were forced to leave the country, and went to what was then Rhodesia. They spoke Zulu fluently and chose Rhodesia because the amaNdebele in the south speak a dialect of Zulu. The year after they arrived, the Ian Smith regime declared independence unilaterally in order to create a white supremacist state. We were compelled to live in a whites-only area and my sister and I compelled to go to whites-only schools. My parents worked constantly to offset the poisonous racism around us. They held church services every Sunday afternoon on the wide wraparound veranda of their old house in Bulawayo for domestic servants in the area who were unable to travel home. The neighborhood echoed with hymns and preaching, and it was almost certainly the only white neighborhood in Bulawayo—most likely, all of Rhodesia—with the soundtrack of an isiNdebele service every Sunday afternoon. Every school holiday my father would take me to stay in several villages in Matabeleland while he was finishing a PhD in anthropology and publishing an isiNdebele newspaper (*Ihawu*, "Shield"). My friends were the sons of these villages, and I learned to speak isiNdebele along with them.

In those villages I heard stories about the great amaNdebele kings Mzilikazi and Lobengula, who had fought the Zulus and established the kingdom of the Matabele. We sometimes went by the grave of Mzilikazi, whom I imagined lying in state, deep beneath the ground, wrapped in purple robes. I had read parts of the biblical books *Samuel* and *Kings*, and I conflated the amaNdebele kings with the kings of Israel. That started my first fascination with history: in my mind, kingship in Africa and Israel occupied the same time. My sense of history was further confused, or enriched, by visits to Khami, the ruins of a medieval city outside of Bulawayo, and Great Zimbabwe, now one of the most famous medieval sites in Africa.

And so I owe being a medievalist to Africa. I took a wrong turn, into Europe, to study its past. Over the years I have been asked repeatedly how I came to be a medievalist when I grew up in Africa. This book is my answer: precisely because I came from Africa. And in Europe's past I found Africa again, because there is so much of Africa in the world.

I
Ancient and Medieval

READING AFRICA

CHAPTER ONE

Egypt, the Exception

The *Ethiopians* likewise say, that the *Egyptians* are a Colony drawn out from them by *Osiris*; and that *Egypt* was formerly no part of the Continent, but a Sea at the beginning of the World.

DIODORUS SICULUS, *Bibliotheca Historica*

Africa, the Continent

Egypt is only in Africa every two years, goes a recurrent joke, when the Africa Cup of Nations is held. The Africa Cup was cofounded by Egypt. It has won the Cup more often than any other nation. Yet when other teams on the continent defeat Egypt, says the Egyptian diplomat Ahmed Haggag, fans lament that "an Egyptian team is defeated by an African one."[1] The contradiction is not just about winning and losing football games. It is about *how* Egypt belongs in Africa—and whether it does at all.

On the face of it, this question shouldn't need to be asked today. Egypt's 2014 Constitution describes Egypt as the "tip of Africa."[2] The second president of Egypt, Gamal Abdel Nasser, was an ardent Pan-Africanist who talked about Egypt as part of "our African land" and about a common "free and one African will."[3] That does not imply that Islam is not a profound part of Egyptian identity, or that Egypt's most predominant identity is not a part of the broader *Ummah* of Islam. There are many overlapping, even sometimes contradictory forms of identity for Egypt and Egyptians—in the modern era, in antiquity, even through the identities attributed to them in European history. Muslim identity need not exclude identity as an African. One of the leaders of the al-Azhar Mosque, one of Cairo's oldest and most important, was Ibrāhīm Niasse, who was also a Senegalese Pan-Africanist. "We are the people of Africa," he wrote in 1960, "so Africa belongs to us, and we belong to Africa."⁴ Much of what is indisputably Africa, indeed, belongs to Islam. There are now nearly as many Muslims in West Africa as there are in North Africa, and more Nigerian Muslims than there are Egyptian Muslims.⁵ Yet newspapers often report persistent racism in Egypt toward Black Africans. As one Egyptian journalist put it, "Egyptians even get offended if you refer to them as African."⁶ Egypt is an exception to Africa in cases that proceed on racial, not geographic, grounds. The vehemence with which that exception is defended suggests that it is less logical than fundamentally incoherent. Zahi Hawass, the charismatic former Minister of State for Antiquities Affairs, once defined that incoherence with paradoxical lucidity (he was defending, not criticizing, it): "Egyptians are . . . not Africans despite the fact that Egypt is in Africa."⁷

Egypt, in other words, is an exception to its geographical situation: its people do not belong to their continent. Hawass was primarily referring to ancient Egypt and its importance to the rest of the world. But behind his comment is a belief about Egypt that began to take hold in the modern era: that because ancient Egyptian culture is so important, it could not really belong to Africa.

My point in this chapter is not to prove the dialectical opposite of Hawass's argument—that, as Afrocentrists argue, Egyptian culture's roots are originally African (although that is where my sympathies lie). My point is that the very debate about where and what Egypt *is* ultimately concerns where, and what, Africa is to the rest of the world. In his magisterial book *The Invention of Africa*, V. Y. Mudimbe points out that the question of where Egypt is says more about the people who raise the question than it does about Egypt's actual location. But it also tells us what they think about Africa.

Egypt has been used for centuries to define what Africa is and is not. In our age, it tends to be a zero-sum choice: it is either the site from which Black African knowledge was disseminated to the world, or it is an exceptional place, the seat of civilization despite its location on an uncivilized continent. Again, Zahi Hawass: "The Ancient Egyptian civilisation did not occur in Africa, it occurred only here."⁸ Egypt, said the philosopher Hegel, is not "Africa proper"; Egypt "is as isolated and singular in Africa as Africa itself appears in relation to the other parts of the world."⁹ Egypt is an exception to an exception. Africa is unlike the rest of the world because of its absences. It "cannot be said to occupy a place in the intellectual history, or in the moral progress, of our species;"[10] "it is no historical part of the world" (Hegel, *History*, 117). It is "unlike" the world because it is *not*; not just different, but the negation (to use Hegel's term) of the world. Yet, to use Hegel's logic, that negation of the world is a way of defining the world, and, in this case, of defining Egypt as part of the intellectual history and moral progress of the world. Africa's limitations define what Egypt *is*: "Something is already transcended by the very fact of being determined as a restriction. For a determinateness, a limit, is determined as a restriction only in opposition to its other in general, that is, in opposition *to that which is without its restriction*; the other of a restriction is precisely the *beyond* with respect to it."[11] Egypt is what Africa is not.

Hegel has less abstract reasons for defining Africa as a limitation. It is the geography of the continent itself, he says, that keeps Africa "shut up." There is a belt of mountains that is difficult, if not impossible, to traverse. Sounding as if he got his information from the Roman poet Lucan's epic *Pharsalia*, which I will discuss in the third chapter, he says that there is a zone of "ravenous beasts" and "snakes of all kinds ... a border tract whose atmosphere is poisonous to Europeans" (*History*, 109). Here the stakes are suddenly clear: Africa is exactly what Europeans cannot tolerate, a geographical other that is also biological and philosophical. In that last phrase, "a border tract whose atmosphere is poisonous to Europeans," Hegel sums up the whole history of what Egypt has meant in relation to Africa, which will be the subject of this chapter. Hegel's summary—to turn his logic back on him—also includes, or even defines, what transcends it: the long history of Egypt as a part of Africa, and even an Africa that is more meaningful, more beneficial to Europeans than Egypt.

We will begin with Alexander the Great's encounter with Egypt and Africa.

Alexander the Great African

Alexandria may have been one of the most illustrious cities of the ancient world, but it was also a hasty stop on Alexander the Great's way to a place he found more important to his own journey. This place was not Europe, although a recent book describes him as the first European, the founder of Western culture.[12] This place was where Alexander founded himself as an institution, the man who was given a divine mandate to reshape the world. This place was in Africa.

It is not surprising that Alexander's act of founding Alexandria has overshadowed the importance of his African journey. Alexandria became the ancient world's preeminent intellectual center. It was not just the place where Plato's Athenian academy reconvened or where the Hebrew Bible was translated into Greek, but also the place where geniuses like Philo of Alexandria and Origen fused Jewish scholarship or Christian doctrine with Platonic allegory and pagan literature (both Greek and Egyptian), opening the way for diasporic Judaism and global Christianity. Western philosophy and literature are unthinkable without Alexandria. Its library contained (or tried to) all written knowledge in the Western hemisphere. It's for that reason that Alexander has been called the first European.

Writing more than 1,700 years after Alexandria was founded, the fifteenth-century Muslim historian al-Maqrizi believed that Alexandria was the city that the Qur'an refers to as a city "that has no like in the world."[13] During that 1,700 years, the fortunes of Alexandria ebbed and flowed, but under the Ptolemies it was the most active place in the world for philosophical and religious thinking. Alexandrian hermetic writings referred to the city as "the temple for the whole world";[14] the historian Dio Chrysostom called it the "crossroads of the whole world."[15] It is probably worth noting that Chrysostom said that standing in front of an audience of Alexandrians, although all of the surviving encomia to Alexandria's cosmopolitanism would fill a large anthology. Yet much, if not most, of the praise of Alexandria's contribution to the world comes from Hellenic writers.

Plutarch, one of the greatest historians and biographers of the ancient world, was also a priest of Apollo at Delphi. His fascination with Egyptian religion led him to write one of the most important sources for it, *On the Worship of Isis and Osiris*, in the first century CE. His main purpose is to write a syncretistic account of the inter-involvement of Greek and Egyptian religion, and at one point he warns Egyptians not to make exclusive, literally territorial, claims for their religion. The Egyptians should help to preserve "our gods that are common to both peoples" and should not "make them to belong to the Egyptians only, and do not include under these names the Nile alone and the land which the Nile waters, and do not assert that the marshes and the lotus are the only work of God's hand, and if they do not deny the great gods to the rest of mankind that possess no Nile nor Buto nor Memphis."[16]

Egyptians, apparently, are preventing their religion from bringing forth a truly universal religion (Plutarch goes on to say that nobody could deny that Isis, at least, is owned "by all peoples"). What Plutarch doesn't say explicitly is that Egyptians should no longer venerate the primal connection between the Nile and their oldest gods. The religion of the Egyptians, that is, will become universal only when it is no longer Egyptian, only when there is no longer an inseparable connection between the gods of Egypt and the territory of Egypt. Plutarch is full of praise for the contribution of Egypt to Greek religion, but only as long as Egyptians don't insist on tying their religion to Egypt.

The revolutionary thinker Frantz Fanon had a response for demands like Plutarch's. Colonized subjects who believe that they will gain dignity by aspiring to become members of a universal humanity, he says, are only capitulating to the destruction of their own local cultures and identities. Plutarch's call to Egyptians to loosen the bonds of their religion with their land is an extension of the original appropriation of Egypt by Alexander's armies, and the remaking of it by the Ptolemies into a new Hellenic domain. As Alain de Boulluec, an eminent scholar of Christian Alexandria, said, any "homage paid to the 'barbarians' [i.e., the Egyptians] was never entirely emptied of the violence they had suffered."[17] Egyptian religion held its preeminent place in the imaginations of devout Greeks and Romans everywhere only because it had been taken from the Egyptians. You no longer had to live near the Nile for your religion to have meaning. It was of Egypt, not in it—just as Alexandria, in the nomenclature of the Roman empire, was *ad Aegyptum*: at Egypt, not in it.

So: Alexandria transcended its place; it became universal. But that place was always highly unstable, both territorially and culturally, sitting on the fault line of theses and antitheses. Alexander marked it out, but its outline was immediately erased (he used barley meal to draw the lines, and birds gobbled it up).[18] Alexandria disappeared as soon as it had been conjured into existence. Even once it had been established, its place continued to be called into question. It was both in and not in Africa, lying, as the novelist E. M. Forster said eons later, "on the verge of civilisation." Not *in* civilization, although it was the first global *civis*, but on the edge of "an enormous desert of limestone that stretches into the heart of Africa."[19]

What Alexander did after founding Alexandria suggests that he wanted to establish himself precisely in that African desert stretching away from Alexandria. He journeyed deep into the Libyan desert, a journey that recapitulated a deep, mythical, history in which Libya, Greece, and Egypt are merged in a fluid whole—fluid, that is, both figuratively and literally. Egypt itself, says the historian Diodorus Siculus, "was formerly no part of the Continent, but a Sea at the beginning of the World."[20] Rivers, lakes, deltas, and the indeterminate nature of swamps interrupt attempts to fix boundaries once and for all. This chapter will show how myth and religion celebrate this very fluidity, a fluidity that has largely been lost in the modern era. The mythic fluidity of the region tends to be diverted into rigid channels: European modernity, in particular, has insisted that Egypt is either *part of* Africa, or *can never have been part*. A fluid Egypt: a fluid Africa.

Alexander's journey from Alexandria took him deep into Africa proper—600 kilometers away to the shrine of the god Ammon in the desert of Libya.[21] There Alexander asked the question that set the course of the rest of his life: whether he would rule the world. Ammon said, of course, that he would. But what Ammon added made Alexander even more excited: Alexander, Ammon said, was actually his son.[22]

Alexander: no longer the son of Philip of Macedon, if he ever was, but the son of a god in the distant African desert. For the rest of his life, Alexander identified as not just divine, but as a true—and not adopted—son of Ammon. Why Alexander wanted this to be true is one of the murkiest and most mysterious episodes of his life, and historians say the whole story is a secret that Alexander kept for the rest of his life. What we do know suggests that Alexander would have been unhappy to be identified as a European. He did not want to be the son of his Greek father Philip. But neither was he entirely and unequivocally Egyptian. He could have proclaimed himself the son of a more central Egyptian god, like Ra, whose honorary son he automatically became when he was proclaimed Pharaoh. His relative indifference to Egyptian religious and political tradition is remarkable, even revolutionary. For centuries, Greek thinkers had admired the complexity, profundity, and antiquity of Egyptian thought. When Solon, the founder of Athenian democracy, visited Egypt, a priest told him that the Greeks were children compared to the Egyptians because they had no ideas or traditions of their own.[23]

Alexander could simply have claimed to be the heir of ancient Egyptian traditions and left to conquer the rest of the world. But, crucially, he imagined that his legitimacy wasn't rooted in Egypt, and the most profound and consequential revelation of his identity and destiny would happen outside of Egypt, in Africa. I do not want to argue that Alexander drew a boundary between what was entirely "Egyptian" and entirely "African." Egypt was not *irrelevant* for him, as the founding of Alexandria attests. It's just that Egypt was not a watertight container with its mouth in Asia. Alexander's journey to the shrine of Ammon suggests that he imagined Africa and Egypt to be integral to each other, making up a continuum of common practices and beliefs.

The Libyan God of Europe

Ammon himself transcends, or blurs, the boundaries between Egypt and Africa—and with the Hellenic world. One of his superpowers as a god was the power of syncretism. He blended first with the quintessential god Ra, then, when the Greeks arrived, with Zeus. Before those grand syntheses, however, he was a highly revered god from several territories. He may have begun as a local Egyptian god in Thebes, where the massive Temple of Karnak was built to honor him. By the Eighteenth Dynasty (ca. 1550–1295 BCE) he had become virtually the national god of Egypt. But starting in the Sixteenth Dynasty, Egyptians traveled in increasing numbers to consult the oracle at Siwa in Libya.[24] Egyptians seem to have assumed that he had a powerful connection to other parts of Africa, too. Queen Hatshepsut traveled to Siwa for the blessing of Ammon before her expedition to Punt, now the Horn of Africa.[25] One of the reasons for her expedition was to open a trading route that bypassed Nubia, which controlled trade from Punt.

Ammon—or at least one part of his complex mythology—was also imagined as a Nubian god, as early as the reign of Rameses II in the Nineteenth Dynasty. To be precise, at first, Ammon was an Egyptian god *in* Nubia: when Rameses extended Egyptian territory far into the land of Kush, he built a temple to Ammon. After the Egyptians retreated to their traditional territory the site, Jebel Barkal (called Napata then), became a capital of the kingdom of Kush and the birthplace of the Twenty-Fifth Dynasty, a Nubian dynasty that ruled Egypt. The presence of Ammon in the Kushite capital became one of the foundations of Kushite political ideology, and one of the ways in which the Twenty-Fifth Dynasty legitimated its rule over all of Egypt. Ammon's most famous temple might have been at Karnak in Egyptian Thebes, but, says one stele, Ammon *lives* in Jebel Barkal. He was the first divine remote worker, the "god of Kush" who was worshipped in Egypt.

The myth that Ammon was a Nubian gained so much traction over time that by the Hellenic period writers referred to him as an "Ethiopian" who came from Meroë, a later capital of Kush even farther south than Napata.[26] Ammon became "originally" Nubian through a combination of myth and politics, a combination that the eminent twentieth-century sociologist Bronisław Malinowski referred to as a charter myth, a myth of origin or foundation that justifies political structures and customs. It's a kind of backstory that not only explains how things got to be the way they are, but also makes them seem too powerful, too ancient, or too transcendent to question. We will see later that charter myths are powerful even in the formation of postindependence African nations like Kenya. Ammon, in particular, was the focus of other important mythic charters in the Hellenic world. The most important is Alexander's declaration that he was Ammon's true son. But Alexander's mythic charter is just another version of a mythic charter involving Ammon written for, and by, the Greek city of Cyrene on the Libyan coast.

The great fifth-century BCE Greek lyric poet Pindar wrote three odes that mention Ammon of Libya. These odes are an important literary archive of the importance of Africa as a mythic place for Greek culture, and they hint at the backstory of the creation of Ammon as a god who is both Libyan and Greek. These odes celebrate the triumph of athletes from Cyrene, a colony on the coast of Libya, at the Pythian Games in Delphi. The beginning of one ode makes it clear that Cyrene is not just an expatriate bubble on the African coast. Its territory extends far south into the Libyan desert: to be precise, as far as the Temple of Ammon at Siwa.

These three odes together tell the story of Cyrene's mythic foundation, and in doing so reveal the persistence of Africa in the Greek mythic and literary imagination. The Fourth Pythian Ode is also the first example of a profoundly important theme in epic literature that we will explore later: landing in Africa. It riffs on an episode in the story of Jason and the Argonauts, in which their ship was stranded on the sands of Libya. The Argonauts carried it on their backs for twelve days to a lake (named Trito) that opened onto the ocean. That journey became the founding myth of the colony of Cyrene. The journey alone was not the myth, however; it was the parade of extraordinary mythical and divine figures that the journey conjures, from mysterious "daughters and warders of Libya" to Athena, Poseidon, and Hercules, all of whom have backstories that link their lives to both Libya and Greece. Indeed, the journey is an itinerary of mythic and divine acts that establish the importance of Libya overall in Greek myth and religion. Libya is named for the daughter of the Titan Oceanus (her sister was Asia).[27] Libya is an important site in many other ways: it was the birthplace of Athena, at Lake Trito; the location of a tree with golden apples, in the Garden of the Hesperides, that the goddess Gaia gave to Hera; the domain of Medusa.[28]

This is the background for Pindar's Ninth Pythian Ode, in which Cyrene becomes the central node of all of these myths. It recalls how the Argonaut Ephemus was given a clod of earth by a mysterious figure (a "solitary god," in one translation, a *daemon*) at Lake Trito, which he later loses overboard once the *Argo* is back at sea. Yet it is not lost: it merges with the sea and becomes "the deathless seed of broad Libya."[29]

This strange story about a piece of dirt echoes a recurrent chthonic theme in the foundation of ancient cities: the myth of the earth-born (*terrigenae*) who helped Cadmus build the Greek city of Thebes, or Kekrops, the hybrid creature born from the earth who founded Athens. It also recalls a relatively recent political trauma, the Persian emperor Darius's demand for a gift of earth and water from all of the Greek city states. Gifts of earth are a synecdoche of possession, so that the solitary god who gives Euphemus that clod is handing over the entire land of Libya to him. To be pedantic, Libya was handed to his fairly distant descendants, not to him. But mythic roots always tell a better, more primordial story and make a far more interesting case for possession of a land than the abstract philosophical ones that the European colonizers of Africa would make centuries later (with some gobsmacking exceptions, as with Great Zimbabwe).

The myth of the dirt clod does sound like an etiology, a retrospective justification for what looks, essentially, like the colonization of Libya by Greeks. And it probably is. In the Ninth Ode, "Queen Libya" gives the newly arrived nymph Cyrene "a portion of land to flourish with her as her lawful possession." Yet the founding myths of Cyrene attest to something that later ideologies of colonization do not: that the land before they arrived was charged with equal, if not superior, divinity and culture. The long historical chain from Euphemus to the actual building of the city was initiated by the "solitary god." Pindar's Ninth Pythian Ode implies yet another version of the founding myth, in which Apollo falls in love with the nymph Cyrene and takes her to Africa, where "queen Libya" is either the daughter of Oceanus or the personification of the land itself.

But the land is not empty, the terra nullius that European colonizers claimed to find throughout the world. Libya already has "golden halls" that shelter Apollo and Cyrene. The myth suggests that Cyrene, who preferred to spend her time hunting beasts in the forests of Thessaly, has been civilized by Africa.

Yet even Pindar's version of the mythic charter of Cyrenian dominance over Libya does not imagine that the arrival of the nymph Libya marked the beginning of civilization in the land of Libya. There may, indeed, have been no beginning in the strict sense, because Libya's history fades beyond time into the realm of divinity. In the Ninth Ode, the nymph Libya is imagined as yet another of the founders of the city of Cyrene, although somewhat distantly, as the person who was the root of the city that would eventually flower. She would eventually be "planted," says the Ode, in a land that had older foundations still. It did not yet have a name, or the name was so thoroughly overwritten by Libya's that it was forgotten. The Ode describes the land as the "sacred precinct" (θεμέθλοις) of Zeus Ammon (Dionysius of Alexandria might echo this when he describes "the precinct of the Libyan god, beneath thick sand").[30] This does not mean that Cyrene was founded on the precise site of the temple of Ammon, but that the cultural and religious institutions of Cyrene and Libya are founded on Ammon. Pindar probably did not mean that literally. Cyrene was very obviously a part of the Greek diaspora, and maintained close ties with Greece. Pindar's odes to Cyrenians victorious in the sacred games in Greece tell us that. At the same time, however, Pindar imagines that Cyrene and Libya are also fundamentally African because of their relation to Ammon. The "sacred precinct" that Pindar describes is the oracle of Ammon at Siwa.

Siwa is, as one study of the Fourth Ode says, "far beyond the Greek zone of settlement."[31] So why did Pindar not only include it, but also make it the very foundation, the base and the boundary of Cyrene and Libya (all meanings included in θεμέθλοις)? Why no Egyptian gods? Because Cyrene, a city founded by Greeks with African roots, and a city culturally part of the Greek diaspora, imagined itself opening onto Libya, and Libya opened onto Africa. The central Temple of the Oracle at Siwa was, in fact, built and designed by Greeks between 570 and 526 BCE. It's likely that the Greeks saw the Oasis of Siwa as a gateway to trade with the rest of Africa, but their investment in the temple opened up Libyan Ammon to the Greek pantheon, and before long he was interchangeable with the greatest Greek god.³² Ammon's shrine at Siwa may have been established by Egyptians, but in Pindar's work he is represented as a primordial presence, located at Siwa since time immemorial. This appeal to immemorial time is one of the tropes of the mythic charter, which sweeps aside any remnants of indigenous claims in favor of a transcendent origin for, and legitimation of, the right of occupiers. Ammon, who was a primordial god in the Egyptian and then the Nubian pantheon, has become a primordial god in the political theology of Cyrene.

Siwa, as a metonym for Libya—Africa—was a space that transcended mere place. The shrine contained the multiple beginnings of the god Ammon, a complex god worthy of being Alexander's father. It contains the beginning point of Alexander's eventual control of the *saeculum*, temporal dominion over much of the earth. Political power has a single point of origin because it insists on it, but stories have multiple beginnings. Ammon is the father of Alexander's divine mandate, but a father who has multiple background stories, stories that include Egypt, North Africa, Greece, Ethiopia, Nubia, and the source of the Nile. And it was from there that Alexander set out to make history. The moment when Ammon adopts Alexander makes the whole Alexander story a kind of repetition, the mirrored reflection of the multiple traditions that come together in Ammon, and Alexander's bringing together the multitudes of the known world into a single empire, collapsing a multitude of places into a single mixed, heterogeneous space.

But that didn't solve the question of where Egypt was. Egypt was fundamentally important to world history, yet slippery, like a bar of soap that Africa, Europe, and Asia have struggled to grasp.

The Fluid Land

For some ancient historians, Egypt began with Africa, or Ethiopia, as they called it. In fact, for some of them *everything* began with Ethiopia. Diodorus Siculus, a Sicilian working in Alexandria, says that the first people were Ethiopians, who were generated from the earth by the sun, which is hottest in Ethiopia. Egypt was, in fact, he reports, first populated by Ethiopians led by Osiris, who founded a colony. These colonists are the first of a number of groups that eventually became melded into the people known as the Egyptians. Diodorus insists that his sources say that the Egyptians *are* the Ethiopian colonists. There could not have been Egyptians ab initio in Egypt because, Diodorus points out, there was no Egypt. There was no territory at all where the Nile eventually deposited enough silt to form the Delta.

Classical geographers wrestled with the problem of Egypt's place, although without the rancor that the question stirs up in the modern era. The line between Egypt and Africa, or Egypt and Asia, or Africa and Asia, moves back and forth. Their answers tended to be either pragmatic or arbitrary, as if it didn't matter a great deal what feature of the landscape you chose as the boundary. The geographer Strabo thought that it was so obvious that Egypt belonged in and with Africa that he never actually said that it was. His *Geography* is full of assumptions that Egypt, Aethiopia, and Libya belong together.[33] Somewhat counterintuitively, Strabo's complicated description of the inhabited African continent is introduced with a description that shows how close the east coast of Africa is to Arabia. This orientation holds together a long and somewhat fidgety itinerary, and his opinion of where Africa is almost depends on where he is at the moment. After his description of Egypt and Ethiopia, which, confusingly, begins in the chapter on the Arabian Peninsula, he stitches back and forth across the Red Sea to compare points in Arabia with points in Egypt and Ethiopia. He then swoops south in Africa down to the farthest known inhabited land he knows about: the "country of the cinnamon-bearers," the Somali peninsula—the Horn of Africa. He says that he "must now set forth the remaining parts that are continuous with these tribes, that is, the parts in the neighbourhood of the Nile" (Bk. 17.1, 3). His account travels up the Nile all the way to its mouths in the Delta and then describes each of the regions of Egypt, starting with Alexandria, where he was writing the *Geography*. At the end of the survey of Egypt, he reminds us that we ought to think of the whole zone of the Nile as one unit: "The description [of Ethiopia] may be said to be included with that of Aegypt" (Bk. 17.2, 141).

Two Alexandrians, who presumably had a better idea than most of where Egypt was, wrote geographical texts that became some of the most influential through the Middle Ages. Claudius Ptolemy, a polymath best known for his theory that the earth lay at the center of the universe, produced the first atlas to use latitude and longitude. It was probably translated into Arabic in the ninth century, and its Latin translation in the early fifteenth century tempted Columbus to think that he could sail west to reach Asia. To the detriment of the Americas, Ptolemy's placement of the earth at the center of the universe was not his only mistake. Yet his was the first ambitious attempt at a "real" atlas, one that shows where cities and natural features (8,000 of them) lie in a world that we can still recognize. Following his atlas, enthusiasts have been able to plot the coordinates of almost all the places he mentions. His placement of Egypt: in Africa, because the Gulf of Suez divides Africa from Arabia. It simply makes more sense, Ptolemy says, to use seas rather than rivers to divide one continent from another.[34]

The other Alexandrian, Dionysius of Alexandria, wrote a text around 125 CE that was less important for travelers, but more important for the educated European's idea of the world. His *Guide to the Inhabited World* circulated widely as a textbook, first in Greek, because its elegant hexameters exemplified a useful range of rhetorical tropes and grammar. The man who wrote the book on Latin grammar, Priscian, translated the *Guide* in the sixth century into Latin, presumably because he thought it would work the same pedagogical magic in Latin classrooms. Dionysius tends to use bodies of water to chart the world. Africa, he says, is called "Libya" because the part of the Mediterranean called the Libyan Sea touches the coast of Africa. Charting the course of the Nile, which he believes rises in the Atlas Mountains, Dionysius literally and metaphorically describes how Libya flows into Egypt, following the course of the Nile: it "creeps from Libya to the east," changing its name from "Siris" as it flows to the "Nile." At that point, the Nile becomes the boundary between Libya and Asia. He doesn't say where Alexandria, which is on the Libyan side of the divide, belongs, but he does put in a plug for its world-historical importance, since the "race of illustrious men" who live there were the first "to distinguish the ways of life" and "to divide the heavens with lines."[35] Alexandria: where the books that divvy up the world are written.

By the time there was enough land in Egypt to be worth colonizing, the Ethiopians had already developed a complex and sophisticated set of political and religious practices, which Diodorus recounts in detail. It all began, though, with what Diodorus says the Ethiopians were the first to discover (or to have shown to them): theology. The very concept of honoring the gods, and the varied sacrifices, processions, and festivals "by which men honor the deity," began with the Ethiopians. Indeed, most Egyptian religious practices (this is presumably what Diodorus means by "νομίμων," observances) are simply the old practices of the Ethiopians.³⁶ Diodorus gives a number of examples, including the Egyptian reverence of kings as gods; the hats worn by the kings; the special care Egyptians take with burials; the shapes of their statues; and the use of hieroglyphics. Diodorus does not have much to say about these, and he trails off near the end ("there is no special need" to write anything more).

Herodotus, the so-called father of history, defined Egypt according to the history of religion in the area. What makes the difference between an Egyptian and Libyan, says Herodotus, is ritual practice. He says that the inhabitants of Marea and Apis, two cities on the border (wherever that is) between Libya and Egypt, decided they wanted to worship the gods of Libya because they were tired of not being allowed to eat the meat that they sacrificed. They "sent to Ammon saying that they had no part of or lot with Egypt: for they lived (they said) outside the Delta and did not consent to the ways of its people, and they wished to be allowed to eat all foods. But the god forbade them: all the land, he said, watered by the Nile in its course was Egypt, and all who lived lower down than the city Elephantine and drank the river's water were Egyptians. Such was the oracle given to them."³⁷

The internal contradictions of establishing the place of Egypt, or the limits of Africa: a gesture that illustrates, again, the tangle of logic that seems to trip up anyone who thinks about Egypt's place in Africa. If the people of Marea and Apis want to reject the Egyptian gods, then why do they accept an African god's command to obey them?

It's the only possible answer a god could give. It's the inverse of the liar's paradox ("I always lie"): disobedience is obedience to the permission to disobey Ammon. Ammon sounds more like a lawyer than a mysterious, enigmatic deity. Although the people of the two cities do not speak the "tongue of the Egyptians," nor do they live in the Delta, they are Egyptians, he says, because "Egypt was the entire tract of country which the Nile overspreads and irrigates." They cannot, therefore, be Libyans, and must continue the ritual practices that he commands.

The implication of this story is that, on the one hand, it is *not* the command of a god that establishes Egypt but the flooding of the Nile. That flooding may, of course, be the work of a god (Isis or Hapi), but Herodotus doesn't say anything about that. Egyptian identity is determined by geography; yet it is also, at the same time, determined by ritual practice. Neither ritual nor territory are sufficient on their own.

Egypt in Medieval Europe

The clearest conviction about where Egypt was located came from medieval thinkers who cared less about the nuances of geography than about the design of the entire world. This conceptual kind of geography was highly influential, because it appeared in the most popular medieval encyclopedias.

These were often compiled by a single person, like Isidore of Seville, a sixth-to-seventh-century Spanish bishop who explained the nature of objects and places by tracing the sources of their names (his encyclopedia is thus known as *The Etymologies*). The pelican, for instance, which is found in Egypt, gets its name from Canopos, an older name for Egypt. Not unusually for Isidore, this was wrong on several scores: Canopos is a mouth of the Nile, and the word "pelican" derives from the Greek πέλεκυς, or hatchet.[38] For Isidore, and everyone except the most pedantic scholars, the world was a beautiful, divine place because it was laid out precisely according to the words with which God uttered it into being. Once we discover how important language is in understanding the world—it is a kind of map of the universe—the other branches of learning will teach us more, and allow us to master it fully. From the beginning the discipline was abstract. Geometry was invented, says Isidore, by the Egyptians because they needed a way to chart and measure the land when it was flooded by the Nile (Bk. 3.13.1, 93). Geometry is a way of conceptualizing land whether or not it is there.

So the map Isidore bequeathed, generally called a "T-O map," was a *conceptual* map, on which the three known continents, Africa, Asia, and Europe, were divided by what looks like a capital T; all three lie within the large O of the world (figure 1). It's a confident vision of the neatness of the world that reduces it to two letters, the basic elements of language. The map was popularized, after all, in an encyclopedia that described everything by its first appearance in language.

These maps place Jerusalem in the center, where the three continents, the three strokes of the capital "T," join. The mouth of the Mediterranean (Gibraltar) is the bottom of the "T." Europe is to the left, Africa is to the right. Asia takes up the entire space above the "T." The right-hand stroke of the "T," which separates Africa and Europe, is the Nile. The basic T-O maps do not include "provinces" (Isidore's term) like Egypt, so it's not possible to tell whether half of Egypt belongs to each continent. The

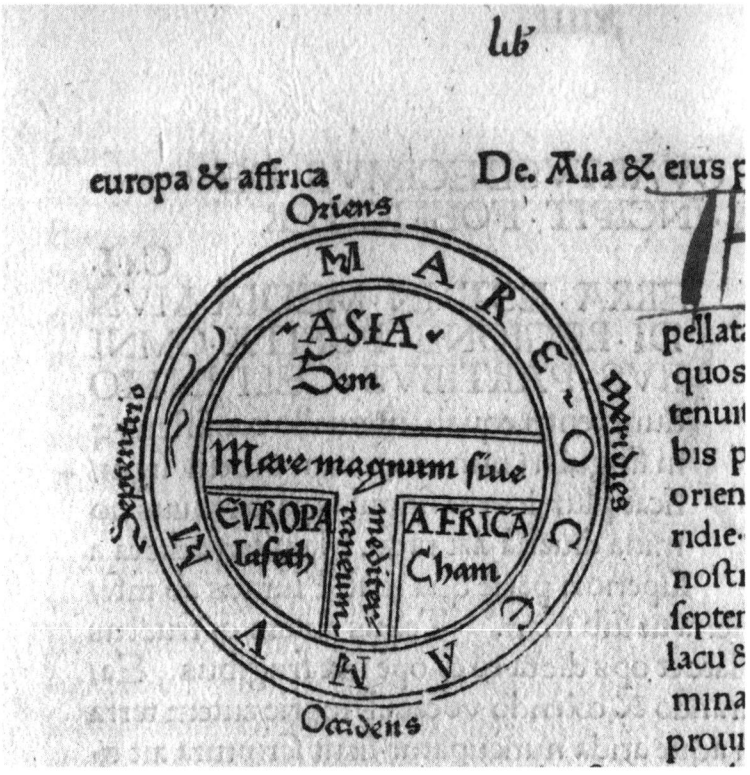

FIGURE 1 · Mappamundi from Saint Isidore of Seville, *Etymologia* (1473).

T-O maps probably don't care, because their purpose is to illustrate the underlying design of the world, how the T and the O are the initials of the very thing that they make up: the *orbis terrarum*, the orb of the earth.

The text of Isidore's encyclopedia puts Egypt explicitly in Asia, along with its miscellaneous provinces, rivers, and towns. Libya, he says, is to Egypt's west. The Canopus mouth of the Nile (the mouth furthest to the west, where Alexandria was founded) marks the end (*finis*) of Egypt and the beginning (*principium*) of Libya (Bk. 14.3.28, 287). Other medieval encyclopedias, such as Ranulf Higden's mid-fourteenth-century *Polychronicon*, tend to back up what Isidore said: that Egypt and Africa are separate. They often include sources other than Isidore. Higden paraphrases the assertion in Pliny the Elder's first-century CE *Natural History* that Africa goes from the West to the boundary of Egypt (*in meridiem* [to the south] *usque in finem Aegypti*).[39] The massive Ebstorf Map, which at twelve feet square was the largest medieval map by far

Egypt, the Exception

until it was destroyed in World War II, integrates quotes like these under the labels for major map features. Under "Africa," the short texts say that the continent stretches from the Nile to the south and west. On most maps, the label "Egypt" appears on the other side of the Nile from Libya/Africa (that is, on the north side). Confident identifications like this are probably why many scholars, even those who work in cartography, assume that everyone in the medieval West thought that Egypt was in Asia, not in Africa.

Yet even in these texts and maps, it is not completely clear where Egypt, in fact, *is*. Even more, it's not always clear where Africa, Asia, and Egypt all begin and end. This is not just because maps might put the boundary in different places. They often seem strategically unclear. Isidore of Seville himself describes different boundaries in another work, *De Natura Rerum*. The Canopic mouth of the Nile, he says, is the boundary between (*disterminat*) Asia and Libya, "with Egypt" (*cum Aegypto*). If this sounds ambiguous, it is: it could mean that "just Libya and Egypt" or that "Asia *and* Libya *and* Egypt all together" decide the border. In the first case, Egypt is in Libya; in the second, Egypt is in *both* Libya and Asia.[40]

Often the same map contains internal contradictions. On the Ebstorf map, Alexandria stands on the east side of the Nile—but the Nile runs from a point almost all the way across Asia, in the *east*. To get around that problem, the Ebstorf map puts the boundary of Africa at Mount Catabathmos, the town of Sallum on the modern border of Libya and Egypt. In other words, the Ebstorf map has to mingle features of Africa with features of Asia, as the course of the Nile runs east. The descriptions of peoples along the Nile in Asia include not only Africans—the Libyans and Ethiopians—but also, in the same group, Egyptians.[41] That mingling either implies that Egyptians were like Libyans and Ethiopians because they were neighbors, although on different continents, or that they are mingled together because they belong to the same territory and the same *ethnos*, the same group of peoples. Either way, the people of Egypt were considered part of the people of Africa, just as in some texts Egypt and Ethiopia were considered the same.[42]

Hugh of St. Victor, an influential twelfth-century theologian, wrote a description of the world that may have been the directions for a world map. Like a good teacher, which he was (he wrote a widely distributed textbook called the *Didascalicon*, which urges students to "learn everything"), he gives the mapmakers options, especially when it comes to

Africa. Writers, he says, sometimes use the names Libya, Africa, Ethiopia, and Egypt interchangeably for the entire southern part of the continent.[43] Egypt, that is, could be as much as three-quarters of the entire continent—at the very least, it is a part of Africa.

Placing Egypt in Asia sometimes upsets the placement of other parts of Africa—particularly in the cases of Nubia and Ethiopia. Some maps and descriptions of the world say that there are two Ethiopias: one in Africa, another in Asia (in the region of Saudi Arabia).[44] That might be the reason the Ebstorf maps and others route the Nile through Asia. But—and here's another internal contradiction—when they do that the source of the Nile is something called the "Gates of Nubia" (*porte Nibie*); the Sawley Map adds the Mountains of Nubia (*Montes Nibie*).[45]

This Nubia, however, is not some mythical city in Asia. Near it is an island in the Nile called "Merohen," or Meroë—the capital of the kingdom of Kush (or, in the Bible, "Cush"), in Nubia. To confuse things slightly, Meroë is sometimes described as the capital of Ethiopia. It could be the Ethiopia in the east: there *is* an Ethiopia on the far southeast of Asia on the Ebstorf and Sawley maps. But Greek, Roman, and Jewish writers left a large archive of evidence that Meroë was always in *African* Ethiopia. Herodotus described Meroë as the capital of Ethiopia, a land that lies fifty-two days south of Egypt, "on the Libyan coast of the southern sea" (Bk. 2.29, 307; Bk. 3.17, 25).

Herodotus mentions Ethiopia because it was a target of the Persian king Cambyses II. Before his invasion, which failed disastrously, he sent spies to the Ethiopian court. What they reported eventually became, in Herodotus's history, the first full—though fabulous—description of Ethiopian culture. Ethiopians have a vast table of meat in a field from which anyone can eat; they live 120 years; they wash in a spring that smells like violets; they restrain their prisoners with gold chains; they use porcelain coffins. Some of these details found their way into Samuel Johnson's fantasy about Ethiopia, *Rasselas, Prince of Abyssinia*.[46]

Moses the African

Herodotus's account of Cambyses's campaign against Ethiopia also had an afterlife in biblical history and interpretation through the Middle Ages. It explains a small but strange detail in the Book of Numbers. Near the beginning of the forty years that the Israelites spend in the wilderness, Moses's brother Aaron and his sister Miriam try to claw back some power from him by accusing him of miscegenation: he has married a Cushite wife. The Bible says nothing about how this happened. There is no backstory, and she is not mentioned again.

How did Moses, a prince of Egypt and the leader of the Israelites, meet a Cushite woman? In Josephus's history of the Jewish people, *The Antiquities of the Jews*, he implicitly compares Moses's journey to Cush to Cambyses's invasion. (Josephus, like other Greek- and Latin-speaking authors, uses the word "Ethiopian," which the Alexandrian translators of the Hebrew Bible into Greek had used).[47] Josephus's account sounds like a mini-quest in a medieval romance. After Ethiopians invade Egypt, the Pharaoh makes Moses his general. The army sets out for Meroë, but overland rather than up the Nile. No one had done that before, because it meant crossing a region filled with keen-eyed snakes that spring out of the ground and can fly through the air. Moses brought with him cages containing ibises, the natural enemies of the snakes, which scared the snakes away. When Moses reaches the Ethiopian capital (at this point called Saba, although Josephus says Cambyses renamed it Meroë),[48] the king's daughter falls in love with him and gives him the city in exchange for marriage.[49] The episode got picked up in Peter Comestor's *Historia Scholastica*, one of the most popular paraphrases of the Bible in the Middle Ages.[50]

That is the backstory of Moses's Ethiopian wife. The whole episode doesn't change much about the history of Moses or of the Israelites in Egypt. That was done by a later medieval Hebrew commentary that turned Moses's adventures in Ethiopia into not only a longer episode but also one that radically recenters the story of Moses in Africa. The *Sefer Hayashar*, or *The Book of Jasher*, is a medieval history of Israel from creation to the conquest of Canaan that fills in many of the gaps in the Torah's history. It turns Moses's adventures in Cush into one of the most important parts of his biography.[51] Instead of fleeing to the land of Midian, as he does in Exodus, Moses, at the age of eighteen, flees to Cush, where he joins a Cushite army besieging a rebellious city. After nine years, the Cushite king dies; Moses is made his successor and uses the ibis stratagem to chase away the snakes that defend the city. In this version, it takes a while: the Cushites have to train the ibises from birth. Moses clearly had time to burn in Cush. In fact, Moses stayed in Cush longer than he ever stayed anywhere else: nine years in the siege, and forty years ruling Cush after that. Moses led the Cushites for as long as he led the Israelites; he lived in Cush more than twice as long as he lived in Egypt. That history explains why Aaron's and Miriam's accusation about Moses marrying a Cushite woman has some traction. Moses is, at that point, just a short time into the Israelites' forty-year journey to Canaan, more Cushite than Hebrew, and more Cushite than Egyptian.

To get around this problem, the *Sefer Hayashar* makes Moses a hero of abstinence, refusing to sleep with his Cushite wife as if he already knows the prohibitions in Exodus against marrying foreign women. But in many other ways, the *Sefer Hayashar* entangles Moses even more deeply in Africa. Its history of Moses's reign in Cush is interrupted by a chapter on war in the rest of Africa. It's a phantasmagoric concentration of important events over the course of 1,200 years: it wraps up Aeneas's stay in Carthage, the Punic Wars, and the Vandal invasion in a single campaign. At this point, the life of Moses becomes a full-fledged history of Africa, both at that moment and across the span of time.

Moses's Ethiopian wife may have been an insignificant detail in the Bible. But by the later Middle Ages, she was at the center of a history that made Egypt and Israel unthinkable without Africa. Rather than explain away, or ignore, the minor Cushite detail in the story of the Exodus, later readers made the role of Cush/Ethiopia—and of Africa—larger and larger. When histories were rewritten in the Middle Ages, Africa often underwent this kind of legendary amplification.

The Old English *Exodus* (ca. tenth century) narrates the Israelites' voyage to the Red Sea and the drowning of Pharaoh's army when they cross it. The Bible plots as many as forty-two points where the Israelites stop, although it doesn't give much information about any of them. The Old English *Exodus*, however, turns this into a heroic battle against a city that stands in their way to the Red Sea. Like Cato's army marching across Libya (about which more later), Moses's army negotiates hazardous terrain on their way, skirting the land to their south where the people are burned brown "by the heated heaven-coal." This is the land of the Ethiopians, a name that in Greek (Αἰθιοπία) means "the burned-face people." Framing the Israelite campaign against the backdrop of a hazardous Ethiopia is certainly a *version* of Moses's apocryphal campaign against the Ethiopians, except without the snakes.

The Old English term for Ethiopians, *sigelwara*, suggests that Ethiopia and Ethiopians conjured almost literal rich associations for an Old English audience.[52] The word is sometimes translated literally as "sun-dweller," but *sigel* also implies a jewel: so sun-jewel dwellers, a mini-puzzle of the kind that Old English literature loves. J. R. R. Tolkien wrote a famous essay on the Old English phrase ("Sigelwara Land") that suggests that there is a wealth of philological and cultural history buried in it—although, he says, we can't now know precisely what it all means.[53] What's not as buried in his essay is a slow-building racism that concludes that the term connotes devilish people "with red-hot eyes that emitted sparks, with faces black as soot."[54] Tolkien might be revealing the racism tangled in European philology itself, in the imaginations of Old English poets, or just his own: one of the most malevolent creatures in *The Lord of the Rings* is the Balrog, a fire-demon shrouded in darkness. It's almost as if Tolkien, although technically an African himself (born in South Africa), pushes Africa into the darkness. In his translation of the Old English *Exodus*, he changes the unambiguous word "African" to "Hebrew." It's a reading that makes superficial sense but erases altogether what Africa means to the story.

At the poem's moment of triumph, just after the Israelites have crossed the Red Sea and Pharaoh's army has been drowned, an African women draped with gold appears.

> It was then easy to find an African woman on the ocean shore
> worthied with gold. Their hands heaving up a necklace,
> they were blithe, seeing their reward, possessing the war-booty—
> their captivity was broken. The sea-surviving began to dole out
> among the tribes on the shore the ancient treasures, spoils and shields.
> She divided up the gold and good cloth by rights, Joseph's riches,
> the glory-possessions of men. Their keepers lay in the death-field,
> the greatest band of people (580–90)[55]

This moment has been a crux in Old English scholarship for a long time. There's no biblical basis for that episode. Most explanations make the African woman an allegory of the church, gathered out of the nations, or the Bride of the Song of Songs. One answer has been that this African woman is the Cushite wife of Moses, but that has been a dead end: why would she show up right then and there?

Mary Dockray-Miller, an Old English scholar, reads the presence of the African woman in terms of what racial difference might have meant to an Anglo-Saxon audience, and sympathetically imagines how the line would have resonated with a person of color in the audience.[56] As with the term *sigelwara* for Ethiopians, the African woman indicates an interest in the complex presence of Ethiopia in biblical and cultural history. In fact, the Old English *Exodus* uses the term *sigelhearwenan* for Moses's wife.[57]

Moses's Ethiopian life was one solution to the question of how he came to have an African wife. The Old English *Exodus* excises, but implies, this backstory, and by doing so makes the presence of the African woman more significant: that is, it signifies numerous things that the fleeting reference to the Cushite wife might not—including the mystery of whether *this* African woman is the Cushite woman herself. One way to understand the abrupt arrival of the African woman—it's both unanticipated and unprecedented in accounts of the Exodus—is, as Dockray-Miller argues, that she embodies racial difference. She confronts Israelite cultural and racial complacency with the "costs of triumph and treasure." And not only the Israelites, of course: the early medieval audience, too, who are reminded of the "lingering horror and violence . . . of war."[58] Indeed, she carries with her the kind of historical and racial trauma that we would recognize after the era of racialized slavery in our time.

But it's not clear that the African woman is a pathological figure. She, and her gold, are the occasion for further celebration. Her arrival marks the *end* of the Israelites' captivity (*hæft was onsealed*). The wealth she brings with her also suggests the complex forms of social organization that the Law will shortly give to the nation of Israel. The poem ends with the Israelites distributing the wealth "by right" (*on riht*), protocols of division that will be the subject of much of the rest of the Torah. The wealth also does not seem to be *just* gold plundered from the Egyptians, but an ancient (*eald*) treasure, which may or may not be the same as Joseph's treasure (*gestreon*). At least part of their treasure is theirs by right of ancestral possession, perhaps even the treasure *of* ancestry. It turns out, in the biblical book of Exodus, that the Israelites also carried with them the body of Joseph, to be buried once they arrived at Shechem. Shechem was where God first promised Abraham that he would give the land of Israel to his descendants (Genesis 12:6).

The African woman suggests (not only) destruction, but (also) an archive of historical wealth: of Israelite covenantal history, of the wealth that Joseph built in Egypt, and of the wealth of Africa. Indeed, another African woman she suggests is the legendary Queen of Sheba, whom

Egypt, the Exception   45

Josephus believed was the queen of Ethiopia. Her visit to Solomon during his reign dazzled the court with its opulence, and she came to be identified with the "black and/but beautiful" Beloved of the Song of Solomon. In the Ethiopian *Glory of Kings*, the *Kebra Nagast*, the Queen of Ethiopia's son with Solomon, Menelik I, became the legendary founder of the Solomonic Dynasty, which lasted until Haile Selassie, and the founding, in turn, of Rastafarianism.

The appearance of the African woman is also a celebration of Africanness, of the indispensable role Africa, or Ethiopia, or Cush had played in the deliverance of the people of Israel, and of Africa's ineradicable presence on the world stage. She is a figure of deliverance, not of the dangers of paganism or miscegenation or captivity—or even merely of difference. It's at that moment that the Israelites realize that their "captivity is broken." Her wealth is a kind of condensation of all that Moses had gone through in rescuing the Israelites. It recalls the vast pile of riches that the Cushites donated to Moses when they crowned him king,[59] the "Egyptian gold" that was repurposed to make the vessels in the Temple (and that became a metaphor for the way that Christians could read pagan philosophy), and the bounty that is freedom itself.

The point is that the presence of an African woman among the Israelites—and by extension in an Old English poem—is not surprising, and does not need to be spelled out. That might be why the poem says that the African woman was "easy to find" (*e[th]fynde*): she's either easy to see because she is African, or it is easy to understand why she might be present at that moment. In either case—whether finding something easily implicates racial difference or hermeneutics—at the moment that the Israelites leave Egypt behind, the wealth of Africa appears in their midst. The African woman is also a reminder of how, in the Middle Ages, Moses becomes *more* embedded in Africa than the glancing reference in Numbers to his Cushite wife. But Moses is far from the only world-historical figure to whom this happens.

One of the lessons of the literary afterlife of the African Moses story is that even passing references to Africa in legendary, mythical, or historical accounts of founding figures of Western culture become *more* extensive and integral to their stories, not less. The story of Alexander is perhaps the clearest and most extensive example of how this happened. His brief encounter with the Libyan god Ammon was already an important—and as we have seen, foundational—part of his biography, even shortly after his death. But in the massive literature about Alexander that developed in the next centuries, Africa's role became even more extensive.

Alexander's African Romance

One of the most popular narratives in the Middle Ages was the story of Alexander's conquest of the "world." It came out of a vast archive of stories about Alexander, some derived from his actual deeds, many completely made up. These were not biographies so much as sprawling imaginative episodes, often referred to collectively with the German term *Alexanderroman*. It spread through much of the known world well into the Middle Ages.[60] The only book in Europe that was translated more than the Alexander Romance was the Gospels. There are versions of it—to name a few—in Syriac, Persian, Hebrew, Armenian, Arabic, Middle Mongolian, and Ge'ez ("Ethiopic," as it was sometimes called), and every medieval European vernacular language. There are often multiple translations and versions in the same language. Some of it is echoed in the Talmud. An Old English version of one part of it—Alexander's letter to Aristotle—is in the same codex as *Beowulf*.[61] Alexander emerges as a complex figure, someone who embodies important but sometimes contradictory aspects of late medieval European culture. In some versions of the Romance, such as the *Roman d'Alexandre*, he appears as what Jonathan Morton describes as an "icon of princely or military power"; in others, he is a bloodthirsty tyrant or a sly, devious trickster.[62] But he is also associated with the transmission and spread of knowledge, both arcane and scientific, from Arabic and earlier Greek (and Egyptian) hermetic writing.[63] The Alexander Romance and its associated texts, along with the art that they inspired, reached almost as far and as deep as the world religions of the era, and further than Alexander's empire itself.

The Alexander Romance itself appears in so many forms and folds that it makes most sense to think of it as the Alexander Universe. Along with sober instruction and philosophy, it includes episodes with Alexander the superhero, under the sea in a diving bell, flying to the moon in a chair carried by birds, and building a wall to keep apocalyptic monsters from destroying the earth. Yet one thing that all the versions of the Romance have in common is that they make Alexander's involvement with Africa more extensive and profound than it is in the standard "canonical" history that we've already discussed. The Ethiopian version makes him a conqueror of almost the entire continent of Africa. It barely mentions

Egypt, except as the site of Alexandria and one of the three regions of Africa he conquered, along with Nubia and Ethiopia itself.[64] On the other hand, the Ethiopian version doesn't have Alexander go to Ammon's shrine: he is a good Monophysite Trinitarian, like Ethiopian Christians.

But that Ammon episode is still crucially important. All versions of the Romance begin in Egypt before Alexander's birth, rather than in Macedonia. But they begin in Egypt *because* of Alexander's birth. In the canonical history, Ammon's sudden revelation of his parentage to Alexander comes as a surprise; indeed, it's such a surprise that the Romance opens with the events that bring that genealogy about. In a sense, the genealogy is also the genesis of the narrative itself. The story, in other words, begins with the puzzle that began this chapter: how did Alexander come to be the son of an African god? How did that work?

The Romance begins, actually, with an ending—with the last originally Egyptian pharaoh, Nectanebo II, who fled to Nubia when the Achaemenid empire invaded. In the Romance, Nectanebo is among the greatest magicians (or "clerks," as medieval romances called them), a kind of conflation of scholar and soothsayer. The first version of the Romance, which was the template for all of the others, is clear about both the divine and geographical source of Nectanebo's power: it is Ammon, "the god of Libya."[65] Some versions of the Romance add additional details that make Libya seem less random in the story, like the Ethiopian version, which says that Nectanebo escaped in a "ship of Libya" (Budge, *A History*, 14–15).

Nectanebo then travels further, to Macedonia, where he causes Alexander's mother, Olympias, to dream that Ammon impregnates her. After she reports the dream to Nectanebo, he tells her to prepare herself for an actual visit from Ammon. The next night, Nectanebo disguises himself as Ammon and sleeps with Olympias. After Alexander is born, the story picks up from the canonical history, but Alexander's visit to the Oasis of Siwa is no longer a surprise. It's a reminder that the Alexander story begins in Africa, because Alexander is a son of Africa.

There are, of course, different reasons that writers thought Africa should play a more important role. It seems obvious that the Ethiopian version, for instance, would want to expand the role of Africa. What's more surprising are the intricate and extensive references to Africa in northern European versions, especially before the so-called age of exploration, although trade connections between Africa and Europe in the Middle Ages were far more extensive than previously assumed. Even in the age of the Crusades, when as Geraldine Heng argues there may have been some hardening of Africa and Africans into caricatures of a Muslim or racial other, European literature imagined in increasing detail and scope the events of an African past.

I'll discuss two closely related European versions of the Romance, the Anglo-Norman *Roman de toute chevalerie* and the Middle English *King Alisaunder*, a loose translation of the *Roman*. The *Roman* uses the story of Alexander to think globally about the history of the world and its future, about climate theory, about the Crusades, about forms of knowledge, and about the diversity of the natural world. Its writer, Thomas of Kent, treats the Alexander legend with a simultaneous magpie curiosity and scholarly rigor. He's skeptical about some events but throws in references to the Latin texts he uses for readers who want to dig deeper. He opens up the possibilities of the story in a number of ways, attuned to the contemporary resonances of the Alexander story with the Second Crusade and the fraught relations among the English king Henry II, his barons, France, and the church. Thomas of Kent's book tries to be a number of things: a heroic epic, a romance, and a history. He follows the cardinal role of improvisational theater: "yes, and," rather than "no."[66]

Except when it comes to Egypt. Rather than exploit the many possibilities that Egypt's ambiguous location among the continents might give it, the *Roman de toute chevalerie* neglects Egypt almost completely. It slides all of the early action of the story out of Egypt and distributes it across Africa. Nectanebo, for instance, is neither a pharaoh nor a ruler of Egypt, but the King of Libya.[67] There's a kind of anxiety that Nectanebo not be associated with Egypt: he himself tells Olympias that she will be impregnated by *Amon le dieu de Libye* (Thomas of Kent, 216.13). Small details in the poem make the role of Africa inevitable, almost unremarkable: the mules that both Olympias and Philip's second wife, Cleopatras, ride, are from "Aufriqke" (Thomas of Kent, 107.10; 686.27). It is Africa, not Egypt—or not Egypt alone—that becomes the first stage for Alexander's world conquest.

In the *Roman*, Alexander celebrates turning fifteen by attacking and destroying a Greek city (Elim), which was ruled by a king (Nicholas) who was born in Carthage. Like the episode of Alexander's visiting the shrine of Siwa, this brief reference seems to have triggered a major revision of the story. In *King Alisaunder*, Alexander travels to attack Carthage itself because its king is an old enemy of Philip's. After landing on the African

Egypt, the Exception 49

shore, Alexander and his army destroy Carthage and return to Macedonia with Carthage's treasure and the *coroune of þe lond*.⁶⁸

The triumphant Alexander with the crown of a destroyed Carthage in his hand echoes two events at Carthage that resonate powerfully through European literature and political thought. The first is the destruction of Carthage in 146 BCE by Scipio Africanus, which opened the way for Roman dominance. The crown that Alexander takes with him from Carthage is a literal version of this process, the so-called *translatio imperii*, the passage of world dominion from one reign to another. As we will see (in chapter 3), the destruction of Carthage is the focus of theoretical reflection of all kinds in the Middle Ages, from political theology to the philosophy of history to dream theory.

The second event that Alexander's attack on Carthage echoes is equally resonant: Aeneas's landing at Carthage after the destruction of Troy. That's the event that kicks off Virgil's *Aeneid*, an epic that celebrates the rise of the Roman empire under Caesar Augustus, and a text that became part of the literary imagination of almost every writer in medieval Europe. There's perhaps an event closer in history to *King Alisaunder* that made Alexander's attack on Carthage an intriguing subject. In 1270, King Louis IX of France launched a crusade (now known as the Eighth Crusade) to retake the Holy Land. His plan was to convert the ruler of Tunis—medieval Carthage—to Christianity, and march on Jerusalem with his help. None of that worked out, because Louis died of dysentery outside the walls of Tunis. To the extent that *King Alisaunder* reflects on the failures of the Crusades, the destruction of Carthage reads like a revenge fantasy.

But in both the *Roman* and *King Alisaunder*, Africa is far more than the site of a historical grudge. It is the real target of Alexander's first phase of conquest. After a blistering campaign through Greece and Italy, Alexander invades Libya and conquers it within two weeks. Egypt is almost an afterthought. In the *Roman*, Alexander pauses briefly on his way to Asia to found Alexandria; *King Alisaunder* doesn't mention Alexandria at all, until Alexander's body is taken there at the end of the poem. It's almost as if both poems imagine the visit to the Oasis of Siwa as the only important event in what was originally Alexander's Egyptian campaign. It becomes a Libyan campaign, with a brief foray into Egypt. It's in part an attempt to rehabilitate Alexander as a proto-Christian subject: he visits a pagan temple in Tripoli where a gaslighting "bishop" tells him that he is not, in fact, the son of Nectanebo. But it also makes Africa, and not Egypt alone, the ground on which Alexander's legitimacy is established.[69]

Alexander's visit to Siwa is the nucleus of another part of the Alexander narrative that distributes "Egypt" into Africa. In the first version of the Romance (the third-century "Pseudo-Callisthenes"), Alexander discovers monuments and graves in Egypt that commemorate the rule of Candace, the Queen of Meroë, and Ammon's support of her campaigns. He writes to Candace, asking her to meet him at the frontier of Egypt and Meroë with the "shrine and statue" of Ammon.[70] She refuses, but sends him the kinds of gifts from Nubia that are often represented as the spoils of victory on friezes. They come in two allotments. The first is for Alexander: one hundred solid bricks of gold, two hundred parrots, two hundred sphinxes, and five hundred young Ethiopians. She makes it clear that these gifts do not indicate her submission to a conquered Egypt. The second batch of gifts is directed to Ammon alone, and is both more lavish and representative of Nubian plenty: an elaborate crown, jewels, ivory caskets, rhinoceroses, elephant tusks, and leopard hides. They are a kind of reverse tribute, in which the regalia of office—represented by the crown—swerve by Alexander only to go to the god who legitimates rule. Candace underlines the gesture by calling Ammon *our* god, who "presides over the boundaries of Egypt."[71] It's a complex gesture of both historical and cultural legitimacy: Candace has a greater right to Egypt than Alexander, having already ruled it under the aegis of Ammon, whose approval Alexander sought. In some versions, Alexander calls Candace to Siwa, as if to stage a transfer of power, which Candace refuses. Candace's gesture also underscores the identity of Ethiopia and/or Nubia: it has wealth that Egypt lacks, and retains the aura, if not the outright presence, of Egypt's chief god. Despite the fictionality of the encounter between Alexander and Candace (and there is much more in the Romance), the story echoes the real history of Nubia and Egypt. The name Candace is actually the title for Queens of Nubia, *Kandake*,[72] and the reference to Candace as a ruler of Egypt may echo the Twenty-Fifth Dynasty, when the rulers of Egypt were Nubian.[73]

The Candace episode in the Romance dramatizes the permeability of Egypt and Nubia: in the story, Egypt is unthinkable without Nubia. The frontier of Egypt is determined not by Egypt's hegemony but by a Nubian god. In the Romance, Alexander's conquest of the world is halted at that point. Candace tells him she will not submit but asks him to return when he has conquered the rest of the world. He never returns to Nubia, although, as we have seen, his body does return to Alexandria. In Thomas of Kent's *Roman de toute chevalerie*, Alexander's career follows three of the four cardinal points of the compass. He does not travel very far west, because, as Thomas says, the Irish, Spanish, and British live in inhospitable territories. Suzanne Akbari suggests that Alexander's body in Alexandria is poised at the cusp of a future westward movement (remember that Dio Chrysostom called Alexandria the crossroads of the world)—indeed, as Akbari says, the future itself, of "the European nations to come." This opening to the future comes at the expense, Akbari says, of the "identity of the traveler himself." The exotic orient in the *Roman*, she suggests, is still signified by Egypt, a "formerly foreign land recently absorbed into the Macedonian Empire."[74] Alexander's body represents the starting point of a process of "domestication and stabilization" that the Romance tradition will continue—and extend—into the far west of Europe.

The return of Alexander's body to Alexandria is not just a return to a city that was a passing thought for Alexander. It's not just a return to Egypt, a country he adorned his trophy case with, as Napoleon was to do centuries later. It's a return to an origin in the profoundest sense: to the place where Alexander found his deepest, African self as the son of a god who was simultaneously a Libyan, Nubian, and Egyptian deity. Alexander's resting place in Alexandria is not just the establishment of a point of stability in a capricious and exotic locale. Even if he had just "acquired" Egypt, it was already a place from which he came. His tomb is one of the many nodes in a network of religious, cultural, and political history that extended across Africa, including Libya, Nubia, Cush, Ethiopia—and, not least, Egypt.

Alexander's tomb was the focus of a cult under the Ptolemies, but it's not clear how long it stood. Accounts contradict each other, and some are downright sketchy. The tomb had either disappeared by 400, when John Chrysostom, on a visit to Alexandria, was told it was gone. Or it was still there when Napoleon invaded Egypt in 1798—at least according to Edward Daniel Clarke, a British antiquities enthusiast who came to Egypt with the British army in 1801, when it drove Napoleon's army out. Following a trail of rumors, Clarke discovered a massive sarcophagus hidden in the hold of a French ship that was poised to carry it off to France. It was, Clarke said, the tomb of Alexander. He backed up his claim in a book with a multitude of citations and quotations from classical and early modern writers that established, Clarke argued, the presence of the sarcophagus in Alexandria since Alexander's death, and its long association with Alexander. Clarke's references include multiple versions of the Romance of Alexander.[75] The sarcophagus was sent to the British Museum, but, despite Clarke's ardent and somewhat petulant lobbying, it wasn't displayed as Alexander's Tomb (another object he gave to the Museum, the Rosetta Stone, was better appreciated). Hieroglyphic writing was fully deciphered shortly after the sarcophagus was installed, and the texts on the sarcophagus were read: it was, it turned out, not Alexander's. It belonged to Nectanebo II.

Whether or not Alexander's body ever ended up in Nectanebo's sarcophagus, the urban myth joined the ends of the Alexander Romance together: Alexander came to rest in the tomb designed for his Egyptian father. Whether or not Napoleon really wanted it for his own sarcophagus, as Clarke hinted, Napoleon knew quite well that the myth of Alexander was a powerful way to legitimate his conquest.

Egyptology's History of Europe

Napoleon thought about Alexander's career throughout his life,[76] and told his army just before it landed in Egypt that the first city they would encounter was built by Alexander. But although his contemporaries certainly framed him as a second Alexander,[77] there turns out to be little evidence that he modeled himself after Alexander. Indeed, for Napoleon, Alexander was a cautionary figure, someone who failed to consolidate his conquests. He did want to emulate Alexander in one regard: to do something like Alexander's visit to the Oasis of Siwa. It was "highly politic," he said, of Alexander to go to Ammon; it was "how he conquered Egypt. If I had stayed in the Orient, I would probably have founded an empire like Alexander, by going on a pilgrimage to Mecca, where I would have prayed and genuflected" (Briant 253).

Napoleon was wrong that Mecca was an analog for Siwa, and almost certainly wrong that his trip would have legitimated his rule in the Islamic world. But it does reveal his profound interest in the Egyptian past. Before he invaded Egypt, he commissioned a virtual scholastic wing of the army whose task it was to produce a massive survey of Egypt and its history. It outlived Napoleon's occupation by a number of decades (even centuries, if you count the Institut d'Egypte, the survey's base, which burned down in the Arab Spring but was rebuilt and reopened in 2012). The survey, the *Description de l'Égypte*, began to appear in 1809, and by its completion in 1828 it was the biggest publishing endeavor in the world. The fusion of knowledge and power that it exemplified made it the perfect case study for another monumental book, Edward Said's *Orientalism*. For Said, the *Description de l'Égypte* was not just a statement of Napoleon's desire to occupy Egyptian territory, but also of the imperial desire to form a system of knowledge that would make Egypt (and the "Orient") an inextricable part of European history—and thus an inevitable extension of Europe. "History as recorded in the *Description*," Said says, "supplants Egyptian or Oriental history by identifying itself directly and immediately with world history, a euphemism for European history."[78]

Said discusses mostly the preface to the entire project, written by its director Jean-Joseph Fourier. The preface is explicitly prescriptive where the ostensible aim of the whole project is to be descriptive. Its goal, Fourier claims, is to "offer the Orient the useful example of European industry" and to procure for the inhabitants "all the advantages of a perfected civilization."[79] Later, Fourier makes it clear that this "industry" is based on firepower and the enslavement of Africans for plantation colonization (the European *génie* has put at its disposal *des habitans de l'Afrique pour la culture des possessions nouvelles*).[80]

The rest of the *Description* is less polemical, but there are moments when one sees precisely how a particular form of knowledge is used either to cordon off Egypt from the rest of Africa, or to link Egypt more closely to Europe. For practical purposes, those are the same thing. The *Description*'s volume on Thebes describes considerable evidence that Egypt had a long involvement with Ethiopia (many writers mention it; hieroglyphs include lions and giraffes). But, the writer asserts, it's not likely that the influence went from Ethiopia to Egypt: there are no comparable ruins in Ethiopia from an older civilization.[81] He uses a more insidious method to support his claim, and one that became the main instrument by which Egypt was carved out of Africa: art history. The style of Egyptian architecture and its ornaments so obviously reflects the flora and fauna of the Nile, the volume argues, that it couldn't be Ethiopian. No, the center, the radiating point, of the arts—and therefore civilization—had to be Thebes (*Description*, 264).

There always seems to be a racist corollary to this division of Egypt and Ethiopia/Nubia/Africa according to artistic forms. If you accept that Thebes is the origin of Egyptian culture, based on the evidence of Egyptian art, says the writer, then you have to stop believing that the ancient Egyptians were of the "Negro race" (*race Nègre*) (*Description*, 265). Besides, says the writer, there's little evidence in sculpture of the "traits" of Black people; the people who live in the area today, he says, don't have the "traits" either—although, yes, it is true that they have a dark complexion; yet that is not the exclusive characteristic of Black people. It is true that some monuments, like the Sphinx of Memphis, might have those "traits," but who are we to say that Egyptian art always aimed at verisimilitude? (*Description*, 264–65). The internal contradictions of this argument are themselves emblematic of how Egypt would be separated from Africa and nudged toward Europe in the next two centuries. Ammon might have once decided where Egypt ended and Libya or Nubia began, but from the Napoleonic conquest on, the decision was made by art.

But art is no more dispassionate in making sovereign decisions than is the oracle that Alexander claimed gave him dominion over the world. That is, it does little more than act as a cover for our own desires and goals—it's what the sociologist Pierre Bourdieu calls an objectifying discourse. "Art" is a particularly insidious kind of discourse[82] because "art" means anything from the work of art itself—whatever that is—to what we are trained to think and say about it. That might sound like a subtle distinction, but it's profoundly important for the role that "art" played in the modern story of where Egypt was placed. In Egyptology, "art" tended to be a strictly formalist discipline, a matter of shapes, styles, and measurements, that stood in for other potential meanings of "art": the free play of the imagination; the expression of desires or fears.

Yet formalism in Egyptology is uncomfortably close to a practice of racial exclusion. The definition of styles was often used to draw the boundary between Egypt and its neighbors along racial lines. Sometimes those Napoleonic scholars of art history sound like modern European xenophobes. The description of Thebes says that it would be absurd to say that the style of Theban art came from Ethiopia: we can't encourage the opinion that the "people to the south in Africa" can again flow (*refluer*) to the north (*Description*, 434).

That might sound almost like a slogan, but the idea that the peoples of the south should not flow into the north still informs the layout of some museums. They themselves partition Egypt off from the rest of Africa, and their narratives of Egyptian history flow, figuratively and literally, always from the north to the south.

The British Museum has two separate areas for its Egyptian artifacts. One is a long gallery on the ground floor with its prestige objects—a large statue of Rameses II, the Rosetta Stone, and the sarcophagus of Nectanebo. What puts these objects together is their bling factor, but also one of the venerable categories of academic art. On the map the gallery is labeled simply "Ancient Egypt: Egyptian Sculpture." That is, these things belong together because they share a genre, not a function or a historical moment. The other Egyptian galleries, on the second floor, collectively labeled "Ancient Egypt," end in a corner room labeled "Sudan, Egypt and Nubia."[83] It feels like a backwater, an afterthought, or, even worse, a deception. How are ancient Sudan and Nubia the same as ancient Egypt?

The text on the cases also supports the insidious absorption of "Africa" into Egypt; there's no question of the rest of Africa, which is situated in the basement, or of "Libya," which is distributed across several exhibition spaces. The labels tend to subordinate the artifacts under the rubric of "Upper Egypt," as if there were and had always been two parts of a whole that was sometimes broken and sometimes repaired. But the objects themselves tell a different story. Many of them are Meroitic (300 BCE–400 CE in what is now Sudan), and use a demonstrably different script from any of the Egyptian forms, one that has not yet been fully deciphered. Solely on the grounds of epigraphy, Meroë would seem to belong to a distinctly different cultural and bureaucratic domain than that of "Upper Egypt," and, by the usual metonymy, all of Egypt. The influence of Upper Egypt on Lower Egypt—and of Meroë on Upper Egypt—is not the subtext of the displays. They do not discuss how elements of southern culture found their way into "Egyptian" culture, or, perhaps more pertinently, how Upper Egyptian culture might have been absorbed into Nubian culture. Instead, they present these elements of "Nubian" culture as traces of *resistance* to a larger, normative Egyptian culture. Conquests of the south by Lower Egypt are presented as cultural missions, evident by the traces they leave behind of recognizably (to us) Egyptian culture.

This presentation of Nubian culture and history still echoes the narrative of Egyptian cultural exclusiveness.[84] In the many rooms devoted to ancient Egypt, this is the only one devoted to Nubia (and/or Kush).

None of these objects is especially spectacular in the way that the gigantic statues in the hall of "Egyptian" sculpture are. The most arresting of these objects is the plaster cast of African goods being presented to Rameses II, which looms over the room as if reminding us how goods from Africa have always been treated: as objects presented to the north, signifying its dominion over Africa. The formalist language of a previous generation of art historians helps to place these objects within the narrative of a certain cultural triumphalism. An ankh on a pot from the Nubian cemetery of Faras in the first century CE is described as "debased," as if the purity of Egyptian forms is contaminated as they travel southward.

The language of debasement in pottery has a troubling genealogy. It begins with one of the most important Egyptologists in the early twentieth century, W. M. Flinders Petrie, who pioneered the technique of dating archaeological levels according to their predominant styles of pottery. Petrie's technique, now commonly known in art history and archaeology as "contextual seriation," assumed that styles "progressed" or "deteriorated" over time. Pottery of a similar quality on the same level must have been made at the same time. But major changes, he believed, only happened when a new "race" moved in. The fundamental importance of pots, for Petrie, was that they identified racial types. He described one style of pottery at Tel Lachish as "Jewish," and used a new style of pottery at another site to posit the arrival of a "cannibal race."[85] The language he uses to describe pottery styles is not just anthropomorphic but jarringly racist. There's an imperceptible difference between pottery and human physiognomy. He talks about "coarse rough faces" in one place, a "face of coarser type" in another.[86] The first quote describes "debased" pottery at Tel Lachish; the second describes the face of a pharaoh who might have been a "foreigner." In the same passage, Petrie uses the term "deterioration" to describe both the quality of art and the "physique" of a degenerating dynasty (*Making*, 141).

The "debased" ankh on a Nubian pot in the back corner of the Egyptian galleries in the British Museum represents the kinds of exclusion that separated the rest of Africa from Egypt in the practice of modern Egyptology, including curatorial practice. The layout of galleries echoes one of Petrie's grand foundational gestures for the field of Egyptology. There have been six races that influenced Egypt, he says, but the first was just "a crude condition, akin to all Africa."[87] The foundational "race" was inchoate, nameless, a "condition" rather than a coherent identity. It's against this degree zero that a coherent story about the history of Egyptian civilization can be told: it is the story of the *difference* from Africa. But it is not just a narrative of evolution away from this "condition"; it is also a continuing exclusion of an Africa that still exists. "Akin to all Africa" refers as much to Petrie's contemporary Africa as it does to the Africa of the distant past. It is Africa, to echo Hegel, that does not change, that does not have a history. Whatever is Egypt is whatever has history—and Africa does not have it.

Against this history of Egypt as an exception to Africa, Afrocentrism has argued that Egypt has a history precisely because it *is* African. Damien Agut's recent important chapter on ancient Egypt opens François-Xavier Fauvelle's monumental *L'Afrique Ancienne* with the forthright assertion that pharaonic Egypt was a *"civilisation africaine."*[88] His argument, indeed the opening phrase of his chapter, is based on the fact that Egypt is on the African continent: "*C'est une evidence géographique*." Agut argues, as have I, that the process of decoupling Egypt from Africa, the process of "de-Africanisation," began with the rise of Egyptology and its deployment of Eurocentric categories of race. But the fit between the discipline of Egyptology and the discipline of "scientific" racism is even tighter, above all in Petrie's work. Indeed, he is its foundational figure.

On the strength of Petrie's reputation for precision and rigor, the polymath scientist Francis Galton, the man who invented the word "eugenics," funded him to produce an 1887 survey called *Racial Photographs from the Egyptian Monuments.*[89] That wasn't their first encounter; in the book in which Galton coined the term "eugenics," he also cited Petrie. Egyptology was there at the birth of eugenics. Petrie followed his photographic survey with a string of papers on cranial measurement, and shared their results, as well as his extensive collection of skulls from Egypt, with Galton for the rest of Galton's career.[90]

Petrie's appreciation of rigor didn't exclude a massive methodological fallacy. In a twenty-five-year-long *petitio principii*, Petrie sorted out racial types according to the categories that Galton gave him; Galton would modify his hypotheses about racial classifications based on the data that Petrie sent him; Petrie would then refine his own classifications accordingly, and so on. Petrie's *Racial Photographs* has almost no text, although the next year he published a short key to the photographs in the journal *Nature*. These photographs represent, he confidently claims, the "four great divisions of mankind," each with a different color: the "red race" of the Egyptians, "the yellow Libyan, the brown Asiatic," and "the black Negro."[91]

Using the measurements of the "skull triangle," Petrie plotted a graph that placed the different "races" in order of intelligence. But nowhere in the article does he discuss how he assesses intelligence. The leaps of imagination between the cluster of facial measurements that he records and his conclusions about the "races" they represent are virtually psychotic: "The long heads have decentralized government, the wide heads slightly centralized, the mean type enjoy a judicious mixture of rule."[92] The sole trace of a method betrays the appeal to supposed common sense and general opinion of the stock racist. He admits to fudging the data so that southern Italians were not rated higher than central Italians, simply because "we could hardly grant that he is a better man than the central Italian" ("Diagrams," 85).

Petrie's photographs and the short pieces he wrote about them had a long and influential afterlife. The Religious Tract Society published a popular book in 1891 by the Assyriologist A. H. Sayce called *Races of the Old Testament*, which used both Petrie's photographs and "intuitive" appeal to what he called the "facticity" of racial difference. "We cannot look at a negro without feeling that he belongs to a different species of humanity than ourselves, to a different race in fact," he proclaims in the third sentence. He argues that the four races that Petrie describes are immutable classifications: the "races depicted by the Egyptian artist four thousand years ago are still to-day what they were then."[93] The one group in the book whose race is unstable is the Egyptians. Sayce's book, which begins with a chapter entitled "The Science of Ethnology," shows unmistakably the unfolding process of "de-Africanizing" the Egyptians. "It is but recently," Sayce says, "that ethnologists have discovered that the Egyptian is a member of the white race" (83). In what became one of the definitive histories of ancient Egypt, the University of Chicago Egyptologist James Henry Breasted (who obtained his PhD at the University of Berlin in 1894 and became the first director of the Haskell Oriental Museum in Chicago in 1901) also talks about the recent racial realignment: "The conclusion once maintained by some historians, that the Egyptian was of African negro origin, is now refuted."[94] The best-selling novelist and travel writer Amelia Edwards tended to be less emphatic about the Egyptians' supposed whiteness, although her accounts always end up affirming it. One remarkable passage in a piece about ancient portraits moves from ancient Egypt to modern Algeria, following a chain of racial logics that topples like a line of dominoes:

> The flesh-tints of Egyptians are rendered of a reddish-brown, and the hair coal-black. The facial angle is quite different from the facial angle of the Asiatics. It is the facial angle of the European races, and it has therefore a certain affinity with that of the typical Libyan. Now, the typical Libyans of ancient Egyptian art were a fair-skinned, red-haired, and blue-eyed race, whose descendants survive to this day eastward of Algeria.... These fair Libyans were doubtless emigrants from Europe or Asia, and were most probably of Pelasgic origin.[95]

The "fair Libyans" are a version of the so-called Kabyle Myth, the notion invented and promulgated by French ethnologists and administrators that the Berbers (later mostly the Kabyle alone) were completely distinct racially from the "Arabs," if not in fact European. "They are handsome," said the Abbé Raynal (who died in 1796, though his study wasn't published until 1826), "with blue eyes and blond hair, which recalls their ancestors from the north," whom Raynal thought were most likely the Vandals.[96] The US Consul in Algiers, William Shaler, wrote breezily to the American Philosophical Society that it "is well known" that the Berbers "are a race of white men," and that the "Kabyles of North Africa are a white people." So entrenched was this notion already by 1825, when he wrote, that he didn't seem to think either assertion needed to be backed up by evidence or further explanation.[97]

But the "Libyans" of ancient Egypt were not a single "race," either. Amelia Edwards, like almost everyone else at the time, depended on the representation of the "four races" in the so-called Book of Gates from New Kingdom tombs. This neat division of the world into easily categorized, subjugated peoples was a prominent trope of New Kingdom art and literature, and did not correspond to the much more complex and heterogeneous reality of social relations. People with the supposedly distinctive traits of "Libyans" (e.g., pastoralism) lived throughout ancient Egypt and in heterogeneous communities. One person could be represented as belonging, at different times, to two or more of the "four races."[98] Juan Carlos Moreno García sums up recent scholarship about the population of ancient Libya: "The archaeological and epigraphic record reveals that the vast area encompassing the Libyan Desert and the territories bordering the Western Delta was home to a diversity of peoples and lifestyles whose 'ethnic' affiliation is difficult to discern."99 But it is precisely the single-mindedness of the trope of the "four races" in New Kingdom Egypt that drives its redeployment by Petrie, Sayce, and Edwards; there appear to be no exceptions or qualifications necessary because the Egyptians did not make any. We cannot be sure that the artists who made the "table of races" found in, say, Seti I's tomb, or indeed Seti I himself, were confident that these "racial" distinctions were self-evident and impermeable. But modern imperial readers of the same depictions certainly do not lack confidence in their own ability to identify race. Edwards says that the peoples in "ancient portraits" can be "surely identified by their racial characteristics [as] unmistakably Roman [or] Greek; while in others we recognize Egyptian, Nubian, and Semitic types" ("Portrait-Painting," 100). Her ordering of races implies (from her point of view) a descending hierarchy, moving from West to East. Even if it does not, she makes the Egyptians into a kind of hinge between "classical" civilization and the Orient (plus Nubia). But she makes it clear where that hinge is most firmly attached: the Egyptians have the "facial angles of the European races." That is, to a modern European, accustomed to looking at other modern Europeans, ancient Egyptian portraits look like they represent modern Europeans.

Nobody at the time questioned how, and whether, it was possible to extrapolate "real" facial features from portraits made by artists whose conventions, ideologies, and religion were, to say the least, incompletely known. The fairly basic problem of how to interpret portraiture remained unexamined to such an extent that the Egyptologist Antonio Loprieno quite recently wrote a large book making the fairly basic point that Egyptologists had failed to distinguish between the "topic" and "mimetic" work of portraiture, the degree to which a representation was rooted in direct observation (however mediated it might be) or in artistic convention (the difference, say, between a photograph and a cartoon).[100] But it wasn't artistic naivete or credulousness that really powered the racisms of nineteenth- and twentieth-century Egyptology. It was a deep-seated faith in the immutability of racial distinction, the simple belief that, in Amelia Edwards's words, these ancient portraits represent "racial types which survive unchanged to the present day" ("Portrait-Painting," 113). The very surface of this racism is the belief that race is an unchanging thing, an immutable quality that determines not just phenotypes but also thought and behavior. The less visible support of this belief is the consistent way in which Egyptologists read back the racism they absorbed from their own world into the unfamiliar and indefinite world of ancient Egypt. And not just professional Egyptologists—also, and perhaps above all, amateur enthusiasts of Egypt.

Petrie occupied the first chair of Egyptology in the United Kingdom. It was endowed, in fact, by Amelia Edwards, whose fascination with ancient Egypt in the last twenty years of her life led her to focus more on Egyptology than on novels. Her travelogue *A Thousand Miles Up the Nile* (1888), which became a bestseller (and is still in print), laments the ongoing destruction of the monuments of ancient Egypt by the growing tourist industry. The tourists who took "wet-paper squeezes," for instance, were removing all of the original colors that still adhered to monuments, and they bought up artifacts from tombs that were rifled for the trade.[101] Someone in her party even bought a fresh corpse that was trussed up as an ancient mummy. But Edwards herself overlooks the traces of other lives in her description of monuments. She sees only herself in the encounter with them. The Hall of Pillars at Karnak is impossible to describe; one can't build up "a recognizable image by means of words. The scale is too vast; the effect too tremendous; the sense of one's own . . . littleness, and incapacity, too complete and crushing."[102] It empties one "not only of words but of ideas . . . I could only look, and be silent" (*Thousand*, 134). This is virtually a paraphrase of Kant's description of the shattering experience of the sublime (the spectator "experiences the feeling of the incapacity of his imagination to present the Idea of a whole; in this the imagination reaches its maximum and, in the effort to surpass it, it is sunk into itself"). Kant's conception of the sublime is haunted in several ways by the general fascination with Egypt in the late eighteenth century (witness Mozart's *Magic Flute* of 1790, set in Egypt in the time of Rameses I). In fact, Kant uses the pyramids as one example of a sublime object.[103]

When Edwards reaches Nubia, she pauses to reflect on what has happened. They have left Egypt by crossing a boundary of nation, race, time, even of humanity.

> Though there exists no boundary line to mark where Egypt ends and Nubia begins, the nationality of the races dwelling on either side of that invisible barrier is as sharply defined as though an ocean divided them. . . . [O]ne comes suddenly into the midst of a people that have

apparently nothing in common with the population of Egypt. They belong to a lower ethnological type; and they speak a language derived from purely African sources.... [T]hey are to this day as distinct and inferior a people as when their Egyptian conquerors, massing together in one contemptuous epithet all nations south of the frontier, were wont to speak of them as 'the vile race of Kush.' Time has done little to change them since those early days (*Thousand*, 181).

As more current scholarship has pointed out, the epithet "vile" or "wretched" was applied also to ancient Israel and Libya, and almost entirely during the New Kingdom. The vilification of traditional enemies was a standard literary topos of the period. Stuart Tyson Smith points out that this vilification did not translate to discrimination against those peoples within the kingdom: some of the most important officials of the New Kingdom were Nubians who identified themselves in portraiture with dark skin and "Nubian physiognomy."[104] More to the point, the representations of Nubians, Libyans, and "Asiatics" that Petrie reproduced are explicitly intended to flatter the Egyptians at the expense of their neighbors—they are deliberately and strategically racist, representing their neighbors as caricatures and stereotypes, sometimes even as animals, barely able to speak Egyptian.[105]

For Petrie, Egypt was a vast archive of racial distinctions that allowed him to construct a grand theory about race across time and space. His 1906 Huxley Lecture for the Royal Anthropological Society describes the "mutations and movements of races" over several millennia of Egyptian and European history. He based the framework of the talk on Egypt's long history because its "racial history" was known best.[106] From Egypt he draws an abstract theory of racial evolution and degeneration, and then tries to apply it to Europe.

Petrie's vision of history is explicitly racist—indeed, he argues that history only makes sense as a history *of* race. Racial history, he argues, can reveal the "true interpretation of those physical changes which are our sole informants concerning most of the past of mankind" ("Migrations," 189). Even where there are other "informants," he pushes them into the background: 238 years before Egypt was conquered by the Arabs in 642, there was "Syrian influence" in eastern Egypt; starting in 287, Saxons "infested" the coast of Gaul, raided England, occupied Normandy, and the "Saxon shore of England" in the first stages of the "great migration" that happened several centuries later (192).

In his Huxley Lecture, the history of Egypt is the story of race in North Africa. It is shot through with the simultaneous nostalgia, fantasy, and anxiety that Fredric Jameson identifies as romance, a genre that "is staged as a struggle between higher and lower realms."[107] Petrie's history of race is precisely a history of that struggle between the "lower stratum of Libyans" and "the new high element [of facial structure]" (200–1). Just as medieval historical, political, and class struggles are staged in the imaginative form of the romance, Petrie's racial history is told in art: old forms of pottery disappear, new ones arise, "fancy forms ... cease to arise" as "ruder races" or "different stock" appear (198). The arrival of "dynastic Egyptians" is the real revolution: they bring figurative art with "spirited carvings." But this art is important also because it sounds so much like Petrie's *use* of Egyptian art. He values this new kind because it has "that minute ethnographical distinction which the Egyptian continued to retain through all his art" (199). Egyptian art is important for Petrie because it is a window onto the history of race—but perhaps more important because, for him, it is also a racist art.

When Petrie speculates about the earliest peoples of Egypt, at a moment before the arrival of dynastic Egyptian art, his method is explicitly impressionist and aesthetic. Not only does he set aside the kind of discipline that made his contextual seriation of pottery an important way for archaeologists to figure out when things happened, he also doesn't seem to care about history—at all. There is not much evidence for the physiognomy of the prehistoric inhabitants of Egypt, but, he says, the earliest graves contain figures with "the Bushman, or Koranna type of steatopygy." The demeaning, racist implications of the first term no longer need to be spelled out. The second term (now more often "Griqua") refers to South African peoples with a complex legacy inseparable from the arrival of the Dutch, and related to San, Xhosa, and Tswana groups. Yet, Petrie says, in these peoples we can see "the last remains of the paleolithic man of Egypt, whom we can thus restore to view as a steatopygous and hairy Bushman" (5). His reasoning is implicitly circular: because figurines with certain body features have been found from prehistoric Egypt, and prehistoric Africa was clearly primitive, they must have been made by the same people who today (in Petrie's eyes) have similar features and who seem primitive: the people targeted by the Dutch and the English as remnants of prehistoric Africa, and supposedly incapable of modernity. Petrie seems to be challenging the Hegelian vision of an Africa without history in some quite radical ways, yet he still turns to contemporary Africa to find a survival of a prehistoric past.

Egypt Theory

At the same time, Petrie is also a faithful Hegelian. Hegel's dictum that Africa had no history depends on the very necessity of an African history. He is deeply ambivalent about the position of Egypt itself in the development of civilization, and frustrated that it came so close to European philosophy yet remained stuck in its past. Egyptian hieroglyphics, in particular, provoke Hegel because they border on what he imagined to be the true philosophical/spiritual work of language, but fail so spectacularly.

Hieroglyphics fail because they still have the shape of "brute form," a "sensuous image, not the letter itself" (Hegel, *History*, 223). They are partially representations of animals (dung beetles or falcons), their "barbarous sensuality" celebrated by people whom Hegel describes as being close to animals themselves, with their "African hardness, Zoolatry, and sensual enjoyment" (239). It is the Africans who keep hieroglyphics partly in the kingdom of the animals, holding the true destiny of writing back like "an iron band" around the "forehead" of Spirit (226). But hieroglyphics are still writing. The "brutish" element of hieroglyphics is remarkable precisely because it somehow is also the kernel of what European languages would later develop into. Hegel marvels over the way hieroglyphs came so close to "pure" writing, despite being in the "vicinity of African stupidity" (223).

Hieroglyphics, in other words, signify something more than the collection of things that the individual signs point to. As a system of signification, they represent Egyptian history, which is *both* history that is defined against Africa's *lack* of it, *and* the legacy of African history. Egypt is and is not Africa. Hegel makes that point in a sentence that is like a hall of mirrors: "Egypt . . . is as isolated and singular in Africa as Africa itself appears in relation to the other parts of the world" (109). Egypt is not like Africa: but it is like Africa because both places share the property of unlikeness. Egypt is as unlike Africa as Africa is unlike the rest of the world, and that is what defines Egypt.

Africa is a kind of specter for Hegel, a ghostly father who sometimes appears, like Hamlet's father, asking to be remembered. It is the father of Egyptian culture, as Hegel reminds us. But the culture of Africa is dead, and all that we remember is the negative qualities, the "brute form," the "barbarous sensuality," the "African hardness." It's a kind of trauma in Egyptian writing that keeps it from achieving its true potential. For one of Hegel's sources, the eighteenth-century writer Constantin Volney, the people of Africa are "today rejected from society" because they have "black skin," yet at the same time they are a people who "discovered the elements of the science and the arts" and the "systems that still govern the universe." They are a "people now forgotten"—forgotten not because they no longer exist physically, but forgotten as the fathers of culture.[108] Hegel implies that they are not completely forgotten. Their trace remains in the origin of writing itself, as a "sensuous" persistence in hieroglyphics.

In Plato's *Phaedrus* Socrates recounts an Egyptian myth that places forgetting itself at the heart of writing. The god Theuth, he says, invented it and went to Thebes to present it to its god-king Thamous. Writing, Theuth says, will improve the wisdom and memory of Egyptians. Thamous contradicts him, arguing that writing will actually "bring about forgetting."[109]

The other name of Thamous is Ammon. His protest against writing will go unheeded and will become prophetic over the long history of the African people. Both Volney and Hegel describe various ways in which the African fathers of writing are being forgotten, although traces of their memory persist. But Ammon himself embodies this ambivalence: he defines writing as just "exterior impressions," not the "real thing" that is memory.[110] On the other hand, the interiority of memory implies something private, something not (yet) revealed to others. Ammon's championing of memory also involves hiddenness, a property that is one of his attributes. Plutarch, the historian and priest of Delphi who studied Egyptian religion, records that when Egyptians call on their supreme god, who is "invisible and concealed" to "make himself visible and manifest," "they use the word 'Amoun'" (Ch. 9, 24ff.) Ammon, who eventually became (also) an African god, embodies what remains hidden in the history of writing, a kind of memory that is paradoxically forgotten in later histories of both writing and philosophy.

Jacques Derrida's 1971 essay "White Mythology" accuses Western metaphysics of forgetting that it originated in Indo-European mythology, which allowed European philosophers to speak as if with the voice of universality, unindebted to time and history.¹¹¹ But there's a second kind of forgetting in Derrida's essay. It is not just that philosophy forgets that it began as Indo-European mythology but also that its own narrative traces show another beginning that is doubly forgotten: the passage from east to west that Hegel plots in his *History of Philosophy*. For "Hegel the light of human knowledge rose in the East, *like the sun*, but the divine Spirit journeyed from there into the West, leaving Eastern nations to the realm of the eternally pre-historical." The history of philosophy is *like* the daily passage of the sun. That analogy is not incidental to philosophy: it creates itself as a metaphor as it develops, so to speak, like a print in the darkroom that reveals the impression of light. Derrida argues that Hegel's history of philosophy is a heliotrope: it follows that passage, but it does so because it discovers points of philosophical illumination in the development of philosophy.

That is a kind of forgetting, too: that philosophy is not just a kind of Indo-Aryan mythology. Hegel's dialectic presents itself as an impersonal logic machine that just happens to have played out across Asia and Europe—with a brief detour into Egypt. As we have seen, the importance of Egypt in Hegel's story for the emergence of philosophy depends on the age-old fluidity of the position of Egypt on the continent of Africa. Hegel's history of philosophy is a T-O map of thought: Egypt could be on either side of the line between Africa and Asia. The larger philosophical scheme, as with the T-O map, is more important than the reality on the ground. For one thing, Derrida forgets the origin of the important metaphor in philosophy of the sun—in Egypt. In "White Mythology" he quotes Hegel for the comparison between the daily course of the sun and the historical course of philosophy. They both travel from east to west: the "History of the World travels from East to West, for Europe is absolutely the end of History."¹¹² The movement between the rising of a literal sun in the east and its setting in the metaphorical west (the "great Day's work of Spirit") is the emergence, over the span of history, of Germany and a "Universal principle" that also gives us "subjective freedom" (Hegel, *History*, 121–22). We learn, those of us in the West watching the sun sink, that we each have our own "inner Sun." Another way of putting this is that the West is where metaphor is invented. Or, to be more precise: the West is where metaphor is revealed to be the passage of time. It is only at the end of the day that we discover that only "we" Europeans understand the full play of the embodied and the abstract that is "our" consciousness. So what does it mean that to tell this story Hegel has to forget that for centuries the sun set in Africa?

This is an ironic, perhaps unintended corollary of Hegel's dictum that Africa stands outside of history. It does not play a part in this "great Day." Hegel's forgetting of Africa doesn't just happen because he doesn't want to ruin a beautiful metaphor (beautiful because it sums up who "we" are, with our inner Suns at the end of history). It happens because Hegel forgets what he almost certainly knew about Egypt's unique position in History, as Hegel imagines it.

Plato argues that the Egyptians were masters of time precisely because of their orientation to the sun. All of the other cultures and civilizations of the world suffer periodic catastrophes—mainly flooding—from which Egypt is immune because of the tempering rays of the sun. At the other extreme, Egypt is protected by the Nile from the sun: Phaeton scorched most of the known world when he stole Apollo's chariot of the sun, except for Egypt. Because Egypt does not periodically have to start all over again, it has accumulated the knowledge and skills of previous civilizations and preserved them intact. The sun marks the years after and before catastrophe in the rest of the world, but it doesn't affect Egypt itself. The Nile, which protects Egypt, makes Egypt immune from time—or, to borrow from Hegel, should make Egypt a metaphor for time, because it is both ancient and enduring. Yet Hegel insists that the sun of philosophy in Egypt is a transient thing, a momentary stop on the way to complete illumination. In his *Philosophy of Religion*, Hegel briefly discusses Egyptian religion as an example of "definite religion," which is still tied to the images and ideas of the natural world, even if somewhat abstractly. Osiris, he says, contains all of the attributes of the other Egyptian gods. The example Hegel uses, the metaphor, is Ammon: the "moment of the sun."[113]

But in many ways, the figure of the river is a more fundamental, less *momentary* and more original, image of Egypt than the sun. It protects Egypt from the diurnal destruction that the sun brings to the rest of the world. And, as Diodorus said, Egypt itself was created by the northward flow of the Nile, depositing the soil of Ethiopia to create it. Like the Nile, the notional boundaries of Egypt have shifted over the centuries, according to bias, ideology, and history. It's possible that the *ur*-metaphor of Egypt is the river, rather than the sun. I'll return to that in a moment: that is another part of the forgetting of the location of the heliotrope in Africa.

To omit the role of Africa in the history of the heliotrope is to leave out a central part of the mythology of the sun in Greek and Roman literature: the western edge of Africa was where the sun set. It was the location of the Garden of the Hesperides, where a tree with golden apples was protected by nymphs (also called the Hesperides). One of Hercules's twelve tasks was to steal one of the golden apples from them. The Hesperides (ἕσπερος, "western") was in the far west of the known world, on the extreme edge of Libya. The Hesperides nymphs were also the guardians of the sunset. One account says that Helios, the Greek sun god, would climb off his chariot at night and set sail from the Hesperides in a golden cup that would travel around the world to Ethiopia for sunrise the next morning.[114] The area of the Hesperides is a bustling site for Greek mythology: it's also the Gorgons' home, where Hercules stole the cattle of Geryon, where Atlas lived.

It's just a coincidence that another part of the mythology of heliotropism that Derrida's essay forgets was written by someone who, like Derrida, was North African. But this writer is well aware of the importance of Africa to mythology and pagan religion in general. Ambrosius Theodosius Macrobius (fl. ca. 400 CE) wrote two works that are immensely important through the Middle Ages and beyond: the *Commentary on the Dream of Scipio*, one of the central texts on geography, cosmography, and dream theory (Freud quotes from it), and the *Saturnalia*, a kind of encyclopedia of classical mythology and cosmology. Macrobius's place of birth is uncertain, but the editor of the *Commentary on the Dream of Scipio* and other scholars believe that he was born in North Africa. North Africa plays a crucial role in both of his works, as we will see here and later.

The *Saturnalia* is a sprawling dialogue about almost everything that takes place over seven days during the Feast of Saturnalia in Rome. It is a kind of contest of erudition, and it contains a treasure trove of classical knowledge that would otherwise have been lost. The speaker in the first book is the mansplaining Praetextus, who pushes the theory that all of the pagan gods are aspects of each other, but that all are also aspects of the same thing: the sun. One of his etymologies, that *sol*, the sun, is taken from *solus*, alone, demonstrates that the ambition of his speech is to consolidate all of the subsidiary meanings that the dozens of gods represent to the single meaning borne by the sun alone. It's an exercise in global metaphor, stripping each of the gods of their peculiar ("proper") meanings, and to refer to them to a single substance. Yet that substance

Egypt, the Exception

turns out to be a metaphor, too. That's more or less what Derrida does with the discourse of Western philosophy. Every utterance turns out to be metaphorical, which means that it refers to a previous or alien utterance, which itself turns out to be metaphorical. For both Derrida and Praetextus, the ur-metaphor, the one beyond which we cannot go, is the sun. So is Derrida merely doing what Praetextus already did 1600 years before? The answer lies not in whether all language is metaphorical and therefore always slippery, but rather where we turn when we follow the passage of the sun.

Praetextus explains that each of the signs of the zodiac expresses something about its relation to the sun during the year. Leo, for example, appears at the hottest time of the year because the sun, like a lion, is fiercest then.[115] Aries splits its time on either side of the sun: on the "left" side during six winter months, and on the "right" side for six months after the vernal equinox (1.21.18., 286, 287).[116] That is why, he says, it is called the Ram: because, just as the power of the sun is its rays, so is the power of the ram its horns (Bk. 1.21.18, 286, 287). All of that explains, Praetextus says, why Ammon is depicted with a ram's horns: because he is "the god the Libyans regard as the setting (or "Western") sun [*solem occidentem*] (Bk. 1.21.19, 286, 287). A North African contemporary of Macrobius's, Martianus Capella, describes the ship of the sun carrying "Hammon, from parched Libya."[117] For both Praetextus, an erudite Roman, and Macrobius, himself likely an African, the sun sets in Libya. But Praetextus slips in his Italocentric perspective: he says that the Greeks called Italy the Hesperides because from their vantage point that's where the sun sets (Bk. 1.3.15, 28, 29). Yet Praetextus also knows that the Libyans' chief god presides over an absolute West. One can go no further, and beyond it is divinity and transcendence: Ammon, the god of the setting sun.

Plutarch says that the "the meaning 'concealed' ... lies in" the name Ammon (Ch. 9, 24). He is "hidden" during the day until his "moment" comes at sunset, when he becomes a god of appearance and visibility. Ammon's "moment" is a more precise instant of what Derrida means when he says that the sun in general makes philosophy possible: the "very opposition between appearing and disappearing, the whole vocabulary of phainesthai [to appear], of alethia [truth/unforgetting] ... of day and night, visible and invisible, present and absent, all this is possible only under the sun."[118]

Yet the Oasis of Siwa also records the passage of the sun during the course of the day. It is the site of what a number of ancient writers called the Fountain of the Sun, which gets cooler as the sun gets hotter and warmer after the sun sets. It's what Derrida would call a "trace," the "mark of the absence of a presence."[119] That, in fact, is the mark of the river, and in particular of the Nile. It carries what comes from Ethiopia to the sea, making Egypt on its way; it marks what is neither Africa nor Asia; it flows either from the east or the south (and may even flow from the west, going underground before turning north); it protects Egypt from the course of the sun. And when Ammon came forth to deliver messages, he was imagined as traveling on a river. The first biographer of Alexander, Kallisthenes, says that the image of Ammon was carried in a golden boat by eighty priests; it did not usually speak, but indicated its decisions by "nods and tokens."[120] The boat of Ammon represents the role of the boat in rituals of burial, when it sailed with the prepared body across the Nile to be buried on the western side, the site of the afterlife. It might be an accident that the first detailed description of how the oracle of Ammon at Siwa worked appears in the first biography of Alexander. But it underlines the remarkable—and transformative—message that Ammon gave to him: not only would he conquer the world, but he was also the son of the Libyan god of the setting sun. And like Ammon, Alexander returned to the West, to enter the afterlife in Africa, in the city he founded on the western side of the Nile.

CHAPTER TWO

Africa, Fulcrum of Epic

> When shall I forget the night I first set foot on African soil?
>
> W. E. B. DU BOIS

> Not yet was it destined for the heroes to set foot on Achaean land, until they suffered still more in the far reaches of Libya.
>
> APOLLONIUS OF RHODES

Mythic Landing: The Iliad, the Argonautica, the Pharsalia, the Aeneid

Alexander's journey to the shrine of Ammon in Libya or the setting of the sun in the African west are not the only things about Africa that tend to be forgotten or overlooked in European literature and philosophy, although they are there in plain sight. Almost every Western classical epic features the heroes landing on the shore of Africa. The most famous instance is in Virgil's *Aeneid*, when Aeneas and his men arrive gratefully on the coast of Africa after a storm has defeated their fleet. Their stay in Africa almost alters the course of European history.

The coast of Africa is important. It marks not just the boundary of a continent, but something more fundamental, even philosophical: the difference between what is land and what is sea, and where one ends and the other begins. Africa plays a kind of essential role in classical epic that may be related to this. In both Homer's *Iliad* and *Odyssey*, the land of the Ethiopians explains the absence of gods themselves from the world of the Greeks. Ethiopia is a land of generosity, where the gods are honored with lavish feasts and sacrifices.[1] In the *Iliad*, the gods are unavailable to intervene in the quarrel between Agamemnon and Achilles because they are at a lavish feast thrown for them by the Ethiopians. During those twelve days, the war in Troy is effectively at a standstill. Far from suggesting otherness or difference, the Ethiopians are a model of everything the Greeks should be but are not: generous, pious, and "blameless" (*Iliad*, Bk. 1.424, 45).

It is the world of the Greeks that is deficient, incomplete. Divine action there is necessary precisely because the Greeks have not achieved what the Africans have. Africa is a space where relations between humans and the gods are restored, a space of ritual and ethical purity. In the *Odyssey*, King Menelaus is trapped in Egypt—after wandering through Ethiopia and Libya—because he did not perform adequate sacrifices to the gods. He will only be released when he goes to the Nile and offers up a hundred cattle. Africa is important in classical epic as a place where, and for which, propitiation needs to be made. One cannot leave for the rest of the world until one has made peace with Africa.

Writers of epic might include scenes of landing in Africa because they want the action to unfold over the entire globe, on all three continents, like tracing all the lines of the T-O map. But these landings reverberate further. They are not just points checked off an itinerary. They also occupy territory, they make a mark—in sometimes quite literal ways—on land; they draw the characters into history. The landings in Africa disturb complacent narratives: they raise the question of what could have been otherwise. Many of the great foundational epics of Western Europe contain, in their nucleus, the possibility that the entire story could have been about Africa instead of Europe. This does not mean that these narratives are a record of ways in which Europeans have triumphed over Africa. Africa is, instead, a reminder of how contingent the heroic actions of foundational European narratives really are. Africa is a continuing presence in them: a promise, an answer, a lack, an archive, a crypt—even a literal monolith, as in Geoffrey of Monmouth's history of Britain.

Alexander's trip to Siwa to consult the oracle of the god Ammon in the Libyan desert shows how important even a brief detour into Africa can be. That was where he received permission to conquer the world from a god, and where he learned that he was also that god's son. His consultation of the oracle was, at least metaphorically, a kind of landing. Siwa was, to rephrase Hegel, singular in Libya, a fertile island in the

Africa, Fulcrum of Epic

Libyan desert. Ammon communicated as if from a river, from a boat carried by eighty priests, which moved forward or back as a sign that the chief priest would interpret. The petitioner thus stood on a metaphorical shore as the boat approached or receded. The approach to Ammon at Siwa is a landing in Africa in an abstract sense, but in epic, landings in Africa are far more precise, concrete, and explicit.

One of the first accounts of landing in Africa appears in the third century BCE epic the *Argonautica*, perhaps familiar from the classic 1963 *Jason and the Argonauts*, which Tom Hanks once declared the greatest movie of all time. Its influence is far deeper than that, of course. It gave us the myths of the Golden Fleece, Medea, Scylla and Charybdis, and the Garden of the Hesperides. As we saw in the last chapter, the latter is a kind of intersection between the divine and the earthly. It is where Hera kept the trees with the golden apples that she was given by Gaia, the goddess of the earth, when she married Zeus. It marks the terminus of Africa, the last point to which one can go before encountering the great Ocean that circles the world. It's where Helios, the god of the sun, launches his boat every evening to travel around the world to the east, where he rises.

One of the twelve labors of Hercules was to steal a golden apple from the Garden of the Hesperides. In the *Argonautica*, he's a forceful figure who wanders off early in the narrative because his strength and talent make the rest of the Argonauts redundant (he can row the *Argo* by himself). We hear about him distantly, as if he is Hamlet and we are the nonentities Rosencrantz and Guildenstern. The Argonauts almost cross paths with Hercules again: they arrive at the Garden of the Hesperides just one day after he had plundered the trees and left the garden devastated. Their own journey to the Hesperides is much less purposeful. It's one of many adventures that makes them seem, especially in comparison with Hercules, a bit hapless and directionless.

In fact, the Argonauts stumble on the garden because they are lost in Africa. They had been blown onto the Libyan shore in a gulf named Syrtis, which will be an important feature of other African landings. Despairing of relaunching the boat, the Argonauts tumble onto the sand, where "each one apart from his fellow" waits to die. They're spared from their own passivity and despair by three goddesses who appear to Jason and announce that they are the guardians, and daughters, of Libya.[2] Rather than help Jason launch the ship, they tell Jason that everything will be fine, and utter something unclear about Poseidon and his horses. Almost as soon as Jason tells his shipmates what he has seen, a massive horse erupts from the ocean and dashes away across the sand. Deciding that they should not only follow the horse but also carry their ship with them, they set out across the Libyan sands. They carry the ship for twelve days and nights, and have virtually crossed Libya before they arrive at a lake named Trito. We will return to this lake later, because it is one of the places that classical mythology recorded as the birthplace of Athena.

The Libyan desert, it turns out, is full of important mythological sites. It's a kind of obstacle course of episodes and figures from the legendary and divine past. The Argonauts always seem to come across these sites belatedly (as they do at the Garden of the Hesperides), or heedlessly, as if these narrative episodes are embedded in the soil like landmines. For example, one Argonaut, Mopsus, steps on a venomous snake and dies rapidly. The snake turns out to have a genealogy that takes as long to recount as it took Mopsus to die: it sprang from blood that dripped from Medusa's head as Perseus carried it over Libya from the place near the Hesperides where the Gorgons dwelled. This is the only account of Perseus crossing Libya, leaving a contrail of noxious toxins behind. The story, however, gives an etiology for the mythological meaning coiled within the snakes of the Libyan desert, who also appear in a number of later epics.

In another episode, an Argonaut tries to steal some sheep for his comrades and is killed by their shepherd. Like the snake, the shepherd turns out to have a very long and important lineage. He is the grandson of Apollo; his grandmother was the daughter of Minos, the king of Crete. His mother was the goddess Tritonis, who presided over Lake Trito; his father was Garamus (also known as Amphithemis), the eponymous founder of the Garamantes, a rising power in southern Libya when the *Argonautica* was written, and who later featured on medieval *mappae mundi* as one of the peoples of Africa.

The territory, the literal soil, of Libya is a large part of the African episode. The first, and most enduring, challenge the Argonauts face is the sheer inhospitality of the sands, too hot and dry to sustain any life except snakes. We have seen with these two examples that what the earth harbors is often deadly, and in ways that the Argonauts cannot know beforehand. Even when they try to read the surface of the land, they're thwarted. At one point they think they can catch up to Hercules, but everyone runs in different directions because the hero's tracks have been erased by the night winds. It is easy to read these events as merely catastrophic, a list of failures that the hapless Argonauts encounter, or even—especially in the case of Africa—demonstrations that the soil they are on will always be a sediment of destruction and collapse.

That, in fact, seems at first to be precisely the point of the Argonauts' encounter with the Garden of the Hesperides. They arrive at the garden to find the Hesperides themselves mourning the devastation that Hercules has left behind. As soon as the Hesperides see the Argonauts approach, they turn into dust (κόνις) and earth (γαῖα). "Dust" here can also mean "ash," and what has just happened seems to be yet another catastrophe: the immolation of the garden of a god. But its turning into earth reminds us that this is a garden that preserves the gift given to Hera by Gaia, the Earth herself. The Africa of the *Argonautica* is not a desiccated, trackless surface, void of history or narrative. The very earth of Libya is the site of renewal, of new initiatives, even of fecundity, precisely where everything seems to be laid waste. Seeing the Hesperides collapse into dust and earth, Orpheus entreats the nymphs who reside there to at least help them with their thirst. Almost immediately, grass springs from the ground and the Hesperides appear as trees. The nymphs tell the Argonauts that there's a spring nearby that emerged from a rock when Hercules—who else—struck it. The Argonauts run to it, and are saved.

The episode demonstrates, again, how there is something in the earth of Africa that waits to be activated—whether a death-dealing snake or a life-giving spring. The earth is both a receptacle and an initiative, a site where the past waits to shape the future. But more precisely, the episode of the spring suggests that this encounter is about the potential of narrative as much as geography. Orpheus, after all, is the ur-poet in Greek literature, the son of Calliope, the goddess of epic poetry. Orpheus's first song in the *Argonautica* is a cosmogony about "how the earth, sky and sea, at one time combined together in a single form," a symbolic ordering of the universe of the epic itself.[3] His prayer to the Hesperides may echo the text of the golden tablets buried with initiates into the Orphic mysteries, an entreaty to enter the afterlife. It is possible, in fact, that the entire episode in Libya follows the course of an Orphic map of the afterlife, shaped by the Egyptian journey in the afterlife, into the Western desert in search of new water.[4] In any case, Orpheus's prayer has the effect of bringing new life after death, young trees where the old had been despoiled by Hercules. In effect, Orpheus conjures a *reverdie*, the topos of spring that is the age-old metaphor for the beginning of poems. Even where there seems to be a new beginning there is nothing new—at least nothing new under the sun, since Homer and since Plato. Or, to contradict Pliny's famous dictum "there is always something new out of Africa," there is nothing new in Africa. It is not a site of incoherence, or collapse, or of unintelligible otherness. Among other things, it is the foundation of narratives *of* foundation.

That is a circular definition, but that is the shape of the Libyan adventure. After they leave the Libyan desert and return to the sea on the Argo, one of the Argonauts becomes the founder of the colony that will eventually rule Libya. They had been sailing on Lake Trito aimlessly, like "a serpent writhing along his crooked path," until Trito reappeared to show them the way to the sea, first giving them a clod of earth (Apollonius, Bk. 4.1570, 399). At night, the Argonaut Euphemos dreams that the clod becomes a woman with whom he sleeps, and that she tells him that the clod—which he should throw into the sea—will become an island, the "gift of Libya," which will be the Greek center of Libyan rule. That is where the poem ends: it has become an epic of foundation precisely because of its tangled traversal of the land of Libya.

Argonautica-style, we have returned to the starting point of our discussion of landing in Africa. We know more about *why* Africa is important as a recurrent site in epic. But the *event* of landing itself, as I have suggested, is equally important. It is often surprisingly specific. A number of landings happen on the same site: the Syrtis, the modern Gulf of Sidra, in the center of the Libyan coastline, an area of sandbanks and fluctuating tides. It has long been notorious for its dangers. St. Paul and his shipmates were afraid of being driven onto the Syrtis, and lowered a sea anchor as a desperate measure to avoid it. Much later, Gaddafi drew a boundary across it that he called the Line of Death. In the classical era and beyond, its danger was amplified by warnings of extreme heat, sandstorms, and snakes. Less dramatically, it is represented as an inhospitable place simply because it is waterlogged. In *Paradise Lost*, John Milton talks about the "boggy Syrtis, neither sea / Nor good dry land."[5]

This prosaic feature of the Syrtis—that it's a swamp—is surprisingly important for the *Argonautica*. It's the subject of one of the longest descriptions of terrain in the entire epic. The Argonauts are driven onto it by a wind that blows for nine days and nights. In the Syrtis, says the

Argonautica, there is "no return for ships." It is overwhelming, unnatural, interminable:

> For everywhere are shallows.... Over them silently washes the foam of the water. Sand stretches along to the horizon and no land animal or bird travels there.... Sorrow gripped [the Argonauts] when they looked at the sky and the expanse of vast land stretching just like the sky into the distance without a break. No watering place, no trail.... Everything was wrapped in a dead calm.... 'What is this land called?' [ask the Argonauts].... 'How desolate is the coast of this vast mainland that stretches before us!' (Bk. 4.1228–58, 429, 431).

The passage is full of the language of indeterminacy: a dim horizon, mist, land like a mist, a vast land, a continuous, limitless land. The land does not have discernible boundaries, either geographically or elementally. There is little difference between it and the water—and even the sky: ἠερίη δ' ἄμαθος παρακέκλιται ("sand stretches away, raised into the air"). Precisely because it is formless, the Syrtis can mean a number of things. The Argonauts obviously despair about ever leaving, and they scatter on the bleak sands to die alone (until Trito appears to Jason). But the poem compares their despair specifically to *civic* collapse—to crowds agitated by war and pestilence, and temples where statues bleed and sacrifices are rejected (Bk. 4.1280ff, 431ff).

This place is not just a geographical marvel or monstrosity; it is also a space of political chaos—what the political philosopher Giorgio Agamben described as a zone of indistinction. He is really describing the rise of the modern sovereign state, which depends both on the existence of people on the margins of life and a powerful administrative apparatus that both continues to exclude these people and to champion regulations for their care. There's a deep and cruel paradox at the heart of this zone of indistinction: politics purports to have everyone's interests at heart, but enforces the codes of these interests *because* there are people that are hurt by them. This, Agamben says, is a kind of chaos, where "exclusion and inclusion, outside and inside, *bios* and *zoē*, right and fact" collapse into a zone of indistinction.[6] The Argonauts find themselves in what seems to be an absence of life, where there is not even the trace of herders (Bk. 4.1248, 429), and they are reduced to individuals left alone to face death. But what triggers their despair is the failure of technological mastery: it's the helmsman who says emphatically that the ship cannot float again, and that everyone "who had knowledge of ships" agrees. *That* is exactly why they despair: their organized knowledge tells them that they are doomed to chaos.

Their despair in chaos also suggests that what amounts, by the end of the poem, to a story that explains the origin of a cultural order—the Greek colonization of Libya—will never happen. The *Argo*, as Trito will hint, is an allegory of the territory of Greece, a "mother" who has borne them before, and whom they will now carry across Libyan soil on the way, in the distant future, to creating a Greek colony in Libya.[7] More broadly, the *Argonautica* is a book written to examine the world of a very specific political order: that of Ptolemaic Alexandria. The author of the *Argonautica* wrote at the very intersection of Egyptian and Hellenic politics and historical knowledge: Apollonius of Rhodes was in fact head of the Library of Alexandria.[8]

Indeed, Egypt haunts even this moment of chaos. Another way of reading the line "sand stretched away, into the air [ἠερίη]" is that the sand stretched far into Egypt. Earlier in Book 4 of the *Argonautica*, Argus says that an earlier name for Egypt, the "mother of men," was "Ἠερίη," the "Morning Land" (Bk. 4.267, 349).[9] Libya will become, in a future Ptolemaic regime, indistinguishable from Hellenic Egypt. And the lurking presence of Egyptian politics and history makes the Argonauts' eventual initiative in carrying the *Argo* across Libya to Lake Trito a very pointed and specific reference to the ritual performance that Alexander witnessed at Siwa: several dozen men carrying a ship.

There is yet another important way of reading the chaos of the Syrtis landing. It is one that the Argonauts might have recognized from Orpheus's earlier song about the beginning of the world: "He sang how the earth, the heaven and the sea, once mingled together in one form, after deadly strife were separated each from other" (Bk. 4.496–97, 369). The Syrtis is a kind of blank space, reminiscent of what Plato called the *chora* or Parmenides the *apeiron*: what was there before the world, neither form nor matter, nor a world with any boundaries.

The way forward through the Libyan desert, as perplexing and frustrating as it is, is also a kind of cosmogony. It records, or makes, writes into being, as Orpheus does, the cultivated spaces of Hellenic settlement in Africa. It is an account of both the world-making importance of Africa and of its indelible influence on the future.

Apollonius tries to write a poem in which the Greek colonization of Libya seems inevitable, recorded for generations on the landscape. For both the Argonauts and the later Greek colonists, everything happens because of what has already happened, and will happen. Although Libya is inhospitable and deadly to them, the mythology implanted in the country turns out to be their own: the Hesperides in their mythic west, the Gorgon, Minos, Phoebus, and, tearing their way across Libya before the Argonauts, Perseus and Hercules. The Libyan earth itself is charged with mythic meaning, in quite literal ways, as we have seen: the Hesperides collapse into dust, the Syrtis is like the primal cosmos. But the Argonauts become part of it. The guardians of Libya send the Argonauts across Libya to their salvation, and also into a future where the Greeks will use that mythic permission to justify their presence in—and possession of—Libya. In later chapters, we will see how the invocation of a mythic history is one of the ways modern colonization justified its appropriation of land. Even fables or myths, like Plato's Atlantis, were cited to justify white rule in places like Rhodesia.

Landing in Africa was not always a precursor to colonization, or an ur-narrative that led to a triumphant historical destiny. It could also be used to point out failures in leadership (as with Jason and his passivity, although he was rescued by divine intervention), or even the underlying structural flaws of an entire political dispensation. The most remarkable example of the African landing as an analytical tool of this kind is Lucan's *Pharsalia* (also known as *De bello civile*), an epic about the war between Pompey the Great and Julius Caesar for domination of the Roman republic.[10] Lucan wrote it during the reign of Nero, who later had him killed. It's a kind of anti-*Aeneid*. Rather than tell the story of how the Roman empire came to be, Lucan tells the story of how the Roman republic fell apart—or, worse, destroyed itself—in violent, senseless acts that the opening line of the poem calls "wars worse than civil" (Bk. 1.1, 1). Most of its characters are vain, arrogant, narcissistic, senile, or clueless—embodiments of the decadent republic. The gods are almost entirely absent. It is a world desolate of divinity, starkly secular, and indifferent to the mythology that structures most classical epics. The only exceptions to the pervasive neglect of mythology are the two landings in Africa by Curio, a supporter of Caesar, and Cato, another supporter of Caesar and the only character in the epic with redeeming features.

Curio sails to Africa to attack the Numidian king Juba I, who is an ally of Pompey, and lands at a place that he is told is the realm of Antaeus. Wondering how it got its name, he asks a passing shepherd, who turns out to be an amateur historian (Bk 4.590ff, 219). This is where Hercules performed his first feat in Africa, the shepherd says, by defeating the giant Antaeus. Antaeus was the son of Gaia, goddess of the Earth, and was invincible as long as his feet touched the soil. Hercules, who noticed that Antaeus sprang up rejuvenated whenever he fell, weakened him by lifting him off the ground, and was able to kill him. That is the source of the region's name, says the shepherd. Lucan's implication is that Curio may imagine himself to be a second Hercules, defeating an African tyrant. Antaeus is rooted in the soil of Africa, and Hercules establishes his dominion by severing his indigenous connection. But, as if realizing that Curio might not have the imaginative capacity to put himself in the position of Hercules, the shepherd gets more obvious. This place, he says, has a more noble name: it was where Scipio Africanus the Elder, who forced Hannibal to return from Italy, first landed in Africa. Curio understands that reference and, indulging in a bit of magical thinking, believes that the "fortune of the place" (*fortuna locorum*) will win the war (Bk. 4.661, 222).

But Curio badly misreads the mythological and historical omens, and he and his army are slaughtered by Juba and the African army. This slaughter, it turns out, is the real historical rhyme. Lucan describes the defeat of a Roman army by Africans as a propitiation for the death of Hannibal and the Punic shades. Carthage is the return of the repressed: so badly does Curio read African history that he reverses Roman history. His defeat is compared to the destruction of the Carthaginian empire. Lucan says it would actually have been a better thing if Africa had not just conquered Curio's army for the sake of Pompey, but for the sake of Rome (*Africa nos potius vincat sibi*) (Bk. 4.793, 232). It would have been better, in other words, if Carthage had won the Punic Wars. This is not the last time we will see Romans looking back at their supposed victory over Carthage with a sense of regret, or fear, or horror.

The second landing in Africa in the *Pharsalia*, and the other extended encounter with mythological history in the poem, is when Cato the Younger arrives after the defeat of Pompey in the civil war. Cato hoped to take his army to Utica (in modern Tunisia), to make a stand against Caesar. It was a harrowing journey, and, although Cato made it to Utica, he committed suicide there rather than accept safe passage when Caesar attacked it. That was his last act of defiance, but not his first. His contemporaries found him stubborn and exasperating, and in the *Pharsalia* he's a fanatical conservative. He would rather destroy himself than deny what he believes are the lost principles that held the republic together. Almost two millennia on, Cato became the symbol of another lost cause. Above the Confederate Memorial in Arlington National Cemetery is Lucan's line *Victrix causa deis placuit sed victa Catoni*: "The victorious cause pleased the gods, but defeat pleased Cato" (Bk. 1.128, 12).

The final stage of Cato's eventual defeat takes him specifically, as with Jason and the Argonauts, to the confusing and deadly Syrtis. Lucan imagines this African shore as an unfinished part of creation, still trying to decide whether it is sea or land, engaged in an unending and fruitless battle—much like Cato. Part of his fleet is shipwrecked, but the remainder struggles through and finds Lake Trito, where Jason and the Argonauts embarked at the end of their journey. Trito is sluggish (*torpentem*), but it is alive with history (Bk. 9.347, 530). It is beloved, says Lucan, by both Neptune and Minerva, who found her first home there after being born from the head of her father Jupiter. Trito offers a safe haven for Cato, but he is simply too impatient to sail across this sluggish lake to attack Utica. He forgets, or deliberately disregards, the story of the Argonauts, who saved themselves from the Syrtis by carrying their ship across the desert to Lake Trito. Cato leaves his ships and marches into the desert with his men.

Cato's journey through the African desert in the *Pharsalia* is an early version of the disregard and condescension that later European explorers had for the traditions and beliefs of the lands they traveled through. The ignominious fate of the sailors—whom Cato leads across the difficult Libyan sands only to meet with devastating attacks by serpents—stands in ironic contrast to the auspicious mythology of Libya. But this contrast, it turns out, is actually one that Cato deliberately cultivates. He may not be aware that Lake Trito is beloved by both Minerva and Neptune, but he is certainly aware of the religious significance of the sites through which he later travels, and which his pigheaded devotion to stoic perseverance causes him to neglect and bypass. Lucan's Cato is a pitiable figure whose desperate and difficult journey through Libya is made all the more ludicrous because of his inattention to the many possibilities of divine intervention that Libya offers.

Cato represents, ultimately, something like the Roman cultivation of cultural purity at the expense of the heterogeneous and exotic—especially African—sources of that very piety. The most revealing episode is Cato's demurral when invited to consult the oracle at the temple of Jupiter-Ammon, which Alexander the Great himself had traveled to consult. Whatever Ammon says has already been decided, says Cato, and it will make no difference to the outcome whether he knows what it is or not. All we can be certain about is death (*me non oracula certum, / Sed mors certa facit* [Bk. 9.582-83, 548]).

To be precise, Cato does not dismiss the power of the oracle, although he might sound a bit dismissive. He says, simply, that consulting oracles is for those who are in doubt about the future, and that we are born knowing everything we already need to know. He is dismissive, though, about the location of the god in this particular place: why would he have buried the truth in this dust, so that only a few could hear him (*Ut caneret paucis, mersitque hoc pulvere verum?* [Bk. 9.577, 548]). Cato objects to the oracle, at least in part, not just because it is irrelevant to the precepts of stoicism, but also because it is so provincial. The narrator's summation of Cato's decision seems to underscore the judgment that it is simply not relevant to the Roman situation. Cato departs, leaving the oracle to the *populis*—a term that implies, paradoxically, the exclusiveness of Cato's relation to the gods: non-populist; Roman, not belonging to the diffuse peoples of the world.

Cato's journey through a Libya immanent with deity reveals a great deal about his character, which is to say, in Roman terms, his *pietas*. His extraordinary fortitude is underscored by his refusal to take solace in the knowledge that the gods offer. Cato makes it clear that he thinks this knowledge is, if not wrong altogether, at least irrelevant. But Lucan's (or the narrator's) apparent attitude to the traces of divinity in the Libyan landscape is more ambiguous. Cato's disparagement of the location of the Jupiter-Ammon oracle does not mean that the oracle is not divine, just that it's bad at real-estate choices. In fact, Lucan is careful to point out that the oracle's sacred importance is confirmed by the green trees that surround it, the only such trees in all of Libya. Where Cato is eager to keep moving, Lucan repeatedly calls attention to the intractable mythological significance of the territory through which Cato marches.

This commentary begins, of course, when Lucan has Cato arrive, after braving the notorious Syrtis, just where Minerva first touched the earth. But for Lucan, the same area is the site of a number of extraordinary events and features in mythology and classical religion. This is where the river Lethe ("Lethon") emerges from the underworld, carrying forgetfulness into the world, and where the Garden of the Hesperides, from which Hercules stole the golden apples, was located. After Hercules took the apples, however, the trees were left impoverished (*inopes*), and the garden seems to have disappeared altogether (Bk. 9.365, 532). This impoverishment is a kind of metonymy for the almost literally impoverished state of North African mythology in Cato's day. The shrine of Jupiter-Ammon, the principal (or only) god of Egypt and Libya (and parts of Asia), is not a rich temple, resplendent with gems. Jupiter-Ammon is a *pauper deus*, a poor god (Bk. 9.519, 542). "The African nations (*Libycae gentes*)," says Lucan, "have built no rich temple there; nor are there treasure-chambers glittering with Eastern gems" (Bk. 9.515-16, 542). The shrine is humble not because the Africans who worship there are poor, however. That poverty is both a part of the cult and the means by which it has protected itself from the devouring machine of Roman theology. The "old ways" of the god persist because those old ways *included* the rejection of lavish displays of devotion (Bk. 9.520, 542). The god cannot be monetized. The particular, African nature of his divinity cannot be assessed in the marketplace of the Roman pantheon.

It makes sense that, as an austere, contrarian Stoic, Cato would admire Ammon's rejection of material grandeur. It is also part of Ammon's nature: remember that Plutarch said that Ammon's very name contained "hiddenness," a name that conceals within it concealment. Something of Africa remains buried within the shrine, something that cannot be turned into another feature of Roman global religion.

Ammon's shrine is a real and historical version (at least for Cato and, perhaps, Lucan) of the nature of mythology in Africa. Perhaps aware that his crowding together of Minerva's birthplace, the river Lethe, and the Garden of Hesperides ignores what most geographers and mythographers have said about their much farther-flung locations, Lucan asks us not to probe too closely: "Churlish is he who robs hoary antiquity of its fame (*fama*) and demands the truth from poets" (Bk. 9.359, 531). Of course, Lucan may have already compromised the possibility of unveiling the truth because he changes the standard poetic locations of these places.[11] But more important are the implications of this for mythology in general. Lucan's warning follows his account of Hercules and the Garden of Hesperides, and so makes the theft of *fama* from antiquity equivalent to Hercules's theft of apples. To search for the truth of myth—whether Lucan means its allegorical significance or what "really" happened—is to strip myth of its significance altogether. Or, more precisely, of its *fama*, its currency in the world. The "truth" of myth ultimately despoils the myth of its importance altogether, or, to change the underlying metaphor, obscures it. The implication is that, if we are to treat myth with the integrity it demands, we must embrace its very nature as falsehood, what the late antique North African mythographer Fulgentius later called the lies of the Greeks.

But it is not clear whether Lucan embraces this paradox in order to make a point about the function of myth or history. This passage is as much about the preservation of the past as it is about the possibility of using allegory to find Christian truth in pagan stories. That is, what it seems to "mean" is that "truth" destroys the background, the context, and the primal ground of myth: the stolen apples leave the garden empty. All of this is one way of underscoring the primal importance of Africa in Lucan's narrative. Its function is not so much to "mean" something (like the opposite of Roman virtue, or stoicism, or empire) as it is to be the primal ground, the chthonic origin, of narrative—as if the poem itself, like Antaeus, needs to touch the earth. What we would now call the willing suspension of disbelief is the same thing as a reverence for the past. Africa, then, is both credulity and antiquity. It's possible that this notion of Africa is an orientalist subtext, but Lucan also invites us, I think, to discover the internal contradictions in thinking about Africa as some kind of mythological realm that overwhelms the actions of Cato and his men.

The integrity of myth, Lucan says, depends on our willingness to respect its integrity. To seek its "truth" is to ruin it. But seeking truth would also make us like Hercules, who despoils a mythic locale in order to become a more important myth himself. To do what Lucan tells us to do is, at least in this case, to continue the work of myth. But in a less abstract, slyer way Lucan's caution against seeking truth in order to preserve myth reveals a contradiction in his version of myth. The importance of African antiquity lies in the extraordinary concentration of mythological scenes and events in the place at which Cato happens to land. As I've already noted, the placement of the river Lethe there contradicts almost all other accounts, which place it in Spain. And the

Hesperides, again in almost all other accounts, are either in the far west of North Africa or are islands even farther west, in the Atlantic. To seek the "truth" of these myths that frame and ultimately indict Cato, then, is to shake the thematic structure of Lucan's poem, or at least of the entire African episode.

Lucan's African landings point to a world beyond the pettiness and narcissism of Rome, which is circling its own drain. The two mythological episodes in Africa point up the weakness and self-delusion of Rome's leaders, whose foothold on the continent, like Antaeus's, seems to be lost. These two episodes, like so much else in Lucan's epic, are bitter and despairing echoes of earlier foreign landings in Africa that shaped history.

As noted, the most important African landing in Western history can be found in Virgil's *Aeneid*, an epic written eighty to ninety years before Lucan's, in the golden age of the early empire under Augustus. Virgil's epic is the story of how this Rome came to be, and is an unashamed comparison of Augustus with the hero Aeneas. Much of the bitterness of Lucan's epic comes from his allusions to, and quotations of, the *Aeneid*. If Virgil's aim is to suggest that his world is ruled by someone comparable to an epic hero, Lucan's is to show how everyone in his world *thinks* they are in Virgil's world, but are really in a hideous mock epic. Curio's and Cato's miserable landings are pitiful echoes of Aeneas's, which was magnificent in either of its implications: if Aeneas had stayed in Africa, he would have ruled it; by leaving Africa, he founded Rome.

But in leaving behind Africa, Aeneas left a complex legacy. Africa was neither an incidental barrier that Aeneas had to cross nor a passing fancy. And as the *Aeneid* records, Africa was anything but merely an exotic, wild site of otherness, a place that contained the opposite of everything Aeneas (and Virgil's emerging Roman empire) strove to be. If anything, the *Aeneid* is a repository of the profoundly mixed feelings that Romans continued to hold for Africa, after the Punic Wars and well beyond: fear, fascination, love, regret, admiration.

The story of Aeneas's landing in Africa, after he and his group of survivors flee the destroyed city of Troy, opens the *Aeneid*. His stay in Africa takes up a quarter of the entire epic (the first four books). The account of the Trojan War is itself a story told in Africa, by Aeneas to the Carthaginian queen Dido. This section of the *Aeneid*—particularly its end, when Aeneas leaves Dido behind in Africa to go to what will become

Rome—was Augustine's favorite part. The love affair between Aeneas and Dido became one of medieval Europe's archetypal love stories, and Aeneas's entanglement with Dido and Africa became a standard allegory of the soul's entanglement in the world before it frees itself in its ascent to heaven/Rome.

Aeneas's landing in Africa is also entangled in references to other texts. Indeed, Aeneas lands in a world familiar to classical literature and drama. The lushness of the harbor—its plentiful trees and abundance of water—alludes to two of Odysseus's landings in the *Odyssey*. The first is on Circe's island, where the men are turned into pigs and saved only when Odysseus agrees to sleep with Circe; and the second is Odysseus's landing on the island of the Phaeacians, who live a blissful life in daily contact with the gods and who offer Odysseus a magical ship to take him, finally, to his home on Ithaca.[12]

Aeneas's landing suggests the frustrations of Odysseus's journey, but also his encounters with beings and places who offer him love and wonder, either at the cost of forgetting his intense nostalgia for his home or, finally, fulfilling his desire to return home. These echoes of the possibility of homecoming makes Aeneas's predicament more poignant because he has no home to which to return.

For all its apparent bounty, Africa, for Aeneas, echoes with deprivation and loss. The harbor hints at a kind of artificiality, even a false appearance: it's a *scaena*,[13] a word that refers to the back wall of the Roman stage. It's possible that this allusion points ahead to the tragic story of Aeneas's abandonment of Dido and her suicide, or even that it suggests a satyr play, which has the structure of tragedy but in a comic mode.[14] But for the purposes of future literary landings in Africa, this scene suggests that Africa is a stage in another sense: a staging ground for the future of European nations and empires.

The scene's suggestion of artificiality also hints at what literary theorists call a pathetic fallacy: the projection of a character's state of mind onto the surrounding landscape. Aeneas does not quite seem to believe—or trust—the security of the landing, and in Virgil's description of its abundance lurk ominous overtones. The harbor seems a little overwhelming, even claustrophobic: "black with gloomy shade" (*horrentique atrum nemus imminet umbra*) (Bk. 4.165. 272–73). When Aeneas climbs to the plateau above, he first finds it *incultus*: wild, with a sense of luxurious abundance that has not been tamed. Yet when he finds out from Venus a little later that he is, in fact, in Africa, in a self-pitying description he describes Libya as a desert in which he is caught between Europe and Asia. He is, he says, *ignotus*, unknown (Bk. 1.384–85, 288). He articulates his sense of desolation in terms of tropes about Africa: it is mysterious, enigmatic, a vast desert. This is a geography of his mood, cast in the othering terms of stereotypes. Aeneas is himself a desert, like Africa, exiled from the two sites that matter: Troy in Asia, where he came from, and Rome in Europe, where he will end up.

In fact, as Aeneas will shortly discover, there is plenty to love about Africa. He is overwhelmed by the magnificence of Carthage and its defenses, and by the speed with which it has been built on what had been recently nothing but fields. At the same time, Virgil suggests that Dido's building program is also metaphorical, a defense against her desire for Aeneas. When she falls into a frenzy of desire for him, she stops building the walls of Carthage (Bk. 4.86–89, 429). Aeneas is on the verge of taking Carthage altogether. If he had, there would have been no reason for the destructive and traumatic Punic Wars centuries later. Aeneas even begins to build this alternative history. Just a hundred lines later Mercury, sent on a mission from Jove, finds Aeneas already laying the foundations for new buildings in Carthage (Bk. 4.260, 439). So much about Aeneas's landing has this centuries-long tail, events that would have changed the very Rome that Virgil celebrates in the *Aeneid*, and that created the very political and emotional charge that Carthage still had for Rome. The most poignant of these is the famous mourning of Dido when Aeneas sails for Rome. It is a scene that echoes through literary history; in Chaucer's summary of the *Aeneid* in *The House of Fame*, the mourning of Dido is longer than the rest of the story. As we will see in a later chapter, Dido's mourning is also a voicing of the complex feelings that Roman subjects had for Carthage. It was a place of both fear and desire, a place that both prevented and made possible the glory of the Roman empire.

But Dido's love for Aeneas also disturbs the position of Carthage in Africa. Founded as a Phoenician colony (by the queen herself), it occupied a delicate position as both a "foreign" city that ruled over Libya, and as a Libyan city. In mythic history, it might be said to be the site that began the complex problem of what—and where—"Africa" is. At least that's part of what Dido's position represents for Aeneas: "The towers of Carthage and the sight of Libyan city charm you" (*te Karthaginis arces, / Phoenissam, Libycaeque aspectus detinet urbis*) (Bk. 4.347–48, 444–45).

Carthage is also a Libyan city, part of the polity and culture of the Africa around it. When Dido and Aeneas begin their affair, the news flashes through the cities of Libya (Bk. 4.173, 434–35) and reaches Iarbas, ruler of the neighboring kingdom of Getulia, whom Dido had rejected as a suitor.

Iarbas is more than a king. He is in fact the son of Jupiter-Ammon, both the greatest Libyan deity and, as it now turns out, the same god who has adjudicated the battle between Juno and Venus over the fate of Carthage and the future Rome. Here he is very much a Libyan god, to whom Iarbas has set up "a hundred" altars and vast temples throughout his vast realm (*templa ... immania*) (Bk. 4.199, 434). In pleading with Ammon to intervene in the affair between Dido and Aeneas, Iarbas stresses the widespread and ongoing piety of the people of all of "Maurisia" (Mauretania, a far wider region than Libya): they are "now" pouring libations to him—suggesting either that they are doing it at that moment, or that widespread worship of Ammon has begun now that Iarbas is king. Ammon listens, and sends Mercury to urge Aeneas onward to his destiny in Rome. But Mercury's flight is a particularly African one. He swoops down on the Atlas Mountains, and, slowing down, makes his own African landing "on Libya's sandy shore" (*litus harenosum Libyae*) (Bk. 4.257, 438). An African god, then, intervenes in the affair between Dido and Aeneas by sending Aeneas away from Africa.

The famous scene of Dido's lament and suicide follows shortly, a section of the poem that, apart from the descent to the underworld in Book 6 (which, because Aeneas encounters Dido in it, is partly a callback to the ending of Book 4), is the part of the *Aeneid* that most influenced literary history. Very shortly after the *Aeneid* began circulating, Ovid (thirty years younger than Virgil) wrote *Heroides VII*, a letter that Dido sends to Aeneas just before her death. Part of Aeneas's legacy as a founder of Rome is to have destroyed the founder of the future Carthaginian Africa, a Mediterranean power that threatened the existence of Rome. Aeneas leaves behind him a trail of ambiguity—of desire, vindication, mourning, and anxiety.

As Dido's sister Anna reminds her just before her death, Africa—a term Anna uses as she evokes territories still outside the nascent Carthage, such as Barca, seven hundred miles away—remains a powerful presence, and one that threatens to overwhelm Dido's carefully maintained polity, precisely because she has scorned Iarbas and other African leaders by loving Aeneas (Bk. 4.40, 424). Iarbas's people are indomitable in war (*insuperabile bello*). Furthermore, Anna reminds Dido that Africa is a land rich in triumph (*triumphis / dives*), that continues to nurture leaders (Bk. 4.38–39, 424).

Africa is not forgotten, although Aeneas leaves it behind. Indeed, as we will see, Aeneas's landing sets a pattern that medieval British epic and history, in particular, will follow.

Britain's African Foundations: Geoffrey of Monmouth

The most British of all British histories, written by Geoffrey of Monmouth in the twelfth century, placed Britain at the center of many of the dominant histories of Europe. In the words of the postcolonial scholar Kwame Anthony Appiah, it "played a significant part in providing a framework within which the different cultural streams—Roman, Saxon, Danish, and Norman—that had come together over the first millennium in Britain could be gathered into a single unifying history."[15] The *History of the Kings of Britain* (*Historia Regum Britanniae*) is also the most British in a literal way: it opens with an explanation of how the name "Britain" came from its founder, Brutus. This is not the friend and betrayer of Julius Caesar, although Geoffrey's history is so imaginative that he probably could have arranged that. But Geoffrey's Brutus is far older, dating back to the early foundation of Rome. He has, in fact, an intimate connection with it: he is the great-grandson of Aeneas. Geoffrey's source just says that Brutus was a Roman consul, but Geoffrey makes him also a (grand)son of Troy, and therefore someone who bequeaths to Britain virtually the same origin story as Rome. Britain, too, is founded by Trojans.

That story became increasingly important in British history, perhaps reaching its pinnacle in the later Middle Ages, when London began to be called New Troy, and its mayor called himself its Duke. Books and public tablets in England dutifully memorialized how long it had been since the fall of Troy and the foundation of Britain. Geoffrey invented, along with the story of Brutus, much of the stories of King Arthur, Merlin, and King Lear. There were numerous translations, paraphrases, rewritings, and romances based on Geoffrey's *History* throughout Europe in the Middle Ages, and in a number of languages: Latin, English, Old Norse, Welsh, French, Castilian, and Catalan. The importance of Brutus to the history of the British—from whom, says Geoffrey, Britain itself got its name—is attested in the titles given to two of the most influential translations: one into Norman French by Wace, the other into Middle English by Laȝamon, both called simply *Brut*.

Yet the first word of Geoffrey's history is the name Aeneas: *Aeneas post Troianum bellum excidium urbis* ("Aeneas, after the Trojan War, [fled] the destruction of the city").[16] The *History* begins with a very brief version of Aeneas's conquest of Latium and Italy, of Aeneas's son and grandson, the father of Brutus. Brutus's birth is preceded by a prophecy that he would kill both his parents, wander through many lands in exile, and end up achieving the highest honor. His wanderings have a spooky parallel to Aeneas's. Brutus kills his father (his mother had died in childbirth) in a reversal both of Aeneas's legendary *pietas* toward his father, and in a callback to Aeneas's shooting twelve stags to feed his men when they land in Africa; Brutus mistakes his father for a stag and shoots him. Driven out of Italy because of the patricide, he ends up in Greece, where he liberates a group of Trojans held in servitude by King Pandrasus. Rather than rule Greece, Brutus and his companions decide to find a place without the specter of subjection. Their first stop is the small Greek island of Leogecia (Leucadia or Lefkada, on the west coast of Greece), where Diana tells Brutus in a dream to sail west until he finds an island, once inhabited by giants and now deserted, where he will build a new Troy. But rather than sail west, Brutus travels *south* for thirty days, until he lands on the coast of Africa, at a place known in classical history (and in fascist Italy, as we will see) as the Altars of Philaeni.

The Altars are significant in several ways. The most important is the story behind them, to which I will turn in a moment. But they also have a literary afterlife. They are the first point in an itinerary through Africa that, itself, becomes a literary trope, almost like a package tour that is available through the centuries. Brutus and his people travel to several specific places that are often obscure, but whose names are repeated in later texts: the "Lake of Salinae" on the border of the Roman province of Byzacena (eastern Tunisia); Russicada in Numidia (modern Skikda in Algeria); the "mountains of Azara" or "Uzarae" (the Aurès Mountains, in northeast Algeria); the Malva River (Moulouya, in Mauretania). The same itinerary first appears in Paulus Orosius's *Historia Adversum Paganos*. Orosius traveled from Spain to become a student of Augustine's; he opens his *Historia* with a description of Africa that is the first statement of this itinerary. It circulated in Latin copies of Orosius's book and also in an Old English translation.

That is not the only thread connecting this Roman North African itinerary with medieval Britain. There is another one, although it's woven in, so to speak, much later. In 1917, Flinders Petrie—whose methods as an Egyptologist and whose cyclical, racist history we discussed earlier—gave a lecture to the British Academy on the Brut legend. He argued that the story was invented not by Geoffrey of Monmouth, but by a "Romanized Briton, brought up in Rome, on the Aeneid."[17] That idea was total speculation built on a mistake. He thought a fifteenth-century Welsh paraphrase of Geoffrey was actually an early medieval record of what this imaginary Roman Briton wrote. Petrie based most of his argument on a minute inspection of the sites in the African landing in Geoffrey's history. He included a table of the longitudes and latitudes of each. Petrie covers the flaws in his argument with a blizzard of erudition, and a palpable confidence in the rigor of his methods. That confidence, however, hides an anxiety that his work might not be considered "scientific" enough. Although he was a polymath—or maybe because he was—he took every opportunity to distinguish his work from mere "literature." In fact, that effort lies at the heart of his argument about the first-century Briton in Rome writing the Brutus story. The very reason people have missed the true origin of that story, he says, is that it has been "discredited" since the twelfth century because Geoffrey of Monmouth wrote "literature" instead of "history." But Petrie doesn't stop there; there's also a racist logic at work. It's not just Geoffrey who "prefers literature to history," but the "Celtic mind" itself. Geoffrey may have buried the real facts in a cavalcade of whimsy, but "Celtic" writers and scholars are still doing that. *That* is why nobody else, he suggests, has discovered the truth about the origin of the Brutus story.

There are still further fundamentally racist reasons that Petrie cares so much about the date of the Brutus story. It confirms a cultural connection between the Britons and the Romans that persists until modernity in the story of Brutus and its Arthurian legacy. Petrie suggests that Geoffrey doesn't *really* believe the whole story; for him it is just historical fiction. For Petrie, however, it confirms racial history. In his short book about the cycles of history, *The Revolutions of Civilisation*, one of the last cycles he traces is the period from 1 to 1500 CE. The low point of the last of the "waves of art" across history comes right in the middle, which corresponds to the arrival of Islam in Egypt and the Saxon invasion of England.[18] That decline, Petrie says, is a lesson for today. He meant the Edwardian era, but his warning is horribly familiar even in the twenty-first century. It's superficially similar to the so-called great replacement theory, the racist fear that immigration will erase white cultures all over the world, except with a classist dimension. The danger, Petrie says, "of a diversity running into two separate groups is notorious in history." He means that diversity can be problematic, but only if racial division is synonymous with class. A "studious Englishman," he says, would rather have a Japanese professor for a neighbor than the "average drinking workingman," even if he were a cousin.[19]

All of that is to say that this random-seeming series of landings in Africa has had a profound effect on European meditations on history, and thus Africa lies at their core. Some of these sites will appear later in this book, but the first of them, the Altars of Philaeni, is especially important because it represents the founding—and the ultimate collapse—of empires. One of the first governors of Africa Nova (eastern Numidia), established in 46 BCE as the second Roman province in Africa, was the historian Sallust. His *Jugurthine Wars* is, in a sense, a history of the Roman failures that led to his position of governor after Caesar had become dictator and defeated Numidia. Sallust argues that Rome failed to conquer Numidia sixty years earlier because the Roman republic had become decadent after the destruction of Carthage, and lacked the capacity to make sacrifices to achieve important victories, a theory that later resonated in Augustine's *City of God* and beyond.

For Sallust, the story of the Altars of Philaeni contains a profound irony. It explains how Carthage first became a Mediterranean power, more than a far-flung colony on the coast of Africa. It's a story that begins with the rise of the Carthage that would threaten Rome's existence, and whose obliteration would in turn make Rome the dominant power in the Mediterranean. For Sallust, the story is profoundly melancholy not just because Carthage is gone, but because the Rome that conquered it is gone, too. It is gone because it failed to emulate what happened at the Altars of Philaeni. All that remains at the Altars is a vast tomb. But later in his book, Sallust says more: It's appropriate, he says, to commemorate (*memorare*) the unparalleled and miraculous story (*egregium atque mirabile*) at this point because the place urges it (*admonuit*).[20]

The story of the Altars of Philaeni marks an event almost as important in Carthage's founding as Dido's legendary marking out of the boundaries of the city with strips cut from a single ox hide. It is a second mythic charter for the empire of Carthage, and one that declares its difference from the Hellenic world. Carthage's chief rival in its early days was the territory of Cyrene, the Greek colony whose origin myth is told in the *Argonautica*, and which opened the worship of Ammon to the larger Hellenic world. Cyrene and Carthage agreed to establish their border in an athletic contest. Two citizens from each city would set out running toward each other at the same time, and the border would be where they met. The Carthaginians, two brothers named Philaeni, ran farther, and won more territory for Carthage. The Cyrenaeans accused them of cheating by leaving Carthage before the agreed time, and would only accept the result of the race if the brothers agreed to be buried alive. They did agree, and their sacrifice was consecrated by altars on the spot (Sallust, 339).

The Altars of Philaeni occupied a strangely complex and persistent place in the Roman historical imagination. The not-so-implicit lesson is that the Carthaginians exhibited the kind of self-sacrifice that builds empires. The site again enters the Roman historical imagination prominently with the advent of Mussolini, who built a grand fascist-style arch on the supposed site of the Altars, again suggesting an important but somehow obscure lesson about the foundation of the Roman imperium. A line from Horace's *Carmen saeculare* that promised that the sun would never see a city greater than Rome was inscribed on it. After Mussolini, however, the arch became a symbol of Italian colonialism, and Colonel Gaddafi ordered it dynamited in 1973.

For Sallust, the Altars were the site of a profound and melancholy lesson for Rome: they suggested the wide gap between Carthaginian determination and Roman decadence. It is not just a story about the abstract moral virtue of sacrifice. Rather, it is quite literally a lesson about how to extend and occupy territory, a reminder that it is bloody, horrible, and almost too unbearable to remember, about which it is "better to be silent," Sallust says, "than to say too little" (211).

The trope of landing in Africa almost always concerns the question of violence, even when it does not seem to. Orosius, the source of Brutus's itinerary, describes how Africa welcomed him "with liberality" to her "undisturbed peace."[21] That is utterly different, he thinks, from the complaint that another shipwrecked group of Trojans makes to Dido.

They are driven "to the cruel seas again" because the Carthaginians "shut up a desert shore to drowning men" (Virgil, Bk. 1.540–14, quoted in Orosius, Bk. 5.2, 209). For Orosius, peace has come because of the universal spread of Christianity. The contrast he makes is between the Christian present—here exemplified by North Africa and a host of Augustine allusions in the same passage—and the pagan past, exemplified by the war and violence of the pagan world in Africa.

Two Africas, then: the violent, pagan one of the past; and the peaceful, universal Africa. Orosius, of course, was in Africa when he wrote about his own landing, and Africa just happens to be in the forefront of his vision while he writes about the spread of Christianity. But even much later, in medieval Europe, these two Africas appear on the world stage.

It is mostly the violent Africa that appears in Geoffrey's history. It is part of a centuries-long economy of destruction that begins with Brutus's landing. For Geoffrey, the profound violence that Brutus inflicts when he lands in Africa is what matters. As we have seen, the Trojans had already plundered an entire country before leaving the continent. On their way along the African coast to Mauretania, they were attacked by pirates, whom they defeated and whose plunder and wealth they took. Geoffrey's text here is intriguingly ambiguous: *spoliis eorum et rapinis ditati sunt*, he says, *either* "the Trojans were enriched by the pirates' spoils and plunder" *or* "the Trojans were enriched by their own spoils and plunder" (Bk. 1.233, 21). And indeed, immediately after this, the Trojans turn into pirates themselves, not only plundering but also laying waste (*uastauerunt*) to the entire country of Mauretania (Bk. 1.326, 21). This devastation, literally and symbolically, echoes an earlier episode, when Brutus's force sheltered on the island of Lefkada, which had been laid waste (*uastata*) by pirates (Bk. 1.278, 19). Brutus and his men are not only left holding the plunder of pirates; they also commit precisely the kind of devastation that pirates commit.

Geoffrey's concern is not necessarily with pirates. It is with what laying waste, beginning with Lefkada and Africa, means in the long history of the foundation of Britain. The action of laying waste runs throughout Geoffrey's history, but it also structures the recurrent involvement of Africa in British history. Five reigns after Arthur, Careticus became king of the Britons. The already precarious polity of Britain fell apart, partly, says Geoffrey, because Careticus loved civil war, but also because the Saxons took the opportunity to lay waste (*deuastabant*) to Britain (Bk. 11.184, 286).

It's at precisely this point that Africa makes its next appearance (Bk. 11.100, 253–54). Realizing that this is their opportunity to conquer the British, the Saxons send for help to Ireland. But it is not the Irish to whom they appeal; it is to Gormund, King of the Africans. An aside mentions that Gormund and the Africans had already subjugated the Irish (Bk. 11.125, 255–56). Geoffrey has said nothing about the Africans since Brutus laid waste to Mauretania, and the only connection in the narrative is the repeated action of laying waste to a land. That, indeed, is what Gormund and the Africans do. They push Careticus and the Britons into Wales and go on to lay waste to Britain as if following a manual written by Brutus and his men centuries before: Gormund "made an utter devastation (*devastavit*, i.e., laid waste) of the country, set fire to the adjacent cities, and continued these outrages until he had almost burned up the whole surface of the island from the one sea to the other (*a mari usque ad mare*)," a violence that is the literal echo of Brutus's ancient violence against Africa as he and his men *uastauerunt patriam a fine usque ad finem* (Bk. 11.137, 257; Bk. 1.326, 21). The Africans give the "greater part" of Britain, named Loegria, to the Saxons.

The African Invention of England

This story marks the turn of British history from the Britons to the Anglo-Saxons—and therefore the invention of "England" ("Anglo"-land). In the story of Britain, Brutus and Africa form a vast chiasmus, two events that are mirror images. Africa is the hinge of Britain's origin civilization: first the scene of Trojan military excess on Brutus's founding journey through Africa; then the campaign to Ireland and Britain by Africans who obliterate the Britain that Brutus founded. From our perspective, it's hard not to read this plot as a revenge fantasy in which the colonies reoccupy the colonizer.

There's another angle to the story of the African role in the Anglo-Saxon takeover of Britain. One of the depredations that the Africans cause is the erasure of Christianity. Not only are priests "laid in the dust" by the Africans, but Gormund is also assisted by the French king's nephew Isembard, who renounces Christianity "out of love" (although Gormund promises to help him take the French throne himself). But this attack on Christianity also paradoxically marks the advent of Christianity among the Anglo-Saxons. The very next passage is the story of how Pope Gregory the Great sent Augustine of Canterbury to convert the English. Geoffrey's account is much briefer than Bede's story in his *History of the English Church*, where Pope Gregory sees two slave boys who he is told are English (*Angli*). No, he says, they are angels (*angeli*), and he launches a mission to the English. But in Geoffrey, rather than bring peace to England, Augustine's Christianity simply keeps the enmity between the Anglo-Saxons and the British alive, only this time in the form of Christian sectarianism. The abbot at the British abbey of Bangor refuses to recognize Augustine's authority over him. The British also believed, says Geoffrey, that Saxon Christianity was just a ruse that would allow them to continue to deprive the British of their land. Christianity just becomes another way in which the ancient violence of Brutus in Africa is perpetuated. At every turn, the result is the act of wasting the land. Freud would probably call this a repetition compulsion, the inevitable reappearance of an early act of violence that cannot be left behind. It begins to be a way that someone makes sense of the world: because it is such a profound experience, it must be a part of life in general. One could call it the waste of life.

The implications of Geoffrey's term *uastare*, to lay waste, are (so to speak) vast (both "vast" and "waste" come from the Latin word *vastus*). The first description of the entire land laid waste may be in one of Geoffrey's important sources, Gildas's *De Excidio Britanniae*, written in the sixth century. Gildas's description of a land ruined by war and heresy is so evocative that, says Lynn Staley, he "inscribed the wasteland upon Britain's imagination."[22] Geoffrey helped to give the wasteland a precise place and name. After the Africans defeat the Saxons and the entire land lies devastated, the part of it named Loegria is given to the Saxons. They possess it for a while, until it is depopulated by war and famine. The few remaining Saxons invite a second wave of Saxons to invade Loegria. They arrive and possess the "empty tracts of land from Scotland to Cornwall" (Bk. 11.204, 278). Loegria, this persistent wasteland, it turns out, is England.[23]

From that point on, this wasteland will haunt England in Arthurian narrative, never quite the same thing, but still not very different. Patricia Ingham calls it England's "elusive shadow."[24] Its centrality runs through Arthurian literature from Chrétien de Troyes's *Perceval*, written just a few decades after Geoffrey's *Historia*, to the most famous version of all, T. S. Eliot's *The Waste Land*. There are many more after Eliot, of course. The wasteland is an obvious precursor to postapocalyptic landscapes in literature and film. But the wasteland is also Africa's elusive shadow, cast by Brutus's original wasting of the land.

Africa and the wasteland remain intertwined in the modern era. In Jessie Weston's *From Ritual to Romance*, a book that Eliot cited as an influence in a famous footnote to *The Waste Land*, Africa plays a crucial part. Weston cites examples from two groups in Africa (the Shilluk of Sudan, about whom more in the chapter on kingship, and the Degema of Nigeria), who believe there is a fundamental link between the vitality of the king and the health of the land. Weston also touches on another important use of the concept of the wasteland in the era of colonization. In an 1891 article about the "Single Women" of Britain, she suggests that they could both become useful themselves and increase the productivity of Britain's possessions by becoming "land owners and enterprising settlers in the Colonies."[25] Weston followed her own advice: she reported from South Africa later in the 1890s. In her study of the legend of Lancelot, she compares Yvain summoning rain by pouring water on a stone to the "sympathetic magic" of South Africa.[26]

Implicit in Weston's advice that women could become useful by making colonial land fertile is the fundamental principle that supports the colonial appropriation of land: the notion of waste. We have seen that it is the effect of invasions in Geoffrey. It is also an explicit instrument of conquest, and Geoffrey would most likely have encountered its results during his life. He grew up on the so-called Welsh Marches, the border between Wales and England that marked the long English attempt to conquer Wales. The tactic of laying waste was common along the Welsh border, employed both by the Welsh and their enemies.[27] William the Conqueror occupied northern England only by laying much of it waste—as he also did to a large part of the Marches. As we will see in the chapter on Kenya below, there is also a more subtle, slow-moving, and fine-tuned way of laying waste that allows the powerful to claim land. The 1235 Statute of Merton allowed lords of the manor to "enclose"—that is, to take for their own purposes—common land that was not being used. The term for this land was wasteland. This statute—the first statute in most medieval English collections of law, and the first in the official record of English statutes—became the bedrock of the British appropriation of land in the colonies. Land could officially be designated as waste, and then given to settlers. The commissioner of the protectorate of Nyasaland (now Malawi) talked about how he had "generally acquired the waste lands for the Crown by means of concessions from native chiefs."[28] The commissioner, Harry Johnston, didn't explain how or why the land was declared waste in the first place. Often the decision was arbitrary. In Kenya, one large area was set aside because a commissioner testified that, on his way to the hearing, he didn't see many people. Harry Johnston and his colleagues in one sense were simply carrying on the eons-old work that Brutus began by first laying waste to Africa.

Yet Africa in Geoffrey's text is more than the other end of a seesaw of devastation. In an almost literal way, Africa provides the foundation of one of Britain's primeval symbols. When King Arthur's uncle Aurelius wins an important victory against the Saxons, he rebuilds the kingdom, restoring both churches and laws. Afterward Aurelius returns to the site of the final, bloody battle and, moved deeply, wonders how to build an appropriate memorial for all of the Britons who had sacrificed their lives there. None of the artisans in Britain take the job, because they do not believe they can build a suitably magnificent monument.

Eventually, someone suggests Merlin. But Merlin does not conjure up a memorial. Instead, he proposes moving the Giant's Ring, a circle of stones in Ireland, to the site of the battle. Aurelius thinks the idea is ludicrous because Britain already has stones. Merlin explains that the stones have medicinal powers that no stones in Britain do, because they were taken to Ireland by giants. Aurelius doesn't talk about the giants, perhaps because, way back at the beginning of the whole history, Diana told Brutus in a dream that his people would inhabit an island "where giants once lived" (Bk. 1.307, 20). The giants were not entirely gone. When Corineus, the progenitor of Cornwall, peeled off from Brutus's force to take Cornwall, he spent his time fighting giants (Bk. 1.466–88, 28–29). What seems most surprising, perhaps, is that no story overtly explains Merlin's identification of these giants: they are Africans, who brought the stones from Africa with them. As far as I know, nobody has really paid attention to the Africans in Geoffrey's history, who not only appear in prominent places but are also responsible for two important items in today's white supremacist brand: the very invention of the "Anglo-Saxon," and the existence of Stonehenge, now a monument to pure "Britishness." It became a symbol of the Brexit movement, indeed the first Brexit monument, creating "the birth of a British identity" through "the first united cultural events of our island."²⁹ Geoffrey himself has been attributed with the myth that Stonehenge is the navel of Britishness—even while he's the very source for stories about the vital role that Africans played in the foundation of Britain and England.³⁰

Most explanations for the long arc of African references in Geoffrey amount to one thing: that Gormund was not really an African. He might be Welsh. Geoffrey, this argument goes, made a linguistic mistake: he misread a reference to Gormunt *ap Ricca* (Arthur's half brother Gormunt, whose father was Ricca, a Cornish elder) as Gormund *of Africa*.³¹ That's theoretically possible, although it depends on several large assumptions (for instance, that Gormunt was already the son of Ricca in Geoffrey's source material, and that Geoffrey read his source in Welsh, but misunderstood the common term *ap*). Another argument has it that Gormund was a Scandinavian pagan, derived from one of several Viking figures.³² If Gormund was originally a Scandinavian, he becomes an "African" because he is a pagan. The Saxons are also pagans, but to ramp up the threat of Gormund and his army, Geoffrey may have decided to make them a more threatening other. Africans would fit the bill (analogous to the Saracen threat in the era of the Crusades). The oldest version of this argument that I have found is in Gustav Storm's 1878 history of the Vikings.³³ It depends on complex arguments about texts that, it turns out, were probably written after Geoffrey's. The now-dominant argument is simpler and depends on several texts that may or may not have been written before Geoffrey, and on the logic of race that contemporary medievalists have uncovered in the medieval period.³⁴

Geraldine Heng's 2018 book *The Invention of Race in the European Middle Ages* reads the opposition between Christian and Muslim as the foundation of modern epidermal racism. The animus that erupted in the First Crusade was cast in both visceral, bodily terms, and in moral terms; cultural and religious difference became as stark as the difference between literal black and white. Carol Lumbley suggests that Geoffrey got the idea to make a vaguely Saracen army African from the chronicler William of Malmesbury's description of King Guthrum as a pagan so stubborn that he was like the Ethiopian who could not change his skin.³⁵ Yet Gormund and his army are not raced in that sense: Geoffrey does not say anything about their physical appearance. As Lumbley suggests, Gormund and his army signal "African alterity." But this alterity may be more complex than just the medieval othering of a racially different group. It may reach into the specific history of Africa's engagement with Europe.

Indeed, Geoffrey's most important successor makes Gormund a more sympathetic character. Wace's *Roman de Brut*, the French version of Geoffrey's history, influenced numerous vernacular versions of the narratives in Geoffrey's history. Wace often adds details that make Geoffrey's text richer in retrospect. He suggests, for instance, that the brutality of the African and Anglo-Saxon conquest of Britain is mostly the fault of the Angles.[36] Gormund himself becomes more a questing hero of a romance than the mere leader of a war machine. He refused his inheritance in the African kingdom because he wanted to prove himself: he took an oath to rule only territory that he himself had conquered. Wace underscores Gormund's commitment to justice (*dreit*) by having him hand over Britain to the Angles, which he had sworn to do if he won the war.[37] If anything, Gormund becomes *more* like a European chivalric hero than a construct of medieval European racial animus.

Racism or misreading may not have turned Gormund and his army into Africans. They may, in fact, always have been African. His name is Germanic, but that does not mean that he would have been perceived as European: he may have been a North African Vandal.[38] Under pressure from the Huns and the Visigoths in the fifth century, the Vandals left their ancestral lands (present-day Poland), making their way through Spain into North Africa in 429. In 430, St. Augustine died during their siege of his hometown Hippo Regius. And by 439, the Vandals had conquered the former Roman provinces of North Africa, including Carthage. Their arrival was violent: even today, thanks to their sacking of Rome in 410, one of our terms for wanton destruction (we could say laying waste) is vandalism. But they established an important culture in North Africa that would influence later developments in European literature (as we will see in the chapters below).

The old idea that the Vandals everywhere wrecked the Roman empire is contradicted by this flourishing of intellectual culture, what scholars now refer to as the Vandal renaissance.[39] In many ways, Vandal culture acquired a distinct African identity.[40] A Romano-African priest flattered an African Vandal that he was a figure more illustrious than any produced by Greece—and that he, too, had come from the "heart of our Africa."[41] The city that became known as the "mother of the Vandals" was not somewhere in the Germanic lands. It was Carthage. North African

Vandal coins used the image of a personified Carthage with the legend *Felix Karthago*—Fortunate Carthage.[42] The Vandals were displaced from Carthage when the Byzantines conquered the city in 533 CE, and rather than cross over to Spain to live with their Visigothic kinsmen, several hundred Vandals escaped to the Mauri in the mountains of Morocco and Mauretania.

The Vandals, then, were Africans. They were also Christians, although Christians caught up in the extensive and violent heresy wars for which North Africa was well known in late antiquity. They were Arians, adherents of a theology that began in North Africa. It was spearheaded by Arius, a charming ascetic from Libyan Cyrene, whose teachings Augustine criticized extensively. Once the Vandals arrived, however, Arianism took over North Africa and became a virtual state religion. The differences between orthodox Christianity and Arianism may seem minute, turning on the precise relationship of the Father and the Son within the Trinity. But the hostility between the two sides was immense, partly because of the association of Arianism with (largely African) state power.

Anti-Arian propaganda exaggerated the difference between Arianism and orthodox Christianity. One author, Victor of Vita, insisted on referring to non-Arians as "the Christians" and Arians as barbarians.[43] Gregory of Tours's sixth-century *History of the Franks* talks about how, shortly after the "dispersal" of the Vandals throughout Africa and Mauretania, the cruelest of the Vandal rulers embarked on a systematic persecution of Christians throughout his African kingdom (*Africanum ... regnum*).[44]

Two of Geoffrey's immediate sources describe Arianism arriving in Britain as an invading horror. In his *Ecclesiastical History*, Bede talks about the poisonous plague of Arianism infecting the Christian churches of Britain. Both Bede and Gildas call Arianism a serpent vomiting poison, a heresy that comes from beyond the sea, but dangerous because it was a threat from within Christianity.[45]

Although Gormund and his Africans do, indeed, come from beyond the sea (in fact two of them, the Mediterranean and the Irish), they are also familiar in ways that the Angles were not. Geoffrey does not *actually* call the Africans pagans. He does say that the French king's nephew Isembard renounced Christianity for the sake of Gormund, but that does not necessarily mean that Isembard became a pagan. Geoffrey's Latin says that Isembard renounced "*his* Christianity," not Christianity in general: he may be giving up one version of Christianity for another.

Elsewhere, Geoffrey freely calls other invaders (e.g., the fifth-century warlord Vortigern) pagans (Bk. 6.101, 126). The Africans are threatening to the Britons, but not necessarily in the way that we now read that threat, as the embodiment of the religious, cultural, and racial other that medieval Europeans feared in the twelfth century. They are people who share a common religion and history, at least in Geoffrey's text, stretching back to the generation after the Trojan War.

At stake here are two ways of understanding the entanglement of Africa with Europe. One way assumes that Africans play a role in the cultural imagination of medieval Europeans that is like Hitchcock's MacGuffin, a more or less irrelevant object that characters search for or desire. Africans appear late in the history of legendary narratives in Britain, it seems, because there is a need for a dialectical opposite, people who could not be more unlike the British. It is not enough to represent the Scandinavians as evil; they become Saracens next—both Muslim and racially different—then, finally, Africans, who are presumably pagan and Black. In medieval terms, this is a kind of allegorical reading. In the Middle Ages, preachers' handbooks provided two ways of understanding objects and events: *in malo*—as an example of evil in the world—and *in bono*—as an example of something good. "Africans," in the allegory of race, are evil, and should (for a medieval audience) be read that way when they appear in narratives.

But the other way of reading the presence of Africa and Africans in Geoffrey's history is *in bono*, as a continual—and not always destructive—presence in British history. The sustained and even foundational roles they play means that they are more than momentary representations of the other. They are not quite embodiments of divine virtue, perhaps, but neither are they demons. For Geoffrey, at least, Africa and Africans are a fundamental part of the legendary British past. At Stonehenge, at the heart of Britain, is African land—or at least a piece of it.

CHAPTER THREE

The Specter of Carthage

A spectre is haunting Europe....

The Communist Manifesto

Carthage is not yet destroyed.

MARY WOLLSTONECRAFT

Carthage the Symptom: Virgil, Silius Italicus, Horace, Freud

No single place on the continent of Africa is more important in the formation of European attitudes about Africa than Carthage, the city that the medieval encyclopedist Isidore of Seville called "the true Africa" (Bk. 14.5.7, 292).

Almost from the moment of its destruction, Carthage came to stand not just for the continent but also for the fate of civilization itself. Polybius reports that Scipio Africanus Minor gazed over the wreckage of the city after he himself had destroyed it, weeping and musing about the eventual fate of Rome. By the time of Augustine, Carthage represented the intractably agonistic nature of the earthly city: having an enemy is necessary for the survival of civil society.[1]

Augustine's account of arriving in Carthage at the age of seventeen is also shot through with other historical memories of Carthage. It is one of the important stops on the itinerary Aeneas follows on his way to Rome in the *Aeneid*, a text that haunts Augustine throughout the *Confessions*. For classical commentators Aeneas's sojourn in Carthage represented the entanglement of the soul in the world, or, as Augustine says, his youthful self in shameful loves. For Virgil, as for the *Argonautica*, Geoffrey of Monmouth, and Geoffrey Chaucer, Carthage is a metonym both of the existential threat that Africa in its entirety posed to the formation of European identity, *and* of the singular importance of Carthage in the formation of the European cultural and political imaginary.

One line in Virgil's *Aeneid* demonstrates the complex part that Carthage played in the Roman historical imagination. When a group of shipwrecked Trojan sailors arrive in Carthage, Dido welcomes them, promising them land in Africa, wealth, and treatment as her equals in the realm. She does this, she says, because she has heard of the destruction of their city (Bk. 1.561–68, 301). Even 150 years after the destruction of Carthage in 146 BCE, Virgil offers a glimpse of what could have been: a balance of power in a joint *imperium*, compassion in place of the destruction of a city. Dido says, to these future founders of Rome, "The city I build is yours" (*urbem quam statuo vestra est*) (Bk. 1.573, 302–03). In the immediate future it will not be theirs, because they sail away from it with Aeneas when he abandons Dido for his destiny in Italy. But later, Dido's offer became devastatingly true, when the Romans took Carthage by force. In an even deeper way, Virgil means that Carthage will *always* be a part of Rome. His epic is testimony to that: it opens in Carthage, and four of the twelve books of the *Aeneid* take place *in* Carthage. But the city that Dido built became Rome's only once it had been destroyed, and had become Rome's traumatic kernel.

Virgil's example of a Carthage that slips through time, provoking Romans despite its destruction—or because of it—is a part of a larger Roman traumatic formation. The longest poem in classical Latin is *The Punic Wars*, written by Silius Italicus. The ghost of Virgil hovers over it, like an early version of Dante's Virgil in *The Divine Comedy*. *The Punic Wars* is modeled after the *Aeneid*, and so the story of Dido haunts its account of the Second Punic War. It is a poem that is remarkably full of ghosts, in many ways a poem about being haunted by history. It's almost as if Silius Italicus's entire poem is set in the underworld of the *Aeneid*, where Aeneas encounters the ghosts of Dido, his father, and the spirits of eminent Romans waiting to be born into the future—including the "destroyers of Libya," the two men named Scipio Africanus (Virgil, Bk. 6, 6.843, 592–93). Silius's poem is haunted, above all, by the *Aeneid*: it shows how the ghost of Dido lingers in Roman literature, and the later ruins of Carthage. Ghosts, like the Freudian unconscious, like Carthage, know no time, and Silius Italicus's characters have a way of saying things about Carthage that apply to its foundation, to its height as an erotic, military, and trade threat to Rome, to its future destruction, and to its refusal to be destroyed completely.

In *The Punic Wars* the destruction of Carthage—before it happens—oppresses even Hannibal, who in reality declined to capitalize on his invasion of Italy to invade the city of Rome itself. At the end of the poem, he bitterly regrets that missed opportunity, now that Carthage is on the verge of destruction. "Rather," he says, "that Carthage had been put to the torch, and the name of Elissa struck out forever!" (*flagrasset subdita taedis Carthago, et potius cecidisset nomen Elissae*).[2] Carthage's destruction is tied to Rome's, and we will see later in this chapter how that becomes a theme of Roman political theory. Carthage's destruction is also an object of complex desire, compounded of the contradictory impulses, as Freud points out, to achieve what one longs for by possessing it, and so destroy it.

I'm using Freud's terms to describe how Carthage haunts Rome because Freud himself was haunted by Carthage. To be precise: he was haunted by Hannibal's desire, and his failure, to defeat Rome. In *The Interpretation of Dreams*, Freud describes a trip to Rome that he cut short just before he arrived at the city, turning back, he says, with "painful emotions." Only when he planned another trip the next year did he realize why he felt so upset about not getting to Rome. He was just like Hannibal, walking in his footsteps, "destined never to see Rome." He recalled that as a boy he had sympathized, if not identified, with Hannibal. Later on, he realized that he may have "bestowed his sympathies on the Carthaginians" because, as Semites, they suffered at the hands of Rome: the Carthaginians under the empire, Freud and Jewish people under Christians. His desire to see Rome, in other words, was mixed with a desire to destroy Rome. Witnessing his father meekly accept an anti-Semitic affront, he wished his father were more like Hannibal's father Hamilcar, who made him swear eternal vengeance on the Romans. Since that time, Freud says, "Hannibal has had a place in my phantasies."[3]

Although Freud does not articulate the connection, two prominent quotations from the *Aeneid* in *Interpretation of Dreams* reiterate the same wish to destroy Rome. The epigraph quotes Juno's words when she sees that Aeneas has arrived in Latium: *Flectere si nequeo superos, Acheronta movebo* ("if I cannot change the things above, I will move the Acheron") (Virgil, Bk. 7.312, 312). Juno is the champion of Carthage in the Aeneid, and in her failure to persuade Jove to thwart Aeneas's foundation of Rome, she is going to turn to the infernal powers. Freud never explains directly why this epigraph is important to the book, but it's not hard to work out why: having failed to find the cause of dreams as merely physical stimuli, Freud will be turning to the unconscious, the underworld of the ego. But he's also identifying his work with Juno's, as an opponent of Rome. That identification is coyly—or unconsciously—ambiguous. Later in the book, Freud says that the epigraph "indicates the tradition to which I prefer to ally myself in my conception of the dream" (80). What he means by "tradition" is a little surprising, and he says it quite indirectly: he means popular opinion, which is not afraid to find a "hidden meaning" in dreams, even while acknowledging that they are illogical and sometimes absurd. But given what Freud says later about the importance of Carthage to him, it's hard not to think that the "tradition" that the epigraph represents is also the tradition of Carthaginian enmity toward Rome.

For Freud, this enmity itself is an example of his own repressed, hidden motives. In a book published the next year, *The Psychopathology of Everyday Life*, he discusses a friend's misquotation from the Aeneid: rather than *Exoriar(e) aliquis nostris ex ossibus ultor!* ("Let someone arise from my bones as an avenger!"), he says *Exoriar(e) ex nostris ossibus ultor!* ("Let an avenger arise from my bones!") (Virgil, Bk. 4.625, 464).[4] Freud unpacks at great length his friend's omission of the word *aliquis* ("someone"). It's one of the first examples of a Freudian slip, and Freud goes on to show how the misquotation reveals a complex of repressions and substitutions. What Freud does not comment on is the quotation's significance: it is what Dido says just before she commits suicide, devoting her body on a pyre to the destruction of Rome, prophesying the rise of Hannibal. For Freud, the enmity with Rome is entangled with the work of the unconscious itself, the insistent but not always clear impulse that we do not fully understand.

Perhaps the deepest irony of Hannibal's fantasy of destroying Carthage because he did not destroy Rome is that it expresses a deep Roman historical wish that persists after the actual destruction of Carthage. Carthage was indeed destroyed by fire, but the name of Elissa/Dido was not blotted out. It becomes not just a reminder of the persistence of Carthage, its haunting by the ghost of its ruler who just stares reproachfully and silently at Rome—as Dido does to Aeneas in the underworld—but also a reminder of how Elissa/Dido is now and always a central figure in the Western literary tradition. Hannibal's fantasy of a destroyed Carthage is Rome's fantasy of the destruction of the *memory* of Carthage.

Virgil's and Silius's poems are the great tragic examples of the haunting of Rome by Carthage. But in Roman literature, Carthage also appears unexpectedly and not always clearly, like a subtle but ominous symptom. Virgil's contemporary Horace wrote a famous series of poems, the *Epodes*, that conjure a world like Evelyn Waugh's *Brideshead Revisited*, elegant and effortless, not terribly interested in the empire that lies beyond. The world is there for the plucking: *carpe diem* is a phrase that Horace coined in the *Epodes*. "When," he asks his patron Maecenas at the beginning of his Ninth Epode, "shall I drink with you?" It ends with a plea for larger cups of wine so they can drink their worries away more effectively. One of the pleasures of Horace's art is the way in which he actually does talk about the larger turbulent world *through* the objects in his charmed world. His poems embody a complicated decadence. They are entranced with luxury brands, like the wines of Chios, Lesbos, and Caecubum, the finest of Horace's day. But the poems hint at historical anxieties that diminish the certainty of victory in war.

Despite its praise of Augustus, Horace's Ninth Epode is also an oblique criticism of Roman decadence and its entanglement with Africa. It laments the shame of Marc Antony's "enslavement" to a woman (Cleopatra) and his indebtedness to a host of "shriveled eunuchs." Where Marc Antony's Romans carry battle standards, the Egyptians display only "degenerate" (*turpe*) gauze canopies (or mosquito nets).

Horace's complaint about degeneracy is, strictly speaking, not about the alteration of Roman culture and institutions, but about its mingling with foreign—specifically African—practices. At the beginning of the Ninth Epode,[5] Horace says that the music that will accompany his drinking bout with Maecenas will be Dorian, played on a lyre, although mingled (*mixtum*) with the barbarian (*barbarum*) sounds of the reed pipe. If the *carmen* that will be heard during the drinking party is mixed with barbarian music, then so will this carmen, this Epode, be mixed with a certain barbarism. In this case, "barbarism" refers more to foreignness than to cruelty, although it considerably disturbs the equilibrium of what should be a battle between two sides in a *Roman* civil war. Marc Antony loses the battle of Actium before it begins because he has been so thoroughly mixed with the barbarisms of Egypt.

But Horace is not just providing an etiology for Marc Antony's defeat. The problem is not just that on this occasion Marc Antony has betrayed Rome by mixing his forces with Cleopatra's, but also that this mixing with Egypt, and with Africa more generally, has been going on for some time. This Epode is a poem not so much about Marc Antony's debasement by Africans as it is about Rome's historic inability to extricate itself from Africa. Marc Antony is ridiculed for his mixing of Roman and African culture, but this poem is fundamentally about the historic mixing up of Roman and African culture since the Punic Wars. In a way, indeed, the poem only makes sense if it is read as a poem about the haunting of Rome by the specter of Carthage.

The poem's description of the flight of Marc Antony after the battle of Actium—to Crete, to the Syrtis, to the coast between Carthage and Alexandria, or "over an uncertain sea"—does not describe what really happened. He actually sailed directly for Egypt, ending up in Alexandria with Cleopatra. But it is possible that Horace is describing a much earlier retreat: that of Hannibal, who in the course of two separate flights touched at Syrtis Minor and stayed on Crete for a while.[6]

Even if one has not committed Hannibal's various itineraries to memory, there is at least one clue in the Ninth Epode to the specter of the Punic Wars. It is actually more than a clue. Horace compares the triumph that Octavian ought to receive after Actium with the glory won by three past generals in African wars: Gaius Marius in the Jugurthine Wars of Namibia and both the elder and younger Scipio Africanus, who defeated Carthage. Horace's call for a formal triumphal entry into Rome for Octavian is not as jingoistic and straightforward as it might seem. Gaius Marius never defeated the Numidians; instead, he negotiated a peace that gave part of Numidia to Jugurtha's father-in-law, Bocchus of Mauretania. Jugurtha was taken to Rome, where he was kept in an empty cistern until he died. And as glorious as the victories of both Scipios were, the elder died in exile and the younger was murdered in his bed. In another poem, the Fourth Ode, Horace criticizes the Romans for never memorializing Scipio's victories on his tomb.[7]

Horace does not pick the Scipios merely because they defeated Rome's greatest enemy, but also because Octavian's victory replays the unresolved Roman *cathexis* in Carthage and its destruction—its Carthage-complex. Although Carthage has been destroyed, it continues to haunt the Roman civil imagination. The Ninth Epode describes Scipio's destruction of

Carthage as lethal and ruinous: his "valor built a tomb over Carthage" (1.25, 295). Horace's choice for "built," however, is *condidit*, a word that suggests foundation more than it does interment.[8] The tomb in effect marks the foundation of a Roman ruefulness over the destruction of Carthage, an ambivalent emotion that Augustine will harden into a choice between the earthly and the heavenly cities.

The ambivalence that Augustine feels compelled to resolve, in psychoanalytic terms, is precisely that of melancholy: the inability to let go of an object or person that is no longer there. In two essays, the Hungarian-French psychoanalysts Maria Torok and Nicolas Abraham describe melancholy as a refusal to change oneself accordingly after a loss, or to do what Freud calls the work of mourning. The Roman relation to Carthage exemplifies with an uncanny literalness what Torok and Abraham say the self does in the melancholic refusal to move on: it builds a "commemorative monument" (or "tomb") over the loss in order to keep it alive rather than to transcend it. More precisely, the self does *exactly* what Roman writers do with Carthage: it builds a tomb in order to "safeguard its *topography*," a topography that it secretly perpetuates.[9] Carthage keeps reappearing, sometimes framed as the only place on earth that matters, as in Cicero's *Dream of Scipio*, where the two Scipios can see only Carthage from their vantage point in the heavens.

Horace's description of Antony putting on a cloak following the battle is more than an example of how a defeated Roman must change his garb. Antony's change makes him more than just vanquished by Octavian: it also suggests that he is another Hannibal—that is, Punic—and Octavian another Scipio. Antony, Horace says, has put on a cloak of mourning instead of the one of *punico*. In this context, a Roman would probably read *punico* as purple or scarlet, and this is overwhelmingly the meaning that Latin dictionaries give it. It is not clear, exactly, what color *puniceus* refers to, but in this poem that is not the main point. In the strictest, literal sense, the poem says that Antony has changed into a cloak of mourning from a *Punic* cloak: *puniceo* would be scarlet or purple (*puniceus*); *punico* is the dative form of *Punicus*, or Carthaginian.[10] As we have seen, the poem casts Antony as a second, defeated, Hannibal. Not only has he discarded the kind of robe any Roman general would wear—probably during a formally awarded triumph—but he has specifically cast off the mantle of a victor of Africa, the symbolic heritage of Africanus. Even if Antony did not do that (and he may not have: Plutarch's *Life* of him describes a scene where he *refuses* to cast it off), Horace's poem effectively deposes him as a Roman victor and sends him skulking back to Africa. Even a hundred years after the destruction of Carthage, Roman shame is expressed in symbols derived from the Second and Third Punic Wars. The final mortification of a Roman is to become a Carthaginian, or at least an African.

Horace's treatment of Antony in these terms is part of his exploration of the origins of decadence. The destruction of Carthage is a recurrent point of comparison. The young men of his days, he says in the Sixth Ode, are not at all like the virile youth of the Punic Wars, who dyed the sea "with Punic blood"—*sanguine Punico* (Bk. 3.6, 162–65), which also means a sea dyed red with blood, like Macbeth's fear that the blood on his hands will "incarnadine" the sea. Horace's Fifth Ode recounts the story of the noble Regulus, a Roman captive whom the Carthaginians sent back to Rome to sue for peace. Instead of delivering the message, Regulus urged the Romans to continue the war at all costs. His determination to return to Carthage (the condition of his mission) to be tortured to death was an example of the kind of determination Rome needed. In Horace's ode, Regulus tells the Romans that the only reason Carthage is mighty is because of Roman decadence: Carthage is great because Rome is already ruined (Bk. 3.5, ll. 39–40, 160–61). Horace's opinion that Carthage was a threat to Rome that needed to be subjugated is merely a more nuanced form of Cato the Elder's recurrent demand *Carthago delenda est* after the Second Punic War: "Carthage must be destroyed."

Carthage and African Identities: Sallust, Tertullian, Augustine

This bellicose Roman attitude toward Carthage was regarded very differently by the historian Sallust, who lived a generation before Horace. For him, it is precisely the destruction of Carthage that started the degeneration of Roman *virtus*. Again and again, Sallust uses Carthage as the locus for crucial decisions that the Romans botched badly. Up until the Second Punic War, Rome's enmity with Carthage united the Romans in a common purpose, he says, and helped to minimize internal dissension. But after Carthage's destruction, the fear of the enemy (*metus hostilis*) (260) was gone, and service to the commonwealth as its organizing principle was swept aside by personal interest, injustice, and wealth. Sallust's understanding of the destruction of Carthage might have something to do with his own partisanship and his status as a *novus homo*, an arriviste (the first in his family to serve in the Roman senate or to be elected as consul).

Sallust discusses the destruction of Carthage and its consequences in his writing on a war that took place thirty-four years later and also in North Africa, although to the west, in the kingdom of Numidia. *The Jugurthine Wars* does not have a villain as unambiguous as Hannibal, and its analysis of Rome and its *hostes* does not offer as clear-cut a lesson as Carthage does. Jugurtha, the king of Numidia, was a sometime ally of Rome—in fact an ally of the eventual destroyer of Carthage, Scipio Africanus the Younger, in the Numantine War in Spain. But after Jugurtha killed some Roman citizens in a war against his brother, Rome declared war on Numidia. Jugurtha was not defeated for seven years in a war drawn out by Roman military incompetence and an alleged susceptibility to bribery. The war ended when Jugurtha was betrayed by his father-in-law Bocchus in exchange for an alliance with Rome. The compromises and corruption that characterized Jugurtha's rule meant that Sallust could hardly make Jugurtha an unalloyed figure of virtue, and he needed to turn elsewhere for a moral anchor in his histories: to Carthage.

In Carthage's relationship to Rome, Sallust found the logic of degeneration that is hidden by the contradictions and opportunism of both the Romans *and* the Numidians. Jugurtha's opportunism only exposes the profound corruption of Rome's patrician class, which is Sallust's real target. Although the wars exemplify Roman degeneration, Sallust traces that degeneration to the time of the Punic Wars.

Carthage thus served as a convenient scapegoat for Sallust because he, too, was near it. As the governor of Numidia, he was acutely aware of the fallout of the Third Punic War. The first Roman territory in Africa, *Africa Proconsularis*, also known as *Vetus Africa* ("Old Africa"), came into being in 146 BCE, precisely because Carthage was no longer in existence. When Sallust became the governor of the formerly independent kingdom of Numidia, it became known as *Africa Nova*. The adjacency of the two Africas was, in fact, one of the reasons for the Jugurthine Wars, which extended a long dispute between the Numidians and the Carthaginians—and later the Romans—over the boundary of the two territories. One of Scipio's largest projects after the war was to dig a large ditch, the Fossa Regia, on the boundary to keep the Numidians out. Sallust's brief history of the settlement of North Africa puts in place a more insidious kind of boundary: he explains that the Numidians arrived *after* Carthage was founded. The areas of what eventually came to be called Numidia, he says pointedly, were *proxume Carthaginem*, next to Carthage (208), which already had a name, whereas Numidia was still a nameless void. This undermining of claims to identity and possession, based on tenure from time immemorial, became a tactic used frequently in the colonization of Africa. As late as the twentieth century, apartheid apologists were arguing that Bantu peoples arrived in South Africa at the same time the first Dutch settlers.

Sallust's history of the Jugurthine Wars is an attempt to trace the tumult of contemporary Roman politics to the fall of Carthage.[11] More precisely, his history is not a banal moralizing of the Roman decision in 146 BCE, but a genealogy of a cultural orientation that was unthought until the political structure of fear was removed. The emergence of a political structure of corruption was what Carthage's fall produced. Tendencies that had been latent since the founding of Rome—greed, dissension, *libido dominandi* (desire for mastery)—had been held in check and corrected, although with some difficulty, until Carthage fell. The strangely displaced lesson of Sallust's history of the Jugurthan Wars and his complaints about contemporary decadence have, in fact, *everything* to do with the fall of Carthage a hundred years before. As the numerous examples I discuss in this book attest, it becomes increasingly difficult to think about what it means to be Roman, to think about what that abstract quality *Romanitas* means, without also thinking about Carthage.

A minor example of this shows how specifically—and concretely—Roman and Carthaginian identities depended upon each other. Around 200 CE, the early church father Tertullian wrote a short treatise (probably delivered as an oration to a Carthaginian audience) on the pallium, a square tunic associated with Greeks, laborers, philosophers, and (by Tertullian) Carthaginians.[12] Whatever its origin, the Romans saw it as a marker of foreign identity, although it was much like a *persona*, the mask worn by Roman actors, and, like this, suggested an identity that could be put on and taken off at will.[13] The emperor Claudius once ordered a man whose Roman citizenship was being challenged to put on a pallium when the prosecution made its case, and a toga when his defense made its own.[14] Tertullian pushes this logic further by having the pallium speak: if clothing signals identity, then it must be the essence of identity itself. In fact, it virtually does not need to speak: its visual presence is a tongueless philosophy (*elingua philosophia*). The pallium transcends its muteness, just as it transcends its nature as a person's *superficies*. *Ipse habitus sonat*, the pallium says: the habit itself speaks. More precisely, it *sounds*, a word that recalls the analogy between the mask and the dramatic *persona*, a word that literally means "to sound through." It is the pallium that sounds through a *persona*, which now means an individual human being, not a mask. This kind of witty inversion is one of the techniques of Tertullian's address. It seeks to destabilize confident and axiomatic assignments of meaning to clothing, and the inversion here makes a further point. It is the *habitus* that speaks: the *custom or habit* of wearing a certain kind of dress is what assigns it its meaning. While the pallium might seem to have an essential identity that changes its wearer, at the same time identity is also assigned by convention, by the long practice of cultural discriminations.

Tertullian argued that the pallium was originally a Carthaginian form of dress that the Carthaginians conveniently forgot about after their conquest by Scipio. Tertullian's address is far more than a plea for authentic dress, however. It is, essentially, a mock epic that casts clothes as the protagonists of events that have changed the course—even the nature—of history. Although Alexander the Great defeated the Medes, for instance, he was made captive by their trousers when he put them on (*in captiua sarabara decessit*). Togas are the gateway drug to civil disorder: if Carthaginians wear this Roman garb, it is not surprising that it has become impossible to distinguish between commoners and knights, slaves and gentlemen, boors and sophisticates. The only hope in all this chaos is the pallium, which can, as it says itself, heal the mores of the commonwealth, the city, and the empire.

But the pallium is also a reminder of Carthage's destruction. It is in danger of repeating the horrible irony of the weapon that demolished its wall—the battering ram. Tertullian argues that the battering ram was once a Carthaginian weapon, but that it had been forgotten by the time of the Punic Wars and was used to destroy its inventors. The battering ram, says Tertullian, "turned Roman." Virgil's older praise of Carthage's cruel study of war (*studiisque asperrima belli*) is now obsolete. The Carthaginians had destroyed Carthage by forgetting what they had been renowned for studying. A second kind of oblivion now threatens the city if the pallium is similarly forgotten.

Tertullian's praise of the pallium involves further layers of irony.

There's a kind of philosophy of the pallium. Changing from the toga to the pallium, or vice versa, is an example of the universe's fundamental law of change. But for Tertullian, the universe gets better as it changes. Change is not just *how* the universe works, but also *why* it works. The pallium, then, isn't a uniform of unchanging essence. It's characteristic of Tertullian's playful wit (which is somewhat surprising, because of his reputation as a fierce polemicist) that he imitates the process of change in the flow of his own argument. The pallium, too, becomes an emblem of the idea of change. It's, in fact, a literal version of that idea. Tertullian discusses how Romans and Carthaginians have literally changed into and out of the pallium across history. The toga might become, someday, a better uniform for Carthage; the pallium might become Roman. And that has, indeed, happened already to the pallium. Tertullian points out that, at one point, it changed from an exotic, declassé kind of dress to one that could be worn on the floor of the Senate. Yet, he says, it was not identified *as* Roman. It was identified with Carthage's most devastating change: its destruction in 146 BCE. The pallium was worn on the floor of the Senate by the man who called for Carthage's destruction, Cato the Elder.

Tertullian turns the pallium, so to speak, inside out. As with the turning inside out of the meaning and references of *habitus*, so too with the pallium. One reason that the pallium does not speak but is silently eloquent is because it does not speak Latin: it cannot speak the language of Tertullian's discourse about it. The second section of the oration switches from a discussion of Carthage's abandonment of the pallium to a general one about the necessity of nature changing its *habitum* incessantly. This turn to philosophy, says Tertullian, is so that "Punic-hood" (*Poenicam*) won't blush for being singled out. At the same time, the entire oration is predicated on singling out Carthage: it opens by addressing the men of Carthage, forever "princes of Africa" (*Principes semper Africae, viri Carthaginienses*). Yet the term he uses for the citizens of Carthage, *viri*, is loaded with connotations of ideal *Roman* citizenship. It is the quality of *virtus*, the particular quality of the Roman *vir*, that has made Rome great. For Cicero, it is not merely a quality that derives from good behavior. It is the very seed (*semen*) of the Roman race, and it has only been further defined by its conquest of the world. Indeed, it is *virtus*, Cicero says, that erased Carthage—whose *viri* Tertullian is even now addressing.[15] It is as if, for Tertullian, Carthaginian identity is inevitably drawn to, and defined by, Rome's historical erasure of it. The opening of the oration calls attention to the double irony of asserting Carthaginian identity. It points out that it is possible to talk about the pallium as Carthaginian in the first place because of the *pax romana*; and it may be an examination of how complex Apuleius's praise of Carthage as the "inspiration of the toga-clad people" is.[16]

The point is not whether Tertullian is earnestly recommending the pallium or not, which is the question that most studies of the oration raise. The point is that the pallium—like any *habitus*—is riddled with internal contradictions when it is taken as a marker of cultural identity. African identity is complicated; but so are all other identities. This modest treatise, whether it's a parody or a satire, is the first sustained account of the contradictions under which an African identity survived in the Roman empire. It is also the first known use of the word *Romanitas*. Tertullian's diatribe against Roman dress, balanced on a precarious sense of the authenticity of his own cultural identity, turns out to produce the term that best sums up the abstract cultural and political unity of the Roman quest for mastery.

The most sustained meditation on what *Romanitas* implied was written by another African: Augustine. He was born in Thagaste, a town in Numidia 150 miles from Carthage. But Augustine was educated in Carthage, and later returned to it after his years in Italy. He wrote his magisterial meditation *The City of God* in Hippo Regius, about 60 miles south of Thagaste. Augustine wrote his *magnum opus* about 450 years after Sallust wrote *The Jugurthine Wars*, the account of the war between Rome and Augustine's own native land. Sallust's theory about the fallout of this war in Numidia is Augustine's most important source for the first three books of *The City of God*, which set out the fall of Rome in 410 as the primary example of the transience of earthly cities. For Augustine, as for Sallust, the fall of Carthage removed the corporate fear that had held the worst impulses of the Romans in check. But, as Augustine often does, he traces these various impulses to a single pathological desire: the *libido dominandi*, the desire for mastery. As with other forms of desire that Augustine discusses in his work, the problem is not so much that this *libido dominandi* itself is the agent of evil as that it achieves its desire.

As with Augustine's puzzled musing over the reasons he stole some pears in his youth, his point is that desire is usually aimed at the wrong object. Carthage's fall is an example of what happens when this *libido* seeks the wrong thing. When Carthage is gone, the desire for mastery turns to self-annihilation: "Romans who, when life had more integrity, feared the evils enemies might bring, now when that integrity of living went by the board, suffered greater cruelties from fellow citizens."[17] The single aim of the Romans during the Punic Wars, to destroy Carthage, fell apart after its destruction into the myriad objectives and desires that culminated in civil war.

Augustine's own objective is different from Sallust's. Sallust calls for the reformation of the moral anarchy that came about after the Carthaginian wars, and urges, as a politician and a member of Caesar's party up to and though the civil wars, the formation of a less destructive polity. But Augustine describes the national pathology as a greedy libido that aims only at destruction:

> [When] Carthage was destroyed, which meant that the great bugbear of the Roman republic had been beaten off and annihilated, these mighty evils sprang up as a sequel to prosperity. First, harmony was crumpled and breached in the fierce and bloody strife of parties. Next, there followed, by a chain of evil causes, civil wars, which brought such great massacres, so much bloodshed, such effervescence of cruelty induced by the craving for proscriptions and plunder (*City*, Bk. 1.30, 127).

The *libido dominandi* does not aim at destruction, but rather takes advantage of chaos. It is true, says Augustine, that someone possessed by this *libido dominandi* could only be satisfied with absolute sovereignty. Yet the *libido* is still just an opportunist, taking advantage of possibilities that happen to fall in front of it. Like a parasite, this *libido* must first be lodged in a proud mind, and this mind must be driven by desperate ambition. But ambition would get nowhere without a population already corrupted by luxury and avarice, which it can exploit.

If this were a sermon from later in the Middle Ages—and even from other parts of Augustine's writing—the rest of the passage would write itself: we must therefore be careful to avoid luxury and avarice. But this is emphatically *not* what Augustine wants us to see in the fall of Rome. The city fell not because of individual greedy urges, but because of the prosperity of Rome itself—the very thing that seemed to demonstrate the fundamental rightness of Rome's conquest of Carthage. Prosperity is not a sign of divine favor, nor the product of a sovereign state that has fulfilled its destiny. Prosperity is the smell of burning insulation. Something in the political economy is malfunctioning. In the case of Rome, one just had to wait a bit to see the seditions, massacres, civil wars, proscriptions, and plunder that followed directly from prosperity.

Prosperity is the symptom of political and moral dysfunction, even a kind of renunciation of responsibility. Scipio Nasica Corculum, the cousin of Scipio Africanus the Younger, argued vehemently against Cato the Elder's desire to erase Carthage because he believed that the fear of the Carthaginians would keep the Romans from greed. It would guard them from themselves (*tutorem necessarium*). It would not only hold back the collective *libido dominandi*; it would also limit the opportunities for the individual libido to attach to whatever objects it saw. This *tutor* is, of course, anything but stable itself. It is not simply restraint or sublimation: it is precisely the uncertainty, the unpredictability, of fear, and that is what makes it an effective instrument of the polity. That is why it makes sense, although it sounds deeply counterintuitive, for Scipio Nasica Corculum to say that what he really fears is security, "the enemy of weak minds" (*infirmis animis hostem securitatem*) (*City*, 1.30, 126).

Augustine's political theology could be weirdly counterintuitive (not to mention its later defilement by thinkers like the Nazi jurist Carl Schmitt). It also shows the remarkable degree to which Carthage resounded in Augustine's memory. In his *Confessions*, indeed, Carthage is an example of how memory works: a memory palace (the classical technique of placing things to be remembered in the windows and niches of an imaginary facade), he says, is just like the way he remembers Carthage. He thinks of the places where he spent time, and thus remembers the people he spent time with.

Augustine's Scandalous Carthaginian Theory

Carthage works, in fact, for Augustine in just the way he laments that it did not for the Roman people. In his *Confessions*, the city of his youthful lusts continues to represent, almost thirty years later, not just a shameful interlude, but a lesson, too: enjoyment is also a chain or a scourge, bringing with it jealousy, suspicion, fear, anger, and contention. In that sense, Carthage is important chiefly as the site of an animus that corrects the natural tendency toward *luxuria*—more or less the same importance that Carthage had for Scipio Nasica.

Carthage allows Augustine to work out another version of the *metus hostilis*, the preservation of something inimical to you that restrains your worst impulses. Augustine is not thinking only of Aeneas's arrival when he writes about coming to Carthage. He is also thinking already about the catastrophe of Aeneas's departure, when Dido, in her rage and grief over his betrayal, kills herself and is cremated on a pyre overlooking the ocean. The point that Augustine makes is that lustful enjoyment is always already a kind of death: the cauldron (*sartago*) of Carthage (*Cartago*) is heated by the flames of lust that also will heat the iron scourges of fear and jealousy, which will correct his waywardness. But Augustine is also describing Carthage's history. As he does in other parts of the *Confessions* (most notably when he writes of leaving his mother behind in Africa on his way to Rome and fame as an orator), Augustine identifies profoundly with Dido's point of view. Just as Dido is ruined by her love for Aeneas, Augustine describes himself falling or rushing (*rui*) precipitately into love: *rui etiam in amorem*.[18] This might be better translated as *collapsing* into love: the word *rui* began to have the connotation of "ruination" about the time that Virgil wrote. In the *Aeneid*, Dido's suicide is framed as the collapse of the city of Carthage itself. She begins her final lament by praising the great city she has built (*statui*); when she falls onto her sword, the poem compares the action, in a simile a bit too real for simile, to the ruination of Carthage (*ruit*) by its enemies.

Augustine's ruination clearly concerns more his moral collapse than any kind of civic malfeasance. Indeed, Carthage is something of the villain, a snare from which Augustine must escape, more like Aeneas than Dido. Yet Augustine's complex entanglement with Carthage suggests that the city is more than a mere allegory for moral progress. If that were all, then a mere recitation of the vices that could be found in Carthage would be sufficient. Yet the city has an imaginative, memorial presence that almost compels Augustine to describe his past life there in terms that are not really his own. It is a city that speaks its history through Augustine's peculiar, even idiosyncratic confession. What seems to be the passage's most frank, mortified, and elemental statement of his enslavement to love—*cupiebam capi* ("I was captured by love") (*Confessions*, III.1, 92)—is essentially a quotation from the *Aeneid*. It echoes the rumor that spreads through all of Libya's great cities: that Dido and Aeneas are neglecting their realms because they have been *cupidine captos*, "captured by love" (Virgil, Bk. 4.194, 434). Even Augustine's most damning self-indictment here is doubly derivative. It uses not just the language of the *Aeneid*, but also the language of a scandal that spread across Augustine's part of Africa.

For Augustine, Carthage carries a thrill that is hard for us to appreciate. It played a pivotal role in the central literary text of his epoch, a text that also happened to be the foundational text of the empire in which he lived. His own youthful enchantment with Carthage is charged with the memory of how close Aeneas came to giving up his world-historical destiny to settle there instead. Rather than represent a possible Carthaginian *imperium*, a world ruled from Africa rather than Rome, for Augustine the city represents historical and moral collapse. In the *Confessions*, Carthage is certainly a figure of Augustine's own moral turpitude, a cauldron of hissing, shameful loves. But Augustine still harbors residual resentment for Carthage's moral environment: he may have made mistakes as a young man, but it was also the fault of Carthage that those mistakes were so easy to make. In *City of God*, Augustine recalls going, as a young man, to "sacrilegious entertainments and spectacles" to honor the gods. Those were the kind of pagan festivities into which a young man in any large Roman town could wander. But Augustine makes it clear that he has festivities of a particularly Carthaginian significance in mind: these were rites for the goddess Caelestis, the chief deity of Carthage, sometimes called its "daemon" or "genius," a newer manifestation of Carthage's ancient goddess Tanit.[19]

So bound up with the city was this goddess that Macrobius repeats the story (almost certainly apocryphal) that, in order to ensure the perpetual destruction of Carthage, Scipio Africanus the Younger performed the act of *evocatio*, calling away the goddess forever from the city.[20] In fact, the goddess became, among other things, a symbol of the endurance of Carthage's illustrious past. The statue that both Tertullian and Augustine saw in Caelestis's temple in Carthage was believed to be, according to the historian Herodian, the same statue that Dido set up when she founded the city.[21] Augustine's shame over his youthful participation in Caelestis's festivals is bound up with his profound ambivalence about the destruction of Carthage. Caelestis's very name is a reminder of the Romanization of the immemorial pagan Carthaginian religion, whose rites simultaneously assert the survival of the goddess Tanit, despite her city's destruction by Rome, and point out her survival as a unit of Roman state religion. But these rites, as Augustine makes clear, are festivities that have a singular importance for Carthage, and for himself as a lover of, and in, Carthage.

In *City of God*, Augustine calls the rites for Caelestis *flagitiosissimae*, "most shameful" (Bk. 2.5, 156). Perhaps a better translation of the word here would be "scandalous"—a violation of public and civic expectations. Augustine might sound like a disapproving moralist, but, in his characteristic manner, he analyses what this shame is in terms that well up from within his own experience—from literature. For him, as he says in *Confessions*, literature itself was a source of shame, because it *seduced* him into loving things that were not true. The *Aeneid* was bad because it made him care more for Aeneas than himself, and weep inconsolably over Dido. It made him, he says, fall in love with love, not with anything real. Theater is worse, perhaps, because it is public and therefore can be mistaken for a general endorsement of shameful behavior. The *flagitiosus adulescens* (the shameful youth) who sees a Terence play in which Jove descends on Danae in a shower of gold will only be encouraged to be more dissolute (*City*, Bk. 2.7, 167).[22]

Augustine draws his more explicit, heavyweight moral criticism of Carthage, as we have seen, from the history of the Jugurthine Wars, and Sallust's argument that the fear of the enemy (*metus hostilis*) and the will to dominate (*libido dominandi*) are like sandbags against the tide of decadence. When they are gone, civic virtue collapses. In two short chapters, Augustine reiterates *six times* that Sallust was talking about the destruction of Carthage, clearly more than a random, disengaged example for him. Augustine repeats several of the same passages from Sallust in those two chapters, again as if demonstrating the Freudian compulsion to repeat: returning to a traumatic event as if to master it. One of the passages he repeats is the succinct formulation of the destruction of Carthage as the origin of the most infamous scandals that beset Rome, once the best and most beautiful of cities (*City*, Bk. 2.16–17, 194–207, quoting from Sallust, Bk. 2.17, 204). Everything seems to return to the scandal of Carthage: it is where Augustine created scandal himself; it was the city of scandal; its loss created scandal in Rome.

So potent is the idea of scandal in *City of God*, Book 2, that it forces together Sallust and the fourth master of the Latin curriculum, Cicero. In their overlapping lives (Sallust may have married Cicero's ex-wife), Sallust and Cicero were ideological and political rivals. They disagreed about many of the things they had in common, although letters in which each heaps invective on the other are probably apocryphal.

Cicero's *On the Republic* is set on the eve of the destruction of Carthage, but it is about what lies in the future, not about the shadow of the destruction. Most of it is a conversation among illustrious Romans of the previous century, including Scipio Africanus the Younger, at whose estate the conversation takes place. Scipio, the host, is the voice of Stoic values. What survives of Cicero's preface indicates that Cicero celebrates this circle of Scipio because of its eventual role in defeating Carthage: without active patriotism, he "could [never] have delivered [our native land] from attack, nor could Gaius Duelius, Aulus Atilius, or Lucius Metellus have freed [Rome] from her fear of Carthage."[23] Rather than organize Roman traditional values, the fear of the enemy is something to be defeated. Yet in *City of God*, Augustine pushes Cicero closer to Sallust's position—and by using what Cicero says about the scandal of theater.

More precisely, Augustine says he is quoting Scipio Africanus from Cicero's book. Scipio, he says, argued that the *flagitia* of comedy would never have been tolerated unless the customs of the time had allowed it (*City*, Bk. 2.9, 170–73). Scipio was talking about the Greeks, who allowed both humans and gods to be mocked in comedies. Romans, who prohibited living people from being singled out in comedies, therefore demonstrate greater respect for justice than the Greeks do. Augustine draws two conclusions from this: that the Romans cared more for their pride than they did for the gods, who could still be mocked; and that gods who could be dishonored like that shouldn't be worshipped.

Scipio's argument, as Cicero presents it, could undermine Augustine's point that the Roman republic fell apart after the destruction of Carthage. Even in the passages that Augustine quotes, Scipio is a fierce moralist, arguing that the republic depends on the common pursuit of justice. Augustine points out that Cicero, speaking in his own person, is even more of a moralist. In the beginning of the fifth book, he says that the republic is safeguarded by its "severe morality," and that observing it will restore the original strength of a republic grown lax and decrepit. Cicero's argument about why the republic has declined, then, contradicts Sallust's—and Augustine's. But in a brilliant rhetorical—and not strictly logical—move, Augustine relativizes both Scipio and Cicero. He implies, first, that Cicero was writing already in a senile republic, and that even if he was right about its early days, the moral strengths he appealed to were gone (*City*, Bk. 2.21, 216–27). His judgment was clouded. Without quite saying it, Augustine suggests that Cicero's argument at this point was deeply compromised by its spokesman, Scipio Africanus himself.

Nowhere in the main body of what survives of *On the Republic* is Scipio described as the destroyer of Carthage. But Augustine frames his discussion of Cicero's republican theory by identifying Scipio specifically as the destroyer of Carthage at the beginning, and then calling him "Africanus" at the end—the name he was awarded for that deed.

The Dream of Scipio Africanus: Cicero and Macrobius

The electrifying exception to Cicero's silence about Scipio as the destroyer of Carthage is at the end of the sixth book of *On the Republic*. Scipio recounts a dream he had in Africa two years before he conquered Carthage, in which Scipio Africanus the Elder conducted him on a flight through the heavens, explaining everything as they went. This dream would become the most influential part of Cicero's entire treatise.

Scipio's grandfather pointed Carthage out to him and told him that, within two years, he would destroy it and become famous. He would, in fact, become known as Scipio Africanus, a name that was, confusingly, bestowed on both men. The dream could be subtitled "On Becoming a Scipio Africanus." The Scipio whom Augustine discusses was given the name Publius Cornelius Scipio Aemilianus when he was adopted by his cousin Publius Cornelius Scipio the younger, the son of Publius Cornelius Scipio the elder. Aemilianus was therefore the adoptive grandson of the original Scipio Africanus—hence his name Scipio, the *cognomen* that belonged to the same branch of a family. Both men named Africanus are tied together by victories over Carthage. Scipio the grandfather defeated the Carthaginian general Hannibal in the Second Punic War and saved Rome; Scipio the grandson destroyed Carthage. Thus, they both became identified by what they had destroyed.

In the dream, Carthage is the only point named on earth. In the time of the dream, it lies between its subjugation by Scipio Africanus the Elder and its final destruction by Scipio the Younger. Cicero suspends Scipio the Younger, and us, in the moment before his actions will lead to his supposed anguish over the destruction of Carthage, a moment before the consequences of Rome's victory will fully be known and the very polity that Cicero is writing about will itself be ended. There's a moral and ethical point here. By showing us Scipio just before he becomes Africanus, Cicero is dramatizing the lesson about transitory glory that Scipio's cosmological voyage gives him: your fame will come to mean as much as if it had never existed.

But there is a further point, and one more deeply rooted in the philosophy of history. Staged on the precipice of destiny, Scipio's dream comes between him—and us—and what will turn him into another—into Africanus. Cicero places us just before the moment at which Rome's imperial destiny will unfurl into the future and asks us not to become creatures of history but to stand outside it, to contemplate, from an ethical standpoint, our own desires for fame, wealth, and power. To extend, logically and spatially, the Roman gaze of Scipio to its fullest extent is also to learn that the space that Rome occupies is insignificant even on the earth, and that the earth itself is insignificant in the cosmos. Rome's domains extend over a mere portion of a mere mathematical point.

But that of course is also not true. The dream exists only because Scipio's actions *were* significant, because the world did become Roman, not African, and Scipio became one of the most famous of those Roman citizens. Even Carthage remains important. From a cosmological perspective it is perhaps even more important than Rome. Above all, the dream affords Scipio the perspective of immortality. Among the stars, he has the privilege of recognizing the insignificance of his own glory, yet contemplating the eventual greatness of his soul, in company with that of his illustrious forebear, the first Roman Africanus. It's only greatness that allows you to embrace insignificance.

Yet Cicero could have made the same point, and arguably more effectively, if he had imagined Scipio having the dream *after* the destruction of Carthage. Instead, Cicero gives us a kind of illicit or nostalgic thrill, knowing that something great is about to happen to Scipio. We are experiencing the presence of someone whose company we are about to lose because their fame will put them out of our orbit. This is no doubt part of what Cicero intended to do as a consummate orator, one who wrote extensively about just this technique.[24]

Cicero's decision not to give us the post-Carthage Scipio is a philosophical decision: the decision to suspend history, and the formation of the *saeculum* of Rome, altogether. Scipio's dream is not one of wish fulfillment but of the deferral of wishes. The real power and significance of the Roman imperium lies not in its realization but in its relativization. It is when we recognize that it is important precisely so that we can stand outside it, or transcend it, that it becomes meaningful. Rome is insignificant, and so is the earth. But that is also its significance. Cicero's narrative gives us precisely the temporal point at which Carthage becomes a symbolic point: about to be obliterated, Africa nevertheless persists.

Scipio the Elder insists in the *Dream* that fame is trivial, because it is just the "speech of men," and the history of *On the Republic* proves that point. Most of it was lost until the nineteenth century, when a palimpsest, a text that was mostly erased so another text could be copied over it, was discovered. Before that, the only part of *On the Republic* that survived is the short *Dream* itself.

The *Dream* was preserved in a commentary on it written by Ambrosius Theodosius Macrobius around 430. Most scholars think he was a North African, but don't know where exactly he came from.[25] Macrobius's commentary uses Cicero's slender text to set out a full-blown Neoplatonic vision of the universe that includes so much information that it became one of the most important academic texts of the Middle Ages. It covers mathematics, music, and astronomy, three of the four disciplines that made up the advanced stage of education, the quadrivium. The fourth discipline, geometry, is arguably the subject of the bulk of the commentary, with five chapters on terrestrial geography. The illustrations for that section shaped medieval maps of the world, the *mappae mundi*: Macrobius's vision of an earth divided into zones was the main alternative to T-O maps, although many *mappae mundi* integrate both models.

Macrobius's preface alone, which explains what type of dream Scipio had, profoundly influenced medieval dream vision literature—in fact, the practice and theory of literature itself. Some texts, such as Alain of Lille's twelfth-century Latin Neoplatonic dream vision *The Plaint of Nature*, Jean de Meun's and Guillaume de Lorris's thirteenth-century French *Romance of the Rose*, and every one of Chaucer's fourteenth-century English dream visions, quote Macrobius and adhere to the conditions that he lays out for certain dreams. Macrobius's theory, that some dreams contained an element of truth while seeming implausible, offered the Middle Ages one of its more capacious theories of fictionality.[26] One of the most influential texts of the last century (although it was actually published in 1899), Freud's *Interpretation of Dreams*, cites Macrobius on dreams. Other modern thinkers as diverse as René Descartes, Robert Boyle, and William Butler Yeats drew from him.[27]

In the rest of this chapter, I discuss how Macrobius's *Commentary* and the specter of Carthage influenced two of the greatest medieval poets, Francis Petrarch and Geoffrey Chaucer. Both Petrarch and Chaucer not only draw from the broad knowledge contained in the commentary, but they also engage with, even grapple with, the central story of the dream—that is, the story of the Roman conquest of Carthage.

Petrarch's Modern Africa

Petrarch inhabits the story in a profoundly personal way that sets his story against the fate of the Rome in his own day, in the early fourteenth century. His story is about him, but about him as the latest in a long line of important Romans, above all the latest poet of Rome in several senses: he wrote about Rome, and maneuvered to become the first Roman poet laureate since the classical era. As poet laureate, he pushed to restore the literary values of classical Rome, and by extension its cultural values, but in a new way: in relation to the new order of Christendom, for which Rome had new importance. That is part of the large project that Petrarch championed—what became known eventually as the "renaissance," the moment at which Europe emerged from the supposed "Dark Ages" or the *medium aevum*, the long interval after the fall of Rome. Petrarch did not use those terms, but they are a compact and powerful way of describing his vision of history and his motivation as a poet and a scholar.

It's easy to forget that Petrarch did not necessarily value the work for which he is most famous, the invention of the love sonnet, still known as the Petrarchan sonnet, without which Shakespeare's famous sonnets would not exist. The sonnets even codified the paradoxes we still use to describe love: it burns like fire, it leaves us cold as ice, it is most noble when unrequited (although this kind of obsessive love isn't as admirable as it used to be). But Petrarch believed his most important work was the epic for which he was awarded the poet laureateship—a work that few people still read. It contains his most extended discussions of a new beginning in history that involves the return, the rebirth (although Petrarch doesn't call it that) of the light of the classical era, a happier age.[28] This epic—and all of the intellectual and cultural work that Petrarch imagined as most crucial to his career and indeed Western European culture—is called *Africa*.

Africa is a retelling of the Second Punic War, in which Scipio the Elder won the title "Africanus." It's the backstory of the events that lead to the vision in Scipio's dream, in which the older Africanus guides the younger through the cosmos during the Third Punic War.

But Petrarch's *Africa* is more than a backstory. It is an explicit prequel to the vision that Scipio Africanus the Younger has at the end of Cicero's *On the Republic*. Petrarch, so to speak, is re-visioning a prequel to *The Dream of Scipio*: its first two books recount a vision in which Scipio the Elder meets his father and uncle, who guide *him* through the heavens and discuss the future of Rome. In doing something that *anticipates* Cicero's narrative, Petrarch is implicitly claiming that Cicero's story depends on his—at least that Cicero's vision, and Macrobius's commentary on it, must now reckon with Petrarch's.

As encyclopedic as *The Dream of Scipio* and its commentary are, its main purpose is to demonstrate that earthly glory is trivial. The heavens and the afterlife are so much greater. Yet Petrarch really compromises the lesson: earthly achievements are a part of the eternal order. Indeed, Africanus's father seems to include Africanus and his own descendants in his opening words, addressing his son as "Eternal glory, honor of my sept" (Bergin and Wilson, Bk. 1.229, 7).[29] Carthage in *The Dream of Scipio* is a kind of irritant that reminds the two Scipios that they may have defeated the Carthaginians, but the idea of Carthage persists. In Petrarch's *Africa*, Scipio the Elder lands on the African shore like a mythic hero, having chased Hasdrubal back to Africa. Scipio takes his place with Hercules and Phoebus in the land of the setting sun. But, says Petrarch, he yearns for more: "While Carthage lives / The splendor of his own exploits is dim" (Bergin and Wilson, Bk. 1.185–86, 5–6). Scipio's father shows him a constellation of illustrious Roman predecessors, who live a glorious afterlife because they were "Romans whose one thought was the defense of their dear country" (Bergin and Wilson, Bk. 1.807–08, 22). They tell Scipio about the glorious future of the Roman empire, but warn him that it will decline—but not die—because "Spaniards and Africans" will eventually encroach on it (Bergin and Wilson, Bk. 2.262, 29). Don't worry, Scipio's father says, Rome will survive, but it is important just the same to remember that everything on earth eventually passes away, including your name and your glory: "Forgetfulness itself will bring forth forgetfulness over the long centuries" (Bergin and Wilson, Bk. 2.589–620, 38–39).

Africa is the sole exception to the earthly rule of oblivion. In a distant future, a Tuscan youth—Petrarch himself—with a love of truth and the greatness of the past will "reflect" the light of the Scipios' deeds in a new age (Bergin and Wilson, 2.450–54, 34). Above all, Petrarch's book will outlive even his own time (Bergin and Wilson, 639ff, 239ff). The poem is literally Petrarch's triumph. He ends it with a description of the formal triumph awarded to Africanus when he returned to Rome after the defeat of Carthage. At his side, wearing a laurel crown like Africanus's, is his poet-companion Ennius, who first wrote about the war in a now-lost book. Petrarch's own book closes in a hall of mirrors: this is the book that will retell the lost story that won its first poet a laurel, and will now win Petrarch a laurel, which will be given to him as he stands in Rome on Easter Sunday, 1341. Petrarch is also a reflection of Scipio throughout the poem: at the beginning of the poem Petrarch promises that *he* will "utterly destroy the cursed race of Africa" in telling the story (Bergin and Wilson, Bk. 1.75, 3) (*sceleratos* funditus *Afros / Eruere* est animus [Pingaud, Bk. 1.54–55, 83; my emphasis]).

Running throughout *Africa* is the metaphor of Petrarch-as-Scipio: writing the poem *Africa* is equivalent to conquering the continent of Africa. Yet Petrarch never did finish the poem, although he did write that triumphant ending where he stands in Rome wearing a laurel, as both Scipio and Ennius did. The poem itself was a provocation—like Carthage for the two Scipios in Cicero's *Dream*—that obsessed Petrarch, although it is something that Petrarch failed to conquer. He has something like an ambivalent Petrarchan love relationship to it. On the one hand, he hopes that the poem will live on long after him and will restore (*renovare*) his name in the future (Bergin and Wilson, Bk. 9.648; Pingaud, Bk. 9.462–63, 361). But on the other hand, the poem seems as threatening an enemy as Carthage. In *Secretum*, a dialogue with an imaginary Augustine, Petrarch talks about burning the whole thing, just like Carthage was burned: "This land of Africa, burned already by that fierce sun to which it is for ever exposed, already three times by the Roman torches devastated far and wide, had all but yet again, by my hands, been made a prey to the flames."[30] Africa, the continent, is a hostile site whose destiny it is to be destroyed, yet, here, at least, the poem *Africa*'s destiny is to be preserved.

But the two objects, continent and poem, do not quite snap together yet. As we have seen, Petrarch begins *Africa* by framing his intent in the poem to destroy not the place but the people, the "*sceleratos . . . Afros*." And he has Scipio's father attribute the fall of Rome to Africans and Spaniards. This might refer to the North African Vandals, but probably is a neat reference to two Carthages: the original one in Africa, and New Carthage, a colony that it founded in Spain and that Scipio the Elder defeated just before his attack on the African Carthage. Africa is not a place that has been obliterated, but rather a repressed *natio* that will always insist on returning.

In the *Secretum*, Petrarch treats his poem and the continent of Africa as if they were the same thing. Part of that is a cheeky reference to the origin of his interlocutor Augustine, who appears to Petrarch in *habitus afer*, dressed as an African (perhaps wearing the *pallium* that Tertullian so vociferously championed as the noble cloak of the Carthaginian) (3). Perhaps because of Petrarch's awe of Augustine, there's none of the racist talk about Africans needing to be destroyed or occupying Rome. Indeed, Africa becomes a site of care and even love, a figure not of a place that needs to be destroyed but of the poem's magnificence. Africa is even the site of truth, or at least of Lady Truth, who comes to Petrarch at the beginning of the *Secretum* to praise him for having built in "our Africa" (*Africa nostra*) such a magnificent poetic dwelling for her on the summit of Mount Atlas (*in extremo quidem occidentis summoque Atlantis vertice habitationem clarissimam atque pulcerrimam mirabili artificio ac poeticis, ut proprie dicam, manibus erexisti*).[31] In conversation with Augustine, at least, Petrarch can think of his work as edifying Africa.

At the same time, there is also a strong animus against Africa in the poem that is part of Petrarch's alignment with Scipio—a stance toward Africa that replicates the ancient *metus hostilis* of the Roman republic. In a textbook example of projection, Petrarch has Scipio say that "all Africa is aflame with hate" toward him and Rome (Bergin and Wilson, Bk. 3.74, 44). But at one point in the poem, Petrarch diverges from Scipio's manichean vision of Africa. Despite the hate that Africa has, says Scipio, it might be possible that the mere glory of Rome could charm (*mulcet*) barbarians (*Barbara*) into siding with Rome (Pingaud, Bk. 3.76, 133). That is a slight modification of a blanket condemnation of Africa, but it still reeks of imperialist arrogance and condescension. Scipio sends an emissary to a western Numidian king named Syphax, to see if his theory of subjugation by cultural glory will work.

Although Syphax eventually joins the Roman cause, his palace is far from the barbarian dwelling that Scipio imagined. Nothing in it is cheaper than pure gold, and on its ceiling is a zodiac sculpted with miraculous skill that describes the mythology behind each figure (Pingaud, Bk. 3.262, 141). It is almost as luminous as the real thing, and a garnet at its center radiates almost as much light as the sun (Pingaud, Bk. 3.100–05, 134). The description of the zodiac itself is 172 lines long, 58 lines longer than Virgil's most extended ekphrasis, a description of Aeneas's shield (Pingaud, Bk. 3.90–262, 134–41; cf. Virgil, Bk. 8.617–731, 102–13). The sheer length of Petrarch's passage makes an implicit claim for poetic importance. Its subject makes another claim: in the earlier vision of Scipio, Petrarch skims the heavens fairly briefly, as if he doesn't want to bother with the detail that Macrobius loads into the dream of Scipio the Younger. But Syphax's palace is the detailed scan of the heavens that is missing from the vision, and it is anchored in a very earthly setting, the throne room of a palace in Mauretania. A point in Africa (Carthage) is the only thing worth mentioning when Scipio views the earth from the heavens in Cicero; in Petrarch the best view of the heavens is in Africa.

Petrarch's zodiac begins with Atlas, who is depicted as placing the seven stars in the heavens that become the Pleiades, his daughters. He is the initiator, at least in this passage, of the zodiac itself, and Petrarch repeatedly returns to the primordial role of Atlas, not only in mythological history but also in the history of the Africans. Earlier in the vision, when Scipio and his father look down on Africa, Scipio's father relates the myth that the gods once dined with the king of the Ethiopians in the shade of Atlas, who is both a mountain and a god, but dismisses the story as a "fiction" made up by ancient Greek poets (Pingaud, Bk. 2.381, 122). But the reappearance of Atlas as the foundational figure of the zodiac suggests that the story is more important in Africa. It might be told by a poet, but the poet is African. A poet in Syphax's court recounts the mythic history of the kingdom, beginning with the defeat of the primal giant Antaeus by Hercules, who thus freed their land from oppression. Hercules is, in fact, the founder (*auctor*) of the land: he also set up the Pillars of Hercules, to mark the world's westernmost point (*terminus orbis*) at the edge of Africa (Pingaud, Bk. 3.398, 146). Atlas also rules all of Libya, holding it in a figurative sense (*cui rura tenenti*) (Pingaud, Bk. 3.402, 146). The story is, in other words, a mythic charter, an account of the genealogy of Syphax's rule that casts him not only as someone who "holds" the lands of Libya and Mauretania, but also as someone who holds the cosmos—hence the zodiac depicted in his throne room.

The mythological and aesthetic richness of Syphax's zodiac suggests how much Petrarch has actually invested in Africa. Petrarch's repeated praise of the skill of the artisans who created Syphax's zodiac suggests that it is a figure for poetry itself, a point that Petrarch underscores by following his own poetic description of the zodiac with the mythological account told by Syphax's poet. Petrarch no longer aspires to destroy Africa; he is, like Hercules, its *auctor*. That is perhaps why Petrarch has Truth praise him for building her that magnificent palace of poetry in what is now "our" Africa, a place with which Petrarch now seems to identify deeply. It is no longer the place of enmity or fear, a place to be destroyed. It is a place that has come to be the habitation of Petrarch's vision of what his art means, and what it can achieve. The dwelling place of Truth is in Africa, in a poem inside a poem written by Petrarch.

Petrarch's deep ambivalence about Africa—as the site of Rome's most ancient enemy and as the site from which his greatest poetic triumph will rise—gives the poem a moral complexity that readers have not often recognized. It is frequently dismissed as a failure, a misguided, puffy excrescence on Petrarch's body of work. There was very little scholarship in English on it until the early 2000s, and little in Italian until the 1920s, when it was celebrated in fascist Italy as a triumphalist account of Rome's glorious future—which may not have helped its reputation.[32] A recurrent take on the poem is that it is a narrative of paralysis: Petrarch was unable to reconcile his vision of a glorious classical Rome with his attempt to write an epic in the Christian era, and he hit an insuperable writer's block.[33]

Petrarch certainly expresses regret about not having finished *Africa*—even though he claims at least once that he went back to it and finished it in a short time.[34] It is possible, as one scholar argues, that Petrarch's advertised inability to finish it is strategic and deliberate, that the poem's apparent incompletion is an important part of its meaning. As we will see, this is one of the recurrent, almost certainly intentional, features of one of Petrarch's most important successors, Geoffrey Chaucer—who was profoundly influenced, too, by *Africa*.[35]

At the very least, Petrarch's expressions of regret for supposedly not finishing *Africa* take on a very different tone from his bellicose statement of conquest and obliteration at the beginning of the poem. He seems to sympathize increasingly with Africa the place, along with his troublesome poem—partly because, as we have seen, he establishes a home for his poetry on the continent. In his imagined discussion with Augustine in the *Secretum*, Petrarch talks about not finishing the poem as a kind of abandonment, but one that has cultural, even world-historical importance. He excuses himself because he was ill for a while but felt most distress over leaving the *Africa* incomplete—*semiexplicatus* (semi-finished)

(*Secretum*, 262). But the word also suggests a term in military strategy that was used by Livy and Caesar, among others, to refer to the deployment or the battle formation of troops (Lewis and Short, s.v., "explico" [1.B]). Petrarch, in other words, is also distressed at leaving Africa—the place—undefended, exposed. Africa—the place—also suggests the *opposite* of what the literal sense of the poem seems to imply throughout: the enemy that triggers a profound Roman fear. Here Africa suggests a kind of desire, or the management of a desire that would be distressing if not regulated or protected. One possibility here is that *Africa* is, in fact, a long allegory of desire in the fashion of allegorized readings of Virgil—and, indeed, in the fashion of Augustine, who read the *Aeneid* as a tempting and destructive celebration of undefended desire.[36]

Africa as a place for, an object of, Petrarch's desire complicates the superficial bellicose reading that Italian fascists glommed on to. But it does explain why Petrarch would talk about it with Augustine, who, as we saw earlier, appears to Petrarch dressed as an African. It is precisely because Augustine felt so deeply about Africa, and Carthage as a symbol of Africa, that Petrarch can finally take leave of the poem. Carthage was for Augustine the early site of his most unbridled, unregulated desires, and Carthage was the site from which he viewed the events of the *Aeneid*, weeping with Dido as she watched Aeneas sail away from Africa.

That is why one of the most powerful moments in all of the hype that Petrarch stirred up around *Africa* is when Augustine tells Petrarch directly what he should do with it. The "deeds of the Romans have been celebrated quite enough by others," Augustine tells him. "You will add nothing to the glory of your Scipio or to your own. He can be exalted to no higher pinnacle, but you may bring down his reputation, and with it your own" (*Secret*, 184). But then Augustine utters one of Petrarch's most poignant lines. It is poignant partly because it echoes a trope of mingled abandonment and desire echoed over centuries (and a phrase that in our age irresistibly conjures up the thousands who have done the same, despite the overwhelming danger): *dimitte Africam*—leave, abandon, Africa (*Secretum*, 274). Coming from Augustine, it does not just mean "abandon the poem *Africa*." In the *Confessions*, Augustine says he left Carthage for the very health of his soul: *Ad mutandum terrarum locum pro salute animae meae* (Bk. 5.8.14, 208). But he describes himself leaving Carthage furtively, leaving his mother behind to weep uncontrollably. He is another, more regretful Aeneas to another Dido. Yet he leaves for spiritual, not earthly, love, and he says with some relief that God forgave him (*dimisisti*) for leaving Africa and his mother behind. Petrarch's Augustine may be echoing that divine pardon in telling Petrarch to leave (*dimitte*) Africa himself: *dimisisti / dimitte* mean *both* to leave and also to forgive, to pardon, to release. Petrarch may eventually have succeeded in moving on from his Carthaginian epic *Africa*, but Carthage seems never to have been left behind in the historical imagination. Leaving Africa is necessary for the soul precisely because of its earthly allure, yet a melancholy thing to do, something you never quite get over—just as Rome never quite gets over Carthage.

And it is not just Rome: far to the north, Petrarch's English fan Geoffrey Chaucer played out the same complex historical psychodrama in his writings about Carthage and Africa. As we saw in the Introduction, cities across medieval Italy had extended and deep trade and cultural connections with Africa. But because Chaucer's—and England's—connection with Africa is, in every sense, more distant than Petrarch's, we now turn, briefly, to how Africa figures in Chaucer's poetry.

Chaucer and the African

Chaucer traveled well, especially for a fourteenth-century English person.[37] He went to France numerous times, to Italy twice, and to Spain at least once. Some of these trips were secret diplomatic ones, so we do not know exactly where he went. It is likely that while in Spain—in Castile, specifically, a kingdom that his patron John of Gaunt would claim in 1372—Chaucer's world was realigned along an axis farther south than that of most Englishmen; even in the fourteenth century cultural and commercial traffic between North Africa and Spain was considerable. The Emirate of Granada still occupied the southeast part of Iberia, and several isolated territories were ruled by the Marinids of Morocco. One of the greatest travelers of the Middle Ages, Ibn Battuta, a Marinid subject from Morocco, traveled to Spain (1349–50) to fight against Alfonso XI of Castile. The great North African intellectual Ibn Khaldun was in Castile just two years before Chaucer.[38] The tribute that Castile received from the Emirate of Granada was paid in part with gold that Granada imported from Mali and Burkina Faso.[39] After John of Gaunt's campaign to take the throne of Castile finally failed in 1387, he agreed to renounce his claim in exchange for an indemnity of 600,000 francs and an annual payment of 40,000 from John of Trastamara, the actual king of Castile.

So some of the gold that circulated in England, and that paid Chaucer, came from Africa, via Granada, Castile, and John of Gaunt.[40]

Since Chaucer doesn't say anything about his trip to Castile, his actual exposure to Iberian and North African culture and history must remain speculative. But Chaucerians have noticed that he cites a surprisingly large number of Iberian figures in his works, and that several Iberian works contain analogs of his own stories.[41] What is certain is that he refers to places in North Africa that would have been beyond the knowledge of all but the most devoted English geographers and policymakers of the late fourteenth century. Chaucer outdoes even the Italian Boccaccio in the specificity of a reference to contemporary Africa. In his *Teseida* Boccaccio talks about a "Libyan" lion, where Chaucer refers to the lions of "Belmarye"—the name he used for the domain of the Marinids[42] in his portrait of the tarnished world traveler, the Knight from the General Prologue of *The Canterbury Tales*. Other references to Africa are clustered in this passage:

> At Alisaundre he was whan it was wonne....
> In Gernade at the seege eek hadde he be
> Of Algezir, and riden in Belmarye....
> At mortal batialles hadde he been fiftene,
> And foughten for oure feith at Tramyssene
> In listes thries, and ay slayn his foo (Fr. 1.23–26, 11.51–63, 24).

Chaucer opens the portrait with a reference to one of the more sordid episodes of the Crusades, an attack on Alexandria by King Peter of Cyprus in October 1365. Peter's army massacred many of the civilians and destroyed both Muslim and Coptic Christian tombs and shrines before fleeing after seven days. They dropped most of the plunder overboard to keep the ships from foundering.[43] Chaucer did not have to travel to Spain at all to find out about the Alexandrian siege: Petrarch wrote a letter to Boccaccio about it in 1365, and the French poet Guillaume de Machaut, one of Chaucer's greatest early influences, wrote a *Prise d'Alexandre*; it's also mentioned in several English chronicles. The fact that Chaucer leads the Knight's portrait with this episode is telling; it may betray the knight's venality, as Terry Jones (of Monty Python) argued. Or it may not; Peter is a chivalric hero—the tenth of the ten worthies—in Machaut's poem, and the contemporary French writer Jean Froissart generally likes

Peter of Cyprus's various attempts at crusading. But it is the only part of the Knight's sojourn in Africa that might have been identified easily back in England, even if mainly by literature nerds like Chaucer. Chaucer scholars have found it harder to explain how Chaucer knew about "Belmarye" and "Tramyssene." The trail gets a little convoluted, and it tends to involve two or three intermediate steps—English participants in minor expeditions who might have been known by people Chaucer knew, or texts that mention either place in passing.

But if we stop thinking within the chamber of medieval English global knowledge, or what we assume it to be, these two places in Africa turn out to be immensely important in Europe. There were extensive trade networks between ports in the Maghreb and Italy, Provence, and Catalonia. "Tramyssene" is modern Tlemcen (in Algeria), which was the principal port for Italian and Spanish gold traders in the thirteenth and fourteenth centuries. Pisa signed a treaty of friendship in the 1130s with Tlemcen. As we have seen, "Belmarye" (Palamon in the *Knight's Tale* is compared to a lion from Belmarye)[44] comes from *Banū Marīn*, the rulers of the Marinid empire in Morocco, under whom extensive trade networks developed with Italy and Spain. In 1337, Tlemcen, with its trans-Saharan trade, came under the control of the Marinids as well.[45] The Marinids also mounted several invasions of the Iberian Peninsula between 1275 and 1340. (Pope Gregory X exempted many Spanish Christians from the crusade that had been preached in 1274 because they were defending Christianity "against the Saracens of Africa").[46] In Africa, the Marinids had captured two of the towns that Chaucer mentions: Tlemcen in 1337; Tunis in 1348.

In his early dream vision the *Book of the Duchess*, Chaucer says that the birdsong he hears is so sweet that he would not give the "town of Tewnes" for it. It is

> a thing of heven;—
> So mery a soun, so swete entunes,
> That certes, for the toune of Tewnes,
> I nolde but I had herd hem singe (329–46, ll. 309–11, 334).

The traditional explanation for the reference is that Chaucer: (a) needs a rhyme for "entunes"; and (b) he is punning on "tunes." But Tunis itself was quite visible on even the English imaginative horizon. It was one of the most significant Mediterranean cities of the medieval period. A thirteenth-century Moroccan writer, Al-'Abdari (fl. ca. 1289), described it as the "high goal of all hopes, a point of convergence for the sight of all, a rendezvous for voyagers from the East and the West."[47] Its wealth attracted Christian invaders in the age of the Crusades: Louis IX of France died besieging it in 1270; in 1390 Chaucer's friend John Clanvowe joined a crusade against Tunis (which was supported by the sultanate of Tlemcen) led by the Genoese and Henry of Bourbon.[48] Tunis had a latent historical importance in medieval Europe, too: it replaced Carthage after the city was destroyed, for a final time, by the Ummayad Caliphate in 698 CE. Carthage in modern history has reemerged as a prosperous suburb of Tunis.

As we have seen, it is Carthage, not Tunis, that persists in the European imagination, precisely because it represents an absence at the heart of history. But to put it this way misrepresents the way that Africa seems to operate in Chaucer's work. In the *Book of the Duchess*, Tunis is part of an economy of enjoyment, perhaps a trope borrowed from chivalric romance, where places like Tunis represent a fascination with the exotic other. In the era of the Crusades, Islamic cities performed the work of the *metus hostilis*: they were objects of both fascination and fear. But Tunis in the *Book of the Duchess* is somehow also part of the music of the birds—that is, part of the structure of the natural and the cosmological worlds. It is both like, or equivalent to, birdsong, and something already inscribed in the music of English (the town of tunes). It is, like Carthage, the one place on earth that is compared with "a thing of heven." Tunis might be in Africa, but it is a suburb of the cosmos.

Chaucer's later dream vision, the *Parlement of Foules*, makes more explicit the strategic location of Carthage at the intersection of history, the cosmos, and music. They are connected, as we have seen, in Cicero, even if only because the attention of the Scipios moves from one to the other. But Chaucer, as he does with Dido and Carthage, radically revises the logic of his source text by summarizing it. At the beginning of the poem, he sits down to read *The Dream of Scipio*, which begins when "Scipioun was come / In Affrike" and dreams that "his aunrestre, Affrican so dere" (that is, Scipio the Elder) appears to him and from the stars "Affrican hath him Cartage shewed." Chaucer condenses the first four sections of *The Dream of Scipio* into seven lines; what remains is the concentrated importance of "Africa" in the text. That concentrate of a continent is perhaps a part of the process of writing a theory of Africa. In her idyll of colonial utopianism *Out of Africa*, Karen Blixen referred to her own farm, lying at an altitude of six thousand feet, as "Africa distilled."[49]

In Chaucer's text, "Africa" is a continent, a city, and a person—a medieval world made of macrocosms and microcosms, all of which are versions of each other. It is both a cosmological vision and a narrative insight: Chaucer's own dream in *Parlement of Foules* begins with a description of how

> Affrican, right in the selve aray
> That Scipion hym say before that tyde,
> Was comen and stod right at my beddes syde (385–94. ll. 96–98, 386).

Africa is written with a poetics of substitution. It is a site where even Chaucer can take the place of the second Africanus in a dream. In other works, Chaucer introduces freewheeling substitutions into the ur-text of the *Dream* that are so wrong that they have to be literary jokes about the transmission of classical texts and their reception in the "modern" era. In the *Book of the Duchess*, the narrator says that the *Dream* was written by Macrobius: "He that wrot al th'avysyoun / That he mette, king Scipioun, / The noble man, the Affrikan." Yet the ambiguous "he"s here tempt the reader into making other substitutions: the writer could be "King Scipioun," the dreamer could be Macrobius. To confuse things further, Chaucer tends to use the name "Affrikan" to refer to Scipio the Elder, not the Younger. And, of course, neither Scipio was a medieval sovereign. Above all, Macrobius did not write the *Somnium*. Even worse, in the *Nun's Priest's Tale*, the rooster Chauntecleer says that Macrobius wrote "the avisioun / in Affrike of the worthy Cipioun" (Fr. 7.253–61, ll. 3123–24, 257). Cicero, in other words, has become the dreamer. That attribution is the work of a pompous fourteenth-century rooster, of course, but it takes to its conclusion the chain of substitutions: anyone could become the dreamer or the author, anyone could be the "Affrikan." That confusion, in fact, and indeed confusion in general, is part of the underlying structure of the *Parlement of Foules*.

The *Parlement* begins with a clear anatomy of the dreamer's confusion, even before we get a dream. In the first stanza, Chaucer says that love has so confounded him (love his "felynge / Astonyeth") that when he thinks about it "Nat wot I wel where that I flete or synke." In the next stanza, it turns out that what he means by "feeling" isn't his experience in love, just his memory of reading about it (ll. 8–11, 385). And one of the sources for this confusion about love is, of all things, *The Dream of Scipio*. It appears after a high-stakes preamble near the beginning of the poem. Chaucer first writes as if he's speaking to us, explaining why he's writing in the first place: "But wherfore that I spek al this?" He then breaks out four lines in a higher register that are cited in almost every study of late medieval hermeneutics:

> For out of olde feldes, as men seyth,
> Cometh al this newe corn from yer to yere;
> And out of olde bokes, in good feyth,
> Cometh al this newe science that men lere.

Chaucer then tells us he's getting back to his "purpos," which is to tell us about this old book, *The Dream of Scipio*. It is not like the *Dream* that medieval readers would have known, however: it is just the original text by Cicero In the Middle Ages, as we have seen, the *Dream* was embedded in the much longer commentary by Macrobius, but Chaucer here, in the *Parlement*, says he's reading "Tullyus [i.e., Cicero] of the Drem of Scipioun." That might *implicitly* include the commentary, except that Chaucer goes on to summarize the dream—and he summarizes just Cicero's part, not Macrobius's. This could be a completely notional book, one that exists only because Chaucer has "forgotten" all of his abundant knowledge of Macrobius's commentary. Or it could be a fragment, just the first part of Macrobius's commentary that contains only Cicero's text. But it is also a book that has been strangely deformed by medieval theology: it has, says Chaucer, seven chapters, "of hevene and helle / and erthe." The *Dream* isn't divided into chapters, and it doesn't say anything about hell, just the orderly Neoplatonic heavens. It is a Ciceronian dream that has been made, without the machinery of allegoresis (finding Christian equivalents in pagan myth), into a Christian text.

In some ways, that seven-book dream is *this* book, the one Chaucer is writing. His summary of it echoes the seven parts of that book: it is exactly seven stanzas of seven lines each. His poem is, in effect, making a new book (as he says in the prologue, poets these days have to make new corn out of old fields, new science out of old books). But this new book exists only in Chaucer's imagination, or in his poem. This impossible book is plucked from the obscurity in which lie the longer works in which it was once embedded (Cicero's *De re publica* or Macrobius's *Commentary*). Cicero in Chaucer's poem even blames Macrobius, strangely, for his carelessness about literary and book history: he "roughte nat a lyte" about his "olde bok totorn." This is a *Nachleben* Scipio, a fanfic Scipio, who also knows something about manuscript transmission. Chaucer might know only the Cicero portion because he's reading a codex with the commentary torn out. But he does seem to go to some trouble to defamiliarize one of the best-known works in late medieval intellectual history. He doesn't defamiliarize just by making it seem exotic and other; he does it by refocusing our attention on a part of its original context that has been there all along—one that we have overlooked.

The middle of the dream in Cicero's original and Macrobius's commentary is taken up by Scipio's description of the habitable and uninhabitable zones of the earth. That's a large part of the commentary, and it's the part that gets illustrated most often in medieval manuscripts. But Chaucer doesn't mention that part at all in his summary. He just cites "the lytel erthe that here is"—and that's it (except for Carthage). Nor does Chaucer (with one exception) mention the list of places that Scipio will go on to in the future (Egypt, Syria, Asia Minor and Greece, the consulship of Rome). Where Cicero's Scipio Africanus the Elder tells Scipio Africanus the Younger that he will destroy Carthage, Chaucer doesn't tell us *why* Carthage is the only place on earth worth noting. It is up to us to remember that Scipio the Elder is called "Affrikan" because he defeated Carthage once, and to remember that Scipio the Younger will go on to destroy Carthage and earn the name "Africanus" for himself. It's up to us to remember that the occasion for the entire dream—for the text that will become a foundation of dream theory, literary theory, geography, music, and astronomy for the Middle Ages—the occasion for all of this is Scipio Aemilianus's meeting with King Massinissa of Numidia in North Africa to strategize against Carthage—two years before Scipio was to destroy it once and for all.

The dream logic of the *Parlement of Foules* works like this: the poem is like the lost book, which is like Carthage. Chaucer's confused about love, but not really love itself, just what he's read about it. So reading is important. But the book Chaucer wants to talk about doesn't seem to be about love at all: it's either about the cosmos, or the insignificance of civilization. The very things that are revealed to us—what Chaucer calls the "new science" that may come from old books—are themselves the things that have come to be lost. We see the earth from outer space for the first time, but what we see, at the same time, is how insignificant everything earthly is. When we see a city it's one whose loss is theorized as the loss of civilization itself by Sallust, Augustine, and, if Polybius's account of Scipio Africanus the Younger's gazing at the ruins of the destroyed Carthage and weeping is to be believed, by no less than the conqueror himself. This chain of substitutions reinforces the *Dream*'s main political and ethical lesson: that nothing we see on earth is significant, not even the greatest Romans.

In *The Dream of Scipio*, Scipio the Younger says he recognizes the elder Scipio in the dream "in that form which I know better from his image (*imagine*) than from the man himself" (Bk. 6.10, 262). Scipio the Younger was only one or two when Scipio the Elder died, so, of course, he does not remember what his grandfather by adoption looked like in person. The "image" he refers to was a mask of Scipio the Elder's face, worn for the funerals of his descendants for at least a hundred years. Such masks commemorated the exceptional achievements of men like Scipio, who was awarded two formal triumphs in his life. Indeed, the poet Horace called them *imagines triumphales* (Bk. 8.11–12, 290).[50] Scipio the Elder's mask was exceptionally important: it is the only *imago* known to have been kept in a temple, and the historian Valerius Maximus says that the citizens requested that the figure be given "triumphal dress."[51] All such masks are images of death and triumph. They commemorate the remarkable achievements of important Romans, but only after they are gone, and are made visible in public to mark the deaths of their notable descendants.

Scipio the Elder tells the Younger: "The outward form does not reveal the man but rather the mind of each individual is his true self, not the figure that one designates by pointing a finger" (76). Scipio the Elder returns to Scipio the Younger's moment of recognition: he is recognized not in person but by a mask, a form, an image. The mask is as remote from Scipio the Elder's true self as his body was. Even the name Africanus, the mark of triumphal distinction for both men, is not who they *are*.

The endurance of the figure of Scipio Africanus rests on its substitutability, its ability to be taken up by other people, by other times, and by other texts. He is the main figure in both Cicero and in Macrobius, the guide in Aemelianus's dream and in Chaucer's. In Petrarch's version of the story of Africanus (based on Macrobius and Cicero), the *dreamer* is Scipio the Elder, because it takes place before the younger Scipio is born. In Chaucer's text alone, Affrikan carries with him traces of other texts (as I'll argue shortly, including Petrarch's), as if partly inhabiting the role of other visionary guides besides the various previous oracular Scipios.

In the *Parlement of Foules*, Affrykan takes Chaucer to a gate that has two inscriptions above it: one that promises a joyful and eternal Maytime of love, and another that threatens the deadly experience of lovelessness. Chaucer naturally wants to go through the first gate, but the second terrifies him so much that he cannot move. The gates might seem like a contrived, amorous paradox from courtly literature (and Petrarch's lyric poems). But they echo two other important gates in Chaucer's literary genealogy: the gates of Dis in Dante's *Inferno*, inscribed with the fateful words "Abandon all hope, ye who enter here"; and the gates of horn and ivory from the *Aeneid*.

In the *Aeneid*, these gates are the way out of the underworld, through the House of Sleep. The gate of horn allows "true shades" (or dreams) to ascend to the upper world; the gate of ivory is for "false shades." Aeneas's father Anchises leads him to the gate of ivory, and Aeneas returns to the upper world through it. Virgil does not explain why, but one implication is that it casts the events of political history—including the recent death of Dido, whose shade Aeneas sees in the underworld—into Virgil's true domain of fiction, the empire of letters. We end Book 6 realizing that *this* is how the book we are reading came about.

Chaucer's allusions to this moment in the *Aeneid* leave behind them tangled threads of dream logic. Affrykan, the first Roman victor over Carthage, is put in the place of Anchises, the father of Aeneas, who betrayed Dido, the Queen of Carthage. Chaucer's poem is put in the place of the *Aeneid*, emerging through the gates of sleep onto the terrain of fiction. And Chaucer, the figure in the poem, is put in the place of Aeneas being led out of the underworld, and, as the callow figure being guided by the elder Scipio, the destroyer of Carthage. But that destruction lies offstage, just as it lies in the future in the original *Dream of Scipio*.

The destruction of Carthage shows up in Chaucer's work twice as an anecdote of feminine trauma (*Franklin's Tale*, Fr. 5, 178–89, l. 1400, 186; *Nun's Priest's Tale*, Fr. 7, 3365, 260). In both cases, Chaucer tells the story of the unnamed wife of Hasdrubal, the ruler of Carthage when

Scipio conquered it, who threw herself into the flames consuming the city, either to protect herself and her children from the Romans, or over grief at her husband's death. Both passages are incidental examples, one (*Franklin's Tale*) part of a spurious attempt to rationalize suicide, the other (*Nun's Priest's Tale*) an analogy in a mock epic involving chickens. The destruction of Carthage, that is, is very much a literary trope, and given the contexts in which each is used, an *example* of a literary trope. It is both a historical catastrophe and a casual reference—a data point in the European literary imagination.

Carthage tends to be represented in literary history as a feminized space, partly as a result of its legacy of destruction. Cato's famous demand to destroy Carthage, *Cartago delenda est*, with its feminine gerundive, was a subtle reminder. After the Second Punic War (won by Scipio Africanus the Elder), Plautus mocked a Carthaginian male character as a woman (*mulier*) because of his clothing and accessories.[52] But Virgil most influentially linked Carthage's destruction, specifically, with Dido's suicide: "A scream rises to the lofty roof; Rumour riots through the stricken city. The palace rings with lamentation, with sobbing and women's shrieks, and heaven echoes with loud wails—as though all Carthage or ancient Tyre were falling before the inrushing foe, and fierce flames were rolling on over the roofs of men, over the roofs of gods" (Bk. 4.665–71, 467, 469).

The muddling of person and city might be a way for Roman writers to "reduce," in the Middle English scholar Randy Schiff's words, "Carthaginian destiny" merely to "Dido's trauma."[53] That reduction is a part of Rome's desire to write its *own* destiny at the heart of imperial history. That destiny, argues Schiff, is not just Rome's economic and military domination of the Mediterranean, but also its formation of a unified culture across the Mediterranean and much of Europe. That unity depends on the murderous erasure of racial difference—hence the genocide Scipio committed at Carthage. Carthage, says Schiff, posed a general and disturbing racial threat to Rome because of Phoenician culture's "ethnic boundary fluidity." Chaucer's failure to mention Dido's Phoenician origins relegates her to the remote and "generalized" site of Libya, cut off from History, in Hegel's sense.

As with everything to do with Carthage after Rome's destruction and rebuilding of it, the opposite is also true, even in Chaucer. Chaucer has a well-known sympathy for Dido (whether real or staged). In a retelling of her life in his *Legend of Good Women*—the longest of all of the stories in it—he stops the narrative briefly to say that he is too filled with grief to relay what Dido said in her suicide note ("I may nat wryte— / So greet a routhe I have hit for t'endyte"). In Chaucer's thumbnail sketch of the *Aeneid* in the *House of Fame*, which is 324 lines long, the story of Dido takes up 202 lines. Most of it is an extended lament over Aeneas's betrayal of her.

But Chaucer suggests that the fascination with Dido is a global phenomenon. Her reign of "greet honour" (588–630, 1.1008, 609) makes her the desire of "kinges and of lords" (1.1012, 609) all over the world. That desire has the distinct quality of a fourteenth-century European male desire, expressed in the terms of courtly literature: "She was holde of alle quenes flour, / Of gentilesse, of freedom, of beautee" (ll. 1009–10, 609). Her palace is filled with the stuff of the greatest European palaces: steeds for jousting, palfreys, falcons, hounds, and cups of gold with florins, the Florentine coin that became a standard currency in Europe and the Mediterranean.

Yet Chaucer also insists on her identity as a ruler in Africa. She is introduced as the founder of Carthage, in the "regne of Libie" (1.992, 609). That is where the story begins, for Chaucer: what she did before she came to Libya, he says, is just a "los of tyme" (1.997, 609). Chaucer's omission of that part of the story makes Dido's identity as an African more important. And Chaucer's additions about her recognizably European qualities suggest that, at the very least, imagining what Africa is like does not demand orientalist and exotic tropes. Dido, and to some extent Carthage, are part of, or are folded into, the European imagination. The part of the Dido story that matters is not her origin story as the queen of the Phoenician city Tyre, who left to found Carthage. What matters is the story of Carthage as the city that Dido founded.

That is true for the Carthaginians themselves. Dido is, after all, inseparably identified with Carthage. She wrote its mythic charter in the strips of ox hide she used to claim the land for the city. As we have seen, mythical charters exist because the act of foundation is both complicated *and* a narrative that is created after the fact. It invents a point of origin that makes the tangled subsequent histories of a place snap into line. A Carthaginian in late antiquity might see a very different Dido than Virgil's, as Tertullian does in his *Apologetica*. He does not even need to use her name; he calls her simply the "founder of Carthage" (*Carthaginis conditrix*). For Tertullian she was a supreme example of chastity because she threw herself into a fire rather than violate her oath not to marry a second time: *Aliqua Carthaginis conditrix rogo se secundum matrimonium dedit: O praeconium castitatis!*[54] Tertullian invokes the sacrifice of Dido precisely to shame the morally lax Carthaginians of his own time: her reputation in Carthage in the third century CE is precisely the opposite of Virgil's crazed and wanton Dido, who ruined her legacy, what she called her *fama prior* (Virgil, Bk. 4.323, 444; Tertullian, 50.5, 220). In his commentary on Virgil, the late antique grammarian Servius also narrates the story: "Dido was first called by her real name Elissa, then after her death she was named Dido by the Phoenicians, that is, *virago* in the Punic language, because when she was urged by her allies to wed one of the African kings [but] was still in love with her first husband, with a strong spirit she killed herself and threw herself on the pyre which she pretended to have built to placate the spirit of her first husband" (my translation).[55] That fame, that reputation, does not seem to have been ruined in the least in Carthage itself. The foundation myth of the original Carthage survives even in the city destroyed and rebuilt by Rome. Tertullian, who strenuously defends the traditions of Carthage, calls his contemporaries to return to the virtues on which Dido founded the city.

Another Carthaginian, the mythographer Fulgentius—whose work we will examine in the next chapter—prefers to remember Dido before she sacrificed herself. He describes himself as a lifelong inhabitant of the city of "Elissa." He does not call it the city of Dido, perhaps because, as Servius said, Dido means *virago*, and so it commemorates her act of self-destruction. Fulgentius seems to avoid the post-Virgilian legacy of Dido deliberately: even in his short commentary on the *Aeneid*, he refers only to Aeneas's lust and does not mention Dido at all. His commentary is a brief version of one of the standard allegorical readings of the *Aeneid*: as the story of the soul, in the persona of Aeneas, developing as it leaves earthly entanglements behind to arrive at its true home.

But in the preface, Fulgentius insists to Virgil himself (his commentary is in the form of a dialogue) that it is Virgil's poetry that he's interested in. He doesn't look for the doctrines of Pythagoras or Plato in it, he says; just the "sweet honey" of the words, "only the slight things that schoolmasters *(grammatici)* expound, for monthly fees, to boyish ears."[56] It's a self-deprecating reference, implying that he's no more than a lightweight dilettante or a dusty scholar. His treatise on obscure Latin words tells us that he's not lying about that last part, but it also makes it hard to believe that he commits a huge, and elementary, blunder in his Virgil commentary. In several manuscripts, Fulgentius dedicates the commentary to Catus or Cantia, a priest in Carthage (143). Please accept this modest "posy," he says, "which I have gathered for you from the flowery gardens of the Hesperides" (120). The editor and translator of Fulgentius's work in English, Leslie Whitbread, suggests that Fulgentius seems to confuse the Hesperides maidens with the Muses. But elsewhere (in *On the Ages of the World and Man*), Fulgentius describes Calliope, the muse of epic poetry, as "one of the maidens of the group on Mount Helicon" (43). Fulgentius's confusion may be strategic, because it makes Africa, the site of the Garden of the Hesperides, the source of the flowers of rhetoric and poetry.

The point here is that writers downplayed or ignored Dido's Phoenician origins in order to make her the originator of a new city, and a city that would be commemorated as a city of origins. Even the group that invaded North Africa at the end of Augustine's life called it the "mother of the Vandals." It is an unforgettable site, even when destroyed—and also, as we have seen with *The Dream of Scipio*, because it is destroyed. Chaucer's Dido is an emphatically Carthaginian (as opposed to Phoenician) Punic figure, precisely because she is such a central figure in Chaucer's poetry. Her grief gives Chaucer the chance to write that extended lament in the *Legend of Dido*, an extraordinary synthesis of different texts and archives. Dido is, as Marilyn Desmond says, "the central figure in this textual experience."[57] For some readers, Dido might be a figure of a vague African other, a blank space in world history created by Roman and European dominion. But she is also a foundational figure in Western literary culture, just as Carthage is a foundational site.

Although Dido's sorrow is a large part of what makes Africa important for Chaucer, the moment at which Aeneas leaves Africa is the focal point of Chaucer's narratives of the *Aeneid*, and also of a long literary attention in history. As we have seen, leaving Africa is a crucial fulcrum of epics, histories, and chronicles from the *Argonautica* to Lucan's *Pharsalia* to Orosius to Geoffrey of Monmouth and beyond. For Chaucer, partly because of the attention that his literary predecessors paid to it—witness the way he's used Ovid's reimagining of that moment—leaving Africa is a dramatization, a condensation, of a set of concerns having to do with the influence of antiquity, the debt to the past, the anxiety of influence, the solipsism of originality.

In the *House of Fame*, Chaucer grudgingly admits that the *Aeneid* tells a different story, that Aeneas might not have been entirely willing to leave Africa: "The book seyth Mercurie, sauns fayle, / Bad hym goo into Italye, / And leve Auffrikes regioun" (348–73. 11. 429–31, 353). But, as usual, when Chaucer sounds most emphatic about what his source says, he's prevaricating. In the *Aeneid*, Mercury doesn't *actually* tell Aeneas to leave Africa. If anything, Mercury's speech is a masterpiece of passive aggression—he just relays some guilt-inducing questions from Jupiter (What do you think you're doing? Don't you care about the future?) The *Aeneid* doesn't say anything about leaving Africa at this point. Indeed, the *Aeneid* uses the name "Africa" only twice—and nowhere in this section.

So why does Chaucer do this?

One answer is that it's a way of reiterating that Carthage *isn't* just a random point on the edge of the frog pond that is the Mediterranean. It's a metonymy for Africa itself, in a way that might have been implicit for readers in Virgil's time, but that Chaucer brings to the forefront for fourteenth-century audiences. The other answer is that Chaucer is— and this may be something of a deep dive—recalling what Petrarch has Augustine say to him in his *Secretum*: *dimitte Africam*. Chaucer's well-known sympathy for Dido reshapes in fundamental ways his retelling of the *Aeneid*. It becomes a story of misogynistic betrayal, an example that Chaucer returns to multiple times in his other work. But Chaucer's citation of Petrarch's deep reluctance to leave his poem *as Aeneas's own reluctance* changes Petrarch's story significantly. Petrarch inserts into an imagined conversation with Augustine his own failure to finish the poem, and has Augustine give him permission to "leave Africa." Chaucer turns that event in Latin literature into an event in world literature. Leaving "Auffrikes regioun" is what makes the future of literature possible. But it also means betraying a past that will always return: a Carthage that is always there, the specter behind eternal Rome.

CHAPTER FOUR

Ghosts of Language: Punic, Lybic, African Myth

> When Immortality saw the writings of these books, she ordered them to be inscribed on certain imposing rocks and placed inside a cave within the sanctuaries of the Egyptians.
>
> MARTIANUS CAPELLA, *The Marriage of Mercury and Philology*

> Our most secret writing, as ancient as Etruscan or the writing of the runes, but unlike these a writing still noisy with the sounds and breath of today.
>
> ASSIA DJEBAR, *So Vast the Prison*

The African Tumor in Language

After the first century, many of the most important works of Latin literature were written by Africans.[1] Although we're accustomed to thinking of Rome as vacuuming up talented provincials like Augustine, who came to embody traditional Roman virtues, leaving the provinces as backward as ever, it is useful to think of Roman intellectual culture at this stage as receding, like the precursor of a tsunami, to the African provinces before returning to wash over Europe. Augustine's *City of God* is a case in point. His vast meditation on ephemeral human accomplishments, triggered by the fall of Rome in 410, and written from his vantage point in Africa, is still being copied, imitated, and cited 1600 years later. Augustine was not the only African writer in late antiquity whose work reached into, and shaped, the future.

This chapter is concerned with several late antique North African writers who both preserved classical myth and shaped the way that it was read in the Christian era. We have already seen how important Macrobius's *Saturnalia* was as an archive of Greek, Roman, and Egyptian mythology. One young attendee at the Saturnalian feast was Servius, who wrote a brief commentary on the *Aeneid* that informed later allegorical readings of it, including one by Fulgentius, whose work is the main subject of this chapter. Virgil himself guides Fulgentius through an allegorical reading of his poem, although Fulgentius often interrupts to supplement Virgil's reading with its Christian implication. It's likely that Fulgentius's dialogue with Virgil gave Dante the idea to make Virgil a guide through the underworld, although Dante is far more deferential to Virgil.

Fulgentius's commentary is deft and witty. He writes an allegory of the *Aeneid* from a pagan point of view, then adds a supplement that nudges it into a Christian one, and then implicitly faults Virgil for not knowing better. At one point, an annoyed Virgil says "I can only set forth what I see" (122). Fulgentius's commentary is formidably learned, drawing on Greek etymologies and Stoic writers. In another work on obscure Latin words, he shows off his knowledge of arcane corners of the Latin language. Like the other North African writers I discuss in this chapter, he gathers mythological information with the zeal of a scholar and antiquarian. Jane Chance's magisterial and magnificent history of mythography begins with these writers, whose work, she says, is shaped by "indigenous religious beliefs and practices" of North Africa. The very comprehensiveness of their work, ranging from what they see around them to the far corners of the known world, caught the eye of scholars in the court of Charlemagne and his successors—because theirs, too, was a world of colliding and merging cultures.[2] Their care for these texts made them the backbone of the literary, allegorical treatment of classical texts through the Middle Ages.

These texts' origins in North Africa, however, have complicated their reception. Their hybridity—their delight in play, obscurity, literary forms, and philosophy all at the same time—has been mistaken for a symptom of the difference of African culture from the rest of the Greco-Roman world, as we will see. But Fulgentius's dazzling conversation with Virgil shows that these writers also clearly enjoy these texts. The obscurity of their knowledge has often been mistaken for flat-footed pedantry, and the playfulness of their writing mistaken for an anxiety about writing in the shadow of the great classical authors. One of those great classical authors—it has to be remembered—was the African Terence (Terentius Afer), who was one of the four core authors in the Latin classroom. Juvenal, too, recommended Africa as the best place to study oratory.[3] Complex ideas about North African writers existed from the late classical period.

One of the greatest of them was Apuleius, the author of *Metamorphoses* (sometimes called *The Golden Ass*). He was a self-described "half-Numidian, half-Gaetulian."[4] He was born in Madaura in present-day Algeria and spent most of his career in Carthage. His *Metamorphoses* sent runners out almost everywhere. It influenced Augustine's style in the *Confessions*, although he later condemned the work in the *City of God*. Boccaccio borrowed from it for the *Decameron* (there is an apocryphal story that Boccaccio smuggled a manuscript of *Metamorphoses* out of the great Abbey of Monte Cassino).[5] Bottom's transformation into an ass in *Midsummer Night's Dream* is based on the main character in Apuleius's work.[6] But it seems to have taken a century or two for the importance of Apuleius's *Metamorphoses* to have been recognized. The only review of it that survives from the fifty years after Apuleius's death is the kind that could kill a career. It excoriates someone who is growing senile by reading "old wives' songs" and the Punic fables (*Milesias Punicas*) of Apuleius.[7] What gives the review its devastating clout, though, is that it was written by an emperor: Septimius Severus, who, just to make the sting a little sharper, was the first and only African emperor.

A judgment that another Roman emperor made about another African writer around the same time suggests that the reputation of African writers in Rome was complicated. A decade or two after Septimius Severus's reign had ended, an African poet and historian, Publius Annius Florus, wrote a short dialogue with some travelers who thought they recognized him as the victor in a poetry contest in Rome long before. Aren't you the one from Africa, they ask, whom the emperor Domitian refused to award the prize because he didn't want the "Crown of Jupiter" to go to an African?[8]

The emperor might have been making a joke. In two of Plautus's plays, taking the Crown of Jupiter means to be foolish or insane: it meant stealing the heavy golden crown off the statue of Jupiter standing on the Capitoline building.[9] It was a difficult thing to do, and it was also an act of sacrilege: the Capitoline Hill was a symbol of Rome, and the statue of Jupiter was its most important part. To take its crown was also to take Rome itself. Domitian may have meant, in part, that to give the prize to Florus was as absurd as turning the province of Africa into the center of the empire. But it is possible that Florus was slyly comparing himself to the great epic poet Statius, who similarly had been denied the prize at the Capitoline Games by Domitian.[10] Domitian might have been incredulous that an African could be good enough to win the poetry prize, or that Florus's attempt to place himself among the best of Roman poets was as foolish as the delusions of a character from one of Plautus's comedies. Yet the fact that Florus himself relates this anecdote suggests that he understood it differently. It was not an insult to his pretensions but a tacit claim that he, and perhaps other Africans, posed a threat to Roman literary dominance. In the centuries after Florus, African writers indeed dominated literature, producing most of the Latin poetry of late antiquity. But beginning in the modern period, their distinctive work was regarded as a problem (or as a symptom) of something gone wrong, rather than a body of work that shaped the history of literature.

In the era of European humanism, scholars recognized that African writers occupied a distinctive place in the tradition of Latin literature but were not completely sure what it was. In the 1530s, the Spanish/Belgian/English humanist Juan Luis Vives identified a particular African "style," which he called *Africitas*.[11] Shortly after, scholars began to refer to a *tumor Africus*, an African bombast.[12] African style suffered against the standard the humanists used—Cicero's prose, which they regarded as elegant and clear.[13] Even then, the *tumor Africus* was blamed on Apuleius, whose influence on subsequent North African writers they recognized. Their judgment of what they might have called a bit more neutrally "Apuleian style" was based solely on the criteria of classical rhetoric. But criticism of *Africitas* is about far more than preferences for different schools of classical rhetoric. Especially in the nineteenth and twentieth centuries, style becomes a proxy for discussions of cultural and racial difference.

As late as 1971, the modern English translator of Fulgentius's works treats his writing as a symptom of the ebbing of the Western empire and the rise of the Eastern: "Fulgentius's Latin is what one would expect of a decadent period, close to the Asianic extravagances of Martianus Capella, strained, pompous, full of tortuous elaborations, infected with Gorgian antithesis, reading like a parody of Ciceronian periods—in sum, what

George Saintsbury called 'a most detestable style, a tissue of appallingly barbarous Latin'" (Fulgentius, 108–9). It's odd, but not unprecedented, for a literary scholar to have such disdain for a writer to whom they have dedicated much of their career. But it's unusual for them to express an invective that is really directed at the world that the author lived in. Fulgentius isn't just a bad writer: he's the product of a "decadent period," guilty of "Asianic extravagance," "infected," "barbarous."

The search for a cause for this literary movement having to do with Africa itself really began with an answer: African style is like that because it is like Africa. The French scholar Paul Monceaux's influential 1894 study of North African Latin literature combines a stylistic analysis with a kind of travelogue: "One grasps well this physiognomy of the African writer, and one understands this style, where order, moderation and often common sense are lacking, but where everything is movement and color, when one has lived this African life, when one has endured this climate of sharp contrasts and one has mingled with these strange crowds, where for thirty centuries so many different races have met, where Europe, Asia and the Sudan collide."[14] There's obvious epidermal racism in his reference to the "physiognomy" of the African writer: their writing is like their facial features and their color. But standard tropes about Africans are also there in plain sight: they are exuberant, chaotic, and love bright colors and rhythm.

As the historian of Carthage Serge Lancel observed, these sweeping generalizations about the fundamental "Africanness" of Apuleian style betray a taste for the "colonial picturesque."[15] The colonialist setting of Monceaux's study is literally up front, in the first sentence of the book: "Roman Africa presents a spectacle analogous to that of French Africa."[16] The dismissal of the writing of these North African writers as barbaric, degenerate, or incompetent sounds remarkably like the judgments about African subjects that settlers and administrators made throughout Africa. The value of these early North African writers, in other words, was largely submerged in the colonial era by the essentialisms that were one of the instruments of imperial ideology and domination in African colonies.[17] Judgments about North African writers might not be an explicit instrument of colonialism, but those judgments have nevertheless assumed that North African writing must be measured against standards that those writers have partially forgotten or poorly understood. Whatever is valuable about them, paradoxically, has been obscured by their mimicry (to use one of Homi Bhabha's terms) of the earlier classical writers at the heart of empire: Virgil, Ovid, Cicero.

When we read these writers on their own terms, as much as possible, as writers anchored in Africa, and interested as much in the African mythological past as in the "purely" Roman and Greek, obscurity actually turns out to be one of their important themes. They're not interested, of course, in how much they've clouded the Roman and Greek pasts that modern scholars are interested in recovering, but in the obscurity and loss of the African past. One of the many functions of allegory, for them, is how to discover what *still remains* of Africa in the loud conversation of Greek and Latin literature and mythology.

Fulgentius, again, is a useful example. Uncovering hidden things is something that Fulgentius loved to do: he wrote a short treatise on obscure and antiquated words, the *Expositio Sermonum Antiquorum*. One of his most elaborate works, *On the Ages of the World and Man*, is built on the principle of hiddenness: it refers to a language that we do not directly encounter in the work but on which the work is built. To a large extent, the exuberance and experimentation of his work, and of his contemporary Martianus Capella, depend on a core of mystery and absence.

Martianus Capella: In the Palace of Myth

Martianus Capella was born, like Apuleius, in Madaura. He was a contemporary of Augustine's, and similarly lived in Carthage for a large part of his life. His great work, *The Marriage of Mercury and Philology*, is an allegory of the union of eloquence and learning, arranged according to the seven liberal arts. It was used both in classrooms through the Middle Ages and by poets, who found it a source of classical stories and a model for imaginative narrative with a philosophical bent—works like Alain of Lille's late twelfth-century Neoplatonic epic *Anticlaudianus*, the thirteenth-century *Romance of the Rose*, or Chaucer's *House of Fame* and John Lydgate's *Temple of Glas*. In the twentieth century, Martianus was often regarded as a pernicious influence on literature, whose precious and labored style, as C. S. Lewis said, was "badness alone."[18] We'll return to modern judgments of the style of these African authors, because it is a part of the reception of older African achievements in general in modern Europe. Lewis tellingly used exoticized analogies in his famous takedown of Martianus's work: "This universe, which has produced the bee-orchid and the giraffe, has produced nothing stranger than Martianus Capella" (78). It might be a coincidence that Lewis compared Martianus to an African animal, but he certainly knew that Martianus was an African (78).

At the end of *The Marriage of Mercury and Philology*, Martianus describes himself as a doddering old man, still in his birthplace, the "town of Elissa"—that is, in Carthage.[19] The biographical notations on Carolingian manuscripts from the fevered intellectual centers that Charlemagne founded, when Martianus's fandom was greatest, spelled out what this meant: he was "African by birth, indeed a citizen of Carthage."[20] A less overt indication of Martianus's cultural context is that the overwrought and vacillating style that C. S. Lewis hated so much goes back to a fellow African—Apuleius.[21]

Martianus's book revels in a deeply embedded knowledge of, and interest in, the mythological and esoteric traditions of Egypt and Libya. He describes what are clearly hieroglyphics, "written with a sacred ink, whose letters were thought to be representations of living creatures," which "Immortality" orders to be copied onto *stelae* in the "sanctuaries of the Egyptians." These, Immortality says, record the genealogies of the gods (46). As with many passages in Martianus, this one is shot through with Easter eggs waiting to be discovered (47nn72–73). But the important point is that Egypt is the site of arcane and ancient knowledge, even if it remains obscure.

The personification "Astronomy" says, for instance, that it has kept itself "secret" "in the sanctums of Egyptian priests" for 40,000 years (318). Sometimes this knowledge is still concealed within the text. At one point, "Philology" says that Egyptian ingenuity conceals, in a sophisticated mathematical riddle, another name for Mercury (35). It wasn't until 1599 that the Dutch scholar Hugo Grotius worked out that when the numbers are mapped onto the Greek alphabet, they spell the name of Thoth, the Egyptian god of mathematics and sacred texts, who was at the same time, as we have seen, skeptical about the usefulness of writing.[22] Other traces of written or spoken language in Egypt glimmer faintly in Martianus's book. "Philology" addresses the ship of the sun, a distinctly Egyptian manifestation, whose true name is also concealed numerically (35). It turns out to be "Phre." The tangle of references gets even more complex: "phre" is a near-pun on the Greek word "phren" or "mind": Martianus is finding an essential continuity, although hidden, between esoteric Egyptian knowledge and the central stage of Neoplatonic philosophy (59n135). And there's more, as this particular riddle may come from local knowledge about the Egyptian sun god. The form of the name may be in the Bohairic dialect of Coptic, used in the western Nile Delta and Alexandria.[23]

The concealment of entire languages and dialects in glancing references is an important part of the relationship these North African writers have to the African past. It may be covered in a cloud of esoteric references and enigmas, but that past is still powerful. Martianus and other writers link the recovery of this past to the academic and philosophical knowledge they are synthesizing and passing on to form the curriculum of medieval classrooms.

Sometimes Martianus situates knowledge and methods more overtly in Africa. In the long procession of divinities at the wedding of "Mercury" and "Philology," Ammon appears with a ram's horns and "showed to the thirsty people the water of a fountain," an allusion to the Fountain of the Sun at the shrine of Siwa in Libya (53). The ship of the sun is also described as Ammon's, the "god of parched Libya" (59). As we have seen, by the era of Alexander the Great, Ammon's oracle at Siwa in Libya communicated by means of a ship carried by priests. The second liberal art, "Dialectic," which is even more important for the structure of the liberal arts that Martianus passes on, comes from the "sands of panting Libya" (108).

"Dialectic," in other words, is an African art. It is a dry discipline, like the desert. But it is specifically Libyan because of the Libyan desert's deep mythological and literary history. Apart from its aridity, it was notorious for its snakes, and long catalogs of the various venomous kinds are a feature, as we have seen, of classical epic's African episodes. Lucan's *Pharsalia* is the longest of these, and Lucan uses the deadly snake attacks as a reproach to the hubris of Cato and his army. Martianus is thinking, in fact, of that particular moment: the "sands of panting Libya" echo Lucan's evocation of the "hot sands of thirsty Libya."[24] Martianus assumes that we know that Libya is the most famous site of serpent lore. We can tell "Dialectic" comes from Libya: her braided hair suggests the venom of serpents. The snake is the attribute of "Dialectic" because being caught in a fallacy is like being bitten with the venom of a hidden serpent (107). "Dialectic" is also described as dark (*furva*), like the obscure traps of dialectical disputation, but also like Lucan's description of the *perustus* ("burned") Garamantes of Libya. An earlier Numidian Christian, Arnobius Afer, used the adjective *furvus*—dark, black—to describe the Garamantians.²⁵

Although Africans like Arnobius use terms like *furvus* to describe fellow Africans like the Garamantians without an apparent pejorative sense, it's possible to read the hostile setting of "Dialectic" and the notice taken of her skin color as the othering of Africa and Africans. From a European perspective, for that matter, it's always possible to read references to Africa and Africans as an automatic othering. That possibility is always latent in passages about the Syrtis and the deserts of Libya and its snakes—or the story of the Gorgon, in the west of Africa, whose head carried by Perseus leaves the drops of blood that coalesce into snakes. There was, indeed, venomous racism in Africa at that moment. Several of the epigrams collected in what is now called the Latin Anthology, a collection of African Vandal poetry, are scurrilous racist attacks on neighboring peoples.²⁶ The point is that Martianus is *anchoring* one of the foundational disciplines of Western intellectual culture in Africa. Its venom and darkness might be African, but they are an integral part of Western thought, part of what makes it up.

Martianus, after all, is imagining the formation of an entire intellectual tradition from his vantage point in one of Africa's most storied cities. His name for it, the "city of Elissa," hints that he takes a very Dido-centric view of its history. Near the beginning of his text, when he describes how the gods enter Jupiter's palace to celebrate the betrothal of "Mercury" and "Philology," he quotes the *Aeneid*, describing how Aeneas's sailors enter Dido's palace: "After they had entered and been given leave to speak" (*Postquam introgressi et coram data copia fandi* [1.520]). The palace of the head of the gods, in other words, is like Dido's palace, and the Trojans are like lesser gods summoned to it. The allusion is a brief glimpse into a place where Carthage is imagined as the foundation of Roman intellectual culture, not an obstacle to it.

Carthage could have taken other directions. Martianus casts "Philology" as a Dido who makes the fateful decision to ally with Aeneas, rather than continue with her project of founding Carthage. Dido consults seers and oracles but pays no attention to them because of her blinding passion for Aeneas. "Philology," on the other hand, knows her union has been blessed by the gods. She is mainly concerned with how to acquire the knowledge necessary to dwell with the gods, while she wanders through an allegorical garden of learning (34). "Philology," it seems, is a do-over of Dido, a figure who pays attention this time to the gods, and to their local habitations. She discerns that Thoth, one of the names of her betrothed, is inscribed at the heart of Egyptian religion and mythology.

Martianus closes his work with an epilogue written in the voice of an old man in Carthage, apologizing for his ramshackle work, although it sounds like a humblebrag. One of its faults, he suggests, is that it takes in too much, piling up heaps of learned information (*docta indoctis aggerans*).[27] As we have seen, part of this large agglomeration covers parts of Africa—but the whole work, at the end, is also framed as a project that begins and ends in Carthage.[28]

Fulgentius: Africa's Mythic Language

Fulgentius, Martianus's great North African contemporary, also inserts bits of autobiographical information that tell us that he is writing in North Africa. He begins his *Mythologies*, which along with Macrobius's *Saturnalia* is one of the most important sources for classical mythology, by telling us that he is somewhere to the west of Alexandria. But where Martianus's revelation that he's writing in Carthage invites us to go back through the massive work to see how Carthage might be relevant, Fulgentius begins by placing the very foundations of Latin poetry in Africa.

Fulgentius's *Mythologies* begins like Virgil's *Georgics* do, in the countryside. Unlike Virgil's, Fulgentius's opening is mostly a dateline: he is writing from the "seclusion of a country estate ... in rustic ease" (41). He is an "exile from city affairs," but is also putting his own estate back in order after it had been invaded by unnamed enemies; the countryside is now restored to its original owners after the "joy of my lord the king's return" (41). Fulgentius doesn't name the king, but most scholars agree that he is probably a Vandal ruler. The ebb and flow of estate ownership was characteristic of the ongoing struggle between the Vandal kingdom and its Libyan neighbors—what Fulgentius calls the "barbarian onslaught."

We could be a number of places in the late Roman empire, but Fulgentius makes it clear in several ways that he is in Africa. The footsteps that the "barbarian" soldiers have left behind are *mauricatos*, "Moorish"—that is, the footsteps of soldiers from Mauretania.[29] The analogy that occurs to him as he wanders through the wreckage of the war is from the first book of the *Aeneid*. He is, he says, like sailors welcomed to the shore after a tempest—specifically the "Trojans of Aeneas." He, too, is landing on the African shore after tempestuous times.

Discouraged and tired, he stops to compose a poem to the Muses, which "draws" (*abstraxit*) them away from Mount Helicon to him. Perhaps because he has just asked for the riches of Homer and Virgil to be given to him, Calliope touches him with a palm branch, giving him the gift of poetry. Overwhelmed at her generosity, the narrator asks why she has come. It turned out that she had already been in Africa. She left Athens long before, she says, for Rome, but had to leave because war came and disturbed even the Capitoline Hill (*Romulae arcis*).[30] She then went to Alexandria, taking with her some of the solemnity and severity of the two Catos and Cicero, but in the new location she was also able to indulge in a wider range of genres and moods.

Calliope's journey is a historical allegory. It is a history of literature imagined as a *translatio studii*, the transfer of learning from one empire to the next—from Greece to Rome to France, as Chrétien de Troyes, who wrote the first great Arthurian romances, said. In language strikingly similar to Fulgentius's, the Latin philosophical poet Lucretius describes how Ennius, the originator of Latin poetry, brought the crown of perennial fronds (*perenni fronde corona*) from Helicon to the Romans.[31] Alexandria thus replaces Athens as the center of philosophy, poetry, and scholarship. Fulgentius likely has in mind Alexandria's *Musaeion*, a scholarly institution modeled after Plato's academy and dedicated to the Muses.[32]

Yet Calliope does not meet Fulgentius's narrator in Alexandria. She meets him outside it, in the countryside. She has had to leave Alexandria, she says, because the city has been taken over by Galen—the most important figure in medicine up through the early modern period. "Galen" is, of course, another metonym: he stands for the whole body of medical knowledge. Most of Galen's work was gathered and disseminated by Alexandrians: the *Summaria Alexandrinorum*, the complete body of Galen's work compiled by physicians in Alexandria, was the basis for the Arabic medicine that was passed on to Western Europe. Calliope objects not to medicine in theory, but to how the knowledge is being put into practice. The streets of Alexandria are "more cruel than wars" because of the many surgeons committing butchery (44). So Calliope flees the city for the African countryside, much as Fulgentius has done.

Calliope, who is a bit of a snob, tells Fulgentius that he shouldn't be afraid to let the muses into his rural house. She has heard that the barbarians ban literature from their houses; it's dangerous even to write the initials of one's name. Calliope invites Fulgentius to become a poet—as long as he stops the trivial jottings that he has been engaged in, recording his dreams and whatever he has been carelessly writing down on "papyrus from the Nile" (44). In the end, what Fulgentius writes down with Calliope's help became one of the most important explorations of how Christian writers could use what Fulgentius calls the "lying literature" of Greek pagans. The *Mythologies* is virtually the handbook for Christian interpretations of classical myth during the Middle Ages. It uses etymologies and incidental details to reveal an underlying principle—usually a moral one—beneath the tantalizing surface of the stories. Fulgentius allegorizes the African giant Antaeus, for instance, as lust, because his name means "contrary"; he's contrary to virtue. And he is rooted to the earth—that is, to the flesh. The Greek fables that Fulgentius excoriates are not so much lies as yet-unrecognized distortions of the truth, a truth that an enlightened and erudite reader might be able to discover.

Fulgentius's work used to be a standard example of clueless or stupidly pious medieval scholarship. In his 1908 *A History of Criticism and Literary Taste in Europe*, George Saintsbury describes it as "sheer serious insanity," the "grovelling allegory" of a "sportive schoolboy."[33] But the Prologue of the *Mythologies* suggests a more complex relationship with the muses of poetry. They are robed—a virtual gimme for readers who are looking for allegories *of* allegory, since the first description of allegory we have, by the Greek writer Demetrius, is that it is like clothing.[34] Yet, precisely because so much of Fulgentius's reading of the myths has to do with the "contraries" of lust and chastity, the muses remain clothed. The only partial exception is Calliope, who lifts her robe to her ankle to protect it from the grass as she walks toward Fulgentius. If there is an erotic subtext in the description of Calliope, as there often is when allegorists describe the unveiling of the surface that hides the truth of myth, Fulgentius carefully, and almost deliberately, forecloses it. He will not discuss, he tells Calliope, myths about adultery and sexual deception—although this is a deception of Fulgentius's, because he goes right on to discuss Zeus, Danae, and Leda anyway. Apart from these blurry and flitting appearances, the metaphors that Fulgentius uses have more to do with *thanatos* than *eros*: before one can get to work on the Greek myths, he says, one must first have buried (*sepulto*) the lies of the Greeks. The recovery of the truth that myths contain, on the other hand, is a work of *exhumation*, bringing to light what has remained untouched for centuries (45).³⁵

Interpretation seems to require an economy of expiation, as if the unearthing of truth leaves a tomb that must be occupied by something, even if it is only lies. At the end of his commentary on Statius's *Thebaid*, Fulgentius explains that Creon's refusal to bury the bodies of the kings who fought against him is the same thing as a refusal to conceal or obscure worldly knowledges that satisfy pride (242). This is another version of the allegory of interpretation: rather than metaphorically bury the lies that a myth contains, here the myth is about its own failure to bury its lies. Both versions, however, grapple with an absence at their very heart. Interpretation, the work of allegoresis, depends on installing an absence in the structure of a myth—there is something missing, which the reader needs to find out. What truth is there in the very lies of the Greeks? Fulgentius's myth of myth, if we can think of the story of Creon that way, thinks about expiation as the work of understanding or comprehending the world.

There is still another version of this story of interpretation, only this time built on the meanings of the voice. The *Fable of Apollo and Marsyas*, near the end of the *Mythologies*, is one of the longest entries. It is the story of how the satyr Marsyas was flayed alive by Apollo for having the temerity to declare that he was a better musician. It is usually read as a story about the demand for free speech, and a number of ancient writers cite the story in discussions of *parrhesia*, or speaking truth to power. In Rome, the central virtue of *libertas* was represented by a statue of Marsyas that stood in the Forum.³⁶ Given Marsyas's well-known identification with the center of Roman power, and the widespread use of the myth in the classical world and in late antiquity, the changes that Fulgentius makes to it are a bit surprising. The story of Marsyas, the bad musician who has an audience with bad taste (Midas), is the point at which Fulgentius chooses to discuss the (mostly Greek) theory of music at considerable length. He divides music into three manifestations: the voice, the stringed instrument, and the wind instrument. Of these, the voice "fulfills all the requirements of music": interval, harmony, modulating harsh tones, linking sounds together, and ornamentation. The lyre falls short, though not badly, because it cannot produce semitones (*limmata*) or the *quilisma*. The flute, however, is far more deficient because it can produce only one and a half scales to the lyre's five.

Fulgentius's discussion of music describes its mathematical ratios, and lists both the Greek and Latin terms. Many of the terms that characterize the abilities of the voice are rare or obscure, and Fulgentius does not explain many of them: a reader who is not already competent in Greek music theory would not know what *distonias mollire* means. *Especially* with the voice, which is the fullest expression of music, Fulgentius becomes obscure and unclear. It's a metaphysical, Derridean joke: as readers we cannot hear the voice. All we can do is read about it, and we will never understand it, never live in what Fulgentius calls, as we will see in a minute, the province of speech.

The voice is, in fact, a serious problem that Fulgentius ultimately relates to the site of Africa. For Fulgentius, the myth of Marsyas is principally about the concealment and disclosure of the voice, and its uncomfortable relation to music. It begins with a failure to make music: Minerva plays a flute she has invented at a banquet for the gods, but she stops when they laugh at her appearance. To find out why they laughed at her, she goes to Lake Trito and, seeing that the flute does indeed make her look ridiculous when she plays it, she throws it away. This is how Marsyas comes to possess the flute.

It is slightly strange that Minerva isn't judged for the quality of her music but the seemliness of her appearance, when the whole subject of Fulgentius's myth seems to be sound and the voice. But it is actually Midas's appearance that is the content of the voice, and the concealment of appearance, so to speak, that makes voice necessary. Midas's servant cannot keep the secret that Midas has been given an ass's ears for judging Marsyas and his flute to be better than Apollo, and, digging a hole in the earth, whispers the secret into it and fills it in. A reed grows on the same spot, and a shepherd makes yet another flute out of it, which sings out the secret "it has absorbed from the earth." The complex play of secrecy and revelation, of speech and music, underpins Fulgentius's interest throughout in music as a kind of analogy for mythology. But I'd like to call attention to the way in which Fulgentius stages this myth in Africa—a story "from the earth"—unlike other versions of the Marsyas and Midas story.

Minerva's return to Lake Trito retraces her origin. According to Lucan, she first touched earth at the lake, after springing from her father's head. Her return to Trito could be seen as a retreat, an attempt to begin again, with a career as the goddess of wisdom. The emergence of Marsyas, however, doesn't fit neatly into the genealogy of gods. He is a shepherd, a rustic barbarian appearing at the edges of empire, and at the fringes of the mythological world, in Libya, where he makes a flute at the marshy edges of Lake Trito. The fulcrum of the entire story rests in Africa.

Or, to be precise, Fulgentius suggests that Africa is where such stories will come to be understood. When Calliope begins expounding myth, Fulgentius says that she "entered into the region of speech" (*prouinciam loquacitatis ingressa*).[37] It is a strange, obscure phrase, and could be one of those examples of "Asianic" preciousness for which Fulgentius has been condemned (indeed, *loquacitas* can also be translated as "talkativeness"). But, as is typical for Fulgentius, it is a pun: Calliope moves to the *prouinciam* of speech, a term that suggests that a Roman North African province is the site where myth can be spoken, and understood, aloud. Everywhere else, myth is merely writing; here in Africa, it is a voice.

What does Fulgentius imply with the phrase the "province of speech"? There are two—not necessarily contradictory—possibilities. The first is that North Africa was known for its eloquence. Augustine is the most famous example of an eloquent North African: from a small Numidian town, he rose to become the official court orator in Milan. North Africans thought highly of their skill at oratory. Their tombstones often praised their skill at oratory, even when they were for children.[38] The North African Apuleius praised Carthage as the inspiration of forensic orators (*camena togatorum*); Juvenal called Carthage their nurturer.[39] Marcus Aurelius's teacher, Cornelius Fronto, a self-styled "Libyan nomad," was known both for his fascination with etymology and for his play with words (short people, he said, should be described with short words). He was also considered an arbiter of Latin vocabulary, somewhat like the *Academie Française* is for French. Aulus Gellius, in his *Attic Nights*, reports that one of Fronto's interlocutors claimed that if Fronto used such words they would be given "citizenship" or a place in a "Latin colony."[40] In every sense, the North Africa of Fulgentius was the province of speech.

Yet Fulgentius's description of speech as *loquacitas* implies that there is something excessive about it: it is garrulous, beyond the decorum of ordinary conversation. The other association that North African speech had in classical literature was the opposite of disciplined oratory. It was often represented as threatening, uncontrollable, even barbaric. News about Dido and Aeneas's affair in the *Aeneid* is personified as "Rumor," a terrifying, monstrous figure who spreads paranoia and outrage through the cities of Libya. In his *Punica*, Silius Italicus describes the speech of Africans (the Mauri, the Gaetulians, the Baniura) as both wild and having the power to tame wild animals (2.439–40; 3.289 [using *loqui*]; 3.305).

These two contradictory aspects of the speech of Africans have one thing in common: on the one hand, as with Fronto, North Africans can be imagined as policing the boundaries of Latin linguistic territory. They admit new members and keep others out. The repertoire of Latin is under attack, but North Africans like Fronto will keep it from utter collapse. Yet, on the other hand, they may be positioned on the borders of Latin *precisely* because they are positioned on the borders of empire, in the province of speech.

In another work, Fulgentius thinks about this African border of two languages—or two kinds of language—from within the system of writing, rather than speech. His *De aetatibus mundi et hominis* is "one of the strangest literary productions of antiquity," and one of the most convoluted of literary texts imaginable.[41] It is an ambitious history of the world up to the emperor Valentinian I, who died in 375 CE, and it works out a vast analogy between the ages of the world and the ages of the individual human. It takes material from sources we have already discussed, including Orosius's world history and the Alexander Romance. It commits itself to a rigorous and difficult set of rules: it is a lipogram, a text that leaves out a particular letter of the alphabet in each section, or throughout the entire work. The most famous modern example is Georges Perec's 1969 novel *La Disparition*, which does not use the letter "e" (neither does its English translation, Gilbert Adair's *A Void*).

In his prologue, Fulgentius says that he plans for his work to have twenty-three chapters, each omitting a letter of the alphabet in turn (only the books up to the letter "O" survived, or else he wrote no further). His first chapter on the creation and fall of humankind, for instance, does without the letter "A," which is featured in some of the most important names in the story: Adam, "Eva," Cain, and Abel. That constraint requires massive and sustained ingenuity, which is only compounded by its rich allusive and punning style. It's not meant to be consulted as a textbook, a window onto the world outside. It is meant to be appreciated as a text that celebrates the system of writing itself.

In his preface, Fulgentius compares his project to the "amazing work" (*opus mirificum*) of "Xenophon," who took away (*diminutis*) one letter in each of his twenty-four books. That is, "Xenophon" wrote a lipogram that omits each letter of the Greek alphabet in each chapter in turn. It's a perfect example, only we are not sure if Fulgentius is using a real example. The only Greek writer we know of named Xenophon was a very serious general, philosopher, and historian, none of whose surviving works is a lipogram. None is close to twenty-four books (the longest is the *Cyropaedia*, which has eight books). One possibility is that Fulgentius is making an obscure academic joke about a reference that the real Xenophon made in his *Symposium* to someone who knew the twenty-four books in each of the *Iliad* and the *Odyssey*.[42] Fulgentius doesn't mention two writers who did make twenty-four-book lipograms out of Homer's work: Nestor of Laranda (the *Iliad*) and Tryphiodorus of Sicily (the *Odyssey*), although there's no evidence he knew them. He may, in fact, be making an elaborate joke about what else is missing from his work besides multiple letters of the alphabet. The most conspicuous absence is a twenty-fourth book, like Homer's poems: he says his work will have only twenty-three books. But this absence itself will be part of the profound structure of his work, an orderly division that will astonish a reader (*emireris*) when he or she discovers it.

That astonishment might refer to the feat of writing such a demanding lipogram. But it may also refer to the mystery of what alphabet he has in mind in the first place. He says his *De aetatibus* will have only twenty-three books because he is not using the Greek alphabet, which has twenty-four letters; but neither is he using the Hebrew alphabet, or there would be only twenty-two books (131). The alphabet he is using, he says, is taken from "our language": *nostra lingua* (130) He is, of course, writing in Latin at that moment, so the obvious extrapolation would be that he means Latin. But right from the start, he identifies "our language" as Libyc (*Oportet deinceps nostre lingue medium ordinem consequi, quo ... unicus ordo Libico monstretur in numero* [131]).

Fulgentius's *De aetatibus* is one of the few late antique sources that names the indigenous language or languages of North Africa. The term "Libyc" is now used to refer to them as a group, or to their relation to modern Amazigh in the term "Libyco-Berber." Fulgentius does not say much about it. It's a kind of uncanny twin of Latin: its alphabet has the same number of letters, but he doesn't say what else about the language makes it *ours*. Gregory Hays suggests that there actually may be no difference: Fulgentius is simply suggesting that the language of the Libyans, too, is Latin—and obviously it was one of Fulgentius's languages.[43] But there is one way in which it seems to be different. The lipogram, Fulgentius says, will be harder to write in "our language" than in Greek, because, unlike Greek, it doesn't allow one letter to be substituted for another (for instance, *i* for *e*, *u* for *o*) (130). Those kinds of substitutions may, in fact, be a characteristic of African Latin, which, as J. N. Adams says, was "in a state of flux with innovation rather than archaism the most decisive determinant of its local characteristics at any time."[44]

Fulgentius's reference to a "Libyan" language that doesn't allow letters to be substituted may be a very oblique reference to a property that the Libyc language did not share with Latin. Like Hebrew, it is an *abjad*—it contains only consonants. Like other consonantal alphabets, Libyc can be read intelligibly only when the reader adds the missing vowels. Thus the ancient Libyan name "ZKTT WYMR," found on a stele, is rendered in Latin as "Sactut Ihimir." There are many words, however, including the last two words of the same inscription, whose vowels remain unknown.[45] It's a language with missing elements, and some may be missing forever.

Libyc, the Purest Language

This is an extraordinary gap in linguistic history, and in the history of Africa. We know almost nothing about what may be the ancestor of the Berber (properly "Amazigh" or "Tamazight") languages that are spoken today in nine countries in North Africa. The largest populations of speakers are in Morocco and Algeria, but it is also spoken in Libya, Tunisia, Mali, Niger, Burkina Faso, Mauretania, and the Siwa Oasis in Egypt—the site where Alexander visited Ammon.[46] It is possible that the Libyc script is related to modern systems of tattooing among Amazigh women, and likely that notational systems used by the Tuareg are directly descended from it.[47] Yet the *language* that the Libyco-Berber script itself represented remains obscure, despite the extensive use of the script.

The script is found throughout North Africa, as far west as the Canary Islands, and may have been used for as long as a thousand years. The earliest surviving examples can't be rigorously dated, but they most likely were written between the seventh and fifth centuries BCE. The script survived the arrival of the Romans and the Latin alphabet, and was used as late as the fifth century CE.[48] It's found in what is now Morocco, Algeria, Libya, Tunisia, and Niger as far south as Abalessa (1,000 miles south of Algiers), where the tomb of a woman identified as Tin Hinan, an ancestral matriarch of the Tuareg, was built sometime around 325 CE.

Libyco-Berber inscriptions found in that tomb are probably older than that, though, because some of them were reused to build the tomb. Libyco-Berber script (including those in the Canary Islands, more than 190 examples remain all told), may have survived into the modern era in Tifinagh, the alphabet used by the Tuareg, and adapted in 1967 by the Berber Academy in Paris as the alphabet for other Berber languages. Since then, "neo-Tifinagh" has been used in Amazigh identity movements; it is the recognized script for Tamazight in Morocco, where it frequently appears on signs along with Arabic.

The Libyco-Berber/Tifinagh script, then, traces a remarkable history of silence and visibility, loss and recovery. It may be the oldest surviving *and* recorded African language, despite significant gaps in historical knowledge. Its modern use to organize a people around its ancient rootedness is similar to the modern revival of Hebrew as a spoken language—except that we do not yet know the ancient spoken language that is now called Libyco-Berber.

Another irony in the history of Libyco-Berber is that the knowledge we have of it depends on one of North Africa's other semi-lost languages: Punic. Around the time of Carthage's destruction, a Numidian prince named Atban was buried in a magnificent tomb. A plaque in the tomb, written in both Punic and Libyc, was discovered in 1631 by Thomas d'Arcos, who sent a transcription to a friend in France, where it lay neglected for a couple of centuries. The inscription's next fateful encounter occurred in 1842, when Thomas Reade, Napoleon's former jailer on St. Helena, noticed it while he was the British Consul in Tunis. Reade, who a British officer once referred to aptly as a "Nincumpoop," tore the tomb down to get at the plaque.[49] He destroyed another plaque in doing so, but the surviving plaque, having been written in both Libyc and Punic, ultimately proved to be the key to deciphering Libyc. He sold it to the British Museum for five pounds. But Reade's single act of vandalism, although it almost prevented Libyc from being deciphered altogether, was almost as nothing compared to the wholesale destruction of Punic literature.

When the Romans destroyed Carthage in 146 BCE, its libraries were either burned or dispersed among nearby Numidian leaders. A few works were later translated into Latin, although none of these have survived, and there are only allusions to what might have been in them. The only exception is a treatise on farming by a Carthaginian named Mago, which was translated into Latin and widely quoted. But Mago's treatise itself has not come down to us. As a spoken language, Punic survived for several hundred years after the destruction of Carthage. Augustine, growing up in what is now Algeria, was certainly acquainted with it, and referred to it later in life as "our" language, the language of we "Africans." He even defended it against some snob in Madaura, where he had attended grammar school: "Many words of wisdom have been committed to memory in Punic books," he said, "as is disclosed by very learned men."[50]

Punic also survived in numerous inscriptions in stone throughout North Africa and the Mediterranean, as far east as the Anatolian plateau in Turkey. Most of these inscriptions are on funerary stelae, stone slabs that marked graves. They tend to name the deceased person (and sometimes his or her ancestry) and include a short prayer or dedication to a god. They may sometimes imply that a child sacrifice has been made to the god of Carthage, Baal Ammon, or to the city's goddess, Tanit.[51] (There is still debate about whether Carthaginians really practiced child sacrifice; explicit accounts are written by outsiders and, because no other texts survive, the only Punic accounts are the brief and enigmatic references on these stelae.) A second, and much smaller, variety of Punic inscription are temple tariffs, which list what portions of animal sacrifices belong to the priests. Because Punic is a Semitic language, it did not take very long for surviving inscriptions to be translated. Somewhere around ten thousand Punic inscriptions have been discovered so far and more are turning up, especially on seals and coins from archaeological digs. These appear frequently on the commercial and gray markets. As I write this, there is a Carthaginian coin, with a single Punic letter on it, for sale on eBay—for under $200(!).

From these meager remnants, the language was reconstructed, although the surviving texts do not really amount to a "literature" as such. The classics scholar Dennis Feeney, in fact, has argued that the destruction of Carthage goaded the Romans into thinking of their language in exceptional terms, as a language that was, after the Punic Wars, the language of an empire.[52] Rome needed texts that befitted the dignity of a world empire, and so by the time of Augustus, the great epic the *Aeneid* was written about the founding of Rome. Its first half is the story of how Aeneas left behind Carthage, whose queen, Dido, destroyed herself out of fury and grief. She embodies the trauma of a culture destroyed in a war that gave Rome supremacy over the Mediterranean.

As Augustine attests, however, Punic did not disappear suddenly in a violent conflagration. It disappeared gradually, under the kind of disdain and neglect for which Augustine called out his colleague. But even Augustine's championing of Punic sounds defensive. He does not talk about *why* he thinks it is important, or even what kind of wisdom he finds in its literature. He has to appeal to unnamed scholars to back him up. Whatever wisdom was in these books remains lost, and Augustine is probably the last writer with any knowledge of Punic to mention it as a spoken, living language. In the middle of the sixth century, the Greek historian Procopius refers somewhat vaguely to people near the Straits of Gibraltar still speaking "Phoenician."[53] After that, Punic passed almost entirely into silence, never to be revived.[54]

Both Punic and Libyco-Berber, then, are languages that have left provocative written traces in history that are more epitaph than living literature. Yet historical witnesses to both languages describe them as worse than unwritten, closer to animal sounds and meaningless babble than to coherent speech. The only fragments of Punic text that were accessible in the Middle Ages and the early modern period appear in a play by the Roman satirist Plautus, whose plays Shakespeare borrowed from heavily for his early comedies. In *Poenulus*, Plautus has the character Hanno, a Carthaginian who speaks Punic, speak ten lines of prayer asking for help in his quest to find some lost relatives. (Other Punic words are said by Latin-speaking characters, punningly mistranslated.) One implication is that enough audience members knew some Punic that they could identify these puns; the play was written between the Second and Third Punic Wars. But the play also implies that there is something elusive and shifty about Hanno and his language. The prologue of the *Poenulus* satirizes Hanno's knowledge of "all languages" (*omnis linguas*), yet he pretends that he doesn't know any. An underlying joke might be that, although he does know Punic, it is not a language, and therefore he still does not know any language. He's therefore "thoroughly Punic"; is there any need to say anything else? No further words: *quid verbis opust*, a phrase that implies that anything to do with Hanno and Punic is beyond language.[55] Plautus's Punic text is part of a complex set of ideas about Carthaginians and their language, yet Hanno is unmistakably someone who speaks the language of a cultural other. Hanno's speech is only a rough phonetic paraphrase. His lengthy prayer in Punic may not have been translated in performance, but even if it were, it would have been a wall of unintelligible sound to most of the Roman audience.

Most ancient representations of the languages of North Africa are more insistent that they are not really languages. They are an unintelligible tangle, not just of varieties, but also of sounds and noises. Herodotus said simply that the language of the Ethiopians was unlike any other and sounded like the squeaking of bats (4.183). Corippus, a poet who may have been what is often now called "Berber," wrote an epic in praise of the Byzantine emperor Justinian's war with the Vandals and their allies. In the second book of his *Iohannis* (ll. 28–161), he writes a catalog of these enemies, which is one of the most important sources for information about the peoples of North Africa before the arrival of Islam. Before he starts, he says, he will need Justinian's eloquence to help him, because his poem will be challenged with the unaccustomed words (*insuetis ... verbis*) and the wild names that bark in a barbaric tongue (*fera barbaricae latrant sua nomina linguae*).[56] Corippus is hardly a disinterested observer. His work, after all, narrates the conquest of Africa by a Byzantine emperor, and the *metus hostilis* shapes the representation of the enemy. It's propaganda, not ethnography or linguistics. Another passage that describes Justinian's opponents as speaking "shrill words in horrible tongues" (*stridentibus horrida linguis verba ferunt*) is sometimes used as evidence for the othering of African languages, but really describes the clamor of competing leaders to answer a challenge to them sent by the emperor's general (Herodotus, IV.352).

Accounts written by even sympathetic writers suggested that these languages were closer to noise than intelligible speech. The great Ibn Khaldun, a fourteenth-century Tunisian who is credited with founding the discipline of sociology, wrote an extended history and description of the Berber groups, a "true people like so many others the world has seen—like the Arabs, the Persians, the Greeks, and the Romans."[57] Yet despite his designation of them as a "true people," Khaldun still situates them at the limits of the human: the "word *berbera* signifies, in Arabic," he says, "a jumble of unintelligible cries; from which one says in speaking of the lion that it *berbère* when it utters confused roars."[58] It's the language itself that remains stubbornly outside the categories of the civilized—and even the human. It is disorderly, confused, *unusual*. Although Khaldun is a sensitive and sympathetic observer, he still situates these languages where Hegel does: close to the bestial, not fully human.

The fate of Libyco-Berber is a bit different. It is identified in scholarly literature as a pure script, the signs of a language that has been supposedly lost, whose sounds are unavailable for condescension and othering. It is not the sounds of the language but the script itself that poses the problem. Just as classical authors heard human speech and denied it the property of language, contemporary scholars have looked at inscriptions among the Tuareg and Berber that echo the Libyco-Berber script and denied them the property of writing. Tifinagh, argues M. C. A. MacDonald, an expert on Nabataean and ancient Arabic inscriptions, is a trivial script, used just for "games and puzzles [and] short graffiti." The Tuareg are, MacDonald says, "an entirely oral society in which memory and oral communication perform all the functions which reading and writing have in a literate society."[59] A 1984 book on the elaborate system of tattooing used by women in Morocco similarly argues that those marks cannot be writing because Berber dialects "are not written down, and in fact never do seem to have been."[60]

Both of these arguments deny inscriptions the property of writing because they presuppose that the language has "not been written down" or that it is "entirely oral." These inscriptions may, indeed, not be writing. But we can't say that they're not writing simply because we begin with the assumption that the speakers of the language don't use writing—or that, if they do use writing, it's not *fully* writing, just graffiti, or that to qualify as writing it has to perform specific functions. In a study of social change among the Tuareg, Jeremy Kennan argues that they don't have "written records of their history" because Tifinagh "has very limited usage."[61] Tifinagh might be writing, but because it doesn't do the kind of work that Westerners find important—the writing of history, for instance—it is not *fully* writing. Tifinagh has no past, in other words, because the past is oral. Even if the forms of traditional Tifinagh might be related to Libyc script, there would be no real linguistic connection, just a hollow repetition of formal patterns.

A similar presupposition governs some accounts of the origin of Libyc script. The two main theories are either that it is derived from Punic, or that it evolved as a script indigenous to North Africa. The second depends on the similarity between Libyc and the numerous ancient designs found on rock walls throughout North Africa. Most contemporary scholars of Libyc inscriptions refer to these as proto-Berber signs, positioned somewhere on the continuum of the development of the script. There are competing theories about the reason that this script developed: was it a spontaneous development, was it derived from Phoenician, or was it brought by people from Spain or elsewhere? All of these theories open onto larger stories about the presuppositions people bring to the story of writing in Africa. Lurking behind all of these, I would argue, is the question of whether Africa is capable of developing writing at all. To argue that it is not may require one to assume, as the French specialist in rock art Jean-Loïc Le Quellec does, that writing requires a certain intellectual sophistication that the earliest rock artists in North Africa lacked. Writing, Le Quellec says, is formed by "conceptual work," not the other way around: inscribing shapes doesn't create ideas. Looking for Libyc script in rock art, he says, is like the pointless exercises of the entomologist Kjell Bloch Sandved, who searched for the shapes of Latin letters in butterfly wings.[62] Again, when writing in Africa comes up, we often start hearing about animals. Le Quellec's argument is not as isolated as it might seem. It is, in fact, one way of articulating an assumption that underlies the work of even eminent thinkers who are sympathetic to the cultures and history of African people.

The Symbolic Violence of Lost Languages: Bourdieu

Libyco-Berber also reveals a more insidious kind of destruction, an *epistemological* violence inflicted by even the best-intentioned Europeans. There are numerous stories of badly educated, arrogant Europeans insisting that Africans not only never had, but never could write, books. Even as sensitive a philosopher as Pierre Bourdieu, who had deep personal ties to Algeria, and who supported the Berber/Amazigh Cultural Movement, could essentially make the same assumption. He insisted that the Kabyle people, among whom he lived and whom he studied for years, were preliterate, although they used (and still do) the characters of Libyco-Berber. Bourdieu's is a cautionary tale for intellectuals who are committed to social activism. The passion—the need—to do what is right is all too often steered by the conviction that, precisely because we are intellectuals, we *know* what is right. For Bourdieu, for example, the very ability to think, to reflect, about what is right is tied to literacy.

But Bourdieu's observational mistake—the idea that the Kabyle were not literate—is actually not his most consequential misapprehension. That would be the idea that literacy is a supreme cognitive and cultural achievement. This is one of the means by which universities shore up the value of their intellectual work. They police grammar, philology, literacy; in short, they define and champion rigor and "standards." For those of us brought up within that system—even brought up, as I was, in a former colony—those standards might appear to be value-neutral. But they are only neutral because they annihilate even the possibility of other values, of other modes of thinking or being. When Bourdieu went from the elite *École Normale Superiéure* to a Kabyle settlement, he saw, ultimately, the *absence* of what made the university, and his own mind, what it was. That supposed absence is the product of intellectual arrogance, yes, but also part of a European cultural heritage.

There is a depressing familiarity to the assumption made by Europeans that Africa is a site of lack. But that supposed lack is something that Europe has counted on since the destruction of Carthage. Indeed, the destruction of Carthage could lay claim to being the lack at the center of European intellectual culture. But that is another story. At one point, Carthage was poised to become the greatest empire on Earth. It failed only because the great Carthaginian general Hannibal did not destroy Rome itself when he invaded Italy. If Hannibal had succeeded, Punic might have been the language of European intellectuals until the post-Enlightenment, rather than Latin. Bourdieu's own language might not have been a "romance" language at all, and his most famous term, *habitus*, might have instead been a word derived from Punic rather than Latin. But then his whole project would not have assumed Africa to be a place deficient of literacy. Bourdieu might have been studying "preliterate" Romans instead—or might never have had the chance, as a member of a preliterate group in the remote mountains of southern France.

Reade's "Nincumpoop" respect for what even he thought was "old African" writing is an egregious example of the violence with which Europeans frame the potential of African premodern writing. Sometimes the violence is more symbolic, as was the case with Bourdieu. His extensive fieldwork among the Kabyle group of the Amazigh formed the basis for theories that would help shape contemporary thought: the *habitus*, the field of practice, symbolic capital, symbolic violence. He was an ardent supporter of the Algerians in their war for independence, and he later assisted with the burgeoning movement of Amazigh identity and self-determination—which included the revival and widespread adoption of Tifinagh.

So it is especially surprising that Bourdieu referred to the Kabyle as a "society without writing."[63] For one thing, the Kabyle had had a written body of customary law for at least 130 years (although it was in Arabic).[64]

French archives contain letters from Kabyle leaders and French colonial officers from the 1840s, decisions recorded by Kabyle hired by and in the *Bureaux Arabes*, and a few poems written in Kabyle Berber. In a later work explicitly concerned with education, *La reproduction: éléments d'une théorie du système d'enseignement* (1970), Bourdieu almost completely ignores Algeria, except to mention that Koranic schools beat their students, and to cite himself in a note on the social capital that a primary or secondary school diploma in Algeria gave graduands.[65] But there is a substantial archive of poems, stories, and texts on religion, grammar, and medicine dating from the seventeenth century from the Anti-Atlas region of Morocco. And, of course, there is the persistent presence of Tifinagh and its ancestral memory of Libyc script.

Why would a thinker as sympathetic to the Kabyle as Bourdieu neglect so much evidence that they were in fact literate? Literacy, for Bourdieu, is not a neutral or inert feature of culture. It is, ultimately, the way that people come to a full consciousness of themselves, the way in which they can develop fully formed symbolic cultures. There is at least a hint of Hegelian teleology behind this: the assumption of an undeveloped literacy among the Kabyle echoes Hegel's declaration that the peoples of Africa could not fully enter into history. Writing, it was long believed, was something that Africans simply could not do. No one stated this more emphatically and confidently than the British explorer Hugh Clapperton, who in 1826 told the Alaafin Majotu, the King of the Yoruba, that he, Clapperton, was "not like a black man, who has no book to write."[66] That declaration is so oblivious and arrogant that it doesn't need a label on its case in the museum of colonial racisms. But other cases do. What I am writing here is, in fact, just such a label on the Bourdieu display. In making the Kabyle a kind of historical artifact, a society from the past, Bourdieu just repeats, in another form, the Hegelian lie that Africans do not have history.

Bourdieu missed, accidentally or not, a lot of evidence of literacy that would have complicated his theoretical work. But it would perhaps have been no more than an inconvenience. After all, proverbial sayings probably contained knowledge old enough to have been unaffected by the arrival of literacy along with colonialism. Proverbs exist because writing didn't. Bourdieu's overlooking the many forms of writing that could be found in modern Kabylia is not just nitpicking, an anecdote about how one of the great thinkers of the twentieth century fudged his work. Bourdieu's blindness to African writing is bound up with ideas about history as progress, ideas that are strangely discordant with Bourdieu's own opposition to colonial domination in Algeria. The denial of a writing that had existed for several thousand years is part of a systematic and philosophical embrace of a European historical vision: history is the movement from the primitive and childlike other to the mature and modern—which is found in Europe.

In one extraordinary passage, Bourdieu uses the metaphor of child development to discuss the supposed awakening that literacy brings:

> The shift from a mode of conserving the tradition based solely on oral discourse to a mode of accumulation based on writing, and, beyond this, the whole process of rationalization that is made possible by (inter alia) objectification in writing, are accompanied by a far-reaching transformation of the whole relationship to the body, or more precisely of the use made of the body in the production and reproduction of cultural artefacts. This is particularly clear in the case of music, where the process of rationalization as described by Weber has as its corollary a 'disincarnation' of musical production or reproduction (which generally are not distinct), a 'disengagement' of the body which most ancient musical systems use as a complete instrument.[67]

Max Weber, the author of *The Protestant Ethic and the Spirit of Capitalism* (1930), was an influential theorist of the hypothesis of "secularization" in European modernity, the idea that contemporary Europe was shaped by medieval institutions, minus their religious content. The implications of Bourdieu's citation of Weber—that history is a dialectical elaboration, a development—are clear. Storytelling is replaced by something like capitalism, the "mode of accumulation" and the "production and reproduction" that writing allow. Bourdieu's citation of Weber implies that what is being developed is more than just economic institutions: it is what Weber called the "process of rationalization." Weber means by this something like the overwhelming array of bureaucratic and technological systems that now seem inescapable. But Bourdieu's use of the term here also implicates a corollary assumption about the Kabyle: that they lack this "rationalization," even that they lack the faculty of fully "developed" reason itself. Bourdieu does not, of course, overtly or consciously endorse the earlier crude historical schemes of cultural development, but those schemes almost inevitably begin to materialize when one thinks about writing as an agent of change. Merely to ask "When does writing begin?" or "How does knowing how to write change things?" is to require some kind of narrative of fulfillment or completion.

To explain how a society possesses knowledge without "rising to the level of discourse" or—as he puts it even more patronizingly—rising to "consciousness" itself, Bourdieu turns to the education of children. He uses them to explain how an entire people could function without having access to "discourse" or "consciousness": children mimic actions, or learn "gnomic riddles, songs, or riddles" that embody a "small number of principles."[68] The seductive sheen of Bourdieu's prose tends to distract one from the surprisingly crude colonialist tropes about Africans in this single passage: they are like children, they lack the capacity for reason, they lack complex institutions, they prefer storytelling to technology, their knowledge base is meager, they are natural mimics, they live much more fully in the body than in the mind.

On this last point, Bourdieu follows a fascinating detour to underscore his notion that Kabyle experience is fundamentally embodied. He attributes his argument about how the body "learns" without the full involvement of the mind to Eric Havelock's 1963 *Preface to Plato*. Havelock argues that the invention of writing transformed the nature of thought, even created "self-consciousness" itself. Traditional education, which depended on the memorization of oral recitations, didn't involve intellectual reflection or dialectical inquiry. It involved just "the surrender to a spell."[69] Havelock has in mind the hieratic quality of Greek poetry and oracular knowledge; but by comparing the Kabyle to preliterate Greece, Bourdieu suggests a very uncomfortable equation of orality with superstition.

The way Havelock's language lurks behind Bourdieu's recalls the silencing of an entire language in Fulgentius's *Ages of the World*. The philosophical precision of Bourdieu's language, a language with which he is clearly talking to specific interlocutors (like Jacques Derrida), suggests that he is trying to justify the study of a "Berber" tribe in a way that will make the subject philosophically respectable.[70] That specific challenge wasn't taken up by Derrida, who was born in Algeria and whose career was built on the traces and absences of language. He briefly discusses Berber in *The Monolingualism of the Other*, where he marvels over the absurdity of the French government's recognizing Arabic but not Berber as an optional language in Algeria. In that book, Derrida's musing about the status of an "other" language concerns Arabic, or Arabic and Berber together, as examples of interdicted or "elided" languages. But the epigraph of the book comes from the writer and philosopher Abdelkebir Khatibi, whose autotheoretical book *Tattooed Memory* meditates on the long ancestral memory of writing in the practice of tattooing among the Berber. Although Derrida's library had thirty-seven of Khatibi's works, Derrida doesn't mention Tifinagh in the essay—and indeed the Khatibi book that provides the epigraph is about the relation only between French and Arabic.

Our Most Secret Writing: Assia Djebar

One of the best accounts of the long modern recovery of Libyco-Berber is in Assia Djebar's 1995 novel *So Vast the Prison*.[71] It is an intricate account, following its many detours and dead ends. It begins with a reference in a letter written in 1630 by Thomas d'Arcos, a Frenchman who converted to Islam after he was captured and enslaved for a time in Tunis. The first two accounts of the inscriptions languished in archives for several centuries, and only Thomas Reade's unfortunate attention began any sustained attempt to decipher the script. Djebar's point in her reconstruction of the fits and starts by which modern Europeans began to pay attention to Libyco-Berber is that we only get an inkling of what the language was by putting together the fragments and abortive attempts to make sense of it from European archives. They are the only way to understand the script, which, in Djebar's telling, will always remain broken and incomplete. But it gets worse: the script will always belong to someone else; it can never be one's own language, precisely because it is recorded in archives written in what she calls languages of power: Arabic, French, English, Latin. Libyco-Berber is both a language that has been lost—"erased in stone" (121)—and that is still, as we will see, everywhere.

Djebar compares the recovery of Berber to the presence of traumatic events and losses in her life. On both the historical and personal levels, it's a kind of haunting, indeed, another version of the specter of Carthage. Djebar imagines Polybius witnessing Scipio Africanus's obliteration of the city in 146 BCE. But she traces—and imagines ("dreams," in her words)—the afterlife of the survival of Libyco-Berber, caught in the wake of the precarious rescue and disappearance of the Punic library in Carthage. On one level, Djebar's is a melancholy reflection on the subjugation of a language and a people—an analogy for the predicament of Berber women in contemporary Algeria. But Djebar's history of the script is not merely what Eve Tuck calls "damage-centered research," which attempts to hold those in power accountable by representing oppressed people as only "depleted, ruined, and hopeless."[72]

For one thing, Djebar finds a kind of beauty, even a miracle, in the very precarity of Libyco-Berber's survival. No one person saved the script. Its survival depended on a number of coincidences and ironies, on the "efforts of so many foreigners (travelers, former slaves, archaeologists) [who had] come to solve the mystery or, by contrast, come simply to gain a very concrete profit."[73] Those who observe the ruins and see beyond them are polylingual, dwelling "between the shores." They have lost both their "own" language and their land. Polybius himself is the main example, an observer of Roman conquest who writes in Greek and witnesses the destruction of languages, at least metaphorically in the ruins of Carthage and, in the same year, an assault on the city of his own language—in Corinth, one of the great Greek-speaking cities. As Djebar suggests, Polybius's own language is no longer his own. Like the writing of Libyco-Berber, too, his own writing disappeared. The bulk is lost, and survives only in quotations and excerpts. It is like the stele at Dougga, which survives despite the ruinations of archaeologists, whom Djebar describes as monolinguists.

The other part of Djebar's story about the recovery of Libyco-Berber is that it is the recovery of her own language as well. "As I wrote," she says, "I recalled myself" (11). That recovery is as complicated and as ironic as the history of scholarship on Libyco-Berber itself. She calls "Berber" her native language, "whose sound is always present, but that, nevertheless, I do not speak" (2). Yet it is a language that allows her to think against the domination of monolinguists: the colonialists who insisted on French, and the Algerian government that recognized only Arabic as an official language until 2002. This language that she does not speak but that is all around her allows her, she says, to say "no." The language is not meaningless: it is the language of "Antinéa, who was queen of the Touaregs at a time when matriarchy was the rule." And it is the language of Tin Hanan, the "fugitive princess" regarded as the ancestor of the Touaregs, whose tomb, built in the far south of Algeria in the third or fourth century CE, contains Tifinagh. Or, as Djebar now calls it, "Libyan," a language that is reunited with itself: an ancient script that was there all the time—and is now the basis for the alphabet of the Maghrebian Amazigh movement. For Djebar, "Libyan" has another crucial feature. It is the language she remembers women speaking among themselves, and a script that is the "secret language" of women. In Tuareg society, she says, "it is the women who preserve writing" (76). This is another way that Djebar's language, which is not her own, is a way to say no: no to the dominance of men, no to the insistence of Arabic or French that they be the only languages.

Djebar's description of the deciphering of Libyco-Berber follows the long archival trail of guesses, intuitions, and coincidences that lead to the revelation that the modern symbols found throughout the Maghreb are in fact the same as the ancient script, and that they may be the same language. But deciphering it prompts a scholarly double-take: the symbols are the same as the script, which must mean that the Amaghizen are not, in fact, illiterate. There has been a written African language for millennia: "Our most secret writing, as ancient as Etruscan or the writing of the runes, but unlike these a writing still noisy with the sounds and breath of today" (122). As for Fulgentius, it is a language that is muted or made silent by a dominant language, but a language that nevertheless gives the world its fundamental, secret order.

II
Medieval and Modern

WRITING AFRICA

CHAPTER FIVE

Allegory of Two African Cities

> No countries ever presented so remarkable a moral and intellectual contrast to each other as the African province of which Carthage was the capital, and Egypt, as represented in the city of the Ptolemies.
>
> FREDERICK MAURICE, *Moral and Metaphysical Philosophy*

Auerbach in Alexandria

As we saw in the last chapter, Fulgentius's *Mythologies* opens with Calliope fleeing west from Alexandria, toward Carthage. Alexandria no longer appreciates poetry; its scholars are much more practical, fascinated by the new discipline of medicine. Carthage had Fulgentius, Martianus, Apuleius—and not long after Fulgentius, an entire school of poets in the Vandal kingdom. Carthage had—or it gave itself—a reputation as a literary center. Apuleius, the author of *Metamorphoses*, called Carthage the "heavenly muse of Africa" and the "muse of the toga-wearers [i.e., the Romans]" (*Karthago Africae Musa caelestis. Karthago Camena togatorum*).[1] There may be several inside references to Carthage here: *Musa caelestis* may refer to the goddess Caelestis, the Roman name for the tutelary deity of Carthage, Tanit. "Camena" is a muse of poetry (technically there were four *Camenae*, but "Camena" is sometimes used to refer to just one of them). The Camenae were also goddesses of wells and fountains; a coin of Septimius Severus depicts Tanit/Caelestis on a lion rearing above a stream.[2] So "Camena" may also suggest that Carthage is the fount of poetry. The term "toga-wearers" for Romans recalls

Tertullian's fierce diatribe on how the *pallium* distinguishes Carthaginians from the "Roman" toga-wearers (Jones, 326). The vast, playful allegorical works of Fulgentius and Martianus would certainly have an outsize influence on medieval and early modern poetry. But arguably Carthage's greatest contribution to literature was the particular kind of allegory that it developed. In modern literary criticism, Carthage's kind of allegory came to be contrasted with the distinctively Alexandrian kind, and the difference between the two shaped one of the most important schools of modern literary criticism.

In 1936, the German scholar Erich Auerbach fled the Nazis for Istanbul, and held a position at the University of Istanbul for the next eleven years. While there, he wrote one of the most influential books of modern literary criticism, *Mimesis: The Representation of Reality in Western Literature*. It was a daunting mix of philology, philosophy, intellectual history, and vast erudition, covering texts from Homer and the Bible to Virginia Woolf's *To the Lighthouse*, which was published just fifteen years before he began writing *Mimesis*. It's often described as a "historicist" book, which shows how the cultural context of a work of literature shapes its style and form. That last part is what makes it such a powerful book: it shows how philology's close attention to language is, in literary work, also a way of understanding politics and culture. It almost singlehandedly supercharged departments of comparative literature in the United States as the motors of political, theoretical, and postcolonial readings, indeed of the dominance of deconstruction in the 1980s, in particular. The postcolonial critic Edward Said's formidable introduction to the fiftieth-anniversary edition of *Mimesis* discusses—and reveals—its importance for political readings of literature, and the formation of the study of global literatures. But for all its vast archive, the book is also famous for not having any footnotes.

There is one exception, however. In a short epilogue that briefly sets out his method and his rationale, Auerbach cites one of his own scholarly works: his "essay on *figura*." The fastidiousness of the citation suggests how intricately bound up the essay is with the book, but also how important it was to follow that trail. The essay, he says, is "reprinted in my *Neue Dante-Studien, Istanbuler Schriften* No. 5, Istanbul 1944, now Berne."[3] In fact, it has been published at least five times in German, and has been translated twice into English.[4] The *figura* essay is a dauntingly scholarly survey of the various meanings and uses of the word over the centuries. It is something like the legal contract—the mythic charter—of the sweeping generalizations that Auerbach makes in *Mimesis*. As we will see, the central figure in Auerbach's study is the cantankerous Carthaginian lawyer, polemicist, and theologian Tertullian.

Perhaps aware that the thicket of citations in his *figura* essay buried his central point, in the *Mimesis* epilogue Auerbach sets out the payoff: the particular meaning of the word he zeros in on concerns nothing less than the "conception of reality"—the main object of *Mimesis* (555).[5] What he means by the "conception of reality" is, really, what the entire book is about, in all of its eclectic collection of (almost arbitrary) texts. (Auerbach himself propagated the story that he had a very limited library in Istanbul.) What is critical about *figura* is the "reality" part. Even though *figura* may be rooted in biblical exegesis and allegory, what attracts Auerbach to its formulation by Tertullian is its care for the historical and cultural context of an event, not just its spiritual significance. Like all allegory, Tertullian's *figura* signifies something else (allegory, after all, comes from the Greek *allegorein*, "other-speaking"). But the literal, surface event is not irrelevant. It "*also signifies itself*," Auerbach says, and does not lose "the power of its concrete reality here and now" (555; my emphasis). That crucial quality of *figura*, its preservation of an event in bodily, historical time, is what Edward Said saw as Auerbach's crucial contribution to literature: it opens the way for *secular* criticism, interpretation that concerns not (just) eternal verities or aesthetics, but also what happens in the *saeculum*, in lived, embodied, political experience.

Auerbach's *figura* essay is bracingly philological, and it doesn't dwell on the larger context in which the word is used in a particular sense—paradoxically, not on the reality that that word reflects. But that context is implicit, standing just outside the philologist's study all along. Auerbach does not so much show *why* Tertullian uses *figura* the way he does as to throw it in relief by contrasting it with the dominant kind of allegory in another African city—Alexandria.

Auerbach identifies Philo of Alexandria as the towering figure of allegorical method in Alexandria, and indeed in late antiquity. Philo's kind of allegory neglects historical events, which he and his followers "interpreted as obscure illustrations of philosophical doctrines."[6] Auerbach's palpable disdain here is a window into his own methods: his criticism very much involves philosophy, in particular classical German idealism, but it is always just offstage. His close reading of texts leads us to philosophical implications, which come *out of* the texts; they do not drive *how* he reads texts (although reality, *Wirklichkeit*, is a term that lies deep at the heart of philosophy) ([ix–xxxii], xii).[7] Auerbach voices a deep suspicion of the forces driving Philo's brand of allegory: it's "clearly spiritual and extra-historical," stripping everything of its "concrete reality." It is "merely," he says, the "most respectable manifestation of an immense spiritual movement centered in Alexandria" (55). The implication is unmistakably that there are manifestations of this spiritual movement that are *not* respectable—even that phrase "*most* respectable" suggests that its best form is still not *quite* respectable.

One explanation for Auerbach's deprecation of Alexandrian spiritual allegory is the "concrete reality" of his world. The *figura* essay was begun in Germany but finished in Istanbul. It inevitably reflects his flight from Nazism, or at least highlights the reasons he finds *figura* so vitally important. In biblical interpretation, *figura* preserves the importance of the original event (usually in the Old Testament) *and* shows its later echo or fulfillment (usually in the New Testament). In other words, the Old Testament—the Hebrew Bible—retains its fundamental importance within Christianity. Christianity's foundation is Judaism, a historical fact that Nazi theology and ideology tried to excise.[8] The *figura* insists both that the immediate meaning of the text is important and that the biblical supertext is ineradicably Jewish.

Some of Auerbach's comments about the nature of Alexandrian spiritual allegory read like a side-eye at Nazism's appropriation of distorted versions of Aryan religions. Alexandrian allegory comes from interpretations of Homer initially, but "later influences, no longer purely rationalistic, but more mystical and religious, were also at work" (54). Auerbach presumably means the myriad mystery religions and cults of late Alexandria, which involved ecstatic (that is, not "rationalistic") practices and half-assimilated influences, like traditional Egyptian religion. At the very least, Auerbach implicitly allows the reader to draw the analogy with the hodgepodge of national socialist lore. His main point, however, is that, at all levels, Alexandrian allegory is profligate and careless with the history and origins of its own influences. Alexandria's eclecticism extracts a spiritual significance without accounting for every part of historical contingency or cultural expression, and aims at a uniformity of meaning that isn't dependent on nuances of idiom. These do not matter at all at the level of the spiritual realm that Alexandrians create out of them. They even stand in direct contrast to them, like the idyllic visions of outdoor-wear brands—the wilderness without humans that is conjured by the desires and the guilt of consumers, and made by exploited laborers. Allegory offers an absolution from history.

At first glance, however, Alexandria would seem to offer Auerbach precisely the kind of history that reflected the world in which he was writing. It was immensely cosmopolitan, a city of intellectual exiles, in which some of the most important developments in Greek and Jewish philosophy took place; the Hebrew Bible was first translated into Greek there. Philo of Alexandria was not only the most influential Jewish philosopher of antiquity and (along with Maimonides, who spent most of his career in Egypt) of the Middle Ages, but also (along with Plotinus) the most important Neoplatonist until the Renaissance. He is important as the figurehead of the "spiritual and extrahistorical form of interpretation" that "competed with the figural interpretation" (that is, the Carthaginian technique, to which I will turn in a moment).

Auerbach devotes more attention to Origen, Alexandria's most important Christian theologian and scholar. His rumored thousands of works included biblical scholarship and commentary, polemics against pagan philosophers, treatises on prayer and martyrdom, and the first Christian systematic theology. It is precisely his importance to the formation of the Christian tradition that drew Auerbach's attention to him as Alexandrian allegory's "outstanding Christian opponent" ("Figura," 55), despite Origen's profound indebtedness to Alexandrian Judaic scholarship and thought. A further paradox is that Auerbach frames the contest between Alexandria and Carthage as a dispute over the role of Judaism in Christianity: in Alexandria, Judaism was irrelevant; in Carthage, it remained foundational and vital. The cosmopolitanism of Alexandria was possible precisely because faith traditions of all kinds could be assimilated under the large and welcoming umbrella of spirituality.

Origen exemplified what was religiously and culturally profligate about Alexandrian intellectual life. His name was conspicuously pagan (and African). It means "child of Horus" or "born of Horus," the Egyptian god who was also an important figure in Alexandrian gnosticism (Horus and Christ were often read as allegories of each other). As a Christian, Origen continued to maintain his ties with the pagan philosophers who trained him, something he encouraged his own students to do. He says to one: "Your natural ability enables you to be made an esteemed Roman lawyer or a Greek philosopher of one of the most notable schools. But I hoped that you would entirely apply your ability to Christianity. Indeed, in order to bring this about, I beg of you to take from your studies of Hellenic philosophy those things such as can be made encyclic or preparatory studies to Christianity."[9] It's an uncanny historical quirk that the Greek-speaking Origen's most influential work on allegory, his commentary on the Song of Songs, survives (with the exception of one fragment) only in Latin. But that quirk is also the logic of allegory. Its idiom doesn't matter because its literal surface will rapidly be peeled away. Indeed, the very process of allegorical reading is the process of acquiring wisdom about things that one did not already know (vastly different, as I will point out in a minute, from the Carthaginian mode of exegesis). In the prologue to his *Song* commentary, Origen says that for novices "it is not given to grasp the meaning of these sayings."[10] He lumps together novices and those who live according to the flesh; for both of them reading these enigmatic passages would actually be destructive: "He, not knowing how to hear love's language in purity and with chaste ears, will twist the whole manner of his hearing of it away from the inner spiritual man and on to the outward and carnal. . . . [I]t will seem to be the Divine Scriptures that are thus urging and egging him on to fleshly lust" (22). This is a more succinct, less elegant expression of the elitism of the abstract, against which Auerbach pitted a reality (*Wirklichkeit*, the Hegelian term that is part of the subtitle of *Mimesis*) built on the everyday and plebian. It is also a hieratic way of reading, as we will see, that Augustine almost spitefully annihilates in the name of charity.

The first observation that Origen makes (in his Prologue to the *Song* commentary) is that the Bible uses homonyms, which he describes as identical terms for different things. For Origen, homonyms are not arbitrary, accidental coincidences, like wearing the same outfit that someone else is wearing at a party. Origen argues that homonyms obscure crucial ontological differences. The word "man" (*homo*), for instance, refers to *both* the outer man (the fleshly, carnal corruptible self) and the inner man (the spiritual one, the soul). If you don't understand that the word "man" refers to two vastly different entities (what he calls the "identity of nomenclature"), you will misunderstand the fundamental nature of reality. To think that the body-man is the same thing as the soul-man is to deny that the spiritual dimension is all that really matters, and you will be left with nothing but "absurd fables and silly tales" (28–29).

Although what Origen means by these fables and tales is not just the idea that we will eat material food after the resurrection, he is also talking about the literary arts in general. He, in fact, had a career as a teacher of literature before and a short while after his conversion. But he turned away from secular literature and sold his library, a gesture that the Jesuit scholar Henri Crouzel describes as "a complete renunciation of secular studies."[11]

Alexandrian theology is pervasively theoretical and philosophical. Even its basic catechetical teaching insisted on the spiritual dimension from the beginning. We "derive," Origen said, "practical wisdom and education from the mystical contemplation of the law and the prophets."[12] But Origen does sometimes seem to read the Bible in a *historical*, even startlingly *secular*, way. The most arresting example is his exegesis of the line from the Song of Songs "I am black but beautiful" (1:5), a line subverted and transformed in the civil rights slogan "Black is beautiful." Toni Morrison's first book, *Song of Solomon*, recognizes the origin of the slogan, and movingly interrogates its adequacy as an agent of transformation and empowerment. But Origen the African, and all Greek readers of the Bible in Alexandria, encountered that line already as an affirmation of the racialized African. In the Greek translation of the Bible, the Septuagint, made in Alexandria in the third century BCE, the line reads "I am black *and* beautiful" (μέλαινά εἰμι καὶ καλή).

Origen locates the beauty of Blackness deep within African history, with the Queen of Sheba and the Ethiopians. Although Sheba at this point was often identified with Arabia, Origen argues that the Shulamite is the Queen of Sheba; using several other biblical verses, he emphatically identifies her as an Ethiopian "from the south" (95). Because of her wisdom, he says, Cambyses (who invaded Egypt in 523 BCE) gave her the name Meroë after she returned from the court of Solomon. Origen doesn't explain what the name means, and that is not what Josephus, his probable source, says. He says that when Cambyses conquered a "royal city" of Ethiopia—Saba—he named it after his sister, Meroë. Meroë was, in fact, a capital of the Kingdom of Kush, in Nubia.[13] Maybe it's not surprising that someone like Origen who, according to Auerbach, doesn't care much for "historicity," would fumble a few historical details. But the important point from Josephus that Origen *does* repeat correctly is that the Queen of Sheba ruled both Ethiopia and Egypt (95).[14]

The Ethiopian Queen of Sheba, in other words, is *also* Egyptian, a historical ruler of the place where Origen lived (although Alexandria itself, of course, did not yet exist in her day). Origen turns to the Book of Numbers to remind us of a further entanglement between Egypt and Ethiopia. In Numbers 12:1, as we saw in the first chapter, Moses's brother Aaron and his sister Miriam complain that he has married an Ethiopian woman (γυναικὸς ... Αἰθιοπίσσης; in Hebrew, "Cushite"). But, Origen points out, their complaint was not actually about the physical marriage. It was about the way God preferred to speak through Moses rather than through them. They understood, says Origen, that Moses's marriage to the Ethiopian woman signified the "Church that is gathered together from among the Gentiles" (97). From their perspective, presumably, the allegorical significance makes the physical marriage, even the race, of the Ethiopian irrelevant—and, perhaps, for Moses, too.

Origen develops his argument along historical/typological lines, returning to the persistence of Ethiopians in biblical history. He draws on an archive of historical reminders that Ethiopia had long been a part of Egypt. Rather than simply impose what Auerbach called the Alexandrian "spiritual and extrahistorical form of interpretation," Origen lingers precisely on the historical level, and its African traces. Moses's Ethiopian wife, he says, is "one and the same" as the Beloved of the Song of Songs, who is also an Ethiopian. In an unexpected turn, Origen has the Shulamite herself defend her Blackness against the "daughters of Jerusalem" who disparage her (it is an allegory, says Origen, of the exclusion of the church by the Jews) (92). Do you not, she says to them, recognize the fulfillment of the "type" in me of Moses's wife? "I am," she says, "that Ethiopian" (*Ego sum illa Aethiopissa*).[15] It's a startling direct address, almost like the "Spartacus" moment in Stanley Kubrick's film. We might not *be* the actual person, but we can all become what the person now *means*: we are all that Ethiopian woman. It's hard to dismiss the resonances of writing those words in Alexandria, words about a figure who proudly claims Ethiopian identity, in a passage that turns her and other Ethiopians into a single archetype of history—the Ethiopian who is we, the world.

Origen, of course, means that the figure of the Ethiopian ultimately echoes through history because she is an allegory of the acceptance of the "spiritual law" and Christ by the gentiles. Origen might not be preoccupied with the particular historical situation of each of these two Ethiopian women, but the fact of their Ethiopian identity remains important. Indeed, he uses the term *figura* to refer to how they signify: the historical foundation is still visible, and Origen finds other Ethiopians still standing on it. Several other biblical passages featuring Ethiopians—above all the Queen of Sheba—bolster his exploration of the significance of Ethiopia as the historical framework of the allegory of the church. The Blackness of the Ethiopians signifies the gentiles in general; symbolically, the Beloved Ethiopian in the Song takes with her to Jerusalem the peoples of the whole world (*totius mundi gentibus*) (*Werke*, 119). It's possible to see Alexandria glimmering behind this as the place to which the world comes for knowledge and enlightenment, just as the Queen of Sheba comes to Solomon with "riddles and with questions" that he answers, sending her back to Ethiopia full of wisdom. In Origen's homily on the same passage in Numbers, Moses's Ethiopian wife is now the figure of enlightenment; her marriage to Moses opens onto a reality no longer hidden by "figures and enigmas," the reality of the spiritual law.[16] Origen's method of stitching together these Ethiopian figures depends on an aspect of Auerbach's *figura*, a certain interest in the vestige of history. But in this passage, as elsewhere in Origen, the *figura* is literally an obstacle to understanding.

When Origen's unpacking of the significance of Ethiopia shifts to the method of allegory proper, this sympathetic glimpse into the historical resonances of Ethiopia heard from Egypt fades away. Ethiopia becomes the site of a Blackness that must be explained away, a problem—the enigma of how it can signify spiritual fulfillment. In two sentences, Origen escalates epidermal racism, giving a "raced" version of the fourfold levels of allegory that were famously associated with Alexandria. On the literal level—sometimes called the historical level—Origen's exposition suggests that Blackness as a marker of difference is geographically determined. The people are called "Ethiopian," he says, because they are burned by the sun (the name is a compound of "burned" [αιθ-] and "face" [ὄψ]). But on the typological level, which links together different historical events by their common reference, Origen's exposition argues that the Blackness caused by the sun is a "certain natural blackness inherited by all" (*naturam quaedam inest ex seminis carnalis successione nigredo*), a genealogical, racial identity. On the tropological level (which signifies moral action), Blackness is a *hereditary moral condition*: "bodies are darkened by innate vices, and passed on" (*infuscata corpora genuini vitii successione permaneant*) (Lawson, 107; *Werke*, 125). The fourth level, the anagogical, concerns the state of the soul. It is darkened for a different reason: because it does not seek the "sun of Justice" out of indolence (Lawson, 108). Once it does turn toward the sun, however, the soul will become "whitened" (*dealbata*), "all her blackness ... cast away" in the "enveloping radiance of the true Light" (Lawson, 107; *Werke*, 107, 165).

Blackness, in Origen's hands, moves from an attribute of desire's object—the beautiful Blackness of the Shulamite—through a series of displacements to something to be discarded as the final stage of allegory reaches the spiritual cosmos. Origen reads race as a shifting allegory, taking on different moral or ontological properties at each level. In a certain sense, it also suggests that the work of allegory is inseparable from racism, at least when it reads the African body. Allegory's dependence on, at the very least, an insuperable distance between body and spirit turns the markers of the body into the body's difference from spirit itself. As Stuart Hall, the cultural theorist and activist, put it, it's because of the slipperiness of the signifier of race "that every identity is also an expulsion, to the constitutive outside, of those who come to be marked as other."[17] That is the consequence of Alexandrian allegory's dallying with the historical, and of its ultimate denial of the significance of history in the light of the soul: it blinds us to what once seemed the very object of desire—the Blackness of the Ethiopian woman.

Although Auerbach does not spell it out as concretely or baldly as I have, for him Alexandrian allegory involved spiriting away, so to speak, markers of the heterogeneity of historical events and representations. The pressing danger, as he wrote *Mimesis* and the essay on *figura*, was the modern repetition of the medieval reception of the Bible in Europe, "from which the Jewish history and national character had vanished" precisely so that "the Celtic and Germanic peoples, for example, could accept the Old Testament" ("Figura," 21, quoted in Zakai and Weinstein, 330–31).[18] Auerbach's self-avowed "historicist humanism" ("Figura," 7) was powered by what he called the "great insight of his life," that "all interpretation of Christian literature" depended on the fundamental connectedness of the Old and New Testaments ("Figura," 59). *Figura* was the seal of the enduring, historical relation between them. To find out how *figura* developed as a historical mode of reading, Auerbach turned to the other great African city—Carthage.

Auerbach in Carthage

Theology in Alexandria, as we have seen, is supremely philosophical. Carthage's theology, on the other hand, comes across as both more polemical and more pragmatic. It sometimes sounds dry and bureaucratic, as if promulgating rules is its main interest. The most influential bishop of Carthage, Cyprian, objected to those who "without any divine arrangement, set themselves to preside [and] appoint themselves prelates without any law of ordination, who assume to themselves the name of bishop, although no one gives them the episcopate." But there is a sharp edge to this pronouncement: this is one of Cyprian's definitions of heresy. One of the biggest of the heresies that superheated North Africa was Donatism, which developed from the question of whether priests who had lapsed during Roman persecutions would be allowed to return to the priesthood (Donatists said no). Violence between Donatists and Catholics escalated over the hundred years of the heresy's existence: toward the conflict's end, Augustine complained that the most militant Donatists, the Circumcellions, had added axes, lances, and swords to their arsenal. Maximian of Bagai, a fifth-century Catholic bishop from the Roman province of Africa Proconsularis, was dragged from his altar and stabbed. He later displayed his scars before the imperial court in Italy.[19] In summing up what Donatism had done to Africa, Augustine employed the rhetoric of satanic panic in Epistle 22.2: the Donatist "evil," which started in Carthage, poured down "over the whole body of Africa."[20]

But Augustine did not blame just Donatism for the state of the African church. It was already mired in carnal filth and illnesses, he said; there were many other heresies and sects that distracted Christians and prompted other acts of violent dissension among them. To reverse the direction of Augustine's metaphor, Carthage was, in part, the poisoned head, because these heresies all flowed there. Carthage was the seat of the presiding bishop of the North African church, and also the center of the anti-heretical polemic that shaped much Carthaginian theology. Tertullian's pronouncement that blood was the seed of Christianity is emblematic of the fierce intensity with which Carthaginians approached theology, and almost any kind of religious dispute.[21]

One of the legacies of these protracted struggles is that Carthage became the site where some of the foundational governing principles of the Catholic church were established. At the Council of Hippo in 393 and the Council of Carthage in 397, the African church established the definitive canon of the New Testament, which was ratified, along with many of the decisions of various Carthaginian councils about church governance and membership, at the Council of Ephesus in 430. Carthaginian theology, as this suggests, is concerned with the *saeculum* of the church on earth—the shape that it must take in *this* life. The scars that heresies left—as on the body of Maximian, or the scars from "Christian battle" that Tertullian praises—are a reminder of the development of theology out of history, and of history's continuing presence.[22]

Carthage's particular kind of allegory, the kind that Auerbach identifies as *figura*, tends, as a consequence, to be mostly about the fulfillment of biblical allegory in the institution of the church. Augustine's interpretation focused mostly on this role of the church: how reading the events of the Bible, its allegories, can yield understanding of the church's contemporary purpose: the work of charity. Unlike the technical and arcane methods of Alexandrine exegesis, Augustine's method (at least as he sets it out in his short manual on interpreting the Bible, *De doctrina christiana*) is radically simple. Whatever interpretation of the Bible "tends to build up love" is ultimately the correct one (even if founded on a mistake at the literal level).[23]

Augustine's mode of reading is egalitarian and inclusive, and is an important aspect of what Auerbach identifies as the Christian championing of plain style in literature. Its sole criterion, its cause and aim, is *caritas*: the twofold love of God and neighbor. What matters is not the details and ornament of language—whether or not we say, in Augustine's nicely self-reflexive example, *inter homines* or *inter hominibus*, or what length (short or long) we give to the third syllable of *ignoscere* (to pardon). These are mere conventions, the "conventions of spelling and syllable division that they learned from those speakers who have gone before them" (*Confessions*, Bk. 1.18, 52–53). The years that Augustine himself spent in becoming an eminent *grammaticus* and court orator in Milan are irrelevant to reading scripture. Learning, indeed, can be an impediment to it, since it too easily triggers pride: men "are weak just in proportion as they wish to seem learned, not in the language of things which tend to edification, but in that of signs, by which it is hard not to be puffed up" (*Doctrine*, chap. 13.20, 859).

It may or may not be an accident that Augustine's main example of his method in *De doctrina christiana* is a passage from Song of Songs, as if to set apart his way of reading the *Songs* as sharply as possible from Origen's. One of his most famous allegorical readings seems almost wantonly arbitrary. The Beloved's teeth, which are "like a flock of shorn sheep / Which have come up from the washing" (4:2), he says, are the teeth of the church—its saints—tearing away people from their errors. It demonstrates how reading need not be constrained by the protocols of Neoplatonic decorum or the Alexandrian erudition formed at the cosmopolitan intersection of Latin, Greek, and Hebrew (one might note that Augustine never felt comfortable in Greek, nor did he much like Greek literature, and he did not know Hebrew beyond a few roots and perhaps miscellaneous cognates in Punic). But this allegory is also about how the church establishes and executes its mission on earth, the administration of penitence by presbyters like teeth biting off the sins of the convert.

Auerbach explores the implications of plain style, of the *sermo humilis* that Augustine at first found highly offputting in the Bible, in his later *Literary Language and Its Public*. Auerbach's attention in the *figura* essay is mainly drawn by Augustine's shaping of figural reading in his great historiographical work, *City of God*. Auerbach uses it as a handy anthology of *figurae*: among others, Noah's ark is the church; Jacob and Esau prefigure the "two peoples of the Jews and the Christians"; Abraham's concubine Hagar is the Old Testament and the earthly Jerusalem; Abraham's wife Sarah is the New Testament and the heavenly Jerusalem ("Figura," 38).

Auerbach doesn't mention that Augustine, in that exegesis of Hagar, reminds us that she is an Egyptian.[24] Egypt, as we will see in a moment, is a hinge in Auerbach's history of the connection between typology and politics, but Augustine's reference is perhaps too incidental for Auerbach to point it out. Yet the discussion that immediately follows is on the subtlety with which Augustine uses typological reading and features a critical passage about Egypt: the beginning of Psalm 114 (for Augustine it was Psalm 113), "When Israel went out of Egypt" (*In exitu Israel de Egypto*). The original, historical reference remains active, to be taken up and reread in time. Augustine views "figures as timeless and *belonging to all times*" (Porter, 89; my emphasis). For Augustine, says Auerbach, the figural fulfillment may still be to come, suspended even until the end of time. In this very passage, too, Augustine explains that Egypt is the figure of the *saeculum*, of the world and of the age (a distinction that is foundational to the entire project of the *City of God*): it is the "image of this age" (*[I]n imagine ponitur huius saeculi*).²⁵ Only when one leaves Egypt (*cum primum huic saeculo renuntiaverit*) can one become a citizen of the heavenly Jerusalem. Auerbach's point is that we have not yet left the saeculum behind; we remain as engaged in, and as determined by, the secular as ever, the Egypt that Augustine says should be understood as the condition of affliction, chastisement, and oppression (*Aegyptus autem, quoniam interpretatur afflictio, vel affligens, vel comprimens*). That is precisely what makes it the "image of this age."

In *Mimesis* Auerbach turns to the departure from Egypt as the moment in which literary history—and implicitly modernity itself—emerged from both the rigid hierarchies of the classical world and the "patriarchal condition" of the earlier Old Testament world in which "nothing pushes up from below" (21). "As soon as the people completely emerges," he says, "*that is, after the exodus from Egypt*—its activity is always discernible, it is often in ferment, it frequently intervenes in events not only as a whole but also in separate groups and through the medium of separate individuals who come forward; the origins of prophecy seem to lie in the irrepressible politico-religious spontaneity of the people" (21; my emphasis). In a sense, this passage is the figural fulfillment of the kind of literary representation that is the subject of the *figura* essay. It conjures the specter of Auerbach's own exile, and the echoes of his world that one hears in this passage, a passage that looks to a world that has moved beyond the suppression of political and religious "spontaneity."

Even the essay on *figura* opens similar windows onto the world of Auerbach, above all in his discussion of the stark difference between Origen and Tertullian. Auerbach illustrates that difference, as it happens, with an example from the departure of the Israelites from Egypt: Origen's explanation of the pretext Moses gives to Pharaoh for their departure, that they are going into the wilderness for only three days, to perform a sacrifice to God (Ex. 3:18). In Origen's reading, says Auerbach, the "mystical and the moral far outweigh the strictly historical elements" (Porter, 84).

Tertullian's resistance to this kind of reading signals a deeper and "well-known" "conflict" between his "more worldly, historical and realistic" way and Origen's "purely spiritual" way that causes the "historical character to evaporate"—"*especially the matter of the Old Testament*" (Porter, 84; my emphasis). Again, Auerbach hints at a figural reading of his own essay. The "conflict" resonates well beyond early Christianity, although it begins there. Ralph Mannheim's English translation calls this a "current" conflict, although Auerbach's German text doesn't say precisely that.²⁶ There is indeed a current conflict at stake, however, which Auerbach hints at portentously. The content of the Old Testament was not spirited away just in Origen's time, but in ours as well: "In the West [that] tendency was the unqualified victor" (Porter, 84). The melancholy of Auerbach's judgment about the history of Alexandrian allegory hides a deeper despair and alarm over how that mode of allegory had become an instrument of Nazi ideology.

Auerbach's pointed comment that the effect of Origen's reading was to "evaporate" the matter of the Old Testament refers as much to his day as to Tertullian's and Origen's own. While Auerbach was writing *Mimesis* in Istanbul, the Nazi medievalist Hennig Brinkmann was appointed to the Chair of German at Istanbul University (1943). Brinkmann, who said at the time that his mission was to undo the "influence of the Jew Auerbach," later wrote one of the definitive treatments of Alexandrian allegoresis, *Mittelalterliche Hermeneutik*.²⁷ It is a study of three- and fourfold exegesis that is still cited along with Henri de Lubac's *Exégèse médiévale* as an obligatory reference in the study of allegory. Well before Brinkmann arrived in Istanbul, he wrote the seminal study on the panegyric given to Origen by his student Gregory Thaumaturgus, which uses the language and metaphor of Origen's prologue to the commentary on the Song of Songs.²⁸ Gregory's panegyric to Origen reads like a cryptofascist celebration of a charismatic leader who possesses a secret that he will impart to his disciples if they are sufficiently dedicated to him. It also reads uncomfortably like the German medievalist Ernst Kantorowicz's fascist-flavored youthful book on Frederick II, which we will later discuss.

More broadly, Nazi theologians and scholars called for the Old Testament to be decanonized. At a Berlin rally in 1933, Nazi Christians called for the "removal of the Old Testament from the Bible" altogether because a "Christianity which still clings to the Old Testament is a Jewish religion, irreconcilable with the spirit of the German people."²⁹ *That* is the tendency that Auerbach says has triumphed in the West, and against which *figura*—in its erudite, oblique way—offers a radically different vision of reality.

At least one influential German scholar had insisted on the connection between allegory's indifference to history in late antiquity and the modern German decanonization of the Hebrew Bible. The Lutheran theologian and historian Adolf von Harnack argued in 1924 that the Hebrew Bible should be dropped from the biblical canon because it does not even rise to the level of "the book of [a] less-worthy, Jewish God." It is not possible, says von Harnack, "to perceive from the Old Testament what is Christian."[30] Von Harnack wrote that not in a manifesto or polemic but in a study of the second-century heretic Marcion of Sinope, who taught that Jesus Christ was an entirely different God from the vengeful God of the Hebrew Bible.

It is not clear whether Auerbach read von Harnack's book on Marcion, although he cites his other work ("Philology," 125). But Marcion is, by negation, one of the most important offstage figures in Auerbach's *figura* essay. It is against Marcion that Tertullian sharpens his insistence that, as Auerbach puts it, the Old Testament was "literally and really true" (Porter, 125). But Marcion and Tertullian had different ideas about what was real, and Tertullian's polemic helps to show how essential representation and figural reading were to Auerbach's discussion of "reality." Marcion, according to von Harnack, rejected allegory more thoroughly than any other theologian at the time. For Origen, he seems to be a cartoonish caricature of figural reading. Marcion, he says, was a "slave to pure history."[31] It was in his polemic against Marcion that Tertullian elaborated the theory of figural typology as a mode that was *both* historical and figurative. Marcion had a pumpkin for a heart, says Tertullian, if he did not believe that Jeremiah was a figure of Christ (Porter, 81). Tertullian's dispute with Marcion shaped *figura* as a kind of reading that looked to the real world, to politics, to history, to the *saeculum*. As with much of Tertullian's work, it is pugnacious and polemical, fiercely territorial in its attention to the heresies raging around and in Carthage. Tertullian doesn't just call Marcion a pumpkin-heart. His full-tilt ad hominem attacks are also *ad nationem* attacks. He begins his devastating takedown of Marcion by placing Marcion's birthplace near the Black Sea, at the limits of the civilized world. So ashamed is it of its barbarism that it has "set itself at a distance," Tertullian sniffs, from "our own more civilized waters." It is cold, foggy, inhabited by promiscuous cannibals. But the saddest and most barbaric thing about it is that Marcion was born there (*barbarum ac triste*). Carthage, like Istanbul was for Auerbach, was a place where Tertullian could write against a distant barbarism that threatened his own world. *Figura* emerged from its place in Africa, its moment in a tumultuous and uncertain history, its insistence on a reality that could not just be spirited away.

Another drama underlying the creation of *figura* in Africa is Auerbach's complex relation to Hegelian *Geistesgeschichte*, the "history of spirit," a philosophical quasi-religious version of intellectual history, which formed a fundamental part of his earlier book on Dante.[32] In a chapter on Dante in *Mimesis*, he acknowledges Hegel's profound influence on his own search to link a philosophy of "reality" with literary criticism. "Over twenty years ago I used [Hegel's ideas] as the basis of a study of Dante's realism (*Dante als Dichter der irdischen Welt*, 1929). Since then I have been concerned with the question what conception of the structure of events, in other words what conception of history, is the foundation for Dante's realism, this realism projected into changeless eternity" (194).

Whether deliberately or not, by locating the crucial turn in literature toward realism in Carthage, Auerbach rewrites Hegel's history of the emergence of representation. For Auerbach, the crucial moments in this history are far earlier, and far away from Dante's Italy—in ancient Egypt and late antique Africa.

Egypt is, in fact, a crucial turning point for both Auerbach and Hegel. As we have seen, history—that is *secular* history—for Auerbach begins once the Hebrews leave Egypt. That is the moment that inaugurates the "spontaneity" of the individual. For Hegel, Egypt remained bound by the "African imprisonment of ideas" (*History*, 226). What Hegel believed was a dead end of representation—and therefore of Spirit—Auerbach discovers is, in fact, a covert way of moving forward. It is covert in two ways: first, it rests on the cultivation and preservation—the *Aufhebung*, the synthesis, that Hegel was unable to execute—of the enigma; and second, it structures history as the "intrinsic historicity" (*Innergeschichtlichkeit*) of *figura* and the fulfillment of types.[33]

Hegel's influence on Auerbach may have shifted over the years, and perhaps even from the start may have been qualified. In an essay published the same year as his Dante book, Auerbach quotes Hegel's entire passage about Dante from his *Aesthetics*, which includes the following: "In the face of the absolute grandeur of the ultimate aim and end of all things, *everything individual and particular in human interests and aims vanishes*, and yet there stands there, completely epically, everything most fleeting and transient in the living world, fathomed objectively in its inmost being, judged in its worth or worthlessness by the *supreme Concept*, i.e., by God."[34] With a lot of squinting, one can see how this might be a kind of figuralism. Something about the secular world, "fleeting and transient," is still a part of the most abstract idea imaginable, just as the historical meaning in *figura* remains in its typological fulfillment: Isaac will always be poised on the edge of sacrifice, Christ will always already be sacrificing himself for us. But Hegel's "end" and Auerbach's "fulfillment" seem very different. For Auerbach, typological fulfillment enriches the meaning of the initial *figura*; it gives the historical event meaning. For Hegel, "aim and end" sound more like the annihilating machine of Alexandrian allegory as Auerbach describes it, making everything human and particular vanish in the "grandeur" of allegory.

There is something about his own fulsome citations of Hegel that puzzles Auerbach. He wonders, for instance, why everyone has forgotten Hegel's "great insight" that Dante "probed deeply and dispassionately into the essence of the secular world" (Porter, 143). The clear answer is: Auerbach may be the only reader who ever saw Hegel as a "secular" critic. Indeed, much of what Auerbach was writing against in Istanbul would seem to be the kind of historically blind spiritualism of the *Geistesgeschichte*, the history of spirit, that dominated German intellectual history. Secularism and spirit do not go well together, and contemporary critics of Auerbach recognized a cognitive dissonance in his work. One reviewer of *Mimesis* said that Auerbach "draws his tools and weapons from the arsenal of German *Geistesgeschichte*; but he has lost his faith in *Geist*."[35] And even while Auerbach claims that Hegel "perfected historicism," he also blames him for obliterating the messiness and unpredictability of the kind of history that begins with the Exodus from Egypt: "It was nevertheless also this philosophy that—precisely in perfecting historicism—also began to undermine it in dialectical fashion when it attempted to reshape the irrationality that lay at historicism's very core into a rational system."[36]

Auerbach's own literary history, founded in Hegel, inevitably follows the melancholy logic that he finds Hegel trapped within. In the introduction to his posthumously published collection of essays, *Literary Language and Its Public in Late Antiquity and in the Middle Ages*, Auerbach recognizes that his project of reforming European literature by refounding it on Hebrew biblical narrative, rather than the Greek canon, is more an end than a beginning. "The European civilization is nearing the limit of its existence (*Grenze ihres Daseins*); its history as a distinct and self-contained entity would seem to be at an end. Already its unity is beginning to be eclipsed by another, more comprehensive unity."[37] This is the moment at which, says Auerbach, the "notion of *Weltliteratur* would be at once realized and destroyed."[38]

Hegel had said that when "we" leave Egypt for Greece "we come home." The world and its representation are lucid and intelligible. Literature makes sense. But no longer writing from his home in Europe (first from Istanbul, then from the United States), Auerbach began to search for the roots of what a "comprehensive unity" that might be outside Europe would look like, for what Hegel's "rational system" of history left out: the resolute individualism and spontaneity of the Hebrew Bible after the exodus from Egypt, and the idea of history forged in an African city.

Auerbach's profound contribution to intellectual history created a way to read the form of literature, indirectly or directly, as a *part* of political and cultural history. It was further developed by Edward Said and Fredric Jameson. Said championed the secular criticism he learned from Auerbach. Jameson, a student of Auerbach's at Yale University, turned to Marx and the historical dialectic—an explicit rejection of *Geist*—to reread world literature as "perfected historicism" without Hegel. One irony of Jameson's work is that it turned to the fourfold method of Alexandrian allegory to uncover the insistent presence of the historical, literal level at the higher levels of allegory. It does not "evaporate," as Auerbach said, but resolves, hides, or conceptualizes the "historical area" that interested Auerbach.

Auerbach was perhaps most explicit about the necessity of that "historical area" in reading literature, and the profound importance of literature in showing us what our own historical area is, in his work on Dante. The phrase "historical area" in fact comes from this. The importance of Dante is that while, yes, using the fourfold method of allegory, he also gave us a modern form of mimesis: "Man, not as a remote legendary hero, not as an abstract or anecdotal representative of an ethical type, but man as *we know him* in his living historical reality."[39] One irony here is that "living historical reality" is still pretty abstract. He ends the book with an approving summary of what the messianic German poet Stefan George said about Dante, that it was Dante's "tone, movement, and *Gestalt*" that made Dante the "father of all modern literature" (175). What is "historical" about Dante's work is something more akin to style and form than what Auerbach calls the "concrete individual." History is really literary history, the story of how "representation" evolves, and not so much what we now call embodied experience. Auerbach *is* fascinated by the worldly, the secular, and the individual, but always in relation to the "unity and wholeness" of the individual—in other words, the individual as they are *represented* in literature.

We have seen that in his later, more melancholy *Mimesis*, Auerbach is less confident about the unity and wholeness of the human subject. But in the 1929 Dante book, Auerbach is channeling a very particular strain of historical anticipation at that moment. Another reader of Stefan George and Dante, the medievalist Ernst Kantorowicz, also finds in Dante the gestalt of the modern moment. But where Auerbach's Dante invents modernity by breaking with the Middle Ages, Kantorowicz's Dante reveals how profoundly modernity is indebted to medieval political theory. Modernity for Kantorowicz, is, if you like, the typological fulfillment of the Middle Ages. But Kantorowicz does not study typology: his subject is sovereignty, an obsession of many of Auerbach and Kantorowicz's contemporaries. Sovereignty is also imagined as a feature of modernity. Rather than, say, a pope's authority, which is distributed among the faithful throughout the world, sovereignty is the supreme authority within a territory—in most cases, the state. The roots of this concept of political theology lie within medieval political theory and its goal of clarifying the relationship between the divine and human actions. Both Walter Benjamin and Carl Schmitt thought of their moment as a medieval moment. Kantorowicz, however, placed the medieval idea of kingship at the center of his theory of the development of modern state power.

CHAPTER SIX

The King's African Bodies

> We hear of African kings who have imagined themselves immortal by virtue of their sorceries.
>
> JAMES FRAZER, *The Golden Bough*

> The king is immortal because legally he can never die.
>
> ERNST KANTOROWICZ, *The King's Two Bodies*

Kantorowicz's African Body

The career of the medievalist Ernst Kantorowicz spanned several of the twentieth century's greatest antagonists: Judaism and Nazism, America and Germany, the Middle Ages and modernity. Kantorowicz left Germany after it became clear that because of his Jewishness his academic career would stall there, even though he was also perceived as an ardent supporter of Nazism. Like Auerbach, he identified himself as a Prussian Jew. His somewhat ironic trajectory after that included later his departure from UC–Berkeley, where he refused to take the McCarthyite anti-Communist oath, although, as he says in a 1938 *curriculum vitae* (possibly written for his application for the Berkeley job), in 1919 he "took up arms once again: against the communists, then in power at Munich, and I was wounded once more."[1] After Berkeley, he accepted a professorship at the Institute of Advanced Study in Princeton, which was founded in 1930 and hosted many intellectual and academic refugees from Germany, including Albert Einstein and the distinguished art historian Edwin Panofsky.

Well into his early career, Kantorowicz was a disciple of the infamous Stefan George, an artsy and charismatic intellectual whose circle (the

George-Kreise) included aesthetes, academics, artists, poets, and musicians. It also included an undercurrent of Aryan racial ideology, even though, like several others in the circle, Kantorowicz himself was Jewish. Although Kantorowicz was aware of the circle's underlying racism, he remained a vital part of it for many years, and in fact became one of the most vocal and erudite formulators of the historical inevitability of German political and cultural superiority.

Kantorowicz's masterpiece was a book called *The King's Two Bodies*, which is both an overwhelmingly learned, sprawling book and one with a good elevator pitch: the notion of modern state power comes from the medieval idea that a monarch had a physical body, and an abstract body that continued to exist when the next monarch was crowned. Hence "the king is dead, long live the king." The idea began with the notion of the church as the "mystical body" of Christ and made its way to theories of rule in the Middle Ages. It eventually became a secular theory of power.

Like Auerbach, Kantorowicz found that Dante was the hinge between sacred theologies and secular reality. Dante, he said, put in place human-centered kingship. And, like Auerbach, Kantorowicz discovered the importance of Dante's "secular religion of humanity" from Stefan George, who often dressed as Dante, complete with a laurel crown.[2] Although *The King's Two Bodies* was published in 1957, its roots go back to Kantorowicz's days in the George circle and the intense debates about sovereignty at that moment. The central text of that debate, by the Nazi jurist Carl Schmitt, was the 1922 *Politische Theologie*; the subtitle of Kantorowicz's book is *A Study in Medieval Political Theology*.[3]

But Kantorowicz was coy about the roots of the book, constructing what the historian Conrad Leyser describes as a myth of origins for it.[4] On the one hand, two years before the book came out, he mentioned that political theology was "much discussed in Germany in the early 1930s," but that it had become popular again because of a 1943 book.[5] His vagueness only increased in the preface to the book, where he cites a conversation in Berkeley in 1946 and a letter from "The Benedictine Order, Inc" (xxxiii–xl). The most obvious reason for his reticence may be that he wanted to dissociate political theology from his conversations about it with Carl Schmitt in the 1930s.[6] He also wanted to decouple this book from his earlier book on the Holy Roman Emperor Frederick II, which was queasily adjacent to Nazism—Hitler kept it by his bedside—yet remained popular through Kantorowicz's lifetime, well after the war.

When his publisher reissued it in 1962 against his wishes, he protested, citing the fascist enthusiasm for it during the war. Such a book, he said, "really ought to be abandoned to oblivion."[7]

Kantorowicz's history of *The King's Two Bodies* has the classic structure of a Freudian disavowal. Disavowals are really affirmations that deny a patent reality because of the difficulty of an underlying truth. On the one hand, Kantorowicz acknowledges the roots of his book in the foment stirred up by Carl Schmitt. On the other hand, he implies his book had nothing to do with that. The account of that 1946 conversation in Berkeley is the book's opening sentence, and in many ways it is the book's charter myth. It begins in a colleague's office in the law school at Berkeley, from which Kantorowicz would resign five years later rather than take the oath that he did not belong to the Communist Party—although, as he pointed out, he had been a fervent anti-communist in his youth. The book begins, that is to say, with a subtle reminder that Kantorowicz himself had become, by the time he finished the book, a symbol of abstract principle over political insistence—or, one could say, of myth over impulse.

The book's subtle mythic charter matters because the book itself is the exploration of a much larger mythic charter, an account of how modern notions of state power began in a very distinctively European medieval and early modern world. Its second chapter, in fact, discusses one of Europe's most influential mythmakers: Shakespeare. Its penultimate chapter is a study of Dante and his invention of "man-centered kingship." The study, Kantorowicz argues at the end, has been all along a study of a "man-made irreality—[a] strange construction of a human mind which finally becomes slave to its own fictions."[8] In other words, the book is a study of the mythic charter of modern Europe, the story of how its current political ideologies and structures originate in the sphere of European Christianity and, above all, of literary imagination.

The myth of the book's beginnings broadens the world of the myth of kingship that Kantorowicz studied in his Frederick II book. That book was explicitly a myth of how the so-called secret Germany that the George circle imagined might come forth into the real world. Like all mythic charters, Kantorowicz's *The King's Two Bodies* works—and indeed exists—precisely because it needs to tell one out of several possible stories. It makes one myth seem more real than others. There are at least three possible stories *The King's Two Bodies* leaves out: the story that *Fred-*

erick II tells; the story about the extensive contemporary conversations concerning sacred kingship in mythology, anthropology, comparative religion, and history; and the story of the single point of the idea's origin, outside what the George circle (and most European and American historians) would have imagined as European: in the city of Carthage.

In lectures Kantorowicz gave at Berkeley shortly after he arrived there in 1939, Carthage is both the place where one of the church's most important theorists lived, and a city that is crucially different from Alexandria. His description of the difference is markedly similar to Auerbach's, and for many of the same reasons. Alexandria "was a thoroughly learned, philosophical and sophisticated city, where Platonism of every tinting was at home"; Origen and his contemporaries were "masters of all the philosophical subtleties."[9] Alexandria was cosmopolitan and also otherworldly; Carthage was intensely polemical and worldly. As with Auerbach, the two cities embody the difference between philosophy and politics. There is also an underlying cultural difference between the two, with Alexandria representing Hellenism in general. What exactly Carthage represents is more complex—again, as it is with Auerbach. For reasons he doesn't specify, Kantorowicz says that in the second and third centuries the "religious or intellectual battlefield" moved West from Alexandria, and that Christianity became "romanized" and "latinized." But that process didn't happen, he says, where you would expect it to: not in Rome or Italy, but "in North Africa, in Carthage, then the Latin center of theological and apologetic disputes." It is the culture of disputation—indeed, violent contention—that ultimately makes Carthage important, as we will see. But that short aside about the precise location of Carthage is like a crack that lets light into a dark room. Kantorowicz's history of the theory of the king's two bodies is really a history of Europe. Carthage, as Kantorowicz describes it here, is on or near the outside of the Roman world, not where one would expect it. It makes his picture of the essentially European idea less sharp, a bit less obvious. Yet Carthage remains important in Kantorowicz's history, largely because he gives one thinker, Cyprian of Carthage, a foundational, recurrent role.

In his Berkeley lectures, Kantorowicz insists that Cyprian's contribution to political theology was so important that he was more than a mere theologian: "not just another Law Father of the Church, he was the Statesman or monarch." Part of what he means by that, I think, is that Cyprian twisted a theological idea into a definition of the church as a secular institution. "The bishop," as he quotes Cyprian in *The King's Two Bodies*, "is in the church and the church in the bishop."[10] This is "where in the last analysis the christological undercurrent" of sixteenth-century juristic theories of monarchy came from. Cyprian's maxim became the guiding analogy for the development of the late medieval and early European theory of the body politic. But Kantorowicz goes on to make an even more comprehensive claim for the influence of Cyprian's formula: that the relation between the bishop and the king was more than just the analogy that it might have seemed at first. It became more of an accurate articulation of the political theology of emergent absolutism, in which the king effectively becomes "pontifical" (441). Cyprian's single sentence contains, then, the past and the future of an institution. Whether or not Kantorowicz's claim for the immense influence of Cyprian's single sentence is absolutely true, one has the sense that the historical scope of the book zooms outward from Cyprian's phrase. But the book also moves the screen to make the light projected by Cyprian fall in just the right places. Although Cyprian's phrase was circulated most widely in Gratian's immensely influential twelfth-century legal collection, the *Decretum*, Kantorowicz refers to it as the "Cyprianic formula" (230).

Cyprian's presence is acknowledged even where it does not need to be. The book's epilogue asks the seemingly belated question "is the origin of the two-bodies idea pagan or Christian?" and quickly marshals evidence from classical sources that sounds very much like the specifically Christian political theology that Kantorowicz has been examining. The evidence culminates with Seneca's maxim that the prince is the soul of the *res publica*, which is in turn his body. This is, says Kantorowicz, very similar philosophically to Cyprian's phrase about the bishop and the church. But there's a strange little hiccup at this point: Seneca's maxim, says Kantorowicz, is "no less antique" than Cyprian's (505). It is, of course, much *more* "antique" (Seneca died almost two hundred years before Cyprian did), but the unexpected litotes lays bare a deep assumption about the nature of Cyprian's maxim. It is important both because it *is* "antique," like Seneca's, *and* because it is *not* located in the classical past, and is therefore *not* pagan. It has the authority of age, and speaks from an age that possesses a legitimate authority over the dispensation of Christian institutions.

Cyprian is an important source for Kantorowicz's political theology precisely because Cyprian was a bishop in Carthage. As we have seen,

Christian North Africa in antiquity was a cacophony of seemingly petty, invidious, and violent adherents to various microtones of Christian theology. To be precise, it was not so much *theology* that was at stake, but ecclesiology. Most of the violent struggles can be reduced to the question of who got to control the church. This question did concern the relation of the North African to the Roman church—was it subordinate, independent, or equal—and it is obvious who won that argument. It is not true, however, that every North African Christian was preoccupied with the status of their church in relation to Rome: in fact, Rome was usually an afterthought, or a rubber-stamping entity that agreed to the principles fought out by the North Africans. The nature of discourse in Carthage, Kantorowicz argues, was essentially legal.

Cyprian is the most important Carthaginian in Kantorowicz's history, but Tertullian is almost as important. It is the two of them, he says, who exemplify how Carthage had such an important influence on the development of an idea about state power that came out of theology. Both of these figures, he says, thought "in the terms of statesmanship and of laws." Tertullian, after all, was a lawyer, and remained one, argues Kantorowicz, all through his career as a theological polemicist. The very roots of his theology, he says, lie in legal arguments about the way Christians had been handled in Roman law courts. His theology was essentially a legal codification of the relations between humanity and God, which he "conceived as a lex, as a Roman law."[11] It is the *political* situation of Christianity in Carthage, in other words, that opened the door to a political theory that borrowed from theology—or, as Kantorowicz would say elsewhere, the secularization of a theological analogy. The very inescapability of disputation and controversy at all levels shaped the particular nature of Carthaginian political theology. At its core is a certain *worldliness* that is lacking in Alexandrian thought.

In this worldliness, Kantorowicz finds another strand that is familiar from Auerbach's study of Carthaginian theories of interpretation. Auerbach's *figura* allows the messiness and spontaneity of human actions to coexist with the more serene, orderly level of the spiritual realm. As we have seen, what is important about this structure is that it gives the Hebrew Bible (the Old Testament) as much importance as it gives the New Testament. One is incomplete without the other. The Hebrew Bible shows up in a markedly similar role in Kantorowicz's account of Tertullian's thought. He talks about Tertullian's "stern severity" and his "cold, logical spirit" as the traces that a career in law leave in his theological work. That could be characteristic of a Roman lawyer, says Kantorowicz, but "maybe it was more the spirit of legislator Jehovah than of the Saviour that inspired" him. It's an unexpected turn in Kantorowicz's history of the European idea of sovereignty. He does not develop a whole theory of sovereignty based on the Hebrew Bible, but this one comment offers a quick look at the other narratives that are left out in his mythic history. The articulation of the founding phrase of the theory of the dual bodies of power takes place not in Europe, but in Africa; it is voiced by thinkers who, Kantorowicz implies, are influenced by the Jewish origins of Christianity, and, like Auerbach's figural readers, place it at the core of their thought.

Kantorowicz's first book, a study of the Holy Roman Emperor Frederick II, is a kind of biography of the idea of sovereignty, without the formidable scholarly apparatus of *The King's Two Bodies*. The infamous thicket of notes in the later book, some scholars argue, is a response to critics of the first book, who questioned to its lack of footnotes. Yet *Frederick II* is clearly a powerfully researched book, and its lack of documentation gives it an Olympian quality. Auerbach might point out that the book's style is generated by its subject: the emperor who, Kantorowicz argued, was the focal point of *Germanitas* and the precursor to the imminent leader of a true Germany. But despite Kantorowicz's efforts to smooth the carpet, there are telltale lumps at the edges of the narrative.

Kantorowicz showed how Frederick consolidated an empire with a mixture of power, politics, and political theology. It is difficult to overestimate how important the book was in the development of a German sense of historical destiny that stretched from the glory of the Middle Ages under Frederick to its reawakening in the present day. Robert Lerner's magnificent biography of Kantorowicz argues persuasively that it is precisely the book's "celebration of authoritarianism" that supercharged its popularity. It was, he says in a very Kantorowicz-like phrase, "a treasury of antiliberal expressions" (106). The book was read and enjoyed by both Hitler and Goering, and it was also the last book read by Wilhelm Canaris, the head of German military intelligence, before he was executed for his part in the resistance against Hitler, at the same time as the theologian Dietrich Bonhoeffer.[12] These highly unusual readers, two of them monstrous, one of them less so, attest to the book's complexity, emotional power, and political importance. It is still treated today as a seminal historiographical study, and it can be read as an *anti*-Nazi, neoliberal, or pro-EU text: David Abulafia argues that it strives to imagine a European state whose virtue derives from a "benevolent universalism."[13] One of Frederick II's canniest strategies, according to Kantorowicz, was to construct an empire based on an exception to, or, to borrow Kantorowicz's quasi-Hegelian terms, a transcendence of, race. Frederick became the "symbol"—"foreign though it was"—of Germany as the successor to, or really, the conserver of, the Roman empire.[14]

But there are also contradictory impulses in Kantorowicz's book. He praises Frederick's policies against intermarriage in Sicily as "profound wisdom" that would prevent "degeneracy of race" and "racial confusion."[15] There is an intermittent bias toward racial purity: Kantorowicz explains that much of the talent of Frederick the Second's administration was drawn from Campania because it "had been less exhausted by racial admixtures than other regions" (292). Kantorowicz is more disingenuous, though, when he describes the relationship between racial universalism and the creation of empire. He praises Frederick for not favoring one race over another because no single race possessed a "world-sense" (385).

But Kantorowicz isn't talking about all the races of Europe. He is talking only about the German races: the Saxons, the Franks, the Swabians, and, "eventually," he says, the Prussians (314). This odd adverb "eventually" is revealing, because it shows that Kantorowicz is not writing a history just of Frederick and the medieval state, but also of the rise of the modern German state, centered on the Prussia of Kantorowicz's birth. That Kantorowicz was also writing about them should have been immediately obvious to his readers, living in a postwar Germany that had lost all of the European and transcontinental possessions that had seemed to qualify it as a burgeoning empire. If it wasn't obvious to everyone, it became so in the book's florid and messianic ending, where Kantorowicz heralds "the fiery Lord of the Beginning [who] ponders how he can renew the 'Empire,'" the "greatest Frederick [who has yet to be] redeemed" (689). Its political meaning is clear, especially to such monomaniacal readers as Hitler. But this ending also has an esoteric overtone that would have been heard only by members of the George-Kreise. To them, the "Lord of the beginning" would be Stefan George himself, an identification confirmed by the passage's allusions to a poem that George wrote in 1918.[16]

Whether the book's readers imagined Hitler or Stefan George as the modern Frederick II, they were goaded to do so by the book's sly address to the contemporary moment. There was little doubt that Kantorowicz's book anticipated a German messianic figure, and the book seemed to set out a map for finding, or an agenda for creating, one. Its vast historical erudition was like a long arrow pointing at a particular living German. Yet the shaft of that arrow is curiously bent, twisting through and around inconvenient or awkward sites in political and cultural history.

Kantorowicz's description of Frederick II's "Italian policy" echoes earlier debates by medievalists over the success of Germany's annexation of Italy in the Middle Ages. For Kantorowicz, Frederick's domination of Italy was incontrovertibly successful. Not only did Kantorowicz give no intimation that the question had been hotly debated, but, against the scholarly consensus at the time, he represents Frederick's actions as the establishment of a "world-monarchy" (488), the "last and greatest Germanic state foundation" (493).[17] Germany's loss of its colonies altogether after the First World War does not strike any chords in Kantorowicz's book. It is almost as if he plays the music of imperial ambition loud enough to drown out the ultimate failures of the Holy Roman Empire and the Second Reich. But Kantorowicz is, in effect, writing about an alien culture, and Frederick's very charisma is the most obvious marker of its difference. It is derived from the otherness that hovers around Frederick, and with something of the air of an ethnographer, Kantorowicz says that "western observers" found him handsome; his charisma has something to do with his "mixed blood," his "brown-tinted skin with rosy cheeks and auburn-blonde hair" (367). But precisely because of those exoticized elements, he is the embodiment of an empire that transcends *ethnos*, collapsing the distances of territory and culture in one body and spirit, which "ranged through all the distances of East and West" (399). For Kantorowicz, Frederick's colonization of Italy is not only a success, but also the condition for Frederick's apotheosis.

In Kantorowicz's account, Frederick's extraordinary charisma is inseparable from its exotic origins. Not only does it have something to do with his "mixed blood," but it originates on soil that is, at least partly, foreign: the island of Sicily. For most of its history, Sicily was a contact zone of religions and cultures, which Goethe famously called "the key to everything." But in the history of imperial rule, Sicily was more than just a Star Wars Cantina of hybrid peoples and traditions at a desert crossroads. Its occupation by Rome marked the beginning of the Roman imperium: it was the first major possession outside the Italian mainland,

and became the first Roman province. In his orations attacking the former governor of Sicily, Gaius Verres, Cicero calls Sicily "the first who made our forefathers perceive how splendid a thing it was to rule over foreign peoples (*exteribus gentibus imperare*)."[18] The *exteribus gentibus*, in the plural, does not refer just to the mixture of peoples on the island of Sicily. As Cicero makes quite clear, the Roman annexation of Sicily had everything to do with the establishment of *imperium* by the eventual conquest of Africa—not merely Carthage. (By "Africa" Cicero most likely means Africa Proconsularis, roughly the territory of modern Algeria, Tunisia, and Libya.) From Sicily, says Cicero, our ancestors "took that great step in their imperial career [*gradus imperii*], the invasion of Africa: for the great power of Carthage would never have been crushed so readily had not Sicily been at our disposal, supplying us with corn and affording safe harborage to our fleet" (*Verrine*, Bk. 2.2.1, 296–97). In perhaps his first use of the trope of Carthaginian ruination as the genesis of Roman cultural accomplishments (the trope that became *The Dream of Scipio*), Cicero goes on to describe how Africanus adorned Sicilian cities with statues and monuments to celebrate his victory (*Verrine*, Bk. 2.2.2, 297).

A more abstract way of understanding that trope is that Cicero is describing the integral role that the presence of, and dominion over, Africa plays in the formation of Roman imperial power. It is thus appropriate that Kantorowicz replays this scene, whether deliberately or not, in describing the emergence of the godlike qualities of Frederick's authority. It was possible only in Sicily because the Sicilians, "half-oriental in origin ... worshipped their ruler as God" (*Frederick*, 219). What he means by "oriental" here is a little clearer elsewhere in the book: he refers to Palermo twice as "half-African" (*Frederick*, 322, 327). The beginnings of Kantorowicz's career-long exploration of sacral European kingship lie in Frederick II's assumption of a regal aura emanating, at least in part, from a distant and barely glimpsed Africa.

To be quite clear, Kantorowicz never attributes the genesis of this concept to Africa, but neither does much of the concrete detail about Frederick's charisma come from medieval sources. In his book, Palermo is the site of a triumphal royal entry that exemplifies the kind of charisma that Frederick possessed by right of office—the kind of charisma whose genesis we have seen Kantorowicz locate in Palermo. But Kantorowicz's example concerns the triumphal entry of Frederick's father, Henry VI, into Palermo. Otto of Blasio's *Chronicle*, Kantorowicz's source, says simply that the people of Palermo bowed their heads (or, possibly, touched their faces to the ground) as Henry rode by.[19] Kantorowicz pumps up the volume considerably, treating this an act of prostration before the king: "When the Emperor Henry VI entered Palermo in solemn state with his victorious army the people flung themselves down with their faces to the ground, shunning the sight of their Lord's majesty" (*Frederick*, 219). Kantorowicz points out in the next sentence that prostration was a common practice in Sicily under the Norman kings, implicitly filling in the gap in the historical evidence. And the *maiestas* that he attributes to Henry does not appear in Kantorowicz's source, which is really focused on the ornamental details of the reception, not as much the magnificence of Henry. The scholarly gaps do not ultimately matter from our vantage point, except that they are a symptom of Kantorowicz's eagerness to begin the genealogy of sovereign charisma at this moment in the Middle Ages.

Mystical Kings, European and African

The Middle Ages is a means of encoding private or secret thoughts about the present. What Kantorowicz referred to in his preface as a "secret Germany" longing for kaisers and emperors was the dream of German cultural and intellectual dominance, in which rulers might be worldly powers but were as much symbols of desires not fully articulated. The Middle Ages as a receptacle for secrecy was a trope that enfolded numerous desires, from the private to the imperial: it could be, for instance, a code for eros or an analogy for Germany's presence in Africa. Both of these, in fact, were used by the first colonial governor of Rwanda, who was also a discoverer of a source of the Nile and Kantorowicz's first cousin, Richard Kandt.

In what follows, I am not suggesting that Kandt's extensive writings about Rwanda and its peoples influenced Kantorowicz directly, although Kandt was an important figure in Kantorowicz's life. Rather, I am using the remarkable careers of these two men to illustrate the proximity of Africa to the Middle Ages among the European intelligentsia in the first years of the twentieth century, and the often unexpressed connections between sovereignty in Europe and rule in Africa that ran through the minds of colonial administrators, anthropologists, and medievalists.

Kantorowicz was twenty-eight years younger than Kandt, but Kandt visited Kantorowicz's family at Posen in Prussia (now Poznań in Poland) every few years, and it would be surprising if Kantorowicz had not read

Kandt's celebrated account of his first journey to Rwanda, *Caput Nili*, which was a bestseller in Germany, first published when Kantorowicz was ten. On his twenty-third birthday, Kantorowicz heard that Kandt had died while away at war. His death, said Kantorowicz, "as a cousin and as a person affected me deeply."[20] The discovery of an unpublished poem by Kandt, addressed to his lover Richard Voss and written while he was in Rwanda, among Kantorowicz's papers suggests that Kantorowicz maintained an affection for Kandt for the rest of his life.

The meaning of the poem that Kandt wrote to Voss while he was governor of Rwanda unfolds when read against the search for the Nile and a medieval mystical text. Its expressions of deep longing begin with slightly abstract references to suffering (*Qual*), to years as chains (*Die Jahr und Jahre mich in Fesseln schlug*), to World, to men in general, to the soul, to bureaucracy (*Amt*), and to ancestry (*Herkunft*). The last lines of the poem, though, reveal more about Kandt's specific desire for Voss, who is clearly the friend (*den Freund*) he finds and who allows him to recover (*genas*). Its erotic meaning isn't terribly hidden, which might explain why Kandt never published it. Richard Voss, however, *did* publish it in his 1920 memoirs, where he describes how he had the poem inscribed on a marble tablet in his Frascati residence, the Villa Franconieri. The inscription was signed "Richard Kandt an Richard Voss. Ruanda."[21]

Kandt's only published poems were printed after his death by his friend Franz Stuhlmann, a noted zoologist and botanist. *Meine Seele klingt*, described as unpublished poems from the War, is different in style from the poem dedicated to Voss. The poems in the collection are simpler and more lyrical, full of more concrete references to trees, birds, and the Fatherland. The poem to Voss, however, begins by naming a suffering (*Wenn in der Qual*) that the poet has long endured, without naming the specific suffering. Its remedy is almost as elusive: although Kandt suggests that it is *Deine Seel*, it is a soul that has no eyes, nor ears, nor any interest in name, office, or pedigree. This spiritual disregard for earthly values echoes medieval negative theology's disengagement from the world; it often enjoins Christians to forget about the objects of earthly love in order to experience a nameless, transcendent love. Kandt alludes to one of the most important German medieval mystics, Tauler, a follower of Meister Eckhart. The phrase *wenn in der Qual* is part of a sermon that Tauler gave on the relation between suffering and love, and the work of self-negation. He says that love is not intense feeling (*grosses*

Empfindung),²² nor sweetness, nor mere pleasure. It can be identified only in letting go (*Verlassenheit*), in a state of serenity (*Gelassenheit*), and if one is in suffering—*wenn in der Qual*—there is a melting away. *Das is Liebe*, says Tauler: this is Love.²³

There is another important dimension to Kandt's poem. His absence from the addressee of the poem is considerable: Kandt wrote it to Voss while he was the Resident of Rwanda, the principal representative of the German government in their new colony. The *Qual* is also the torment of separation in a *fremde* land from Voss, his *Freund*.²⁴ Writing in his diary shortly after Kandt's death, Voss calls the love he has had for Kandt for fifteen years the *Liebe und Treue troß einer Qual* (love and fidelity despite torment), and thinks back to the *alte Qual* he felt when longing to exchange letters with Kandt while he was in Rwanda.²⁵ In a sense, then, whether he thought about it deliberately or not, Kandt turns to the Middle Ages as an analog of the vast and seemingly unbridgeable distance between himself and Voss, between Germany and Africa. Africa might as well be the Middle Ages.

Several years before he became the *Residentur* of Rwanda, Kandt had traveled there in 1898 on a precariously funded expedition to find the source of the Nile. His account of the expedition, *Caput Nili*, is as much an ethnography as it is a travelogue. The book became a bestseller, and his obvious knowledge of the people of Rwanda—he had been the first European to meet the ruler of the area, Mwami Musinga²⁶—made him an obvious choice to represent Germany's colonial interests there. He helped to lay the foundation of modern Rwanda in a quite literal way. His house became the nucleus of what became the new city of Kigali, the eventual capital of Rwanda. His book is quite clear that modernity was not to be found among the Rwandans any more than multicultural tolerance was to be found among bourgeois Prussians: the "Negroes and we," he says several times in the book, "do not live in the same century" (*Die Neger und wir leben nicht in dem Gleichen Jahrhundert*) (Kandt, 219; my translation).

Kandt never tells us exactly what century the Rwandese still lived in, but his many allusions, hints, and insinuations make it clear that it lay somewhere in the Middle Ages. The passage I just quoted comes immediately after Kandt compares the burning alive of a woman to the burning of heretics in the past. It must be said, however, that Kandt's implicit relegation of Africa to the Middle Ages is anything but a way of separating Africans absolutely from Europeans: he points out that there would still be countless Europeans who would tolerate burning people alive if it were sanctioned by the state. The *geisteger Verfassung*, the *mentalité*, of the Middle Ages remains, although rendered latent by the emergence of the modern nation-state. This double consciousness is a striking anticipation of the latency of medieval institutions within emergent modern institutions that his cousin Ernst was to make the subject of his greatest study. Kandt's recognition that an anti- or ante-modernity still lurked beneath the surface of Europe is an arresting departure from the absolute divisions most colonial writers tended to make between European and African, and it is also a convoluted rationale for his role as an agent of empire in the colony of Rwanda. What is missing here is the confident, brazen faith in cultural progress that compelled most colonial administrators to justify their mission as straightforward modernization, to fast-forward Africa from the Middle Ages to the twentieth century. Kandt seems to imply that the role of any administrator is to extend the ability of the state to repress the medievalism lurking in the minds of even modern Europeans.

Kandt's alignment of Rwanda with the historical imaginary of the European Middle Ages implies the work of a subtle and complex intelligence, although the *equation* of Africa and the European Middle Ages was one of the basic building blocks of colonial policy. Another colonial official in Rwanda said that the Resident, in particular, needed to be "open to feudal manners" in order to deal effectively with the local chiefs.[27] Indeed, as Reinhart Bindseil, a modern German ambassador to Rwanda and a scholar of Kandt, points out, "Kandt described the political and social situation of the country using the *termini* of feudalism, with the king (*mwami*) as ruler [*Herrscher*], the Tutsi as the aristocracy of the country [*Aristokratie des Landes*], and the Hutu as common subjects [*Untertanen*]. Even after taking office, he regarded this political and social system as the best basis for German authority."[28]

Yet Kandt's remapping of the political landscape of Rwanda is activated by both a particular imaginative investment in the Middle Ages and by a kind of analogous enchantment with the Tutsi, in particular. He introduces his readers to the Tutsi in a strangely bookish way, recording not his own observations but a paraphrase by the only other German to have traveled to Rwanda, Count Gustaf Adolf Graf von Götzen: "He found the country divided into provinces and districts, which were under the auspicious administration of the Watussi, whose huge figures, up to two meters high, reminded him of the world of fairy tales and sagas [*Welt der Märchen und Sagen*], and at their head a king who travelled the country restlessly and built his residences sometimes here, sometimes there" (Kandt, 258). I'll say more about "fairy tales and sagas" in a minute, but I first want to highlight the peculiarly *German* medieval flavor that this description gives the court. There is the evocation of a highly elaborate feudal administration, but also the description of a peripatetic king, a particular feature of medieval German monarchy, the so-called *Reisekönigtum*, the itinerant monarchy.[29] There's also some of the flavor of King Vortigern in the twelfth-century *Roman de Brut*, who cannot build his castle because the work is undone every night, or the strange story that the chronicler Walter Map tells of the army of the undead doomed to wander forever (which Map compares to the peripatetic court of Henry II of England) after they make a pact with the king of the dwarfs, the *pigmeus*.[30] Kandt's next sentence, in fact, goes on to the describe the land of the Twa, the so-called pygmies, at the borders of the "Watussi" land, a "race of dwarfs . . . who were believed to live in caves on volcanoes . . . in the North" (258). Kandt's account locates them also in relation to a remote antiquity; they are the "remains" (*Reste*) of a race who hunt the beasts of a primeval forest (*Urwaldwildes*). This "race of dwarfs" may fit Kandt's placement of the Tutsi in the world of legends and sagas even more closely: he may be evoking the Nibelungen, the race of dwarfs in the *Nibelungenlied* (and in Wagner) who live in caves. Indeed, the violence of a war of dynastic succession that Kandt describes prompted one scholar to describe Kandt's book as an "African *Nibelungenlied*."[31] But for Kandt, the echoes of the European Middle Ages in the center of Africa, and his imaginative investment in the Tutsi as facsimiles of European feudal rulers, might be stronger than an accidental resemblance.

Kandt begins his paraphrase of Götzen's account with a version of a racial fantasy that has become known as the Hamitic hypothesis. Götzen found the Hutu "in servile dependence (*knechtischer abhängikeit*) on the Watussi, a foreign Semitic or Hamitic noble caste (*adelskaste*)" (Kandt, 257). This strange hypothesis, invented and amplified by European racial theory, is a quite literally outlandish theory, which argued that taller peoples with purportedly finer features and "nobler" modes of living, from the Maasai of Kenya and Tanzania to the Tutsi, were really the descendants of the "Hamitic" branch of the Caucasian race. The modern form of the theory was first articulated, seemingly, by John Hanning Speke, another explorer of the source of the Nile, whose encounter with the equally "feudal" kingdom of Buganda prompted him to muse that the ancestors of the rulers must have been "semi-Shem-Hamitic."[32] The horror of the eventual genocides in Rwanda and Burundi can be traced directly to this hypothesis. The "rulers" that European explorers encountered in the two countries, according to this poisonous theory, came from different racial "stock" that gave them a primal, almost ontological right of sovereignty over the surrounding peoples, whom this theory denigrated (darkened, in the literal, original sense of the word) as inferior. How brutally admirers of this theory imagined the inferiority of non-Hamitic peoples can be seen in the writing of one of the most important sociologists of central Africa, C. G. Seligman, the teacher of both Bronisław Malinowski and E. E. Evans-Pritchard, who became the most authoritative ethnographer of the peoples of Sudan. In his 1930 book *The Races of Africa*, which was in print until 1979, Seligman says bluntly that "the civilizations of Africa are the civilizations of the Hamites, its history the record of these peoples and of their interaction with the two other African stocks, the Negro and the Bushman. . . . The incoming Hamites were pastoral 'Europeans'—arriving wave after wave—better armed as well as quicker witted than the dark agricultural Negroes."[33] This deference to the "Hamitic" qualities of ruling classes is a foundation for the practice of indirect rule in African colonies, most fully expressed in Frederick Lugard's *The Dual Mandate in British Tropical Africa*, but also in the German administration of Rwanda, eventually presided over by Kandt himself.[34]

One crucial scene in Kandt's *Caput Nili* is a kind of dramatization of the European recognition of the hieratic quality of kingship among "Hamitic" peoples. Actually, Kandt describes it literally as a drama, a "comedy," in which the Tutsi court attempts to pass off an old man as the king, who, by all accounts Kandt has heard, is just a boy. He seems outraged principally at the poor judgment of the "director" who made such an unlikely actor wear a *Königsmaske* (271). But Kandt realizes only belatedly that someone else has been passed off to him as the king: the whole scene, he says, was well-acted (*gemimte*) but badly staged (*inszenierte*), and he uses the language of drama in part because he recognizes that something more than mere deceit is operating. Another "Mtusi," he says, "was required to play the role" of the king for "Whites." But not just for them: by the end of the passage, he has recognized that what he witnessed is probably something inscribed in the ritual of sovereignty itself, not just among the Tutsi, but also among the Buha of Tanzania and the "Urundi," the Hutus and Tutsis of what is now Burundi. Kandt now describes the hidden leader as a "mystic king" (*mystische König*), whose presence is concealed from the people because to see him "eye to eye" would mean death.

The phrase "mystic king" shows up in German literature most often in relation to King Arthur, as in Carl Vehse's popular history of "national cultures," which explains Arthur's mystical quality as the mingling of *sang royal* and the blood of the Savior.[35] The "mystical king" was also a casual trope of nineteenth-century medievalism, perhaps best known in English from repetitions of the phrase "mystic, wonderful" in Tennyson's *The Idylls of the King*. Kandt offers nothing like a systematic analysis of the nature of the power that such kings exercise, but, in another passage, he describes the widespread myth of an absent king who might return to redeem the people of Rwanda from the oppressions of the current royal court. There are various versions of who, and where, this king is, says Kandt; but he ultimately thinks that this king never lived, that opponents of the Tutsi court used this specter (*Gespenst*) as a "symbol" of their political hopes. Kandt says that the only thing the various, conflicting versions of stories about this absent king who will return have in common is that they are the inventions of Märchen- oder *Liederdichter*, the writers of fairy tales and songs (265). Kandt does not simply relegate the myth to the realm of anonymous, unthinking orality; these terms suggest something of the expertise behind recorded German folk tradition, exemplified recently for Kandt in the work of Novalis and the Brothers Grimm, and even of the songwriters of the medieval *Minnelied*.

At the same time, the study of comparative mythology was zeroing in on the topic of sacred kingship. The proverbial key to all mythologies was *The Golden Bough*, a vast collection of myths compiled by the folklorist J. G. Frazer; it was initially published in two volumes in 1890, but he kept gathering material until his third edition topped out at twelve volumes. It profoundly influenced twentieth-century literature (T. S. Eliot cites it in the first note to his masterpiece *The Waste Land*), but its reception by anthropologists was mixed. Some anthropologists in the next generation dismissed Frazer's apparently indiscriminate hoarding as an "embarrassment,"[36] but the great British anthropologist Bronisław

Malinowski once said that he was "enslaved by it" and "bound to the service of Frazerian anthropology."[37]

By the third edition of *The Golden Bough*, Frazer was citing the work of contemporary academic anthropologists. The most notable of these was Malinowski's teacher Seligman (which might explain Malinowski's odd language of fealty), who gave Frazer his then-unpublished work on the execution of the "divine kings" of the Shilluk in South Sudan (and material on the rainmakers of the Dinka). Another of Seligman's students, E. E. Evans-Pritchard, said that it was Seligman, in fact, who first introduced the idea of the ritual killing of sacred kings to Frazer, and from there "into the mainstream of ethnological theory."[38] Seligman published the information he gave Frazer that same year in an obscure scientific journal in Khartoum. In that article, "The Cult of Nyakang and the Divine Kings of the Shilluk," he attributes the term "divine kings" to Frazer.[39] Seligman's article became the scientific foundation of future anthropological work on divine kingship in Africa, but it's so entwined with *The Golden Bough* that the theory's origin is a hall of mirrors: Frazer read Seligman on sacred kings, then Seligman read Frazer on sacred kings, and Frazer in turn used Seligman to support his arguments.

Frazer's presence haunted the work like a king's mystical body. In 1933, Seligman traced the African history of divine kingship in a lecture series named for Frazer; fifteen years later Seligman's student Evans-Pritchard gave a Frazer lecture that questioned whether Shilluk "sacred kings" were ritually put to death at all. At its close he argued that the work on divine kingship had primarily focused on Africa, and that it had not been "well-founded." He called out, in particular, Leo Frobenius and C. G. Seligman. But his biggest target was Frazer himself, whose "method of interpretation" he said he himself had not followed: that would involve the uncritical and "superficial review of the whole field."[40]

The whole lecture is a polite rejection of the comparative mythology that had driven the study of divine kingship. But it doesn't replace mythology with gimlet-eyed participant observation. Instead, it deftly acknowledges that kings "everywhere and at all times" have seemed divine: they represent the whole society, yet must stand outside it. The "mystical" aspect of kingship is really a political, not a religious, symbol. But to illustrate that universal principle, Evans-Pritchard quotes a maxim that puts us back in the world of medieval and early modern Europe: *Rex est mixta persona cum sacerdote*—the king's person is mixed with the priesthood.⁴¹ It's a maxim from early modern English law, the archive with which Kantorowicz begins *The King's Two Bodies*. In two sentences, Evans-Pritchard takes us through the argument of Kantorowicz's book: the theory of kingship has its origins in religion, but is useful in a secular world as a way of organizing and representing power. The theory of European and African kingship across disciplines in the twentieth century is a conversation that pretends to be a monologue: divine kingship originates in Africa (in either Egypt or Nubia); it is also universal; it also originates in Europe; it is specifically Christian; it is superstitious and uncivilized; it is a discovery by anthropologists; it the discovery of medieval historians.

These competing monologues appear at the same time in European intellectual history for two reasons. At the same time that European powers were working out the policies and ideology of colonial administration, the nature of monarchy was under intense interrogation. There were assassination attempts against almost every European monarch in the nineteenth century, which triggered in turn demonstrations of support for the symbols of monarchy. The failed European revolutions of 1848 only seemed to entrench the institution further in the Middle Ages. Karl Marx called them a "cardsharp's trick," by which the state had "returned to its oldest form, to a shamelessly simple rule by the sword and the monk's habit."⁴² The Scramble for Africa, in other words, was shaped partly by more visibly medieval—but weakened—forms of monarchy that depended on dominion over colonies to replicate those earlier forms of state power.

Anthropology's Divine Kings and Colonial Rule: Leo Frobenius and Max Gluckman

The famous German ethnographer Leo Frobenius is one of the clearest examples of the connections between anthropological inquiry in Africa and the institution of the monarchy. One of Frobenius's direct backers was Kaiser Wilhelm II, who followed Frobenius's publications closely, and who authorized a payment of 25,000 marks to Frobenius in 1913. From 1914 to 1915, Frobenius led an expedition in which ethnographic inquiry was garbled with an attempt to enlist Ethiopia on the side of Germany against Britain. After Wilhelm's abdication in 1918 (and the loss of Germany's colonies in the Treaty of Versailles), Frobenius carried on an extensive correspondence with him, which fills an entire volume.⁴³

Frobenius was quite clear that his numerous research voyages in "the large sociological laboratory of Africa" were motivated by his desire to find explanations, and perhaps remedies, for the weakening of monarchical institutions in Europe.[44]

The racist thread of Frobenius's work is directly linked to the notion that the monarchy is a primevally "white" institution. He explained his discovery of the similarities between monarchical institutions in Africa and in Europe with a particular form of the Hamitic hypothesis, the belief that "Hamitic" people, who were more or less European, had migrated into Africa and dominated the indigenous pastoral peoples (whom Frobenius referred to as "Ethiopians"). For many other anthropologists, the Hamites were unequivocally white; for Frobenius they were as much Semitic as Aryan. In many passages, Frobenius falls into the anti-Semitic tropes that circulated everywhere around him in Germany of the 1920s and 30s, while at the same time giving to the Hamites what we could describe as the structural position of Europeans.

In short, Frobenius's racialization of Africa said as much—probably everything—about ambivalences and fantasies about German and Aryan identity as it did about Africa. The Hamites embodied the traits of Western civilization, but only in degenerate, almost barbaric forms. They were the limit case for European civilization, a sped-up experiment in the "sociological laboratory" that showed the decay that lay ahead. Frobenius explicitly compares the Lemba of modern-day Zimbabwe and South Africa to "Galician Jews," deploying such a cartoonish anti-Semitism that he explains, in a mind-bogglingly contradictory footnote, that he does not want to "give the impression that [the Lemba] resembled the Jews." Nevertheless, the Lemba, he says, have a "permanent readiness to wander . . . remarkable tendency to breed . . . hooked nose, sensually formed thick lips . . . unmanliness of the race . . . devout and submissive . . . money-grabbing . . . incredible miserliness."[45] In Africa, Frobenius finds a reflection of the lurid anti-Semitism around him, and uses that reflection to confirm what he believes to be the essential, underlying structure of social organization throughout Africa.[46]

But it is, somewhat surprisingly, with the "Ethiopians" that Frobenius moves beyond implicit racism to a more horrific and approving kind. It is horrific partly because he embraces it as a vision of an ideal German future, a future that Kantorowicz, for one, was imagining at the same time in the form of an ideal *Führer*. Frobenius finds in the African institution of sacral kingship not just the interesting mythic analogy with medieval European institutions that his contemporaries had found. He believes there is a primeval connection between them and that sacral kingship diverged historically on the two continents. What Frobenius finds most striking about African sacral kingship is very much like what Kantorowicz finds in medieval kingship: it offers a glimpse of rejuvenated sovereign institutions in an age of popular democracy. Frobenius's description of the political utility of *Königsmord*, the ritual killing of kings, could be a passage from Kantorowicz's *Frederick II*: "After the dread and horror of the day of the downfall there followed a joyous celebration of the appointment of the new ruler and the return to strict discipline and order."[47]

Kantorowicz's solution to the longing for a new kind of leader to replace the monarchical void that the Weimar Republic brought with it was to imagine a philosopher-artist-king like Stefan George—and inadvertently to facilitate the absolutist imaginations of Goering and Hitler himself. Frobenius's solution was more concrete: to restore Wilhelm II to the throne in a German monarchy. He maintained a very close intellectual relationship with Wilhelm II though the 1920s and 30s.[48] A lecture that Frobenius gave to the Kaiser in exile in October 1923 transformed Frobenius's strange version of the Hamitic hypothesis into a political theory of German conquest. The Kaiser enthusiastically seized on the hypothesis as a more or less workable strategy to reinstall the German monarchy: "Once we have proved to the Germans that the French and English are not Whites at all but Blacks—the French e.g. Hamites—then they will set upon this rabble."[49] More starkly than Frobenius himself had, the Kaiser articulated how the kind of anthropological "discoveries" that Frobenius was making were coterminous with both monarchical nostalgia and the imperial colonization of Africa.

The similarities between African practices of kingship and those of the European Middle Ages are an implicit justification for German imperial rule: it would not disrupt African "constitutional" structures, and—seemingly counterintuitively—might even arrest the "degradation" of African cultures by contact with the West. The structures of governance in other European countries might not, after all, be as compatible as those of imperial Germany. After Germany lost its colonies and its Kaiser following World War I, the supposed primal connections between not just the cultures of the "Nilotes" and of the Germans, but also their uncanny echoes in political theology, made the "example of the holy African kingdom" "more than a mere consoling metaphor" for Frobenius.[50]

Even before the end of World War I, Frobenius was shoring up arguments for the continuity between ancient African and medieval practices of kingship. At one point in the 1913 *The Voice of Africa*, he quotes the impression of a German ethnographer, Siegfried Passarge, that the medieval German court and the contemporary Cameroonian African court are similar. The "ceremonial institutions at a Soudanese [sic] Royal court," says Passarge, "are exactly similar to those of the courts of Germany in the Middle Ages."[51] Frobenius leaps back and forth across time and space to give Passarge's observation historical heft. He first argues that the "constitution of the Nubian Imperial Court . . . corresponds with that of the Imperial Court of Byzantium" (631). The qualifier "Imperial" for both courts says more about Frobenius's immediate object of interest, the Germany of the Kaiser (although precarious at that point), than Nubia or Byzantium. Indeed, in the next sentences, he refers to the "kingdom" and the "king" of Nubia, rather than an emperor. He invokes his theory of cultural transmission from "the East" to explain how Byzantium might have spread its political institutions to Nubia, and how Nubia must have spread *its* institutions to central Africa when it "extended its sway" (632). His brief discussion of a possible history for the relation between medieval African and imperial German courts ends with an extraordinary medievalist fantasia: "The same Lord High-Stewards and the same cupbearers performed the same office at the Round Table of a King Uther or a King Arthur as at the Imperial Byzantine Court" (632).

The similarities among courts in far-flung parts of the world fascinated him for abstract and academic reasons: it was a demonstration both of his theory of the diffusion of culture and also the distinctive characteristics that each culture took on, its *paideuma*. That medieval Nubia, Byzantium, and the France and England of King Arthur were so similar demonstrated the corresponding theory that cultures followed similar stages of development independently, following the logic of organisms—his famous theory of cultural morphology.

It's worth dwelling a bit further on this passage from Passarge's work. In the early twentieth century, Passarge was widely respected as an ethnographer, even mentioned admiringly by Bronisław Malinowski as one of the early "participant observers" he urged ethnographers to become. Passarge wrote ethnographies of the Khoisan and Bantu-speakers of

South Africa that are still cited for information about those groups in the nineteenth century, although with qualifications about his facts. He participated in an expedition to Cameroon in 1894, and Frobenius's quote about the medieval German similarities to the courts of Cameroon comes from his narrative report.[52] Frobenius himself called Passarge a "careful observer" (435). But Passarge was a poisonous and influential anti-Semite, whose work helped form the racial policies of the Nazi Party.[53] His ethnographies of African peoples are shot through with anti-Semitic tropes. Even the ethnography that Frobenius quotes from described Black Africans as parasites on white culture, and argued—despite the evocation of medieval German courts—that Africans were incapable of self-rule.[54] Conclusions like that about the governance of African territories reveal a direct pipeline between ethnographic work and potential colonial policy if Germany had won World War II and reacquired its lost colonies. Indeed, Passarge was appointed professor of colonial geography in Hamburg in 1908, where he ran the Geographical Seminar at the Hamburg Colonial Institute (sponsored by the Imperial Colonial Office, it became a founding part of the University of Hamburg). He became chairman for geography in the National Socialist Teachers League (NSLB) in 1933.[55] Passarge's may be the most reprehensible embodiment of the implicit and explicit connections between ethnography and imperial colonialism. Like Frobenius, however, his invocation of the Middle Ages betrays his explicit imperial sympathies, although unlike Frobenius his motives were far more than merely academic. The trope of medieval kingship is a kind of conduit between academic study and administrative interests in colonial-era ethnography (and even beyond).

In English anthropology, the interest in divine kingship throughout African anthropology "became part of the intellectual universe of European indirect rule," the policy first formulated by Lord Lugard, the High Commissioner of the Protectorate of Northern Nigeria and an important figure in the British appropriation of Uganda and Kenya.[56] Lugard had an unusual engagement with indigenous customs: he famously made a blood brotherhood with the Gĩkũyũ leader Waiyaki wa Hinga. That pact incidentally illustrated one of the major flaws in indirect rule: the Gĩkũyũ practiced a form of distributed rule that was not compatible with Lugard's theory that power was embodied in just one person, and Waiyaki was merely one of several leaders. Indirect rule, in the words of Robert Gordon, "stressed the ancient authority of tribal chiefs and their importance for local governance, precisely those individuals who best embodied divine kingship."[57] Behind that theory lies the mostly unconscious assumption that the best model of rule for African colonies is the medieval theory of sovereignty. Ethnographers believed, thanks to confirmation bias, that they had discovered those theories in the African groups they studied. That story would take another book to tell, but as an example of the insidious force of the theory of divine kingship, I will discuss a later ethnographer praised for his progressive sympathies for the people he studied: Max Gluckman, the South African anthropologist whose Marxism "upset" his mentor Evans-Pritchard (Gordon, 347).

Gluckman was born in 1911, the year that Seligman's article on divine kingship came out. Gluckman's personal and scholarly irreverence disturbed many in the field. The American anthropologist David Schneider said that he had "almost no intellectual position of any coherence, and even as a buffoon I think he was pretty bad" (Gordon, 7). His work tried to bracket the assumptions about social and religious structures that European anthropologists brought to their field, focusing instead on the "social processes" of class and economy in the age of global capital (Gordon, 3). Gluckman's personal commitment to anti-colonialism often led to trouble. At one point, he was accused of sedition for discussing the war with Lozi people in Barotseland (present-day Zambia) (Gordon, 191). Both of the institutions he directed, the Rhodes-Livingstone Institute (RLI) in Lusaka, and the Department of Anthropology at the University of Manchester, had reputations for being left-leaning and anti-colonial. Colonial officials were deeply suspicious of members of the RLI, and many members had difficulty getting jobs later.[58] It's possible that Gluckman foresaw the helpfulness of institutes devoted to local study to nascent movements for independence.

On the other hand, one of the guiding policies behind the RLI was indirect rule. Its purpose was to develop forms of colonial administration that would be compatible with local groups. That purpose was hidden, perhaps, behind a screen of good intentions: the "improvement" of "African conditions"—now a recognizably neoliberal motive, devastatingly described by Teju Cole as the work of a white savior industrial complex.[59] Gluckman, in fact, enthusiastically supported anthropology's complicity in developing colonial administration, and saw it as a way to extend the clout of the discipline. In a 1944 memorandum, he outlined the ways in which RLI would support "government."[60]

There is a related blind spot in Gluckman's anthropological work in Zambia, as well. He argued that anthropology should begin by studying particular situations, working out from them to an understanding of the social structures that they reveal. A famous paper—later known as the "Bridge Paper"—analyzed a single day in Zululand that included a court hearing and the opening of a bridge.[61] It closes with a catalog of the social relations that the day revealed: between groups of Blacks and whites, Christians and pagans, Europeans and Zulus, the Zulu court and Zulu subjects, government and nongovernment employees, kinsmen and neighbors. It is, in effect, a complex Venn diagram of one day that helps to draw a more enduring Venn diagram of underlying social structures. Gluckman's method aims to prevent the prejudice of the "*a priori* speculations about early stages of forms of organization" that plagued previous work.[62] One of the circles in the Venn diagram is the Zulu regent and his court, and it is a sign of Gluckman's commitment to radically observing just what is in front of him that he doesn't turn this into a discussion of sovereignty or sacred kingship. The catch is his invocation of "early stages" of organization, indeed a kind of a priori speculation: if a day reveals almost everything we need to know, why do we need to think about what came decades, if not centuries, before that?

There are two reasons for that bias: Gluckman came to Zambia with the a priori idea that the basic form of group organization in Africa was the tribe. He takes it for granted that one of the main concerns of social anthropology is "stability and change in *tribal* societies" (*Politics*, xxi; my emphasis). When Gluckman and his colleagues hit the ground in Zambia, they were sent, as Kate Crehan observes, "clutching a bundle of RLI index cards," to groups that the RLI had already categorized as tribes.[63]

Gluckman's comment about "early stages" of social organization reveals his continuing interest in history as an analogy—even an explanation—for the present forms of social organization that he records. He uses the term "tribe," he says, "since 'tribe' was used to describe most of the communities of Europe, virtually up to feudal times. And forms of social organization akin to those communities, are what I am dealing with" (*Politics*, xv). In other words, Gluckman imports a medieval concept that shapes his empirical, day-to-day observations about the way people live in the present.[64] Because the "tribe" was such an important tool in the extension of colonial rule, postcolonial scholars often assume the word didn't become potent until the era of colonialism, that it was "rarely used during the Middle Ages of European history."[65] It is true that the term, with that specific sense, is not common in medieval sources. But in the nineteenth century, medievalists began to think of it in terms of economic development. The most important work here was Frederic Seebohm's 1883 *The English Village Community Examined in its Relations to the Manorial and Tribal Systems and to the Common or Open Field of Husbandry*. It was a major work of economic history, which was published in several editions for the next forty years.[66] Seebohm intended colonial administrators (the "statesmen," he says, "of the new Englands across the ocean") to use it as a guide to hurry colonies from the tribal stage to the modern political economy.[67] A work of medieval economic history—published by the Society of Antiquaries, no less—was meant as a handbook for the construction of the modern colony. As we will see in the next chapter, Seebohm's was far from the only medieval textbook to have that outsize influence.

Another of these texts is Frederick Pollock and Frederic Maitland's *The History of English Law Before the Time of Edward I* (1898), a standard text in law and history for English undergraduates for more than fifty years. It's not clear that Gluckman ever cited Seebohm, but he would have read Pollock and Maitland when he was a law student. He cites the text in an important 1955 article, "The Peace in the Feud" (he also cites *The Shorter Cambridge Medieval History*), which argues, based on his work in Africa, that feuds are central to social cohesion, not ongoing threats to order, as *Cambridge Medieval History*, in particular, had argued.[68] Gluckman recognized that his argument would be valuable for medievalists, and that article is still cited in almost all work on medieval feuds.[69] Gluckman, the anthropologist who shaped medieval studies, is the bookend of Kantorowicz, the medievalist who shaped anthropology.

But Gluckman's idea of the importance of the tribe also seems to have been shaped by Pollock and Maitland's history of medieval law, which relates tribes to blood feuds. The blood feud, they say, is a direct result of the "tribal system whence it springs."[70] Particularly when they talk about tribes, Pollock and Maitland anticipate Gluckman's argument about the social importance of conflict. In the "face of strife," they argue at the beginning of the book, the importance of the family appears "in the war of tribal factions, and more specifically in the blood-feud" (7). For Gluckman, too, the feud reveals important social structures, although his description of what these are is more complex. A feud will reveal different allegiances and interest groups, not just a single group like the family. That is part of the more complex understanding of feuds Gluckman bequeathed to medieval studies.

But Maitland and Pollock also discuss the relation between tribes and feuds specifically in a context with which Gluckman was familiar from experience: peoples subjugated in conquest. Maitland, who wrote the following passage, breaks the fourth wall of the academic stage and seem to address directly the students who will shortly be entering the Colonial and Foreign Offices to imprint English legal systems on the colonies. It is so unusually topical; reveals so much about the *reasons* medieval studies was important in the era of colonialism; and maps medieval British history so well onto contemporary colonial policy, that I will quote most of it:

> In different ages and circumstances the pride of a conquering race will show itself in very different forms. Now-a-days the victor may regard the conflict as one between civilization and barbarism, or between a high and a low morality, and force his laws upon the vanquished as the best, or the only reasonable laws. Or again he may deliberately set himself to destroy the nationality of his new subjects, to make them forget their old language and their old laws, because these endanger his supremacy. We see something of this kind when Edward I thrusts the English laws upon Wales. The Welsh laws are barbarous, barely Christian, and Welshmen must be made into Englishmen. . . . The conquerors will show their contempt for the conquered by allowing such of them as are not enslaved to live under their old law, which has become a badge of inferiority. The law of the tribe is the birth-right of the men of the tribe, and aliens can have no part or lot in it (68–69).

This is an articulation of what Lord Lugard would later call the Dual Mandate, and indeed he alludes to this passage in a 1933 lecture on colonial administration.[71] But it is hardly an endorsement. Before it had really become a coherent policy or practice (which it eventually did, with the significant contribution of anthropologists), Maitland wrote this outraged but somehow also wry critique of it—wry, perhaps, because he is, as he implies, writing about what is going on at the moment. This form of indirect rule is as damaging to the rulers as it is to the ruled, and the brilliant ambivalence of the "law of the tribe" applies as much to the English as to the Welsh: everyone is held back, kept tribal, under this system of rule by conquest.[72] The stage of mere tribal law is primitive in the sense that it comes early, but it is also retrograde in the development of what Maitland calls the "modern and political point of view." And, after all, as Maitland says, the "tribal system," like the blood feud, is "doomed to die." This passage also clarifies the tension between Gluckman's progressive politics and his codification of tribal groups: tribes are an intermediary step to what he called the "improvement" of "African conditions." Nevertheless, Gluckman always had an eye to the medieval past, even on an impressionistic level. He talks about how Shakespeare's history plays (which are about the medieval struggles between the York and Plantagenet royal households over the throne of England) remind him of Zulu and Barotse discussions about the "politics of rebellion" (*Custom*, 48).

Rebellion, as Gluckman argued, is a persistent feature of kingship, not a violation of it. It is just as medieval as it is African. All successions of leadership are traumatic, but not ritually traumatic, as with the case of the murder of divine kings. They are traumatic because they expose the political—and arbitrary—grounds of rule. Gluckman, as an observer of the way systems work rather than of the things people believe (or wanted to believe) about them, brought these beliefs down to earth. He did this quite literally. Feuds are settled, he argues, by what he calls "men of the earth," ritual experts who remind combatants of the mutual importance of the earth, often merely by digging it up ("Peace," 10). These men of the earth invoke a law that is otherwise too "weak" to override personal and family grudges. Invoking the earth works because it has a mystical importance. He does not explain what that is. But it has, above all, a secular importance, he says, because it is the very basis of society: people farm it, live on it, dance and die on it, and must be friendly to each other to use it.

Gluckman's theory of sovereignty is, in other words, literally, a secular, worldly one, based in and on the earth. In the same passage, he conspicuously snubs the theory of divine kingship when it might come up. Kings in Central and South Africa (the site of Seligman's work) "symbolize the political unity of the tribes" (they are implicitly not divine ancestors or gods) and "are identified with the earth" ("Peace," 10). Like his mentor Evans-Pritchard, Gluckman was skeptical about the claims that earlier anthropologists made for the practice of divine kingship, especially regicide.[73] As we will see in the next chapter, Gluckman's description of the importance of land is strikingly similar to another of his mentors, Malinowski. Evans-Pritchard and Malinowski might have showed Gluckman how to shift the paradigm of divine kingship, but his emphasis on the way social relations are continually formed and deformed is what really drives his theory of kingship. In another significant article, Gluckman argues that kingship—and rule in general—is always precarious. Part of the role of a leader is to provoke hatred in at least some of his followers; not everyone wants the same thing, and the leader must disappoint someone. Conflict is part of the system of government not because that is the ontological nature of leadership or monarchy, but because leaders facilitate or deny what each person wants. Gluckman quotes a Barotse maxim: "Every man thinks that the king has one subject."[74] Leadership is the convergence of a multitude of competing interests; an amateur Freudian (as Gluckman was) might say the monarch is the ego's check on the id's impulses. For Gluckman, these impulses come first, even in the case of divine kings: they are challenged not because of violations of ritual but because they have failed a large enough group of interests. Ritual is important as a way of reinforcing the leader's authority, or as a way of covering up the real reasons for deposing a leader.

Gluckman's point is not that African groups altered forms of government because of dissent or insurrection, but that conflict reinforces the form of government. Gluckman replaces the a priori theory that spiritual authority shapes a society with what may be another a priori theory: that a long series of compromises creates a particular form of constitutional government. It's exactly the story that the central texts on English constitutional history, like Pollock and Maitland's, tell. In an article about the analogies between the Barotse people and medieval English law, Gluckman says that Barotse who could speak English "define the kingship as a 'constitutional monarchy.'"[75] The very focus on law as the main event of a people's history is an echo of the importance of medieval constitutional history in the development of colonial rule. The medieval English analogy runs through the entire essay, from the epigraph, which comes from *Macbeth*, to Gluckman's comparison between the "history of African states" and the fifteenth-century Wars of the Roses. In the case of the Wars of the Roses, he draws a counterintuitive lesson: that the tumultuous period of rebellions against temporary monarchs was precisely what united the "nation about the kingship." Perhaps Gluckman had Shakespeare's *Henry VIII* in mind; it presents Henry as the union of the two factions, creating what would become under his daughter the strong Elizabethan state.

But Gluckman's attention was primarily on African leadership, of course. What he traces are the often contradictory forces that are the very structure of rule itself, at the particular moment that there was an administrative need to understand how British rule would work in African colonies. Gluckman's much vaunted breadth of analysis takes in not just the people of a "tribe" but also everyone who interacts with them, including (perhaps, especially) the Europeans who interact with them. Yet the *formation* of his method puts Europeans at its very center. In the article on law among the Barotse, he discusses the medieval "analogy" at length. The article is a kind of constitutional history of the Barotse, but again and again in it he turns to important historians of the Middle Ages—Maitland, Paul Vinogradoff, Marc Bloch, J. E. A. Jolliffe—to articulate principles he then discovers among the Barotse and the Zulu. At one point, Gluckman quotes all of chapter 61 of the Magna Carta and a commentary on it by Noel Dowling (*Cases on Constitutional Law*). Chapter 61 concerns armed insurrection, which Dowling, Gluckman points out, had characterized as a revolutionary action. Gluckman argues, using Jolliffe, that it is really rebellion, which does not aim at a new form of rule, just at replacing the ruler, that is, the "right to revolt" ("Power," 1535). As we will see in the next chapter, the Magna Carta was often invoked in English colonies by settlers as a precedent for diminishing the power that the Crown had to regulate their lives. Here Gluckman uses the Magna Carta as a medieval precedent for what has happened in Africa—or at least in the field of cultural anthropology: the abstract power of the king has been diminished by political struggle.

The repeated conflicts over the succession of monarchs in medieval England caused what Kantorowicz called the individual *dignitas* of the king to fade as the political structures of distributed power in the modern state developed. In European ideas about Africa, by contrast, the early medieval form of *dignitas* still existed, precisely because it was needed to unify factions. A group's weakness, argues Gluckman, makes the "kingship's symbolic and ritual value" more important ("Power," 1539). That weakness, he implies, is caused by colonialism: the Barotse king passed a statute in 1929 regulating the use of royal insignia. Gluckman doesn't mention that 1929 was when indirect rule was put in place everywhere in

Northern Rhodesia—except for Barotseland. The king, Yeta, interpreted that concession as a veiled threat, and worked to align his kingdom with the governor's interests.[76] In a sense, reverence toward the royal regalia is also a symptom of indirect rule, or of its imminence.

Gluckman's general interest in theoretical terms might be the secularization of power, but his sharpest interest is in how secular forces work in the colony. His analysis of the frailty of leadership closes with an example that is really the entire point of the essay: that of the "village headman." Headmen were authorities appointed by colonial administrations who were not necessarily traditional leaders. In fact, it usually worked better when they weren't. They had split, often impossible allegiances: they made sure government laws and regulations were enforced, but they were also supposed to enforce customary, indigenous law without the traditional right to do so. It's as if they were forced to moonlight at a job that their day jobs depended on. As Gluckman says, the village headman "takes the greatest strains of the dual pulls of political representation" ("Frailty," 52).

In the end, Gluckman's larger story is the ebb of the old days, in which divine kingship was regarded as a mystical political force. Even when it might exist, he showed how the myth really covered dynamic political forces, forces that could be understood because they were so apparently similar to the rules of medieval kingship. But Gluckman's work also provided a means of relativizing—i.e., secularizing—kingship, in order to subordinate it to colonial administration. Power was distributed to village heads and chiefs, whose power was torn between the "dual pulls" of indirect rule. Anthropology was one means by which Britain and other imperial powers extended their power into the colonies more effectively, even while it emerged as a discipline that tried to record cultures that were being lost. With some exceptions, it kept the groups it studied frozen in time and place. The not unforeseen consequence was that anthropology made groups easier to register and administer, kept in their place literally and figuratively, frozen in a time that was not modernity.

CHAPTER SEVEN

Kenya's Medieval Charter

> One of our real needs *is the application of a little more historical spirit.*
>
> SIR EYRE CROWE, on the reform of the Foreign Office in 1905

> African traditions have no parallel to the European feudal society.
>
> TOM MBOYA

The Feudal Metaphor

In 1938, well before he became the first president of independent Kenya in 1963, Jomo Kenyatta published a book that ended with an elegantly veiled threat: "The African is conditioned, by the cultural and social institutions of centuries, to a freedom of which Europe has little conception, and it is not in his nature to accept serfdom for ever."[1] For Kenyatta, and the rising generation of African leaders of independence movements, "serfdom" was not only a term that described precisely how colonial governments oppressed Africans economically and politically. It was also, as Kenyatta hints, something altogether alien to Africans, not in their "nature." Kenyatta was not wrong: "serfdom" was a term that came from the so-called feudal institutions of medieval Europe.

"Feudalism," as the hugely influential nineteenth-century historian William Stubbs described it, was "a complete organization of land tenure." The king "was the original lord"; below him, based on their possession of land, "every lord judged, taxed, and commanded the class next below him [and] abject slavery formed the lowest."[2] This lowest class was serfdom. The concept of feudalism was far more than an idea that Victorian medievalists spun, however. It was also the model that British colonies used for land policy and land law (and much of the law in general).

I quote a nineteenth-century historian to describe this system because it was a creation not of the Middle Ages but of the eighteenth and nineteenth centuries. "Feudalism" was an Enlightenment idea *about* the Middle Ages, not a widespread, uniform system active *during* the Middle Ages.[3] Part of the appeal of the concept was that it gave historians and political economists a neat way to describe what they had moved beyond—into an era of towns, cities, capitalism, imperialism. Yet one of the deep ironies of the concept of feudalism was that it became a crucial instrument of colonialism. Indeed, one of the most influential historians who taught the concept to colonial rulers and administrators was William Stubbs.

The particular kind of feudalism that Stubbs (and a few other contemporaries) taught was a fundamental part of the Kenya Colony from its establishment in 1920. The terms "feudal" and "feudalism" appear frequently in the policies and position papers of settler colonization, and like "serfdom" is used in a sense defined by historians in the colonial era. Land law, the main instrument that colonial officials used to appropriate much of the most fertile land in Kenya for white settlers, was not based on the current law in Britain. It was based on selective readings of medieval land laws, written largely before the end of the thirteenth century. These laws allowed the colonial government to install and support a small class of landowners who had extraordinary powers over a large, disenfranchised population. In short, colonial Kenya reproduced the ruling classes of the English Middle Ages (or at least some version of it).

The project of colonizing Kenya was elitist and racist from the start. The novelist Elspeth Huxley unabashedly argued that the colonization of Kenya would only succeed if it was "entrusted to the best among the colonising race."[4] And, indeed, initially it largely was. In 1907, Hugh Cholmondeley, the 3rd Baron Delamere, became the leader of the white members (the majority) of the Kenya Legislative Council, and also the President of the Colonists' Association. Numerous earls, counts, countesses, barons, baronets, and younger sons of the aristocracy moved to Kenya in the 1920s. Forming the notorious "Happy Valley Set," by most reckonings they were *not* the "best among the colonising race." They became infamous for heavy drinking, drug use, infidelities, brutality, and murder. Nevertheless, Kenya's aristocratic ethos was so pronounced by 1929 that the anti-colonial historian Margery Perham wrote that "ordinary" whites "could have the intoxicating sense of belonging to a small ruling aristocracy."[5] Isak Dinesen's famous book *Out of Africa*, which is the original vision board for the offhand but luxurious safari-wear aesthetic of the vast tourism industry in sub-Saharan Africa, takes this intoxication to almost metaphysical levels: "Everything that you saw made for greatness and freedom and unequalled nobility."[6]

In Dinesen's book, nobility and aristocracy are not just a fantasy of a numinous bygone era. Her book traces the feudal metaphor in her relations with (perhaps better, *to*) the non-white people who work and live on her Kenyan farm. "*My* squatters," she says, "were born on the farm, and their fathers before them, and they very likely regarded me as a sort of superior squatter on their estates." The placid distancing of "sort of" and the condescending deployment of the word "estates" simultaneously gives them a feudal aura and deprives them of it. Dinesen's is a thought experiment: imagine, although it is too ludicrous to be true, that *we* were the real feudal subjects; imagine, although it is too ludicrous to be true, that feudalism were an indigenous African institution. Dinesen's feudal analogy is extraordinarily insidious (and this is part of the reason why Ngũgĩ wa Thiong'o called it Africa's most dangerous novel): in extending, and then denying, feudalism to Africans, Dinesen is also extending, and then denying, the suitability of the feudal metaphor to describe her own position. That is, if we were to begin to think of land occupation in terms of hereditary right, we would arrive at an embarrassing contradiction. European claims for land tenure would begin to appear nonsensical, because the logic of land tenure leads to the nonsensical image of Dinesen as herself a squatter.

Yet this is precisely what she is, in every sense of the word. Karen Blixen—Dinesen was her maiden name, used as a pen name—is occupying land appropriated from the Gĩkũyũ, and her claim is supported by a shaky scaffolding of dubious claims and murky title exchanges. The 6,000 acres of land underlying the farm was acquired, before the Blixens bought it, from the Gĩkũyũ chief Kinyanjui wa Gathirimu, who owned about 16,000 acres in the area. Kinyanjui's claim to the land, however, was still under suspicion as late as 1932, when the Kenya Land Commission (convened to settle land claims and land rights once and for all) recorded three different accounts of who owned the land, and of how it was acquired.[7] Recent accounts of Kinyanjui tend to cast him as an opportunist who came to power precisely because he helped the British to appropriate Gĩkũyũ land.[8] But even if the land was acquired legitimately from Kinyanjui, Dinesen was *still* a kind of superior squatter, at least according to her definition of squatting. Two years before she and her husband Baron Bror Blixen bought the farm, the Crown Lands Ordinance of 1915 effectively converted all land in Kenya into Crown land. Groups like the Gĩkũyũ became mere tenants-at-will, as an infamous court ruling of 1923 put it, and settlers became leaseholders from the Crown.

Part of the underlying incoherence of Dinesen's concept of "squatting" is betrayed by another definition she gives for it: "The squatters knew that in order to stay on the land they had got to work for me one hundred and eight days out of each year, for which they were paid twelve shillings for every thirty days" (358). This account is from the end of the book, when Dinesen is about to lose her farm, and financial transactions obviously loomed larger than in the reconstruction of the early bucolic days. At the beginning of the book, the relationship with the squatters was imagined as "purely" feudal (the squatters "hold a few acres on a white man's farm, and in return have to work for him a certain number of days in the year"). By the end of the book, however, Dinesen's relationship with the squatters is represented as something closer to Dinesen's own leasehold arrangement for the farm—except that Dinesen's obligation to her landlord involved, in feudal terms, a strict commutation of services for cash instead of the mélange of labor market and feudal obligation that enabled her own tenants to occupy their land.[9] Nevertheless, Dinesen was indeed a kind of serious squatter, although not just because of the underlying claims of the Gĩkũyũ in the fantasy she dismisses, but because all tenancy under the Crown has an uncomfortable proximity to squatting, as Dinesen defines it here.

The magic of settler land appropriation in Kenya was that it used the logic of medieval law to get around present-day paradoxes like this one. Dinesen might be a squatter, but she really was a different kind of squatter. If she were not, the law would have to decide whether Dinesen perched on top of a shaky pile of claims to land on which her squatters had always lived. But the law had already done that—precisely by making the arbitrary decision to redefine, or to neglect, what it means to occupy ancestral land. Dinesen's difficult leavetaking of the farm is complicated precisely because the burden of the Gĩkũyũ past is becoming heavier:

she recognizes that "her" squatters will be forced to move, and that the notional, nostalgic alienation from land that she imagined earlier for them will become all too real: "It is more than their land that you take away from the people, whose Native land you take. It is their past as well, their roots and their identity" (359). This is the indulgent side of feudal fantasy, the enjoyment of a past totality that enfolds and embraces the present. The other side is renunciation, the recognition that this totality is belated, that it may be, in fact, the very obstacle—and the path—to modernity, however terrible the cost may be.

If you take away land from "the people," Dinesen says, you may "as well take their eyes." It is precisely this vivid championing of indigenous land rights—however momentary it might be—that makes the next sentence so shocking: you find this attachment to the past, she says, "in a higher degree [with] the primitive people than [with] the civilised" (368). To the degree that they maintain an attachment to their land, people fail at modernity, caught forever in a feudal or prefeudal moment. For the Gĩkũyũ, Dinesen implies, the condition of the primitive might not be just a stage of development. She compares these "primitive people" to animals who will "go back a long way" and suffer "to recover their lost identity." Historicity is not just a primitive condition—the condition of primitivism—it is an instinctual, primary drive. It is not clear whether Dinesen recognizes this animality in herself. She does not acknowledge that going back a long way to recover lost identity, an identity specifically tied to land, is precisely what she has just done throughout her book. "I had a farm in Africa," she famously intones in the opening lines; "here I am, where I ought to be" (3–4). Dinesen's nostalgia demonstrates that the European's desire for a farm in Africa brings with it a host of unexamined, unanalyzed debts and obligations to the European past, a past imagined more often than not as a feudal substrate. It is a past that one leaves behind in Europe, yet a past that irresistibly and unconsciously reconstitutes itself in Africa.

Medieval Land Law in Africa

In case after case in Kenyan colonial commissions, the officers inquire into the deep history of land use, even soliciting expert opinion about the cultural value of land. The eminent paleontologist Louis Leakey wrote an entire monograph on the Gĩkũyũ and their use of land for the Carter Land Commission, appointed in 1932 to ratify the large-scale alienation of lands from Africans. Leakey's monumental work, so daunting that it was not published until 1977, shows no trace of having influenced any of the commission's decisions. In fact, the Kenya Colony imposed land law fitfully and haphazardly, through spasmodic policy, miscellaneous court rulings, and the arbitrary decisions of individual land commissioners. The result was a bewildering catalog of property rights that still existed as late as a report published by a commission on land rights (the "Ndung'u Commission") in 2003. That confusion, of course, was not the goal most colonial administrators had aimed for. Many of them—if only because it made their jobs easier—wanted property boundaries in their areas demarcated clearly, both on the ground and in theory. Indeed, the entire purpose of land legislation in colonial Kenya was to simplify and rationalize land ownership, although the project of making sense of property rights was not necessarily a symptom of modern state efficiency. It was driven, in fact, by a profoundly medieval agenda.

There are a number of reasons that the Middle Ages powerfully influenced those who shaped land policy. In a profound but forgettable way, the common law is, of course, essentially medieval. At the base of the medievalization of Africa by the British is the radical restructuring of land ownership into a totalizing "feudal" structure: all land was held by the Crown. One of the most significant court rulings in Kenyan history decided that all Kenyans were "tenants-at-will of the Crown." Each of the various ordinances, statutes, and commissions that assigned land in colonial Kenya rested on fundamentally medieval principles of land law, just as they had in other British colonies in Africa. The summary of the Southern Rhodesian Morris Carter Commission from 1925, which served as a trial run for the 1932–33 Carter Commission in Kenya, was an especially lucid statement of the appropriateness of law derived from the European Middle Ages: "As regards agriculture the rights enjoyed by the natives, although of a somewhat precarious nature, in many respects resemble our conception of individual rather than communal tenure.... Taken as a whole the system bears a close resemblance to that obtaining in feudal times in Europe, where a copyholder had a holding of land and enjoyed rights of commonage over parts of his lord's domain."[10] Sydney Olivier, a Labour peer and former colonial official, mordantly pointed out that, rather than justify the imposition of a feudal law that would ultimately disenfranchise Africans, medieval English precedent would actually have legitimated their legal rights: "If there were equitable rights of natives who, from year to year, occupied and cultivated land belonging to the tribe, those rights ought to be taken into account. They should be taken into account in the same way, I presume, as William the Conqueror took account of the rights in manors which were annexed by him."[11] But Olivier's statements of outrage did not discernably restrain the weaponization of medieval English land law against the African inhabitants of Kenya.

The very institution of a royal commission on land (and arguably of commissions of any kind) dates to the first massive registration of land in Britain, the compiling of the Domesday Book. William I appointed commissioners who had to sort out tangled claims about ownership using both written and oral evidence.[12] One of the most intractable problems that the commissioners faced, however, was determining the numbers of peasants on holdings. The terms that witnesses used came from different languages and described different functions; the only way to decide how to describe land use (at least in this respect) was to ask for further oral testimony.[13] Three separate land commissions were held in the thirteenth century, but the largest was the Hundred Rolls inquiry of 1279–80, part of Edward I's huge project of legal and administrative reform. Although Edward I's commissions were motivated by a desire to overhaul and exercise the "feudal machinery ... under royal control," colonial commissions aimed not at reforming feudal prerogatives but at extending them into places they had never been. Yet the commissions used procedures and forms remarkably similar to the ones medieval land commissions used: the beginning of each Land Commission Report records the names of the commissioners, the jurors, a general statement of the objective of the commission, the articles of inquiry (that is, the questions they asked), and the dates of each inquisition. That is precisely the same information, and in the same order, as in the medieval patent roll.[14]

The medieval genealogy of these commissions is too rich to discuss fully here, but I want to call attention to just one strand of the DNA of colonial commissions: the question of how many cattle the people of Kenya could have. The Commission of 1934 was ostensibly concerned about sustainability: too many cattle will ultimately ravage the land. The commission knows, it says, that cattle are important because they are, effectively, currency. But that is as far as the exercise in cultural relativism takes them. Cattle are "*debased* currency [because] a bad cow has the same value as a good cow."[15] The report makes no attempt to explain this logic of equivalence, which is apparently so inscrutable and intractable that Africans don't even recognize that the quality of their cattle matters. "Government," it says, "has tried to educate the natives in better husbandry, but these efforts have been largely ineffective in the backward tribes where the evil is most persistent" (3). But the report's worry over the bad cattle ravaging Africa is really a kind of concern trolling, masquerading as a desire for modern efficiency. Since even education has failed, the commission recommends that the Government resort to the drastic measures of culling "surplus" livestock so that, as it says in characteristically anodyne language, the population will stay "within the limits which the grazing facilities from time to time dictate" (4).

What the report doesn't explain is why Africa has not yet been ravaged by bad cattle. The problem may be that land that farmers and pastoralists used to depend on to support a cattle economy is now not available to them, a fact that the commissioners who are, in fact, at that moment taking away more land do not bother—or need—to mention. Indeed, the recommendation that they make, framed for some reason as a direct quote, has the structure of classic Freudian disavowal: "'It is definitely not a problem which can be solved by an increase of land'" (3). This is not just the starting of a guilty conscience. The concern with overgrazing and their recommendation of the "principle of compulsion in reducing the numbers of stock" is triggered by the 1235 Statute of Merton. The first statute printed in the authoritative *Statutes of the Realm*, Merton established that a lord had the right to exclude neighbors from wastes, woods, and pastures "saving sufficient pasture to their men (*i.e.*, tenants) and neighbours, so that the lords of such wastes etc. might approve themselves of the residue."[16] In other words, if his neighbors had enough land to pasture their livestock, a lord could keep them from using his land. The Statute of Merton is widely regarded as the basis for the infamous Acts of Enclosure, but I do not think its importance in the expropriation of land in the colonies has been recognized.

The 1934 Land Commission clearly recognizes that colonial land policy is crowding out pastoralists. But rather than adjust the extent of colonial encroachment onto traditional pastures (implicitly blaming the problem on poor land management), it blames the problem on the "backward" management techniques of the owners of the cattle. The report does not explain how "better" cattle would mean fewer cattle, of course, but its point nonetheless is that the problem lies with the number of cattle, not with the size of the land: "If the uncontrolled increase of stock be permitted to continue, then the whole of Africa would be insufficient to satisfy the wants of the future" (4). This hysterical Malthusian dystopia is conjured not just because the commission wants to grab land, or because it is resorting to scare tactics, but also because it is hewing to the constraints of the Statute of Merton. It cannot adhere to the core principle that land can only be excluded if there is enough pasturage for neighbors: if bad cattle are going to take over Africa, then everyone needs all of the land all of the time. But if there are fewer cattle, then there does not need to be as much pasturage. That is the reason for the commission's tactical terror of bad cattle: they are evidence that Africans don't actually *value* cattle, and, therefore, by extension, that they don't value the land.

Even the underlying principle of "efficiency" here has its roots in the Statute of Merton. While there are more "modern" rationales for land appropriation, including John Locke's argument that the "industrious and rational" have an inherent right to land, the commission often decided whether or not to alienate "waste" land, based on sketchy evidence that the land wasn't being adequately exploited and therefore was surplus to the needs of Africans—that is, that the commission's "neighbors," to use the terms of the Statute of Merton, had sufficient pasturage.[17]

A large part of Gĩkũyũ territory, for instance, was appropriated in 1902 because of a Provincial Commissioner's vague impressions after driving through the area: "In travelling through the Gĩkũyũ country south of the Thika, the main point that strikes the traveller is the sparsity of population and the large areas of good land uncultivated. It is very evident indeed that there is ample room for very extensive settlement in the country without in any way unduly encroaching on native occupation" (*Report*, 13). His impressionistic vagueness, enabled, no doubt, by the fact that he was actually the Provincial Commissioner for another district altogether, makes him seem clueless, except that it hews so cannily close to the Merton Statute considerations about the adequate supply of land for the neighbor. The 1934 commission quotes this letter to justify its ruling that, while the population in the area of Nairobi has increased pressure on the land, the original decision was equitable. Its rationale for granting more land to the Gĩkũyũ elsewhere, rather than restoring it in the Thika area, is a tangled account of how the ameliorations of an urban area—a market economy, urban efficiency, improvements in health—implicitly make the rural presumptions of the Merton Statute irrelevant. It "would be ridiculous," the *Report* says, "for the Kikuyu to make grievance out of circumstances from which they have benefited so greatly" (14).

In numerous ways, feudal law provided technical justifications for what were, in the scale of imperial expansion, thousands of instances of micro-appropriation. But the master theorist of English land appropriation in African colonies was Frederick Lugard, an explorer of East Africa and Governor of Nigeria. His 1922 book *The Dual Mandate in British Tropical Africa* set out the rationale for, and the mechanisms of, indirect rule, the form of colonial governance most associated with the British Empire. Its ethical foundation was the rationale for land appropriation: that colonial rule was justified by the inability of Africans to use their resources efficiently. But Lugard added an extra ounce or two to the ethical burden by arguing that colonial powers in turn had an obligation to "develop" Africa out of its original inefficiency. It is true that he saw the end point of his own logic: eventually Africans would become "developed" enough to warrant independence. But that was not his sole rationale for English rule. It rested partly on the technicalities of the law of waste, introduced by the Statute of Merton.

In practice, the law of waste was one of the explicit precedents for land expropriation. The Crown law officers ruled in 1899 that, because Kenyan landholders are "practically savages," using land almost randomly, "in such regions the right of dealing with waste and unoccupied land accrues to Her Majesty by virtue of her right to the Protectorate."[18] To be fair, Lugard sometimes sounded as if the law of waste possessed innate logical difficulties. In Nigeria, "The assumption of the right to dispose of waste land and unoccupied lands was not in conflict with the theory that all land has an owner, since, as I have shown, there were derelict lands in Northern Nigeria."[19] His logic in the larger passage here is just as difficult to follow, but his equivocation about the authority of the law of waste ultimately does not matter, because *The Dual Mandate* fiercely defends what Lugard regarded as an older justification for expropriation: the right of conquest, precisely what the Crown law officers meant by the Queen's "right to the Protectorate." His history of land rights in Africa is a breezy and brutal statement of a fact far easier to grasp than the numinous economics of the law of waste: "Title to land accrued to the latest conquerors" (283).

Right by conquest is an important legal principle for Lugard, however, not because it is the engine of precolonial land expropriation, but because it is the basis for English land rights—in general. Although not as prominent a feature in rationales for William the Conqueror's invasion of England as one might suppose, medieval chronicles occasionally invoke it. The king's chaplain, William of Poitiers, for example, mentions it as one of the legitimations of William's sovereignty, but almost as a passing thought: William possesses English land "by lawful succession over the English land, which he possesses both by hereditary designation confirmed by the oath of the English, and by right of conquest. He was crowned by the consent, indeed by the wish of the leaders of the same people."[20] Right by conquest might be why anyone took William's right "by hereditary possession" more seriously than those of the Anglo-Saxon king Harold, or the Norwegian king Harald Hardrada, but here it hides between the more fulsome descriptions of the act of legitimation, the oaths that attest to the acceptance of a regime. The principle of right by conquest was used very little, if at all, until Edward I enacted the statue of *Quo Warranto* ("by what warrant"). Aimed at restoring royal lands to Edward I, *Quo Warranto* required landholders to show by what authority—by what warrant—they held the land. Charters were, of course, the best evidence, but possession "by right of conquest" could also be claimed: the land had been held by the possessor's ancestors since the Norman Conquest (the date at which "time immemorial" begins).[21]

In *The Dual Mandate*, Lugard repeatedly uses the principle of right by conquest as the ultimate justification for the Crown's jurisdiction over land. But, as in feudal law—which this, more or less, was—ultimate sovereignty looked more theoretical than real. It was bound by the laws and customs of land tenure that preceded a conquest. The famous Domesday Book is nothing more than an attempt to reconcile land that was held by the English before the Conquest with the land that the Norman invaders were claiming: it did not start as a tabula rasa any more than the land was unoccupied. This paradox helps to explain many of the difficulties that land commissions faced—or made for themselves—in the first half of the twentieth century. It also explains why, when Lugard is setting down his ideas about the administration of land law in the British colonies, he veers from a weirdly bellicose celebration of naked force to prim, nationalist self-admiration: "Conquest vests the control of the land in the conqueror, who in savage warfare also disposes of the lives and chattels of the conquered, but he usually finds it necessary to conform largely to the existing law and custom. In civilised countries conquest does not justify confiscation of private rights in land" (281).

This is the foundation myth of Anglo-Norman law: its historical foundation is naked force (what Marx mockingly calls "primitive accumulation"), but, at least in terms of property, it treats that force not only as an abstraction but also as something else altogether: a *ius nudum*, a law without a practical content. That is, the sovereign's dominion is theoretically absolute—the king ultimately owns all the land—but in practice he does not exercise that right. In Roman civil law, a creditor's claim over what he has lent is a *ius nudum*: theoretical and abstract, because he doesn't actually *have* the property at the moment. But Lugard isn't interested in abstract legal quibbles, even though he's taking for granted the complex Anglo-Norman notions of dual ownership. A conqueror *could* be as brutal, greedy, and arbitrary as he wanted, but in practice probably would not be, because "he usually finds it necessary to conform to the existing law and custom" (281). It's interesting that Lugard doesn't explain why a conqueror finds it necessary to conform to the customs and laws of conquered groups. An explanation would only highlight how strong and persistent the original law remains, and would threaten to turn the law of the conqueror and indigenous law into a zero-sum game. The more extensive and powerful the original customs and laws remain, the more constrained is the actual power and dominion of the conqueror. But that's what so sly about Lugard's description: the recognition that it's "necessary" to preserve indigenous laws isn't forced on the conqueror by practical considerations. It is not that a conqueror will find it easier to rule when he uses preexisting institutions, nor that by preserving indigenous institutions, customs, and social relations a conqueror makes dissent or rebellion less likely. It is because that restraint is itself part of the legitimation of conquest.

Lugard's brief description of the *dominium* of a conqueror is brutally disingenuous. On the one hand, it may be necessary for practical reasons for even savages to concede something to the people they conquer. On the other hand, the constraint that "civilised nations" experience is utterly different: it is not driven solely by a *libido dominandi*, nor by the "need" to conform to preexisting customs, for whatever reason. The kind of conquest Lugard is talking about—an obviously *British* kind of conquest—is motivated and disciplined by the seemingly unimpeachable, self-evident superiority of civilization. What "civilised nations" do is conquer, but not *use* conquest to legitimate the appropriation of land—although any apparently acceptable justifications are, in fact, acceptable, only because of the fact of conquest in the first place. The concealment of the secret of the authority of land law in colonies is both a way to formulate conquest as an ethical, even salvific mission, and a way to continue the appropriation of land with the hidden authority of conquest.

But the most important part of Lugard's argument for the necessity of British rule does not come from medieval law. It comes from nineteenth-century assumptions that history is a long course of steady improvement, culminating in the achievements—cultural, political, material—of imperial modernity, or, in a pinch, of the modern state. Lugard's work is shot through with—or, in actuality, it is built out of—his axiomatic belief that European culture is simply more "advanced" than African. He looks at any marker of difference through the monocle of evolutionary theory: characteristic features of African culture are simply belated, not yet developed into what Europeans had made of them. African conceptions of land are "primitive" because they fail to distinguish adequately between communal and private ownership. They lack even the definiteness of the medieval English concept of "tenure in common" (285). The Bantu groups, for instance, "have reached a degree of social organization which, in some cases, has attained to the kingdom stage under a despot with provincial chiefs of the feudal type" (68).

There is a deep and intractable racism at the foundation of his argument, and that is where the insidious catch in the dual mandate lies. Lugard's isn't a universal theory of economic determinism. The conditions of production are not the only influences on the developmental stage of a group. There are also the innate characteristics of the group itself—that is, its race. Once Lugard opens the lid on his racism, it comes boiling out: the "Bantu groups" he applauds for developing as far as the feudal stage have managed it not because of any inner logic of culture or economy, but because they must have "in prehistoric times assimilated alien blood" (68). This would be ludicrous if it weren't for the corollary he doesn't draw, but doesn't need to: only "alien blood" is capable of developing feudalism. Despite his gestures toward the second part of the dual mandate, "improving" the conditions of Africans, Lugard envisions a "natural" limit to their development, somewhere on the threshold of the Middle Ages—not able to cross it unless they are actually descended physically from, say, the European Middle Ages.

Lugard's estimation of the feudal stage as an exceptional level of development for Africans, and indeed one just out of their reach, is slightly more belittling than the stage at which most writers about the political economy of African colonies place African cultures. For most of them, Africa is manifestly and securely at the medieval—feudal—stage, which for them simply meant that, like the Middle Ages, Africa was backward. But for those who knew more about what the Middle Ages were like, the analogy was a tool of analysis and prediction, an actual instrument of governance. One of the leading economists in the Kenya Colony, Vincent Liversage, wrote a short book in 1945 to educate the officials who were to make the crucial decisions about land tenure in the years to come. An advertisement for it in the *Journal of the Royal Economic Society* says it provides "the essential facts [of land tenure in various parts of the world] for those who must know them before making decisions of profound consequence for the rest of the world."[22] Responding to the basic ignorance of the administrators who would make decisions about land (Liversage tactfully says "they have not had the opportunity of making a comparative study of the subject"),[23] his short survey is lanced with the terms of medieval land tenure: the term "tenure" itself, "right of usufruct" (4), "seigniory" (7), "freehold rights" (8), "common of pasture" (12), "tenant-at-will," (15), "demesne land" (24). He writes a thumbnail sketch of the medieval manor economy in England drawn from Ephraim Lipson's authoritative three-volume study (21–22). Unlike Lugard, he believes that the evolution of a feudal system is a universal response to economic conditions, and he compares the medieval system with the "almost exactly similar land code" of the Ashanti and the practice of feudal obligations among four African groups, in Fiji, and in India (24–26). Elsewhere, he says that "usufruct and seignory are the very warp and woof of the *Githaka* system" in Kenya.[24]

A substantial part of the rationale for the imposition of common law in land ownership rests on the kind of analogy that Liversage draws with the manorial economy. But Liversage's work is subtly different. It explicitly uses comparative methods drawn from economic anthropology and justifies the model of feudal tenure precisely because it seems to be a near- universal form of social relations. The point of his wide-ranging comparisons is that land tenure follows a universal logic, even if its forms around the world are affected by variations in material and economic conditions. He is patently concerned, though, with a particular moment in the development of economic forms: with feudalism. The *point* of all of his comparisons is to predict what will happen to the form of feudalism in colonies like Kenya. Although that form seems, to him at least, incontrovertibly present, it is also implicitly unstable. Unless it is carefully controlled, the system of feudal tenure ends in private ownership (52), which will almost immediately monetize the value of land (58). The problem with that is the inevitable cycle of borrowing that follows: "Sooner or later debt overhauls prosperity" and agriculture may no longer be economically sustainable. That debt, in Liversage's account, seems to be the primary reason the feudal system disappeared in Europe: "Debt was largely instrumental in causing the disappearance of the yeomen and small squires in England, and letting in the large landlord" (78). Debt, in other words, led England out of the Middle Ages into modernity, which, for Liversage—at least for his interest in efficient farming—is not necessarily better than the feudal stage.

Liversage's problem is not how to keep Africa in the Middle Ages, though. It is how to move Africa into modernity without destroying its most important "feudal" institutions. Keeping those institutions intact—to push the analogy, keeping Africa medieval—is precisely what he means when he says that "uncontrolled evolution" will end in private ownership (52). What controls—by restricting and inhibiting—the potentially catastrophic emergence of modern forms of capital is the supple, intricate, and enduring feudal institution.

The relative sophistication of Liversage's appropriation of the feudal analogy is due to his training as an agricultural economist at the University of Wisconsin, where he took an MSc (he did a BSc at the University of London at Wye, which specialized in agriculture). Wisconsin had one of the first departments of agricultural economy in the world, and one that would remain among the best. Liversage's training there made him almost uniquely suited to decisions about land policy. His decision to write *Land Tenure in the Colonies* suggests that he was well aware of his virtually singular expertise in land policy.

The relative nuances of Liversage's work show, by contrast, how close a party line on feudalism most other colonial administrators followed. Their understanding of feudalism, and of the suitability of feudalism for the governance of colonies, was a fundamental part of the training most of them had. A remarkable number of them were, in fact, medievalists, and a remarkable number of these medievalists were trained at Balliol College, Oxford.

How Oxford Medievalists Ruled the World

The first British High Commissioner of Palestine, Lord Samuel, supposedly once said that "life is one damn Balliol man after another." He was, of course, a Balliol man himself. If by life he meant the expropriation of land in the colonies and the study of the Middle Ages, then it describes pretty well how things worked between the 1890s and the 1940s. This is a list of just a few of the most significant colonial administrators from Balliol: three successive viceroys of India—Henry Petty-Fitzmaurice, Marquess of Lansdowne (1888–1894), Victor Bruce, Earl of Elgin (1894–1899), and George Curzon (1899–1905), who won the Marquis of Lothian Historical Prize in 1883 (half of the first 18 winners were from Balliol);[25] four of the chief officials of the Kenya Colony and its predecessor—Frederick Crawford, governor of Uganda (1967–1961) and deputy governor of Kenya (1953–1957, the "Mau Mau" years), Geoffrey Alexander Stafford Northcote, Assistant Colonial Secretary in Kenya (1904–1927) before becoming chief official in Northern Rhodesia, Gold Coast, British Guiana, Arthur Hardinge, Commissioner of the East Africa Protectorate (1896–1900), and Charles Norton Edgecombe Eliot, Commissioner of Kenya (1900–1904), who alienated land for British settlers so extensively that he was forced to resign; and Eliud Mathu, the first African member of the Kenya Legislative Council, twenty-one years before independence.

One reason so many important administrators came from Balliol was because Ralph D. Furse, the head of the Colonial Service (he was, of course, a Balliol man), set up a pipeline from the college to the Colonial Office. His accomplice was a Balliol tutor, Kenneth Bell, whom Furse described as the Colonial Office's talent scout at Oxford. Bell identified bright, competent, athletic public school men he thought would be suitable for the Colonial Service and encouraged them to apply to the Office after graduation.

There was yet another reason that Balliol sent so many candidates to both the Colonial Office and the Foreign Office. In a mark of the influence that Balliol had in shaping those two branches of the Civil Service, the Master of Balliol, James Leigh Strachan-Davidson, told the Civil Service Commissioners in 1905 both what type of man they wanted *and* what he should study: they "should select ... certain subjects, i.e. practically the Modern History subjects, for these men to be examined in.... What you want is the type of man who is born to competence and has been to a public school.... If you want to get this man decently educated you must look to the Modern History School."[26]

The public school desideratum does not need to be explained. But Modern History does, especially in an age that is suspicious of the practical utility of the humanities in general. Administrators should study administration, but there was no such thing at Oxford in the colonial era. The next best thing, indeed, the only really suitable thing, was the study of history, which offered examples of empire and rule through the ages that students could draw from when they became colonial administrators. The study of "modern" history (as opposed to classical history) as a discipline at Oxford closely tracks the burgeoning demand for administrators in a ballooning empire: formal study began in 1853, and it became a subject in its own right in 1873. An 1895 student handbook says that the degree in Modern History is meant "for those who devote themselves to the active duties of life," sounding a bit like a dog whistle for the Colonial Service.[27] That year Modern History was the second biggest subject in the Honours School (*Handbook*, 175).

But "Modern History" is not what we tend to think of as modern. Any candidate for the degree had to study the largely medieval events of English constitutional history and sit for a paper on English political history up to 1485 (*Handbook*, 175). Apart from having to sit one paper on history covering the Tudors, Stuarts, and Hanovers, a student could study nothing but medieval history for the rest of the course. He (and occasionally she) could even take as special subjects "The Age of Dante, the *Purgatorio* to be studied minutely" or "Mediaeval Latin Palaeography and Diplomatic, to be studied with special reference to MSS. of English origin" (*Handbook*, 178). It was entirely possible to study Modern History and emerge as a medievalist.

That, in fact, was how many of the important medievalists at Oxford learned their subject. But medieval studies was emphatically not just for those seeking quiet and arcane *otium*. Medieval studies happened to be one of the centers of intellectual power at Oxford, and *its* center was Balliol. Some of the tutors and professors (and their texts) shaped a considerable part of the mental, moral, and legal terrain of the British Empire. The preeminent figure was the medieval historian William

Stubbs, Regius Professor of Modern History, Master of Balliol, and eventually Bishop of Oxford. His three-volume *Constitutional History of England* (1875–78) became the foundational text for the Modern History course. The *Constitutional History*, along with Stubbs's other book, *Select Charters and Other Illustrations of English Constitutional History from the Earliest Times to the Reign of Edward the First*, made up precisely one-third of the books recommended for the English and European History portions of the course.

Besides Stubbs, several of the most influential Oxford historians in the nineteenth and twentieth centuries either taught at Balliol or were trained there: Richard Southern, V. H. Galbraith, T. F. Tout, W. P. Ker, Maurice Keen, and Rodney Hilton. Hugh Trevor-Roper snarkily complained about the obvious domination not just of medieval studies, but the study of history generally, by "a close oligarchy of medievalists trained at Balliol college."[28] The Balliol medievalist oligarchy did not just control the field of academic history. They also shaped a significant part of the real history of the colonies and the postcolony. Ralph Furse's talent scout for the Colonial Office, Kenneth Bell, was one of those Balliol medievalists. He wrote a general history of medieval Europe, *Mediaeval Europe 1095–1254* (1911), and lectured primarily on medieval and early Reformation topics. But he also published and taught in his other area of concern. His *Documents on British Colonial History*, which he edited with another Balliol man, W. P. Morrell, was published in 1928, and he was the Beit Lecturer in Colonial History at Oxford from 1924 to 1927.[29]

One of Richard Southern's distinguished students who did not go on to become a medievalist was Max Gluckman, the anthropologist who founded the controversial Rhodes-Livingstone Institute in what is now Zambia. The RLI was ambiguous from the start: technically free of interference from the colonial government, one of its tasks was to conduct research that would help the British rule more effectively. It acquired a reputation for staunch anti-racism and implicit anti-colonialism, and the Northern Rhodesian authorities found it an increasingly less important part of their program of governance. As we saw in the last chapter, unlike Liversage, and most economists and administrators, Gluckman placed the cultures he studied—he insisted on the word "tribes"—in a *pre*-feudal moment, characterized by an almost mythic egalitarianism. The word "tribe" was, for him, an acceptable alternative to "primitive," "preliterate," or "preindustrial," and it was also the word, he said, that described European communities "*up to feudal times.*" In Gluckman's perhaps quixotic attempt to sidestep any influence by theories of political economy on him and on "tribes," an attempt that comes disturbingly close to placing Africans outside of history altogether, we get a glimpse of what form a refusal to think of culture in the terms that medievalists used might take. It is possible to read Gluckman's work as a resistance to, and a critique of, the very initiatives that funded the RLI and that it was intended to facilitate.

My point is not that the medievalist origin of colonial land policy can be recognized easily, or undone quickly. The structures of feudalism were so deeply entangled in the appropriation, allotment, and management of land that it turned out to be impossible, or at least difficult, simply to disavow feudalism after independence.

Independent Feudalism

First, the most obvious irony: in the decades following independence, Jomo Kenyatta and his family came to own more land than almost anyone else. By 2005 they had acquired more than 15,000 square kilometers, an area larger than several countries.[30] This accumulation of land was certainly not something that just the Kenyatta family achieved. Most of the prominent political families of postindependence Kenya pursued it, and the drive to acquire land, which eventually became the frenzy now known as land grabbing, structured much of independent Kenya's politics. A great deal of the acquisition of land came at the expense of what is known in Kenya as the *wananchi*, the common people, literally the people of the earth. Land allocated for people who had been squatters on European-owned land—those people subjected to what Kenyatta called "serfdom"—and who formed collectives to purchase it, was often instead bought up by people who already owned extensive land and could marshal both the financial and political capital to outmaneuver marginally educated and poor groups of subsistence farmers. Even when collective purchase arrangements remained intact, the poorest were neglected because they could not afford to pay the 10 percent deposit. When ex-squatters received land, it was often far less than an acre, barely enough for subsistence farming. These people were forced, despite Kenyatta's prophecy, to continue to accept serfdom. They remain so entrenched in that old economic order that even progressive scholars continue to refer to them as the "peasantry."[31]

But how did the structure of governance after independence end up reproducing the conditions of serfdom? In a 1952 speech, Kenyatta seems to demand economic equity for Kenyans, "that is equal pay for equal work.... Those who profess to be just must realize that this is the foundation of justice. It has never been known in history that a country prospers without equality."[32] Kenyatta means primarily that Africans should be paid the same salaries as Europeans, but it is also clear that he envisions equal pay as a universal right, the first step in dismantling the system of colonial subjugation. On the other hand, his criticism is directed at a system that seems here more capitalist than feudal, a system founded on wage labor and not tenant service. Indeed, a position paper issued by the ruling Kenyan African National Union (KANU) party, and signed by Kenyatta in 1965 (but probably written by Tom Mboya, Kenyatta's brilliant finance minister), argued that its platform of "African socialism" was not predicated on a Marxist critique, precisely because Marx wrote in the wake of European feudalism, and "African traditions have no parallel to the European feudal society, its class distinctions, its unrestricted property rights, and its acceptance of exploitation. The historical setting that inspired Marx has no counterpart in independent Kenya."[33] The notion that class division belonged to a specific moment of European history, and was not a universal condition, is one of the characteristic features of midcentury African Marxist critique. It didn't reject Marx per se, just his assumption that historical materialism, the dialectical development of economic, social, and political structures, had the specific shape of European history. African Marxists argued that historical materialism could tell other stories: Africans need not be kept on the outside of the materialist dialectic. As the Guinea-Bissau revolutionary leader Amilcar Cabral said, imperialist domination inhibits or prevents the "development" of the aspects of African culture that do not conform to recognizable analogies with European history. Pan-Africanists needed to discover and reinforce the elements of African cultures that preceded or escaped any theory that used Europe as the model for what history fundamentally *is*. That is where the true dialectical struggle lies. As Cabral says, it is "within the culture that we find the seeds of opposition."[34]

The first step, then, was to recognize that feudalism isn't helpful because it obscures the field of history rather than enlightens it. From the vantage point of the twenty-first century, the Pan-African critique of Marxist historiography is a tragic one, not because it was wrong but because it was so right. Cabral was shot in 1973; Tom Mboya, the writer of the KANU "African socialism" paper, was shot in 1968.³⁵ It still isn't clear who was ultimately responsible for either assassination, but Mboya's death itself marked a significant change in the structure of governance in Kenya. Kenyatta began to develop increasingly obvious tendencies toward autocracy, precisely the kind of arrogation of power that Mboya and Kenyatta had argued over for several years. Kenyatta effectively suppressed the trade union movement in 1965 because he thought of it as Mboya's most important base of power.³⁶ Just a few days before Mboya's killer was executed in 1969, Kenyatta declared Kenya a one-party state. During the remainder of his rule, and to an even greater degree that of his successor Daniel arap Moi, Mboya's call to forget feudalism was itself forgotten in the systematic reinscription of feudalism in the laws of Kenya. To be blunter, Kenyatta reproduced the very conditions of the feudal system that he inveighed against in his 1938 ethnography of the Gĩkũyũ (which he wrote at the London School of Economics), *Facing Mount Kenya*.

As John Lonsdale puts it, Kenyatta consolidated his power though a policy of "ethnic feudalism," which "relied for loyalty on political tribalisms that competed for an abject dependence on the state."³⁷ In a 1996 speech in the Kenyan Parliament urging a new constitution, the opposition MP Kiraitu Murungi denounced both Kenyatta and Moi for creating the office not of president but of "a feudal monarch" with powers "greater than the powers of the governor at the height of colonialism." That declaration was followed by what the Hansard report notes as "*Loud applause.*"³⁸ The burgeoning sense by 1996 was certainly that feudalism still existed in Kenya, whether as a historical survival or as an analogy. Murungi blamed the survival of the colonial constitution, whose purpose was to protect British interests (Hansard, 946), a critique that was abundantly supported by the massively documented 2013 *Report of the Truth, Justice and Reconciliation Commission*, which argued that Kenyatta and Moi centralized power by institutionalizing the state's power of compulsory acquisition of land. This power, the *Report* argued, "was derived from the feudal notion that as sovereign, the state holds the radical title to all land within its territory."³⁹ Paul Ndung'u, the chair of the 2004 commission charged with investigating the theft of public lands in Kenya, suggested that this reoccupation of a feudal political order happened through "the deliberate mis-interpretation of the law by those in authority, by confusing the powers of an absolute Monarch with those of a President in a Republican State."[40] But, given the widespread condemnation of feudalism by figures like Kenyatta and Mboya as self-evidently irrelevant to Kenya's history, how did feudalism end up becoming part of its future?

It is possible to think about the persistence—or emergence—of serfdom in Kenya in two ways. The first is its appearance in metaphorical or literary work, in the immense attraction of feudal nostalgia to the colonial and postcolonial imagination. The second is the reproduction of actual feudal conditions—or at least such conditions as historians imagined them at the time—in pre- and postindependence writing about land. As the Ndung'u report demonstrated copiously, the system of land ownership was essentially one of feudal patronage; what the report didn't show was how extensively land in Kenya was already intractably configured as feudal, bearing with it the technical, legal, and ideological apparatus of a medieval system that had been refined in English courts and universities for centuries.

We will never know how Mboya might have overseen the dismantling of feudal law at the heart of colonial land ownership in Kenya. He still embodies the hope that Kenyatta betrayed so devastatingly. Kenyatta's betrayal of African socialism remains difficult to account for, unless we impute to him a greed so overwhelming that it obliterated his early vociferous defense in *Facing Mount Kenya* of traditional forms and rights of land ownership as a fundamental part of his own identity. Indeed, that book might not have been written had it not been for his commitment to defending traditional Gĩkũyũ land rights. Kenyatta first went to London in 1929 as the representative of the Kikuyu Central Association to try to press their case for land rights with the Secretary of State but returned in 1931 to testify before a Parliamentary Commission on East Africa. In 1932, he testified before the Carter Land Commission itself, whose report was published in 1934—the year that Kenyatta started studying at the London School of Economics with one of the most influential anthropologists and ethnographers of the twentieth century: Bronisław Malinowski. Kenyatta wrote *Facing Mount Kenya* while attending Malinowski's seminar, and Malinowski wrote an approving introduction, praising it as the first "competent" ethnography of Africa by an African.

Kenyatta and Malinowski Imagine Land

Facing Mount Kenya is, among other things, an ethnographical sublimation of Kenyatta's intense advocacy for Gĩkũyũ land rights. The first words of the preface are "The country of the Gĩkũyũ"; the third sentence mentions the 1,110,000 Gĩkũyũ who, at the time, were squatters on European farms because of the "alienation of agricultural and pastoral land" (xv). The preface describes Kenyatta's personal involvement in the various land commissions that have enabled him to "speak with more than ordinary knowledge . . . on the vitally important question of land tenure" (xv). He cites his expertise in land cases and commissions again at the start of the book's second chapter, "The Gĩkũyũ System of Land Tenure." His scrupulousness in defining his status as a participant-observer is partly due to Malinowski's own methodology, but it also underscores Kenyatta's larger point, which is that Gĩkũyũ culture is unthinkable without an orientation to the land. Land tenure, he argues, is "the most important factor in the social, political, religious, and economic life of the tribe." The earth is the "'mother' of the tribe . . . the most sacred thing above all that dwell in or on it" (21). For anyone "who wants to understand Gĩkũyũ problems," he says at the end of the preface, "nothing is more important than a correct grasp of the question of land tenure. For it is the key to the people's life" (xxi).

In demonstrating the importance of land, Kenyatta follows the explicit example of Malinowski's work. The book is so faithful to Malinowski's methods that it has been described as "a deadpan exercise in the functionalism of the later Malinowski," a description that wedges open a considerable difference between Malinowski and Kenyatta over what a functionalist reading of the book itself would be.[41] But even where Kenyatta asserts a reading of the singularity of the Gĩkũyũ origin of land ownership, its utter and mythic exceptionalism, it hews surprisingly close to the contours of Malinowski's theory of mythical function.

Kenyatta begins his description of land ownership with the myth of the creation of the first man, named Gĩkũyũ, by Ngai, who gave him "a territory full of the good things of nature" and who built his first house in a grove of fig trees "at a place called Mokorwe wa Gathanga, and had many children" (23). Kenyatta doesn't mention what Wangari Maathai and Ngũgĩ wa Thiong'o do in their versions of the myth: Mumbi, the wife's name; the fact that she was given the land at the same time; and that the "many children" were the ten daughters who were the mythic progenitors of the ten Gĩkũyũ clans.[42] And although Kenyatta doesn't explicitly say so, Mokorwe wa Gathanga is a real place—today generally called Mukurwe wa Nyagathanga—and the subject of intermittent struggles over its status as a uniquely Gĩkũyũ shrine.[43]

Kenyatta's myth of origin is not just an account of when Gĩkũyũ land ownership began. It is both a synchronic account of ownership—the first possession of land by Gĩkũyũ is just one kind of possession—and a diachronic account of the *evolution* of land rights. The originary moment is not an absent degree zero; rather, it is a localized inscription of a particular site that continues to legitimate all of the forms of land ownership. The story of origin that Kenyatta writes is precisely what Malinowski called a mythic charter, a narrative with a historical and legal function for communal owners of land. "Their territory," Malinowski says, "is related to them through mythological or historical legends which also establish their legal right to ownership."[44] The origin story reinforces the "conviction that only common descent and emergence from the soil give full rights to it." In fact, Kenyatta's deployment of the myth in *Facing Mount Kenya* follows Malinowski's description of the overall function of mythic charters so closely that one begins to wonder whether Kenyatta wrote it to conform to Malinowski's description of them. For Malinowski, the "traditional feeling of a real and intimate connection with the land; the concrete reality of seeing the actual spot of emergence in the middle of the scenes of daily life; the historical continuity of privileges, occupations, and distinctive characters running back into the mythological first beginnings—all this obviously makes for cohesion, for local patriotism, for a feeling of union and kinship in the community."[45] Kenyatta's origin account is a mythic version of the entanglement of land and history, in which "[c]ommunion with the ancestral spirits is perpetuated through contact with the soil in which the ancestors of the tribe lie buried" (*Facing*, 21). But it is a myth that situates itself at the specific site of the "actual spot of emergence," in the midst of the complex mechanisms of Gĩkũyũ culture. As if to enact in narrative its persistent importance in daily life, Kenyatta recounts the story twice: at the very beginning of *Facing Mount Kenya*, and at the beginning of the chapter on land tenure. The repetition only highlights its importance as the *form* of the mythic charter—that is, a specifically functionalist narrative, a story whose importance is its general social utility.

That is a slightly obscure way of saying that Kenyatta's account of land ownership owes a great deal to Malinowski. The mythic charter is not the only point at which there are clear filiations between the two thinkers. There are similar examples that could be taken from Malinowski's great work *Coral Gardens and Their Magic*, which he published in 1935, the year Kenyatta started taking his seminar. There are two moments in particular in *Coral Gardens* that seem to have legitimated Kenyatta's foregrounding of land in his ethnography. Although land is not as important, proportionately and affectively, in Malinowski's work, he still asserts that "land tenure enters very deeply into every aspect of human life, and it is the integral expression of all the ways in which man uses his land and surrounds it with the values of avarice, sentiment, mysticism and tradition."[46] But where this reads as a statement of a general functionalist principle for Malinowski, *Facing Mount Kenya* uses Malinowski's terms to argue that land for the Gĩkũyũ does more than just conform to one of the principles of contemporary ethnography: land tenure is "the most important factor in the social, political, religious, and economic *life of the tribe*" (21; my emphasis). The paradox here is that Kenyatta's vociferous and justified defense of the exceptionality of Gĩkũyũ land rights—its complex excess of conventional feudal categories—is "formulated," as Malinowski says in the preface to *Facing Mount Kenya*, "with the full competence of a trained Western scholar" (vii).

I want to suggest that there's something more than a methodological bind here. It is not just that Kenyatta would ideally use terms that are not infected or distorted by the language of land tenure in Western Europe. It is that the discourse of land itself is irremediably prejudiced by its origins in medieval land law. Thus, when Kenyatta clearly means to talk about original, or traditional, or precolonial land practices, he calls it "the question of land tenure," using the very language of inquiry from land commissions, a language that already destabilizes the originary legitimacy of primal land occupation. Land is a "question," once one invokes the category of "land tenure," because "tenure" is an imposition on a system of ownership already elaborated on its own terms, and in which "tenure" literally makes no sense.

Kenyatta, then, did not accidentally use the technical language of land inquiry, despite his training in ethnographic observation. Rather, the very training he received reproduced the discourse of feudal land tenure. Malinowski's enthusiasm for land as a kind of total social fact is a symptom of the lurking influence of that medieval legal tradition. Both legal and historical texts on land tenure in Malinowski's day taught that land law was the most important part of English law in general.[47] Indeed, the two chapters on land tenure (the second called simply "Land Tenure") are a substantial part of the two-volume work, and a moment at which Malinowski thinks through the larger questions of historical bias. Malinowski faults both himself and others for shaping their conceptions of culture according to normative European temporalities. But in perhaps less guarded moments, Malinowski resorts to progressivist notions of history, and unfurls the old feudal analogy: "In the various parts of our globe, there exist phases of civilization as far removed from ours as the Middle Ages."[48] It is probably easier now to see the biases that Malinowski tried to expunge. Michael Young, the author of a biography of Malinowski and editor of a collection of his fieldwork photography, faults him for the "rhetorical usage" in his early work, especially, of words like "aristocrat," "commoner," "vassal," "court, "tribute," "insignia of rank," and "hereditary office," words that are "redolent of feudal Europe rather than Melanesia."[49]

There is also the matter of the "mythic charter," a concept that, as we have seen, is thematically and structurally central to *Facing Mount Kenya*. Partly because it concerns land, the mythic charter is one of the most significant tenets of functionalism. Malinowski's theory shows how narrative is deeply instrumental (not in Max Weber's sense, nor quite in Fredric Jameson's, either). It establishes legitimacy by restating the past: the myth of origin that explains how a group came about, or how it possesses what it does, and that also asserts an inner historical logic that must be accepted as the principle of causation itself. Stories of origin, says Malinowski, "are to the natives a statement of a primeval, greater, and more relevant reality, by which the present life, fates, and activities of mankind are determined" ("Myth," 86). But this inner logic is not one that compels the observer, who is not called on to assent to the "greater, and more relevant reality" in what Malinowski would call the "legal" sense. In a trivial sense, the laws of land use do not really apply to the observer because he or she is not there to establish a land claim. In a more covert way, the ethnological bracketing of this "more relevant reality" also entails, for Malinowski, the rejection of historiographical causation—or, really, of the content of history itself. The content of the myth does not matter; what matters is the work that it does in the present, in recreating a narrative of origin that gives the patina of deep history to the group's claims of legitimacy. For Malinowski, a myth is *historia*, not *res*. It might determine "the present life, fates, and activities of mankind," but always a small subset of mankind—the natives or the "primitives" (in his diaries and letters Malinowski sometimes called them far worse). Malinowski is always interested in how the function of history is perceived, and in how that *perception* determines social activities, not in seeking out a historical explanation for behavior.

That is why Malinowski's governing metaphor for the function of myth—the charter—raises some problems. The charter is a peculiarly belated instrument of authority, developed in the Middle Ages for the establishment of rights to land. Malinowski sometimes calls it a "warrant," a term that comes directly out of Anglo-Norman land law ("Myth," 85). The authority of a charter sometimes rested on a form of mythic origin. In many cases, legitimate rights were inscribed in the charter because ownership could be traced to a time before history, or at least a time before Norman law, "beyond which the memory does not run." But its authority also rested on two implicitly antithetical principles. On the one hand, its status as a written instrument gave it an innate authority, which was further protected by the practice of indenture (two copies cut from an original parchment that had to be matched to establish their legitimacy). Charters were often seen as an instrument enabling oppressions, exclusions, and expropriations that were very real. In the Great Rising of 1381, for example, the rebels famously targeted charters, burning all of those belonging to the Abbey of Bury St. Edmunds, one of the largest landholders in medieval England.

The charter's written-ness was not, technically, what made it authoritative—writing just gave it the form of authority. What established its legitimacy was the event to which signing it attested, not the event of signing itself. As a medieval technology of ownership, it points back to the original sociological and local unity of the small group—the ceremony of conferring rights on a borough and its soon-to-be citizens, or subinfeudation and its witnessing by friends and relatives. It was often accompanied by a literal conveyance: the handing over of a piece of dirt. A charter is, then, in several senses, already mythic, already an assertion of something that happened in the past, something that we ourselves cannot witness. What commands our assent to that event is the written instrument—the form, and not the content, of history.

The self-cancelling nature of the charter embodies, or reifies, a larger contradiction in Malinowski's concept of the mythic charter. To reiterate: the mythic charter recounts an event of origin that gives it the authority to legislate—its meaning; but the authority to legislate actually comes from the structural demands of a group—in this case, the "land question," which gives the form of the mythic charter its urgency. The mythic charter is important because land is so important, not because the charter endows the land with significance. That might not be the logic that the Trobriand islanders would endorse, but it is precisely Malinowski's logic. Although Malinowski and his LSE medievalist colleague Eileen Power had significant issues with Weber's work, Malinowski's charter also shows how his synchronic, somewhat utopian functionalism gets dragged into Weber's logic of capitalist rationalization. Once "land tenure" is foregrounded, it becomes an end toward which everything else is organized and driven. The taxonomies of land possession that Malinowski and his students (including Kenyatta) routinely provide are precisely a capitulation to the demand that land be both legible and abstract. The mythic charter is itself an attempt to rationalize—or to mediate between—an ideology that, despite all of its disavowals, champions the primitive, the original, the feudal (or prefeudal), and the imperative to make sense of it in terms that modernity would recognize. Malinowski's charter does the work of Weberian instrumentality. It is driven toward an end that makes sense out of its means: it attempts to install an originary unity in order to assert that its meaning is land. This reified end, the "question of land," is both what legitimates the function of myth and, for the sociologist, what is actually missing in the socially symbolic work of the mythic charter. The charter is, essentially, what legitimates the ends of sociology: to supply not just what is missing in the symbolic, but to unearth the ends, the instrumentality, of cultural work.

One could say much more about the deep vitality of nostalgia in Malinowski's aspirations for a synchronic sociology, but the word "primitive" itself is a metonym of the repressed return of history in his work. It has two apparently antithetical senses: in ethnographic description (essentially, his early work), he uses the term indiscriminately for the people he is writing about. In his late work (especially in *Freedom and Civilization*), the word is emptied of its content as a signifier of historical development in general. He still talks about peoples and groups as "primitive," but his overarching purpose in the book is to show the formal similarities between "civilized" and "primitive" groups. History is the irrelevant domain of content and inner meaning, the site from which otherness and radical alterity emerges. What can be understood and, above all, written about are the formal similarities of social organization. In *Freedom and Civilization*, Malinowski argues that the charter performs the same function for every group, whether it mobilizes collectively to go fishing, or whether it divides the ends, the "collective purpose," of the group into factories and laboratories (161).

This leveling of history was a bit of an LSE thing. In her remarkable inaugural lecture, Eileen Power strongly contested the narrative that equates the emergence of capital with modernity: "The fundamental institutions and functions of modern times are found to be in existence far back in the Middle Ages."[50] Compared with other versions of historiography in England at the time, Power's is synchronic, pitched more to the sociologists at LSE than the medievalists at Oxford and Manchester. In many ways, *Freedom and Civilization* reads like an extended gloss on Power's lecture and its skepticism of teleological explanation, especially what she called "the application of an economic system to an economic epoch." Even history at LSE, then, was explicitly cynical about older Marxist teleology and, at the very least, agnostic about the existence, and the importance, of epistemic rupture. The only real exception for Malinowski, at least, was Nazism and fascism, which were the result of a nation's inability to read its own "sovereign charter" and the eventual submission to "the machine" of violent totalitarianism (*Freedom*, 222).

But, surprisingly for someone who wrote an article on violence and social organization, Malinowski does not have much to say about the violent domination of one group by another, even while he was writing the book in the middle of World War II. And, surprisingly for someone who wrote about land issues in East Africa, and who mentored Jomo Kenyatta, he has almost nothing to say about modern colonialism. What he does say is risibly utopian and depressingly familiar. He envisaged a "federation of nations" after the war that would "produce an enormous quantity and quality of liberties for each institution, each cultural group, each region, and the whole of humanity" (*Freedom*, 334). Even "preliterate peoples" "would enjoy an even greater amount of autonomy, tribal or national, than they now have" (335). That would be nice, but, as always, there are conditions. These "preliterate peoples" would have to accept "minimum tutelage" (335); Malinowski does not say how literacy fits into the program of autonomy, either negatively or positively (i.e., are we not really free unless we can read?), but presumably it is so that we can read our own charters, mythological or otherwise. What is really unaccountable is that the other condition of literate autonomy is *precisely* the condition under which the British ruled East Africa: indirect rule, the very system that Kenyatta was about to return to Kenya to fight. And Malinowski goes further than that: there would have to be an "exception," of course, to the autonomy of preliterate peoples "where raw materials exist which are necessary for mankind as a whole" (335). Malinowski's vision of hero anthropologists who would make up a "special colonial committee" to "advise and assist" these exploited preliterate groups does not really atone for the fact that he has just endorsed the British rationale for colonization and the method of its implementation.

Malinowski's vision is of a postwar world that has not changed so substantially that it cannot be put back together even better than before. That is not true of Kenyatta's study of the Gĩkũyũ. Although it is ostensibly a synchronic ethnography, it is deeply riven, indeed constructed, by the event of colonialism. His project is all about a diachronic devastation that made it impossible not to think of a "before" and "after" in Gĩkũyũ history, that made it, indeed, impossible not to think historically, although it is a history constituted as interruption. The analytical aspect of Kenyatta's chapter on land tenure, its Malinowskian method, comes to an abrupt end with the arrival of the Europeans. A brief paragraph refers to the "foregoing analysis" of "how the land was formerly acquired" (*Facing*, 44). The division of the book at that point signals the division of land by the Europeans, the point at which Kenyatta's narrative enters into history not by recounting just how Europeans made modern Kenya by expropriating the land, but by entering into the cultural terrain suggested by the nostalgic tone of that transitional paragraph.

It's a melancholy story, but it also partly concerns the possibility of a Gĩkũyũ mastery of history through the agency of prophecy. The story of the seer Mugo wa Kabiru, who prophesied the coming of the Europeans "many moons" before 1890, concerns precisely the legitimacy of narrative (*Facing*, 83). Mugo's prophecy was devastatingly accurate, and offered no apparent solution to the coming catastrophe. Its minimal effect, however, is to legitimate Kenyatta's interruption of Malinowskian method, and to interpose a mythic story before he recounts the end of Gĩkũyũ history. Its maximal effect is to legitimate Kenyatta's own version of prophecy.

The chapter ends, just a few pages later, with a beast fable—how an elephant stole an accommodating man's hut by gradually edging into it—that is also a devastating, hilarious parody of the bureaucratic forms and rationales of the Land Commission. There is a list of commissioners ending with "(4) The Rt. Hon. Mr. Fox to act as chairman; and (5) Mr. Leopard to act as Secretary to the Commission" (*Facing*, 49). Appealing to the principles of waste and efficiency, the elephant explains that he was entitled to space in the man's hut because, due to "unoccupied space in the hut, I considered it necessary, in my friend's own interests, to turn the undeveloped space to a more economic use by sitting in it myself" (50). The commission rules that the man's complaint was just the result of "a regrettable misunderstanding due to the backwardness of your ideas." The underlying problem is that the man had "not yet reached the stage of expansion which would enable [him] to fill it" (51).

Kenyatta's "traditional" analysis of how land was used "formerly" is halted, then, not by one narrative, but by two: one, mythical or legendary; the other, a combination of a supposedly traditional African genre and Swiftian satire. We could read the two stories as a sly indictment of the whole validity of the mythical charter, since it doesn't do much good if no one pays any attention to it. But it's also possible that Kenyatta intended a reading thoroughly within the horizon of functionalism, proposing that the content of the stories doesn't matter as much as the forms of legitimacy they confer. That, I think, is the ostensible lesson of Mugo's prophecy. Although it didn't change anything, it still told the truth. The *function* of the mythical charter, then, is to legitimate prediction—specifically the prediction of what would happen when the current forms of legitimation and law fail. In Kenyatta's narrative, it is fundamentally a question of what form a *legitimate* charter of possession can take. It can be neither the former modes of the Gĩkũyũ, nor the modes of feudal conveyance that Kenyatta lampoons.

The brilliant finale to the beast fable is somehow about both the way in which the violence of primitive accumulation is turned against itself and also the literal dead end of the European occupation of land. The man builds a large hut into which all the animals move. They then begin disputing about who has the "rights of penetration" to it (51). While they're occupied in the hut, the man burns it to the ground, "jungle lords and all" (52). The chapter on land tenure ends with the man's expression of what sounds like a proverb: "Peace is costly, but it's worth the expense"

(52). That proverb is also a prediction of what was to come in Kenya's future, with the so-called Mau Mau Uprising, for which Kenyatta was jailed by the British. The proverb can't quite be described as a call to revolutionary action, but along with the book's dedication to the "dispossessed youth of Africa [in] the fight for African Freedom, and in the firm faith that the dead, the living, and the unborn will unite to rebuild the destroyed shrines," it amounts to a pretty strong implication about what the book's real end is.

Ngũgĩ wa Thiong'o: Land before Time

For the great Kenyan novelist Ngũgĩ wa Thiong'o, Kenyatta's story remains predictive, a kind of mythic charter for the work of narrative after independence. Several of his novels are structured by, or feature importantly, the literal and metaphorical building of houses. But several of them also feature houses being burned down, most notably in *Petals of Blood*, *Wizard of the Crow*, and *Matigari*. The arson in the first two novels, especially in *Petals of Blood*, is a complexly signifying act—the flames of a brothel *are* the petals of blood, in a sense the mythic charter of the novel. In *Matigari*, the burning of the house belonging to the neocolonialist sell-out John Boy Junior comes at the end of the novel, occupying the same structural position as the man burning his hut does in Kenyatta's account of land tenure. Political leaders immediately confuse the burning of John Boy's house with insurrection, virtually doing the reader's work of turning the act into a national allegory for them. But where Kenyatta is circumspect, using traditional proverb rather than straightforward declaration, *Matigari*'s end is all about how the burning is an eminently political act of resistance. Rather than proverb, the crowd breaks into political slogan: "The property of those robbing the masses must burn!"; "Nationality-chauvinism must burn!"[51] That these slogans hover on the edge of parody is part of the complexity of Ngũgĩ's writing; the recurrent refrain that "Parratology" must burn becomes a parroting that either suggests the self-cancelling of political speech, or the inevitable self-indictment of all political speech. Part of the ambiguity of the ending—is Matigari alive or dead?—is a kind of metafictional game, but part of it, and perhaps the most important part, is the problem of whether a revolutionary act is ever dispositive.[52] Matigari emerges from the forest of the Mau Mau Uprising into modern Kenya, a reanimated figure of the revolutionary struggle that bought independence. But he has also been there all along: his name means, among other things, "remnant," and by the end of the novel the unresolved question of his presence becomes the question of whether the struggle will continue (the preface to *Petals of Blood* says simply *A luta continua!*). There *is* an answer in the book: the boy Muriuki, whose name means "resurrection," digs up the AK-47 that Matigari buries at the beginning of the book. There is more to that already overdetermined symbolism: the book ends with Muriuki standing under the tree where Matigari buried the gun, a tree that Ngũgĩ very pointedly reminds us on the last page is a *mugumo* tree.

The gun, in other words, is buried at either the literal or figurative site where Gĩkũyũ and Mumbi took possession of the land, and where Mugo prophesied—under the *mugumo* tree, whose other name *mukuyu* (Kenyatta spells it *mokoyo*) is the derivation of the name of the Gĩkũyũ people themselves. In other words, the entire novel is structured by the mythical charter of *Facing Mount Kenya*, although the means of its legitimacy, by the end of the novel, is quite clearly and literally the end of a gun. On the other hand, Kenyatta's portrait for the frontispiece of his own book does show him pointing to the end of a spear.

This is far from the only point at which Ngũgĩ takes up the feudal remnants of Kenyatta's ethnographic project, even amid his own revolutionary one. But Ngũgĩ's indebtedness to the remnants of feudal tenure is betrayed most explicitly when he reimagines the importance of land before the arrival of Europeans. The third sentence of the novel sets a standard for idealization that could hardly be exceeded: the river between two ridges is in "the valley of life."[53] But "life" is oddly constrained, bordered. The ridges are hermetic, "isolated," leaving the people "undisturbed by what happened outside or beyond . . . pure and intact, [the country] left alone, unaffected by turbulent forces outside" (1). The ridges are not yet part of a land administration so far beyond them that its origins lie in the European Middle Ages. They are resistant to the imposition of any history other than their own. Yet there already is a kind of creeping alienation going on of the kind that Marx calls commodity fetishism. The land has almost as much agency as the people: the ridges are like "sleeping lions which never woke. They just slept, the big deep sleep of their Creator." They "faced each other, like two rivals ready to come to blows in a life and death struggle for the leadership of this isolated region" (1). It's hard not to hear echoes of Hegel's account of the struggle for recognition, and its constitution of the historical process—and its explicitly feudal setting. The point here, of course, is that none of this has happened yet: the ridges still sleep the "big deep sleep of their Creator" and have not awoken into history, or at least the version of history from the European medieval past.

There is in fact history on the ridges. Here is where Gĩkũyũ and Mumbi stopped on their way to the original grove (Mukuruwe wa Gathanga), and where the great Mugo wa Kibiro was born. But to acknowledge the birth of Mugo is already to acknowledge, to some degree, the historical catastrophe that will eventually occur, even if the moment at the novel's opening is a precolonial idyll. And there is the history that is underwritten by a theology of origins, the work of creation that remains immanent but unactivated—the slumbering lions in the sleep of their Creator. There is history, but, to slightly misalign a term, it is not woke.[54] This history of origins contains its own negation, as all origins do: their legacy is an essential passivity in which any action undermines the theological postulate of an origin. The origin becomes, instead, a beginning, an entrance into "secular" history (a form of history we discussed earlier in the chapter on Auerbach). That is, history begins to be made up of stories that could begin almost anywhere.

This possibility, in fact, is staged in the first few pages of *The River Between*. Lurking behind the story of the ridges is the unitary story of Gĩkũyũ origin (noted above). But from the start, the novel presents the story as a potential antagonism between the two ridges. Both claim to be the place Gĩkũyũ and Mumbi stayed on their way to Mukurwe: on those grounds, the Kameno ridge claims that "spiritual superiority and leadership had been left there," while the ridge Makuyu claims that "leadership had been left" to it (2, 1). The claim that each makes ultimately undermines the originary force of the myth of origin. Why does the myth of origin need to be a zero-sum game? Why couldn't Gĩkũyũ and Mumbi have stopped at both places? It is not the content of the myth that is at stake, but the legitimizing function it performs: it determines which ridge will be the leader. The unitary mythic origin becomes precisely a mythic charter, a story that supports the evidence of a specific site. As the novel says, "Kameno had a good record to bear out this story" (2). Its two main exhibits are a sacred grove and a long string of heroes, including Mugo wa Kibiru; Makuyu has a small hill where Gĩkũyũ and Mumbi stood, and where God (Murungu) promised them the land.

Even the mythic origin of land use is replaced by possible stories based on the evidence about when possession, ownership, or sovereignty began. It is true that the novel suggests that the leadership disputes between the two ridges were only latent, slumbering just like the ridges themselves. Yet the novel also suggests that these claims have been troublesome enough that they have been adjudicated, and that the *form* of this evidence is an important part of their meaning. The list of heroes who come from Kameno doesn't bring to light some subterranean connection between the divine origin of Kameno's authority and its heroes, which each of them confirms in turn; rather, it is a genealogy that attempts to insert an authoritative beginning in the place of a divine origin.

Similarly, the grove in Kameno is described as a "good record," a term that describes the value of a piece of evidence in a forum of juridical inquiry. Perhaps because it lacks the legitimizing force of heroic genealogies, Makuyu must resort to displaying its small hill and reiterating the claim that Murungu gave the land to them, through Gĩkũyũ and Mumbi. But—and this is the point toward which I have been aiming—Makuyu demonstrates its claim in the form of a medieval legal charter. Murungu, say the people of Makuyu, told them "This land I give to you, O man and woman. It is yours to rule and till, you and your posterity" (3). It is a record that contains the three elements of a gift or conveyance of land in the Middle Ages: the formulas "I have given and granted" (*dedi et concessi*); the concession to future generations as well (*heredibus*, to heirs); and the formula "to rule and till," which repeats one of the most popular conceptions about land ownership under the "feudal" system, that tillage is a primal marker of the right of possession. Speaking on the feudal nature of the "land question" in Ireland, John Stuart Mill argued that the Irish people believe that "the right to hold the land goes as it did in the beginning with the right to till it."[55]

A medieval charter, just like a mythic charter, is powerful because it is a record that can perpetually repeat the original event. Ngũgĩ's novel, too, is a charter that reasserts the primal moment of land ownership. In the fourth and fifth chapters, the protagonist, Waiyaki, is taken by his father to a hill, from which they look down at the ridges, a sly repetition of the master-of-all-I-survey trope of European exploration narratives.[56] But this moment also conjures the originary moment of human (that is, Gĩkũyũ) occupation. There is "no sign of life" on the ridges they look down on— because of the distance, perhaps, but also because they are situated at the moment before there was anyone alive to settle the land (*River*, 16–17).

This scene repeats two of the significant episodes in the history of the expropriation of Gĩkũyũ land. Waiyaki is also the name of the Gĩkũyũ leader who made an agreement to lease land to then-Captain Lugard in 1890, which was the moment when Kenyatta's elephant was allowed to enter the hut—and the year that Kenyatta gives for the fulfillment of Mugo wa Kibiru's prophecy. Chege, Waiyaki's father in the novel, is another name for Mugo wa Kibiru, whose prophecy the novel's Chege recounts at that precise moment. Indeed, Chege goes on to reveal to Waiyaki that his own genealogy begins with Mugo wa Kibiru, but concludes with the melancholy observation that Waiyaki is "the last in our line" (19). This originary moment before time is also the eschatological moment, the end of time. The anxiety about the double demand of temporality runs through this moment, and structures the charter at its heart.

Chege seems to repeat Kameno's mythic charter at this point: "In the beginning of things . . . Murungu brought the man and woman here and . . . gave the country to them and their children and the children of their children, *tene na tene*, world without end" (18).[57] While subtly different from the first, this version of the mythic charter adheres at least as closely to the forms of the medieval charter. In Ngũgĩ's novel, there is the *dedi* formula (he "gave the country") and the *heredibus* formula ("their children and the children of their children"). But this version adds a final formula: "*tene na tene*, world without end." The translation here, "world without end," conjures, perhaps, Cranmer's phrase in the Book of Common Prayer. But in the context of possession rather than theology it echoes the closing clause of many medieval charters, *per saecula saeculorum*.[58]

Yet perhaps the best-known instance of it is not in the legal archive but in a novel that Ngũgĩ most surely knew. Walter Scott's *Waverly* satirizes a baron obsessed with the arcane Anglo-Norman and Latin minutiae of the charters that granted his ancestors their land. He argues, for example, that the barony had to be a male fief, because the original charter grants land in exchange for pulling off the king's boots after battle (*in servitio exuendi, seu detrahendi, caligas regis post battaliam*), which, he says, a woman obviously could not do. He grieves over the loss of part of his estate, which, he says, now "passes from the lineage that should have possessed it in saecula saeculorum."[59] The charter formula is invoked by its failure, by the loss of something that should have remained forever—just as the possession of the land of the Gĩkũyũ "*tene na tene*, world without end" is reiterated precisely because of the tragedy at the heart of *Facing Mount Kenya* and *The River Between*.

In *The River Between*, the moment of creation—the moment at which land comes into being—is hedged with repetitions: the threefold repetition of the sleep of the ridges after creation; the several places where Gĩkũyũ and Mumbi stopped, each of which is the beginning of different genealogies of leadership, but each of which is not the final; and the original grove of Mukuruwe wa Gathanga. The bestowal of land itself comes as a repetition, the charter that creates land ownership, but which also presupposes the entire genealogy of a technology of land registration. As Simon Gikandi says of the myths of origin in the novel, they are "haunted by the language of the Bible and the colonial event."[60] These myths of origin are quite literally mythic charters, using the very language of medieval land registration, a technology that preexists colonization but that made it thinkable. And it now means that the concept of land is unthinkable without those feudal terms, not just haunting it but calling it into being.

Kenyatta's account of Mumbi and Gĩkũyũ taking possession of the land became the canonical account of creation after the publication of *Facing Mount Kenya*, but Godfrey Muriuki argues that there are multiple accounts of the origin of the Gĩkũyũ. The genealogical evidence of the clans suggests a number of different points of origin beside Mukuruwe; there is the story of Mumbi and Gĩkũyũ; and there is a story about a dying man giving each of his sons a choice of a place to live. None of the sources Muriuki cites for the Mumbi story is before Kenyatta's book (although I could add to the list a book that came out in in 1933, Gathigira's *Miikarire ya Agĩkũyũ*); all of the sources for the last story are from 1910 or before.[61] Those early studies were written before British land settlement had really begun; land was allocated, but the Protectorate had been unable to interest settlers. The 1919 land settlement scheme for soldiers was perhaps the point when the land that had merely been "scheduled" by the Protectorate began actually to be occupied. That is perhaps the reason that the 1910 ethnography of the Gĩkũyũ by William Scoresby Routledge and Katherine Routledge devotes only two pages to land ownership, following sections on "Snuff" and "Raiment," and an earlier sentence on the possibility that land could be "entailed."[62] The book uses the term "tenure" just once, in Katherine Routledge's short conclusion, which frames the conclusion as the "fulfillment of a solemn promise" to tell the English public that Gĩkũyũ land is private property and cannot be "given away" (329).

In retrospect, the conclusion is situated at the exact moment when "land" begins to become a political reification in Kenya, conjured into existence by the encroachment of the discourse of feudal tenure. That is precisely why Routledge uses the term "security of tenure" here: to urge the English to respect a right that will already have existed only once it is recognized. But that recognition will bring with it the whole compressed historiography of the struggle between lord and bondsman. Routledge intuits that this will happen, but also dismisses it as unlikely: "It seems highly improbable that the Akikúyu . . . would ever achieve sufficient combination for a united attempt to throw off British rule; but it is quite conceivable that, if unwisely dealt with from headquarters, the native might be inspired to make trial of strength in a way that would issue in terrible tragedy in the case of isolated settlers" (332).

Routledge was wrong that the Gĩkũyũ would never unite against the British, but she was right about the scale of the violence that resulted from the British expropriation of land. Kenyatta's fable invoked not a physical hut that would be burned down to achieve peace, but the burning hut as a national allegory. In many ways, the conflagration of the "Mau Mau" struggle was also the means by which a form of unity was achieved: one of the recurrent motifs in the oaths that fighters took was a pledge to "the movement of Unity."[63] The oaths were often inflected by the particular version of Gĩkũyũ history found in Kenyatta's book: they made the oath takers children of Mumbi and Gĩkũyũ who swore never to sell their land to any white man.[64] The oath is perhaps the quintessential anti-charter: it pledges to undo what the technology of the charter has done, yet its object is still at least partly constituted by that charter. Land remains something that it had not been before: something that can be sold, and something that can be expropriated or stolen.

The figure of a burning hut that makes peace possible is, of course, deeply ambiguous. The irony of Kenyatta's rule is that the man in the allegory discovers that he can never occupy the land where the hut once stood because another man is already living there. Kenyatta's former personal secretary, J. M. Kariuki, who took an oath to protect the land as a child of Mumbi, called him out publicly for land grabbing in the 1970s.[65] Kariuki's body was discovered by a roadside in 1975, burned. A sacred *mugumo* tree had fallen the day before.

CHAPTER EIGHT

Fanon Outside History: Manicheism, Augustine, and Hegel

> When I look for man in European techniques and styles I see a succession of negations of man, an avalanche of murders.
>
> FRANTZ FANON

> Hear first, if you please, what happened before the constitution of the world, and how the battle was carried on, that you may be able to distinguish the nature of light from that of darkness.
>
> MANI, quoted by Augustine

Which Manicheism?

It is because of Frantz Fanon that an esoteric gnostic religion that was last popular in late antique North Africa became an important part of the lexicon of revolutionary struggle and postcolonialism. Manicheism, probably best known to medievalists because of its formative, and then adversarial, role in the thinking of Augustine of Hippo (354–430), provided Fanon with an analogy for white supremacism in his massively influential 1952 book *Peau noire, masques blancs* (*Black Skin, White Masks*). For the person of color, the world is divided into the stark oppositions of "Good–Evil, Beauty–Ugliness, White–Black," and for Fanon this is a "genuinely Manichean concept of the world."[1] Fanon uses the term "Manichean" only twice in *Black Skin, White Masks,* although he underscores its importance, asking his readers to commit it to memory: "the word [Manichean] has been spoken, it must be remembered" (31).

But what kind of remembering are we asked to do? The answer, as often with Fanon, is both immediate and more complicated than it seems: "White or black, that is the question." It's an answer that is literally a question, and it's a question that really does not demand an answer, because, and this is Fanon's whole point, the answer is predetermined, already decided: once the question is even asked, the answer is "white." So why bother to remember, and remember something as arcane as Manicheism? In an important sense, Fanon does just that kind of remembering when he comes back to the concept of Manicheism in his later, incendiary *Les damnés de la terre* (*The Wretched of the Earth*), published in 1961, nine years after *Black Skin, White Masks*. He not only refines the concept of manicheism, but he also seems to have engaged in historical remembering of the late antique phenomenon of Manicheism. It is not incidental that the last important arena of Manicheism was the part of North Africa where Fanon was living, and that its most important conduit was through the writing of another North African thinker: Augustine.

Much of the "manicheism" of *The Wretched of the Earth* seems informed by a deeper knowledge of Augustine's anti-Manichean polemic. It was Fanon's presence in Algeria, and his involvement in the struggle for Algerian independence, that seems to have activated the latent metaphors that manicheism already held in his writing. In fact, one of Fanon's colleagues in the resistance was to become one of the most important Augustine scholars of the twentieth century: André Mandouze, whose writings on both Augustine and the Algerian struggle are almost equally voluminous. Mandouze published two resistance journals, *Consciences algériennes* and *Consciences maghrébines*, that printed Fanon's articles. And Fanon's wife, Josie Fanon, attended Mandouze's seminars on Augustine at the University of Algeria at the same time.[2]

At the very least, I want to show that Fanon's use of the concept of manicheism in *The Wretched of the Earth* is extraordinarily attuned to the work of remembering, as well as to the historical and Augustinian resonances of Manicheism, resonances that have been overlooked in the assimilation of the term to a general, globalized, and vague theory of postcolonialism. Perhaps more than any single work, Abdul JanMohamed's important 1983 book *Manichaean Aesthetics: The Politics of Literature in Colonial Africa* made "manicheism" part of the necessary kit of tropes in postcolonial theory, but that book quotes Fanon on manicheism in just one place and does not discuss what Fanon might have meant beyond a superficial paraphrase.[3]

Fanon's ironic fate, although it is one he predicted, is that his own thinking tends to be confused with the absolute polarizations that he identified in the colonial world. This misreading has been a common way to dismiss Fanon's critique in general. Malvern van Wyk Smith, using mostly secondhand quotations of Fanon, criticizes Fanon's "naive dramaturgy of racial conflict" and his "morality-play version of racial contestation."[4] But deeper, more sophisticated, readers of Fanon also misread him in this way. Paul Gilroy's *Against Race*, which uses an epigraph from Fanon at the beginning of each section, and which acknowledges the complexity and subtlety of Fanon's thought, also argues that "his thinking remains bound to a dualistic logic" and a "binary code almost as pernicious as the manichean dualism that he sought to supplant."[5] In what follows, I hope it will become clear that, while Fanon certainly thinks in terms of oppositions, his thinking should not be confused with the erstwhile object of colonial racism. With devastating rigor and honesty, he shows, again and again, how experience in the colonial world is reduced to the subjugation of the colonized by the colonizer, of Black by white. But part of his horror over this situation, if only a somewhat detached and abstract part, is motivated by his distaste for the implacable but sophistical logic of this reduction, its refusal to move beyond a primary—yes, even primitive—confrontation.

It might help to think of Fanon as a deeply Hegelian thinker, for whom oppositions, denials, and negations are not just the way thought works, but also a part of thought itself. Fanon's work, I think, is especially attuned to what Hegel described as absolute negation, "the innermost source of all activity, of all animate and spiritual self-movement, the dialectical soul that everything true possesses and through which alone it is true" (*Science*, 169, 836). At one point, Hegel calls the negative the power of thinking itself. What is horrifying for a Hegelian is when thought comes to an end, when an opposition never moves beyond itself. Fanon's Hegelian loathing of colonialism centers on its fixity, what Fanon referred to as petrification or "substantialisation," of the past as a frozen statue, a "stagnation where gradually dialectic has changed into the logic of equilibrium" (*ce mouvement immobile où la dialectique, petit à petit, s'est muée en logique de l'équilibre*).[6] At the end of *Black Skin,*

White Masks, Fanon rails against the past, to which Black people, he says, are slaves. Another part of Fanon's contempt is reserved for bourgeois culture, but precisely because of its fixation on the past: it is "rigidified in predetermined forms, forbidding all evolution, all gains, all progress, all discovery" (175).[7]

While this might sound as if Fanon is rejecting any orientation toward the past—and there are many passages in both of his major books that do, indeed, sound like that—his work is shot through with references to history. While he might say that "the past can in no way guide me in the present moment," or that he does not have the "right" to allow himself "to be mired in what the past has determined," he does indeed draw from it throughout his work (*Skin*, 175, 179). He certainly draws from it in order to critique that bourgeois, colonialist "petrification," but he also draws from it as an active thinker himself, steeped in Hegelian ways of conceiving history as an active, creative, synthetic phenomenon—as change itself (*Skin*, 179). At the end of *Black Skin, White Masks*, Fanon seems to embrace a kind of humanist universalism that he does not necessarily countenance, at least not as directly, in *Wretched*, in which the possibility of future action lies in a reconfiguration of a past that is exterior, somehow, to the petrified history given to us by the pedagogy of colonialism. "I am a man," Fanon states in one moment, "and what I have to recapture (*reprendre*) is the whole past of the world" (*Skin*, 176).[8] In another, he declares "I am not the slave of the Slavery (*l'Esclavage*) that dehumanized my ancestors" (*Skin*, 179; *Peau*, 186). The echo of Hegel's *Phenomenology of Spirit* here, amplified by the capitalization of *l'Esclavage* in the French edition, is not accidental. These two sentences read as a virtual restatement of the crux of the most influential reading of Hegel's "master/slave" dialectic in Fanon's day, Alexandre Kojève's *Introduction à la lecture de Hegel*: "In transforming the world through his work, the slave (*l'Esclave*) transforms himself and thus creates the new conditions which allow him to recapture (*reprendre*) the liberation struggle."[9] Where Kojève is full of optimism about recapturing the struggle for liberation, Fanon only holds out the possibility that there is a past that has, thus far, escaped the machine of *l'Esclavage*. That past that could be recaptured, at the same time, is nothing less than the past of the entire world.

Fanon is full of surprising reversals and demurrals like this, reversals that seem to turn into a corner where only bitter despair lies, yet also open onto possibilities far beyond the mere recuperation of the moment.

Notice that Fanon remembers the passage from Kojève not for its celebration of the inevitable renewal of the struggle for revolution, but for its endorsement of the underlying vitality of history—for the possibility that a history beyond the enforced polarizations of manichean colonialism can still be recaptured.

Nevertheless, *The Wretched of the Earth* begins with an infamous chapter on violence, which seems to reject resoundingly the kind of optimism for a universal humanity that Fanon imagines at the end of *Black Skin, White Masks*. Perhaps more than his deployment of the term "manichean," this work has been responsible for Fanon's reputation as an uncompromising, polarized, binary thinker. The first copies of *The Wretched of the Earth* were confiscated because of that reputation, and Fanon's former assistant in Tunis says that after its publication even those supposedly close to him regarded him as a "bloodthirsty maniac."[10] Almost a decade later, Hannah Arendt acknowledges the complexity of Fanon's theory of violence, and points out (although in a footnote) that "Fanon himself . . . is much more doubtful about violence than his admirers" and that "only the book's first chapter, 'Concerning Violence,' has been widely read."[11] Yet the prominence of that first chapter of *Wretched* seems to pull her irresistibly toward a cruder characterization of Fanon's total theory. She puts Fanon together with thinkers who "glorify violence for violence's sake," a position manifestly different from her more balanced assessment of Fanon in her book's notes (65). Sartre's own reading of Fanon, and his preface to the first edition of *Wretched of the Earth*, may have helped to shape Arendt's cruder version of Fanon—and that of many in her wake. Sartre's preface, Arendt implies, has reduced Fanon's argument to a simpler but even more pungent version: "'Violence,' he now believes, on the strength of Fanon's book, 'like Achilles' lance, can heal the wounds it has inflicted'" (20).[12] Even if Sartre has simplified Fanon's argument, Arendt's rhetoric suggests that Fanon's theory of violence exerts a malevolent influence, a "strength" that implicitly exculpates Sartre from total responsibility for the more totalizing violence he advocates in that preface. Later in the book, Arendt implies that Fanon's theory of violence necessitates an ontology of primal *agon*, the notion that "where we have life we have struggle and unrest" (69). She links this worldview to the French right-wing thinker Georges Sorel, whose vision of uncompromising struggle, she implies, sprang out of his disillusionment with the supporters of Alfred Dreyfus and his subsequent disgust with democracy and embrace of anti-Semitism. Arendt attributes Fanon's immediate acceptance of the possibility of violence to his involvement in the Algerian War, which is what seems to have given him "an infinitely greater intimacy with the practice of violence" (71). What is surprising, given Arendt's deployment of the language of cosmological struggle here, and her own sympathy for intellectual history, is that she does not mention, in her genealogy of the Fanonian theory of violence, the primal importance of struggle in Manichean cosmology.

All but one of Fanon's invocations of manicheism in *The Wretched of the Earth* come in the initial chapter on violence, and the link between manicheism and violence is tacit, if not always spelled out plainly, as when he says that the colonialist's slogan—"it's them or us"—is the result of the "organization of a Manichean world" (43). In "classical" Manicheism, the battle between light and dark began even before the creation of the world, and the most fundamental fact about the world we live in is that the elemental struggle still continues.[13] As it happens, one of the best sources for this information is Augustine, who was a Manichean disciple for a time, and who spent a large part of his career debunking Manicheism. One of the ironies of Augustine's struggle against Manicheism is that his quotations became our important sources for its worldview. It is possible to see the entirety of Augustine's work, in fact, as a response to his earlier dalliance with Manicheism.[14] In what follows, I would like to explore the possibility that Fanon's use of manicheism, especially in his late work *The Wretched of the Earth*, is bound up with Augustine's own struggle with Manicheism, and the not-irrelevant fact that much of this struggle happened just about where Fanon was engaged in his own struggle, in modern-day Algeria and Tunisia.[15]

I have already suggested that Fanon's manicheism is more complicated and elusive than the static dualism he is credited with in postcolonial shorthand. One of the many ironies of this fate is that Fanon's use of the term "manichean" is deceptively complex, hedged around with qualifications that make it difficult to pin down what, exactly, manicheism actually is. Fanon writes in a seductively simple style, and many of his sentences come as virtually ready-made apothegms. Yet almost every one of them contains depths that betray his intense engagement with intellectual history. Read properly, Fanon's texts prompt the reader to pause frequently, to think about the layers of irony that wrap a sentence, or about the way in which Fanon invokes a complex aspect of the Hegelian dialectic. So when Fanon uses the term "manichaean" to describe what only seems to be a simple binary, the death struggle of white and Black race relations in the colonial era, that simple opposition is rapidly subsumed.[16]

Indeed, his description of this supposed binary unravels even as he writes:

> The people who in the early days of the struggle had adopted the primitive Manicheism of the colonizer—Blacks versus Whites, Arabs versus *Roumis*—realize en route that some Blacks can be whiter than the Whites, and that the prospect of a national flag or independence does not automatically result in certain segments of the population giving up their privileges and their interests. The people realize that there are indigenous populations like themselves (*des indigènes comme lui*) who, far from missing the chance (*lui ne perdent pas le nord*), seem to take advantage of the war to better their material situation and reinforce their burgeoning power. These profiteering elements realize considerable gains from the war at the expense of the people (*Les indigènes trafiquent et réalisent de véritables profits de guerre aux dépens du peuple*) who as always are prepared to sacrifice everything and soak the national soil with their blood (*Damnés*, 138; *Wretched*, 93–94; translation modified).

Note that Fanon describes this colonizer's perspective as "primitive" manicheism. He seems to define it as a kind of manicheism different from an evolved, sophisticated, or complex manicheism, a manicheism that has nothing to do with the people (as yet); a colonial import. But it also bears the sense of "original," a sense that becomes increasingly ironic in the next two sentences. Fanon talks about the dawning realization on the part of the "people" that some of their own exploit others during crises, becoming "whiter than the Whites." Yet these exploiters, initially part of the people, are distanced as *des indigènes comme lui*, sharing an identity but somehow different precisely because of the need to compare them with the rest of the people. It is a phrase, too, that makes clear that these are not "people" in general, but the *indigènes* of the French *Code de l'indigènat*, excluded in perpetuity as a group "inapt for politics," in the words of the Algerian philosopher Sidi Mohammed Barkat.[17] Reinforcing this sense, Philcox translates the phrase as "indigenous elements in their midst," while Constance Farrington's 1963 English translation uses the word "natives" for *indigènes*, retaining some of the reactionary flavor of the word but losing the French connotations of legal status and, ultimately, of autochthonous identity.[18] The irony that emerges in these three sentences is that the part the Whites played in the first "primitive Manicheism" is now played by *indigènes*, by people who come to occupy the place of the primitive, in every sense, in the dynamic of exploitation. These exploitative *indigènes* reinscribe the narrative that domination is originary, that colonization is legitimate because domination is an indigenous phenomenon. It is not just that Blacks now do it, so the culpability is diffused, but that their emergence as a dominating class creates the fiction that exploitation itself is an indigenous phenomenon. It is a much subtler version of the argument that colonization is justified by the strife that preceded it, but it is the same argument. What I want to call attention to, however, is the way that Fanon twists the connotations of the word *indigène* here. It first appears as a synonym for "people"—but a people that is not *all* the people. It next appears as a term that differentiates itself from the people (*Les indigènes trafiquent et réalisent de véritables profits de guerre aux dépens du peuple*). Indigeneity, in Algeria both the marker of autochthonous identity and of subjugated status, is also, in this passage, ultimately the marker of a colonized mentality. When war came along, these emergent indigenous oppressors, Fanon sarcastically says, *ne perdent pas le nord* (translated in 1963 as "did not lose sight of the main chance" and more recently by Philcox as "far from being at loose ends") (Farrington, 144; *Wretched*, 93). The literal sense of the French ("they did not lose the north") idiomatically suggests that they maintained their sense of direction. But the devastation of the irony lies in their emergence, in this passage, as the "true" *indigènes* who are oriented (so to speak) away from Algeria, north toward France.

This passage shows how rich Fanon's critique of colonialism is. It does not just argue that colonialism takes away a people's identity; it also shows how that identity gets taken away within the unfolding of language itself. It is almost impossible to write about the phenomenon of the colonial mentality from the outside, precisely because it is so inescapable a phenomenon that it shapes perception itself. But this passage also reveals how diegetic, diachronic, and historical Fanon's indictment of colonialism can be. Not only does it account for the ways that the perception of the colonized and colonizers changes according to the unfolding of the historical dialectic—that is, Fanon's is also a phenomenological account of domination—but it continually points back to the deep historical roots of colonial domination.

From the outset of this passage, Fanon makes it impossible to think of this "primitive manicheism" as a simple binary outside of time. There are *les Blancs et les Noirs*, yes, but there are also, immediately and inseparably from them, *les Arabes et les Roumis*; the Farrington translation called this last group "Christians" (144) while the more recent translation by Philcox opts for "Infidel" (93). It is not clear how the two groups relate to each other: are they simply two opposing pairs in parallel? Is there no difference between them? Is the second group a subset of the first, a more particularized, Maghrebian version? If so, where do the people who are neither Arab nor Christian, the people who were imagined by colonial ethnographers to be the true *indigènes* of Algeria, the Berbers, belong? There is also a complex play of deterritorialization behind the word *Roumis*: usually identified as originally an Arabic word, it arrived in Arabic from Ottoman Turkish, and was originally used to describe members of the Byzantine empire (who were not, to confuse things further, *Italian* Romans). Fanon's point here, of course, is that this manicheism might be primitive, but it is not simple. It is adaptable but contradictory and immensely versatile at hiding those contradictions. That is, it does not stand outside of history—in fact, it is a certain aspect of the writing of history itself. Fanon's sly exposure of the rootedness of "manicheism" in history is a way of calling attention to its very reinscription of history. Indeed, as I will argue later, the very term "manicheism" is an example of Fanon's insistence on colonialism's entanglement in history.

The term "Roumis" hints at the historical force of "manicheism" for Fanon. As the first English version of Fanon attests, its primary sense in Algeria is "Christian," but French colonial historiography believed that the term survived from the Roman colonization of North Africa. Henri Leclercq, an eminent historian of the early church in Africa, argued that the ruined churches of late antiquity had not just an archaeological significance, but also a political use (*utilité politique*). Those who the *indigènes* have named the *Roumis*, he says, "are in their eyes, and must be in reality, the descendants and the inheritors of those who so long ago so gloriously and so efficiently governed the land."[19] The *perception* of this connection by the *indigènes* is partly what legitimates the rule of these new masters, but, as Leclercq goes on to say, so does the re-appropriation of the Roman past by the new colonizers. It is the very respect that these successors of the Romans have for the ancient monuments of Christian North Africa that legitimates their larger cultural work, which is to restore *l'oeuvre de civilisation* itself (1073).[20] The opposition between Arabs and *Roumis* is thus, like all of Fanon's manichean oppositions, the product of a historical narrative. But it is a narrative that doubles back on itself: the new colonizers are the *Roumis*, who are called that because they are the inheritors of the old colonizers, who preceded the Arabs, the people they now colonize. To compound the complexity, the *indigènes* are not even a term in that opposition: the Berbers are neither Arab nor *Roumi*, unless one considers the isolated testimony of colonial-era travelers that the Kabyle occasionally saw themselves as *Roumis*.[21] The opposition is hardly dualist, or at least not the same intractable colonial opposition that Fanon is primarily talking about. What is "primitive" about this manicheism, according to the fantasized historiography that Fanon is critiquing, is that it now seems to be an *original* manicheism, a dualism that existed before the Arabs arrived and thus so antique that it has begun to edge into an ontology.

This process of making history more solid and certain than it actually was is what Fanon refers to as petrification. It is not just history, strictly speaking, but a politics that shapes the present in the image of a supposed past, even—and especially—when national parties are attempting to break free of the colonial past. The urban elites, says Fanon, act on the assumptions they have inherited from the colonizers about the rural masses: they have only the *impression* that the latter are "bogged down in their inertia and futility" (*s'enliser dans l'inertie et dans l'infécundité*) (*Damnés*, 109; *Wretched*, 65; translation modified). It is not so much, speaking precisely, that the elites put in place policies to reinforce the backwardness, the atavism of the countryside, but that colonization has already subjugated the rural populace "by an organized petrification of the peasantry" (*Wretched*, 65). The countryside, then, is not just backward; it is a historical artifact, although it remains one only because it is actively preserved. Colonial officials are thus like a frame around the rural masses they supervise. Fanon's word for supervision is *encadrer*, which also means "framing": the metaphor implies that colonial officials are a defensive barrier that, like a new frame around an old picture, sets off the quaint antiquity of the countryside (*Damnés*, 109; *Wretched*, 65). Historicity, then, is something that is both exhibited and actively maintained and guarded. The colonial frame of the past guards both inside and outside: it keeps those within its borders in a suspended state of development—it keeps them "historical"—and it reassures the urban elite, the national parties, of their place, by contrast, in the outside of modernity.

Manicheism and Dialectic

It is precisely the opposition between modernity and premodernity that is at stake for Fanon, an opposition that colonialism stages as a recapitulation of the Marxist development of urban capitalism out of, and beyond, rural economies. The rural and the medieval merge inside the frame. The masses of the countryside, in Fanon's words, "still live in a feudal state (*stade féodal*)" in an all-powerful "medieval structure (*structure moyenâgeuse*)" (*Damnés*, 109; *Wretched*, 65). Although Fanon does not spell this out explicitly, the "feudal" and medieval quality of the countryside is an invention, a back-formation of the whole colonial enterprise: the feudal metaphor. The economic and cultural history of the European Middle Ages is written onto the Algerian landscape, the rigid lines of its discourse enforced at every level of administration. These "feudal overlords" defend their power by keeping the countryside feudal, by resisting the modernity represented by the "young Westernized nationalists" of the towns and cities because it will "threaten the fundamental sustainability of feudalism (*le principe même de la pérennité des féodalités*)" (*Damnés*, 110; my translation). The enemy is not, ultimately, the colonial occupier, but a historical one; or, rather, the forces of history themselves: the *modernistes* who intend to dismantle *la société autochtone*, the autochthonous, true indigenous society that, in this alternate history, has not been altered by the arrival of colonialism. Yet it is colonialism itself that designates its members as *indigènes*, people who have both a primary claim to the land and virtually none, precisely because their historical status has made them, so to speak, miss out on modernity.

Fanon's lucid summary of the historical dialectic of colonialism hides, at almost every turn, dizzying contradictions and reversals like this. It is precisely the simplicity of his prose that leads readers into thinking that manicheism is a straightforward process. We tend to think: yes, it is; it's simply a matter of dividing the world into black and white. But having identified that division, with Fanon's help, as the primary process of colonialism, we also discover that there is no other process. Once we divide the world, it is too late to think of other divisions, or of a world without any. The *masses rurales* become the backward agrarian populace of the capitalist, urban revolution; the original people become the indigenous excluded from full, legal representation; the nationalist leader becomes a mere bourgeois disrupter of tradition. The horror of colonialism is not just that it is a dualistic world, in which everything is cruelly and irrevocably divided between white and black by one event or one decree, but a world in which thought itself seems always to bend back to that original division and confirm it. In *Black Skin, White Masks*, the delirium of manicheism is described with something of the detached perspective of the clinician describing what a person in the throes of the pathology tends to do. But in *Wretched*, the delirium infects—no, it *is*—the writing of the critique of colonialism itself. It is not the description of a pathology, but the very language of the pathology itself, inside the delirium, that it is also attempting to deactivate.

In *Wretched*, "manicheism" has become a world-transforming system, not just the pathological effect of colonialism but also the very logic of the machine of domination. Unlike some later critics of colonialism, however, Fanon is always clear that the work of domination is psychic as much as anything else, that it depends on a transformation of worldview and not just of the world itself. It may be that this interior dimension is missing from later uses of the term in postcolonial studies, which ironically treat the binaries of colonial racism as essentially lodged in the world (although Achille Mbembe introduces Lacan to Fanon in his *Critique of Black Reason*). Part of the force of Fanon's critique of the "manichean" world, however, is the tone of bemused outrage with which he describes the imposition of this worldview and the acquiescence to it of the colonized: "When we consider the resources deployed to achieve the cultural alienation so typical of the colonial period, we realize that nothing was left to chance and that the final aim of colonization was to convince the indigenous population it would save them from darkness" (*Wretched*, 149). Fanon's point is not just that colonialism presents itself as a system of intellectual enlightenment and spiritual salvation, but that the very concept of the "darkness" that colonialism illuminates and from which the indigenous are being saved exists only within the narrative of colonial domination. The myth is that this narrative is like a Hegelian determination: before it comes into being, there is no way of understanding what its opposite is, and that the darkness before colonialism anticipates, or even demands, the light that colonialism brings. But that light is always the *fulfillment* of the darkness, the reason that can explain away and dispel the night of unreason. The belief that colonialism demands is a belief that there was no belief before it arrived.

Why does Fanon's use of "manicheism" become so subtle and complex in *Wretched*? Part of the reason is because Fanon's own understanding of it has moved from the universal to the particular. In *Black Skin, White Masks*, it was a pathology, or an ancient view of the cosmos. It described, in psychiatric literature, someone who divides the world into absolutes. The psychiatric manual that Fanon drew from, Maurice Dide and Paul Guiraud's 1922 *Psychiatrie du médecin praticien*, begins by summarizing the belief held by the "Sect of the Manicheans" in an eternal struggle between "the principle of Good and that of Evil, between God and the Devil." Yet the struggle could be between almost anything, depending on the "color of delirium": between revolutionaries and counter-revolutionaries, freemasons and Jesuits, entire nations.[22] In the complex unfolding of Fanon's analytic, the terms of manicheism do seem occasionally to change—for example, the pairings "Good–Evil, Beauty–Ugliness"—but they are always subordinated to the originary dualism: "White and black represent the two poles of a world, two poles in perpetual conflict" (*Skin*, 31).

Fanon's manicheism seems haunted by the historical content of the practice of Manicheism in the period of late antiquity, with its recurrent emphasis on light and dark, terms that Fanon treats as refractions of that primal dualism. The colonized, for instance, begin life in "opacity," but with the arrival of the colonists discover a "great thirst for light." Indeed, the whole enterprise of colonialism is designed to convince the *indigènes* that colonialism came to "snatch them from the night" (*arracher à la nuit*) (*Damnés*, 201; my translation). The archives of historical Manicheism are full of the same imagery. For instance, take this passage from Mani, quoted, of course, by Augustine:

> In one direction, on the border of this bright and holy region, there was a land of darkness (*tenebrarum terra*), deep and vast in extent, where abode fiery bodies, destructive races. Here was boundless darkness flowing from the same source in immeasurable abundance, with the productions properly belonging to it. Beyond this were muddy, turbid waters, with their inhabitants.... And similarly inside of this, a race full of smoke and gloom, where abode the dreadful prince and chief of all,

having around him innumerable princes.... Such are the five natures of the region of corruption.²³

Wretched echoes the topography of this Manichean vision quite closely. Fanon describes the towns (which he refers to as both *zones* and *villes*) of the colonizers as "a sector of lights," the towns of the colonized as "hungry for ... light," opposed but not complementary to the town of the colonizers (4). Fanon is describing not an ideal, abstract set of oppositions, but the real world of colonial Algeria, where one town is asphalted and its inhabitants wear shoes, the other starved of coal, bread, and shoes. In one sense, writing about the manichean world in Algeria brought Fanon, quite literally, down to earth. The very oppositions of colonialism are made visible in and on the landscape: the difference is apparent even if you don't know anything about Manicheans or colonialism or theories of mastery. One town is well-fed, the other hungry; one town is spacious and built to endure, the other is cramped and shoddy.

Yet even as Fanon gets down to earth there is another register, another kind of reference, hovering behind his text. The very notion that two towns represent two consequences of governance echoes the basic opposition of Augustine's *City of God*, which pits the earthly city against the heavenly one, the opposition framed in terms reminiscent of the Manichean opposition of light and dark. The earthly city is "dark, beclouded," while the heavenly city shines with the "light of the Lord."²⁴ Fanon's ironic appropriation of Augustine's trope makes the town of the *indigènes* the all-too-earthly city, squalid in its materiality, all matter without form; the town of the colonizers is a parodic heavenly city, where the inhabitants' "feet can never be glimpsed," as if, like angels, they float from point to point (*Wretched*, 4). Indeed, Fanon's next paragraph sounds almost like a bald restatement of Augustine's central argument: "This compartmentalized world, this world cut in two (*coupé en deux*), is inhabited by different species" (*Damnés*, 41; *Wretched*, 5; translation modified). An important difference between the two texts, of course, is that Augustine is writing about the eschaton itself, about the difference between the here and now and the afterlife; Fanon is writing about a deeply riven here and now. But Fanon's language is unmistakably *eschatological*, bordering on the kind of language that Mani uses in the passage above, which is ultimately about the difference between the land of light and the land of darkness, the *tenebrarum terra*.

The paradox of Fanon's use of manicheism is that when he moves from Europe, where he wrote *Black Skin, White Masks*, to a colony (Algeria)—when he moves from a theory about colonialism from a distance to a practice of resistance on the ground—his rhetorical, philosophical, and historical use of manicheism gets more complex. As I have suggested, this is partly because Fanon realizes that manicheism has already done this work, and on the same terrain. Its historical alterity, the very strangeness of using an arcane term taken from late antique religious history to analyze the contemporary colonial world, is part of what gives it its affective force: it renders a phenomenon, a psychosis, that its adherents almost by definition overlooked, through an objectifying term that makes it at least partially apprehensible. Ultimately, of course, it *is* a psychosis, as Dide and Guiraud had classified it in the psychiatric handbook where Fanon first encountered it, and an analysis of its logic is as irrelevant to reality as the conspiracy maps of *A Beautiful Mind*. But the rootedness of manicheism in North Africa, and Augustine's powerful and sustained contempt for it, give Fanon's use of the term the force of a genealogical critique not yet possible in *Black Skin, White Masks*. Manicheism is not just a psychiatric pathology but also a recurrent, historically inflected phenomenon.

Fanon demonstrates the same kind of historical attunement with his appropriation of other systems of thought that he uses, in turn, to think through manicheism. Take Hegel, for instance. The colonial master that Fanon talks about is different from Hegel's master. For Fanon, the master/slave opposition is not dialectical, because one term is always contained within the other. The bondsman has no opportunity for the self-consciousness that would allow him to recognize himself as a term in an opposition; he is simply the deprivation of the self-consciousness of the master. In Hegel—especially in Hegel, according to his first great French popularizer, Jean Hyppolite—the struggle for recognition gives the bondsman recognition of his other, his opposite, his negation in various ways, each of which allows him to recognize different abstractions of which he is part. In the opposition to death, the primal fear, he recognizes life—not quite his life, but a life given to him by "external thingness."[25] He knows that there is an abstraction called "life" that makes him different from the material world around him. But he does not fully know or experience this life as his, because the object of his "life" is to labor for the sake of others who can enjoy the things he makes fully, and so experience life fully. Their life is a continual demonstration that they have the ability to turn the things that have "independent being" for the bondsman into things that no longer have being because they are fully enjoyed, used up, in fulfilling their desire.

For Hegel, Hyppolite, Kojève, and Sartre (Fanon's most important sources for the dialectic of servitude), work is precisely what will liberate the bondsman.[26] He notices the power of his instrumentality in the world, and discovers how fully he shapes the world, and in doing so discovers the fuller extent of his being-in-the-world. "In the product of the work," says Hyppolite, "he finds himself" (176). This stage (or "moment," as Hegel calls it) is exactly where Fanon argues that the colonial subject's struggle for recognition peters out. In an important footnote in *Black Skin, White Masks*, Fanon spells out precisely why work cannot be the road to self-consciousness, and ultimately liberty, for the colonial subject. The Hegelian slave (*esclave*) "loses himself in the object and finds in his work the source of his liberation" (221n8). His work allows him to discover his own power and independent being in the objects he transforms. Because they once represented for him the independence of being as an abstraction, his capacity to alter them proves to him his *own* independence. Work makes the recognition of this liberatory idea possible, and, by strengthening the slave's engagement with the independence of being, is also the way in which he can realize that idea.

But because the "Negro wants to be like the master," says Fanon, he does not ultimately find his identity in what he does, but in what he is told. Of course, every slave begins working because he is told to, but for Hegel the slave's work is the first step away from the inter-animation of the master-slave relationship. As a result of the Black man's desire to be like the Master, in Fanon's view,

> he is less independent than the Hegelian slave.
> In Hegel the slave turns away from the master and turns toward the object.
> Here the slave turns toward the master and abandons the object (*Skin*, 221n8).

Fanon's argument asks us to rethink how capitalism alienates workers from the product of their labor. Workers' own involvement in the process of production is what ultimately causes their alienation from the product:

because they submit themselves to the process of specialization, they are a part of an abstract labor machine in which their labor is measured in abstract units and in which the thing they make is not their own.

The question of how liberation can come about in these circumstances is largely the story of how Marx has been understood and used. This is not the place to explore how Marx understands Hegel's dialectic of liberation and applies it to the moment of capitalism. What I want to emphasize is that the subjection of the worker in the capitalist West is fundamentally different from subjugation in the colony. Indeed, as Ato Sekyi-Otu argues, Marx's is simply one of the many Western narratives of domination and subjugation that fail in the colony because they are "predicated on relations of reciprocity, benign or malignant, [that] are incapable of capturing the 'originality of the colonial context'" (62). The alienation of the worker, which is both the result and the consequence of the specialization of labor, also produces multiple spheres of social relations in which specialization becomes a form of identity.

In an oblique and ingenious way, the very title *Les damnés de la terre* underscores this difference. Most of Fanon's readers, and certainly those who fell more on the *colon* side of the equation than on the *colonisé* side, would have assumed that the title alludes to "L'Internationale," the stirring communist hymn that celebrates the universal worker. The supposed allusion of Fanon's book to the first line of "L'Internationale" (*Debout! les damnés de la terre!*) has misleadingly suggested that Fanon is engaging with a kind of universal colonial subject. But this is a book that ends with a potent critique of the recourse to universalism by the colonial subject, which Fanon argues is only a capitulation to the colonial obliteration of distinctive local histories and cultures. In fact, the title comes through Jacques Roumain's "Sales nègres," a poetic litany of places and races that is a vociferous denial of a universalism that would only be racist.[27] It devastatingly parodies the slippage between *terre* as a specific (piece of) land and *terre* as "Earth." The colonist insists, according to Fanon, that he has made the *terre*: he is the "absolute beginning," and without him the *terre* would return to the Middle Ages. "We made (*faite*) this land.... If we leave, all will be lost, and this land will return to the Dark Ages (*cette terre retournera au Moyen Âge*)" (*Damnés*, 53; *Wretched*, 15).[28] Indeed, "The colonist makes (*fait*) history and he knows it" (*Damnés*, 53; *Wretched*, 15). Land and history: the very elements of Marxist economic historiography are marshaled against the colonized subjects cut off from the land that now acquires a history from which they are removed.

Or the decision is made that there was no history before the colonizers came. The abstract version of this decision is Hegel's infamous declaration that Africa "is no historical part of the world; it has no movement or development to exhibit" (*History*, 99). The brutally pragmatic version of this argument holds that the land was vacant before Europeans occupied it. It did not matter whether people were, in fact occupying it. If the land was not possessed in accordance with the rules of the French Civil Code, it was declared *terre vacant et sans maître*. The decision of *terre vacant* makes opposition to the master a vacant space; the worker is doubly annulled. The dialectic of recognition can't even commence because no term is the negation of the master. This manicheism only *appears* to be the emergence of two opposites; it really is the establishment of a single category, which, in Aristotelian fashion, can be known by its accidents: whiteness, the master, the colonizer. The colonized, by contrast, is not a category, so what appear to be the accidents of an underlying substance are really an impossibility.

In the section of *The Wretched of the Earth* where Fanon makes the famous, and notoriously misunderstood, pronouncement that the colonial world is "cut in two," he also makes it quite clear that he is not talking about dueling binaries, each of which has a chance to become the term that dominates the other (*Damnés*, 41; *Wretched*, 5; translation modified). The kind of "cutting" that he means is more radical than that: it creates a split in which only one part can have the attribute of existence. The "'native' sector" cannot vie with the "European sector," because the former is not really an alternative to the latter (*Wretched*, 4). As Fanon says, both sectors are "governed by a purely Aristotelian logic," and both "follow the dictates of mutual exclusion" (*Wretched*, 4). In the language of Aristotle, the opposition between them is not that of "relation." The European is not afraid that the native town will supplant his town, but that the natives "want to take our place" (*Wretched*, 5). There is only *one* place, and only one party can occupy it. But, as I have suggested, the logic is even more existential: if one party (the European party) does not occupy that place, it does not exist.

The text behind Fanon's analysis here is the fundamental handbook of the Aristotelian system, the *Categories*. Its main purpose is to set out the ten principal ways in which being can be analyzed (substance, quantity, quality, relation, location, time, position, possession, doing, undergoing). Fanon's reading of Aristotle here makes the issue of the relation between Black and white not just one of political rights but also of the *right to be in the first place*.[29] Under colonialism—that is, under racist regimes of occupation—the question never arises. The Aristotelian logic that Fanon invokes makes it quite clear that the issue is not whether the native is defined as a set of attributes that does not fit into one of the ten categories of being. It is crueler than that. The cut that divides the world in two is the cut that creates racial difference, the opposition between Black and white. Once this cut is made, Fanon argues, it can only be understood as the Aristotelian principle of "mutual exclusion" (*Wretched*, 4). This principle is quite specific, and is spelled out in one small section of the *Categories*. It is clear, too, that Fanon is referring to just one condition of this Aristotelian principle. Aristotle says that "with contraries it is not necessary if one exists for the other to exist too."[30]

To apply this logic to Fanon's argument: it is possible that the category "black" could exist independently of the category "white." It is possible that "white" could be inferred from the existence of "black." But that seems like a speculative exercise. What Fanon means is that one category has *made* the existence of the other category impossible. It is possible, even likely, that Fanon was attracted to Aristotle's discussion of reciprocal exclusivity by the example that Aristotle uses of one category's existence making the other's impossible. I will quote from the French translation of the *Categories* made by J. Tricot in 1936 and in print ever since: *Si tous les êtres sont blancs, la blancheur existera, à l'exclusion de la noirceur* ("if all of *being is* white, white *will exist* to the exclusion of blackness") (§11, 77; my emphasis). What is stake here is not just white or Black people, but being (*l'être*), existing as white or black. More than that: it is not a question of white beings and black beings existing, but of the abstract quality of *whiteness* existing, *as a category of being* on its own terms. Thus, in a sense, it is not white people in the colony who exclude Black people—though that is certainly true—but whiteness itself that makes the existence of Blackness impossible. That is one reason why the only kind of imaginary identification possible for the native seems to be the place of the settler. Aristotle is talking about an extreme instance, the limit cases of these categories. But Fanon is talking about precisely this extreme instance, the limit case, that Aristotle uses as a mere example. The difference is that, in Fanon's world, the "reality" of being itself becoming white, has actually come about.

The possibility that whiteness could become an abstraction that makes it impossible to attach being to Blackness is not a recent one, nor is it restricted to the colony. It is the result of a centuries-long habituation to thinking of color as abstract that begins with passages like this one from Aristotle. The most common example used in analyses of logical problems throughout the High Middle Ages was that of Socrates himself (sometimes Plato) "becoming white."[31] One of Aristotle's recurrent examples of qualities that imply their opposites is—along with heat and cold, and to a lesser extent, health and sickness—white and black. Although his ultimate point is not that whiteness is a self-subsisting entity, Thomas Aquinas says that a "white man" can be understood as a man *and* something "composed of itself and another, just as a white thing is composed of that which is white and whiteness."[32] Nicholas Oresme uses "whiteness and perhaps some flavors" (*albedo et forte quidam sapores*) as the key example of one of the few qualities that follow from one of the four primary qualities.[33] The analysis of whiteness makes its way outside the intramural limits of scholasticism: Dante compares justice to whiteness (although as something that cannot have degrees), and the Middle English poem *Pearl* concerns an object that refers to varying degrees of whiteness.[34]

Not only is the difference between white and black one of the most common subjects of research into the nature of the qualities that make up bodies, it is, again and again, whiteness that is used as the primary and often exclusive example. I am not arguing that the analysis of *albumen* in medieval scholasticism created racism in Europe on its own.[35] I just want to suggest that whiteness was often treated as an abstract, self-subsisting category, and one frequently without relation to its opposite, blackness. In the colony, says Fanon, the European is defined by this abstract quality, which not only reinforces—or rather, legitimates—itself but impoverishes other categories: "You are rich because you are white, you are white because you are rich" (*Wretched*, 5).

I think this is what Fanon means when he says that the received version of the Hegelian dialectic of the master and bondsman works differently in the colony, or that Marxist analysis "should always be slightly stretched" (*Wretched*, 5). For Fanon, Hegel's "master" is not defined or transformed by his relation with the slave because, as with the "white thing" of scholasticism, it is composed out of itself "and another"—except the other ("whiteness," in the case of the "white thing") is its own abstraction. Fanon's comment about Marxist analysis may be a little more straightforward, because (as he does not do with his Hegelian use of the master/slave dialectic) he states succinctly what would be involved, what would need stretching. The abstract force of whiteness is what compartmentalizes the world, and so what is usually regarded as the epiphenomenon, the superstructure of the underlying economic activities that actually alter the world, becomes more important than the substructure.

The validity of a critique of the superstructure was one of the points of contention in French academic Marxism after the war, and it is arguable that the reason it becomes acceptable to use the superstructure as an object of analysis is related to the conditions that Fanon describes in the colony. The logic of white mastery, and its cost in the Algerian War, perhaps, made the domination of the symbolic a phenomenon that needed to be addressed outside of purely economic conditions. It may be significant that one of the earliest thinkers to treat the superstructure as an "instituting institution," and one of the earliest to be criticized for his focus on symbolic capital, was the anthropologist Pierre Bourdieu, whose main work concerned the Kabyle of Algeria, and who supported the struggle for Algerian independence in many ways. But Fanon, at this point, is not primarily concerned with the future of Marxist analysis. His argument conveys the insistence of history—not the protocols that Marxist analysis has established—in the problem of dealing with the historiography that Marxism itself has created: "It is not just the concept of the precapitalist society, so effectively studied by Marx, which needs to be reexamined (*repensé*) here" (*Damnés*, 43; *Wretched*, 5).

On the one hand, colonialism "petrifies" medieval governing structures; on the other, a return to the Middle Ages is the threat that the colonizer makes when the colonized threatens insurrection (*Wretched*, 53 and 72). It legitimates the governing structures of the colony, and also is what the colonies will collapse into without those governing structures. The arrival of the Middle Ages signals the imminence of modernity, but the Middle Ages is also the negation of modernity. In at least one moment of *The Wretched of the Earth*, the medieval gives Fanon a way of imagining a history that unfolds outside of the Marxist materialist historical dialectic. It is not strictly true that Fanon is such a committed Marxist that, to keep him relevant, one must first jettison (or to be kinder, "bracket") his commitment to Marxist dialectic. He certainly hews close to it throughout his work. But even in such a crucial place as his chapter on revolutionary violence, Fanon says that it is inadequate to account for the phenomenon of colonial domination. A strictly economic account of colonialism does not work, he says, because race is an even more fundamental category. It calls for nothing less than a reconfiguration of Marx's concept of the precapitalist moment: that is, it calls for a reconfiguration of the way Marx has taught us to think about the place of the medieval in the modern—that is to say, colonial—world. The fabled relation of the master and the bondsman (*chevalier* and *serf*), so central to Hegel's and Marx's placement of the genesis of modern economic history in the European Middle Ages—as Andrew Cole has argued—is simply irrelevant in the colony.[36] The problem is that there is no intimacy, no relation in the physical, familial, or philosophical senses. The *serf* is "essentially different from the knight," for they are "different species (*espèces différentes*)" (*Damnés*, 43; *Wretched*, 5). Fanon underscores the *serf*'s lack of economic and political substance by describing him only in relation to the colonizer's *essence*. The colonized lacks being, in a fundamental sense, in the colony.

A simple, "allegorical" manicheism might map out a distinction between the "people of the shadows" (the evil of Manichean opposition) and those who dwell in the light. But Fanon's point is both less and more than that. On the one hand, even the people of the shadows possess being in the original, historical, Manichean system, a kind of substantiality that weighs against those in the light; in modern colonial manicheism, the colonized lack even the attribute of being. But on the other hand, of course, they do not. Fanon's point here is that it is really the entire philosophical delirium that lacks being. Or, to bring closer to the surface the metaphor that Fanon is using in this passage, the other is really the one that imagines the colonized as other: no matter what the colonizer does, despite all his work of *l'appropriation* (a word that folds into one the theft of property and the assertion of self-identity), he will remain always a stranger. The ruling "species" will remain one that comes from elsewhere, and the fundamental incoherence—the real delirium—of the system will never change: there will never be a true relation, a real resemblance, between the ruling species and the *autochthones, 'les autres'*

(*Damnés*, 43). Those last words wreck the extended irony that Fanon has been tracing; they close the bracket that colonialism first opened. The earth that the colonized first inhabited is no longer theirs. They are the other of their own territory. Fanon's ultimate point is not just that the colonized lack being, but that the entire system is a vast delusion, ludicrous precisely because people still believe in its supposed substance, despite its patent and derisory contradictions.

Struggling with Augustine, Then and Now

Augustine and Manicheism turn out to be far more significant in the struggle against colonialism than Fanon's *Black Skin, White Masks* had intimated. Fanon may have discovered all of these resonances himself in his wide reading, although the remaining books in his library do not include any by Augustine.[37] A likelier nexus for information about Augustine and Manicheism is probably the occasion of the Algerian War itself. Two of France's greatest Augustine scholars were deeply involved in opposing the war: one from France itself and another a leading leftist Catholic intellectual in Algeria.

The first of these is Henri-Irénée Marrou from the Sorbonne, still the greatest authority on education in late antiquity. Although Marrou was a critic of Marxism, he opposed France's conduct of the war in Algeria on moral, political, and religious grounds. Marrou and Fanon even published articles in the same issue of the leading journal opposed to the Algerian War, *Esprit* (February 1955). Marrou's most visible intervention was an editorial, "France, ma patrie . . . ," published in *Le Monde* (April 5, 1956), which blasted the French government's use of torture in conducting the war. (It was not until September 2018, when President Emmanuel Macron acknowledged that torture had been used in at least one case, that anyone in the French government admitted to its widespread use in Algeria.) While Marrou was motivated by a sense of outraged morality, he was not exactly a revolutionary. The heart of his column argues that absolute good and evil cannot easily be separated in the real world, and in those terms, he seems to reject the dualist world that Fanon had three years before seemed to portray in *Black Skin, White Masks*. Marrou says that, as a historian, he must reject all "Manichean classifications."[38] But while he may have opposed Marxism and Marxist-Leninist revolutionary action, he does not reject Fanon's critique as bluntly as it might seem. After all, Fanon does not exactly argue that we ought to accept "Manichean classifications" either—just that they are imposed by colonialism. Part of Marrou's point, to be sure, is that Fanon's revolutionary violence is predicated on a conviction that it is virtually impossible to overturn the division of the world into Black and white. But in 1956, Fanon had not yet written the chapter on revolutionary violence in *The Wretched of the Earth*. Marrou's invocation of "Manichean classifications" is therefore inspired, most immediately, by Fanon's analysis in *Black Skin, White Masks*.

But as Marrou says, he is speaking as a historian, and, to be specific, one who studies Augustine. His rejection of "Manichean classifications" is also a deliberate echo of Augustine's own rejection of Manicheism. Indeed, when Marrou describes what the Manicheism to be rejected in Algeria and France looks like, he turns not to Fanon but to Augustine himself, drawing from precisely the passage I discussed earlier. Marrou does not believe that there has ever really been a party of the Pure confronting the *Puissances des Ténèbres*, the powers of darkness or the *gens tenebrarum*.[39] Instead, like his teacher Augustine, Marrou believes that we have always lived in an inseparable jumble of the City of Good and the City of Evil. The immense difference between Marrou and Fanon lies partly in the ease with which Marrou sets aside a fissure in the world so profound that Fanon sees violence as the only truly effective response. Marrou's Enlightenment confidence in the virtues of French republicanism (he appeals throughout his *Le Monde* editorial to the importance of the ideals of *la patrie*) is the kind of confidence that Fanon attacks as a symptom of Manichean delusion. To believe either that we must accept colonial manicheism because we live in a mixed world, or to believe that we can improve the situation, is ultimately to be trapped within that delirium. What is perhaps most important about Marrou's editorial for the elaboration of that critique of colonial manicheism, however, is that Marrou, like other Augustine scholars who opposed the war in Algeria, sees a profound historical connection between the world of Augustine and the world of the anti-colonial movement. For Marrou, the Augustine who opposed the delusional division of the world into light and dark is a contemporary *indigène*: *ce Berbère*, *this* Berber, as if he is standing right there before him.

During his time in Algeria, Fanon also had continual contact with André Mandouze, another leading scholar of Augustine, who would go on to publish *Saint Augustin: l'aventure de la raison et de la grâce* (1968) and would eventually compile the indispensable archive of North African Christians, the *Prosopographie de l'Afrique chrétienne*, with a preface by Marrou. Mandouze was also a committed and active anti-colonialist, engaged with the resistance in Algeria throughout the war. He advised, organized, and published two anti-colonial journals, *Consciences algériennes* and *Consciences maghrébines*, for which Fanon wrote a number of articles. Mandouze and Fanon met frequently to discuss strategies of resistance, and Fanon's wife, Josie, attended his seminars on Augustine. For Mandouze, the war in Algeria against French colonialism was an extension of the resistance to the Nazis during the war, in which he had also been an active participant. The title of the first volume of Mandouze's memoirs—*D'une résistance à l'autre*—attests to the deep continuity he saw between the struggle against fascism and the struggle against colonialism.

But, as an Augustine scholar, for Mandouze Algeria also irresistibly summoned up the particular struggles of late antique North Africa. In his memoirs, Mandouze laments that his plan to commemorate the 1600th anniversary of Augustine's birth was interrupted by the beginning of the Algerian War. His complaint is not about his interrupted scholarly career, of course. It is about the misery that the war brings, a misery that has the shape of historical irony. Not only did the war break out exactly 1600 years after Augustine's birth, it also broke out in the same month and, above all, *dans son pays*, in his own land, the *malheureuse terre de saint Augustin*.[40] For Mandouze, Augustine haunts the war like a specter. "Wherever the war is, there Augustine is also," he says at one point in his memoirs.[41] As it happens, these words come from Mandouze's recollection of his reaction to Marrou's famous 1956 editorial in *Le Monde*. Wherever the war is, there Manicheans are also. And there was Fanon, too, writing about the land that the Manicheans themselves had inhabited. Manicheism is not just a remote and arcane theology, but the worldview of a large number of the people who once lived where Fanon was writing.[42] In some ways, Fanon may have seen Manicheism as a forerunner of colonialism, with its imposition of foreign belief; in other ways, it represents a form of belief prior to the arrival of modern colonialism, a belief that is, or becomes, characteristically African. François Decret's great study of Manicheism in North Africa argues that it survived so long as an African "church" precisely because it dropped features of Manicheism that seemed alien to North African culture: it "became indigenous."[43]

But indigeneity is not simple. Where "indigenization" now is virtually synonymous with decolonization, and where the first cultural push of the postindependence FLN Government of Algeria was a deliberate strategy of indigenization, Decret's use of the term implies a colonial context. It echoes, indeed, the long rule of France over Algeria, and the attempt to imagine a white settler identity that was French, while also distinctly Algerian, expressed, for example, in a literary movement sometimes called *Algérianisme*. This attempt sometimes exposed the desire for a phantasmatic foundational legitimacy among the settlers, a desire that leaped right over the work of becoming *like* an indigenous population to the invention of a myth of originary presence. The *Association des ecrivains algériens* thus awarded Paul Achard's 1931 novel *L'Homme de Mer* its Grand Prix Littéraire de l'Algérie for its celebration of France's millennium of domination over North Africa: Achard imagines modern France as the inheritor of Rome, recreating "a new France" in Algeria "from the debris of the Roman Empire." But the real importance of this historical fantasy is that it forges a narrative of legitimacy from the earth: the French are, as the descendants of the Romans, autochthonous Algerians, not invaders. As Achard says, the "land of Africa was therefore not new for them." But neither was France: the settlers of Algeria derived their political legitimacy precisely from their status as French citizens, although known as *Latins d'Afrique* or *Français d'Algerie*.[44]

Decret's observation about the indigenization of Manicheism may also carry with it a completely antithetical sense, a trace of the deprecation implied by the *Code d'Indigenat*, under which non-white residents of Algeria were second-tier citizens. White settlers in colonial Algeria have been described as oscillating between "the need, on one hand, to maintain the privilege of the coloniser, and the appeal, on the other, of a process of indigenisation."[45] The final irony of Fanon's life is that in spite and because of what Homi Bhabha calls his "consummate self-fashioning of himself as an Algerian," he died in the United States; his body had to be smuggled across the Algerian border to be buried. Fanon's final wish, as reported by the ALN commandant who spoke the final words at the funeral, was to lie with his brothers *en terre algérienne*.[46] He performed in death the most radical act of indigenization: to share the earth with the damned of the Algerian colony, the earth that had long been the resting place of the original Manicheans.

Like Fanon, Manicheism originated elsewhere, yet became African once it arrived. It preceded Islam and the modern form of Christianity, but in its spread throughout Northern Africa it also anticipated some of the ductile adaptability of the system of colonial belief. However Fanon would have mapped the historical phenomenon of Manichean religion onto his topography of the dualistic colonial world, he would have absorbed from his most likely sources two things: that Manicheism was a powerful explanatory tool; and that it demanded such a suspension of credulity that Augustine spent a large part of his career marveling over how thoroughly he had been deceived by it.

If recent arguments that Augustine remained entangled in Manichean epistemological modes are accurate, it is not enough simply to name, and to repudiate, heretical (or racist) ontologies. Augustine's anti-Manichean polemic also shapes his Christian apologetics, which is summoned, across the course of his conversion, by the need to resolve, and then repudiate, incoherencies in Manichean metaphysics. In Augustine's work, Christian theology is what Hegel would call a determinate negation, a truth that is discernible only in the ruination of a previous belief, because it is the truth that both destroys it and, in doing so, brings itself about. For Augustine, determinate negation led to Christian orthodoxy; for Fanon, or, rather, according to Fanon's critique of the colonial world, it led to the articulation of precisely the supposedly primitive superstitions that colonization was meant to bring to an end. The myths of the colonized, says Fanon, "especially their myths, are the very mark of . . . indigence and innate depravity" (*Wretched*, 7). The attribution of mythic immediate experience to the colonized serves three functions simultaneously: it annuls the modernity of the colonized as potential participants in modern liberal democracy; it performs a coercive and inhibitory function, allowing the colonized to redirect their urge for reciprocal violence into fantasized powers of far greater malevolence—and force—than those of the colonizers; and, most consequentially, it continues to articulate, and produce, forms of counterviolence. The symbolic machines of colonial domination, says Fanon, "serve not only as inhibitors but also as stimulants. . . . [U]nder certain emotional circumstances an obstacle actually escalates action" (*Wretched*, 17). Because the colonizer forces the colonized to dwell in the negative, in other words, the colonized have at their disposal the tremendous power of the negative.

In Fanon's intellectual heritage—and in the biographical trajectory of *Black Skin, White Masks* and *The Wretched of the Earth*—the negative does the work that Manicheism does for Augustine: it contains the negation of the beliefs he inherits, and propels the way forward. In many ways Fanon's earlier book, which is founded on the personal trauma of being a Black person in a world dominated by whites and whiteness, narrates the ruination of the knowledges, and self-certainty, that he may at one point have believed that he could hold fast. *Black Skin, White Masks* holds out the possibility, perhaps outlined a bit more firmly in *The Wretched of the Earth*, that this experience of negation could be an act of ethical cleansing and of radical beginning. For Fanon, the absolute night is a beginning. For Augustine, the utter speciousness and phantasmatic content of Manicheism is also the means to drive thought forward out of the night of ignorance.

What is vastly different about Fanon's work, of course, is that rather than write about the slow recuperation from a world of *darkness* and superstition, as Augustine does, he is writing about the formation of a world of phantasms and nightmares by the totalitarian machinery of colonization. Turning the ideology of the civilizing mission of colonization on its head, Fanon argues that, rather than bring modernity and post-Enlightenment reason into the world, colonization produces, instead, a re-enchantment of the world. Fanon is not describing the mere inversion of the process by which Weber says industrialization displaces older, "enchanted" modes of belief. He means something more like what Theodor Adorno and Max Horkheimer describe in *The Dialectic of Enlightenment*. They argue that the vestiges of primeval superstition, magic, or religious belief have not disappeared, and that these vestiges explain why it is that we so willingly accept relations of domination that we might otherwise find intolerable: "Justified in the guise of brutal facts as something eternally immune to intervention, the social injustice from which those facts arise is as sacrosanct today as the medicine man once was under the protection of his gods."[47] What is powerful in Fanon's critique is the exposure of the magical world behind the discourse of enlightened colonial domination: it really is founded not on rationality but on a primitive fear of the other, on the mythical, mystified, structure of race, which masquerades as race science, but also as the rational apparatus of colonial administration generally. The mythmaking of the colonized is a critique—and an exposure—of the dominations that global capital employs, but, above all, of the demonization that fuels the engine of colonization.

In Fanon's account, superstition and myth are produced by a determinate negation that is the reflex action of the colonized. This particular act of negation, however, is the result of the prior acts by which the colonizers have negated their right to exist. Reasserting that right can only be by means of that first act of negation, not by a simple act of opposition: "Yes, I have the right to exist" can only be said once you acknowledge that the right to say that—the very concept of rights and of political self-assertion—is a part of the juridical operations of European sovereignty. The right to exist can therefore only become a primordial right in the form of ancestral, indigenous prohibition. The right to exist is expressed *as* the threat of annihilation, a threat made tolerable only by a negative guarantee of existence in a world that is the determinate negation of the colonizer's ontology.

Determinate negation, however, is simply a way of describing the unintelligible and intolerable situation of the colonized, and therefore another way of framing the necessity—because it is the only action that is left—of violence. What makes the situation of the colonized intolerable, at least outside the sphere of violence, is that it cannot be repudiated. The colonized cannot simply walk away, or decide to choose another belief system. That is the difference with historical Manicheism, which was not a machine of total domination. Augustine did not have to contemplate violence, because he could use debate and polemic in a public sphere that was actually Manichean, in the sense that one opposite could in fact overcome the other—which is what Augustine and his followers believed was the outcome of Augustine's public disputations. But mere opposition and contradiction are meaningless as strategies for the colonized; they are constitutive annulments of Aristotelian categories of being, not transitional moments in a dialectic. Unlike Augustine's, Fanon's *remains* a manichean world—except that white and Black, colonizer and colonized, are not true antagonists, struggling against each other. In the history that colonization writes over the land it appropriates, the colonizer is always already transcendent.

But Fanon argues that there is a price for this transcendence: it is achieved by a determinate negation ("a *systematic negation* of the other person and a *furious determination* to deny the other person all attributes of humanity" (*Wretched*, 250; my emphasis). Although this transcendence is not a resolution, synthesis, or *Aufhebung* in the movement of a Hegelian dialectic, it preserves one important feature: the negative, which Hegel associates, in fact, with the work of preserving ("something *preserves* itself in the negative determinate being").⁴⁸ In logics and history that might unfold outside the manichean world of colonialism, negations would continue to imply all of the previous moments that have been passed over, transcended, left behind. But in the colonial world, even the *implied content* of the negative is utterly annulled. What does remain, ineradicable and powerful, is negation itself, which, for Fanon, is not nothing; far from it. Lurking behind, or, rather, outside, the text of colonialism is an absolute negative, a negation that can only be invoked in terms that themselves demand further cancellations and negations, names of what cannot, in the text of colonialism, fully be named. The most provocative term—in every sense of the word—is, of course, violence. But another is death, a condition and an act that, in a fragment by Césaire that Fanon quotes, is the apprehension of both hate and love, "evil and pernicious" but also "verdant and sumptuous" (*Wretched*, 45).

Readings of Fanonian violence that reduce it to mere murder cannot account for the multitudes in Césaire's vision of death, partly because it is the only mode of being left to the colonized, the one that Fanon calls their "absolute praxis" (*Damnés*, 82; *Wretched*, 44).⁴⁹ The strange adjective "absolute" points to what cannot be named (why would Fanon not refer to praxis as final, or only, or necessary?): violence as a praxis of death. To put this in different terms, but terms that are haunting Fanon's text on violence, the absolute is precisely an absolute negation, what Hegel in the Preface to the *Phenomenology* calls the "monstrous power of the negative." Hegel's word is *ungeheuer*, which is also translated as "tremendous" in English and *prodigieuse* in French. It is unnamable, and Hegel is slightly coquettish about what to call it (spoiler alert: he calls it death): "Death, if that is what we want to call *this non-actuality*, is of all things the most dreadful, and to hold fast to what is dead requires the greatest strength."⁵⁰

The story of violence in *The Wretched of the Earth* is the story of a continually deforming agent, one that first produces the non-reality (as both a subjective and objective genitive) of the colonized, and then turns a transformed violence against that agent. In the opening pages of *The Wretched of the Earth*, Fanon says that the manichean world of colonization produces the colonized as the mere "quintessence of evil," "absolute evil" (*mal absolu*) (*Damnés*, 44; *Wretched*, 6). But the force that produces this determinate negation of the colonized becomes, in turn, an absolute negation, a form of pure, uncontained force. The colonized, Fanon says, is "an agent (*dépositaire*) of malevolent powers, an unconscious and incurable instrument of blind forces" (*Damnés*, 44; *Wretched*, 6). There is an important ambiguity here, a glimpse behind the scenes of the tremendous power of the negative itself: *dépositaire* means "agent," but its literal sense is someone who receives, someone with whom something is deposited. The colonized is demonized by the unfathomable forces that stand outside the modern machine of colonialism (presumably forces of darkness, superstition, antiquity), yet forces that are themselves, of course, the fantasized deposit of white supremacy. Yet in the manichean world that the colonizer has driven into being, these forces cannot be contained as merely backward, superstitious customs; they are the tremendous power of the absolute negative, of manichean delirium—what the colonizer immediately experiences as unconscious, implacable, blind force: violence.

CHAPTER NINE

Zimbabwe and the Fear of the Medieval

If you want independence, take it and return to the Middle Ages.

FRANTZ FANON

Southern and South Central Africa has been named the country without a past.

SIR RIDER HAGGARD

The Specter of Carthage, Again

Frantz Fanon analyzed the image of the Middle Ages in colonies as both a threat and a desire. On the one hand, colonizers resisted the fall into the "barbarism" of Africa, which they imagined would drag them back in time, to the premodern era from which they had evolved. On the other hand, the colonies were mapped according to a "feudal" ideal that placed colonizers in the position of medieval feudal lords. They placed their supposed subjects in an equally incoherent historical position. Africans could not possess a Middle Ages of their own, although Europeans often thought of them as "medieval," precisely because that would align them too closely in history to Europe. Africans, that is, were "medieval," but did not actually have a Middle Ages. This is another consequence of Hegel's fantasy that Africans did not have history. Even for colonial figures who certainly did not read Hegel, there was a good reason to deny history to Africans: to "have" a history is to leave marks behind, and those marks might be the traces of a story that was different from the ones that colonialism needed to tell.

Perhaps the most awkward historical artifact in colonial Africa was the medieval ruin of Great Zimbabwe. This was a walled, urban complex that once covered 1,800 acres; the central structure, the Great Enclosure, is a thirty-foot-high wall of freestanding granite blocks that curves around in an ellipsis for 820 feet. This complex was the center of a vast trading network, exporting prodigious quantities of gold and receiving goods from as far as China and Persia. The ruined site was so impressive that it encouraged Europeans to make wild leaps of historical imagination: it was the city of the Queen of Sheba, the gold mines of Ophir, the mines of King Solomon, a city built by Carthaginians, Arabs, Vikings, or the survivors of Atlantis.

Great Zimbabwe, indeed, was the background for three novels by the Victorian writer Sir Rider Haggard: *Elissa*, *King Solomon's Mines*, and *She*, one of the biggest-selling novels of all time. All three influenced Arthur Conan Doyle, Rudyard Kipling, Sigmund Freud, Edgar Rice Burroughs, J. R. R. Tolkien, Graham Greene, and Ian Fleming. And all three describe a "superior," clearly white civilization in the distant past that is invaded by Black Africans and destroyed. Part of the fantasy Haggard spread was founded on a European skepticism that Black Africans could have built structures like Great Zimbabwe. But the other part was motivated by Haggard's role in inspiring the colonization of the country named after Cecil Rhodes: Rhodesia. Haggard is clear about the connection between his historical fantasies and the violence that accompanied the invasion of the country by Rhodes's British South Africa Company. In an earlier adventure romance based on the role missions played in the colonization of Rhodesia, *The Wizard*, Haggard dedicated the novel "To the Memory of the Child, Nada Burnham, who 'bound all to her' and, while her father cut his way through the hordes of the Ingobo Regiment, perished of the hardships of war at Buluwao on 19th May, 1896, I dedicate these tales—and more particularly the last, that of a Faith which triumphed over savagery and death."[1]

As with faith itself, there is so much at stake in this dedication that it is difficult to unpack. The dedication reflects the plot of *Elissa*, a story about a Phoenician priestess in the city of "Zimboe," a barely veiled Great Zimbabwe. She and a visiting Israelite prince fall in love, and she rejects the suit of Ithobal, the son of a Phoenician and an African queen, "absolute king" of a large, vague area surrounding the cities of the "white men."² The story ends with Ithobal and his horde of "savages" destroying Zimboe and leaving it ruined. It's an obvious reflection of the embattled feelings of the small settlements of whites in Rhodesia in 1900, when Haggard wrote *Elissa*, and an origin story for Great Zimbabwe itself: whites have been there since time immemorial, and are still embattled. The dedication insinuates the siege into that mythic history: Nada was the first white child born in Bulawayo and the first to die there, a modern, but short-lived, avatar of Elissa.

Elissa's name points to another city in the mythic charter of a white Zimbabwe: Carthage. Before she was known as Dido, the founder of Carthage was called Elissa. The earliest account of her life says that the name Dido was given to her by the "Libyans," and that Elissa was her "Phoenician" name. As we will see, the belief that it was Phoenicians who founded Great Zimbabwe was promoted by both white politicians and serious academics (e.g., the German sociologist Leo Frobenius). Haggard's choice of the name instead of Dido may have been to avoid the too-obvious connection with Carthage, but it may also reflect his desire to make the lineage of Great Zimbabwe unmistakably Phoenician, and not to entangle Carthage in its Libyan heritage. Elissa's death in the story— she commits suicide rather than marry the African king Ithobal—reflects Dido's suicide when Aeneas leaves. But the earlier version of the Dido story is even more on point for Haggard: in the pre-Aeneid version, Dido commits suicide rather than marry a Libyan king.³ Haggard's naming of Elissa as the priestess of Zimboe is not just a historical rhyme. It's the novelization of an alternate history that whites believed fervently—or perhaps desperately—for eighty years or more. It's one in which the specter of Carthage, again, plays a fundamental role.

The Southern Rhodesian government's publicity department frequently used images of Great Zimbabwe to attract tourists and settlers. One 1930 pamphlet, "Zimbabwe the Mysterious," incongruously featured a picture of the large conical tower at Great Zimbabwe with the caption "Rhodesia's Climate Calls."⁴ The cover image included the winding passage behind the Great Tower with a menacing African figure peering around the corner. The pamphlet begins the tour with a stop at the former site of the graves of the members of a British South Africa Company patrol who were killed by King Lobengula (they were reburied alongside Cecil Rhodes in southern Zimbabwe). The original burial site is in what the pamphlet calls the Elliptical Temple, "patently designed for a site of worship" (11). Although the pamphlet doesn't explicitly say so, it presents the empty graves of the patrol members as a revival of the site of worship: Rhodes's dead soldiers are gone, like the original builders of Zimbabwe, but they have left a sacred space. They are the ghosts of the original Phoenicians.

The mystery the pamphlet promises is really just the lack of absolute certainty that the Phoenicians built Zimbabwe. "Nobody yet knows," it says, who the builders were, yet "the very ancient and prehistoric conception is by far the most satisfactory from every point of view" (11). It gets even more specific about Zimbabwe's origin: "The fact remains that there is a most remarkable similarity in both structure and design between the ancient ruins of Carthage and those of Zimbabwe; and this factor cannot be ignored" (12). Another appearance of the specter of Carthage, which, in the European imagination, haunts the opposite end of Africa centuries later.

Haggard's stories, as fanciful as they seem, were poured from an imperial-era concoction of the Dido story and unfounded speculation about the origins of Great Zimbabwe. In the preface to *Elissa*, Haggard says that it is "beyond question" that Zimbabwe was "once a Phoenician city" (although he immediately goes on to raise questions about it) (8). There are powerful reasons that explorers and amateur archaeologists created this myth, as we will see. But Haggard's historical fantasies were just as much about the present as they were about the past. As the dedication to Nada Burnham shows, his stories were motivated by what was happening at the moment, as much as by a mythic dream of the past. They sometimes influenced events, from the expansion of Rhodes's dreams to individual tragedies. Nada, for instance, died partly because of Haggard's stories. Her father, the famous adventurer Frederick Burnham, was so entranced with Haggard's tales that he and his wife moved from Arizona to Rhodesia. Haggard himself said that Burnham "in real life is more interesting than any of my heroes of romance."[5] He, more or less, followed the script of Haggard characters (like Allan Quatermain), at one point declaring that his one last "romantic adventure" in Rhodesia was to find the buried treasure of King Lobengula of the amaNdebele.[6] Nada, named for the protagonist of Haggard's novel *Nada the Lily* (1892), was born in Bulawayo just after the British South Africa Company's defeat of the amaNdebele in the First Matabele War in 1894 allowed whites to settle there. She died two years later, during the siege of Bulawayo in the Second Matabele War.[7]

The ending of *Elissa* also projects a future of Black sovereignty, where Ithobal's absolute kingship is both vague and overwhelming. Both that vision, and the fall of Zimboe, are a kind of alternate history of what could have happened if the siege of Bulawayo had been won by the amaNdebele, led by Lobengula. Haggard's dedication is the lurid pin on a map of appropriation, but in fact the subjugation of the amaNdebele happened gradually, by a series of deliberate misreadings of agreements that Lobengula made with the Crown. The vagueness of the conquest prompted Crown agents, as it did Haggard, to punctuate pivotal moments. Most of these had to do with rulings made by colonial officials and judges, but the most consequential legal maneuver established Lobengula's sovereignty in order to legitimate what the British South Africa Company hoped would be his submission to the Crown.[8] That is, he was recognized as a king in order to be able to dethrone himself. After Lobengula's death, constitutions were drafted that would impose some kind of direct rule on the amaNdebele, and which did not include any theory of amaNdebele sovereignty. It was simply ignored—except by Leander Starr Jameson, a doctor and politician whom Lobengula had made an iNduna, an Ndebele adviser. Jameson helped to persuade Lobengula to grant mining concessions to Rhodes, which ballooned into Rhodes's full-scale occupation of the area. Shortly after Lobengula's death, Jameson took it on himself, while the legal pretexts were being drafted, to stage a formal transfer of power. He chose the late medieval formula of succession related to the theory of the king's two bodies, but altered it significantly: "The King being dead, the white Government had taken his place."[9] Almost from the start, white rule in Rhodesia depended on situating African cultural and political institutions at a medieval level of "development." The amaNdebele lost sovereignty as if they were medieval subjects.

In more persistent ways, the Africans of Rhodesia were entangled with the Middle Ages more insistently than in any other colony, precisely because of the importance of Great Zimbabwe. It was easier for colonists to imagine that the magnificent city had been built by Phoenicians from the Mediterranean two thousand years earlier than it was to believe that it had been built by Africans in the Middle Ages. But that turns out to be what actually happened, and it was a possibility that Europeans suspected and defended against. In the preface to *Elissa*, Haggard asserts that medieval Zimbabwe was the "seat of a barbarous empire," which had nothing to do with the ancient city (8).

Europeans had known about this empire for some time. The Portuguese encountered it in its late stages, and claimed to have converted its ruler to Christianity. There are numerous surviving accounts. John Ogilby's atlas of Africa, commissioned by Charles II and published in 1670, includes a compilation of what was known about the empire. It extended as far as the Cape of Good Hope in the south to Congo in the north, and the Zambezi river to the west. Its royal court was called Banamatapa (present-day Monomatapa), located six days away from a "great House call'd *Simbaoe*, or *Zimbaoch*." The empire, Ogilby reports, is anything but "barbarous":

> The Palace of the Emperor carries a vast extent, having four Eminent Gates, and very many large Chambers, and other convenient Apartments, guarded round about with Watch-Towers, and within hung with Cotton Hangings of divers Colours, wrought with Gold, and richly Embossed; as also overlaid with Tin gilt, or, as others say, cover'd over with Plates of Gold, and adorn'd with Ivory Candlesticks, fastned with Silver Chains: The Chairs gilt and painted with several Colours: The four chiefest Gates of the Court richly Embossed, and well defended by the Life-Guards of the Emperor.[10]

The atlas describes an elaborate feudal system in which subsidiary kings pay tribute to the "Chief Sovereign." As in the court of Louis XVI, the most powerful lords of his own kingdom are kept close to the sovereign to prevent insurrection (600). The sovereign has all of the attributes of a mystic king: everyone must kneel in front of him; no one can speak unless he asks them to; when he drinks, the entire court sings praise songs. A train of attendants accompanies the king with an embroidered pavilion and a canopy set with gemstones, like the canopy of state in European courts (599). Royal protocols like that would have been familiar to Ogilby: access to Charles II was hedged with elaborate and shifting rules of behavior and ceremonial spectacle.[11] Ogilby, in other words, describes an empire that would have been familiar to early modern Europeans.

Most of this information also appears in John Wilmot's 1896 book *Monomotapa (Rhodesia): Its Monuments, and Its History from the Most Ancient Times to the Present Century.* Haggard knew the book; he wrote its preface and cites it in *Elissa*. Cecil Rhodes hired Wilmot to research European archives to confirm the Phoenician hypothesis, and Wilmot read the Portuguese records of a late medieval African civilization with an uncharitable eye. He scoffs at the "absurdly inflated descriptions" of the Portuguese accounts of the royal court's sumptuousness; he sarcastically dismisses their descriptions of a "wonderfully civilised empire ruled over by a monarch."[12]

This sarcasm has political implications. It sweeps aside any hint that the area might be organized by anything that Europeans would recognize as sovereignty, and from the perspective of jurisprudence encourages colonists to think of it as almost a terra nullius—not perhaps a land without people, but one without a king. It is important, too, that the bafflement of modern rediscoverers of Zimbabwe is scrupulously recorded. Great Zimbabwe is immediately recognized as a mystery: there is no possible connection between the people who live there now and the obvious evidence of a sophisticated polity. The characterization of it as a mystery, an enigma, or a riddle still persists: who isn't intrigued by a mystery? But it was a historical myth that propelled white rule from Cecil Rhodes through the end of the Ian Smith regime in 1980: the terra nullius of the Middle Ages.

One of the first studies of Great Zimbabwe, Theodore Bent's *The Ruined Cities of Mashonaland* (1892), declared that "the ruins and the things in them are not in any way connected with any known African race," and called the activity of the African people around Great Zimbabwe before the arrival of the Europeans a "desecration" of the past.[13] But the first Europeans to visit Zimbabwe committed desecrations that are now used as examples of imperial greed and destructive archeology. The British South Africa Company licensed prospectors to dig in the numerous ruins in Rhodesia, including Great Zimbabwe. The first semi-systematic excavation of the ruins, led by Richard Nicklin Hall from 1902 to 1904, discovered recent bottles and pipes several feet down. Hall did more than dig, however. He cleared away several meters of "rubbish" that he thought covered Zimbabwe's original Phoenician level, and therefore destroyed several centuries' worth of stratigraphic and cultural evidence.

Bent was motivated by a racist myth that was created at the same moment that the first modern European to write about the ruins heard about them. Karl Mauch, an amateur German geologist and explorer, said he heard about the ruins from a local person, who himself claimed that the ruins "could never have been built by blacks."[14] Bent echoed Mauch in a speech to the Royal Geographical Society when he declared that the ruins were "not in any way connected with any known African race."[15] There may have been archival and art-historical arguments going on among explorers and academics about what group of people actually did build Great Zimbabwe, but the political shape of the myth was already fully developed: no matter who the builders were, they were white.

Cecil Rhodes's visit to the ruins in 1891 made the racial politics of that myth clear. His group was met by several hundred armed men, who had heard that the "great master" was coming to kill them. The standoff was defused when they were told that Rhodes was simply coming "to see the ancient temple which once upon a time belonged to white men." When the group inspected the ruins up close, the politics became even clearer: Rhodes's companion writes that it was clearly not just a place built just by white "men," but "by a white nation."[16] Symbolic conquest came before military conquest; even before Rhodes subjugated the Mashona, he had rewritten the history of Great Zimbabwe, and with it the territory that he was about to claim. He was not taking something that had never belonged to whites; he was restoring a sovereign right that had existed since a white race built Great Zimbabwe.[17] Rhodesia was a once and future white nation.

By the 1970s, the motive for the literally outlandish claims about the origin of Great Zimbabwe's builders had become patently—and unsurprisingly—clear. An MP demanded in Parliament that the guidebook for the ruins stop suggesting that Great Zimbabwe had been built by "indigenous peoples," because it was more likely that it had been built by "light-skinned" people.[18] His demand reveals instantly what is at stake in the twofold desire to attribute the building of Great Zimbabwe to non-Africans: that technological achievement depends on racial characteristics; and that evidence that whites were in the area before any of the present groups justified white dominion over the country of Rhodesia. Rather than confirm the assumption that Europe's Middle Ages were, indeed, the best mirror for Africa, the existence of Great Zimbabwe troubled its surface—and ultimately revealed its incoherence.

Picturesque Archaeology

The iconography of Zimbabwe is central to the image of both the white colony and the independent Black nation—which is, of course, named after it. Rhodesia prominently featured one of the magnificent soapstone birds from Great Zimbabwe on the crest of the first Rhodesian coat of arms, granted in 1924; it appeared on the shilling coin from 1932 to 1952 and on the twenty-cent coin of the Rhodesian Front government. Its legacy as a symbol of European sovereignty was established almost from the moment of its discovery. It was the focus of an extraordinary act of historical fetishization that was founded not on physical evidence but on the impressionistic techniques of art-historical criticism.

From the beginning, Europeans used the shapes of structures and details of design to connect Zimbabwe with cultures flung far in time and space. Richard Nicklin Hall specifically credits the "true artist" Thomas Baines, an explorer and well-known painter, for "reducing from chaos to method" the general and hasty information about the ruins that the early missionaries David Livingstone and Robert Moffat had given. It is Baines's work, claims Hall, that prepared the way for all subsequent archaeological work on Great Zimbabwe. It is telling enough that Hall puts Baines's paintings on the level of systematic archeology. The paintings themselves, however, look as if they are motivated more by a quest for the sublime than for scientific truth. A painting of the upper ruins (the so-called Acropolis) has the high-contrast play of light (bright patches in front, darkening shadows becoming clouds in back) and dramatic diagonals of contemporary representations of medieval ruins in Europe and England. Its aesthetics belong as much to the appeal of the romantic fragment as they do to the canons of scientific method.

The 1930 tour guide to Great Zimbabwe includes a virtual outline of how to imagine its history. Once we accept the theory that Great Zimbabwe shipped gold to either Babylon or ancient Palestine—although, to be sure, "*Nobody really knows!*"—then "all the barriers would appear to be demolished which might prevent the imagination from wandering in a field more picturesque perhaps than strictly archaeological, but not altogether fanciful. It is only a step further to connect the Zimbabwe Ruins with the Phoenicians, and the ancient gold workings of Rhodesia with the King Solomon's Mines of romance" (13, 14; emphasis in original).

But it's precisely the case that archaeology at Great Zimbabwe worked by imagination and the cultivation of the picturesque. Another painting by Baines shows a vast circle of worshippers around a priest standing in front of the conical tower—except here it stands by itself, unconstricted by the thirty-foot-high walls that actually surround it. Baines has opened up a vast space of worship and spectacle that could only have existed in Great Zimbabwe's distant past (that is, if the conical tower had been built before any other structure).[19]

Baines's source for the ceremony in the second painting was Karl Mauch, the first modern European to write about the ruins. Mauch relates that he was told that up until forty years before his arrival great gatherings were held after harvest in which two oxen and a heifer were sacrificed in the upper ruins. The "high-priest" was assisted by "2 virgins, 2 young women," and one man.[20] Baines's painting in some ways is a precise rendering of the ritual. The priestly figure is accompanied by four women (two of them shorter, presumably to represent youth, the graphic equivalent of virginity), and three cattle stand in the foreground, to the left. But in two ways, the painting deviates significantly from Mauch's account. The "high-priest" in the painting is also a woman, with her arm outstretched accepting the sacrificial gifts. She presumably represents the inhabitant of what Mauch was told was "The House of the Great Woman." Baines may be trying to reconcile the two conflicting accounts of the nature of the priesthood that Mauch gives. He simply makes the "high-priest" the Great Woman, and thus tantalizingly hints that this is really the domain of the Queen of Sheba.

Another significant change is to the scene of the ceremony. The conical tower is misshapen, but that may be just because Mauch's description of it was unclear. There is one conspicuous element that does not appear in Mauch's diaries, however. The foreground is taken up by baskets of maize and grain, and a gourd, perhaps containing beer. Baines's addition makes concrete Mauch's general, abstract impression that there were "Jewish" elements in the ceremony: it corresponds almost exactly to the specifications for the Feast of Weeks (the festival of the first fruits) laid down in the Book of Numbers:

> Also on the day of the first fruits, when you present a new grain offering to the LORD in your Feast of Weeks, you shall have a holy convocation; you shall do no laborious work. You shall offer a burnt offering for a soothing aroma to the LORD: two young bulls, one ram, seven male lambs one year old (Num. 28:26–27).

Baines's painting is the first concerted attempt to imagine a connection between Great Zimbabwe and the ancient non-African past. The so-called Hamitic hypothesis persisted long after Baines, and became more elaborate, but Baines's profound changes to Mauch's account depict a present that can only be understood in terms of an alien past, no matter how distant that past is. Baines uses the distant participants to enact this point. In the first ranks of the vast circle of people, you can make out a few figures jumping with arms outstretched, but everybody else is part of an undifferentiated mass. The crowd disappears rapidly into the sides and background of the painting. By the third tier of the crowd, people are indistinguishable from the background, victims of perspective, dwindling light, and ideology. The context of Great Zimbabwe is enigmatic and shadowy, yet it is an enigma provoked, paradoxically, by the clear and abundant presence of elements from the past. Much of the work on Great Zimbabwe that followed concerned the question of what, or, more precisely, when, that past was. It might be recent—within the last forty years—or it might be ancient, from King Solomon's time, Queen Dido's, or Hatshepsut's. But it could not have been from the Middle Ages.

The prejudice that sophisticated structures like Great Zimbabwe could not have been built by Africans was so strong that much of the evidence that would have contradicted that prejudice was completely disregarded. It was literally thrown away. The second European to investigate Great Zimbabwe, Richard Nicklin Hall, assumed that the remnants of what seemed local vernacular architecture got in the way of his investigation. For him, they were simply evidence of the occupation of Great Zimbabwe after its fall by people who moved in much later. What this really meant was that Hall, as we have seen, began his excavation by throwing away six to twelve feet of stratigraphic layers, which he thought of as mere debris, from the most important parts of the site. As he put it, the first task was to "remove the filth and decadence of Kaffir occupation."[21] To a large extent, Hall destroyed the archaeological evidence altogether; modern archaeologists often describe what he did as stripping the flesh off and leaving only the skeleton.

Hall's racism, like that of all the early Europeans who visited the site, is repellent and obvious. But he yoked his theories about the site to his racism more thoroughly than most. He classified the buildings at Zimbabwe according to their complexity and finesse and, without any stratigraphic or other evidence, sorted them into periods based solely on his own aesthetic preferences. The best buildings were erected in the first period; successive periods built increasingly less impressive buildings, until the "decadent period," during which the art of building in stone was lost altogether. The gap between the end of the "decadent" period and the present was the period when, he assumed, the ruins had been taken over by unsophisticated peoples who left behind them the detritus that he cleared away.

Hall's description of removing the "filth and decadence" that had piled up in Great Zimbabwe's ruins repeats precisely the rhetoric used by nineteenth-century humanist scholarship in speaking of the Middle Ages. The nineteenth-century classicist, economic historian, and politician James Thorold Rogers imagined that the "first task" of scholars in the renaissance was to "clear away the barbarisms which long negligence had suffered to grow over Latin speech."[22] In a fusion of the two tropes—of the "rubbish" created by "degenerate" peoples and the decline of culture—an 1853 encyclopedia, *The Great Cities of the Middle Ages*, compares the Oxford sheriff's attempt to "remove" the "great store of filth" laying on the streets to the University's "neglect, or rather decay of learning": "Their Latin was barbarous, and what they spoke or wrote was in a common or hackney style. . . . [W]hat they acquired was also laid upon an unsure foundation."[23] Hall's removal of "filth and decadence" was legitimated by one of the founding assumptions of the philosophy of culture in post-Enlightenment Europe, which was also one of the a priori principles that produced the notion of "culture" in the first place.

Barbarian Invasions: Rhodes's Gibbon

The problem was how to account for the refinement, in the sense of a progressive amelioration, of modern culture with the evidence of historical regressions and ruptures like the so-called barbarian invasions of Rome. The solution was to reimagine the supposed degeneration of Greco-Roman culture, not as a regression but as a supersession—that is, in the terms that Hegel made famous, as a cancellation that was also a preservation. Barbarian influences became, at one and the same time, the final degradation of Roman culture and its reanimation in an entirely new form. This supersession is emphatically not a universal, or logically necessary, mechanism, however. In the hands of eighteenth-century philosophers, it is driven by an implacably racist, supremacist logic: the barbarians, often described with the grab-bag term "Goths," are the very German races that turn out to save Europe. In Schlegel's words, "After

Christianity, the character of Europe has, since the beginning of the Middle Ages, been chiefly influenced by the Germanic race of northern conquerors, who infused new life and vigor into a degenerated people."[24] In other words, modern Europe emerges out of the simultaneous collapse of Rome and the integration and redeployment of its wreckage in the European—principally Germanic—Middle Ages, which also marks the terminus of the "degenerated" Roman culture.

In a study of the figure of the "barbarian" in eighteenth- and nineteenth-century European art history, Éric Michaud defines this narrative as an explicitly ameliorist narrative of historical development. He argues, indeed, that the "barbarian invasions" themselves were "in large part a romantic invention, inseparable from the formation of the nation states and the rise of nationalism in Europe."[25] The Gothic style became both a signifier of "national pride" and of racialized identity: it expressed the "genius" of the mixture, specifically, of "northern" and "southern" European races. Charles Herbert Moore's study of Gothic art (first published in 1899) argued that this "fusion produced a superior race, a race equal in artistic capacity to any of those of ancient times, and in which the genius of the North supplied a fertile imagination and a daring spirit of innovation, while that of the South contributed a disciplined sense of beauty and an inheritance of classic culture."[26]

The corollary of the "racial improvement" theory of the development of modern European culture rests on the seemingly contradictory notion of cultural and racial internal entropy, the ticking away of degradation within the machine. In 1794, Friedrich Schlegel used Alexandria as the example of the internal logic of decadence. From its height in the Doric school, which had refined the Ionian pure appropriation of "nature," Greek poetry lost its beauty in Alexandria's exhausted imitation of earlier models ("making new wreaths of old flowers," he says, riffing on what is in fact a favorite trope of late antique North African writers). In Alexandrian poetry, "art became artificiality, and was finally forsaken for barbarism."[27] Nine years later, also writing from the University of Jena, Hegel wrote about the devolution of the Roman empire in similar terms, in a dry run of the famous master/slave dialectic in the later *Phenomenology of Spirit*. The "degradation of the class of the nobility," he says, resulted in the disappearance of slavery but the appearance of "the people," a concept ultimately, or initially, rooted in the relation of slavery itself. Hegel was a close reader of Gibbon; at this point, he turns to Gibbon's six-volume *The History of the Decline and Fall of the Roman Empire* for a concrete depiction of the historical process:

> This long peace, and the uniform government of the Romans, introduced a slow and secret poison into the vitals of the empire. The minds of men were gradually reduced to the same level, the fire of genius was extinguished, and even the military spirit evaporated.... [T]he deserted provinces, deprived of political strength or union, insensibly sunk into the languid indifference of private life.[28]

Hegel's historical dialectic unfolds in a different direction than the explicitly racialized salvation of the West by the "barbarian invasions," but by no stretch of the imagination is Hegel's vision of how history unfolded in the rest of the world free from a fundamental, annihilating racism.

Hegel's universal history culminates in the emergence of modern Europe, but a Europe that appears at the end of the long passage of civilization from "Oriental" through Greek and Roman to German. Although his history ends at the same point where "barbarian invasion" histories end, there is a difference between them. For Hegel, the Germans emerge because of the objective work of the historical dialectic, which a posteriori legitimates the racial superiority of the Germans; "barbarian invasion" histories treat race as an a priori category that explains the mechanism of cultural emergence. Both philosophies of history depend on an exclusively Eurocentric vision of history, however. Other cultures and places might perform transitory roles along the way. As we have seen with Kantorowicz's study of Frederick II, places like Africa might even step out of the wings for a brief moment on the world stage. In the case of Africa, in particular, either version of the nineteenth-century historiography of culture inevitably puts Europe in the place, paradoxically, of the barbarians who reanimate culture after Rome, or the Hegelian fulfillment of historical dialectic. The "barbarian" narrative, however, acknowledges that Africa possesses a quantum of "culture," even if only at a minimal level. The choice is grim: either Africa embodies a failure of history, or the utter, and primal, absence of history.

Somehow, colonizers managed to hold both opinions simultaneously. Hegel set the viciously nihilistic tone: "Blacks are wholly unruly, and not on the way to any culture; theirs is a gold-filled land of children, lacking any culture."[29] There is so much for racist dialectic to unfold here:

the invention of property, the emergence of theories of legitimacy and sovereignty, the contradiction of a nullity of culture (not) belonging to a people who are also represented as standing at the infantile stage of the timeline of civilizational development, who will never move on that timeline because they stand outside historical dialectic altogether. They possess both the potentiality of culture and its annulment.

Yet the discovery of Zimbabwe in 1871, forty-one years after Hegel completed *The Philosophy of History*, from which those words above are taken, constitutes a powerful riposte to Hegel's claim that history was simply impossible in Africa.[30] Zimbabwe did not change the minds of Europeans overnight, however. Rider Haggard, for one, dug in deeper. Echoing Hegel, he wrote in the preface to Wilmot's book about the Phoenician origins of Zimbabwe that "Southern and South Central Africa has been named the country without a past" (Wilmot, xiii). He meant that the Africans around Zimbabwe did not have a past, and therefore that Zimbabwe had to have had an ancient past that really belonged to outsiders from the North. If Africans *did* have any past, it was simply a story of the degradation and erasure of a past that did not belong to them.

The man driving the English invasion of Zimbabwe, Cecil Rhodes, understood the decline of Great Zimbabwe's culture as the fall of a great civilization into the barbarism of the Middle Ages. His favorite reading at the very moment that he was conquering Rhodesia was a vast melancholy meditation on how a great civilization had declined: none other than Gibbon's *The Decline and Fall of the Roman Empire*. Gibbon's monumental accomplishment itself was a declaration of the return of order and learning to the field of Rome. So taken was Rhodes with Gibbon's recovery of long-neglected sources that he commissioned a London bookseller to translate all of Gibbon's sources into English. Rhodes stopped the project when he had spent about 8,000 pounds, roughly what his company spent every two days on the Second Matabele War.[31] During this war, which effectively gave his British South Africa Company control of the territory of Rhodesia, Rhodes was seen reclining and reading Gibbon. Rhodes was able to conjure up parallels between his own situation and even arcane sections of Gibbon's history quite readily. Stung by accusations that he had instigated the war in order to subjugate the amaNdebele completely, Rhodes countered with an argument from Gibbon: that his accusers were like the *delatores* in the Roman empire who were paid to make accusations against public officials.[32]

But a larger question is what Rhodes got out of reading Gibbon while he was subjugating the peoples of southern Africa in order to create a new empire. A clue might lie in the other literary work Rhodes always had with him, the *Meditations* of Marcus Aurelius. *Decline and Fall* obviously functioned as a long cautionary tale for Rhodes: a kind of handbook on what to avoid in creating empire again. But Marcus Aurelius, from the perspective of Gibbon, furnished a positive example of a ruler who got things right, even if for the last time in Roman history. *Decline and Fall* begins just after the death of Marcus Aurelius, which marked, says Gibbon, the end of "the period in the history of the world during which the condition of the human race was most happy and prosperous."[33] Rhodes emphatically identified himself with Roman emperors: he believed he looked like Titus and thought like Hadrian.[34]

The ruins of Great Zimbabwe offered both a justification for Rhodes's invasion of the area and a powerful arena for his historical imagination. Rhodes not only sponsored the first excavations of Zimbabwe but also took its most valuable discoveries as his personal property, most notably the large soapstone birds that the excavators and first white custodians of Zimbabwe argued were Phoenician. Rhodes's wholesale appropriation of Zimbabwe and its artifacts is a metonymy of what he did with the rest of what became a country named after him: it was invaded and held not by the British government, but by Rhodes's private corporation, the British South Africa Company. Indeed, their archives show that the company influenced developments in the archaeology of Zimbabwe in order to exploit the myth of originary Phoenician occupation.[35] Ultimately, however, Rhodes would have adopted the Phoenician myth as official dogma without evidence. He once defiantly said that it didn't matter what archaeologists thought about the Phoenician origins of Great Zimbabwe: "That is not the way empires are founded."[36]

But Cecil Rhodes's interest in Great Zimbabwe went further than exploiting it as a justification for the appropriation of the entire country. Great Zimbabwe represented a kind of restaging of the story of Rome, in which Rhodes could become another Marcus Aurelius, or even, although there is no evidence that he imagined this, the Germanic, northern stock coming to reanimate the degenerated ruins of a civilization. His traveling companion, David Christiaan de Waal, says that when he and Rhodes first stood before the walls of Great Zimbabwe, "A strange feeling ran through me.... [I]t was the same sensation I felt when I beheld the remains of ancient Rome."[37] De Waal or even Rhodes himself may have been the visitor whom Theodore Bent, during his Rhodes-funded excavation of Great Zimbabwe, reports as saying that the ruins "reminded him forcibly of Rome."[38]

These more or less inchoate feelings of identification with ancient Rome were fleshed out five years later by Rhodes's collaborator Alexander Wilmot, a member of the Cape Colony Legislative Council, who contributed to the cost of Bent's expedition and conducted archival research on Great Zimbabwe at a number of European archives. Wilmot's book *Monomotapa* combined the theory of self-driven decadence with the theory of a cataclysmic barbarian invasion. Throughout *Monomotapa*, he speculates that the original builders of Zimbabwe—in his mind, most likely Phoenicians—intermarried with local Africans and dropped into historical, economic, and cultural oblivion: "The great vicissitudes of the world do not seem to have materially affected the mixed race which dwelt around the ancient forts. Their country was fertile and their wants simple. The luxury which the use of their gold promoted seems to have been relegated to other climes. In the absence of any record we have to consult the histories in stones which have been left us" (119–20). For Wilmot, the descendants of the builders were certainly incapable of compiling or maintaining an archive of any kind. Their history, indeed, was a process of becoming alienated to themselves—aliens in their own country, shut out from a history that is no longer theirs. Wilmot found among them, he says, only mystified silence about the traces of the (foreign) civilization around them: "Strange to say, we cannot even find any traditions unless of a most obscure and doubtful character. . . . [T]hey lived in huts and gazed upon the colossal ruins of the Phoenicians as the works of strangers from whose religion and comparative civilisation they were alienated" (166). If this sounds as if Wilmot is looking for evidence in the wrong places, and the wrong kind of evidence—excluding altogether anything that didn't appear to echo Phoenician culture—it is because his work on Great Zimbabwe is shaped almost completely by his conviction that the answers could only lie in literal archives. Only documents could speak, and even the living voices of the present-day inhabitants of the area around Great Zimbabwe were silent to him. What actual historical evidence he used in the book was taken from Jesuit archives in Lisbon and the Vatican: accounts from Portuguese travelers, traders, and missionaries starting at the beginning of the sixteenth century.

The rest of the book relies on his own subjective, impressionistic comparisons to establish the "Phoenician" history of Great Zimbabwe, circulating around phrases like "compares curiously" (7), "They remind one" (7), "strikingly like" (11), "We divine the idea and the sentiment" (26). He floats the idea that the ruins of Zimbabwe themselves might constitute an archive, and even talks about the "sermons in stones" that they might yield. Even rocks, for him, are more voluble about history than Africans. Yet those "sermons" are, in reality, mostly made up of his own tendentious discoveries of formal similarities between the ruins of Great Zimbabwe and both Phoenician and Arabian ruins. The real archival substance lies in almost thirty pages of appendixes listing relevant manuscripts in Rome and Lisbon, and translations of Portuguese impressions of the area. Those archives are important because they imitate the form of what an archive for Great Zimbabwe would look like, but they do not have its content. The Portuguese merely happen to be the earliest visitors to Great Zimbabwe who left written records, and in Wilmot's book they both provide the form of a scriptural history and appear as interlopers in the historical record—in a sense, as invaders who form part of the chronicle of Great Zimbabwe's long deterioration.

Because Wilmot forecloses the value of any kind of local, "African" evidence, he has to construct geographically and chronologically far-flung archives from among the Phoenicians, the pre-Islamic Arabians, and the Portuguese. Somewhere in the immensely large period between the first and the third is the lacuna where Great Zimbabwe flourished. Wilmot can't be any clearer about when, precisely, Great Zimbabwe was at its height, but what he leaves out of his timeline is more revealing. It excludes three historical epochs: classical Greece and Rome, for the most part Islamic Arabia, and the European Middle Ages.[39] This last omission is especially telling: that is precisely the period when later—competent—archaeologists established that Great Zimbabwe flourished.

Yet the moments of rupture and collapse that Wilmot points to in Great Zimbabwe's history happen to chime with the conventional beginning, middle, and end of the European Middle Ages. The "barbarian invasion" of Rome hovers over Wilmot's historiography like a founding traumatic event. In his preface to the book, Sir Rider Haggard tacitly admits that this is an overdetermined trope: "A new incursion of barbarians took place—how many such have those ruins witnessed?" (Wilmot, xiv). Their innumerability is both an implicit admission of the fundamental incoherence of the historiography that Haggard and Wilmot are pursuing, and the necessary structural repetition of the same originary trauma: the barbarian invasion of Rome.

Wilmot compares three moments—and two kinds—of collapse repeatedly to the fall of Rome. The first is the original collapse of the civilization of Great Zimbabwe, which had already declined somewhat from the heights of its Phoenician founding: "To Europe the land was a *terra incognita*. . . . [F]or more than two thousand years a partially civilised people mined and traded with Arabia, whose only records are the ruins of towers and temples scattered throughout a land whose inhabitants were eventually subjugated by the most cruel barbarians who have ever disgraced the name of man in Africa" (101). What is striking about the passage is its historical vagueness. While evoking the figure of barbarian invasion, he situates this moment somewhere around CE 800–1000 (depending upon when he imagines Monomotapa was founded by the Phoenicians): either in the "Dark Ages" or the beginning of the High Middle Ages in Europe, according to what version of medieval chronology he followed at the time. It is not clear, either, what barbarians he means. There is a final, cataclysmic invasion, but elsewhere in the book he implies that there was a series of invasions over the centuries before the Portuguese arrived (and that, as we have just seen, constitutes a symptomatic awkwardness in Haggard's preface) (Wilmot, 137, 142, 145, 166).

While the invasion of Rome is a vague specter in the background of the various, ultimately unknown invasions of Monomotapa over the centuries, both Haggard and Wilmot put a vigorously reanimated Fall of Rome in the foreground when they discuss (what is for them) the final and dispositive invasion: the arrival of the "Zulus," "who rushed on the Mashonas of Monomotapa as the Huns and Goths hurled themselves on European civilization" (Wilmot, 69). By "Zulu" Wilmot means the amaNdebele, the group led by Lobengula who fought against Rhodes in the two Matabele Wars. But misnaming the amaNdebele is the least inaccurate thing in Wilmot's account. The supposed subjugation of the "Mashonas" is a colonial exaggeration (perhaps even invention). Rhodes's British South Africa Company propagated the myth of amaNdebele cruelty and ferocity—in the words of the company's secretary, they were a "cruel, damnable race"—in order to justify its invasion of Matabeleland in 1893.[40] The bellicosity of the amaNdebele was something of a trope. The missionary David Carnegie wrote about them in terms that seemed like a justification for the British South Africa Company takeover: amaNdebele government "really is no government worthy of the name, but a patched-up combination of heathen laws and customs."[41]

Wilmot makes a strange historiographical mistake. It is not one patently motivated by greed, as with the narrative of Zulu invasion. It is motivated by deeper structural assumptions about what the shape of history should be: that is, African history ought to bend in accordance with the events of European history. Wilmot places the arrival of Mzilikazi and the amaNdebele not in the years immediately after 1823, but—quite bizarrely—"late in the fifteenth or early in the sixteenth century" (69). As I will argue shortly, that moment conflicts with other events that Wilmot documents copiously. But this elementary timeline mistake on its own suggests condensations of meaning as rich as a Freudian dream. First, there is the explicit comparison of Great Zimbabwe with Rome and its invasion by the "Huns and Goths," the European-lite builders of Zimbabwe finally subjugated by barbarians. This is the repetition compulsion of European civilization, the drive to restore an earlier order of things—an ideology that Wilmot was in the process of helping to impart to the British South Africa Company. Second, there is the location of this event either in the Middle Ages or the moment of the Reformation in Europe.

For a Catholic like Wilmot, this allusion implied very different things than it did for most of his readers, who were British Protestants: it would have suggested the destruction of ancient ritual and belief, not their correction. A symptom of that identification with the abolition of a system of belief may be the nostalgic tone that creeps into his description of the traces of the primeval religion of Zimbabwe: "the religion of the people who built their fortresses was as much destroyed and passed out of use as the great edifices constructed by them. [Their successors] gazed upon the colossal ruins of the Phoenicians as the works of strangers from whose religion and comparative civilization they were alienated" (166).

Third, there is the contradictory deployment of the trope of Reformation *as* the restoration of a former order. The business of the British South Africa Company was to detect the echoes of a long-gone and virtually destroyed European civilization in the ruins of Africa and reanimate it with a new vigor and purity. As Rhodes's fascination with the textual sources of Gibbon and his sponsorship of Wilmot's search of European archives for the witness of early African trade and exploration attests, he was well aware of the potential of written archives to change—or to supposedly complete—history.[42]

Wilmot's reassignment of the amaNdebele arrival to a moment three hundred years before it actually happened is a triumph of ideology over archive. Not only does Wilmot ignore what he knew the archives had to say about the amaNdebele arrival, but the date of the invasion suggests a corollary about Great Zimbabwe that the colonizers resisted all the way through the Ian Smith regime: that Great Zimbabwe flourished during the European Middle Ages. Wilmot cites Portuguese accounts as early as 1516 that mention the long-standing trade in gold in the interior of Mozambique and Zimbabwe (133). He insinuates, in fact, that Portugal's interest in southern Africa dates from the Middle Ages. Henry the Navigator and his great-nephew King John II of Portugal sponsored expeditions that were at least in part, Wilmot suggests, intended to discover the mythical realm of Prester John. Wilmot reports that when Vasco da Gama anchored off Mozambique on March 10, 1498, he was told "that Prester John (about whom the Portuguese were specially ordered to inquire) lived at an immense distance inland" (128).

Because Wilmot associates the realm of Prester John with Great Zimbabwe, his book has an appendix titled "Complete List of Documents in the Archives of the Vatican Concerning Africa," a peculiar undercount, since the list is only twenty-six items long. But its purpose is really to locate Europe's interest in that part of Africa in the Middle Ages: the first item on the list begins not with an *incipit* or a shelf-mark, but with a date: 1282 (Wilmot, 225).

The Inconvenience of the Medieval

The chapter in which Wilmot discusses these documents locates the discovery of Great Zimbabwe and its wealth in gold firmly in the Middle Ages—indeed the *English* Middle Ages. His chapter opens with Henry IV and Edward III of England, not because they played any role in exploring southern Africa but simply because Henry IV, the grandson of Edward III, was the uncle of Henry the Navigator. Wilmot's beginning implies that the British claim to sovereignty over Zimbabwe begins with British medieval monarchs, not necessarily the Portuguese. Indeed, he subtly but resolutely compares the Portuguese with the barbarian invaders he believed had plunged Zimbabwe into its own *medium aevum*. The Portuguese perform, in Wilmot's account, something of the ambivalent work of Freudian identification. On the one hand, like Wilmot they were Catholic, and mark the arrival of Europe in Africa. On the other hand, Wilmot distances himself from them by a resolute application of racism. Without explicitly stating it, he insinuates that there is some kind of overlap between them and invaders like the Zulus in the Venn diagram of racial characteristics. The Portuguese are not destructive and violent, nihilistic like Africans, but they are still incapable of sustaining civilizations. "The Portuguese, like all the Latin races, are really not colonizers," he says, completely forgetting about the vast and long-lived Spanish empire, not to mention the ancient Romans (the French at this time were still, like the British, acquiring colonies) (136). Like his egregious misstatement of the date of the Zulu invasion, this one is a kind of tell, an indication that some kind of dreamwork is taking place.

In one moment, and in one group, the Portuguese embody both the invasion and the entropy theories of civilizational collapse. There was clearly, in Wilmot's mind, nothing at Great Zimbabwe that could still *be* collapsed, and he gently mocks the Portuguese implication that they had conquered any kind of empire. Wilmot frames the "absurdly inflated descriptions" in Portuguese accounts of the "Emperor" of Monomotapa by using scare quotes around the title throughout the book, and corrects Portuguese references to royal figures with a sneer: "Such grandiloquent titles as Emperor, King, Queens, and Princes, are perfect misnomers" (165).

Although the Portuguese map onto the inhabitants of Zimbabwe the social structures of medieval Europe, they are not, for Wilmot, fully European. They do not arrive in Africa with the purported intention to civilize: the news that gold was mined at Monomotapa "roused," Wilmot says with a stunning lack of self-awareness, "the attention, the cupidity, and the activity of the Portuguese" (130). The Portuguese are not the British, if only—and that presumably was enough—because they belong to a race that is incapable of colonizing. They are also archaic, driven (despite, and alongside, their "cupidity") by medieval motives. They are searching—"specially ordered to inquire"—for Prester John; their missionaries are like the Augustinian monks that Gregory the Great sent to convert England (161); they produce a "proto-martyr" according to the protocols of medieval hagiography.[43] They are distinctly Catholic, yet different enough from Wilmot because of their supposed racial difference that he is not implicated in their medievalized version of his own faith. The Portuguese dominion over Africa fails because of continual "decadence" (209), accompanied by not just strategic errors but structural failures, a "sad system of maladministration and degradation of character" (196). In the end, they are, he says, simply "a weak and waning nation" (221).

Wilmot's history reveals the sidesteps, silences, and fantasies that are necessary to write a history of Great Zimbabwe as originally European. Its very attempt at historiographical sophistication reveals the fundamental incoherence of Rhodes's—and Rhodesia's—insistence on the impossibility of a medieval Great Zimbabwe. What their literature on Great Zimbabwe referred to for the next ninety years as the enigmatic "silence" of Great Zimbabwe was, in fact, their own refusal to allow African voices out of the past to speak.

Another problem that mapping Rome and Carthage onto Great Zimbabwe resolved was why—and how—it fell. The crucial difference between the fall of Great Zimbabwe and the fall of Rome is that Rome fell because its unchallenged power, after the fall of Carthage, incubated a fatal moral decadence in the conqueror. Without significant external challenges to the Roman *imperium*, without what Sallust and Augustine called the *metus hostilis*, nothing prevented the catastrophic "disasters arising from prosperity." Its very dominance is what undid Rome, and, since Sallust, the powerful irony of success has dominated the historiography of the fall of Rome. The early historiography of the fall of Great Zimbabwe, however, from the 1850s on, assumed that its decline happened because the people who came after its peak simply didn't have the intelligence or cultural sophistication to maintain Great Zimbabwe's achievements. This casual assumption, almost treated as an axiom, lies behind the colonial argument that everything that looked characteristically "African" simply obscured the original achievements of Great Zimbabwe.

Other historians were even more openly racist. Hall, who was appointed the Curator of Great Zimbabwe in 1902 by Rhodes's British South Africa Company, asserted that the "decadence" of the Bantu "has been in operation for very many centuries." They were firmly stuck in the Middle Ages. It is not "possible," he says, "that the primitive Bantu of mediaeval times had the capacity to suddenly evolve . . . the *renaissance* which resulted . . . in the Zimbabwe Temple." That is because, he says, the Bantu experience a "sudden arrest of intelligence" at the onset of puberty.[44] To put this in the reprehensible terms of racist historiography:

the reason that there is no history in southern Africa is that its occupants are intellectually incapable of making it.

This monomaniacally circular argument more or less dominated the racist historiography of Great Zimbabwe until the end of the Rhodesian state. Structures like Great Zimbabwe are extraordinary; that means that they must have been built by an extraordinary intelligence; the people hereabouts do not seem to have extraordinary intelligence; that means they must not have built Great Zimbabwe; these structures therefore demonstrate how inferior their intelligence is to the extraordinary intelligence of the builders. In other words, the ruins of Zimbabwe could not be medieval because the only people in the area then were Africans, and they could not have built them.

The explicit target of this self-sustaining argument is any claim to sovereignty that Africans might make. Great Zimbabwe supposedly demonstrated that non-African peoples established a sophisticated civilization well before the political organization of Africans. Because these builders were more or less white (Phoenician, Egyptian, Arab, or Israelite), the newly arrived white occupiers were simply taking up a continuity that had been broken in the Middle Ages. The legitimation of sovereignty, too, is circular: the order of modernity depends on its intimate relation to antiquity. Cecil Rhodes's vision of a modern empire in southern Africa generated a library of poems, novels, and romances about this supposed pre-African past. All of it without exception portrays Great Zimbabwe as a historical and cultural void after the disappearance of the builders, and that disappearance as a powerful and imponderable historical mystery. The poem *Zimbabwe* by Andrew Lang, a friend of Rider Haggard's, is one of the most succinct examples of this sweeping romanticization:

> Into the darkness whence they came,
> They passed, their country knoweth none,
> They and their gods without a name,
> Partake the same oblivion (Wilmot, xix–xx).

There are actually two kinds of oblivion at work here: our own lack of information about the supposedly ancient inhabitants of Zimbabwe, and the acts of historical erasure that succeeding groups of Africans supposedly committed, wittingly or unwittingly. Yet both kinds of oblivion can be identified precisely because they did not work. Lang still "knows" that there were ancient inhabitants, and that they had gods—although we don't know what they were called—and that they disappeared, rather than being the ancestors of the people who still live in the area. Not only is oblivion not total—not really oblivion, that is—but it works to make historical fantasy legitimate. We can know nothing of the site's "real" history because it has been erased, but we know about it because it has been erased. The degree of erasure, in other words, is what guarantees the grandeur and importance of the culture that was erased. That culture must therefore have been magnificent, and, by definition, different from the later historical period in which it was erased.

Lang's poem was quoted by Haggard in his introduction to Wilmot's *Monomotapa*. A poet quoted by a novelist introducing a work by an historian: that convergence is one instance of a coterie that produced narratives yoked together by an ideology that supported Rhodes's conquest. It also suggests how many genres of writing flowed into the creation of that myth. The year before *Monomotapa* was published, Lang edited a collection of adventure stories for children called *The Red True Story Book*. It interrupted Lang's long-running series of fairy stories, and in the preface he apologized, suggesting that "real facts" could also "sometimes, be curious and interesting."[45] Its first story was by Rider Haggard, about the so-called Shangani Patrol, an attempt to capture Lobengula that ended in the deaths of almost all of the participants. The Shangani Patrol became a Rhodesian national myth; the bodies were first buried at Great Zimbabwe, as we have seen, and later reinterred near Cecil Rhodes's grave, outside of Bulawayo. Already in 1895, Haggard was shaping the story as a kind of mythic charter. For him, the last stand of the Shangani Patrol established its place in both indigenous and imperial history: "The fame of this death of theirs has spread far and wide throughout the native races of Southern Africa, and Englishmen everywhere reap the benefit of its glory."[46] Haggard's source for the story was one of the few men who escaped from the Shangani Patrol: Alexander Burnham, the American adventurer lured to Zimbabwe by Haggard's stories, whose daughter Nada (named after a heroine of a Haggard novel) died the next year in Bulawayo—as Haggard recorded in the dedication to his novel *Elissa*.

Again and again, these narratives loop back upon themselves and their authors, always circling around both the mythic ideology behind Rhodes's conquest and its political and military execution, like planets orbiting a black hole. Individual narratives also worked the same way, anxiously distracting observers from the void at their core. In his preface to Wilmot's *Monomotapa*, Haggard is convinced that, despite the "oblivion that covered the land and its story" the Phoenicians (or "some race intimately connected with them") first built the town at Great Zimbabwe. His frank admission at this point of two obstacles to the theory is telling. First, he concedes that there is no "testimony" that the Phoenicians were present there; and, second, "no inland Phoenician town is known to history." But, he says, this does not mean that the Phoenicians could not have built Great Zimbabwe. Apart from this syllogistic shred, his primary evidence is, essentially, that the Phoenicians were adventurous, and that the adventurousness of the English proves that Phoenician settlement was possible. In other words, because the English were now exploiting Great Zimbabwe and the land around it, it must have been originally exploited by non-Africans.

The shakiness—no, the incoherence—of this argument is closer to the logic of dreams than to real historical inquiry. The ease and nonchalance in the assumption that the original settlers could have been Phoenician, Egyptian, Israelite, or refugees from Atlantis is like the loose associations in what Freud calls condensation. In dreams, condensation brings together contradictory ideas and treats them as if they contain no contradictions. The argument that Great Zimbabwe, for instance, was founded by "whites" depends on the actions of peoples that the contemporary English would not consider "white": Egyptians, Phoenicians, Israelites. The concept of "civilization" in writing about Great Zimbabwe is a condensation: it is English and "white," and is the product, if not the marker, of modernity. Yet this argument also assumes, at the same time, that there was something very much like "civilization" in the ancient past. The claim that *English* civilization has some kind of right to possess Great Zimbabwe rests on the assumption that English and bronze-age civilizations share some kind of profound similarity that African culture does not share with either of them. The credulity of Europeans about the African past seems virtually limitless—at least about the past that was *not* the one that belonged to Africans. In the case of Great Zimbabwe, that past was the Middle Ages.

The fantasy of extraneous occupation always contained, to some degree, the *end* of that past. There is almost as much speculation about how Great Zimbabwe ended as there is about how it began. The work of fantasy is just as much about contemporary imperialism as it is about the imperialism of the "ancient" rulers of Great Zimbabwe. The aggression behind many of the fantasies of the destruction of past imperialism (witness Haggard's evocation of "hordes of invading savages stamping [Zimbabwe] out of existence with their blood-stained feet" [*Elissa*, 9]) betrays the intensity of a fear that the past contained both the possibility of oblivion and the answers to it. It is yet another contradiction in the fantasized European origin of Great Zimbabwe. If the "Bantu" were capable of creating a cataclysmic historical event, then that meant that they also had a history. To contradict Hugh Trevor-Roper, something really did happen in African history.

Even two of the proponents of the theory that Great Zimbabwe was built more than two thousand years before admitted privately, as did Theodore Bent, and publicly, as Hall did in a book published in 1905, that none of the artifacts or buildings was older than a few centuries.[47] The history of Great Zimbabwe, in other words, included the ancestors of the Africans who still lived around it (although Hall still thought it was built by Arabs). In 1906, David Randall-MacIver, an archaeologist trained in Egypt by W. M. Flinders Petrie, published a book with the trenchant title *Medieval Rhodesia*. It summarized his 1905 excavations at Great Zimbabwe and other ruins in the area, and systematically demonstrated that there was nothing older than the medieval period. It devastates other arguments about Great Zimbabwe's age with donnish wit: they "professed, as might be expected, a knowledge of lost ancient history which the most learned Orientalists do not dream of claiming"; "if it has been necessary to abandon that dream, it is because it has proved to be incompatible with any respect for science and the logic of observed facts."[48] In Randall-MacIver's book, the medieval period was suddenly regarded as sophisticated *because* it was medieval. The study of the African Middle Ages was no longer the study of ruination, oblivion, and ignorance. It was the study of the historical depth of Indigenous people, their extension backward in time to the roots of their own sovereignty.

Randall-MacIver's is one of the rare cases of a European describing the period of the Middle Ages in Africa as a period of African *sophistication*, rather than an epoch of backwardness in comparison with modern Europe. He anticipates some of the recent work recuperating a powerful and momentous, often "medieval," African past—such as Henry Louis Gates's television series *Africa's Great Civilizations*. There were also some sporadic, and not very widespread, attempts to recuperate the Middle

Ages in the period of independence. D. T. Niane's edition of the *Sundiata* epic, the story of the founder of the Malian empire in the thirteenth century, for instance, celebrates the preservation of the glorious African past in oral history; several of Léopold Sédar Senghor's poems meditate on the same period.[49]

But as Sylvie Kandé argues, this attention to a medieval African past was criticized by other African writers as falling into the history already dictated by Europeans. Niane himself "urged African intellectuals not to define their modernity as postmedieval."[50] Several years after Niane's edition came out, Yambo Ouologuem's novel *Bound to Violence* devastatingly satirized Frobenius's kind of medievalism, which in Ouologuem's book is a distinctly European fantasy. The barely disguised "Shrobenius" profits academically and monetarily from his celebration of Africa's "grandiose empires of the Middle Ages." He sells more than 1,300 African artifacts to European institutions, sparking a frenzy of antiquities extraction by Europeans. The supply of genuine pieces quickly runs out, and copies are rapidly created that are supposedly *"charged with the weight of four centuries of civilization."*[51] In some ways, what happened with "Shrobenius" is what happened with the first European encounters with Great Zimbabwe. Artifacts like the great stone birds were saved as evidence of ancient art. But the gold was literally extracted, by the Ancient Ruins Company, formed by W. G. Neal in 1895 for the purpose of ransacking ruins in Zimbabwe.[52] Neal reused the term "Ancient" in the book he cowrote with Hall in 1904: *The Ancient Ruins of Rhodesia*. Some of the pillaged gold may have paid for the book.

Randall-MacIver was well aware of the intense investment that most Europeans had in the myth of ancient settlement, but also carefully and deliberately calls it a "romance that has been destroyed" (87). He suggests that there is a newer, better romance to be written: "Were I a Rhodesian I should feel that in studying the contemporary natives in order to unravel the story of the ruins I had a task as romantic as any student could desire" (87). In a witty subversion of the convention that European modernity has corrected the ignorance and degeneration of the Middle Ages, Randall-MacIver accuses the makers of popular opinion about Great Zimbabwe of being no better than medieval chroniclers (vii). Like these chroniclers, popular opinion has demonstrated "an uncritical credulity that would have been as admirable in their days as it is unworthy in our own" (vii). It began with the off-the-cuff speculations of the Portuguese explorers of the early sixteenth century, and with the zany fantasies of Karl Mauch in 1871. You can hear the frustration in Randall-MacIver's book about having to address the implausible ideas about Great Zimbabwe that had already lodged in the popular press by 1906. Yet investigators who presented themselves as serious and qualified archaeologists continued to defend the discredited theory for the next seventy years.

Many of these, admittedly, were "pseudo-archaeologists" hired by the white supremacist Ian Smith regime to shore up that theory, because, just as it did for Rhodes, it supported the historical claims that whites made for their earlier sovereignty over the area.[53] In 1970, the Rhodesian Front government decreed "that no official publication may state unequivocally that Great Zimbabwe was an African creation."[54] In 1965, the year that Rhodesia declared unilateral independence from Britain because it refused to change its racist policies, a South African economist, A. J. Bruwer, dedicated his defense of the Phoenician hypothesis, *Zimbabwe: Rhodesia's Ancient Greatness*, to Ian Smith.[55] Its title, said one review, might "tempt the unwary into believing this was a work of historical scholarship."[56] No Phoenician graves had been found, Bruwer argued, because they were too deep; the gold mines could not be "Bantu" because they had no word for gold. It was more than frank about its sympathies for the Smith regime and its dependence on the myth of a Phoenician Great Zimbabwe. Bruwer uses the histrionic language that sympathetic Rhodesians at the time used: archaeologists had "whipped up" "ruthless propaganda" into a "destructive hurricane." Opponents of the Phoenician hypothesis were really, Bruwer said, "politico-archeologists." Sadly, that label was taken seriously by the Smith government, except it was used to discredit serious archaeologists. In 1970, the Rhodesian Inspector of Monuments, Peter Garlake, a highly respected archaeologist who was later to refound the discipline in independent Zimbabwe, was forced to resign and leave the country because he refused to endorse the Phoenician myth. His 1973 book *Great Zimbabwe* argued not just that there was an absence of evidence from before the medieval period, but that Great Zimbabwe had been built by the ancestors of the modern Karanga people.

The term "politico-archaeologists" made its way into one of the bestsellers of 1972, Wilbur Smith's *The Sunbird*.[57] The novel is set in an ancient city on the border of Botswana and Rhodesia, but is clearly a version of Haggard's Zimboe. The story is split between the narrative of the city's fall and the present, when archaeologists rediscover the site. After they discover a wall painting of a mysterious figure that one of them calls the "portrait of our wonderful white king" (60), they talk about how no one will now be able to deny their hypothesis that the city had been built by a white race (68). Nevertheless, they imagine how the evidence will be distorted, and that the entry for the site in the *Encyclopedia Britannica* will claim that it was "the work of some Bantu group" (61). That distortion would be the work, says the novel's hero, a brilliant, misunderstood archaeologist named Benjamin Kazin, of "the debunkers, the special pleaders, the politico-archeologists, who could twist any evidence to fill the needs of their own beliefs, the ones who had castigated me and my books" (61). Smith had clearly been reading A. J. Bruwer. Kazin has written a book called *Ophir* that essentially follows Bruwer's argument: Carthaginians left Carthage around 200 BCE and settled the area. In Smith's novel, Kazin discovers a gold scroll in the ruins of the city that resoundingly confirms his hypothesis: Carthaginians who survived the destruction of Carthage by Scipio Africanus sailed to southern Africa and built a new city named Opet.

Wilbur Smith later claimed that he did not really believe the Phoenician theory; in his autobiography he claims that "any schoolboy" could tell that the ruins were built by "African natives."[58] Yet a few pages later he talks about how he had developed "my own theories" about Great Zimbabwe—the notion that it had been founded by Carthaginians (164). Smith is more subtle about the consequences for the present day of this story than the Rhodesian government at the time was. But one of Smith's characters in *Sunbird* says, "we white Africans are like the old Carthaginians" (167). Africans, however, tend to be compared to animals, described as dirty or coarse, demented or savage. The main villain is an African protégé of Kazin's, who turns out to be "one of the most dangerous terrorists in Africa" (122). The fall of Opet under the pressure of a "solid mass of black humanity" migrating from the north and the war of independence currently going on in Rhodesia—during which opponents of the Smith regime were described as "terrorists"—are clearly linked (169). The city of Opet finally falls under what is named only as "Blackness" (439).

Smith's story bookends two empires: the Carthaginian empire of Opet and the present-day racial "empire" of white-ruled South Africa and Rhodesia. The word "empire" is used to describe both the immense influence and wealth of the Cecil Rhodes figure in the story and the hegemony of the people of Opet. Smith uses *Indaba, My Children*, an oral history by the Zulu writer Credo Mutwa, for information about a rock painting, the White Lady of the Brandberg, that is clearly a model for the white king of Smith's story. The painting, says Mutwa, is a "young white man, one of the great emperors who ruled the African Empire of the Maiti [Phoenicians] for nearly two centuries."[59]

Credo Mutwa's first books are collections of narratives about the Zulu past, which tends to stand in for an African past in general. They've been used for archival and ethnographic research, and for recreating a Zulu past. In the 1980s, Mutwa built a series of "heritage" villages to bring the past he recorded to life. His work is widely pointed to as a powerful example of indigenous knowledge, and Mutwa appeared on conference panels worldwide as one of its most powerful champions. Yet his legacy is ambiguous: toward the end of his life, he coauthored books with David Icke, a reputed Holocaust denier and a popularizer of conspiracy theories, including the so-called lizard theory conspiracy—the notion that the earth is secretly governed by alien reptilian beings. That doesn't necessarily compromise Mutwa's earlier work, but much of it hasn't been corroborated by other accounts. In the interests of respect to a Zulu elder, what I can do is simply to point out that Mutwa's history of the Phoenician settlement matches the accounts of Haggard, Bent, and other white visitors to Great Zimbabwe, although Mutwa's history is vastly more detailed, including painstaking reconstructions of Phoenician kings and warriors drawn from "Bantu" descriptions.

Mutwa's politics, too, line up with the political motivations—or consequences—of the Phoenician myth. He was an explicit supporter of apartheid. The final chapter of a 1969 collection of his historical narratives argues that apartheid is "what the Bantu want" because "it is a law of nature" (Credo Mutwa, 253). Mutwa also supported the creation of so-called Bantustans, regions in which the government cordoned often-displaced members of what they designated as separate tribes. What Mutwa objected to was social discrimination, the kind of daily insults of epidermal racism that Fanon describes. But apartheid, Mutwa says, "distinguishes *without* deciding which is better" (253; emphasis in original). The Bantustans will allow people to recreate or preserve their traditions, including tribal law. The term "tribal law" is, as we have seen, one of the creations of indirect rule, and Mutwa argues for it as a permanent system of governance. His reason, surprisingly, dips into colonial representations of Africans as constitutionally incapable of modernity: one of the "faults of my race," Mutwa says, is susceptibility to bribery (256). But there's a fundamental incoherence in his vision of governance, which implies a centralized, sovereign rule, and it's one that he says includes "every black man" of Africa—for whom the European system of government is "utterly incomprehensible"—although his preferred system is explicitly Zulu: "rulership by a single chief and his indunas" (257).

That form of centralized government may have existed in past centuries among the Zulu—and Mutwa's work may still be an important source for the indigenous knowledge of Zulu social relations. But recent work on indigenous knowledges suggests that many other forms were either erased or remade by colonial policy. The "chiefdoms" it defined often coincided with the political history of an area. But sometimes things were more complicated. The Zimbabwean historian Gerald Chikozho Mazarire shows how a chiefdom imposed on the Mapanzure/Hera people, just south of Great Zimbabwe, has led to multiple conflicting accounts of its origin, mostly because the name the colonial administration imposed, Chishanga, described a district in the long-gone eighteenth-century Rozvi confederacy. The name was used *in* the area by groups who later moved there, but it was not used as the name *of* the area. It is now more what Mazarire calls an imagined geography than a territory marked by Native Reserves Commissions.[60] Underlying this geographical fluidity, he argues, are indigenous Shona concepts of time and space that spill out of the colonial box, and that suggest ways to decolonize geography—ways that have nothing to do with feudal England.

But imagining how to do that begins with understanding how profoundly the imagination of European colonizers shaped the land, the laws, and the histories of former colonies. That imagination did not just invent things that did not exist before in Africa. It invented things that never existed in Europe, but which came, through the multifarious pressures of colonialism, to seem more and more real in medieval scholarship, anthropology, political theology, and colonial governments. What was once a dream of a medieval Europe, a feudal metaphor, often assumes the identity of important contemporary beliefs that are represented as authentic, even precolonial, principles in law and politics.

In profound, sometimes destructive ways, someone else's dream became Africa's. But we do not need more dreams about Africa. We just need to wake up to what it has always been.

CODA

The New Divine Kings

I keep asking myself, what will happen to divine kingship in modern Africa.

MONICA WILSON, 1959 Frazer Lecture

Our present rulers in Africa are in every sense late-flowering medieval monarchs.

CHINUA ACHEBE, *Anthills of the Savannah*

As we saw in the last chapter, African scholars are discovering ways to imagine what an Africa that was not remapped by the European feudal analogy could look like. As a medievalist, however, I am doomed to hear the echoes of that past in Africa. When the life of Robert Mugabe, the fiercely anti-colonialist but authoritarian leader of independent Zimbabwe for thirty years, was drawing to an end, I unavoidably thought of Kantorowicz. Mugabe's wife Grace said that he could run as a corpse in the 2018 elections and still win. Even as a corpse he would still have the mystical body of a sacred king. At Mugabe's funeral, a priest declared "this man lives forever."[1]

In fact, Mugabe was deposed shortly before he died, and that modern test of the medieval legal principle didn't happen. But there was a bitter contest over where his corpse was to be buried. The king, says Kantorowicz, still "seems to will after his death," and whoever controlled Mugabe's burial would be seen as Mugabe's chosen successor.

The government of the Second Republic wanted Mugabe to be buried at National Heroes Acre, a burial site for Zimbabwe African National Union–Political Front (ZANU–PF) officials; a coalition of Shona chiefs wanted him to be buried according to traditional practice, in a sacred cave; Grace Mugabe wanted a private burial at his country house. In the end, he was buried at his house in a Catholic ceremony. But shortly afterward, rumors began that either a "Shona chief" or Emmerson Mnangagwa, Mugabe's successor, wanted to retrieve a symbol of authority that Mugabe has supposedly been buried with: a club called a *tsvimbo yaMambo*, the chief's (or king's) staff. It soon began to be called a scepter, and a Pentecostal prophet described it in terms that are closer to medieval political theology than Shona or Ndebele customs. The scepter would "ensure the complete transfer of power," he said, and must be "surrendered to the next person, according to the Holy Spirit." It was not a physical thing, he said, "it's a spiritual thing."[2] As Kantorowicz points out, quoting Shakespeare's *Richard II*, Richard's stripping of his royal regalia (including the scepter) is a spiritual process: it marked the forfeiture of Richard's mystical body, the *corpus politicum*, and its assumption by Henry IV (Kantorowicz, 34–40).

Handing over a *tsvimbo* is a traditional way to designate the next head of a household or group, but the language of succession here comes from medieval political theology, via the discourse of Pentecostalism, one of the largest and most dynamic forms of Christianity in sub-Saharan Africa. African Pentecostalism arrived first in South Africa in 1908, and expanded in several waves, forming organized groups, like the Assemblies of God and many independent churches, often unaffiliated with any Western organization. It features ecstatic worship, a focus on the end times, prosperity, and spiritual warfare, often with a nationalist flavor. It is often not just politically oriented, but increasingly integrated into the political life of a nation. When Kenyan President William Ruto, an ardent Pentecostal, ran for office in 2022, he signed an agreement with a coalition of Evangelical and Pentecostal churches. It promised budgetary allocations for pastors, allocations of land to churches, appointments to commissions, state corporations, Cabinet positions, and a Cabinet-level office for religious affairs. Implicit and explicit agreements like that have been described as Pentecostal state capture, but they are also rearticulations of the medieval sacral functions of the state.

The political language of state-linked Pentecostalism tends to be taken from biblical monarchical imagery and medieval political theology. Godfrey Nzira, a prophet in the African Independent Church, proclaimed that Mugabe was the "divinely appointed king of Zimbabwe."³ That language of divine rulership frequently becomes part of the discourse of a ruling party, not just of independent Pentecostal leaders. Leaders of Uganda's ruling National Resistance Movement have described Yuweri Museveni, the autocratic leader of Uganda since 1986, as "heaven sent and a messiah in Uganda," who, like Christ, had "left his comfort zone of heaven and opted to come down to earth to die for sinners."⁴

In his massive book, Kantorowicz traced the thousand-year process by which the language and imagery of Christ's divinity was wrapped around kings. The theological language became, to use a word Kantorowicz employed, secularized. The process of secularization usually implies the way we became modern: as the West became less religious, it was "disenchanted," in Emile Durkheim's famous phrase. Institutions became separated into religious and state entities; the forces of industrialization created jobs that required specialized skills and fragmented occupations. Max Weber, in tracing the process by which capitalism developed out of Calvinism, described it as the "withdrawal or release" of institutions from ecclesiastical or spiritual discipline.⁵ Or, in Carl Schmitt's barbed formula, "All significant concepts of the modern theory of the state are secularized theological concepts."⁶

Some African states opted for secularism at independence. Mozambique, for example, explicitly defined itself as a secular state.⁷ But former English colonies in Africa had their constitutions effectively handed to them. The British Colonial Office negotiated with the soon-to-be-independent colonies, whose representatives often included settlers. The outlines of these constitutions were similar, and came to be known as the Lancaster Template after Lancaster House, in London, where the conferences were held. The Lancaster Template didn't demand separation between church and state, but it avoided religious language and allowed religious pluralism. Rather than unfold over several centuries, in other words, secularization happened to African states within a few years.

Zimbabwe's 1980 constitution does not mention God, except in the formula for oaths of office ("So help me God"). It put in place a head of state (the president) and a head of government (the prime minister). Mugabe was the first prime minister, but seven years later he also became the president. Mugabe increasingly mingled power and ceremony, and he eventually became a theocrat, a virtual divine king. In the years since independence Zimbabwe, like several other states, went through a process of *de*secularization. In December 1991, the president of the southern African state of Zambia, "on behalf of the nation," declared his country a "Christian Nation."[8] Governments are increasingly endowed with spiritual and religious functions, from which they also draw their legitimacy. In 2013, Zimbabwe's new constitution included a preamble acknowledging "the supremacy of Almighty God, in whose hands our future lies."

In the later Mugabe years, as we have seen, his state supremacy and the supremacy of God began to coalesce. ZANU-PF officials said that following politicians other than Mugabe was a sin like idolatry, and that Mugabe's politics had made him "close to the son of God" (Nyahuma, 175). In an infamous speech, the ZANU-PF youth leader Kudzanai Chipanga said that Mugabe would be seated next to God, deciding who would be admitted to heaven. But he wouldn't do it alone: Zimbabwe's finance minister, Ignatius Chombo, would be "Secretary of Administration," and would hand names to Mugabe for approval; women would be vetted by Grace Mugabe; and Chipanga would approve the youth who worked with him in ZANU-PF. Heaven was recast in the image of the ZANU-PF bureaucracy. Mugabe's government may have inherited a secularized state, but by the end of his regime it had resacralized, at least in the obsequious imaginations of ZANU-PF party members, the dignity of office. It was the government of a sacred king.

But Chipanga's vision of Mugabe at the right hand of God leading a heavenly bureaucracy is also, precisely because it is a modern bureaucracy, a secular vision. It is not a theology of kingship as much as it is a theology of Lord Lugard's indirect rule. Mugabe might make the ultimate decisions, and sit next to God, but the petty, individual work of "approving" is delegated to officials who judged people according to the rules—customs, if you will—that applied to them. Thus, Grace Mugabe judges women; Chipanga judges people according to how well they had worked for ZANU-PF. It's a feverish version of the two tiers of judicial administration in the colonial system, with government-appointed chiefs overseeing areas with subordinate "customary" laws.

Rather than erase it, Zimbabwe ultimately strengthened forms of indirect rule in revisions of its constitution.[9] The 2013 constitution strengthened the authority of customary law and recognized customary law courts. It kept the system of chiefs inherited from the 1980 constitution intact, but took out the term "tribespeople," referring to "traditions" and "traditional leaders" instead. As with indirect rule, the selection of chiefs is a bit murky: they are elected; they are appointed by the President on the recommendation of the Council of Chiefs; they should be chosen "in accordance with the prevailing culture, customs, traditions and practices of the communities concerned."[10] This murkiness is a symptom of what Mahmood Mamdani describes as the legacy of indirect rule: a way to govern by division.[11] Customary law can't extend beyond the tribe, and so it is difficult to build political alliances among tribal divisions. But customary law, and the governing structures it left behind, keep the idea of the tribe as a specifically political thing alive.

The reemergence of the divine king in authoritarian regimes may depend on the maintenance of tribal divisions. But it also uses, as we have seen, the language and analogies of the political theology of both medieval Europe and traditional religion. Even the socialist President of Senegal, Léopold Sédar Senghor, Africa's most famous poet and leading thinker of Négritude, used the analogy of medieval and early modern monarchism to define the modern African presidency:

> The president personifies the Nation as did the Monarch of former times his peoples. The masses are not mistaken who speak of the "reign" of Modibo Keita [Mali], Sekou Toure [Guinea] and Houphouet-Biogny [Ivory Coast], in whom they see above all, the elected of God through the people.[12]

The idea that the monarch "personifies" the people is best articulated in Thomas Hobbes's *Leviathan*, a work written during the English Civil War that advocates for rule by an absolute sovereign. The idea that the king emanates, or stems, from the people, however, is a principle in medieval political philosophy. Senghor's definition of the sovereign is a strange mishmash of early modern absolutist theories of power and medieval theology. His pun on "election" is telling: it means both the popular vote of the people and the choice of God (*eligo*, "I choose"). The question of who, precisely, decides thus recedes into the shadows cast by the charismatic ruler.

But "election" has increasingly become a thing irrelevant to modern African presidencies. Even where constitutions have not been amended to make the presidency a term for life, elections take place in one-party states, or the election apparatus has been captured by the ruling party.

The strongman appointing himself president for life is often pointed to as an example of the chaos of the modern African state, or, even worse, as an example of the premature nature of independence. But it is also a holdover of the fundamentally medieval structure of governance and jurisprudence that colonizers put in place. In one sense, it is a literalization of the idea that the *dignitas* of the sovereign does not die, that the mystical and personal bodies converge in the postindependence leader. Another source is the idea of sovereign immunity, the principle that the king is not subject to the laws of his own courts. English law is famous for its capacity to tolerate institutional checks on royal power, notably in the Magna Carta. But Roman civil law, which continued to profoundly influence English law, enshrined the principle that the sovereign is not bound by the laws (*Princeps solibus solutus est*). In practice, the monarch was not subject to the courts in medieval English law: Pollock and Maitland called the idea that the king could be hauled into court "a pious legend of Westminster Hall."[13]

Constitutional revisions since independence in Africa have increased the extent of presidential immunity, either by amendments or in entire new constitutions. Life terms and the principle of immunity tend to strengthen each other in constitutions: as long as one is president, one cannot be charged with a crime, even when the constitution might allow the president to be prosecuted after he or she leaves office.[14]

Presidents have created a kind of *corpus mysticum* by a process of church capture, as we have seen with the president of Kenya, William Ruto. In Zimbabwe, the relation has been a mutually beneficial "theodicy of legitimation," especially, although not exclusively, among the African Initiated (or Indigenous, or Independent) Churches (AICs).[15] Rallies to support ZANU-PF and their leaders would defend Mugabe against critics; in turn, ZANU-PF officials would steer disputes through courts and commissions in favor of AIC interests.

The particular appeal that ZANU-PF had for AICs, and that AICs had for ZANU-PF, was the common ideology of liberation and indigenization. Both emerged in opposition to colonialism, and staunchly defended the importance of African traditions. In the Mugabe era, both used the rhetoric of the anti-colonial struggle to define what a "true" politics or a "true" Christianity might be. One of the tragic ironies of the ZANU-PF capture of AICs is that it depended on their *resistance* to state institutions and their orientation toward local traditions. It was only when Mugabe's land reforms lost him the support of Western governments that he began to co-opt the AIC history of celebrating indigenous traditions in the face of Western oppression. In Mugabe's rhetoric, this became a struggle of "African" values against imperialism: "We as chiefs in Zimbabwe," he said, "should fight against such Western practices and respect our culture."[16]

It was precisely the independence of AICs from Western denominations that was part of their political appeal. They represented African forms of experience that did not depend upon structures left by colonial missionaries and administrators, and did not need to conform to doctrinal or ecclesiological statements drafted outside Zimbabwe. They could be exuberant, worshipful, deeply spiritual, and entirely African. Some AIC members integrated practices and beliefs from traditional religion more thoroughly than others; some paid more attention to the historical points of global Christian orthodoxy. But the Mugabe regime was extremely nervous about both AICs and Pentecostal Churches of Christ (PCCs) participating in global Christian movements. Mainline Christian denominations clearly divided their loyalties between their local parishes, congregations, presbyteries, meetings, synods, dioceses, and governing bodies outside the country. But independent churches did not—except that many saw themselves as part of a global movement that transcended the petty divisions of denominational Christianity. Part of the theological imagination of Pentecostal Christianity, in particular, is that it is fulfilling the call of the Gospels to evangelize the whole world, to make disciples of all nations. That is why tiny churches in the African countryside often have names like "Worldwide Ministries" or "International Gospel Group."

The independent churches were politically useful for the Mugabe regime, and paradoxically the regime had to enforce that independence. When the Zimbabwe Assemblies of God, Africa, eventually one of Mugabe's staunchest supporters, tried to hold a rally with other denominations in 1988, the ministries of both Foreign Affairs and Home Affairs banned it and deported the invited speakers. The intervention of the two ministries demonstrates the double threat of the rally: "trans-denominational public gatherings" opened the way to alliances between independent churches, and with mainline denominations; and those alliances had "international repercussions."[17] The government is sacralized by churches that are both independent from each other and from political and global structures; but the consequence for those churches is that this independence becomes a politically enforced condition of their existence.

These churches in turn can take on the very political structures of the regime they support. After they came to embrace the Mugabe regime, the Zimbabwe Assemblies of God adopted the same leadership structure as ZANU-PF, and Mugabe in turn used the Assemblies of God's charismatic techniques to control ZANU-PF (Nyahuma, 183). Mugabe's leadership eventually incorporated a literal, Pentecostal version of charisma, the gifts of the Holy Spirit. It is yet another form of the desecularization of government in the Mugabe era. In the 1920s, the sociologist Max Weber analyzed the innate force that leaders seemed to acquire, or that their power was based on, as a secularization of charisma. He wrote amid the same intellectual ferment in Germany over political theology that involved Carl Schmitt, Walter Benjamin, and Ernst Kantorowicz.[18] We have already discussed Kantorowicz's imputation of Frederick II's charisma to Stefan George as a "future leader" of Germany. But while he was working on *The King's Two Bodies*—which the anthropologist Clifford Geertz described as a history of the "vicissitudes of royal charisma"—Kantorowicz also explored the vast network of ancient and medieval influences on the nature of charisma in medieval and early modern kingship.[19] He worked on this for some time. He gave a talk in 1951 that was a fleshed-out version of a 1945 paper; before his death in 1963, he corrected proofs for a long article based on the 1951 talk, which was not published.[20] It traces the relation between the throne and the conferral—and demonstration—of the sovereign's charisma: the throne represents divinity seated with the sovereign. The accuracy of Kantorowicz's argument is demonstrated in Chipanga's vision of Mugabe in heaven, seated beside God.

Kantorowicz predicted, that is, the very forms by which Mugabe's divine kingship would be represented. As with his work on kingship generally, there are subterranean but extensive reverberations from and in African anthropological work. Clifford Geertz's characterization of *The King's Two Bodies* as a history of royal charisma reminds us, citing Evans-Pritchard's "The Divine Kingship of the Shilluk," that "anthropological studies, especially those done in Africa, have of course been sensitive to such issues for a long time."[21]

The mystification of Mugabe's corpse reminds us of another connection with divine kingship: its definition *as* the capacity to die, as it was defined in work like Seligman's and Evans-Pritchard's—and popularized in Frazer's *Golden Bough*. And, it turns out, in Kantorowicz's work as well. His unpublished essay on enthronement and charisma exposes one of the central themes of *The King's Two Bodies*: that the notion of the continuity of rule takes place over the corpse of the king. As Alfons Puirgarnau, in his study of Kantorowicz's enthronement essay, puts it, "The death of the king is a key fact for understanding the notion of charisma in Kantorowicz."[22]

Of all the many sources that flow into the resacralization of leadership—medieval and early modern political theory, modern ethnography, comparative mythology, indigenous practices—the most active is the Pentecostal and charismatic church (and, to the degree that they incorporate charismatic practices, AICs). They form a circuit, as we have seen, with the charismatic leader, and respiritualize the secular metaphor of the king's political body. But their very independence, their innate spontaneity, poses a problem of governance: how to restrict their political power when that very power bolsters a regime, and when the basic ideology of Pentecostalism is trans-national, global evangelism.

In African regimes that are less repressive than Mugabe's, one of the instruments of control is a "Christianized" discourse of anti-homosexuality. The political discourse—one could say the sovereign discourse—of homophobia invariably twins the accusations that it is un-biblical and un-African: President Daniel arap Moi of Kenya claimed that homosexuality is "against African tradition and biblical teachings"; Nigerian President Olusegun Obasanjo said that it is "clearly un-biblical, unnatural, and definitely un-African."[23] Yet political homophobia in Africa has distinctively un-African roots.

The Ugandan anti-homosexual legislation, for example, has multiple trails back to fundamentalist organizations in the United States. The Christian Right activist Scott Lively addressed the Ugandan Parliament during an anti-homosexual conference that he organized in Kampala; the Fellowship Foundation spent somewhere around $20 million in Uganda, and its associate, the Ugandan cabinet minister David Bahati, introduced the bill in Parliament.[24] After it was passed, Janet Museveni, the Minister of Education and the wife of President Yoweri Museveni, commended the legislation and reported that she had just met with Sharon Slater from the conservative Mormon group Family Watch. She and Slater agreed, she said, about the importance of "safeguarding African culture and family values against emerging threats."[25]

Museveni's own homophobia has deeper philosophical and historical layers. He has tended to focus on the "natural law" argument about procreation, a bulwark of conservative Catholic teaching on sexuality, with its roots going back to Thomas Aquinas. He does argue that homosexuality is promulgated by a Western neocolonial agenda, but at the same time he admits that it has a precolonial history in Africa. In one speech before Christian (primarily Catholic) leaders he admitted that it was "there before you [i.e., Christianity] came," but that it was a "deviation from the teaching of the Bible."[26] Museveni wraps his package of homophobic arguments in political opportunism: it gets its real luster from the larger, and very real, goals of establishing national sovereignties in Africa, and the fight against neocolonialism and neoliberalism. Once you open the package, however, the things inside fall apart: homosexuality is an instrument of neocolonialism; it is authentically African; it was there before Christianity arrived; it is non-biblical; therefore it is not African, because it is non-Christian.

There are a number of historical ironies in Museveni's arguments that homosexuality is "imposed" by Western countries, and that homosexuality is un-African. Kabaka Mwanga II, the colonial-era ruler of Buganda (a kingdom within Uganda), was famous both for his nonnormative sexuality, and for his opposition to Christianity. His execution of a number of Christians in his court fueled gossipy reports about his thwarted sexual desires, and the innate "barbarism" of his sexual preferences.[27] Most of those reports came from British missionaries, so that is where the Christian anti-homosexuality that Museveni ultimately taps into begins. But colonial administrations developed much of the ideological and legal framework for anti-homosexuality, which became an explicit part of colonial mechanisms of control. The perception that homosexuality was not only an "oriental vice" but also one that was endemic in the tropics prompted administrators to adapt medieval and early modern statutes that concerned sodomy.[28] The Indian Penal Code was the kernel for more expansive legislation in other colonies; one of the strictest and most comprehensive was the Penal Code of Uganda. The Penal Code was explicitly a biopolitics, a form of government that seeks to control populations in order to maximize the life—to increase the efficiency—of populations.

In the colonial context, this meant a wide array of laws that regulated "native" life in ways that did not apply to settlers: native labor ordinances, pass and land laws, restrictions on crops that could be grown. Land laws that were tied to the "efficiency" of "native livestock" are uncomfortably on the nose, almost too explicit about the regulation of reproduction in general. The Dangerous Diseases Ordinance of 1907 in Uganda responded to the declining population of Uganda by restricting the circumstances under which syphilis might be transmitted.[29] Colonial regulation against homosexuality, in other words, implies a concern that homosexuality preceded the arrival of European law. And it most likely did—at the very least, argues the anthropologist Marc Epprecht, precolonial sexual practices were more diverse and permissive.[30] The restrictive Western and Evangelical notion that anti-homosexuality is central to the message of the Bible was repackaged as a version of "Africanness" that became increasingly central to the cultural identity of many African churches.

This crabbed reading of what is central to biblical Christianity obscures rather than amplifies the particular nature of *African* religion—and not just Christianity or Islam—on the continent. What is now imagined as central to indigenous African Christianity is the product of modern American fundamentalism. It is ultimately a way to subordinate African Christianity to distinctly right-wing, nationalist forms of Western Christianity.

But, as this book began by observing, African theology can also claim its roots as an ancient African religion. Africa runs through biblical history itself—Moses's Cushite wife and his long sojourn in Nubia in the *Sefer Hayashar*; Mary and Joseph's flight to Egypt; the Libyan Simon of Cyrene carrying the cross for Jesus; the Ethiopian eunuch in the Book of Acts encountering Philip the Apostle; the Coptic tradition that the Apostle Mark launched the church in Africa. And Carthage and Alexandria: the cities that shaped so much theology, allegory, political theory, literature. And Carthage alone: the ruined, sacrilegious, desirable city, the African city that led to the city of God.

Acknowledgments

This project reaches back into the earliest days I can remember, and my debts are both profound and extensive. In more or less chronological order: my father, Donald K. Smith, and my mother, Faye G. Smith, whose resistance in the face of apartheid has become my bedrock. Both of them taught me about biblical and African history in parallel. S. E. Motsoko Pheko, who, like my mother, passed away while I was finishing this book, didn't bow under the suffering of apartheid. He was one of the great Pan-Africanists, whose deep and inspiring pride in Africa's history gave me the conviction that Africa comes first. Reader Ncube, my other father when I was a boy in Matabeleland, who gave me my first lessons in deep history, with the amaNdebele people. As for this book specifically, Patrice Nganang, who one evening said, "You should write about Africa." I did, and his generous conversations have helped to shape and sharpen the book. Maybe even before that, Simon Gikandi, who encouraged me since I first discussed my interest in working on, and teaching about, Africa. I read African literature on the Kenyan curriculum all through high school, but it wasn't until I read Simon's early books while I was still in graduate school that I saw how important and urgent African literature really is. It's especially meaningful that he read through the manuscript and offered important advice.

Kenyan friends, especially Humphrey Njoroge, for his extraordinary memory and archival skills, Githinji Gikonyo, Aggrey Kadenge, Jack Kionga, Frank Kinama Musyimi, Andrew Ndegwa, Simon Njoe, George Ooko, Jacob Osogo, J. Paul Ramoya, and many others of my fellow Laibons from Lenana School for years of conversation, information, and friendship; and Wandia Njoya, Mordecai Ogada, and Najar Nyakio Munyinyi.

Academic colleagues and friends here at Princeton and around the world: Sarah Anderson, Wendy Belcher, Kathleen Biddick, Eduardo Cadava, Zahid Chaudhary, Celia Chazelle, Suzanne Conklin Akbari, Rita Copeland, H. M. Cushman, Patricia Dailey, Jacob Dlamini, Jeff Dolven, Daniel Donahue, Diana Fuss, William C. Jordan, Beatrice Kitzinger, Joshua Kotin, Claire Lees, Russ Leo, Sierra Lomuto, Mark Miller, Jane Newman, Kinohi Nishikawa, Rob Nixon, Julie Orlemanski, Ryan Perry, Helmut Reimitz, Emily Rose, Gayle Salamon, Benjamin Saltzman, Nigel Smith, Susan Stewart, Nicholas Watson, Cord Whitaker, and Jessica Wolfe. David Wallace was one of the readers for Chicago, and I am deeply grateful for his powerful strategic and conceptual advice about the book.

I explored these ideas with students in several graduate seminars. I'd particularly like to thank Lina Abashouk, Nathan Ashe, Lawrence Chamunorwa, Janet Chow, Rachael Clifford, Catie Crandell, Kierra Duncan, Andrew Finn, Anthie Georgiadi, rl Goldberg, Michael Harrington, Julia Hori, Mumbua Kioko, Matthew Kumar, Izzy Lockhart, Isaac Harrison Louth, Thembelani Mbatha, Sean McFadden, Ali Mctar, Meseret Oldjira, Sylvia Onorato, Chase Padusniak, Jason Ray, Kristen Starkowski, and Josephine Wang. I owe Chase Padusniak thanks at least twice over for his heroic work in completing my incomplete citations and editing the footnotes.

The cover image is courtesy of the Ben Enwonwu Foundation and Sotheby's. I'm grateful to Chika Okeke-Agulu for his help in obtaining both images and permissions.

I wrote several chapters with the opportunity that the Princeton Humanities Council Old Dominion Professorship gave me. Juliana Dweck, Kristen Windmuller-Luna, and a Mellon Foundation Faculty Development Grant generously enabled work in the Princeton Art Museum collection. Additional research was made possible by an Mpala Foundation Grant, for which I thank Aly Kassam-Remtullah and Daniel Rubenstein.

Of all the publishers interested in this project, only Randy Petilos and University of Chicago Press imposed the condition that I not water down the argument and the citations. That sold me. Randy was the best of editors, enthusiastically supporting the project from start to finish, reading and re-reading it with amazing care for matters both global and minute. I'm grateful to him. For editing, shaping, and focusing parts of the project, Sam Dresser at *Aeon*, Anne Sevarese at Princeton

University Press, and William Callahan at InkWell Management. For their amazing editorial work on an earlier version of the Fanon chapter, Benjamin Saltzman and Ryan Perry. Above all, huge thanks and gratitude to Catherine Osborne for her acute and thoughtful editing, which made the process feel more like a conversation than an awkward reunion with my own mistakes.

I had some kind invitations to give talks while working on the book from Suzanne Akbari, at the Institute for Advanced Study; Wendy Belcher, at the 2016 Modern Language Association conference; Carly Boxer, Jack Dragu, and Luke Fidler, at the University of Chicago; Taylor Cowdery at the University of North Carolina at Chapel Hill, for the Dorothy Ford Wiley Lecture; Michael Raby, at McGill University; Larry Scanlon, at Rutgers University; Lynn Staley, at Colgate University, for the Annual Humanities Lecture; and Ahmed Seif, at Harvard University.

To Lucia, *mpendwa wangu*, who taught me how to be American without losing Africa.

Notes

Preface

Ovid, *Metamorphoses, Volume I: Books 1-8*, trans. Frank Justus Miller, rev. G. P. Goold (Harvard University Press, 1916) IV: 657–662.
Derek Walcott, *Omeros* (Farrar, Straus and Giroux, 1990), 297.

Introduction

Ousmane Sembène, in *Caméra d'Afrique*, dir. Férid Boughedir (1983).
1. Patriot Front Manifesto, c. 2017. I do not want to disseminate their link, so I quote from the Southern Poverty Law Center, https://www.splcenter.org/fighting-hate/extremist-files/group/patriot-front (accessed June 14, 2022).
2. F. X. Fauvelle, *The Golden Rhinoceros* (Princeton University Press, 2021); the collection of essays *Great Kingdoms of Africa*, ed. John Parker (University of California Press, 2023); Michael Gomez, *African Dominion: A New History of Empire in Early and Medieval West Africa* (Princeton University Press, 2018); and Howard W. French, *Born in Blackness: Africa, Africans, and the Making of the Modern World* (Liveright, 2021).
3. See Abdul Sheriff, "The Persian Gulf and the Swahili Coast: A History of Acculturation over the *Longue Durée*," in *The Persian Gulf in History*, ed. L. G. Potter (Palgrave Macmillan, 2009), 173–88.
4. For the history of how this happened during the Middle Ages, see Geraldine Heng's important book *The Invention of Race in the European Middle Ages* (Cambridge University Press, 2018). Hereafter, "Heng" with page numbers in the main text.
5. "What is Sub-Saharan Africa?," The Economist, March 7, 2019, https://www.economist.com/the-economist-explains/2019/03/07/what-is-sub-saharan-africa.
6. Martin Mühleisen, Dhaneshwar Ghura, Roger Nord, Michael T. Hadjimichael, and E. Murat Ucer, "Introduction," in *Sub-Saharan Africa: Growth, Savings, and Investment, 1986–93*, Occasional Paper 118 (International Monetary Fund, 1995), https://doi.org/10.5089/9781557754585.084.
7. Martin Heidegger, *What Is Philosophy?*, trans. Jean T. Wilde and William Kluback (Yale University Press, 1958), 27–32.
8. Quoted in Jacques Derrida, "The Pit and the Pyramid: Introduction to Hegel's

Semiology," in *Margins of Philosophy*, trans. Alan Bass (University of Chicago Press, 1982), 8.
9. Translation by Bill Thayer, https://penelope.uchicago.edu/Thayer/E/Gazetteer/Periods/Roman/_Texts/Ptolemy/4/8*.html.
10. Strabo, *Geography*, trans. H. C. Hamilton and W. Falconer (London, 1857).
11. C. L. F. Panckoucke, ed., *Description de l'Égypte* (France: Commission des Monuments l'Égypte, 2022 [1821]), 3:77.
12. Quoted in Daniel F. McCall, review of Cheikh Anta Diop, *The African Origin of Civilization: Myth or Reality*, ed. and trans. Mercer Cook (Lawrence Hill and Co., 1974), in *Journal of Asian and African Studies* 9 (January 1974): 91–92.
13. See Cheikh Anta Diop, *The African Origin of Civilization: Myth Or Reality*, trans. Mercer Cook (Lawrence Hill, 1974); Cheikh Anta Diop, *Precolonial Black Africa: A Comparative Study of the Political and Social Systems of Europe and Black Africa, From Antiquity to the Formation of Modern States* (Hill, 1986); Martin Bernal, *Black Athena: The Afroasiatic Roots of Classical Civilization* (Free Association Books, 1987); Mary R. Lefkowitz, *Not Out of Africa: How Afrocentrism Became an Excuse to Teach Myth As History* (Basic Books, 1996).
14. Sierra Lomuto, "White Nationalism and the Ethics of Medieval Studies," *In the Middle*, December 5, 2016, https://www.inthemedievalmiddle.com/2016/12/white-nationalism-and-ethics-of.html.
15. Cord J. Whitaker, *Black Metaphors: How Modern Racism Emerged From Medieval Race-Thinking* (University of Pennsylvania Press, 2019). The monumental study by St. Clair Drake, *Black Folks Here and There: An Essay in History and Anthropology* (Center for Afro-American Studies, UCLA, 1987 and 1990) anticipates much of this work, but it has been unjustly overlooked.
16. *A History of the Expedition to Jerusalem, 1095–1127*, ed. Harold S. Fink, trans. Frances Rita Ryan (University of Tennessee Press, 1969).
17. The other categories Fulcher names are Syrians and Armenians, a grouping that falls, perhaps, in between race and ethnicity, the vague space of the medieval category of *natio*.
18. See Janet McIntosh, *Unsettled: Denial and Belonging Among White Kenyans* (University of California Press, 2016), 118–19.
19. Matt King, "Perceptions of Islam in the *Carmen in Victoriam Pisanorum*," in *Hortulus* 11, no. 2 (2015): 3–25, p. 7.
20. Rosamond E. Mack, *Bazaar to Piazza: Islamic Trade and Italian Art, 1300–1600* (University of California Press, 2002), 2.
21. Mack, *Bazaar to Piazza*, 181–82n5.
22. Robert Sabatino Lopez, *Medieval Trade in the Mediterranean World: Illustrative Documents* (W. W. Norton, 1967), 384–86.
23. Froissart describes the raid in his *Chronicles*.
24. "Negabat"; or killed ("necebat," the manuscript reading). See King, "Perceptions of Islam in the *Carmen in Victoriam Pisanorum*."
25. See H. E. J. Cowdrey, "The Mahdia Campaign of 1087," *English Historical Review* 92 (1977): 1–29, p. 17.
26. A. Metcalfe, *Muslims and Christians in Norman Sicily: Arabic Speakers and the End of Islam* (Routledge, 2005), 57.
27. The notable example of this is Peter the Venerable's *Summa totius haeresis ac diabol-*

icae sectae Saracenorum siue Hismahelitarum and his *Contra sectam siue haeresim Saracenorum*. Peter worked from translations of Mozarabic texts he commissioned, including the first translation of the Qur'an into Latin, by Peter of Ketton. But Peter the Venerable did not begin this work until 1142–43, when he traveled to Spain, fifty-five years after Pisa's invasion of Mahdia. See John Victor Tolan, *Saracens: Islam in the Medieval European Imagination* (Columbia University Press, 2002), 155ff. It's likely that the writer of the *Carmen* depended on work like that of the ninth-century scholars and polemicists Eulogius of Cordoba and Paulus Alvarus of Cordoba. An excellent study of the careers of the two is Charles L. Tieszen's *Christian Identity amid Islam in Medieval Spain* (Brill, 2013).

28. For a useful survey of the Arianism of the Vandal ruling elites, see Jonathan Conant, *Staying Roman: Conquest and Identity in the Africa and the Mediterranean, 439–700* (Cambridge University Press), 130–95, 202.
29. For a review of the uses of the name "Africa" for Mahdia, including this 1088 Pisan reference to "Africa," see Carlo Ottavo Castiglioni, *Mémoire géographique et numismatique sur la partie orientale de la Barbarie . . .* (Milan, 1825), 5–23.

Chapter One

Diodorus Siculus, *The Historical Library of Diodorus the Sicilian*, trans. George Booth (London, 1700), Bk. 3.1.86.

1. Shaun T. Lopez, "Race, Place and Soccer: Egypt, Morocco, and 'African' Identity in the Competition to Host the 2010 FIFA World Cup," in *Soccer in the Middle East*, ed. Alon Raab and Issam Khalidi (Routledge, 2015), 30.
2. The quotation is from the preamble to the Egyptian Constitution, available at https://sschr.gov.eg/en/the-egyptian-constitution/.
3. Gamal Abdel Nasser at the First Summit of the Organization of African Unity, May 1963, 127–43, p. 129, https://au.int/sites/default/files/speeches/38523-sp-oau_summit_may_1963_speeches.pdf.
4. Ibrāhīm Niasse, "Ifrīqiyā ilā al-ifrīqiyīn." In Sa'ādat al-anām bi-aqwāl shaykh al-islām (Cairo: al-Sharika al-Dawliyya, 2006), 65–66, translated in Zachary Valentine Wright, *Living Knowledge in West African Islam: The Sufi Community of Ibrāhīm Niasse* (Brill, 2015), 253.
5. "African Countries with the Highest Share of Muslims," https://www.statista.com/statistics/1239494/share-of-muslim-population-in-africa-by-country.
6. Abdel Rahman Sherif, quoted in *al-Araby al-Jadeed* (*The New Arab*), July 23, 2015, https://www.newarab.com/analysis/being-black-egypt.
7. Zahi Hawass, quoted in *The Brisbane Times*, September 25, 2007, https://www.brisbanetimes.com.au/world/tutankhamun-was-not-black-antiquities-chief-20070926-ge94td.html.
8. Zahi Hawass, quoted in *Daily News Egypt*, April 14, 2014, https://www.dailynewsegypt.com/2021/04/14/claims-that-ancient-egyptians-were-african-untrue-zahi-hawass.
9. Georg Wilhelm Friedrich Hegel, *The Philosophy of History*, trans. J. Sibree (Batoche, 2001), 110. Hereafter, "Hegel, *History*" with page numbers in the main text.
10. Karl Wilhelm Friedrich Schlegel, *The Philosophy of History*, trans. James Burton Robertson (London, 1846), 1:76.

11. George Wilhelm Friedrich Hegel: "The Science of Logic," trans. George di Giovanni (Cambridge University Press, 2010), 106, I.I.I.265. Hereafter, "Hegel, *Science*" with page numbers in the main text.
12. Pierre Briant, *The First European: A History of Alexander in the Age of Empire*, trans. Nicholas Elliott (Harvard University Press, 2017). Hereafter, "Briant" with page numbers in the main text.
13. Henri Riad, "Egyptian Influence on Daily Life in Ancient Alexandria," in *Alexandria and Alexandrianism: Papers Delivered at a Symposium Organized by the J. Paul Getty Museum and the Getty Center for the History of Art and the Humanities and Held at the Museum, April 22–25, 1993* (Getty, 1996) [29–39], 29.
14. *Corpus Hermeticum*, II. To Asclepius, sect. 24, quoted in Françoise Dunand, "The Factory of Gods," in *Alexandria, Third Century BC: The Knowledge of the World in a Single City*, ed. Christian Jacob and François de Polignac, trans. Colin Clement (Harpocrates, 2000) [152–62], 152.
15. Dio Chrysostom, "Discourse 32," in *The Complete Works of Dio Chrysostom*, trans. J. W. Cahoon (Delphi Classics, 2017) [293–316], 301.
16. Plutarch, *Isis and Osiris*, in *Moralia*, trans. Frank Cole Babbitt (Harvard University Press, 1936) [5:3–191], 5:153. Hereafter, "Plutarch" with page numbers in the main text.
17. Alain le Boulluec, "Alien Wisdom," in Jacob and Polignac, *Alexandria, Third Century BC* [56–72], 57.
18. Plutarch, *Alexander*, in *The Age of Alexander: Nine Greek Lives by Plutarch*, trans. Ian Scott-Kilvert (Penguin, 1973), 282.
19. E. M. Forster, *Alexandria: A History and a Guide* (Whitehead Morris, 1922), 190.
20. Diodorus Siculus, *The Historical Library of Diodorus the Sicilian*, trans. George Booth (London, 1700), 86. Bk. 3.1.
21. The site, the Oasis of Siwa, was considered to be in Libya, not Egypt, until the first century CE. See Robert B. Jackson, *At Empire's Edge: Exploring Rome's Egyptian Frontier* (Yale University Press, 2002), 242. Pausanius, in *Description of Greece*, the first mention of the shrine in Greek literature, says that Pindar sent a hymn to the "Ammonians of Libya;" see Pausanias, *The Description of Greece*, vol. 1, trans. W. H. Jones (Harvard, 1918), 9.16.1, p. 239. The movement of Siwa between Libya and Egypt is a specific example of the fluidity of "Africa" and "Egypt" that this chapter discusses.

    The definitive study of the shrine at the Oasis of Siwa is Klaus P. Kuhlmann, *Das Ammoneion Archäologie, Geschichte u. Kultpraxis d. Orakels von Siwa* (von Zabern, 1988). See also Robert Jackson, "Siwa Oasis," in *At Empire's Edge*. On Alexander and Ammon, see A. B. Bosworth, "Alexander and Ammon," in *Greece and the Eastern Mediterranean in Ancient History and Prehistory: Studies Presented to Fritz Schachermeyer on the Occasion of his Eightieth Birthday*, ed. K. H. Kinzl (Walter de Gruyter, 1977) [51–75], 51. See also A. B. Bosworth, *Conquest and Empire: The Reign of Alexander the Great* (Cambridge University Press, 1992), 282ff.
22. See Quintus Curtius Rufus, *Historiarum Alexandri Magni Macedonis libri qui supersunt*, ed. Edmund Hedicke (Teubner, 1908) [4.7.32], 68; and Diodorus Siculus, *Library of History*, vol. 8, trans. C. Bradford Welles (Harvard University Press, 1983), 265, Bk 17.51.

23. Plato, *Timaeus*, in *Plato*, vol. 7, trans. R. G. Bury (Harvard University Press, 1929), 31, 21e. Diodorus Siculus claims that Athens was an Egyptian colony (see Bk. 1.29).
24. *The Cambridge Ancient History*, vol. 2, pt. 1, ed. I. E. S. Edwards, C. J. Gadd, N. G. L. Hammond, and Edmond Sollberger (Cambridge University Press, 1973), 323; Klaus P. Kuhlmann, *Das Ammoneion: Archäologie, Geschichte und Kultpraxis des Orakels von Siwa* (P. von Zabern, 1988), 42–48.
25. See Kuhlmann, *Das Ammoneion*, 133; J. H. Breasted, *Ancient Records of Egypt* (University of Chicago Press, 1927), 5:285.
26. Luc Gabolde, "The Amun Cult and Its Development in Nubia," in *The Oxford Handbook of Ancient Nubia*, ed. Geoff Emberling and Bruce Beyer Williams (Oxford University Press, 2021), 343–67, 26n1.
27. See *Early Greek Mythography, Volume 1: Text and Introduction*, ed. Robert L. Fowler (Oxford University Press, 2000), 42; *Early Greek Mythography, Volume 2: Commentary*, ed. Robert L. Fowler (Oxford University Press, 2013), 13; Jan Bouzek and Denver Graninger, "Geography," in *A Companion to Ancient Thrace*, ed. Julia Valeva, Emil Nankov, and Denver Graninger (Wiley-Blackwell, 2015) [12–21], 12. Fowler (2013, 15) calls Pompholyge, a name found nowhere else, "an *ad hoc* invention." Libya has multiple genealogies in classical sources; that complexity might be another aspect of the "multiplicity" of Africa as a site of origins. For a discussion of the classical myth of Libya and nineteenth-century philology's use of it in representing "Africa," see V.Y. Mudimbe, "In the House of Libya: A Meditation," in Daniel Orrells, Gurminder K. Bhambra, and Tessa Roynon, eds. *African Athena: New Agendas* (Oxford UP, 2011)190-209.
28. See, for example, the episode in which Cato's army is attacked by snakes, a passage prefaced by the legend of Perseus and Medusa along with a catalogue of the snakes of the Libyan desert, in Lucan, *Pharsalia*, trans. Jane Wilson Joyce (Cornell University Press, 1993), Bk. IX. 11. 734–846, pp. 256–59.
29. Line 42. Translation from Peter Agócs, "Pindar's Pythian Four: Interpreting History in Song," *Histos* Supplement II (2020) [87–154]: 106.
30. Line 211. Translation from Y. Z. N. Khan, "A Commentary on Dionysius of Alexandria's *Guide to the Inhabited World, 174–382*" (PhD diss., University of London, 2002), 220.
31. Agócs, "Pindar's Pythian Four," 102.
32. See K. P. Kuhlmann, "Roman and Byzantine Siwa: Developing a Latent Picture," in *Life on the Fringe: Proceedings of a Colloquium Held on the 29th Anniversary of the Netherlands Institute for Archaeology and Arabic Studies in Cairo*, ed. O. E. Kaper (Brill, 1998) [159–180], 175; and K. P. Kuhlmann, "The Preservation of the Temple of the Oracle," *ASAE* 75 (2000): 63–89.
33. See, for example, Strabo, *Geography*, trans. Horace Leonard Jones (Harvard University Press, 1917), vol. 1, Bk. 1.2, 51. Hereafter, "Strabo" with book and page numbers in the text.
34. J. Lennart Berggren and Alexander Jones, *Ptolemy's Geography: An Annotated Translation of the Theoretical Chapters* (Princeton University Press, 2000), 95. Like most Greek geographers, Ptolemy used "Libyē" to refer to Africa, although they also referred to the region west of Egypt as Libya.
35. Khan, "A Commentary," 1. 221, 236.

36. Diodorus Siculus, *The Library of History*, Bk. 3.3, 86.
37. Herodotus, *The Histories*, vol. 1, trans. A. D. Goodley (Harvard University Press, 1920), Bk. 2.18, 297. Hereafter, "Herodotus" with book and page numbers in the main text.
38. Isidore of Seville, *The Etymologies of Isidore of Seville*, trans. Stephen A. Barney, W. J. Lewis, J. A. Beach, and Oliver Berghof (Cambridge University Press, 2006), Bk. 12.7.25, 265. Hereafter, "Isidore" with book and page numbers in the main text.
39. Ranulf Higden, *Polychronicon Ranulphi Higden monachi Cestrensis; together with the English translation of John Trevisa and of an unknown writer of the fifteenth century*, vol. 1, ed. Churchill Babington and J. Rawson Lumby (London, 1865), bk. 1.6, 48.
40. *Asiam autem et Libyam cum Aegypto disterminat os Nili flumnis quod Canopicon appellatur.* Isidore of Seville, *Traité de la nature*, ed. Jacques Fontaine (Féret, 1960), Ch. 48, 325. See also *Isidore of Seville: On the Nature of Things*, trans. Calvin B. Kendall and Faith Wallis (Liverpool University Press, 2016): "The mouth of the river Nile, which is called the Canopic mouth, determines the boundary between Asia and Libya together with Egypt" (175).
41. *Gentes Libye Ethyopie. Nomen Ethyopum late patet. In partibus Egipti, Lybie, Africe quam plurime sunt nationes.* A downloadable, interactive version of the map may be found at https://www.bl.uk/alexander-the-great/activities/interactive-ebstorf-map.
42. As far as I can tell, the first writer to use "Egypt" and "Ethiopia" interchangeably was, in fact, an African: Augustine of Hippo. In his commentary on the Psalms, he says that the "name of Egypt or Ethiopia signifies the faith of all peoples" (*aegypti, uel aethiopiae nomine, omnium gentium fidem significauit*) (my translation). See Augustinus Hipponensis, *Enarrationes in Psalmos (CPL 0283)*, Library of Latin Texts: BREPOLiS (online), 67:40, CCSL 39. 1. 2. The first example might, in fact, be the Bible, in the Psalm Augustine is commenting on: in most contemporary Bibles, now Psalm 68 (verse 31), which uses "Egypt" in apposition with "Ethiopia" ("Cush" in the Hebrew Bible). The *Glossa Ordinaria*, essentially the footnotes that accompanied the text of the Latin Vulgate Bible in the Middle Ages, quotes Augustine at that point. For "Egypt" alone, it cites the definition *for Ethiopia* from St. Jerome's glossary of Hebrew names (*tenebris gentium*, "people/nation of darkness"); see *Saint Jerome's Book of Hebrew Names (Old Testament): A Translation and Introduction*, trans. Sidney Korzenik, in *Philosophy Department Masters' Essays* 2.1 (1933) [1–112]: 13. Hugh's prize student, Richard of St. Victor, similarly uses the *Glossa*'s definition of Ethiopia for Egypt. See A. B. Kraebel, "*The Apocalypse of St. John* (selections)," in *Interpretation of Scripture: Theory, A Selection of Works of Hugh, Andrew, Richard, and Godfrey of St. Victor and Robert of Melun*, ed. Franklin T. Harkins and Frans van Liere (Brepols, 2012) [327–370], 369n45.
43. Hugh of St. Victor, *La "De Descriptio Mappe Mundi" de Hughes de Saint-Victor: Texte Inédit avec Introduction et Commentaire*, ed. Patrick Gautier Dalché (Études augustiniennes, 1988), 151.
44. For a survey of the various placements of Ethiopia, and the two Ethiopias, in the Middle Ages, see Suzanne Conklin Akbari, "Where is Medieval Ethiopia? Mapping Ethiopic Studies within Medieval Studies," in *Toward a Global Middle Ages: Encountering the World through Illuminated Manuscripts*, ed. Brian C. Keene (The J. Paul Getty Museum, 2019), 80–91.

45. Hugh of St. Victor's *Descriptione mappe mundi* says the Gates of Nubia are on the border of Egypt: *Usque ad portas Nubie deserta Egypti sunt* (Dalché, "*De Descriptio Mappa Mundi*," 148). See also Robin Seignobos, "Nubia and Nubians in Medieval Latin Culture," in *The Fourth Cataract and Beyond: Proceedings of the 12th International Conference for Nubian Studies*, ed. Julie R. Anderson and Derek A. Welsby (Peeters, 2014) [989–1004], 990.
46. See Wendy Laura Belcher, "Habesha Discourse in Johnson's Sources for *Rasselas*," in *Abyssinia's Samuel Johnson: Ethiopian Thought in the Making of an English Author* (Oxford University Press, 2012), 189–211.
47. Another strain in biblical exegesis argued that "Cushite" referred to the people of Cushan (referred to only in Habakkuk 3:7) as a way to assimilate the Cushite woman with Zipporah, Moses's Midianite wife. See Steven McKenzie, Elad Filler, and Elizabeth McGrath, "Moses' Cushite Wife," in *Encyclopedia of the Bible and Its Reception* (de Gruyter, 2021), 1154–62. The Septuagint and the Vulgate translate "Cushan" as "Ethiopian."
48. An earlier version of the story by an Alexandrian named Artapanus says that Meroë was founded by Moses. See Donna Runnalls, "Moses' Egyptian Campaign," in *Journal for the Study of Judaism in the Persian, Hellenistic, and Roman Period* 14, no. 2 (1983) [135–56]: 138.
49. Josephus, *Jewish Antiquities*, vol. 1, trans. H. St. J. Thackeray (Harvard University Press, 1930), Bk. 2.243, 273.
50. Peter Comestor, *Historia Scholastica* (Strasbourg, 1500), 28r. See heading: "De uxore Mosyi Aethiopissa."
51. On Moses's adventures in Ethiopia, see *Sefer Hayashar: The Book of the Generations of Adam*, trans. Nachum Y. Kornfeld and Abraham B. Walzer (Yosher, 1993), 184–90. The *Sefer Hayashar* isn't the only medieval Jewish source for the narrative: there are at least two others, as well as Josephus's source, Aretanus, and a ninth-century Byzantine history. For a detailed account of the routes of transmission of the story, see Tessa Rajak, "Moses in Ethiopia," in *The Jewish Dialogue with Greece and Rome: Studies in Cultural and Social Interaction* (Brill, 2002), 257–72.
52. See Jasmine Kilburn-Small, "The Figure of the Ethiopian in Old English Texts," *Bulletin of the John Rylands Library* 86, no. 2 (July 2004): 69–85. I translate *-wara* as "guardian," based on Bosworth-Toller's dictionary entry for *-wara*. J. R. R. Tolkien's famous essay "Sigelwara Land" emends it to "Sigelhearwan." See note 54 below.
53. In two parts: J. R. R. Tolkien, "Sigelwara Land," in *Medium Ævum* 1, no. 3 (December 1932): 183–96; J. R. R. Tolkien, "Sigelwara Land," *Medium Ævum* 3, no. 2 (June 1934): 95–111.
54. Tolkien, "Sigelwara Land" (1934), 110.
55. This translation is by Ophelia Eryn Hostetter, https://oldenglishpoetry.camden.rutgers.edu/exodus.
56. Mary Dockray-Miller, "*Afrisc Meowle*: Exploring Race in the Old English *Exodus*," *PMLA* 137 (2022): 458–71.
57. Cf. *Old English Version of the Heptateuch*, trans. S. J. Crawford (Oxford University Press, 1922), Numbers 12:1, 313.
58. Dockray-Miller, "*Afrisc Meowle*," 458.
59. Kornfeld and Walzer, *Sefer Hayashar*, 185–86.
60. On Alexander and Ammon, see A. B. Bosworth, "Alexander and Ammon," in *Greece*

and the Eastern Mediterranean in Ancient History and Prehistory: Studies Presented to Fritz Schachermeyer on the Occasion of his Eightieth Birthday, ed. K. H. Kinzl (Walter de Gruyter, 1977) [51–75], 51. See also Bosworth, *Conquest and Empire*, 282ff.

61. For this and the following, see Richard Stoneman, "Formation and Diffusion of the Alexander Legend," in *A History of Alexander the Great in World Culture*, ed. Richard Stoneman (Cambridge University Press, 2022), 1–14.

62. See Jonathan Morton, "*Engin*: Creativity, Invention, and *Knowledge* in the Medieval Romance Tradition of Alexander the Great," *Romanic Review* 111, no. 2 (September 2020) [205–226]: 207.

63. The *Secreta Secretorum*, which purports to be advice that Alexander's tutor Aristotle gave to him, is an especially rich mélange of this scientific and hermetic knowledge. My thanks to Jonathan Morton for this point.

64. E. A. Wallis Budge, *A History of Ethiopia: Volume One* (Routledge, 2014), 71–72. That version says that the inhabitants of Africa to the West of Egypt brought him gifts but weren't conquered. Hereafter, "Budge, *A History*" with page numbers in the main text.

65. Some versions of the romance don't mention Ammon, e.g., the Ethiopian *Zena Eskander* just mentions "the gods of Egypt" (*The Life and Exploits of Alexander the Great*, trans. E. A. Wallis Budge [London, 1896], 8).

66. For more, see Charles Russell Stone, *Roman de toute chevalerie: Reading Alexander Romance in Late Medieval England* (University of Toronto Press, 2019), 50–76; and Venetia Bridges, "Insular Alexander? The *Roman de toute chevalerie* and the *Roman de Horn*," in *Medieval Narratives of Alexander the Great: Transnational Texts in England and France* (D. S. Brewer, 2018), 145–93.

67. From the rubric for the section on Nectanebo in MS Durham Cathedral Library C.IV.27.B. See Thomas of Kent, *The Anglo-Norman Alexander*, vol. 1, ed. Brian Foster (Anglo-Norman Text Society, 1976), heading 3, p. 8. Hereafter, "Thomas of Kent" with line and page numbers in the main text.

68. *Kyng Alisaunder*, vol. 1, ed. G. V. Smithers (Early English Text Society, 1952), l. 985, p. 57.

69. For a survey of the extensive material on Africa in the first Greek versions of the Alexander romance, see Corinne Jouanno, "The Fate of African Material in the Greek and Byzantine Tradition of the *Alexander Romance*," in *Acta Classica*, Supp. (January 2014): 128–42.

70. Pseudo-Callisthenes, *The Life of Alexander of Macedon*, trans. Elizabeth Hazelton Haight (Longman, Green, and Co., 1955), Bk. 3.8, 109. For a translation of the Armenian version, see Pseudo-Callisthenes, *The Romance of Alexander the Great*, trans. Albert Mugrdich Wolohojian (Columbia University Press, 1969), Bk. 3.18, 131; for a translation of the Syriac version, see Pseudo-Callisthenes, *The History of Alexander the Great*, trans. E. A. Wallis Budge (Cambridge University Press, 1889), Bk, 3.8, 118; or, in the original Greek, Bk. 3.18. An online comparative version is available (with both original texts and translations) at https://www.attalus.org/info/alexander.html.

71. Pseudo-Callisthenes, *The Life of Alexander of Macedon*, 109.

72. Carolyn Fluehr-Lobban, "Nubian Queens in the Nile Valley and Afro-Asiatic Cultural History," in *Nubian Studies 1998: Proceedings of the Ninth International*

Conference for Nubian Studies, August 21–26, 1998, Boston, Massachusetts, ed. Timothy Kendall (Northeastern University, 2004), 256–64.
73. See Julia Budka, "Nubians in Egypt during the 25th Dynasty," in *The Oxford Handbook of Ancient Nubia*, ed. Geoff Emberling and Bruce Beyer Williams (Oxford University Press, 2021), 475–90.
74. Suzanne Akbari, "Alexander in the Orient: Bodies and Boundaries in the *Roman de toute chevalerie*," in *Postcolonial Approaches to the European Middle Ages: Translating Cultures*, ed. Jahanara Kabir and Deanne Williams (Cambridge University Press, 2005) [105–126], 123, 121.
75. Edward Daniel Clarke, *The Tomb of Alexander: A Dissertation on the Sarcophagus Brought from Alexandria and Now in the British Museum* (Cambridge University Press, 1805), 68–71.
76. See Agnieszka Fulińska, "Alexander and Napoleon," in *The Brill Companion to the Reception of Alexander the Great*, ed. Kenneth Royce Moore (Brill, 2018), 545–75.
77. Fulińska, "Alexander and Napoleon," 546ff.
78. Edward W. Said, *Orientalism* (Vintage, 1979), 86.
79. *D'offrir à l'Orient l'utile exemple de l'industrie européenne, enfin de rendre la condition des habitans plus douce, et de leur procurer tous les avantages d'une civilisation perfectionnée* (my translation). See Jean Baptiste Joseph Fourier, *Description de l'Égypte: Preface Historique* (Paris, 1821), 9. Said's translation uses "Napoleon" where Fourier's doesn't. The pronoun "il" throughout refers to the expedition.
80. Fourier, *Description de l'Égypte: Preface Historique*, 41.
81. *Description de l'Égypte: ou, Recueil des observations et des recherches qui ont été faites en Égypte pendant L'expédition de L'armée française*, vol. 3, ed. Edme-François Jomard (Paris, 1821), 2nd ed., 263. Hereafter, "*Description*" with page numbers in the text.
82. Pierre Bourdieu, *Distinction: A Social Critique of the Judgement of Taste* (Harvard University Press, 1984).
83. See https://www.britishmuseum.org/visit/museum-map.
84. One major exception to the top-heavy Egyptian bias in museums is the Museum of Fine Arts, Boston, which has the largest collection of Nubian artifacts outside of Khartoum. In 2018 it mounted an exhibition specifically to correct the misapprehension that Nubian art was merely debased Egyptian art. As the catalogue put it, the exhibition aimed to introduce the "glorious cultures of Nubia, seen and appreciated for themselves, rather than through the lens of Egypt." See *Arts of Ancient Nubia*, ed. Denise M. Doxey, Rita E. Freed, and Lawrence M. Berman (Museum of Fine Arts, 2018), 14.
85. W. M. Flinders Petrie, *Tel El Hessy (Lachish)* (London, 1891), 47; Debbie Challis, "Skull Triangles: Flinders Petrie, Race Theory and Biometrics," in *Bulletin of the History of Archaeology* 26, no. 1 (2016): 1–8. On Petrie's use of "Jewish" as a racial term, see Neil A. Silberman, "Petrie's Head: Eugenics and Near Eastern Archaeology," in *Assembling the Past: Studies in the Professionalization of Archaeology*, ed. Alice B. Kehoe and Mary Beth Emmerichs (University of New Mexico Press, 1999), 74.
86. Petrie, *Tel El Hessy*, 48; W. M. Flinders Petrie, *The Making of Egypt* (Sheldon Press, 1939), 139 (hereafter, "Petrie, *Making*," with page numbers in the main text), quoted in John D. Ramsey, "Petrie and the Intriguing Idiosyncrasies of Racism," *Bulletin of*

History and Archeology 14, no. 2 (2004) [15–20]: 15. Petrie uses the terms "debased" and "deteriorated" to describe pottery in "Pottery of Ancient Egypt," *Archeological Journal* 40, no. 1 (1883) [269–280]: 273, 280, as well as "degradation" (and the "reduction of useful elements to mere ornament") in *Methods and Aims in Archaeology* (Macmillan, 1909), 128.

87. W. M. Flinders Petrie, *The Wisdom of the Egyptians* (British School of Archeology in Egypt, 1940), 1.
88. Damien Agut, "L'Egypte, oasis africaine," in *L'Afrique Ancienne*, ed. François-Xavier Fauvelle (Belin, 2018) [33–57], 33.
89. Petrie traveled under the aegis of the British Association for the Advancement of Science, which, inspired by Galton, began a racial survey of the British Isles in 1878. Galton had already tried to extract data about facial measurements and race from composite photographs of coins of Alexander the Great and Cleopatra VII. See Debbie Challis, *The Archaeology of Race: The Eugenic Ideas of Francis Galton and Flinders Petrie* (Bloomsbury, 2013), 65, 66, 74.
90. For a useful discussion of the collaboration between Petrie and Galton, see Kathleen L. Sheppard, "Flinders Petrie and Eugenics at UCL," *Bulletin of the History of Archaeology* 20, no. 1 (May 2010): 16–29.
91. W. M. Flinders Petrie, "The Earliest Racial Portraits," *Nature* 39 (1888) [128–130]: 128.
92. W. M. Flinders Petrie, "On the Use of Diagrams," *Man* 2 (1902) [81–85]: 84. Hereafter, "Petrie, 'Diagrams'" with page numbers in the main text.
93. Archibald Henry Sayce, *The Races of the Old Testament* (London, 1893), 24. Hereafter, "Sayce" with page numbers in the main text. For a useful discussion of Sayce's work in relation to Petrie's, see Challis, *Archeology*, 113–19.
94. J. H. Breasted, *A History of Egypt: From the Earliest Times to the Persian Conquest* (Scribner, 1909; 2nd ed. 1937), 26. In 1919 Breasted founded the Oriental Institute (later the Institute for the Study of Ancient Cultures) at the University of Chicago.
95. Amelia B. Edwards, "Portrait-Painting in Ancient Egypt," in *Pharaohs, Fellahs, and Explorers* (Harper and Brothers, 1891) [70–112], 83–84. Hereafter, "Edwards, 'Portrait-Painting,'" with page numbers in the main text.
96. G. T. Raynal, *Histoire philosophique et politique des établissemens et du commerce des Européens dans l'Afrique septentrionale / ouvrage posthume de G. T. Raynal; augmenté . . . par M. Peuchet* (Paris, 1824), 2:144 (my translation). For more information, see Patricia Lorcin, *Imperial Identities: Stereotyping, Prejudice, and Race in Colonial Algeria* (I. B. Tauris, 1999); Edmund Burke III, "The Image of the Moroccan State in French Ethnographical Literature: A New Look at the Origin of Lyautey's Berber Policy," in *Arabs and Berbers: From Tribe to Nation in North Africa*, ed. Ernest Gellner and Charles Micaud (Lexington, 1972) [175–99], 175.
97. William Shaler, "On the Language, Manners, and Customs of the Berbers," *Transactions of the American Philosophical Society* 2, no. 1 (1825) [438–65]: 438, 447.
98. See Stuart Tyson Smith, "Ethnicity: Constructions of Self and Other in Ancient Egypt," *Journal of Egyptian History* 11 (2018): 113–46.
99. Juan Carlos Moreno García, "Elusive 'Libyans': Identities, Lifestyles and Mobile Populations in NE Africa (late 4th–early 2nd millennium BCE)," *Journal of Egyptian History* 11 (2018) [147–84]: 173; Juan Carlos Moreno García, "Invaders or Just Herders? Libyans in Egypt in the Third and Second Millennia BCE," *World Archaeology* 46 (2014): 610–23; Seth Richardson, "Libya Domestica: Libyan Trade

and Society on the Eve of the Invasions of Egypt," *Journal of the American Research Center in Egypt* 36 (1999):149–64.
100. Antonio Loprieno, *Topos Und Mimesis: Zum Äuslander in Der Ägyptischen Literatur* (Harrassowitz, 1998).
101. Amelia B. Edwards, *A Thousand Miles Up the Nile* (New York, 1888), 322. Hereafter, "Edwards, *Thousand*" with page numbers in the main text.
102. Quoted in John Marx, *The Modernist Novel and the Decline of Empire* (Cambridge University Press, 2005), 104.
103. Immanuel Kant, *The Critique of the Power of Judgment*, trans. Paul Guyer and Eric Matthews (Cambridge University Press, 2000), 135–36. Technically the pyramids are an example of the mathematical sublime: the other is another sacred space, St. Peter's in Rome, whose immensity causes a "bewilderment or sort of embarrassment." For more on Kant's recurrent allusions to Egyptian religion, see Christine Battersby, "Egypt, *Parerga* and a Question of Veils," in *The Sublime, Terror and Human Difference* (Routledge, 2007), 85–104.
104. Stuart Tyson Smith, "Ethnicity: Constructions of Self and Other in Ancient Egypt," *Journal of Egyptian History* 11 (2018) [13–146]: 128–29. See also Stuart Tyson Smith, *Wretched Kush: Ethnic Identity in Egypt's Nubian Empire* (Routledge, 2003), and the book Smith credits as his influence: Antonio Loprieno, *Topos Und Mimesis: Zum Äuslander in Der Ägyptischen Literatur* (Harrassowitz, 1988).
105. Smith, *Wretched Kush*, 4.
106. W. M. Flinders Petrie, "Migrations (The Huxley Lecture for 1906)," *Journal of the Anthropological Institute of Great Britain and Ireland* 36 (1906) [189–232]: 189. Hereafter, "Petrie, 'Migrations'" with page numbers in the main text.
107. Fredric Jameson, "Magical Narratives: Romance as Genre," *New Literary History* 7, no. 1 (Autumn 1975) [135–163]: 138.
108. Constatin Volney, *Les Ruines ou méditation sur les révolutions des Empires* (Paris, 1791), 22, quoted in R. Bernasconi, "Hegel and Egypt's African Element," *Hegel Bulletin* online (2024:1–17; doi:10.1017/hg1.2024.2).
109. Plato, *Phaedrus*, ed. and trans. Chris Emlyn-Jones and William Preddy (Harvard University Press, 2022), 515 (275a).
110. Plato, *Phaedrus*, 515 (275b).
111. Jacques Derrida, "White Mythology: Metaphor in the Text of Philosophy," trans. F. C. T. Moore, *New Literary History* 6, no. 1 (1974): 5–74.
112. Derrida, "White Mythology," 71n64, quoting Hegel, *Philosophy of History*, 121.
113. Georg Wilhelm Friedrich Hegel, *Lectures on the Philosophy of Religion*, trans. E. B. Speirs and J. Burdon Sanderson (Humanities Press, 1968), 2:105. Hegel mentions Ammon a few more times; in the *Aesthetics* he refers to "the Libyan Ammon" (*Aesthetics: Lectures on Fine Art*, trans. T. M. Knox [Oxford University Press, 1975], 1:451).
114. Athenaeus, *The Learned Banqueters*, vol. 5, ed. and trans. S. Douglas Olson (Harvard University Press, 2009), Bk. 11.470, 279, 281.
115. Macrobius, *Saturnalia*, vol. 1, ed. Robert A. Kaster (Harvard University Press, 2011), Bk. 1.21.16., 285. Hereafter, "Macrobius" with book and page numbers in the main text.
116. Hegel echoes this twice in *Philosophy of History*: "Amman is regarded as a great divinity, with whom is associated the determination of the equinox" (210, 278).

117. Martianus Capella, *Martianus Capella and the Seven Liberal Arts: Volume II: The Marriage of Philology and Mercury*, ed. and trans. William Harris Stahl, Richard Johnson, and E. L. Burge (Columbia University Press, 1971), Bk. 2.193, 59.
118. Derrida, "White Mythology," 52.
119. Derrida, *Of Grammatology*, trans. Gayatri Chakravorty Spivak (John Hopkins University Press, 1976), esp. viii and 47.
120. Kallisthenes, quoted in Strabo, *Geography*, Volume VIII: Book 17, trans. Horace Leonard Jones (Harvard University Press, 1932), Bk. 17.1.43, 115; and Diodorus Siculus, *Historical Library*, Bk. 17.50, 6–7.

Chapter Two

W. E. B. Du Bois, *Dusk of Dawn: An Essay Toward an Autobiography of a Race Concept* (Schocken, 1968), 117.

Apollonius of Rhodes, *Argonautica*, trans. William H. Race (Harvard University Press, 2009), Bk. 4.1127, 427.

1. Homer, *Iliad*, trans. A. T. Murray, rev. William F. Wyatt (Harvard University Press, 1924), Bk. 1.423–24, 45; hereafter, "*Iliad*" with page numbers in the text. Homer, *Odyssey*, Vol. 1, trans. A. T. Murray, rev. George E. Dimock (Harvard University Press, 1919), Bk. 1.22–26, 15.
2. Apollonius of Rhodes, *Argonautica*, trans. William H. Race (Harvard University Press, 2009), Bk. 4.1323, 435. Hereafter, "Apollonius" with book and page numbers in the main text.
3. Jacqueline Klooster, "Apollonius of Rhodes," in *Speech in Ancient Greek Literature: Studies in Ancient Greek Narrative, Volume Five*, ed. Mathieu de Bakker and Irene J. F. de Jong (Brill, 2021) [100–119], 103, 108.
4. See Boris Kayachev, "The So-Called Orphic Gold Tablets in Ancient Poetry," *Zeitschrift für Papyrologie und Epigraphik* 180 (2012): 17–37.
5. John Milton, *Paradise Lost: The Biblically Annotated Edition*, ed. Matthew Stallard (Mercer University Press, 2011), Bk. 2, 939–40, 80.
6. Giorgio Agamben, *Homo Sacer: Sovereign Power and Bare Life*, trans. Daniel Heller-Roazen (Stanford University Press, 1998), 9.
7. William G. Thalmann, *Apollonius of Rhodes and the Spaces of Hellenism* (Oxford University Press, 2011), 81–83.
8. For a reading of the entire poem in its political context, see Anatole Mori, *Apollonius of Rhodes' Argonautica* (Cambridge University Press, 2008). Mori summarizes how Susan Stephens, in *Seeing Double: Intercultural Poetics in Ptolemaic Alexandria* (University of California Press, 2003), explores how Apollonius sets up "competing centers of authority in his text by deploying Egyptian mythology in the epic as a conscious articulation of a new idea of kingship" (9). See also Jacqueline Klooster, "Argo Was Here: The Ideology of Geographical Space in the Argonautica of Apollonius of Rhodes," in *The Ideologies of Lived Space in Literary Texts, Ancient and Modern*, ed. Jo Gabby Marc Heirman and Jacqueline Klooster (Gingko Academic Press, 2013), 159–73.
9. See also Thalmann, *Apollonius of Rhodes*, 79n6.
10. Lucan, *The Civil War*, trans. J. D. Duff (Harvard University Press, 1928). Hereafter, "Lucan" with book and page numbers in main text.

11. On the other hand, Pliny does locate the river Lethon and the Garden of Hesperides near Lake Triton. See Pliny, *Natural History*, vol. 2, trans. H. Rackham (Harvard University Press, 1942), Bk. 5.5, 221ff.
12. On these and other allusions, see Veronica S. R. Shi and Llewelyn Morgan, "A Tale of Two Carthages: History and Allusive Topography in Virgil's Harbor (*Aen.* 1.159–69)," *TAPA* 145, no. 1 (2015) [107–133]: 110n8 and n9.
13. *Virgil: Eclogues, Georgics, Aeneid, Books 1–6*, trans. H. R. Fairclough, rev. G. P. Goold (Harvard University Press, 1916), Bk. 4.164, 272. The rest of the epic can be found in *Aeneid: 7–12; Appendix Vergiliana*, trans. H. R. Fairclough, rev. G. P. Goold (Harvard University Press, 1918). Hereafter, both cited as "Virgil" with book and page numbers in the main text. For this and other metaphors from theater, see J. A. S. Evans, "'Aeneid' 2 and the Art of the Theater," *The Classical Journal* 58, no. 6 (1963): 255–58. One of Julia Hell's central arguments in *The Conquest of Ruins: The Third Reich and the Fall of Rome* (Chicago: University of Chicago Press, 2019) is that the stage metaphor animates the "ruin-gazing" politics of spectacle through history.
14. George W. M. Harrison, ed., *Satyr Drama: Tragedy at Play* (Classical Press of Wales, 2005).
15. Kwame Anthony Appiah, *My Father's House: Africa in the Philosophy of Culture* (Oxford University Press, 1993). 49. For the complex historical and cultural significance of Africa in Lucan, see Paolo Asso, "The Idea of Africa in Lucan," in *African Athena: New Agendas*, ed. Daniel Orrells, Gurminder K. Bhambra, and Tessa Roynon (Oxford University Press, 2011) 225-238.
16. Geoffrey of Monmouth, *The History of the Kings of Britain*, ed. Michael D. Reeve, trans. Neil Wright (Martelsham: BOYE6, 2009), 6. Hereafter, "Geoffrey" with page numbers in the main text.
17. W. M. Flinders Petrie, "Neglected British History," in *Proceedings of the British Academy, 1917–18* (Oxford, 1918) [251–78], 260.
18. W. M. Flinders Petrie, *The Revolutions of Civilisation*, 3rd ed. (Harper, 1922), 85.
19. W. M. Flinders Petrie, *Janus in Modern Life* (Archibald, Constable & Co., 1907), 70–71.
20. Sallust, *The War with Jugurtha*, in *The War with Catiline; The War with Jugurtha*, trans. J. C. Rolfe, rev. John T. Ramsey (Harvard University Press, 2014), 337. Hereafter, "Sallust" with page numbers in the main text.
21. Orosius, *Seven Books of History against the Pagans*, trans. Andrew T. Fear (Liverpool University Press, 2010), Bk. 5.2, 209. Hereafter, "Orosius" with book and page numbers in the main text.
22. Lynn Staley, "Landscape and the Identity of the Realm," in *Law, Governance, and Justice: New Views on Medieval Constitutionalism*," ed. Richard Kaeuper (Brill, 2013) [87–310], 287.
23. See John D. Niles, "The Wasteland of Loegria: Geoffrey of Monmouth's Reinvention of the Anglo-Saxon Past," in *Reinventing the Middle Ages and the Renaissance: Constructions of the Medieval and Early Modern Periods*, ed. William F. Gentrup (Brepols, 1998), 1–18.
24. Patricia Clare Ingham, *Sovereign Fantasies: Arthurian Romance and the Making of Britain* (University of Pennsylvania Press, 2001), 220.
25. Jessie L. Weston, "Hints for the Single Women of the United Kingdom," *National Review* 17, no. 98 (April 1891) [279–85]: 280.

26. Jessie L. Weston, *The Legend of Sir Lancelot du Lac: Studies upon its Origin, Development, and Position in the Arthurian Romantic Cycle* (David Nutt, 1901), 72.
27. See Sean Davies, *War and Society in Medieval Wales, 633–1283: Welsh Military Institutions* (University of Wales Press, 2004), 89–111.
28. Clement Ng'ong'ola, "The State, Settlers, and Indigenes in the Evolution of Land Law and Policy in Colonial Malawi," *The International Journal of African Historical Studies* 23, no. 1 (1990) [27–58]: 29.
29. Quoted in Gordon J. Barclay and Kenneth Brophy, "A Veritable Chauvinism of Prehistory: Nationalist Prehistories and the 'British' Late Neolithic Mythos," *Archeological Journal* 178, no. 2 (2021) [330–60]: 334.
30. Barclay and Brophy, "A Veritable Chauvinism of Prehistory," 332.
31. E. C. Southward, "Gormont, Roi d'Afrique," *Romania* 69, no. 273 (1946–47) [103–112]: 110.
32. For a summary of the scholarship, see Jean Blacker, "Arthur and Gormund: Conquest, Domination and Assimilation in Wace's *Roman de Brut*," in *Si sai encor moult bon estoire, chançon moult bone anciene: Studies in the Text and Context Of Old French Narrative in Honour of Joseph J. Duggan*, ed. Sophie Marnette, et al. (Oxford: Society for the Study of Medieval Languages and Literature, 2015) [261–282], 263n5.
33. Gustav Storm, *Kritiske Bidrag til Vikingetidens Historie* (Oslo, 1878), 193–96.
34. For a more recent example, see Blacker, "Arthur and Gormund." For a study of how Scandinavians elsewhere become Saracens, see Diane Speed, "The Saracens of *King Horn*," *Speculum* 65 (1990): 564–95.
35. Carol Lumbley, "Geoffrey of Monmouth and Race," in *A Companion to Geoffrey of Monmouth*, ed. Joshua Byron Smith and Georgia Henley (Brill, 2020), 391.
36. Blacker, "Arthur and Gormund," 271.
37. Wace, *Roman de Brut*, ed. and trans. Judith Weiss (University of Exeter Press, 1999), 11.13638–40, 342–43.
38. See Ernst Erich Metzner, "Wandalen im Angelsäschsischen Bereich? Gormundus Rex Africanorum und die Gens Hestingorum," *BGDSL* 95 (1973) 219–71. An earlier version of this argument is Edward Williams Byron Nicholson, "Gormund and Isembard: A Postscript to the 'Vandals in Wessex,'" *Y Cymmrodor* 22 (1911).
39. Cf. Jonathan P. Conant, "The Vandals," in *A Companion to North Africa in Antiquity*, ed. R. Bruce Hitchner (Wiley, 2022) [375–90], 380; and Frank Clover, "Felix Carthago," *Dumbarton Oaks Papers* 40 (1986): 1–16.
40. Andrew Merrills and Richard Miles, *The Vandals* (Wiley-Blackwell, 2010), 91. In *Staying Roman: Conquest and Identity in Africa and the Mediterranean, 439–700* (Cambridge: Cambridge University Press, 2012), 56, Jonathan Conant suggests that Procopius describes them in terms usually used to describe African culture elsewhere.
41. Parthemius praising Sigesteus is cited in Conant, *Staying Roman*, 55.
42. Clover, "Felix Carthago," 3.
43. Victor of Vita, *History of the Vandal Persecution*, ed. and trans. John Moorhead (Liverpool University Press, 1992).
44. Gregory of Tours, *History of the Franks*, trans. Ernest Brehaut (W. W. Norton, 1969), Bk. 2.3, 25.

45. Bede, *Bede's Ecclesiastical History of the English People*, trans. A. M. Sellar (G. Bell and Sons, 1912), Bk. 1.8, 20.

Chapter Three

Karl Marx and Friedrich Engels, *Manifesto of the Communist Party* (Pluto Press, 2017), 47. Mary Wollstonecraft, quoting the Marquis de Mirabeau, in *An Historical and Moral View of the Origin and Progress of the French Revolution* (London, 1794), 1:268.

1. For an important reading of the staging of this scene, see Julia Hell, *The Conquest of Ruins*, where she begins with the example of Carthage in the history of imperial sovereignty but focuses ultimately on Rome and the trope of ruin-gazing in general. Her earlier article, "Imperial Ruin Gazers, or Why did Scipio Weep?," in *Ruins of Modernity*, ed. Julia Hell and Andreas Schönle (Duke University Press, 2010), 169–92, informed some of my early thinking about Carthage. I had not yet read her book until I finished writing this one; we discuss some of the same texts and figures (notably Virgil, Lucan, and Freud) but in different passages and in quite different ways.
2. Silius Italicus, *Punica*, vol. 2, ed. and trans. J. D. Duff (Harvard University Press, 1934), Bk 17.223–24, 454 (my translation). Hereafter, "Silius" with page numbers in the text.
3. Sigmund Freud, *The Interpretation of Dreams*, trans. A. A. Brill (Macmillan, 1913), 164–65. Hereafter, "Freud" with page numbers in the text.
4. Quoted in Sigmund Freud, *The Psychopathology of Everyday Life*, trans. Anthea Bell (Penguin, 2003), 43.
5. See *Odes and Epodes*, ed. and trans. Niall Rudd (Harvard University Press, 2004), 292–95. This edition contains the entirety of both the Latin text and the translation. Hereafter, "Horace" with page numbers in the main text.
6. Francis Cairns, "Horace's Epode 9: Some New Interpretations," *Illinois Classical Studies* 8 (1983) [80–93]: 85, 87.
7. Cf. Livy, *History of Rome*, vol. 11, ed. and trans. J. C. Yardley (Harvard University Press, 2018), Bk. 38.53, 189; Seneca, "Epistle 86," in *Epistles*, vol. 2, ed. and trans. Richard M. Gummere (Harvard University Press, 1920), 311; Valerius Maximus, *Memorable Doings and Sayings*, ed. and trans. D. R. Shackleton Bailey (Harvard University Press, 2000), Bk. 5.3.2, 479.
8. Although Charlton T. Lewis and Charles Short list burial as one of the meanings, the other senses overwhelmingly refer to foundation, preservation, or founding. The first sense refers to the foundation of a city or the establishment of a people. See Lewis and Short, *A Latin Dictionary* (Nigel Gourlay, 2020), s.v. *condo*. Hereafter, "Lewis and Short" with page numbers in the text. The entire dictionary is available online: https://www.perseus.tufts.edu/hopper/text?doc=Perseus:text:1999.04.0059.
9. Nicolas Abraham and Maria Torok, *The Shell and the Kernel: Renewals of Psychoanalysis*, ed. and trans. Nicholas T. Rand (University of Chicago Press, 1994), 1:131; also "a *secretly perpetuated* topography" (1:125).
10. Lewis and Short, s.v. *puniceus, punicus*. Horace uses the form *puniceus* in the Fourth Ode (10.4). Pliny suggests that the name comes from the "Carthaginian apple" (the *punica granatum*), whose flowers provided the dye, but the dye actually comes from Lydian shellfish.

11. It is often assumed that Sallust had little knowledge of Numidian history. But, in *The Jugurthian Wars*, he cites as one of his sources the Punic books (*libri punici*) of the Numidian king Heimpsal II. Some of the inaccuracies in Sallust's description of Africa, often used as evidence that he was not involved much in Numidian affairs, may in fact come from Heimpsal II, who was Sallust's source for much of his information about the origins of the various peoples in the area. See Erich S. Grue, *Rethinking the Other in Antiquity* (Princeton University Press, 2010), 272–76.
12. For an exhaustive discussion of the work, see Vincent Hunink, *Tertullian, De Pallio: A Commentary* (Gieben, 2005).
13. See Andrew Wallace-Hadrill, "The Creation and Expression of Identity: The Roman World," in *Classical Archaeology*, 2nd ed., ed. Susan E. Alcock et al. (Blackwell, 2012) [370–93], 371.
14. Cited in Wallace-Hadrill, "The Creation and Expression of Identity," 371. See also Suetonius, *Lives of the Caesars*, vol. 2, ed. and trans. J. C. Rolfe (Harvard University Press, 1914): Claudius 15, 27.
15. Cicero, *Philippics*, vol. 1, ed. and trans. D. R. Shackleton Bailey, rev. John T. Ramsey and Gesine Manuwald (Harvard University Press, 2010), 4.13, 235.
16. Cited in Carly Daniel-Hughes, *The Salvation of the Flesh in Tertullian of Carthage: Dressing for the Resurrection* (Palgrave Macmillan, 2011), 137n22.
17. Augustine, *City of God against the Pagans*, vol. 1, ed. and trans. George E. McCracken (Harvard University Press, 1957), Bk. 1.30, 127. Hereafter, "Augustine, *City*" with book and page numbers in the text.
18. *Confessions, Volume I: Books 1–8*, trans. Carolyn J.-B. Hammond (Harvard University Press, 2014), III.1, 92. Hereafter, "Augustine, *Confessions*" with book and page numbers in the text.
19. See Stephen Benko, *The Virgin Goddess: Studies in the Pagan and Christian Roots of Mariology* (Brill Academic, 1993), 25–26.
20. Macrobius, *Saturnalia*, vol. 2, ed. and trans. Robert A. Kaster (Harvard University Press, 2011), Bk. 3.9.7–11, 66–71.
21. Herodian, *History of the Empire*, vol. 2, ed. and trans. C. R. Whittaker (Harvard University Press, 1970), Bk. 5.6.4–6, 48–53. The statue was certainly no longer there when the temple was commissioned as a *cathedra* in 399–400. See Gareth Sears, "Augustine in Roman North Africa (Thagaste, Carthage)," in *Augustine in Context*, ed. Tarmo Toom (Cambridge University Press, 2018) [37–43], 42–43.
22. See James J. O'Donnell, "Augustine's Classical Readings," *Recherches Augustiniennes* 15 (1980): 144–75. Terence was an African—indeed, Carthaginian—playwright, whose full name, Publius Terentius Afer, bespoke his origins. His work became a model for Latinate elegance, and he was one of four central authors in the Latin classroom. Augustine would have been trained with his plays. The other three—Virgil, Sallust, and Cicero—are intertwined throughout Augustine's discussion of decadence in *City of God*, Bk. 2.
23. *On the Republic; On the Laws*, ed. and trans. Clinton W. Keyes (Harvard University Press, 1928), Bk. 1.1, 13. Hereafter, "Cicero" with page numbers in the text.
24. *Ethos*, in his *De Oratore*, on the importance of character in orations. His idea of *ethos* is different from Aristotle's. See James M. May, *Trials of Character: The Eloquence of Ciceronian Ethos* (University of North Carolina Press, 2009), 1–12.

25. William Stahl, "Macrobius," in *Complete Dictionary of Scientific Biography*, vol. 9, ed. Charles Coulston Gillespie (Scribner, 2008); and for citations, see Macrobius, *Commentary on the Dream of Scipio*, trans. William Stahl (Columbia University Press, 1990), 4–5.
26. See A. C. Spearing, *Medieval Dream Poetry* (Cambridge University Press, 1976).
27. On Descartes: Jan Rothmann, *Institutio Oratoria: Bacon, Descartes, Hobbes, Spinoza* (Brill, 2009), 396. On Boyle: Robert Boyle, "Some Considerations Touching the Usefulness of Experimental Natural Philosophy," in *The Works of Robert Boyle*, ed. Edward B. Davis (Routledge, 1999), 3:236. On Yeats: *The Collected Poems of W. B. Yeats*, ed. Robert J. Finneran (Scribner, 1997), 1:6.
28. Petrarch, *Africa*, trans. Thomas G. Bergin and Alice S. Wilson (Yale University Press, 1977), Bk. 9.454–58, 234–35. Hereafter, "Bergin and Wilson" with book and page numbers in the text.
29. For the Latin: Petrarch, *Africa*, ed. Léonce Pingaud (Paris, 1872), Bk. 1.168–69, 99. Hereafter, "Pingaud" with book and page numbers in the text.
30. *Petrarch's Secret; or, The Soul's Conflict with Passion, Three Dialogues between Himself and S. Augustine*, ed. and trans. William H. Draper (Chatto and Windus, 1911), 170. Hereafter, "Petrarch, *Secret*" with page numbers in the text.
31. Francis Petrarch, *Secretum*, ed. Enrico Fenzi (Murcia, 1992), 94. Hereafter, "Petrach, *Secretum*" with page numbers in the text.
32. S. A. A. Agambu, "The Reception of Petrarch's *Africa* in Fascist Italy," in *International Journal of the Classical Tradition* 29 (2022): 83–102.
33. See J. Christopher Warner, "Petrarch's Culpa and the Allegory of the Africa," in *The Augustinian Epic, Petrarch to Milton* (University of Michigan Press, 2005) [20–50], 23–24.
34. Francesco Petrarca, *Posteritati*, in Francesco Petrarca, *Prose*, ed. Guido Martellotti, Pier Giorgio Ricci, et al. (Ricciardi, 1955), 16.
35. On the poetics of incompletion in Petrarch, see Warner, "Petrarch's Culpa," 24ff.
36. For a discussion, see Warner, "Petrarch's Culpa," 24ff.
37. For a full discussion of Chaucer's cosmopolitanism, see Marion Turner, *Chaucer: A European Life* (Princeton University Press, 2019).
38. María Rosa Menocal, *The Ornament of the World: How Muslims, Jews, and Christians Created a Culture of Tolerance in Medieval Spain* (Little, Brown and Company, 2002), 149.
39. For a brief discussion of the sources of Granada's gold, see Sarah M. Guérin, "Exchange of Sacrifices: West Africa in the Medieval World of Goods," *The Medieval Globe* 3, no. 2 (2017) [97–123]: 99–100.
40. Claire Gilbert, "The King, the Coin, and the Word: Imagining and Enacting Castilian Frontiers in Late Medieval Iberia," in *Authority and Spectacle in Medieval and Early Modern Europe: Essays in Honor of Teofilo Ruiz*, ed. Yuen-Gen Liang and Jarbel Rodriguez (Routledge, 2017), 33–45.
41. See R. F. Yeager, "Chaucer Translates the Matter of Spain," in *England and Iberia in the Middle Ages, 12th–15th Century: Cultural, Literary, and Political Exchanges*, ed. María Bullón-Fernández (Palgrave Macmillan, 2007), 189–214.
42. Giovanni Boccaccio, *The Book of Theseus: Teseida delle nozze d'Emilia*, trans. Bernadette Marie McCoy (Medieval Text Association, 1974), 151; *The Knight's Tale*, in

The Riverside Chaucer, 3rd ed., ed. Larry D. Benson (Houghton Mifflin, 1986), Fr. 1, 37–66, l. 2630, 60. Hereafter, "Chaucer" with page numbers in the text.

43. Celia M. Lewis, "History, Mission, and Crusade in *The Canterbury Tales*," *Chaucer Review* 42, no. 4 (2008): 353–82.
44. Chaucer, *General Prologue*, 1.57, 24; *Knight's Tale*, 1.2630, 60.
45. For more, see Roland Anthony Oliver and Anthony Atmore, *Medieval Africa, 1250–1800*, 2nd ed. (Cambridge University Press, 2001), 51–54.
46. Quoted in Joseph F. O'Callaghan, *The Gibraltar Crusade: Castile and the Battle for the Strait* (University of Pennsylvania Press, 2011), 66. For the Marinid invasions, see specifically 60–94 and 262–63; and for the end of the Marinid presence, 262–63.
47. Quoted in Allen James Fromherz, *The Near West: Medieval North Africa, Latin Europe and the Mediterranean in the Second Axial Age* (Edinburgh University Press, 2016), 115.
48. Celia Lewis, "History, Mission, and Crusade in *The Canterbury Tales*."
49. Isak Dinesen, *Out of Africa* (Putnam, 1968), 13.
50. See Lewis Webb and Lovisa Brännstedt, "Gendering the Roman Triumph: Elite Women and the Triumph in the Republic and the Early Empire," in *Gendering Roman Imperialism*, ed. Hannah Cornwell and Greg Woolf (Brill, 2023) [58–94], 73; and Hell, *The Conquest of Ruins*, 124–26.
51. Quoted in Chiara M. Mazzeri, "Ancestors at the Gate: Form, Function and Symbolism of the *imagines maiorum*: A Comparative Analysis of Etruscan and Roman Funerary Art," *Opuscula: Annual of the Swedish Institutes at Athens and Rome* 7 (November 2014) [7–22]: 12n29. See also Harriet Flower, *Ancestor Masks and Aristocratic Power in Roman Culture* (Oxford University Press, 1996), 48–52.
52. Patrycja Matusiak, "The Other as a Woman: Polybius and Appian on the Swapping of Gender Roles Among the Carthaginians," in *Beyond Borders: Transgressions in European Literatures*, ed. Agnieszka Adamowicz-Pośpiech, Renata Dampc-Jarosz, and Andrzej Rabsztyn (Vandenhoeck and Ruprecht, 2022) [19–27], 21.
53. Randy P. Schiff, "On Firm Carthaginian Ground: Ethnic Boundary Fluidity and Chaucer's Dido," *Postmedieval* 6 (2015) [23–35]: 29.
54. Tertullian, *Apology*, in *Tertullian: De Spectaculis; Minucius Felix: Octavius*, trans. T. R. Glover (Harvard University Press, 1931), 50.5, 222. Hereafter, "Tertullian" with page numbers in the text.
55. Servius comments on *Aeneid* 1.340: *Dido vero nomine Elissa ante dicta est, sed post interitum a Poenis Dido appellata, id est virago Punica lingua, quod cum a suis sociis cogeretur cuicumque de Afris regibus nubere et prioris mariti caritate teneretur, forti se animo et interfecerit et in pyram iecerit, quam se ad expiandos prioris mariti manes extruxisse fingebat.* See *Servii Grammatici qvi fervntvr in Vergilii carmina commentarii*, ed. Georg Thilo and Hermann Hagen (Leipzig, 1881), 1:120. The entire commentary is available online at http://www.perseus.tufts.edu.
56. *Fulgentius the Mythographer*, trans. Leslie George Whitbread (Ohio State University Press, 1971), 121. Hereafter, "Fulgentius" with page numbers in the text.
57. Marilyn Desmond, *Reading Dido: Gender, Textuality, and the Medieval "Aeneid"* (University of Minnesota Press, 1994), 130.

Chapter Four

Martianus Capella, *The Marriage of Philology and Mercury*, trans. W. H. Stahl and Richard Johnson, in *Martianus Capella and the Seven Liberal Arts* (Columbia University Press, 1977), 2:47.

Assia Djebar, *So Vast the Prison*, trans. Betsy Wing (Seven Stories, 1999), 167.

1. Silvia Mattiacci, "Apuleius and *Africitas*," 88, in *Apuleius and Africa*, ed. Benjamin Todd Lee, et al. (Routledge, 2014).
2. *Medieval Mythography: From Roman North Africa to the School of Chartres* (University of Florida Press, 1994), 16.
3. Juvenal, *Satire 7*, in *Juvenal and Persius*, ed. and trans. Susanna Morton Braund (Harvard University Press, 2004), 7.148–9.
4. "Seminumidam et Semigaetulum," in "Apology," in *Apuleius: Apologia; Florida; de deo Socratis*, ed. and trans. Christopher P. Jones (Harvard University Press, 2017), esp. chap. 24.
5. Robert H. F. Carver, *The Protean Ass: The Metamorphoses of Apuleius from Antiquity to the Renaissance* (Oxford University Press, 2008), 108–12.
6. Carver, *The Protean Ass*, 428–45.
7. *Historia Augusta*, vol. 1: *Clodius Albinus*, trans. David Magie, rev. David Rohrbacher (Harvard University Press, 2022), 464.
8. For an edition, see Michiel Verweij, "Florus and His 'Vergilius Orator and Poeta': The Brussels Manuscript Revisited," *Wiener Studien* 128 (2015) [83–105]: 93.
9. See *The Trinummus of Plautus*, ed. H. R. Fairclough (Macmillan, 1910), 6 (I.82–87); and *The Menaechmi of Plautus*, ed. Joseph H. Drake (Macmillan, 1916), 102 (V.941–45).
10. Statius blamed his defeat on *saevum ingratumque ... Iovem*. "Jupiter" signified at once the god in whose name the games were held; the embodiment of Jupiter on the Capitoline hill; and Domitian himself, who was associated with the god Jupiter. See *The Silvae of Statius*, trans. Betty Rose Nagle (Indiana University Press), 23.
11. *De tradendis disciplinis* (1531), I.II (*Opera*, Basel, 1555), 1.482, cited in Mattiacci, "Apuleius and *Africitas*," 103n6.
12. Mattiacci, "Apuleius and *Africitas*," 130n7.
13. See John F. D'Amico, "The Progress of Renaissance Latin Prose: The Case of Apuleianism," *Renaissance Quarterly* 37, no. 3 (1984): 351–92.
14. *On saisit bien cette physionomie du lettré d'Afrique, et l'on goûte ce style, où manque l'ordre, la mesure et souvent le bon sens, mais où tout est mouvement et couleur, quand on a vécu de cette vie d'Afrique, quand on a subi ce climat aux ardents contrastes et qu'on s'est mêlé à ces étranges foules où depuis trente siècles se rencontrent tant de races diverses, où se heurtent l'Europe, l'Asie et le Soudan* (Paul Monceaux, *Les Africains: Étude sur la littérature latine d'Afrique* [Paris, 1894], 96). My translation.
15. "Y-a-t-il une Africitas?," in *Revue des etudes Latines* 63 (1985), 161–82, quoted in Mattiacci, "Apuleius and *Africitas*," 89. For a brief discussion of other racist explanations of Africitas, see J. N. Adams, *The Regional Diversification of Latin, 200 BC–AD 600* (Cambridge University Press, 2007), 516–18.
16. *L'Afrique romaine présentait un spectacle analogue à celui de l'Afrique française* (Monceaux, *Les Africains*, 3). My translation.

17. See Homi Bhabha, *The Location of Culture* (Routledge, 1994), 70: "The objective of colonial discourse [was] to construe the colonized as a population of degenerate types on the basis of racial origin, in order to justify conquest and to establish systems of administration and instruction."
18. C. S. Lewis, *The Allegory of Love: A Study in Medieval Tradition* (Oxford University Press, 1963), 89.
19. *Martianus Capella and the Seven Liberal Arts*, vol. 2, ed. and trans. William Harris Stahl (Columbia University Press, 1971), 382. Hereafter, "Martianus," with page numbers in the main text.
20. *Martianus iste genere Afer, civis vero Carthaginiensis*. See Natalia Lozovsky, "Perceptions of the Past in Ninth-Century Commentaries on Martianus Capella," in *Carolingian Scholarship and Maritianus Capella: Ninth-century Commentary Traditions on "De nuptiis" in Context*, ed. Mariken Teeuwen and Sinead O'Sullivan (Brepols, 2011), 130n28, quoting Remigius of Auxerre. For other examples, see p. 129.
21. See Ahuvia Kahane, "Apuleius and Martianus Capella: Reception, Pedagogy, and the Dialectics of Canon," in *The Afterlife of Apuleius*, ed. F. Bistagne, C. Boidin, and R. Mouren (London University Press, 2021), 109–23.
22. See Leslie S. B. MacCoull, "Coptica in Martianus Capella De Nuptiis 2.193," *Classical Philology* 90, no. 4 (1995) [361–66]: 365.
23. MacCoull, "Coptica in Martianus Capella De Nuptiis 2.193," 362–63.
24. Martianus: *ex harenis Libyae anbelantis*; Lucan: *per calidas Libyae sitientis harenas*. See Stahl's comment in Martianus, 108n20.
25. *Furvos Garamantas*: see Arnobius, *Adversus Gentes*, ed. H. Dodwellus, *Dissertationes Cyprianicae. Patrologia Latina* 5 (Paris, 1844), col. 1171a, Bk. VI.5.
26. See John H. Starks Jr., "Was Black Beautiful in Vandal Africa?," in *African Athena: New Agendas, Classical Presences*, ed. Daniel Orrells, Gurminder K. Bhambra, and Tessa Roynon (Oxford University Press, 2011).
27. *Martianus Capella*, ed. Adolf Dick (Teubner, 1925), Bk. 9.998, 553.
28. This assertion is more complex, however: Martianus says the whole work is composed by Satire (*Satura*), and he has inadequately followed its lead—but that declaration is *also* satirical.
29. For a discussion of this, see Gregory Hays, "The Date and Identity of the Mythographer Fulgentius," in *Journal of Medieval Latin* 13 (2003) [163–252]: 245–47.
30. As we saw in the case of Statius, the Capitoline was associated in complex ways with the civic role of poetry.
31. *De Rerum Natura*, trans. W. H. D. Rouse, ed. Jeffrey Henderson (Harvard University Press, 1992), 117–19. Fulgentius might have the phrase *perreni fronde coronam* in mind when Calliope describes how she brought *nouellos ... frutices* whose tops will reach the stars (8–9). In *Georgics* 3 (10–12) Virgil claims, echoing what Lucretius said about Ennius a hundred years before, that he will be the first to bring the Muses from Helicon to Italy. See Stephen Hinds, *Allusion and Intertext: Dynamics of Appropriation in Roman Poetry* (Cambridge University Press, 1998), 52–63.
32. Edward Jay Watts, *City and School in Late Antique Athens and Alexandria* (University of California Press, 2008), 145–48.
33. George Saintsbury, *A History of Criticism and Literary Taste in Europe* (Dodd, Mead, 1908), 1:394.

34. Demetrius, *On Style*, trans. W. Rhys Roberts (Cambridge University Press, 1902), I.100, 119.
35. Fulgentius, *Opera: Mitologiarum Libri Tres*, ed. Rudolph Helm (Leipzig, 1898), 11.
36. J. L. Richardson Jr., *A New Topographical Dictionary of Ancient Rome*, s.v., "Statua Marsyae" (Johns Hopkins University Press, 1992). See also Jocelyn Penny Small, *Cacus and Marsyas in Etrusco-Roman Legend* (Princeton University Press, 1982), 70–74.
37. Fulgentius, 47; *Mitologiarum*, 14 (my translation).
38. Anna Dolganov, "Nutricula causidicorum: Legal Practitioners in Roman North Africa," in *Law in the Roman Provinces*, ed. Kimberley Czajkowski and Benedikt Eckhardt (Oxford University Press, 2020), 387.
39. Apuleius, *Florida* 20.10, in *Apuleius: Rhetorical Works*, ed. S. J. Harrison, John Hilton, Vincent Hunink (Oxford University Press, 2001); for Juvenal see Dolganov, "Nutricula causidicorum," 358.
40. See Jo-Marie Claasen, "Cornelius Fronto: A 'Libyan Nomad' at Rome," *Acta Classica* 52 (2009) [47–71]: 52.
41. Gregory Hays, "A World Without Letters: Fulgentius and the *De aetatibus mundi et hominis*," in *Journal of Medieval Latin* 29 (2019): 303–39, esp. 338. The Latin edition is Rudolf Helm, *De aetatibus mundi et hominis*, in *Fabii Planciadis Fulgentii v.c., Opera* (Teubner, 1970). Hereafter, "Helm" with page numbers in the text.
42. See Barry Baldwin, "Fulgentius and His Sources," *Traditio* 44 (1988) [37–57]: 57.
43. See Gregory Hays, "Romuleis Libicisque Litteris: Fulgentius and the 'Vandal Renaissance,'" in *Vandals, Romans and Berbers: New Perspectives on Late Antique North Africa*, ed. A. H. Merrills (Routledge, 2016) [101–32], 105. Hays suggests that "Libyc" allows Fulgentius to avoid saying "Latin" in a section that removes the letter "A." This and Hays's article "World Without Letters" are indispensable studies of the *De aetatibus*.
44. Adams, *The Regional Diversification of Latin*, 541; on Africa, 516–76. On vowel substitutions, see J. N. Martin, *Social Variation and the Latin Language* (Cambridge University Press), 37–70.
45. María José Estarán Tolosa, *Epigrafía Bilingüe del Occidente Romano: El Latín y las lenguas locales en las inscriptiones bilingües y mixtas* (Prensas de Universidad de Zaragoz, 2016), 52. RIL 151, Pl. V.2=CIL 5220/17395 (from Kef Beni Feredi in the Cheffia valley in northeastern Algeria).
46. See Bruce Maddy-Weitzman, *The Berber Identity Movement and the Challenge to North African States* (University of Texas Press, 2011), 2–3.
47. See M. Aghali-Zakara and J. Drouin, "Écritures libyco-berbères: Vingt-cinq siècles d'histoire," in *L'aventure des écritures: Naissances* (Bibliothèque Nationale, 1997), 99–111; R. Elghamis, "Le tifinagh au Niger contemporain: étude sur l'écriture indigène des Touaregs" (PhD diss., University of Leiden, 2011), https://scholarlypublications.universiteitleiden.nl/handle/1887/16532; and L. Galand, "The Problem of the Libyan Alphabets in Ancient North Africa," in *Sahara-Studien* (H. Nowak, 1988), 59–64.
48. See Werner Pichler, "Origin and Development of the Libyco-Berber Script," *Berber Studies* 15 (2007).
49. Jo Wright, "Sir Thomas Reade: The 'Nincumpoop' Collector of Arabic Manu-

scripts,'" in *Qatar Digital Library*, https://www.qdl.qa/en/sir-thomas-reade-'nincumpoop'-collector-arabic-manuscripts.

50. Letter 17, in *The Works of Saint Augustine: Letters, 1–99*, ed. Boniface Ramsey, trans. Roland J. Teske (New City Press, 2001), 49.

51. Matthew M. McCarty, "The Tophet and Infant Sacrifice" (310–25) and Madadh Richey, "Inscriptions" (222–40), in *The Oxford Handbook of the Phoenician and Punic Mediterranean*, ed. Brian R. Doak and Carolina López-Ruiz (Oxford University Press, 2019).

52. Denis Feeney, *Beyond Greek: The Beginnings of Latin Literature* (Harvard University Press, 2016).

53. James Allan Stewart Evans, *Procopius* (Twayne, 1972), 142; David Wilhite, *Ancient African Christianity: An Introduction to a Unique Context and Tradition* (Routledge, 2017), 53.

54. The only fragment of Punic text that anyone could claim to understand for the 1,200 years after Procopius last mentions it appears in Plautus's *Poenulus* (see below), although Plautus wrote only a phonetic equivalent of Hanno's speech. Nevertheless, Plautus's translation provided the only knowledge of what Punic might have been like for over a millennium. Punic script itself remained undeciphered until Jean-Jacques Barthélemy published an alphabet in 1758.

55. On the Punic text in the play, see A. S. Gatwick, "Hanno's Punic Speech in the *Poenulus* of Plautus," *Hermes* 99 (1971): 25–45; Erin K. Moodie, "In Defense of Milphio: Aggressive Puns and Status Transactions in Plautus' *Poenulus*," *Classical World* 111 (2018): 321–50; and George Fredric Franko, "The Characterization of Hanno in Plautus' *Poenulus*," *American Journal of Philology* 117, no. 3 (1996): 425–52.

56. Flavius Cresconius Corippus, *Iohannidos*, ed. James Diggle and Francis Goodyear (Cambridge, 1970), ll. 26-27, 27. See Andy Merrills, "Corippus' Triumphal Ethnography: Another Look at Iohannis II.28–161," *Libyan Studies* 50 (2019): 153–63.

57. Quoted in Ramzi Rouighi, *Inventing the Berbers: History and Ideology in the Maghrib* (University of Pennsylvania Press, 2019), 79. Rouighi's book has a useful exploration of the history of the name "Berber" and its relation, or lack of it, to the originally Greek term *barbaros*, "barbarian."

58. Quoted in Richard Smith, "What Happened to the Ancient Libyans? Chasing Sources across the Sahara from Herodotus to Ibn Khaldun," *Journal of World History* 14 (2003) [459–500]: 478.

59. M. C. A. MacDonald, "Literacy in an Oral Environment," in *Writing and Ancient Near East Society: Essays in Honor of Alan Millard*, ed. Elizabeth A. Slater, et al. (T&T Clark, 2005), 60.

60. Susan Searight, *The Use and Function of Tattooing on Moroccan Women* (Human Relations Area Files, 1984), 292.

61. Jeremy Keenan, *The Lesser Gods of the Sahara: Social Change and Contested Terrain Amongst the Tuareg of Algeria* (Frank Cass, 2005), 22.

62. Jean-Loïc Le Quellec, "Rock Art, Scripts, and Proto-Scripts in Africa," in *Written Cultures in a Colonial Context*, ed. Adrien Delmas and Nigel Penn (UCT Press, 2011), 26.

63. Pierre Bourdieu, *Outline of a Theory of Practice* (Cambridge University Press, 1977), 40.

64. For these examples, see *Bourdieu in Algeria: Colonial Politics, Ethnographic*

Practices, Theoretical Developments, ed. Jane E. Goodman and Paul A. Silverstein (University of Nebraska Press, 2009), 111–12. For a discussion of records of customary law, see Judith Scheele, "A Taste for Law: Rule-Making in Kabylia (Algeria)," *Comparative Studies in Society and History* 50, no. 4 (2008): 895–919. See also two important articles by L. Galand: "Du berbère au libyque: une remontée difficile," 3–28, and "La notion d'écriture dans les parers berbères," 409–13, in *Études de linguistique berbère*, Société de linguistique de Paris, Collection Linguistique 83 (2002).

65. Pierre Bourdieu, *Reproduction in Education, Society and Culture* (Sage, 1977), 16, 211.
66. Hugh Clapperton, *Journal of a Second Expedition into the Interior of Africa* (London, 1829), 46.
67. Pierre Bourdieu, *The Logic of Practice* (Stanford University Press, 1990), 73.
68. Bourdieu, *The Logic of Practice*, 4.
69. Eric A. Havelock, *A Preface to Plato* (Belknap, 1963), 207. The question that governs this passage in Havelock has even more deprecatory consequences for Bourdieu's application of it to the Kabyle: "How did the Greeks ever wake up?" (208).
70. Jeremy F. Lane argues that Bourdieu's deployment of philosophical language stems from the institutional subordination of sociology to philosophy in French academia. I'm indebted to his discussion. See "Returning to Kabylia," in *Pierre Bourdieu: A Critical Introduction* (Pluto Press, 2000), 86–113.
71. Assia Djebar, *Vaste est la prison* (Albin Michel, 1995); trans. Betsy Wing, *So Vast the Prison* (Seven Stories Press, 2001). Hereafter, "Djebar" with page numbers in the text.
72. Eve Tuck, "Suspending Damage: A Letter to Communities," *Harvard Educational Review* 79, no. 3 (2009): 409–27, 539–40, esp. 409.
73. Assia Djebar, *Ces voix qui m'assiègent* (Albin Michel, 1999), 148; Ronald Bogue, *Deleuzian Fabulation and the Scars of History*, vol. 1 (Edinburgh University Press, 2020).

Chapter Five

Frederick Maurice, *Moral and Metaphysical Philosophy* (London, 1890).

1. From *Florida*, in *Apologia; Florida; De Deo Socratis*, ed. and trans. Christopher P. Jones (Harvard University Press, 2017), 20.10, 326. Hereafter, "Jones" with page numbers in the text.
2. David R. Sear, *Roman Coins and Their Values*, vol. 2 (Spink, 2002), 6285.
3. Erich Auerbach, *Mimesis: The Representation of Reality in Western Literature*, trans. Willard R. Trask (Princeton University Press, 2003), 555. Hereafter, "Auerbach, *Mimesis*" with page numbers in the text.
4. *Archivum Romanicum* 22 (1938): 436–89; reissued in 1939 by Leo S. Olschiki in Florence as a self-standing offprint. Reprinted in Erich Auerbach, *Neue Dantestudien* (Istanbul, 1944), 11–71, and in his *Gesammelte Aufsätze zur romanischen Philologie* (Berlin, 1967), 55–92; *Mimesis und Figura: mit einer Neuausgabe des 'Figura'-Aufsatzes von Erich Auerbach*, ed. Friedrich Balke and Hanna Engelmeier (Wilhelm Fink, 2016), 121–88. The first English translation was by Ralph Manheim in Auerbach, *Scenes from the Drama of European Literature: Six Essays* (Meridian,

1959), 11–76; also in *Time, History, and Literature: Selected Essays of Erich Auerbach*, ed. James I. Porter, trans. Jane O. Newman (Princeton University Press, 2016), 65–113. Hereafter, this version is cited as "Porter" with page numbers in the text.
5. He does add "in late antiquity and the Middle Ages," but the concept is the zero degree of his study of modernity, as well.
6. Erich Auerbach, "Figura," in *Scenes from the Drama of European Literature* (University of Minnesota Press, 1984) [11–76], 54. Hereafter, "Auerbach, 'Figura'" with page numbers in the text.
7. From Edward Said's introduction: "Auerbach says explicitly that his work 'arose from the themes and methods of German intellectual history and philology; it would be conceivable in no other tradition than in that of German romanticism and Hegel'" (571).
8. See Avihu Zakai and David Weinstein, "Erich Auerbach and His 'Figura': An Apology for the Old Testament in an Age of Aryan Philology," *Religions* 3 (2012): 320–38 (hereafter, "Zakai and Weinstein" with page numbers in the text); and Avihu Zakaj, "Exile and Interpretation: The Struggle Against Aryan Philology and Nazi Barbarism," in *Eric Auerbach and the Crisis of German Philology: The Humanist Tradition in Peril* (Springer, 2017), 59–82.
9. Quoted in Edward Jay Watts, *City and School in Late Antique Athens and Alexandria* (University of California Press, 2006), 165.
10. *Origen: The Song of Songs: Commentary and Homilies*, trans. R. P. Lawson (Paulist Press, 1957), 22. Hereafter, "Origen" with page numbers in the text.
11. Henri Crouzel, *Origen: The Life and Thought of the First Great Theologian*, trans. A. S. Worrall (Harper and Row, 1989), 8.
12. *Contra Celsum*, trans. Henry Chadwick (Cambridge University Press, 1980), Bk. 2.6, 71.
13. Josephus, *Jewish Antiquities*, vol. 1, trans. H. St. J. Thackeray (Harvard University Press, 1930), Bk. 2.249, 273.
14. Josephus, *Jewish Antiquities*, vol. 3, trans. Ralph Marcus (Harvard University Press, 1934), Bk. 8.165, 305.
15. Translation in Lawson, *Origen*, 93; Latin from Origen, *Werke Bd. VIII: Homilien zu Samuel I, zum Hohelied und zu den Propheten. Kommentar zum Hohelied, in Rufins und Hieronymus' Übersetzung*. ed. Wilhelm A. Baehrens (J. C. Hinrich, 1925), Bk. 2.21–22, 114. Hereafter, "Werke" with page numbers in the text.
16. English from Origen, "Homily Seven," in *Homilies on Numbers*, ed. Christopher A. Hall, trans. Thomas P. Scheck (IVP Academic, 2009) [24–32], 26; *in figuris*, Origen, *Werke Bd. VII: Homilien zum Hexateuch in Rufins Übersetzung*, ed. Wilhelm A. Baehrens (Leipzig: J. C. Hinrich, 1899), Bk. 7.17, 39).
17. Stuart Hall, *The Fateful Triangle: Race, Ethnicity, Nation*, ed. Kobena Mercer (Harvard University Press, 2017), 72–73.
18. The essay is a valuable exploration of the "spiritualizing" tendency of Nazi theology, and its attempt to excise the Old Testament altogether.
19. Matthew Alan Gaumer, *Augustine's Cyprian: Authority in Roman Africa* (Brill, 2016), 125–26.
20. *Select Letters*, trans. James Houston Baxter (Harvard University Press, 2014) [40–55], 47), quoted in Gaumer, *Augustine's Cyprian*, 34.
21. E.g., *semen est sanguis Christianorum*: see *Apology*, in *Tertullian: De Spectaculis;*

Minucius Felix; Octavius; trans. T. R. Glover (Harvard University Press, 1931), 50.12, 226.
22. Tertullian, *De pudicitia*, in *De paenetentia; De pudicitia*; ed. G. Krüger (Freiburg, 1891), 19–75; 22.15, 75.
23. Augustine, *On Christian Doctrine*, in *St. Augustine's City of God and Christian Doctrine*, trans. Philip Schaff (New York, 1890), chap. 36, 846. Hereafter, "Augustine, *Doctrine*" with page numbers in the text.
24. *City of God*, vol. 5, trans. Eva M. Sanford and William M. Green (Harvard University Press, 1965), Bk. 16.34, 159.
25. See Augustinus Hipponensis, *Enarrationes in Psalmos (CPL 0283)* (Library of Latin Texts: BREPOLiS), 113:1, CCSL 40. 1. 1.
26. Erich Auerbach, "Figura," in *Archivum Romanicum* 22 (1938): [436–89], 456.
27. Kader Konuk, *East West Mimesis: Auerbach in Turkey* (Stanford University Press, 2010), 122.
28. August Brinkmann, "Gregor des Thaumaturgen Panegyricus auf Origenes," in *Rheinisches Museum für Philologie* 3, no. 56 (1901): 55–76.
29. Zakai and Weinstein, 321; see also James I. Porter, "Auerbach and the Judaizing of Philology," *Critical Inquiry* 35 (2008): 115–47, 122–25, for a reading of Odysseus's scar that situates it in the *Entjudung* movement (hereafter, "Philology" with page numbers in the text).
30. Adolf von Harnack, *Marcion: The Gospel of the Alien God*, trans. John E. Steely and Lyle D. Bierma (Wipf and Stock, 2007), 138. Porter discusses this passage, with a slightly different reading than mine ("Philology," 125).
31. Harnack, *Marcion*, 46–47.
32. Auerbach fully acknowledges Hegel's influence on his work. He finds Hegel's expression "changeless existence" to describe the experience of Dante's inhabitants of the three realms "one of the most beautiful passages ever written on Dante" (*Mimesis*, 191). See also Avihu Zakai, "Constructing and Representing Reality: Hegel and the Making of Erich Auerbach's *Mimesis*," in *Digital Philology: A Journal of Medieval Cultures* 4, no. 1 (Spring 2015) [106–33]: 110.
33. I take the translation of *Innergeschichtlichkeit* from John David Dawson's useful discussion of the philosophy of history in Origen and Auerbach in "The Preservation of Historical Reality: Auerbach and Origen," in *Christian Figural Reading and the Fashioning of Identity* (University of California Press, 2001), 118.
34. Erich Auerbach, "The Discovery of Dante by Romanticism," in Porter, *Time, History, and Literature*, 134–43, 142; my emphasis.
35. Norbert Fuerst, "*Mimesis*: Dargestellte Wirklichkeit in der abendländischen Literatur by Erich Auerbach," in *Journal of English and Germanic Philology* 47 (1948) [289–90]: 290, cited in Karl F. Morrison's important study *The Mimetic Tradition of Reform in the West* (Princeton University Press, 1982), 410.
36. Erich Auerbach, "The Idea of the National Spirit as the Source of the Modern Humanities," in Porter, *Time, History, and Literature* [56–62], 57.
37. Erich Auerbach, *Literary Language and Its Public in Late Antiquity and in the Middle Ages*, trans. Ralph Manheim (Princeton University Press, 1993), 9–10; quoted in Veli N. Yashin, "Euro(tro)pology: Philology, World Literature, and the Legacy of Erich Auerbach," *Yearbook of Comparative Literature* 57 (2011) [269–90]: 275.
38. Quoted in Yashin, "Euro(tro)pology," 281.

39. Erich Auerbach, *Dante, Poet of the Secular World*, trans. Ralph Manheim (University of Chicago Press, 1961), 174–75; my emphasis.

Chapter Six

James Frazer, *The Golden Bough* (Macmillan, 1922), 265.
Ernst H. Kantorowicz, *The King's Two Bodies: A Study in Medieval Political Theology* (Princeton University Press, 2016), 4.

1. Ernst Kantorowicz Collection, Leo Baeck Institute, Box I, Folder I/1/2. See Robert E. Lerner, *Ernst Kantorowicz: A Life* (Princeton University Press, 2018), 221.
2. See Victoria Kahn, "Political Theology and Fiction in *The King's Two Bodies*," *Representations* 106, no. 1 (2009): 77–101.
3. Ernst H. Kantorowicz, *The King's Two Bodies: A Study in Medieval Political Theology* (Princeton University Press, 2016), 4. Hereafter, "Kantorowicz, *King's*" with page numbers in the text. Robert Lerner discounts a direct connection between Schmitt's and Kantorowicz's uses of the term "political theology" (*Ernst Kantorowicz*, 247–48).
4. Conrad Leyser, introduction to the Princeton Classics Edition of *The King's Two Bodies: A Study in Medieval Political Theology* (Princeton University Press, 2016) [ix–xxiiii], xiii.
5. Ernst H. Kantorowicz, "Mysteries of State: An Absolutist Concept and Its Late Mediaeval Origins," *Harvard Theological Review* 48, no. 1 (January 1955) [65–91]: 67.
6. See Victoria Kahn, "Sacred Kingship and Political Fiction: Ernst Kantorowicz, Carl Schmitt, Ernst Cassirer, and Walter Benjamin," in *The Future of Illusion: Political Theology and Early Modern Texts* (University of Chicago Press, 2013), 55–82.
7. Eckhart Grünewald, *Ernst Kantorowicz und Stefan George: Beiträge zur Biographie des Historikers bis zum Jahre 1938 und zu seinem Jugendwerk* (Franz Steiner, 1982), 165, cited by Joseph Mali, "Ernst H. Kantorowicz: History as 'Mythenschau,'" *History of Political Thought* 18, no. 4 (1997) [579–603]: 585.
8. On the debates among German historians about the role of myth in the writing of history, see Mali, "Ernst H. Kantorowicz," 603.
9. Ernst Kantorowicz Collection, Leo Baeck Institute, AR 7216 / MF 561, "Medieval Institutions: History 125a," Box III, Folder III.9/1, 47–48.
10. Cyprian, as quoted in Kantorowicz, *King's*, 440. Kantorowicz gives this as Letter 68; in other editions, 66. See also Kantorowicz, *King's*, 440n409, in which he argues that, despite similarities between John 14:10 and Athanasius of Alexandria's formulation, Cyprian was the first to deploy the verse from John in this context.
11. Ernst Kantorowicz Collection, Leo Baeck Institute, AR 7216 / MF 561, "Medieval Institutions: History 125a," Box III, Folder III.9/1, 48.
12. See Eberhard Bethge, *Dietrich Bonhoeffer: A Biography*, ed. Victoria J. Barnett (Fortress, 2000), 927–28; and Martin A. Ruehl, "'In This Time without Emperors': The Politics of Ernst Kantorowicz's *Kaiser Friedrich der Zweite* Reconsidered," *Journal of the Warburg and Courtauld Institutes* 63, no. 1 (2000) [187–242]: 188n5. Ruehl argues, with considerable justification, that *Frederick II* is deeply sympathetic to the currents of racism and hypernationalism that the Nazi party exploited.
13. Cited in Ruehl, "In This Time," 188n10; see David Abulafia, "Kantorowicz, Frederick II, and England," in *Ernst Kantorowicz: Erträge der Doppeltagung Institute for*

Advanced Study, Princeton, Johann Wolfgang Goethe-Universität, Frankfurt," ed. Robert L. Benson and Johannes Fried (Franz Steiner, 1997), 124–43, esp. 132.

14. Ernst Kantorowicz, *Frederick the Second, 1194–1250*, trans. E. O. Lorimer (Frederick Ungar, 1922), 385. Hereafter, "Kantorowicz, *Frederick*" with page numbers in the text.

15. I don't mean to imply that David Abulafia neglects this contradiction (see "Kantorowicz, Frederick II, and England," 131–32).

16. This final paragraph can be read in a number of ways, including as an esoteric description of George and his circle. This "Lord of the Beginning" is also "the deceiver, the radiant, the merry, the ever-young, the stern and mighty judge, the scholar, the sage who leads his armed warriors to the Muse's dance and song" (Kantorowicz, *Frederick*, 689). George famously encouraged Kantorowicz to write about Frederick. Abulafia compares the messianism of *Frederick II*'s final paragraph with a 1918 poem of George's. For further discussion see David Abulafia, "Kantorowicz and Frederick II," *History* 62, no. 205 (1977): 193–210.

17. On Kantorowicz's disregard of scholarly and historical evidence on this point, see Martin Ruehl's excellent discussion of Kantorowicz's thought in the context of the George-Kreise in "'Imperium transcendat hominem': Reich and Rulership in Ernst Kantorowicz's *Kaiser Friedrich der Zweite*," in *A Poet's Reich: Politics and Culture in the George Circle*, ed. Melissa S. Lane and Martin A. Ruehl (Camden House, 2011) [204–248], 213.

18. Cicero, *The Verrine Orations*, vol 1, trans. L. H. G. Greenwood (Harvard University Press, 1928), Bk. 2.2.1, 296–97; translation modified. Hereafter, "*Verrine*" with page numbers in the text.

19. *Viso augusto iuxta morem illius terre prono vultu in terra coram eo corruente*: Otto von St. Blasien, *Ottonis de S. Blasio Chronica*, ed. Adolf Hofmeister (Hahnian Library, 1912), 63. The phrase originally described the deference paid to David by Bathsheba when she asked that Solomon be David's heir (1 Kings 1:17), and Araunah the Jebusite when David asked to build an altar on his threshing-floor (2 Samuel 24:21). It's not clear that *prono vultu in terram* necessarily means "prostrate," however: it literally means "bent the face forward to(ward) the ground." The phrase is sometimes modified by *se prostraverunt* (Henricus Canisius and Jacques Basnage de Beauval, *Thesaurus monumentorum ecclesiasticorum et historicorum, sive Henrici Canisi lectiones antiquae* [Amsterdam, 1725], 132); or the first of a series of acts of adoration, which include prostration: *prone vultu et corpora in temple pavimento prostratum* (Dynamius Patricius, *Vita Sancti Maximi episcopi Reiensis. Patrologia Latina* 80 [1863]: coll. 31–40, esp. 40).

20. Berlin, May 3, 1918: *In meinen Geburtstag ist übrigens noch ein sehr bitterer Tropfen gefallen, und zwar las ich in der Voss. Ztg., dass Richard Kandt gestorben ist. Ganz abstrahiert, dass mir sein Tod als Vetter und als Mensch sehr nahe gegangen ist, hat mir dieses Ereignis wieder vor Augen geführt, auf wie schwachen Füssen die Dynastie 'Kantorowicz' steht* (quoted from Robert Lerner, personal communication, November 17, 2015).

21. Richard Voss, *Aus Einem Phantastischen Leben* (Engelhorn, 1920), 254–55.

22. Cf. the title of Kandt's book: *Caput Nili: eine empfindsame Reise zu den Quellen des Nils* (Berlin: Dietrich Reimer, 1904). Hereafter, "Kandt" with page numbers in the text.

23. Wilhelm Preger, *Geschichte der deutschen Mystik im Mittelalter* (Leipzig, 1893), 3:207. Preger used Julius Hamberger's edition of Tauler's sermons, *Johann Taubers Predigten* (Frankfurt, 1864). In his published poem, "Trost der Namenlosen," Kandt echoes both the secrecy of his love and its transcendence of corporeal attributes. He dedicates *meine tiefste Liebe* to "you, the nameless one" (*Euch Namenlosen*), and ends with the narrator laying a white rose on the grave of the *Namenlosen*. See Kandt, "Trost der Namenlosen," in *Meine Seele klingt: nachgelassene Gedichte aus dem Kriege* (Dietrich Reimer, 1918), 17–18, l. 23.
24. See Marita Keilson-Lauritz, "Lauter schwule Reisen? Ein Versuch zu einer Theorie der Homosexualität am Beispiel von Richard Kandt, Wolfgang Corden und Hubert Fichte," *Arcadia* 46 (2011) [378–95]: 383–86.
25. Voss, *Aus Einem Phantastischen Leben*, 448–49.
26. See Heinrich von Bethe, "Bericht über einem Zug nach Ruanda," *Deutsches Kolonialblatt* 10 (1899): S 6–12. Previous explorers had met a stand-in, a subterfuge that Kandt saw through.
27. Bundesarchiv Berlin-Dahlem, R1001/1029: Götzen an Auswärtiges Amt, Kolonialabteilung, July 4, 1905, Appendix: Die innenpolitischen Verhältnisse im Bezirke Bukoba von Regierungsrat Haber, quoted in Michael Pesek, "Cued Speeches: The Emergence of Shauri as Colonial Praxis in German East Africa, 1850–1903," *History in Africa* 33 (2006) 395–412: 406n30.
28. Reinhart Bindseil, *Ruanda und Deutschland seit den Tagen Richard Kandts* (Dietrich Reimer, 1988), quoted in Horst Gründer, "Reinhart Bindseil, *Ruanda und Deutschland seit den Tagen Richard Kandts*," *Militärgeschichtliche Mitteilungen* 1 (January, 1989): 255–56 (my translation).
29. See Hans Conrad Peyer, "Das Reisekönigtum des Mittelalters," in *Vierteljahrschrift für Sozial- und Wirtschaftsgeschichte*, vol. 51, ed. Hermann Aubin (Wiesbaden, 1964), S. 1–21, and Ferdinand Opll, *Das itinerar Kaiser Friedrichs Barbarossa (1152–1190)* (Böhlau, 1978).
30. Map uses the word *pigmeus* ("pygmies"). See Walter Map, *De Nugis Curialium*, ed. Montague Rhodes James (Clarendon, 1914), Bk. 1.11, 13.
31. Peter Scholl-Latour, *Afrikanische Totenklage Der Ausverkauf des Schwarzen Kontinents* (C. Bertelsmann Verlag, 2001), 85.
32. John Hanning Speke, *Journal of the Discovery of the Source of the Nile* (London, 1863), 123.
33. Charles Gabriel Seligman, *The Races of Africa* (Thornton Butterworth, 1930), 96, 100.
34. Lugard believed that "Hamites" possessed "powers of social organisation and intellectual development in advance of the pure negro stock." See Frederick Lugard, *The Dual Mandate in British Tropical Africa* (Blackwood, 1922), 68.
35. *Die Weltgeschichte: aus dem Standpunkte der Cultur und der nationalen Charakteristik*, vol. 1, ed. Carl Eduard Vehse (Dresden, 1842), 486. See also *Conversationslexicon für bildende Kunst*, vol. 5, ed. Friedrich Faber (Leipzig, 1850), s.v. "Gral."
36. Godfrey Lienhardt, "Frazer's Anthropology: Science and Sensibility," *JASO* 24, no. 1 (1993) [1–12]: 2.
37. Quoted in Edmund Leach, "Frazer and Malinowski: On the 'Founding Fathers,'" *Encounter* 25, no. 5 (November 1965) [25–36]: 25.
38. E. E. Evans-Pritchard, "The Divine Kingship of the Shilluk of the Nilotic Sudan:

The Frazer Lecture, 1948," *HAU: Journal of Ethnographic Theory* 1, no. 1 (2011) [407–22]: 407; cf. James Frazer, *The Golden Bough: A Study in Magic and Religion* (Macmillan, 1911), 3:17–33.

39. Charles Gabriel Seligman, "The Cult of Nyakang and the Divine Kings of the Shilluk," in *Report of the Wellcome Tropical Research Laboratories at the Gordon Memorial College*, vol. 4, pt. B, ed. Andrew Balfour, et al. (Khartoum, 1911) [216–38], 221.
40. Evans-Pritchard, "The Divine Kingship of the Shilluk," 420.
41. Evans-Pritchard, "The Divine Kingship of the Shilluk," 420.
42. Saul K. Padover, *Marx on Revolution* (McGraw-Hill, 1977), 247. I've substituted "habit" for "cowl" (Marx uses the word *Kutte*).
43. See Suzanne Marchand, "Frobenius and the Revolt against the West," *Journal of Contemporary History* 32, no. 2 (1997) [153–170]: 161, 166; and Christoph Johannes Franzen, Karl-Heinz Kohl, and Marie-Luise Recker, *Der Kaiser und sein Forscher: Der Briefwechsel zwischen Wilhelm II und Leo Frobenius (1924–1938)* (Kohlhammer, 2012).
44. Michael Spöttel, *Hamiten: Völkerkunde und Antisemitismus* (Peter Lang, 1996), 134.
45. Spöttel, *Hamiten*, 137.
46. Marchand, "Frobenius," 168–69. Nevertheless, much of Frobenius's work is distinctly anti-colonial and even, in very qualified ways, anti-racist. Indeed, he was championed by the first wave of African nationalists. Léopold Sédar Senghor wrote an effusive essay on the powerfully positive influence of his work in 1973; W. E. B. Du Bois called him "the greatest student of Africa."
47. Quoting (and translating) from Leo Frobenius, *Kulturgeschichte Afrikas* (Zürich: Phaidon-Verlag, 1933), 34. As Spöttel says, this passage is "clearly a comment on current events in Germany" (*Hamiten*, 135).
48. For the extensive correspondence between the two, see Christoph Johannes Franzen, Karl-Heinz Kohl, and Marie-Luise Recker, *Der Kaiser und sein Forscher: Der Briefwechsel zwischen Wilhelm II und Leo Frobenius (1924–1938)* (Kohlhammer, 2011).
49. John C. G. Röhl, *Wilhelm II: Into the Abyss of War and Exile, 1900–1941*, trans. Sheila de Bellaigue and Roy Bridge (Cambridge University Press, 2014), 1229.
50. Karl-Heinz Kohl, "Der sakrale Königsmord: Zur Geschichte der Kulturmorphologie," *Paideuma* 45 (1999): 63–82, esp. 78 (my translation).
51. Leo Frobenius, *The Voice of Africa, Being an Account of the German Inner African Exploration Expedition in the Years 1910–1912* (Hutchinson and Co., 1913), 632. Hereafter, "Frobenius" with page numbers in the text.
52. See Siegfried Passarge, *Adamau: Bericht über die Expedition des Deutschen Kamerun-Komitees in den Jahren 1893/94* (Berlin, 1895).
53. Most infamously, in Siegfried Passarge, *Das Judentum als landschaftskundlich-ethnologisches Problem* (Munich: Lehmanns, 1929). The English translation of the title is "Judaism as a landscape-ethnological problem."
54. Christian S. Davis, *Colonialism, Antisemitism, and Germans of Jewish Descent in Imperial Germany* (University of Michigan Press, 2012), 112–13.
55. W. S. Barnard, *Encountering Adamastor: South Africa's Founding Geographers in Time and Place* (African Sun Media, 2016), 39; Boris Michel, "Anti-Semitism in Early 20th Century German Geography," *Political Geography* 65 (2018) [1–7]: 4.

56. David M. Gordon, "(Dis)embodying Sovereignty: Divine Kingship in Central African Historiography," *Journal of African History* 57, no. 1 (2016) [47–67]: 60.
57. Robert J. Gordon, *The Enigma of Max Gluckman: The Ethnographic Life of a "Luckyman" in Africa* (University of Nebraska Press, 2018), 60. Hereafter, "Gordon" with page numbers in the text.
58. Marian Kempny, "History of the Manchester 'School' and the Extended-Case Method," *Social Analysis: The International Journal of Anthropology* 49, no. 3 (Winter 2005) [144–65]: 154.
59. Teju Cole, "The White Savior Industrial Complex," *The Atlantic*, March 21, 2012. On the RLI principles, see Kate Crehan, *The Fractured Community: Landscapes of Power and Gender in Rural Zambia* (University of California Press, 1997), especially 2.2.1, "Max Gluckman and the Rhodes-Livingstone Institute."
60. Richard Brown, "Passages in the Life of a White Anthropologist: Max Gluckman in Northern Rhodesia," *Journal of African History* 20, no. 4 (1979) [525–41]: 532–34; Terence Ranger, "White Presence and Power in Africa," *Journal of African History* 20, no. 4 (1979): 463–69.
61. Max Gluckman, "Analysis of a Social Situation in Modern Zululand," *Bantu Studies* 14, no. 1 (1940): 1–30.
62. Max Gluckman, *Politics, Law, and Ritual in Tribal Society* (Basil Blackwell, 1965), 10. Hereafter, "Gluckman, *Politics*" with page numbers in the text.
63. Crehan, *The Fractured Community*, 2.2.1.
64. See Crehan, *The Fractured Community*, for further discussion of the tensions of Gluckman's methods.
65. Abbas Gnamo, *Conquest and Resistance in the Ethiopian Empire, 1880–1974: The Case of the Arsi Oromo* (Brill, 2014), 88.
66. Seebohm's work was part of the "village community" debate begun in Henry Sumner Maine, *Village-Communities in the East and West: Six Lectures Delivered at Oxford* (London, 1871). See Maura B. Nolan, "Metaphoric History: Narrative and New Science in the Work of F. W. Maitland," *PMLA* 118, no. 3 (2003) [557–72]: 570n8.
67. Frederic Seebohm, *The English Village Community Examined in its Relations to the Manorial and Tribal Systems and to the Common or Open Field of Husbandry* (Longmans, Green, and Co., 1915), vii–viii.
68. Max Gluckman, "The Peace in the Feud," *Past and Present* 8 (1955) [1–14]: 13. Hereafter, "Gluckman, 'Peace'" with page numbers in the text. A different version appears in Max Gluckman, *Custom and Conflict in Africa* (The Free Press, 1963), 1–26. Hereafter, "Gluckman, *Custom*" with page numbers in the text.
69. For its influence on medievalists, see Stephen D. White, "'The Peace in the Feud' Revisited: The Feuds in the Peace in Medieval European Feuds," in *Making Early Medieval Societies: Conflict and Belonging in the Latin West, 300–1200*, ed. Kate Cooper and Conrad Leyser (Cambridge University Press, 2016), 220–43.
70. Sir Frederick Pollock and Frederic William Maitland, *The History of English Law Before the Time of Edward I*, 2nd ed. (Cambridge, 1898), 1: 200. Hereafter, "Pollock and Maitland" with page numbers in the text.
71. Frederick Lugard, "Colonial Administration," *Economica* 13/41 (August 1933) [248–63]: 259. Lugard discusses the "feudal analogy" between England's feudal system and African groups.

72. The rest of the passage goes on to argue that the law of the tribe represents "personal" and "racial" law, rather than the law of territory.
73. Joseph Eddy Fontenrose, *The Ritual Theory of Myth* (University of California Press, 1966), 11.
74. Max Gluckman, "The Frailty in Authority," in *Custom* [27–53], 37. Hereafter, "Gluckman, 'Frailty'" with page numbers in the text.
75. Max Gluckman, "Civil War and Theories of Power in Barotseland: African and Medieval Analogies," *Yale Law Journal* 72, no. 8 (July 1963) [1515–46]: 1517. Hereafter, "Gluckman, 'Power'" with page numbers in the text.
76. Gerald Lewis Caplan, "A Political History of Barotseland 1878–1965" (PhD diss., School of Oriental and African Studies, University of London, 1968), 325. Available at https://www.proquest.com/docview/2185912663?pq-origsite=gscholar.

Chapter Seven

Sir Eyre Crowe, Memorandum of January 5, 1905, National Archives T 1/10369/4480, quoted in E. T. Corp, "The Transformation of the Foreign Office, 1900–1907" (PhD diss., University of Kent, 1976), 227.

Tom Mboya, *African Socialism and its Application to Planning in Kenya*, Sessional Paper no. 10 (Government of Kenya, 1965), 7.

1. Jomo Kenyatta, *Facing Mount Kenya* (Mercury Books, 1961), 306. Hereafter, "Kenyatta" with page numbers in the text.
2. William Stubbs, *The Constitutional History of England* (Oxford, 1883), 1:274, 1:278.
3. See Elizabeth A. R. Brown, "Reflections on Feudalism: Thomas Madox and the Origins of the Feudal System in England," in *Feud, Violence and Practice: Essays in Medieval Studies in Honor of Stephen D. White*, ed. Belle S. Tuten and Tracey L. Billado (Ashgate, 2010), 135–55, at 145–49. See also Susan Reynolds, *Fiefs and Vassals: The Medieval Evidence Reinterpreted* (Oxford University Press, 1994); and Kathleen Davis, *Periodization and Sovereignty: How Ideas of Feudalism and Secularization Govern the Politics of Time* (University of Pennsylvania Press, 2008).
4. Elspeth Huxley, *White Man's Country* I, 64, quoted in Will Jackson, "White Man's Country: Kenya Colony and the Making of a Myth," *Journal of Eastern African Studies* 5, no. 2 (2011) [344–68]: 348.
5. Quoted in Ngũgĩ wa Thiong'o, *Wrestling with the Devil: A Prison Memoir* (New Press, 2018).
6. *Out of Africa* (Putnam, 1968), 19. Hereafter, "Dinesen" with page numbers in the text.
7. See Robert Tigor, *Colonial Transformation of Kenya: The Kamba, Kikuyu, and Maasai from 1900–1939* (Princeton University Press, 1976), 49.
8. See Ndirangu Mwaura, *Kenya Today: Breaking the Yoke of Colonialism in Africa* (Algora, 2005), 48.
9. Technically, the "squatters" on her farm were not squatters; they were "labor-tenants." Squatting was a practice unrecognized by law, except that it had the barest sense of "occupying."
10. Southern Rhodesia, *Report of the Land Commission*, 1925 (Salisbury: Government Printer, 1925).

11. United Kingdom, *Hansard Parliamentary Debates*, vol. 64, House of Lords (23 June 1926), cols. 542–64, sect. 549.
12. See Sally Harvey, "The Domesday Book and Its Predecessors," *EHR* 86 (1971): 73–75.
13. See David Pelteret, "Slavery in Anglo-Saxon England," in *The Anglo-Saxons: Synthesis and Achievement*, ed. J. Douglas Woods and David Pelteret (Wilfrid Laurier University Press, 1985), 132.
14. For a good overview of the Hundred Rolls commission, see Sandra Raban, *A Second Domesday? The Hundred Rolls of 1279–80* (Oxford University Press, 2004).
15. *Report of the Kenya Land Commission* (HMSO, 1934), 3; my emphasis. Hereafter, "*Report*" with page numbers in the text.
16. William Stubbs, *The Constitutional History of England* (Oxford, 1883).
17. "The land ought to be accounted fully used if the population . . . was living at or beyond the optimum density. Where such conditions prevail, the tribe is entitled to be compensated up to the full value of any of its land which is taken. But the greater the margin by which the population fall short of this requirement, *the greater is the justification of Government for regarding unoccupied land as waste land*" (*Report*, 12; my emphasis).
18. Quoted in Nicholas Githuku, *Mau Mau Crucible of War: Statehood, National Identity, and Politics of Postcolonial Kenya* (Lexington Books, 2016).
19. Frederick Lugard, *The Dual Mandate in British Tropical Africa* (Blackwood, 1922), 290. Hereafter, "Lugard" with page numbers in the text.
20. *The "Gesta Guillelmi" of William of Poitiers*, ed. R. H. C. Davies and M. Chibnall (Oxford University Press, 1988).
21. Donald W. Sutherland, *Quo Warranto Proceedings in the Reign of Edward I, 1278–1294* (Clarendon Press, 1963).
22. *The Economic Journal* 56, no. 221 (March 1946), n.p.
23. Vincent Liversage, *Land Tenure in the Colonies* (Cambridge University Press, 1945), ix. Hereafter, "Liversage" with page numbers in the text.
24. Vincent Liversage, report for the Department of Agriculture of the Colony and Protectorate of Kenya, quoted in Githuku, *Mau Mau Crucible of War*, 64.
25. *The Historical Register of the University of Oxford* (Oxford, 1888), 163–64.
26. Quoted in T. G. Otte, *The Foreign Office Mind: The Making of British Foreign Policy, 1865–1914* (Cambridge University Press, 2011), 15.
27. *The Student's Handbook to the University and Colleges of Oxford* (Oxford, 1895), 175. Hereafter, "*Handbook*" with page numbers in the text.
28. See *One Hundred Letters from Hugh Trevor-Roper*, ed. Richard Davenport-Hines and Adam Sisman (Oxford University Press, 2014). These historians "maintained that 'there is no History but Medieval History': that is, that non-medieval history . . . was a less exacting discipline, a second-class kind of history, in fact not history at all but trivial dilettante chit-chat" (214). Trevor-Roper mentions Manchester as well as Balliol, but its dominant figure, T. F. Tout, was trained at Balliol. This isn't just a Balliol "thing," however. A 1922 article for undergraduates planning to study in England warned that it was difficult to study anything *but* medieval history at Oxford, Cambridge, or London: "It is somewhat exasperating if you do not happen to be a medievalist to find how completely the term 'medieval history' is regarded as synonymous with history." See Elma Gillespie Frances, "Historical Research in England," *The Arrow of Phi Beta Phi* 38, no. 4 (1922) [620–27]: 623.

29. See Summary List of Papers of Kenneth Norman Bell, Balliol College Historical Collection Centre.
30. Luxembourg and Jamaica, for instance. See *Challenging the Rulers: A Leadership Model for Good Governance*, ed. Okoth Okombo, et al. (East African Educational Publishers, 2011), 8.
31. See, for example, K. Kanyinga's important article, "The Legacy of the White Highlands: Land Rights, Ethnicity and the Post-2007 Election Violence in Kenya," *Journal of Contemporary African Studies* 27 (2009) [325–44]: 335.
32. "Speech at the Kenya African Union Meeting at Nyeri, July 26, 1952," in *Colonialism: An International Social, Cultural, and Political Encyclopedia*, ed. Melvin E. Page (ABC-Clio, 2003), 1:936.
33. Sessional Paper no. 10, p. 7. Mboya introduced it in Parliament; there may have been contributions from Mwai Kibaki, the future Finance Minister and President of Kenya.
34. Amilcar Cabral, *The Weapon of Theory: Address Delivered to the First Tricontinental Conference of the Peoples of Asia, Africa and Latin America Held in Havana in January* (1966), https://www.marxists.org/subject/africa/cabral/1966/weapon-theory.htm.
35. On Cabral's assassination, see Patrick Chabal, *Amílcar Cabral: Revolutionary Leadership and People's War* (Cambridge University Press, 1983).
36. See M. Tamarkin, "The Roots of Political Stability in Kenya," *African Affairs* 77, no. 308 (July 1978).
37. John Lonsdale, "Moral and Political Argument in Kenya," in *Ethnicity and Democracy in Africa*, ed. Bruce Berman, et al. (Boydell and Brewer, 2004), 91.
38. *Kenya National Assembly Official Record* (Hansard), June 12, 1996, 946. Hereafter, "Hansard" with page numbers in the text.
39. *Report of the Truth, Justice and Reconciliation Commission*, Vol. IIB (Nairobi, 2013). 211.
40. Paul Ndung'u, "Tackling Land Related Corruption in Kenya," http://siteresources.worldbank.org/RPDLPROGRAM/Resources/459596-1161903702549/S2_Ndungu.pdf, p. 6.
41. It has to be pointed out that this comes from one of the infamous "reviews from the future" in the *American Journal of Sociology*—witty, irreverent, but also deeply thoughtful mini-studies of important anthropologists written by the pseudonymous "Barbara Celarent" (a name taken from the first two words of the mnemonic that medieval students used to memorize the moods of the Aristotelian syllogistic). For a review of *Facing Mount Kenya*, see *American Journal of Sociology* 116 (2010): 722–28, esp. 724.
42. See also Wangari Maathai, *Unbowed: A Memoir* (Anchor, 2007), 4–5; and Ngũgĩ wa Thiong'o, *The Perfect Nine: The Epic of Gĩkũyũ and Mumbi* (The New Press, 2020).
43. See, e.g., the debate in Parliament on whether gazetting it as a protected area amounted to an endorsement of "devil worship." Question 22, "Maintenance of Worshipping Places," May 9, 1996, in Hansard, 737–78. The question was whether the administration of these Gĩkũyũ shrines could be taken over by the Kenya National Evangelism Fellowship Church, or not.
44. Bronisław Malinowski, *Freedom and Civilization* (Allen and Unwin, 1947), 120. Hereafter, "Malinowski, *Freedom*" with page numbers in the text.

45. "Myth in Primitive Psychology," in *Malinowski and the Work of Myth*, ed. Ivan Strenski (Princeton University Press, 1992), 93. Hereafter, "Malinowski, 'Myth,'" with page numbers in the text.
46. Bronisław Malinowski, *Coral Gardens and Their Magic* (Indiana University Press, 1965), 319–20.
47. See, e.g., William Searle Holdsworth, *An Historical Introduction to the Land Law* (Oxford University Press, 1927), 300; and Pollock and Maitland, 1:14.
48. "Ethnology and the Study of Society," in Strenski, *Malinowski and the Work of Myth*, 49. To be fair, Malinowski goes on to mention as well "Classical Antiquity . . . the Homeric Epoch or the Neolithic times."
49. Michael Young, *Malinowski's Kiriwina: Fieldwork Photography, 1915–1918* (University of Chicago Press, 1998). Malinowski's resort to the feudal analogy, while not overt in his work, may be symptomatic of his close work with the London School of Economics's famous medieval historian Eileen Power around this time. They collaborated on administrative and curricular projects at LSE, and both were members of a collaborative project from 1928–34 to explore "historical inquiry into the family." See Eileen Jacobs, "Eileen Power (1889–1940)," in *Medieval Scholarship: Biographical Studies on the Formation of a Discipline*, ed. Helen Damico et al. (New York: Garland, 1995), 1:219–31.
50. "On Medieval History as a Social Study," *Economica* 12 (1934) [13–29]: 26.
51. Ngũgĩ wa Thiong'o, *Matigari*, trans. Wangui wa Goro (Heinemann, 1987), 168.
52. That Matigari's name can also mean "remnant" implicates Matigari in Ngũgĩ's complex dance between Christianity's work as the ideology of colonial oppression and the liberatory message implicit in it. "Matigari" is the word that Gĩkũyũ translations of the Bible use in Isaiah's distinctive formulation of the theology of the remnant, the ruins of a people that will refound it.
53. Ngũgĩ wa Thiong'o, *The River Between* (Heinemann, 1965), 1. Hereafter, "Ngũgĩ *River*" with page numbers in the text.
54. This isn't as frivolous a play as it might sound. The novel's opening is shot through with reference to the potential antagonisms of the two ridges, hints of a specifically dialectical struggle to come. (For instance, the antagonism between the two ridges disappears when seen from a distance—specifically, from the site of the original mugumo tree). The novel is, in fact, about the dialectic of traditional and Christianized culture; but the opening suggests that the dialectic could be filled with any content.
55. John Stuart Mill, *England and Ireland*, 4th ed. (London, 1868), 12.
56. See Mary Louise Pratt, *Imperial Eyes: Studies in Travel Writing and Transculturation*, 2nd ed. (Routledge, 2008), 201–08.
57. Ngũgĩ's first novel, *Weep Not Child*, uses a similar form for the mythic charter.
58. E.g., Charter of Aethelwulf, in *A Handbook to the Land-Charters, and Other Saxonic Documents* (Oxford, 1888), 339; charter of Guy de Thouars, in Everard Judith and Michael Jones, *The Charters of Duchess Constance of Brittany and Her Family 1171–1221* (Boydell Press, 1999), 152. In *Devil on the Cross*, Ngũgĩ uses the phrase *per omnia in saecula saeculorum*, a longer phrase found both in the Mass and in medieval charters. See *Rotuli Chartarum In Turri Londinensi*, ed. Thomas Duffy Hardy (London, 1837), xxxiv.
59. Sir Walter Scott, *Waverly: or, 'Tis Sixty Years Since* (London, 1831), 1:185.

60. Simon Gikandi, *Ngũgĩ wa Thiong'o* (Cambridge University Press, 2000), 50.
61. Godfrey Muriuki, *A History of the Kikuyu, 1500–1900* (Oxford University Press, 1974), 46–47; S. K. Gathigira, *Mĩikarĩre ya Agĩkũyũ* (C. M. S., 1933). In the interval between 1937 and 1910, there is C. W. Hobley's 1922 study, which says only that the Kamba and Gĩkũyũ "attribute the existence of the world and of its inhabitants to creation by Engai." See *Bantu Beliefs and Magic* (Witherby, 1922), 26.
62. William Scoresby Routledge and Katherine Routledge, *With a Prehistoric People: The Akikuyu of British East Africa* (Arnold, 1910), 21. Hereafter, "Routledge" with page numbers in the text.
63. Marshall S. Clough, *Mau Mau Memoirs: History, Memory, and Politics* (Lynne Rienner, 1997), 99.
64. Donald L. Barnett and Karari Njama, *Mau Mau from Within* (Modern Reader, 1966), 131–32.
65. Clough, *Mau Mau Memoirs*, 98–99.

Chapter Eight

Frantz Fanon, Les damnés de la terre (Éditions La Découverte et Syros, 2002), 302. My translation.
Augustine, *Against the Epistle of Manichaeus*, trans. Albert H. Newman, in Philip Schaff, ed., *St. Augustin: The Writings Against the Manichaeans and Against the Donatists. Nicene and Post-Nicene Fathers*, vol. 4 (Edinburgh, 1887), Chap. 12, p. 135.

1. *Black Skin, White Masks*, trans. Charles Lam Markmann (London: Pluto, 1986), 141, 31. Hereafter, "Fanon, *Skin*" with page numbers in the text. I will use lower-case "manichean" when I talk about Fanon's use of the concept, upper-case "Manichean" when I refer to the late antique religion. In the French originals, Fanon typically writes it in lower case, although English translations are inconsistent.
2. See David Macey, *Frantz Fanon: A Biography*, 2nd ed. (London: Verso, 2012), 258.
3. In a single paragraph, JanMohamed quotes two passages from Fanon's *The Wretched of the Earth* in *Manichean Aesthetics: The Politics of Literature in Colonial Africa* (University of Massachusetts Press, 1983), 3–4.
4. Malvern van Wyk Smith, *The First Ethiopians: The Image of Africa and Africans in the Early Mediterranean World* (Wits University Press, 2001), 19–20.
5. Paul Gilroy, *Against Race: Imagining Political Culture beyond the Color Line* (Harvard University Press, 2000), 253, 248. Gilroy's main criticism of Fanon is that his notions of race are outdated, and that contemporary "race-thinking" contaminates the possibilities of liberal democracy: "Today, in Europe, at least, there is less justification for this stark dualistic diagnosis" (249). A more recent example of the attribution of stark dualism to Fanon is David Jefferess, *Postcolonial Resistance: Culture, Liberation, and Transformation* (University of Toronto Press, 2008). Although Jefferess's discussion is more nuanced elsewhere, he closes the book by characterizing "Manichean or binary thought" (implicitly, Fanon's own) as calling for a "simply reversed ... structure of material relations of power and identities" (185).
6. *The Wretched of the Earth*, trans. Richard Philcox (New York: Grove, 2004), 237; translation modified. Hereafter, "Fanon, *Wretched*" with page numbers in the text. Unless otherwise noted, all translated text from *Wretched* will be quoted from the Philcox translation.

7. Fanon's condemnation applies not just to "the petrification of... colonial meanings and institutions" but also to the "*anticolonial* practico-inert"; decolonization is every bit as much subject to petrification unless it takes a critical relation to history. The postindependence leader, in Fanon's words, "*brings the people to a halt and persists in either expelling them from history or preventing them from taking root in it.*" See Douglas Ficek, "Reflections on Fanon and Petrification," in *Living Fanon: Global Perspectives.*, ed. Nigel C. Gibson (Palgrave, 2011), 83 (quoting Fanon, *Wretched*, 136; emphasis in original).
8. *Peau noire, masques blancs* (Editions du Seuil, 1952), 183. Hereafter, "*Peau*" with page numbers in the text.
9. Kojève, *Introduction à la lecture de Hegel* (Gallimard, 1979), 34 (my translation).
10. For the first, see Homi Bhabha, "Forward: Framing Fanon," in Frantz Fanon, *The Wretched of the Earth* (Princeton University Press, 2004), viii; for the second, see the interview with Marie-Jeanne Manuellan, "Dans l'ombre de Fanon," *Le Monde*, September 12, 2017.
11. Hannah Arendt, *On Violence* (Harcourt, 1960), 14n19. Hereafter, "Arendt" with page numbers in the text. Fred Moten in *The Universal Machine* (Duke University Press, 2018) suggests that "to reread *Les damnés de la terre* against the grain of Arendt's nonreading of it is to consider that we don't and can't either know or fight the murderous brutality of the settler's weakness with our own; rather, we think and struggle from and with our own potency" (184). In glossing "potency" here, Moten notes that it is not, "contra Arendt, a political thing; that her relegation of the social in favor of a regulated and specifically political publicness is, in fact, inseparable from her commitment to an already given structure of power in which both acknowledged and unacknowledged constituents subsist in a shadow they cast but cannot control" (265–66n50).
12. In Alice Cherki's preface to Fanon's *Les damnés de la terre*, she argues that Sartre was responsible for shaping the interpretation of Fanon as an advocate of violence, noting that "*Sartre justifie la violence alors que Fanon l'analyse*" (11).
13. See, for example, Augustine, *Contra epistulam Manichaei quam uocant fundamenti*, cap. 14 and 15.
14. See Johaness van Oort, *Mani and Augustine: Collected Essays on Mani, Manichaeism, and Augustine* (Brill, 2020); and Jason BeDuhn, *Augustine's Manichaean Dilemma, Volume 1: Conversion and Apostasy, 373–388 C.E.* (University of Pennsylvania Press, 2009), and *Augustine's Manichaean Dilemma, Volume 2: Making a "Catholic" Self, 388–41 C.E.* (University of Pennsylvania Press, 2009) (a third volume is projected).
15. S. Ney, in "Teleology and Secular Time in Armah and Ngũgĩ: Augustine, Manichaenism, and the African Novel," *Research in African Literatures* 48, no. 2 (Summer 2017), finds analogies between the anti-Manichean strain of Augustine's *City of God* and the manicheism described by (largely) JanMohamed.
16. Only two major readings of Fanon that I know of fully express this aspect of Fanon's work. Ato Sekyi-Otu's scintillating and profound excavation of the analogy of drama in Fanon's work in *Fanon's Dialectic of Experience* (Harvard University Press, 1997) insists on the contingent, propaedeutic nature of almost every statement in his work, which can only be grasped as an unfolding totality—or as unfolding toward an already ruined totality (80). What Sekyi-Otu describes as the spatialization of

Notes to Chapter Eight   387

dialectic in Fanon is another aspect of the "stagnation" of dialectic in Europe generally (*Wretched*, 237): "The critique of domination becomes an analysis of the spatial structuring of positions." I choose to believe that Fanon's dialectic works more as a chordal, interposed *negation* of dialectic. It insists, as I will argue later, both on the irresistible, diremptive, scopic regime of dialectic, *and* on the force—the violence—of negation, and the immanent destruction of a dialectical *skopos*. The other brilliant and essential reading is by Fred Moten, who is also attuned to the multimodal nature of Fanon's dialectic, but I would argue is a doubly *symptomatic* reading: first, it is founded on Fanon's attention to the physical and psychic symptoms of the oppressed; and second, it leaves us with a symptomatic Fanon, one who unwittingly comes up against aporia rather than one who, as I argue here, dwells cannily and forcefully in the negative.

17. Sidi Mohammed Barkat, *Le corps d'exception: Les artifices du pouvoir colonial et la destruction de la vie* (Editions Amsterdam, 2005), 40.
18. Frantz Fanon, *The Wretched of the Earth*, trans. Constance Farrington (Grove, 1963), 144. Hereafter, "Farrington" with page numbers in the text. For Philcox's phrasing see p. 93.
19. Fernand Cabrol and Henri Leclercq, *Dictionnaire d'archéologie chrétienne et de liturgie*, s.v., Lambèse, Vol. 8, 1073: *Ceux qui les indigènes nomment les roumis sont à leurs yeux et doivent être en réalité les descendants et les héritiers de ceux qui ont si longtemps, si glorieusement et si utilement gouverné le pays*. Hereafter, "Cabrol and Leclercq" with page numbers in the text. I was pointed to this passage by Walter Kaegi, *Muslim Expansion and Byzantine Collapse in North Africa* (Cambridge University Press, 2010), 22.
20. *Y ont restauré l'oeuvre de civilisation, et ont montré dans leur intelligence et leur respect pour les anciens monuments leurs titres de propriété, leurs droits à les ramener à la lumière et à ne pas souffrir qu'on les détruise*.
21. Examples quoted in Michael Greenhalgh, *The Military and Colonial Destruction of the Roman Landscape of North Africa, 1830–1900* (Brill, 2014), 33. The Kabyle are today the largest Berber/Amazigh group in Algeria.
22. Dide and Guiraud, *Psychiatrie du médecin praticien, refondue en Psychiatrie clinique* (Le François, 1956), 164.
23. Augustine, *Against the Epistle of Manichaeus Called Fundamental*, trans. Dods, cap. 15, 113; Augustine, *Contra epistulam Manichaei quam uocant fundamenti*, ed. Zycha, cap. 15, 212.
24. Johannes van Oort, *Jerusalem and Babylon: A Study into Augustine's "City of God" and the Sources of His Doctrine of the Two Cities* (Brill, 2015), 118–23.
25. Jean Hyppolite, *Genesis and Structure in Hegel's "Phenomenology of Spirit,"* trans. Samuel Cherniak and John Heckman (Northwestern University Press, 1974), 173. Hereafter, "Hyppolite" with page numbers in the text.
26. For more on Fanon's engagement with Kojève's and Sartre's versions of Hegel, see Sekyi-Otu, *Fanon's Dialectic of Experience*, 32, 73 (Kojève); 61–70 (Sartre).
27. See Macey, *Frantz Fanon*, 175–76, who suggests that, while the phrase originates in *L'Internationale*, that reference is mediated through Roumain's poem. See also Miguel Mellino, "The *Langue* of the Damned: Fanon and the Remnants of Europe," *South Atlantic Quarterly* 112, no. 1 (Winter 2013).
28. Medievalization is the threat that the colonist also makes against independence

movements: "If you want independence, take it and return to the Dark Ages (*retournez au Moyen Âge*)" (*Damnés* 94; *Wretched*, 53). And what the colonist uses to justify the use of corporal punishment: "We need to use the lash if we want to take this country out of the Dark Ages (*sortir ce pays du Moyen Âge*)" (*Damnés* 116; *Wretched* 72). In fact, references to *Le Moyen Âge* are always only in the voice of the colonist. A slight exception appears in the very last sentence of the chapter on "The Grandeur and Weakness of Spontaneity," but even here it is used as an adjective and sardonically placed in quotation marks: "All that is left is a slight readaptation, a few reforms at the top, a flag, and down at the bottom a shapeless, 'medieval' mass, which continues in its perpetual movement" (*Un minimum de réadaptation, quelques réformes au sommet, un drapeau et, tout en bas, la masse indivise, toujours 'moyenâgeuse,' qui continue son mouvement perpétuel*) (*Damnés* 141; *Wretched*, 96; translation modified).

29. For a crucial reading of Fanon's Aristotelian logic here, see Sekyi Otu (*Fanon's Dialectic of Experience*, 55–56). Sekyi Otu argues that Fanon "avers that it is in the formal logic of Aristotle's *Categories*, not in the dialectical logic of Hegel's *Phenomenology*, that we will find the open secret of the colonial relation" (72).

30. Aristotle, *Categories*, ed. Jonathan Barnes, trans. J. L. Ackrill (Princeton University Press, 1991); *Categories*, trans. J. Tricot (J. Vrin, 2004), §11, 24.

31. See the numerous examples in *Medieval Commentaries on Aristotle's Categories*, ed. Lloyd A. Newton (Brill, 2008).

32. Thomas Aquinas, *Quodlibet* II, §2.1, 80.

33. Nicholas Oresme, *Questiones super Physicam*, Bk. II, §5, 11, 193–94, 203, quoted in Robert Pasnau, "Scholastic Qualities, Primary and Secondary," in *Primary and Secondary Qualities: The Historical and Ongoing Debate*, ed. Lawrence Nolan (Oxford University Press, 2011), 48.

34. Dante, *De Monarchia*, Bk. I, §11, 53.

35. For an extended examination of the metaphorical applications of blackness and whiteness, see Whitaker, *Black Metaphors*, 79–104.

36. Andrew Cole, *The Birth of Theory* (University of Chicago Press, 2014).

37. He did have the popular 1940 biography of Augustine by Gustave Bardy. See "Frantz Fanon's Library," in Frantz Fanon, *Alienation and Freedom*, ed. Jean Khalfa, et al., trans. Steven Corcoran (Bloomsbury, 2020), 726.

38. "*Historien, je me refuse à toute classification manichéenne*," quoted in André Mandouze, *Mémoires d'outre-siècle* (V. Hamy, 1998), 243.

39. See Marrou, "*France, ma patrie. . . .*" The latter phrase is Augustine's, used throughout *Contra epistolam Manichaei quam vocant fundamenti* (§§ 18, 20, 24, 25, 32).

40. Mandouze, *Mémoires*, 1:226, 1:242.

41. "*Encore une fois, si la guerre est là, Augustin l'est aussi*" (*Mémoires*, 1:243).

42. See Macey, *Frantz Fanon*, 6.

43. Decret, *L'Afrique manichéenne* (Etudes Agustiniennes, 1978): *La grande originalité des Africains dans l'Eglise de mani est d'avoir ecarté, autant que possible, tout particularisme qui les ferait se singulariser parmi les populations de leur pays. . . . Il est hors de doute aussi que cette 'indigénisation' du manichéisme africain explique sa longue survie* (1:210).

44. Quoted in David Cummings, "Civilising the Settler: Representations of French Settler Colonialism in Algeria," *Settler Colonial Studies* 8, no. 2 (2018): 177, 178, 181.

45. Fiona Barclay, Charlotte Ann Chopin, and Martin Evans, "Introduction: Settler Colonialism and French Algeria," *Settler Colonial Studies* 8 (2018) [115–40]: 119.
46. Krim Belkacem, "Frantz Fanon, notre frère," *El Moudjahid* 88 (December 21, 1961) [646–51]: 648; the phrase was repeated on several other occasions, e.g., in Bertène Juminer, "Hommages à Frantz Fanon," *Présence Africaine* 40 (1962) [118–41]: 129.
47. Theodor Adorno and Max Horkheimer, *Dialectic of Enlightenment: Philosophical Fragments*, trans. Edmund Jephcott (Stanford University Press, 2002), 21.
48. G. W. F. Hegel, *Science of Logic*, trans. A. W. Miller (Routledge, 2002), 119. Miller's 1969 translation is something of a gloss, though accurate. George di Giovanni's more recent translation from 2010 gives "The something *preserves* itself in its non-being" (92).
49. Two recent accounts of the "absolute" version of afropessimism are Frank B. Wilderson III, *Afropessimism* (Liveright, 2021) and Achille Mbembe, *Necropolitics* (Duke University Press, 2019). Also see Calvin L. Warren's recent intervention *Ontological Terror: Blackness, Nihilism, and Emancipation* (Duke University Press, 2018), which, in part, challenges the metaphysical investments of afropessimism.
50. G. W. F. Hegel, *Phenomenology of Spirit*, trans. A. V. Miller (Oxford University Press, 1977): Preface, 33; 19.

Chapter Nine

Frantz Fanon, *The Wretched of the Earth*, trans. Constance Farrington (Grove, 1963), 96–97.
Sir Rider Haggard, Preface to John Wilmot, *Monomotapa (Rhodesia): Its Monuments, and Its History from the Most Ancient Times to the Present Century* (London, 1896), xiii.
1. *The Wizard*, in *Arrowsmith's Christmas Annual* (Bristol, 1896), n.p.
2. H. Rider Haggard, *Elissa: The Doom of Zimbabwe* (Longmans, Green, and Co., 1900), 33. Hereafter, "Haggard, *Elissa*" with page numbers in the text.
3. Karen Haegemans, "Elissa, the First Queen of Carthage, Through Timaeus' Eyes," *Ancient Society* 30 (2000) [277–91]: 279.
4. "Zimbabwe the Mysterious: Southern Rhodesia," Southern Rhodesia Publicity Bureau (1928).
5. Quoted in John Hays Hammond's preface to Frederick Burnham, *Scouting on Two Continents* (Doubleday, 1926), xi.
6. Andrew Offenburger, *Frontiers in the Gilded Age: Adventure, Capitalism, and Dispossession from Southern Africa to the U.S.-Mexican Borderlands, 1880–1917* (Yale University Press, 2019), 225n57.
7. See Steve Kemper, *A Splendid Savage: The Restless Life of Frederick Russell Burnham* (W. W. Norton and Co., 2017), esp. chap. 9.
8. See *Empire and Legal Thought: Ideas and Institutions from Antiquity to Modernity*, ed. Edward Cavanagh (Brill, 2020), 529.
9. Cavanagh, *Empire and Legal Thought*, 534.
10. John Ogilby, *Africa: being an accurate description of the regions of Ægypt, Barbary, Lybia, and Billedulgerid* ... (London, 1670), 598. Hereafter, "Ogilby" with page numbers in the text.
11. See Brian Weiser, *Charles II and the Politics of Access* (Boydell and Brewer, 2004).
12. John Wilmot, *Monomotapa (Rhodesia): Its Monuments, and Its History from the*

Most Ancient Times to the Present Century (London, 1896), 142–43. Hereafter, "Wilmot" with page numbers in the text.

13. J. Theodore Bent, *The Ruined Cities of Mashonaland; Being a Record of Excavation and Exploration in 1891* (Longmans, Green, and Co., 1895), 122.
14. Karl Mauch, *The Journals of Carl Mauch; His Travels in the Transvaal and Rhodesia, 1869–1872*, trans. E. Bernhard (National Archives of Rhodesia, 1969), 139.
15. J. Theodore Bent, "The Ruins of Mashonaland, and Explorations in the Country," *Proceedings of the Royal Geographical Society and Monthly Record of Geography* 14, no. 5 (1892) [273–98]: 288.
16. David Christiaan de Waal, *With Rhodes in Mashonaland* (Cape Town, 1896), 271, 276.
17. Roger Luckhurst writes that "for Rhodes, the ruins of Great Zimbabwe were a kind of legitimation of imperial expansion: it had happened before that a superior northern race had been in the region; now it was happening again." See Luckhurst's introduction to Rider Haggard, *King Solomon's Mines* (Oxford University Press, 2016).
18. Quoted in Henrika Kuklick, "Contested Monuments: The Politics of Archaeology in Southern Africa," in *Colonial Situations: Essays on the Contextualization of Ethnographic Knowledge*, ed. George W. Stocking Jr. (University of Wisconsin Press, 1991), 158.
19. Thomas Baines, *The Gold Regions of South Eastern Africa* (London, 1877), facing p. vi.
20. Mauch, *The Journals of Carl Mauch*, 215.
21. R. N. Hall, *The Ancient Ruins of Rhodesia (Monomotapae Imperium)* (Methuen and Co., 1904).
22. James Thorold Rogers, "Philological and Historical Criticism: Its Place in Modern Life," *Princeton Review* 56 (1880) [205–224]: 215.
23. Theodore Alois Buckley, *The Great Cities of the Middle Ages* (London, 1853), 320. The quotation is actually from the seventeenth-century antiquarian Wood's *The History and Antiquities of the Colleges and Halls in the University of Oxford*, ed. John Gutch (Oxford, 1791), 1:371.
24. Quoted in Éric Michaud, *The Barbarian Invasions: A Genealogy of the History of Art* (MIT Press, 2019), 155.
25. Michaud, *The Barbarian Invasions*, 3.
26. Charles Herbert Moore, *Development and Character of Gothic Architecture* (New York, 1899), 22.
27. For a fuller discussion, see Asko Nivala, *The Romantic Idea of the Golden Age in Friedrich Schlegel's Philosophy of History* (Routledge, 2017), 102–6.
28. G. W. F. Hegel, *Natural Law: The Scientific Ways of Treating Natural Law, Its Place in Moral Philosophy, and Its Relation to the Positive Sciences of Law*, trans. T. M. Knox (University of Pennsylvania Press, 1975), 102.
29. *Die Neger sind ganz unbändig, und zu keiner Kultur zu bewegen; es ist das Kultur entbehrende, goldgefüllte Kinderland.* See G. W. F. Hegel, *Die Philosophie der Geschichte: Vorlesungsmitschrift Heimann (Winter 1830/1831)*, ed. Klaus Vieweg (Fink, 2005), 67. My translation.
30. "Discovery" here, of course, is a fundamentally Eurocentric invention, and it's mud-

died in this case from the start. The first possible European mention of Zimbabwe dates from the Portuguese traveler António Fernandes, ca. 1513 to 1515.
31. See David Wardle, "Cecil Rhodes as a Reader of the Classics: The Groote Schuur Collection," in *South Africa, Greece, Rome: Classical Confrontations*, ed. Grant Parker (Cambridge University Press, 2017), 341.
32. John Hilton, "Cecil John Rhodes, the Classics and Imperialism," in Parker, *South Africa, Greece, Rome*, 98.
33. Edward Gibbon, *The History of the Decline and Fall of the Roman Empire* (London, 1777), Bk. I, chap. 3, 96.
34. Robert I. Rotberg, *The Founder: Cecil Rhodes and the Pursuit of Power* (Oxford University Press, 1990), 387.
35. Joost Fontein, *The Silence of Great Zimbabwe: Contested Landscapes and the Power of Heritage* (Left Coast Press, 2006), esp. 17n3.
36. The exchange is in Mountstuart E. Grant Duff's famous diary: "'Why does not Mr. Theodore Bent say that the Zimbabwe ruins are Phoenician?' [asked Cecil Rhodes]. Lord Acton answered, 'Because he is not quite sure they are.' 'Ah,' replied the proconsul, 'that is not the way that Empires are founded.'" Bent's book, published five years later, would argue for the Phoenician theory—but he had off-the-record doubts about it. See Mountstuart E. Grant Duff, *Notes from a Diary, 1896 to January 23, 1901* (John Murray, 1905), 1:185.
37. Quoted in Rotberg, *The Founder*, 427.
38. Bent, *The Ruined Cities of Mashonaland*, 64.
39. "'The Arab accounts are few, full of evident errors, and more occupied sometimes with efforts of imagination than with a sober record of facts' he said, quite unironically" (111).
40. Quoted in D. N. Beach, "Ndebele Raiders and Shona Power," *Journal of African History* 15, no. 4 (1974) [633–51]: 633n2. See also T. O. Ranger, "The Rewriting of African History During the Scramble: The Matabele Dominance in Mashonaland," *African Social Research* 4 (1967).
41. Carnegie, *Among the Matabele* (London, 1894), 18, quoted in David Chanaiwa, "The Army and Politics in Pre-Industrial Africa: The Ndebele Nation, 1822–1893," *African Studies Review* 19, no. 2 (September 1976) [49–67]: 50.
42. Another Catholic, the French philosopher of history Michel de Certeau, identifies the Reformation as the moment at which the writing of history began most crucially to exert its power: "Reason must be able to establish or restore a world, and ... it is no longer a matter of deciphering the secrets of an order or a hidden Author, but of producing an order so that it can be written on the body of an uncivilized or depraved society. Writing acquires the right to reclaim, subdue or educate history." See *The Practice of Everyday Life* (University of California Press, 1984), 144.
43. Father Silveira was credited with calming a storm at sea and engaging the King of Monomotapa to experience a vision of the Virgin for five successive nights; his body was venerated by wild animals. Wilmot includes what Rider Haggard calls some "interesting legends" (xxi) of Silveira's martyrdom in an appendix (167–76).
44. R. N. Hall, *Pre-Historic Rhodesia* (Fisher Unwin, 1909), 13.
45. Andrew Lang, *The Red True Story Book* (London, 1895), vii.
46. Lang, *The Red True Story Book*, 18.

47. Richard Hall, *Great Zimbabwe: Mashonaland, Rhodesia* (Methuen, 1905), xxvi–xxix. But in the foreword, A. H. Keane stubbornly insisted that the site was developed by Phoenicians and "Jews," and provided gold to King Solomon (xxxii).
48. David Randall-MacIver, *Mediaeval Rhodesia* (Macmillan and Co., 1906), viii. Hereafter, "Randall-MacIver" with page numbers in the text.
49. These examples are taken from Sylvie Kandé's important "African Medievalisms: Caste as a Subtext in Ahmadou Kourouma's *Suns of Independence* and *Monnew*," in *Medievalisms in the Postcolonial World: The Idea of the "Middle Ages" Outside Europe*, ed. Kathleen Davis and Nadia Altschul (Johns Hopkins University Press, 2009), 301–24. See also Simon Gikandi's remarks in the same volume: "Africa and the Signs of Medievalism," 360–82.
50. Kandé, "African Medievalisms," 312.
51. Yambo Ouologuem, *Bound to Violence*, trans. Ralph Manheim (Heinemann, 1971), 94, 96; emphasis in original.
52. William Stiebing, *Uncovering the Past: A History of Archaeology* (Oxford University Press, 1994), 222.
53. Innocent Pikirayi, "Peter Garlake (1934–2011), *Great Zimbabwe* and the Politics of the Past in Zimbabwe," *Azania: Archaeological Research in Africa* 47, no. 2 (2012): 223–25.
54. Peter S. Garlake, *Great Zimbabwe* (Thames and Hudson, 1973), 204; Peter S. Garlake, *Great Zimbabwe: Described and Explained* (Zimbabwe Publishing House, 1982), 64.
55. A. J. Bruwer, *Zimbabwe: Rhodesia's Ancient Greatness* (Hugh Keartland, 1965).
56. Merrick Posnansky, review of *Zimbabwe: Rhodesia's Ancient Greatness*, *Journal of Asian and African Studies* 8, no. 1 (1973): 107–9.
57. Wilbur Smith, *The Sunbird* (Heinemann, 1972), 60. Hereafter, "Smith, *Sunbird*" with page numbers in the text.
58. Wilbur Smith, *On Leopard Rock: A Life of Adventures* (Zaffre, 2019), 161–62. Hereafter, "Smith, *Leopard*" with page numbers in the text.
59. Credo Mutwa, *Indaba, My Children: African Folktales* (1999), Kindle ed. 298. Smith slightly misquotes Mutwa's "*five* great emperors." Cf. Vusa'mazulu Credo Mutwa, *My People, My Africa* (John Day, 1969), 115; hereafter, "Credo Mutwa" with page numbers in the text.
60. Gerald Chikozho Mazarire, "Changing Landscape and Oral Memory in South-Central Zimbabwe: Towards a Historical Geography of Chishanga, c. 1850–1990," *Journal of Southern African Studies* 29, no. 3 (2003) [701–715]: 704.

Coda

Monica Wilson, "Divine Kings and the 'Breath of Men': The 1959 Frazer Lecture," *HAU: Journal of Ethnographic Theory* 7, no. 2 (2017): 563–75.
Chinua Achebe, *Anthills of the Savannah* (New York: Anchor Books, 1987), 68.
1. "'This Man Lives Forever': Zimbabwe's Mugabe is Buried," *Associated Press*, September 28, 2019, https://apnews.com/article/fb35fda9b877426e9a24705ea75eacb2.
2. Ian Ndlovu, *Divine Kingdom Baptist Ministries*, February 24, 2019. Discussed on the Gospel Zigo channel on Facebook.
3. Blessing Nyahuma, "Robert Mugabe's Role As a Man-god in Zimbabwe and the

Notes to Coda   393

Final Judgement," in *Politics and Religion in Zimbabwe: The Deification of Robert G. Mugabe*, ed. Ezra Chitando (Routledge, 2020) [173–87], 175. Hereafter, "Nyahuma" with page numbers in the text).

4. "Messiah": Reported on Spectre Media, Facebook (September 16, 2021), quoting Namajana Rose Nsereko, NRM Deputy Secretary General; also "like Christ": on the Daily Monitor, Facebook (March 26, 2018), quoting Jacob Oulanyah, Deputy Speaker of Parliament.

5. Ernst-Wolfgang Böckenförde, Mirjam Künkler, and Tine Stein, "The Rise of the State as a Process of Secularization [1967]," in *Religion, Law, and Democracy: Selected Writings*, ed. Mirjam Künkler and Tine Stein (Oxford University Press, 2020), quoting Hermann Lübbe, *Säkularisierung: Geschichte eines ideenpolitischen Begriffs* (Verlag Karl Alber, 1965), 23.

6. Carl Schmitt, *Political Theology: Four Chapters on the Concept of Sovereignty*, trans. George Schwab (MIT Press, 1988), 36.

7. Daniel D. Nsereko, "Religion, the State, and the Law in Africa," *Journal of Church and State* 28, no. 2 (1986) [269–87]: 271.

8. Quoted in H. Kwasi Prempeh, "Presidential Power in Comparative Perspective: The Puzzling Persistence of Imperial Presidency in Post-Authoritarian Africa," *Hastings Constitutional Law Quarterly* 35, no. 4 (2008), 761.

9. As a company nation originally, Southern Rhodesia was one of the few British colonies to exercise direct rule. But by the 1950s, the administration began to introduce structures of indirect rule, first with the creation of a Chiefs' Assembly in 1951, and then with recognition of customary law within the legal system in the African Law and Tribal Courts Act of 1969. See George Hamandishe Karekwaivanane, *The Struggle over State Power in Zimbabwe: Law and Politics since 1950* (Cambridge University Press, 2017), 47–90. As Karekwaivanane argues, the commission relied on the work of Max Gluckman because it attributed Weberian "rationality" to "tribal" systems, which were nevertheless othered precisely because "they were not 'modern'" (60).

10. Karekwaivanane, *The Struggle over State Power*, 57–58. One of the main objections that chiefs raised about their constitutional role in the early 1960s was that elections would undermine their customary right of appointment. See Chapter 15.282.4, *Constitution of Zimbabwe Amendment (No. 20)*, https://www.veritaszim.net/sites/veritas_d/files/Constitution%20of%20Zimbabwe%20Amendment%20%28No.%2020%29.pdf.

11. Mahmood Mamdani, *Define and Rule: Native as Political Identity* (Harvard, 2012).

12. Quoted in Prempeh, "Presidential Power in Comparative Perspective," 766.

13. Quoted in Guy I. Seidman, "The Origins of Accountability: Everything I Know about the Sovereign's Immunity, I Learned from King Henry III," *Saint Louis University Law Journal* 49, no. 2 (2005): 435.

14. On this development in African constitutions, see C. M. Fombad and E. S. Nwauche, "Africa's Imperial Presidents: Immunity, Impunity and Accountability," *African Journal of Legal Studies* 5 (2012): 91–118. On the relation between impunity and the mystical foundation of the law, see Zahid Chaudhury, "Impunity," in *Political Concepts: A Critical Lexicon*, https://www.politicalconcepts.org/impunity-zahid-r-chaudhary.

15. See Joram Tarusarira and Bernard Pindukai Humbe, "The Ambivalence of African

Independent/Initiated Churches in Colonial and Postcolonial Politics," in *Religion in Rebellions, Revolutions, and Social Movement*, ed. Warren S. Goldstein and Jean-Pierre Reed (Routledge, 2022), 158–72.

16. Quoted in *Human Rights Watch*, "This Alien Legacy: The Origins of 'Sodomy' Laws in British Colonialism," December 17, 2008, https://www.hrw.org/report/2008/12/17/alien-legacy/origins-sodomy-laws-british-colonialism.
17. David Maxwell, "'Catch the Cockerel before Dawn': Pentecostalism and Politics in Post-Colonial Zimbabwe," *Africa: Journal of the International African Institute* 70 (2000) [249–77]: 259.
18. On the interrelations of Weber and Schmitt's thought, see Pedro T. Magalhães, "A Contingent Affinity: Max Weber, Carl Schmitt, and the Challenge of Modern Politics," *Journal of the History of Ideas* 77, no. 2 (2016): 283–304.
19. Clifford Geertz, "Centers, Kings, and Charisma: Symbolics of Power," in *Local Knowledge: Further Essays in Interpretive Anthropology* (Basic Books, 1983), 123. Hereafter, "Geertz "with page numbers in the text.
20. The history of the essay, and an invaluable summary of its argument, is in Alfons Puirgarnau, "Ernst Kantorowicz's *Synthronos*: New Perspectives on Medieval Charisma," *Religions* 14, no. 7 (2023): https://doi.org/10.3390/rel14070914.
21. Geertz, "Centers, Kings, and Charisma," 123n5.
22. Puirgarnau, "Ernst Kantorowicz's *Synthronos*," np.
23. Quoted in Human Rights Watch, "This Alien Legacy."
24. "U.S. Evangelical Leaders Blamed for Uganda Anti-Gay Sentiment," *NPR*, December 18, 2009, https://www.npr.org/templates/story/story.php?storyId=121605529.
25. *Ghana Web*, April 7, 2023, https://www.ghanaweb.com/GhanaHomePage/africa/I-commend-parliament-for-anti-homosexuality-bill-Ugandan-First-Lady-1745213.
26. *Uganda Christian News*, February 17, 2023, https://www.ugchristiannews.com/homosexuality-it-is-a-deviation-from-bible-teachings-says-museveni.
27. See John Blevins, "When Sodomy Leads to Martyrdom: Sex, Religion, and Politics in Historical and Contemporary Contexts in Uganda and East Africa," *Theology and Sexuality* 17 (2011): 51–74.
28. See Robert Aldrich, *Colonialism and Homosexuality* (Routledge, 2003), 31.
29. See Carol Summers, "Intimate Colonialism: The Imperial Production of Reproduction in Uganda, 1907–1925," *Signs* 16, no. 4 (1991): 787–807.
30. Marc Epprecht, *Hungochani: The History of Dissident Sexuality in Southern Africa* (McGill-Queen's University Press, 2004), 39.

Index

Aaron, 40, 42, 188
Abalessa, 164
'Abdari, Al-, 135
abjad, 164
Abraham, 15, 44, 193
Abraham, Nicolas, 109
Abulafia, David, 208
Achaemenid empire, 47
Achard, Paul, 296
Achebe, Chinua, 335
Actium, battle of, 107, 108
Adair, Gilbert, 162
Adorno, Theodor, 298
Aeneas, 85–88, 89, 90, 103, 104, 105, 118, 140, 161, 162, 166. *See also* Virgil
Aeneid. *See* Virgil
Africa: as belated, 5, 63–64, 237, 245–46, 325, 334; history of, 1–4, 6–9, 13, 50, 129, 164–65, 187, 303; landing in, 30, 48–49, 72–79; leaving, 6, 85, 94, 118, 131–32, 144–45; maps of, 4, 37–39; and the Middle Ages, 2, 10, 13, 34, 42, 46, 89, 124, 200, 202, 213–15, 221–23; "proper," 4, 7, 25, 64–65; provinces of, 7, 92, 111, 150, 160–63, 182, 191, 192, 210; sub-Saharan, 5–6, 235, 336; *tumor* of, 148, 150–52; as whole continent, 4–5, 7, 8–10, 16, 23–26, 57, 103. *See also* Ifriqia
Africa, Horn of, 34
Africa and Byzantium (exhibition), 3
Africa Cup, 23
African Independent Church, 337
African Initiated (or Indigenous, or Independent) Churches, 340–41, 343
Africans: as belated, 63, 63, 213, 237, 245–46; as degenerate, 107, 151–52, 220, 314, 315, 318, 370n17; development of, 237, 245–46, 252, 307; as feudal, 214–17, 225–31, 308, 380–81; and lack of history, 1, 2, 64, 228, 317, 325–26, 329; as medieval, 10, 136, 220–29, 233–48, 251–54, 307; othering of, 10, 11–12, 48, 85, 99, 102, 127, 155; "primitiveness" of, 10, 63–65, 173, 228, 237, 245, 250–51, 259–61, 278, 297, 325
Africitas, 150–52
Afrocentrism, 7–9, 24, 57. *See also* Pan-Africanism
Afropessimism, 4, 389n49
Agamben, Giorgio, 77
Agareni, 14
Agut, Damien, 57
Akbari, Suzanne, 51
Alaafin Majotu, 172
Alain of Lille, 124, 152
al-Azhar Mosque, 23
Alexander, Romance of, 46–52, 162
Alexander the Great, 25–29, 33, 46–52, 70, 72–73, 113; tomb of, 51–52; and visit to Ammon's shrine, 27–29
Alexanderroman. *See* Alexander, Romance of
Alexander's letter to Aristotle, 46

Alexandria, 26–27, 34–35, 38, 49, 51, 78, 133, 156–57, 181; and allegory, 183–90; and Auerbach, 181–86, 188, 191; and style, 315
Alfonso XI, 132
Algeria, 11, 14, 164, 166, 170–77, 178, 210, 272, 276–79, 281, 284–85, 291, 293–96
allegory, 26, 43, 78, 84, 86, 102, 131, 157, 158, 182–200
alphabets, 153, 162–65, 177, 372n54
Altars of Philaeni. *See* Philaeni, Altars of
amaNdebele, 18–19, 306–7, 317, 321–22, 323
Amazigh, 163, 164–65, 170, 171. *See also* Berber
Ammon, 27–30, 32–33, 36, 47, 48, 49, 52, 65, 67, 69, 72, 154, 164; Alexander's visit to, 27–29; as Jupiter-Ammon, 81–84, 88; oracle of, 70. *See also* Theuth
Amun. *See* Ammon
Anchises, 140
Angles, 100
ankh, 56
Antaeus, 80, 84, 158
anthropology, 204, 218, 219, 223–31, 246–47, 334, 342. *See also* ethnography
anti-homosexuality, 343–45
anti-Semitism, 220, 276
apartheid, 112, 333–34
Apollo, 31–32, 67, 159–60
Appiah, Kwame Anthony, 89
Appolonius of Rhodes, 71
Apuleius, 115, 149, 150, 153, 161, 181
Arabic, 14, 34, 46, 157, 165, 168, 169, 171–72, 174–75, 177, 279
Arabs, 34, 35, 59, 277, 279–80, 320–21
Arendt, Hannah, 275–76, 386n11
Argo, 31, 73, 76, 78
Argonautica (Apollonius of Rhodes), 73–79
Argonauts, 30–33, 73–79
Argus, 78
Arianism, 16, 101
Aristotle, Alexander's letter to, 46
Aristotle, *Categories*, 288–90, 388n29

Arius, 15, 31, 101
Arlington National Cemetery, 81
Arnobius Afer, 155
Arthurian literature, 94, 96–97, 98–99, 222
Asia, 29, 31, 33, 34, 35, 39, 40
Atban, 165
Athena, 30, 31, 74
Athens, 31, 157, 355n23
Atlantis, 79, 304, 328
atlas, xii, 34–35, 308
Atlas: mountains, xii, 35, 68, 88, 128, 129; myth of, xii, 68, 129
Auerbach, Erich, 182–200, 206, 375n32; and Alexandria, 183–90; and Carthage, 191–200; *figura*, 182–84, 190; *Literary Language and Its Public*, 193, 198; *Mimesis*, 182–83, 186, 190, 194–200
Augustine: and *Aeneid*, 131; as African, 1, 115, 131–32; and Carthage, 16, 100, 103, 109, 115–22, 131; *City of God*, 115–17, 119–21, 193, 148–49, 282; *Confessions*, 117–19, 131, 148–49, 161, 166, 192; *De doctrina Christiana*, 192–93; and Donatism, 191; on Ethiopia and Egypt, 356n42; and Manicheism, 271–73, 276, 283, 284–85, 293–95, 297–99; in Petrarch's *Secretum*, 128, 130–32; on Psalm 114, 193–94; and Punic, 166–67; and Song of Songs, 192–93
Augustine of Canterbury, 96
Augustus, Caesar, 7, 49, 107
Aulus Gellius, 161
Aurelius, Marcus, 98, 161, 318

Baal Ammon, 166
Baines, Thomas, 311, 312
Balliol College, 248–50, 382n28; colonial administrators from, 248
Bangor, abbot of, 96
Bantu, 112, 223, 245, 325, 329, 331, 332, 333
barbarians, 107, 156, 168, 314–15, 320–21, 323, 333
Barca, 88
Barkat, Sidi Mohammed, 277

Barotse, 224, 228–31. *See also* Zambia
Bede, *Ecclesiastical History*, 96, 101
Béjaïa, 14
Bell, Kenneth, 248, 250
Belmarye. *See* Marinids
Benjamin, Walter, 200, 342
Bent, Theodore, 309–10, 319, 333, 391n36
Berber, 164, 168, 170, 174–75, 279
Berber Academy, 165
Berkeley, University of California, 201, 202
Bernal, Martin, 9
Bhabha, Homi, 296
Bible: Acts, 3; canon of, 192; Hebrew, 193, 194–95, 199, 206–7; Isaiah, 3; New Testament, 193, 206; Numbers, 40–41, 188, 189, 312; Old Testament, 190, 193, 194–95, 206, 374n18; Psalm 114, 193–94; *Song of Songs*, 43, 187–90, 192–93
Bindseil, Reinhart, 214
black and white as categories, 289–90
Black Athena. See Bernal, Martin
Blackness, 4, 7, 188–90, 289–90
Blixen, Karen, 136. *See also* Dinesen, Isak
Bloch, Marc, 230
Boccaccio, Giovanni, 133, 149
Bocchus of Mauretania, 108
Book of Gates, 59
Book of Jasher, 41–42
Boston, Museum of Fine Arts, 359
Boulluec, Alain de, 27
Bourdieu, Pierre, 54, 170–75, 291, 373n70
Boyle, Robert, 124
Breasted, James Henry, 58
Brexit, 98–99
Brinkmann, Hennig, 195
Britain, 89–91, 94–102
British Museum, 1, 52, 55, 56, 165
British South Africa Company, 304, 305, 307, 309, 310, 317, 318, 321, 322, 325
Brutus, 89–90, 94–95, 98
Bruwer, A. J., 331
Buganda, 216, 344
Bulawayo, 304, 305, 307, 327
Burkina Faso, 132, 164

Burnham, Alexander, 306, 327
Burnham, Nada, 304, 306
Burundi, 217
Butterfield, Ardis, 16
Byzantium, 222

Cabral, Amilcar, 252
Cadmus, 31
Caelestis, 119, 120, 181. *See also* Tanit
Caesar, Julius, 79
Calliope, 75, 144, 157, 161
Callisthenes. *See* Kallisthenes; Pseudo-Callisthenes
Cambyses II, 40, 41, 187
Camena, 181
Cameroon, 223
Canaris, Wilhelm, 207
Canary Islands, 164
Candace, 50
Capella, Martianus, 148
Capitoline Hill, 149–50, 157
Caravans of Gold (exhibition), 3, 11
Careticus, 94
Carmen in Victoriam Pisanorum, 13–16
Carthage: in the *Aeneid*, 49, 87–89, 104–7; and Auerbach, 181–82, 185, 191–92, 197; destruction of, 2, 48, 92, 109–10, 120–21, 113, 140–41, 165, 175–76; in *The Dream of Scipio*, 138–39; as fantasized origin of Great Zimbabwe, 305–6, 325, 332; and foundation of Europe and Rome, 104–24; founding of, 92–93, 142; historical significance of, 16–17, 92–93, 103–45, 345; in *The House of Fame*, 142; and Kantorowicz, 204–7; in *The Marriage of Mercury and Philology*, 156; and *metus hostilis*, 16, 110, 117–88, 120, 128, 325; "mother of the Vandals," 100–101; in *The Punic Wars*, 104–5; as return of repressed, 80, 105–6; in Romance of Alexander, 48–49. *See also* Tunis
Carthage, New (Cartagena), 127
Castile, 132
Catabathmos, Mount (Sallum), 39
Cato the Elder, 110, 114, 117, 141

Cato the Younger, 79, 80–84
cattle, 239–41
Certeau, Michel de, 42
Césaire, Aimé, 300
Chance, Jane, 148
charisma, 195, 210–11, 339, 342–43
Charlemagne, 148
Charles II, 308
charter, 259–60, 267
Chaucer, Geoffrey, 11, 132–33; *Book of the Duchess*, 134–35, 136; *The Franklin's Tale*, 140–41; *General Prologue*, 11, 133; *House of Fame*, 87, 142, 145, 152; Knight, 133–34; *Legend of Dido*, 144; *Legend of Good Women*, 141–42; *The Nun's Priest's Tale*, 136, 140–41; *Parlement of Foules*, 135–39
chiefs, 98, 214, 223–24, 231, 235, 245, 308, 334, 336, 338–39, 341, 393n9, 393n10
Chipanga, Kudzanai, 338, 342
Chombo, Ignatius, 338
Chrétien de Troyes, 157; *Perceval*, 96–97
Christ, 14, 196, 198, 337, 393n4
Christianity, 14, 16, 26, 49, 94–96, 99–101, 133, 134, 148, 185–86, 191–92, 203–7, 212, 279, 297, 314–15, 336, 340–41, 343–45
Chrysostom, John, 51
Cicero, 120, 210; *Dream of Scipio*, 109, 122–24, 126, 135–40 (*see also* Macrobius, Ambrosius Theodosius: *Commentary on the Dream of Scipio*); *On the Republic*, 120–21, 126
Circumcellions, 191
Civil Code, French, 288
civil law, 244, 340
Clanvowe, John, 135
Clapperton, Hugh, 172
Clarke, Edward Daniel, 51, 52
Claudius, 112
Cleopatra, 107, 108
Code d'Indigenat, 296
Cole, Andrew, 292
Cole, Teju, 224
Colonial Office, 227, 248, 250, 337. *See also* Foreign Office

colonialism, 93, 172, 223–24, 226–27, 230, 231, 234–70, 273–75, 278–79, 281–85, 289, 291–95, 298–301, 304, 334, 340. *See also* feudalism; land
Comestor, Peter, 41
Commentary on the Dream of Scipio. *See* Macrobius, Ambrosius Theodosius
communism, 202, 203, 287
Communist Manifesto (Engels and Marx), 103
conquest, right by, 242–43
constitutional history, 221, 229–30, 249–50, 340
constitutions, 23, 229, 253, 254, 339–40, 393n10
Coptic, 154
Corineus, 98
Corinth, 176
Corippus, 168
Cornwall, 96, 98
Crehan, Kate, 225
Creon, 159
Crouzel, Henri, 187
Crowe, Eyre, 232
Crown lands, 98, 236, 238, 242, 243, 307. *See also* land
crown of perennial fronds, 157, 370n31
Crusades, 10, 14, 48, 49, 133, 135
Curio, 79–80
Cush. *See* Kush
Cushite ("Ethiopian") woman, 41–46
Cyprian of Carthage, 191, 205–6
Cyrene, 30–33, 93, 101

Danae, 120
Dangerous Diseases Ordinance, 345
Dante, 104, 140, 148, 197–99, 202, 290, 375n32
d'Arcos, Thomas, 165, 175
Darius I, 31
De bello civile (Lucan). *See Pharsalia*
de Waal, David Christiaan, 318
decolonization, 13, 296, 334, 386n7
Decret, François, 295–96
Decretum, 205

Degema, 97
Delamere, Baron (Hugh Cholmondeley), 234
Delphi, 65
Demetrius, 158
Derrida, Jacques, 65–66, 68–70, 174–75
Descartes, René, 124
Description de l'Égypte (Panckoucke), 7–8, 53–55
desecularization, 338, 342. *See also* resacralization; secularization
Desmond, Marilyn, 144
development, economic, 5–6, 226, 228, 230, 237, 245–56, 281
dialectic, 4, 66, 154–55, 173, 174, 199, 252, 273, 274, 276, 278, 281–93, 316, 384n54, 386n16, 388n29
Diana, 90, 98
Dias, Bartolomeu, 7
Dide, Maurice, 283, 285
Dido, 86–89, 93, 104, 106–7, 118–20, 131, 135, 140, 141–44, 145, 155–56, 161, 162, 166, 305, 306. *See also* Elissa
dignitas, 230, 340
Dinesen, Isak, 235–37. *See also* Blixen, Karen
Dinka, 218
Dio Chrysostom, 26, 51
Diodorus Siculus, 23, 28, 33–36, 67
Dionysius of Alexandria, 32, 35
Diop, Cheik Anta, 8–9
Dis, 140
Djebar, Assia, 148, 175–77
Dockray-Miller, Mary, 43–44
Domesday Book, 239, 243
Domitian, 149–50
Donatism, 191
Dowling, Noel, 230
Dreyfus, Alfred, 275
du Bois, W. E. B., 72
Dual Mandate, 216, 227, 243–45. *See also* indirect rule
Durkheim, Emile, 337
Dutch Reformed Church, 3

Ebstorf map, 38–39
education, 120, 124, 114, 138, 124, 154, 143, 149, 172, 174, 187, 240, 293, 366n22, 382n28
Edward I, 227, 239, 243
Edwards, Amelia, 58–59, 61–62
Egypt, 23–70, 153; and allegory, 193–94; and art, 54–61; constitution of, 23; location of, 7, 23–24, 33–40, 53, 57, 64, 66; Napoleon's invasion of, 52–54; and philosophy, 64–70; and race, 8–9, 24, 54–64; and religion, 35–36; as river, 67–68, 70; as symbol, 197, 198. *See also Description de l'Égypte*; Egyptians; Egyptology
Egyptians, 15, 44–45, 107
Egyptology, 8, 54–64; and formalism, 54–58
Einstein, Albert, 201
Eliot, T. S., *The Waste Land*, 97, 217
Elissa, 105, 143, 153, 155, 305. *See also* Dido
eloquence, 151, 161–62. *See also* oratory, North African
empire, 33, 46, 47, 49, 84, 86, 92–93, 107, 151, 162, 207–9, 214, 249, 318, 326, 332–33; Alexander's, 46, 51, 52; British, 242, 249; Carthaginian, 80, 92–93, 171; of Great Zimbabwe, 308–9; Roman, 27, 49, 79, 85, 87, 100, 115, 126, 166, 296, 315–17
England, 96, 324, 334, 380n71
Ennius, 127, 157, 370n31
Ephemus, 31
Ephesus, Council of, 192
Epprecht, Marc, 345
Ethiopia, 3, 8, 33–34, 35–36, 40, 41, 53, 67, 71–72, 187–90, 356n42
Ethiopians, 39, 40, 41, 42, 45, 168, 188–90, 220
ethnography, 63, 213, 216, 219, 224, 253, 254–55, 257, 260, 262, 265, 269, 279, 333, 343. *See also* anthropology
Etruscan, 177
eugenics, 57–64, 360n89
Euphemos, 76
Evans-Pritchard, E. E., 216, 218, 224, 228, 342

Exodus, Old English, 42–46. *See also* Cushite ("Ethiopian") woman

fairy tales, 215, 217
Family Watch, 343
Fanon, Frantz, 27, 271–301; *Black Skin, White Masks*, 271–75, 282–83, 285–86, 293–94, 297–98; and dialectic, 273, 274, 276, 278, 281–94, 385n54, 386n16, 387n28; and history, 274–75, 279, 280–82, 287–88, 291–92, 387n28; and Middle Ages, 281, 287, 291–92, 387n28; and negation, 271, 299–301; and violence, 275–76, 294, 297, 300–330; *Wretched of the Earth*, 272, 274–78, 280–84, 287–92, 294, 297–301
Faras, 56
Fauvelle, F. X., 3, 57
Feeney, Dennis, 166
feud, 226, 228
feudal analogy, 225, 230, 233–35, 281, 334, 384n49
feudalism, 214–15, 216, 223–28, 242, 251–54, 258, 281, 303, 308, 335; and land, 246, 247, 255–62, 267–69. *See also* Middle Ages
Fibonacci sequence, 14
figura, 182–85, 190–200, 206
Foreign Office, 227, 324, 248. *See also* Colonial Office
formalism in art, 53–61
Forster, E. M., 27
Forum, Roman, 159
Fountain of the Sun, 70, 154
"four races," 59–60
Fourier, Jean-Joseph, 53
Frazer, J. G., 201, 217–18, 343
Frederick II (Holy Roman Emperor), 195, 208, 209
French, Howard, 3
French Civil Code, 288
Freud: and Carthage, 105–6; and disavowal, 203; *Interpretation of Dreams*, 105–6, 124; *Psychopathology of Everyday Life*, 106; and repetition compulsion, 96, 120
Frobenius, Leo, 218, 219–23, 305, 330, 379n46
Froissart, Jean, 133
Fronto, Cornelius, 161, 162
Fulcher of Chartres, 12–13
Fulgentius, Planciades Fabius, 143–44, 152, 156–64, 177, 181; *Mythologies*, 156–62; *On the Ages of the World and Man*, 162–64, 174
Furse, Ralph D., 248, 250

Gaddafi, Muammar, 76, 93
Gaia, 31, 73, 75, 80, 80
Gaius Marius, 108
Gaius Verres, 210
Galbraith, V. H., 250
Galen, 157
Galton, Francis, 57, 360n89
Gama, Vasco da, 323
Garamantes, 74, 155
García, Juan Carlos Moreno, 59
Garlake, Peter, 331
Gates, Henry Louis, 3, 329
gates of horn and ivory, 140
Gathigira, S. K., 269
Gaunt, John of, 132
Geertz, Clifford, 342
Genoa, 13, 14, 135
Geoffrey of Monmouth, *History of the Kings of Britain*, 89–92, 94–102
George, Stefan, 199–200, 201–2, 208
Germanitas, 207
Germany, 184, 201, 202, 203, 207–9, 211, 212, 213, 219–20, 221–22, 223, 342, 379n47
Getulia, 88, 149
giants, 98
Giant's Ring, 98
Gibbon, Edward, 315–18, 322
Gikandi, Simon, 269
Gĩkũyũ, 223, 235–37, 241–42, 253–57, 262–63, 265–70
Gĩkũyũ (first man), 255, 265, 266, 270
Gildas, *De Excidio Britanniae*, 96, 101

Gilroy, Paul, 273, 385n5
Gluckman, Max, 224–31, 250–51
Goering, Hermann, 207, 221
Goethe, Johann Wolfgang von, 209
golden apples, 31, 68, 73, 83
Gomez, Michael, 3
Gordon, Robert, 223–24
Gorgon, 68, 74, 155
Gormund, 95, 99–100
Gothic art, 315
Goths, 314–15, 321, 322
Götzen, Gustaf von, 214–15
Granada, 132
Greece, 6, 78, 90, 174
Greek: language, 153, 163–64, 186, 315; literature, 30, 75, 84, 129, 152, 154, 174; mythology, xii, 30–31, 68, 71, 148, 158; religion, 26–27, 32–33, 354n21
Greeks, 78, 79, 84, 112, 121
Gregory X (pope), 134
Gregory of Tours, 101
Gregory Thaumaturgus, 195
Gregory the Great (pope), 96, 324
Grimm, Brothers, 217
Griqua, 63
Grotius, Hugo, 153
Guide to the Inhabited World. See Dionysius of Alexandria
Guillaume de Lorris. See *Romance of the Rose*
Guiraud, Paul, 283, 285

habitus: Bourdieu's term, 171; as clothing, 113–14, 115, 128
Hadrian, 319
Hagar, 192
Haggard, Sir Rider, 303, 304–9, 317, 320–21, 326, 327–29, 331, 333, 391n43
Hall, Richard Nicklin, 309, 311, 313–14, 325, 329, 330
Hall, Stuart, 190
Hamilcar, 105
Hamitic hypothesis, 215–16, 220, 221, 311, 313, 378n34. See also race; racism

Hannibal, 80, 105, 106, 108, 109, 171
Hanno, 167
Happy Valley Set, 234–35
Harald Hardrada, 243
Harold (king), 243
Hasdrubal, 126; wife of, 140
Haskell Oriental Museum, 59
Hatshepsut, 29
Havelock, Eric, 174, 373n69
Hawass, Zahi, 24
Hays, Gregory, 163
Hebrew, 26, 41, 42, 43, 46, 163, 164, 165, 184, 185, 188, 193, 198, 199
Hegel, 282, 314, 315–16; and African lack of history, 172, 288, 303, 316; and Africans, 4–5, 64–65, 197, 316; and Dante, 197–98; and division of Africa, 4, 6; and Egypt, 24–25, 64–67, 197; *Geistesgeschichte*, 197, 198; and Gibbon, 315–16; on hieroglyphics, 64–65; and history, 1, 25, 198–99, 274, 316–17; and history of philosophy, 66–67; and master/serf, 274, 285–86, 290–93, 315–16; and negation, 4, 25, 273, 297, 300, 386n16; and "proper" Africa, 4, 7, 25, 64–65; and race, 64–65, 316; and "reality," 186, 197; and Rome, 315–17. See also dialectic
Heidegger, Martin, 6
Helicon, 144, 157
Helios, 68
Hell, Julia, 365n1
Heng, Geraldine, 10, 12, 48, 99
Henry II (king of England), 48, 215
Henry VI (Holy Roman Emperor), 210–11
Henry of Bourbon, 135
Henry the Navigator, 323
Hera, 31, 73
Hercules, 30, 68, 73, 80
Herodian, 119
Herodotus, 36, 40, 168
Hesperides, 31, 68, 75, 83, 144
hieroglyphics, 31, 52, 53, 64–65, 153
Higden, Ranulf, 38

Hilton, Rodney, 250
Hippo, Council of, 191–92
Hippo Regius, 100
history: of Africa, 1–4, 6–9, 13, 50, 129, 164–65, 187, 303; as art, 53–54, 56, 315; cultural, 43–44; cyclical, 91–92; dialectical, 316; of Egypt, 52–64; in Fanon, 274–75, 279, 280–82, 287–88, 291–92; intellectual, 199, 219, 276; invented, 320–25; of kingship, 201–11, 218; and land, 233–48, 251, 253–70; literary, 87–89, 141, 154, 157, 194, 198–201; medieval, study of, 226–30, 249–52, 259, 382n28; as myth, 258–59, 260–62, 266, 269–70, 305 (*see also* mythic charter); oral, 333; and philosophy, 66, 123, 142, 144, 150, 197, 198, 316–17; as progress, 2, 173, 245–46, 259; as racial, 62–64, 91–92; and writing, 65, 165–69, 176, 391n42. *See also* feudalism; Hegel; land; Middle Ages
Hitler, Adolf, 202, 207, 208
Hobbes, Thomas, 339
Holy Roman Empire, 202, 207, 209
Homer, 163, 184; *Iliad*, 71–72; *Odyssey*, 72, 86, 163
homosexuality, anti-, 343–45
Horace: *Carmen saeculare*, 93; *Epodes*, 30, 31, 107–10
Horkheimer, Max, 298
Horton, Africanus, 8
Horus, 185
Hugh of St. Victor, 39–40
Hundred Rolls inquiry of 1279–80, 239
Hundred Years War, 16
Huxley, Elspeth, 234
Hyppolite, Jean, 285, 286

Iarbas, 88, 89
Ibn Battuta, 132
Ibn Khaldun, 168
Ifriqia, 13, 16
indigeneity, 13, 33, 80, 277, 294, 296–99, 310, 327, 329, 333–34, 340–41, 343, 345, 387n19
indirect rule, 216, 222–23, 227, 231, 242, 262, 333, 393n9. *See also* Dual Mandate; Lugard, Frederick
iNduna, 307
Institut d'Egypte, 52
Institute of Advanced Study, 201
International Monetary Fund, 5
Ireland, 95, 98
Isembard, 95, 101
Isidore of Seville, 37, 103
Islam, 14–17, 23–24, 52, 92, 135, 168, 175, 320
Israelites, 40–46, 194
Istanbul, 182, 183, 184, 195, 196, 198, 199
Italy, 90, 209
ius nudum, 244

Jameson, Fredric, 63, 199, 258
Jameson, Leander Starr, 307
JanMohamed, Abdul, 272–73
Jason, 30, 73–74, 77, 79, 81
Jason and the Argonauts (film), 73
Jean de Meun. See *Romance of the Rose*
Jebel Barkal, 29
Jeremiah, 196
Jerusalem, 194
John II (king of Portugal), 323
Johnson, Samuel, 40
Johnston, Harry, 98
Jolliffe, J. E. A., 230
Jones, Terry, 133
Joseph (son of Jacob), 44
Josephus, Flavius, 41, 187
Jove, 87, 106, 120. *See also* Jupiter
Juba I, 79
Judaism, 15, 26, 184–85, 207
Jugurtha, 108, 111
Jugurthine Wars, 108. *See also* Sallust
Juno, 105
Jupiter, 87, 149–50. *See also* Ammon
Justinian, 168
Juvenal, 161

Kabaka Mwanga II, 344
Kabyle, 59, 170, 171–74, 280, 291, 373n69, 387n21
Kallisthenes, 70
Kandake, 50

Kandt, Richard, 211–17; poem for Richard Voss, 212–13, 378n23
Kant, Immanuel, 61, 361n103
Kantorowicz, Ernst, 195, 200, 201–11, 220, 336, 342, 337; and Alexandria, 204; and Carthage, 204–7; *Frederick II*, 202–3, 207–11, 226, 230, 316, 336; *The King's Two Bodies*, 202, 203–4, 205, 219
Kariuki, J. M., 270
Karnak, 29, 53, 54, 61, 65
Kebra Nagast, 45
Keen, Maurice, 250
Kekrops, 31
Kennan, Jeremy, 169
Kenya, 234–70, 340
Kenyan African National Union, 252
Kenyatta, Jomo, 233, 251–65, 268–70; *Facing Mount Kenya*, 253, 254, 256, 258, 262–64, 265, 269, 270
Ker, W. P., 250
Khatibi, Abdelkebir, 175
Khoisan, 222
Kigali, 213
Kikuyu. *See* Gĩkũyũ
King Alisaunder, 48, 49
kingship, 203, 215–19, 221–31, 307, 336–37; and mystical body of king, 202, 217, 218, 309, 335, 336, 339, 340; and sacred body of king, 204, 217, 218, 225, 336, 338. *See also* sovereignty
Kinyanjui wa Gathirimu, 235–36
Kojève, Alexandre, 274–75, 286
Kush, 29, 30, 40–42, 55, 62, 187, 357n47

Lady Truth, 128, 130
Lancaster Template, 337
Lancel, Serge, 151
Lancelot, 97
land, 27, 31–32, 36–37, 77, 129, 142, 229, 233–49, 251, 253–60, 265–67, 269–70. *See also* Crown lands; feudalism; land laws; waste
land, occupation of, 12, 54, 209–10, 235–37, 241, 257, 263–64, 267, 289, 307, 313, 318, 328. *See also* feudalism; land; tenure, land

Land Commission: Kenya (Carter), 235–40; Rhodesia (Carter), 238
land laws, origin in Middle Ages, 234, 235, 237–44, 246, 259, 261, 265, 267. *See also* Crown lands
land settlement scheme of 1919, 269
Lane, Jeremy, 373n70
Lang, Andrew, 326
Latin, African, 164
Latin Anthology, 155
Latium, 90, 105
Laȝamon, 90
Le Quellec, Jean-Loïc, 170
Leakey, Louis, 237–38
Leclercq, Henri, 279–80
Lefkowitz, Mary, 9
Legislative Council of Kenya, 234
Lemba, 220
Leogecia (Lefkada), 90, 94
Lerner, Robert, 207
Lethe, 83, 85
Lewis, C. S., 152–53
Leyser, Conrad, 202
libido dominandi, 112, 115–17, 120
Libya, 7–8, 30, 31–33, 35, 36, 38, 47, 48, 49, 55, 68, 69, 73–74, 78, 83, 87–88, 104, 141, 154, 162, 164, 305, 355n27. *See also* Cyrene; Siwa, oasis of
Libyans, 59–60
Libyc (Libyco-Berber), 163–70, 176–77
"L'Internationale," 287
lipogram, 162–64
Lipson, Ephraim, 246
literacy, 170–75, 261–62
Lively, Scott, 343
Liversage, Vincent, 246
Livingstone, David, 311
Lobengula, 18, 305, 306, 307, 321, 327
Loegria, 95, 96
Lomuto, Sierra, 10
London School of Economics (LSE), 260, 261, 384n49
Loprieno, Antonio, 60
Louis IX, 49, 135
Lozi, 224
Lubac, Henri de, 195
Lucan. *See Pharsalia*

Lucretius, 157
Lugard, Frederick, 216, 223, 224–26, 227, 268, 338. *See also* indirect rule
Lumbley, Carol, 99
Lydgate, John, 152

Maasai, 215
Maathai, Wangari, 255
MacDonald, M. C. A., 169
Macedonia, 47, 49, 51
Machaut, Guillaume de, 133
Macrobius, Ambrosius Theodosius: *Commentary on the Dream of Scipio*, 68, 119, 124–25, 136, 137, 138; *Saturnalia*, 68–69, 148
Madaura, 149, 152–66
Maecenas, 107
Magic Flute, The (Mozart), 61
Magna Carta, 230
Mago, 165–66
Mahdia, 13–16
Maimonides, 185
Maitland, F. W., 3, 226–28, 229, 340
Malawi, 98
Mali, 11, 132, 164
Malinowski, Bronisław, 30, 216, 217–18, 222, 229, 254, 255–62, 384n49
Mamdani, Mahmoud, 339
Manchester, University of, 224, 261, 382n28
Mandouze, André, 272, 294–95
Mani, 271, 283, 284
Manicheism: and delirium, 282–83, 292, 293, 294, 301; postcolonial concept of, 272–73, 276–83, 285, 288, 292, 294, 385n5
Manicheism, religion of, 271–73, 276–78, 281, 283, 285, 293–99, 386n15
Mannheim, Ralph, 195
Mansa Musa, 11
Map, Walter, 215
mappae mundi, 37–40, 74, 124
Maqrizi, Taqi al-Din al-, 26
Marc Antony, 107–10
Marcion, 196
Marcus Aurelius, 161
Marinids, 11, 132–34

Mark (apostle), 3
Marrou, Henri-Irénée, 293–94, 295
Marsyas, 159–61
Martianus Capella, 69, 150, 152–56, 181
Marx, Karl, 103, 199, 219, 224, 252–53, 261, 265, 281, 287, 290–93
Mashona, 310, 321
Massinissa, 138
Matabele Wars, 321; First, 306; Second, 307, 317
Mau Mau Uprising, 264, 270
Mauch, Karl, 309–10, 312
Mauretania, 7, 88, 94, 95, 101, 164
Mauri, xii, 101, 156
Maurice, Frederick, 182
Maximian of Bagai, 191, 192
Mazarire, Gerald Chikozho, 334
Mbembe, Achille, 282
Mboya, Tom, 233, 252, 253
medicine, 157
medievalization, 238, 324, 387n28
Medusa, 31
Meister Eckhart, 212
melancholy, 92, 109, 195, 198, 200, 317
memory palace, 117
Menelaus, 72
Menelik I, 45
Mercator, Gerardus, xii
Mercury, 87, 88, 145
Merlin, 98
Meroë, 30, 40, 41, 50, 55, 187, 357n48
Merton, Statute of, 240, 241
Metus hostilis, 16, 103, 110, 117–18, 121, 128, 135
Michaud, Éric, 315
Midas, 160
Middle Ages: as belated, 10, 221–22, 245–46, 258, 288, 292, 314, 315, 317, 326; and desire, 211–14, 303; historians of, 230, 233–34, 249–50 (*see also* Kantorowicz, Ernst; Maitland, F. W.); and history of Africa, 321–25, 329–30; and race, 10–13, 245–46, 351n4. *See also* Africa: Middle Ages; Alexander, Romance of; education; Fanon, Frantz: and Middle Ages;

Index   405

feudalism; land laws; Macrobius, Ambrosius Theodosius; medievalization; modernity; Zimbabwe, Great: as medieval
Milan, 192
Mill, John Stuart, 267
Milton, John, 76
Minerva, 81, 160
Miriam, 40, 42, 188
Mnangagwa, Emmerson, 336
modern history course, 249–50
modernity, 28, 64, 91, 125, 173, 194, 200, 213–14, 231, 237, 245, 247, 260–61, 281, 291, 297, 298, 326, 328, 330, 331, 334
Moffat, Robert, 311
Moi, Daniel arap, 253, 343
monarchy. *See* kingship
Monceaux, Paul, 151
Monomotapa, 308, 319, 321, 324, 327–28, 391n43
Monte Cassino, 149
Montecassino Chronicle, 14
Moore, Charles Herbert, 315
Moors, xii, 156
Mopsus, 74
Morocco, 101, 164, 169, 172
Morrell, W. P., 250
Morrison, Tony, 187
Morton, Jonathon, 46
Moses, 40–46, 188, 357n51; Ethiopian wife of, 40–45, 188–90
Moten, Fred, 386n11, 386n16
Mudimbe, V. Y., 24
Mugabe, Grace, 335, 336, 338
Mugabe, Robert, 336–38, 340–44
Mugo wa Kabiru, 262, 263
mugumo tree, 265, 270
Mukure wa Nygathanga, 256
Mumbi, 255, 265–67, 269–70
Muriuki, Godfrey, 269
Murungi, Kiraitu, 253
Musaeion, 157
Muses, 144, 157, 158
Museum of Fine Arts, Boston, 359
Museveni, Janet, 343
Museveni, Yuweri, 337, 344

music, 107, 135, 159–60, 173
Mussolini, 93
Mutwa, Credo, 333–34
Mwami Musinga, 213
myth, 83–85, 258–59. *See also* Greek: mythology
mythic charter, 30, 32–33, 93, 142, 203, 256, 258, 263, 264, 266, 305
Mzilikazi, 18, 332

Napata. *See* Jebel Barkal
Napoleon, 7, 51–53, 165
Nasser, Gamal Abdel, 23
Native Reserve Commissions, 334
Nazism, 184, 195, 202–3, 208, 223, 261
Ndebele. *See* amaNdebele
Ndung'u Commission, 238, 253–54
Neal, W. G., 330
Nectanebo II, 47, 48, 52, 55
neocolonialism, 264, 344
neoplatonism, 154
Neptune, 81
Nero, 79
Nestor of Laranda, 163
Ney, S., 386n15
Ngai, 255
Ngũgĩ wa Thiong'o, 235, 255–70; *Matigari*, 264–65; *Petals of Blood*, 264, 265; *The River Between*, 266–69
Niasse, Ibrāhīm, 23–24
Nibelungen, 215
Niger, 164
Nigeria, 242
Nile, 34–36, 37, 38, 39, 53, 67, 70, 158, 213. *See also* Egypt: as river
Nilotes, 221
Normans, 211, 245
nostalgia, 86, 221, 237, 254, 260, 263
Novalis, 217
Nubia, 8, 29–30, 33, 40, 47, 49, 55, 60, 62, 222
Numantine War, 111
Numidia, 7, 79, 92, 108, 111–12, 138, 149, 155, 165
Nyasaland, 98
Nzira, Godfrey, 336–37

Obasanjo, Olusegun, 343
Octavian, 108
Ogilby, John, 308
Olivier, Sydney, 238–39
Olympias, 47, 48
oracles, 29, 32, 36, 54, 70, 72, 82
orality, 169
oratory, North African, 118, 149, 161
Oresme, Nicholas, 290
Origen, 26, 185–90, 194, 196, 204
Orosius, 90–91, 93–94, 162
Orpheus, 75–76, 78
Orphic mysteries, 75
Osiris, 33
Otto of Blasio, 210
Ovid, *Heroides VII*, 88, 144
Oxford, medieval history at, 248–50, 382n28. *See also* Middle Ages: historians of; modern history course

paganism, 14, 15, 26, 45, 49, 68, 84, 94–96, 99, 101–2, 119, 148, 158, 185, 187, 205
pallium, 112–15
pan-Africanism, 8, 23, 252
Pandrasus, 90
Panofsky, Edwin, 201
Parmenides, 78
Passarge, Siegfried, 221, 223
Paul, Saint, 76
Pearl (poem), 290
peasantry, 239, 251, 280
Penal Code: of India, 344; of Uganda, 344
Pentecostalism, 336–37, 341–43
Perec, Georges, 162
Perham, Margery, 235
Perseus, 74, 155
persona, 112–13
Peter of Cyprus, 133–34
Peter the Venerable, 352n27
Petrarch, Francis, xxi, 2, 6; *Africa*, 125–32, 133, 140; and Italian fascism, 130; as laureate, 127; and modernity, 125; *Secretum*, 127–28, 130–32, 145

Petrie, W. M. Flinders, 56, 57–59, 62, 91–92, 329
Phaedrus (Plato), 65
Phaeton, 67
Pharsalia (Lucan), 79–85, 154
Pheko, S. E. M., 18
Philaeni, Altars of, 90, 92
Philip of Macedon, 28, 48
Philo of Alexandria, 26, 183–84
philology, 68–69, 148, 155–56, 158, 182
Phoenicians, 87, 141, 142–44, 167, 169, 304–7, 309, 311, 317, 318, 319, 320–22, 328, 331–33, 391n36
Pindar, *Pythian Odes*, 30–33
Pisa, 13–16
Plato, 65, 67, 78, 79, 290
Plautus, 141, 149–50, 167
Pliny the Elder, 38, 75
Plotinus, 185
Plutarch, 26–27, 65, 69, 83, 109
political theology, 33, 49, 117, 200, 202, 204, 205, 207, 222, 336, 339, 342, 376n3
Pollock, Frederick, 226–28, 229, 340
Polybius, 16, 139, 175–76
Pompey the Great, 79, 80
Portuguese exploration, 308, 309, 319–20, 323–25, 331, 390n30
Poseidon, 30, 74
postcolonialism, 9, 89, 182, 225, 254, 272–73, 276, 282
pottery, 56, 63, 359n86
Power, Eileen, 260, 261, 384n49
Prester John, 323, 324
primitivity, 173, 228, 237, 244, 250–51, 259–61, 277, 278, 280, 325
Priscian, 35
Pritchard, E. E. Evans. *See* Evans-Pritchard, E. E.
Procopius, 167
prostration, 210–11, 377n19
Prussia, 208, 211
Pseudo-Callisthenes, 50
Ptolemy, Claudius, 7, 34–35
Publius Annius Florus, 149–50
Punic, 114, 149, 165–67, 171, 175, 193, 372n54

Punic Wars, 80, 87, 110, 125–30, 141
Punic Wars, The (Silius Italicus), 104–5, 162
puniceus, 109–10
Punt, 29
Pythian Games, 30

Quo Warranto, Statute of, 243
Qur'an, 15, 26

Ra, 28, 29
race: as allegory, 102, 188–90; in art, 54–61; and Aryanism, 202; and degeneration, 107, 151, 220, 314, 315, 318, 370n17; and eugenics, 56–64, 208; of Europeans, 91–92, 208, 227, 315, 324; as history, 62–64; and land, 245; in Old English *Exodus*, 43–45; and pottery, 56; and Sicily, 210. *See also* eugenics; Hamitic hypothesis; Middle Ages: race
racism: and denigration of Africans, 4–5, 7–8, 11, 54, 64–65, 155, 316, 325–26, 334; division of Africa by, 4–6, 53–54; epidermal, 10, 59, 62, 65, 99, 155, 188–90, 209, 272, 277–78, 286, 287, 289–90, 310. *See also* Hamitic hypothesis; Middle Ages: race
Rameses II, 29, 55, 56
Randall-MacIver, David, 329, 330, 331
Rastafarianism, 45
Raynal, Abbé, 59
Reade, Thomas, 165, 171, 175
reality (*Wirklichkeit*), 183–84, 186, 196
Regulus, 110
Report of the Truth, Justice and Reconciliation Commission, 253
reproduction, regulation of, 345
resacralization, 338, 342, 343. *See also* desecularization; secularization
Rhodes, Cecil, 304, 305, 306–7, 309, 310, 317–18, 319, 325, 327, 331, 332, 390n17; and Gibbon, 317–19, 322
Rhodes-Livingstone Institute (RLI), 224–25, 250
Rhodesia, 304, 305, 306, 307, 310, 311, 393n9

Rhodesian Front, 311, 331
ritual, 35–36, 119, 312
Rogers, James Thorold, 314
Roman d'Alexandre, 46
Roman de Brut (Wace), 215
Roman de toute chevalerie, 48, 49, 51
Romance of the Rose (Jean de Meun and Guillaume de Lorris), 124
Rome, 79; defined against Carthage, 80; fall of, 320–21, 325; in Gibbon, 315–18, 322; and *imperium*, 209–10; sack of, 100. *See also* empire: Roman; Holy Roman Empire
Roper, Hugh Trevor, 250, 329
Rosetta Stone, 52, 55
Roumain, Jacques, 287
Roumis, 277, 279–80
Routledge, Katherine, 269–70
Routledge, William Scoresby, 269–70
Royal Anthropological Society, 62
Royal Geographical Society, 310
Rozvi confederacy, 334
Ruto, William, 336, 340
Rwanda, 211, 213–16

Saba. *See* Meroë
Sahara, 5, 7. *See also* Africa: sub-Saharan Africa
Sahel: Art and Empires on the Shores of the Sahara (exhibition), 3
Said, Edward, 53, 182, 199
Saintsbury, George, 151, 158
Sallust, 92, 110–12, 116, 120; *Jugurthine Wars*, 92–93, 111–12, 366n11
Sandved, Kjell Bloch, 170
Saracens, 12, 14, 134
Sarte, Jean-Paul, 275, 286, 386n12
Saturnalia. *See* Macrobius, Ambrosius Theodosius
Sawley Map, 40
Saxons, 92, 95, 98–99
Sayce, A. H, 58
scepter. *See tsvimbo yaMambo*
Schiff, Randy, 141
Schlegel, Friedrich, 314–15
Schmitt, Carl, 117, 200, 203, 342, 337
Schneider, David, 224

Scipio Africanus the Elder, 80, 104, 108, 122, 124, 126, 135–36, 139; *imago* of, 139
Scipio Africanus the Younger, 16, 103, 104, 108, 111, 119, 121, 122, 126, 135–36, 139
Scipio Nasica Corculum, 117
Scipio, Dream of. See under Cicero; Macrobius, Ambrosius Theodosius
Scott, Walter, 268
script: Libyc, 164–65, 168–70, 172, 175–77; Meroitic, 55; Punic, 166, 372n54
secularization, 173, 206, 231, 337–38, 342. *See also* desacralization; resacralization
Seebohm, Frederic, 226
Sefer Hayashar, 41–42
Sekyi-Otu, Ato, 287, 386n16, 388n29
Seligman, C. G., 216, 218, 224, 228, 342
Sembène, Ousman, 1
Semites, 60, 105, 220
Seneca, 205
Senghor, Léopold Sédar, 339
Septimius Severus, 149, 181
Septuagint, 187
serfdom, 233–34, 251–52
Servius, 148
Seti I, 60
settlement. *See* land settlement scheme of 1919
Shakespeare, 203; *Henry VIII*, 230; *Macbeth*, 229; *Midsummer Night's Dream*, 149; *Richard II*, 336
Shangani Patrol, 327
Sheba, Queen of, 44–45, 187–90, 312
Shilluk, 97, 218
Shulamite. *See* Sheba, Queen of
Sicily, 4, 209–11
Silius Italicus, 104–5, 162
Siwa, oasis of, 29, 30, 32–33, 47, 49–50, 52, 69–70, 72–73, 154, 164, 354n21
Slater, Sharon, 343
slavery, 11, 274, 285–86, 291, 316
Smith, Ian, 309, 323
Smith, Malvern van Wyk, 273

Smith, Stuart Tyson, 61
Smith, Wilbur, 331–33
Smuts, Jan, 3
Socrates, 65, 290
Solomon, 45, 31, 87, 190, 304, 311, 377n19
Solon, 28
Sorel, Georges, 275
South Africa, 97
Southern, Richard, 250
Southern Rhodesia. *See* Rhodesia
sovereignty, 16, 54, 77, 116, 200, 202, 207, 211, 228, 243–44, 253, 261, 267, 299, 307–11, 317, 323, 326, 329, 331, 334, 336, 339–40, 342, 343, 344. *See also* kingship
Speke, John Hanning, 216
Sphinx of Memphis, 54
squatter, 235–37, 251, 255, 389n9
Staley, Lynn, 96
state capture, 336, 339–40
Statute of Merton, 97
Stonehenge, 98–99, 102
Storm, Gustav, 99
Strabo, 7, 34
Strachan-Davidson, James Leigh, 248–49
Stubbs, William, 233–34, 250
Stuhlmann, Franz, 212
style: and *Africitas*, 148, 150–53, 161–62; and Auerbach, 182, 192–93, 199; and Egyptian art, 53–57; gothic, 314, 315; and pottery, 56
Sudan, 55, 97, 151, 216, 218, 222
Suez, Gulf of, 35
sun: as heliotrope, 66–70; as symbol, 33, 43, 66–70, 93, 129, 153–54, 189–90
Sundiata (Niane), 330
Syphax, palace of, 128–30
Syrtis, Gulf of, 73, 76–78, 81, 108

Tamazight, 164. *See also* Amazigh; Berber
Tanit, 119, 166. *See also* Caelestis
Tauler, 212–13
Tel Lachish, 56

tenant, 236, 238, 240, 246, 252, 389n9. *See also* tenure, land
Tennyson, Alfred Lord, 217
tenure, land, 112, 233, 235, 238, 243, 245–47, 255–58, 260, 262–65, 269–10. *See also* tenant
Terentius Afer, 120, 149, 366n22
terra nullius, 32, 309
terre vacante, 288
Tertullian, 112–15, 142–43, 182, 183, 191, 194, 206–7
Thagaste, 115
Thamos, 65
theater, 86, 121
Thebes (Egypt). *See* Karnak
Thebes (Greece), 31
Theuth, 65, 156. *See also* Ammon
Thomas of Kent, 48, 51
Thoth. *See* Theuth
Tifinagh, 165, 169, 176
Tin Hinan, 164–65, 176
Titus (emperor), 318
Tlemcen, 11, 134, 135
T-O map, 37–39, 66, 72, 124
Tolkien, J. R. R., 43
tomb, 51–52, 60, 92, 108–9, 159, 164–65, 176
Torok, Maria, 109
Tout, T. F., 250
trade: between Europe and Africa, 13–14, 47; trans-Saharan, 11, 134
Tramyssene. *See* Tlemcen
translatio studii, 157
Trastamara, John of, 132
tribal law, 224, 228, 334, 338–39, 382n28
tribe, 225, 228, 251–52, 333
Trinity, doctrine of, 14, 101
Tripoli, 49
Trito, Lake, 30, 31, 74, 76, 78, 81, 160–61
Tritonis, 74
triumph, 30, 108, 109, 127, 139, 210–11
Trojans, 89, 90, 93–94, 155, 157, 155, 157
Troy, 72, 85, 87
Truth, Lady, 128, 130
Tryphiodorus of Sicily, 163
tsvimbo yaMambo, 336

Tuareg, 164, 169, 176
Tuck, Eve, 176
Tunis, 49, 134–35, 165, 168. *See also* Carthage
Tunisia, 4, 13, 164. *See also* Carthage
Turner, Marion, 367
Tutsi, 214–17

Uganda, 337, 343
University of California, Berkeley, 201, 202
Utica, 80, 81

Valerius Maximus, 139
Vandals, 15, 100, 144, 155, 156
Venus, 87
Victor of Vita, 101
Vikings, 99
Vinogradoff, Paul, 230
Virgil, 148; *Aeneid*, 71, 85–89, 91, 94, 104, 105–6, 118, 131, 140, 142, 143, 145, 148, 155, 161–62, 166; *Georgics*, 156
virtus, 110, 114
Vives, Juan Luis, 150
Volney, Constantin, 65
von Harnack, Adolf, 196
Voss, Richard, 212

Wace, *Roman de Brut*, 90, 100–101
Waiyaki wa Hinga, 223
Wales, 91, 95, 97, 99
warrant, 243, 259
Wars of the Roses, 229
waste, 94–98, 100, 240–42, 263
Weber, Max, 173, 258, 298, 337, 260, 342, 393n9
Weimar Republic, 221
Welsh Marches, 97
Weston, Jesse, 97
Whitaker, Cord, 11
Whitbread, Leslie, 144
whiteness, 289–91
Wilhelm II, Kaiser, 219–22
William of Malmesbury, 99
William of Poitiers, 243
William the Conqueror, 97, 239, 243

Wilmot, John, 308–9, 317, 319–25, 326, 327, 328, 391n43
Wilson, Monica, 336
Wolcott, Derek, xii
Wollstonecraft, Mary, 103
World Bank, 5
writing, 65, 158, 162–63, 168–75. *See also* script

Xenophon, in Fulgentius, 162–63

Yeats, William Butler, 124
Young, Michael, 258
Yvain, 97

Zambia, 225, 250, 338. *See also* Barotse
ZANU-PF (Zimbabwe African National Union–Political Front), 336, 338, 340
Zeus, 29
Zimbabwe, Great, 304–34; as ancient, 321–22; compared to fall of Rome, 320–21; as medieval, 321, 323–25, 329–33
Zimbabwe, Republic of, 310–11, 331; constitution of, 337–38
zodiac, 69, 128–30
Zulus, 225, 228, 230, 334, 335–42